SOCIALIST TRANSFORMATION OF INDIAN ECONOMY

SOCIALIST TRANSFORMATION OF INDIAN ECONOMY

A Study in Social Analysis,
Critique and Evaluation

GYAN CHAND

ALLIED PUBLISHERS

BOMBAY   NEW DELHI   CALCUTTA   MADRAS
LONDON   NEW YORK

First Published 1965

ALLIED PUBLISHERS PRIVATE LIMITED

15 Graham Road, Ballard Estate, Bombay 1
13/14 Asaf Ali Road, New Delhi 1
17 Chittaranjan Avenue, Calcutta 13
38-C Mount Road, Madras 6

REPRESENTATIVES ABROAD

GEORGE ALLEN AND UNWIN LIMITED

40 Museum Street, London W.C. 1

© *Allied Publishers Private Limited*

PRINTED IN INDIA
BY D. P. SINHA AT NEW AGE PRINTING PRESS, RANI JHANSI ROAD,
NEW DELHI 1, AND PUBLISHED BY R. N. SACHDEV FOR ALLIED
PUBLISHERS PRIVATE LIMITED, 13/14 ASAF ALI ROAD, NEW DELHI 1.

TO JAWAHARLAL NEHRU

for all that he meant and
means to our people
and in memory of three years (1948-51)
of close association of the author
with him in the work of planning and development

PREFACE

THIS book assumes that India has unreservedly and rightly adopted socialism as her goal; and has to find her own road to it. It endeavours to answer the question as to what this road should be and how we can travel on it. Having been convinced over thirty years that socialism is the key to India's future I have watched with increasing concern how, in spite of our professions, we have in practice departed from the path of socialism and created enormous difficulties for ourselves. The position, as it exists today, is full of contradictions. On the one hand socialism makes a strong and wide appeal to our people and the new compulsions in favour of socialism are growing, and on the other anti-socialist forces are gaining strength, there is a wide and deep penetration of our economy by the international forces uncompromisingly opposed to the advance of socialism everywhere. And what is much worse, a large and growing section of our own people are not aware of the dangers looming ahead on this account and are playing a very hazardous game. Socialist forces in this country are more divided than ever and the split in the world communist movement is a serious set-back from the point of view of advance of socialism everywhere.

The outlook in the immediate future is on that account not at all bright for the realization of socialism; and yet as there is no other way of conquering the age-old hunger, poverty and social iniquity in this country, the attainment of socialism has to be made an act of faith, and men of socialist conviction have to muster all their strength to defeat the forces arrayed against socialism and think as clearly as possible what socialism should mean in theory and practice. It is the purpose of this book to help in this process of thought and action. The issues which it raises are so basic and so many that it has to be assumed that the views stated in this book are necessarily to be clarified, further developed and their inadequacy reduced and removed by similar earnest efforts of mind of other socialists. It is hoped that this will actually happen. In spite of the wide ground which this book covers it does not aim at or achieve anything like comprehensiveness on this very complex subject. It is hoped that the general pool of ideas, to which this book is meant to be an earnest contribution, will grow in depth and richness and it will be possible to draw upon it for understanding and solving the problem of socialist transformation of Indian economy. On my seventy-second birthday this book is my reverent offering to the socialist India of Jawaharlal Nehru's dreams, hopes and arduous endeavours.

I have to thank my wife for helping me in writing this book and by struggling as valiantly as ever with my beautifully illegible handwriting and in other ways.

20 June 1965   GYAN CHAND

CONTENTS

Chapter One

SOCIAL HORIZONS I

CROSS-ROADS

The post-Nehru era has commenced. The country having paid its magnificent tribute to his memory and achievements, has now to face the future without him. The spirit of Nehru would, it may be hoped, guide all—the leaders and the people —in the accomplishment of the tasks which, everyone is agreed, are truly stupendous and would require unity of purpose and action and the individual and collective qualities of the highest order. The fact that in the seventeen post-independence years the country has come through severe ordeals and has borne the shock of his death with fortitude, dignity and maturity is a matter of the deepest gratitude; and the fact that the succession has been smooth and orderly—to many very much unexpectedly so—is again due to the impact of his death on the minds of the people and a sense of responsibility which it has created. Fortunately the fears of friends and hopes of opponents have been all belied and the new era has been well launched. Irreplaceable as he was, there is very good reason to look ahead without undue diffidence or even with subdued optimism. The situation is far from easy and our difficulties have just begun. But the end of one era has to mean the start of another. It is not certain that the people will be equal to the needs of the situation and the men with the necessary courage, strength, understanding and constructive ability will be found who can steer the country through the rocks and the shoals which cannot be avoided.

At this great turning point in our history, we have to proceed with faith in ourselves and our future—but more than everything else faith in the path which Jawaharlal Nehru—

more than anyone else—showed with great depth of conviction and fervour particularly in the last few months of his
life.[1] It appears that even before his serious illness he knew
that a re-affirmation of principles was called for and even with
failing health a few days before his death he fully participated
at Bombay in the discussion of the basic issues.

The most fundamental task of the nation to which he drew
our attention is the task of building a socialist society in this
country—the more so because he knew and stated very clearly
that in the post-independence period, in spite of bold declarations and resolutions, socialism still remains a hope and a dream
and in fact the position makes it more and not less difficult to
realise our social objectives. This is largely due to the people
having failed to develop the necessary understanding and
strength to carry out a task which no one—not even Nehru—
could have accomplished without full and intelligent support
of the people. This makes the present turning point all the
more momentous; the whole nation has to realise that imperative obligation, which our grave shortcomings and lapses of the
past have created for us, has to be met with the strength which
we have not been able to summon so far. His death does not
and could not alter the objective reality which has impeded
development and social transformation or reduce the strength

---

1. The view that political democracy without social democracy (by which
Jawaharlal Nehru explicitly stated he meant socialism) had no meaning was
affirmed by him on a number of occasions. At Jaipur, some months before
his death he once again stated: "Socialism is the inevitable outcome of
democracy. Political democracy has no meanng if it does not embrace economic democracy. And economic democracy is nothing but socialism." He
added, "monopoly is the enemy of socialism. To the extent it has grown
during the last few years, we have drifted away from the goal of socialism."
He did not, it is true, make any very distinctive contribution in the formulation of his faith in socialism, but the latter was with him a matter of
deep conviction and in it were fused inspiration of Marxism and, as pointed
out later in the text, a belief in an elusive but very real sense in "the meaning of life"—in verity of all verities. This accounted for his not being a
dogmatic socialist but also at times for his lack of clarity and firmness in
the enunciation of his views on a number of crucial occasions.

of the forces arrayed against socialism. It is only natural that these forces should feel that they have to use the opportunity provided by his death to their advantage and the grievous disadvantage of the people as a whole. It is, therefore, essential to assess the basic facts with the utmost clarity and apply our mind and energy to the new challenge that has to be faced. The architects of our nation, ever since Rammohan Roy, have felt that our people have a role of their own in the new dispensation and they can perform it with success only if they are true to themselves. Nehru, it is clear, also shared this belief. It may be that this view in some inscrutable way is in accord with our historic destiny. Even if it is, it makes the need for a true social vision of the future, i.e. vivid understanding of socialism and all that it implies, all the more inescapable. Without socialism, as Nehru repeatedly pointed out, we will not only not fulfil ourselves but not even survive as an independent country. We are really at the cross-roads and have to know it in the innermost depth of our being.

INCREASING SOCIAL PURPOSE

The processes at work in the country can be traced to the early beginnings of our national movement and a continuity of growth of an increasing social purpose indicated. It is, however, the entry of Mahatma Gandhi into Indian politics in 1920 and the post-1914-18 was impact on the progress of events in the country which made this social purpose more and more explicit and articulate and led to the emergence of new social horizons. The progress of events has, in more than four decades, produced effects which have given greater unity and coherence to the social outlook of our people and direction and force to their common urges. These (urges) cannot be defined easily or framed in basic terms, yet it is undeniably true that wide permeation of these social purposes has taken place and given them a dynamic of their own. The basic facts of Indian economy—abject poverty of the masses on the one hand and extreme social inequalities on the other, very low

level of national income, backward technique and low productivity, an enormous mass of unutilized man power, increasing pressure of population—are in themselves such stark
realities as to indicate vividly the direction in which we have
to go and the pace of development that has to be set. The
logic of these facts is, however, very strongly reinforced by
the effect of world forces and of expectations aroused in the
course of the struggle for national freedom by the alignment
of forces which occured even before independence and has
after it become much more marked and differentiated and by
the growth of social ideas which, though a part of the common
pool of mankind today, have in the context of facts of our
national life and social processes at work acquired a content of
their own and have on that account to be assessed and evaluated
in terms of our own experience, needs and social trends. The
processes at work in this country are essentially the same as
are producing extreme imbalance, which is in effect the search
for a new balance, all over the world. The crucial issue of
poverty in face of potential abundance, which it is so clearly
possible to realize by the application of the available knowledge
and technique and the utilization of the existing resources, has
to be faced, and it has to be understood that continuance and
even aggravation of poverty at present of over nearly two-
thirds of the world is mainly due to the rigidity of social
structure and men's inability to change it, to utilize fully the
potential of knowledge, technique and organization. It is when
the interests of the community, i.e. those of the dispossessed
masses, become paramount, forces are brought into operation
which would make them (masses) the means and the end of an
entirely new social dispensation that hunger and poverty would
be conquered and an abundance-based economy with scope for
a culture, in which the people participate and to which they
contribute in full measure, would be established. Abundance
itself will not produce abundant life—life of real fellowship,
true grace and internal poise and tranquillity, and abundance
without abundant life would create inner poverty and therefore

social disequilibrium worse than that created by extreme inequalities and poverty which have always gone together.
Abundance is not an end in itself and has to be a means by
which a rich individual and social life has to be realized. This
fact, however, does not affect the fundamental issue that the
co-existence of extreme poverty and potential abundance in
our country and other underdeveloped countries is the cardinal
issue and the main hindrance in the way of realizing the
latter and abolishing the former is the inadequacy of our
understanding, common effort and social organization and
therefore our inability to use the available opportunities and
resources. In other words, in India, as in other retarded countries, we can have the means to create conditions in which
the process of growing from more to more and producing and
accumulating resources for growth can be started and developed
on a cumulative basis if appropriate social motives, norms and
relations can be created and made progressively adequate and
effective.

GENERAL ATMOSPHERE

This view is the basis of socialist approach all over the world
and in India it has gained currency, and even ascendancy as a
part of world process but also owing to the clear indications
thrown up by our own experience, pressure of urgent needs of
our people and possibly some elements in our social inheritance.
Socialist approach in India, as it will be made abundantly clear
later, is still lacking in clarity, coherence and depth and has
yet to be defined fully and developed in terms of our conditions
and needs; but it is, all the same, a very significant factor in the
remaking of our country and shaping the basic policies. The
climate of public opinion is distinctly favourable for adopting
and applying this approach increasingly in the development of
social philosophy and formulation and implementation of policies. There is, it is true, a large element of make-believe in the
prevailing trends of opinion and apparent conformity on a
considerable scale, for reasons unrelated to honest convictions

and analysis of facts and forces, is being commonly practised and accounts for the avowal of socialism as a common goal of policies and programmes; and yet it is true that socialism has a very wide appeal and is gaining increasing hold over the minds of our people. Implications of socialism are not clearly understood on a wide basis and organized support for it by men, for whom it is a real faith to live and work for, is limited to, relatively speaking, a small section of the people. Socialism, however, is a great moving force and opposition to it has on that account in most cases to pay homage to it by disguising itself in a pseudo-socialist garb. Subtle erosion of this general support of socialism is being organized and has to be consciously and resolutely counteracted. Though the general atmosphere is favourable for socialism, unless it is strengthened by clear and coherent thinking and an increasing measure of organized support of the people for the implementation of socialist policy in an unmistakable and conclusive manner, it can and will be converted into a miasma of wooly sentiment of welfarism and demagogic exhortations in the name of the people intended more to defeat rather than promote the advance of socialism.

INDIAN NATIONAL CONGRESS

The most important party in India is now avowedly a socialist party. Though now a political party it has been greatly benefitted by prescriptive advantage that it has acquired by its having put on the mantle of the national movement which it led and by the continued close association with it of most of the veteran leaders of the struggle for national freedom. Mahatma Gandhi's advice to it that it should cease to be a political organization and become essentially a social service institution was disregarded partly because of the understandable reluctance of its leaders to abdicate their position of power after independence, but more because there was no other organization which could have maintained and developed the newly won freedom of the country for consolidating its political integrity and facing and solving the very complicated problems of shaping its future. The socialist creed of the Indian National Congress has been adopted not only because of its wide electoral appeal but also because in the pre-independence period socialist trend was becoming increasingly articulate and effective and thinking of the leaders was being more and more influenced by it. This trend has become stronger since independence, but its content bears the mark of tentative, empirical adjustment under the pressure of political tactics and strategy. The view that socialism in India has to grow out of the specific needs, experience, history and ethos of the people is a rational view and is now advanced and supported by even the most radical exponents of international socialism; and yet specificity of socialism in India remains a search for national uniqueness in social thinking rather than a clearly defined social goal or a way of thought. This point will be further examined later, but in indicating the content of social thought today in India the fact that it has been shaped by the plastic stress of events, earnest desire for making it as authentic as possible from the Indian standpoint and, of course, the influence of the world socialist thought has to be taken into account and duly allowed for. The result is that, in the words of Jawaharlal Nehru, "now we face the future with all the burden of the past upon us and the confused dreams and stirrings of the future that we seek to build". We cannot possibly have an absolutely clear picture of the future that we want to build; but we should reduce the confusion of our dreams and stirrings and attain large measure of clarity in our thoughts, plans and action as far as possible. The Congress, though committed to socialism as a goal, is at present of divided mind in its total acceptance of this goal as a social imperative and even much more so in relation to its pursuit with earnestness of purpose and a sense of urgency so clearly indicated by our immediate needs and tasks. This is so because the Congress, in spite of Bhuvaneshwar, still presents not a variety but contradiction of views and as an organization it is being subjected to pulls and counterpulls of forces which cannot possibly remain long in harness together. That they are being contained in the same organizational framework is partly due to the confusion of dreams and stirrings but much more to the alliance not of convictions but of convenience which is being maintained by purely opportunistic considerations and accounts for increasing internal conflicts and growing import- ance of unprincipled moves and manoeuvres in the struggle for power at all levels. The immediate result is that even Jawaharlal Nehru's unifying and sustaining role in our uneasy balance of forces was being seriously impaired in spite of his undiminished hold on the masses. Though for the time being the issue of succession has been fortunately settled with a great deal of general goodwill, the struggle for power has not and cannot be ended. Powerful interests, persons and even foreign powers are deeply involved in this struggle and present a challenge which has to be resolutely met. The prospect for the future of India is obviously disturbing and the challenge, which the fact poses, has to be faced and met. This has to be met on the plane both of thought and action; and thought has to be clari- fied and developed with full appreciation of the meaning and bearing of the concrete situation.

SOCIALIST OBJECTIVE

The starting point of this process has to be the assessment of current thinking on socialism. The Congress, the Sarvoday- ists, the socialist parties, including small splinter groups, the communists and a few independent socialists represent the various currents of thought which are relevent for this purpose. The Congress approach on socialism, however, has, owing to its pre-eminence and practical importance, first to be considered. In spite of the Congress being a combination of divergent trends and subject to internal stresses on that account, its adoption of socialism as its creed and therefore, as the avowed basis of social objectives, policy and programme of Govenment at all levels has, it is obvious, a point of very real significance and has to be given its due consideration in the appraisal of current trends. The Congress, as a whole, it is well known, avoided the use of the word socialism before independence, and Mahatma Gandhi and most of the prominent congressmen regarded it as an imported concept and unsuited to the tradition and genius of our people. Though Jawaharlal Nehru openly avowed socialism, he took care not to identify himself with the Congress Socialists or any other specific social trend. After independence until 1954 again non-commital phrases like "Welfare State" and "Cooperative Commonwealth" were used to describe the goal of economic development and social change in India. After 1954 the phrase "Socialist Pattern of Society" was brought into currency to make a distinction between socialism and the social goal of India, though it became increasingly difficult to distinguish the latter from the former or treat socialism as an exotic approach and stress its incompatibility with Indian culture or the inner spirit of the historical experience of the people. The Gandhian approach has been and is a real force in the country and its influence is widely diffused even though it is not unoften used as a cover for social conservatism and a means by which the real issues, as stated later, are often evaded. The Gandhian approach in its recent developments has, however, been radicalized and its revolutionary meaning, which has always been implicit in it, been brought to the fore. As this and its relation to socialism will be more fully examined later, it is only necessary to point out here that Sarvodaya, as this point of view is now commonly described, instead of being antagonistic to the advance of socialism would very likely contribute to its realization and in some measure enrich its content. Rigid or dogmatic interpretation of socialism, avoidance of which is rightly emphasized not only by Jawaharlal Nehru but also the socialists and since 1956 by the communists, would of course hamper and distort its growth and has to be guarded against. The point, however, which matters is that socialism is now not a heresy to be avoided or denounced, but an integral part of the working faith of the vast majority of politically minded people. As a matter of fact the ease with which the Congress has, since 1954, formally made socialism its creed, indicated quite often more a formal conformity rather than a genuine conversion, and profession of socialism even by those, who are at heart opposed to it, is in fact a cloak for resistance to its advance. Insidiousness of these tactics does not, however, change the fact that socialism is, owing to the compulsion of our needs and wide permeation of the ideas for which it stands, a view which has its gravitational pull, and the Congress has acceded to it because it represents the time spirit and is a force generated by the deep, even though semi-articulate, urges of the masses in this country. Political strategy is an important factor in bringing about this change, but that is only another way of saying that impacts of the needs and aspirations of the masses make it necessary to profess allegiance to socialism as a means of winning and retaining the confidence of the people. It is well known that the Congress's commitment to socialism, such as it is, was largely due to the enormous weight which Jawaharlal Nehru's own views had been carrying and still carry in the counsels, deliberations and decisions of the organization and that he threw his weight in favour of socialism was due partly to his deep conviction that without replacement of acquisitive society by a socialist society the most vital problems of India and the world could not be solved; and it is a matter of the highest importance that they should be if India and the world are to create conditions on which the fulfilment of their future depends. The other reason which accounted for Nehru's personal support of socialism is his vivid perception of the fact referred to above that in substance that is what the masses really wanted, and unless socialism became a reality, democracy in India would be blown up by the explosions which otherwise would be inevitable. The overwhelming importance of Nehru's support for the Congress adopting socialism as its basic objective was, however, a mixed advantage because his conception of socialism and personal attributes and limitations practically became the determinant of the socialism of the Congress and the Government and the extent to and the manner in which it has been implemented. Socialism, as a world force, like all

momentous movements, owes not a little to the personal contribution of its outstanding builders and exponents and Nehru's
tremendous importance for socialism in India is no exception;
and yet the fact that in the Congress without Nehru its socialism would be of little consequence is its serious weakness, for
though there are in the Congress some very ardent and sincere
socialists they by themselves as a group could not generate or
sustain any impetus from within. The position in this respect
was being changed for a short while before Nehru's death and
volume of independent opinion within the Congress in favour
of socialism was becoming more and more articulate and even
effective. The future is still unpredictable, but it is not unlikely
that consolidation and growth of socialist forces within the
Congress would take place and the chances of their being able
to give battle to reaction and even win it have considerably
improved.

NEHRU AND SOCIALISM

Nehru's support of socialism, to repeat, has been a mixed
advantage, and unless socialist movement within and outside
the Congress gains strength, contributes to its clarification and
coherence and utilizes the experience of building up socialism
in the country for co-relating it directly to the actual needs and
problems of the people, congress socialism will have no enduring
value and would only leave behind a trace of feeble and ineffective effort, in spite of its having been backed by a very
vital personality to make socialism as a working faith for taking
the country forward to its destiny. Affirmation of faith in socialism by Nehru had had practical significance, but apart from
flexibility of approach, which in effect has meant its eclecticism
and emphasis on the importance of means as much as of ends,
which is Gandhism in a diluted form, Nehru did not strike any
note which could give to his approach any distinctive characteristic of its own. That it is desirable to realize socialism without
violence is a proposition which even the most ardent communist
can well subscribe to without any reservation, and that it is

possible to do so under a parliamentary system and therefore without using coercive methods is also now conceded by them (communists). Whether it would be realized this way would depend upon whether it (parliamentary system) can respond to the urgent needs of the people and become an instrument in their hands for their highest well-being and social liberation from their existing bonds in the present conditions of an undeveloped country like India. There is no warrant for the view that this would happen as a matter of course, provided there is a system of free and fair elections and rules of the parliamentary game are adhered to. It is often said that political (ballot box) democracy without social democracy is only an empty shell. In other words, without social revolution parliamentary democracy cannot fulfil itself and has, therefore, to be re-enforced by a dynamic technique of social change which is not inherent in parliamentary democracy itself. Nehru did not give any serious consideration to this vital point and exhortation to avoid violence in social transformation, in spite of its profound importance, had the ring of a counsel of perfection about it and cannot ensure that violence or counterviolence could in fact be avoided in building up the social pressures needed for advance towards a socialist society. This is not the only one of the unresolved perplexities inherent in this approach, but it is one of the most fundamental, and the fact that it is not being faced as it should be illustrates how this approach—apart from not being shared with due intensity by the large majority of persons who are, because of being within the Congress or owing allegiance to it, formally committed to it—is not conclusive for practical purposes and has failed to create any dynamic of its own. It is, therefore, not possible to build any great expectations on the prospects of socialism on the basis of this approach.

TRENDS SINCE 1920

These are serious limitations and have to be given their due weight in the assessment of the present position and its relation to the future; and yet it is necessary to take into account

that progressively the Congress has since 1920, when the movement was launched by Mahatma Gandhi, been developing
quasi-socialist trends and an inner logic which has made it
necessary for it to visualize the future of India in terms of a
new social order based on equality and social justice, i.e. in
essence in socialist terms. The non-co-operation movement
itself, having made a breach with old constitutional methods,
had to depend upon the masses, stir them to action and identify
itself with their needs and interests. This itself was not only
a far cry from demands like having simultaneous civil service
examination or introduction of permanent settlement but
involved a fundamental departure in thought not only in relation to the British Government but also to the people of the
country. A sense of deep concern for them, which was devout-
ly felt by Mahatma Gandhi himself and in some inscrutable
manner transmitted to them, was widely diffused and made the
attainment of political freedom look clearly like a means—an
essential means but all the same means—to the end of realizing
the good of the masses, i.e. attaining for and through them
freedom from dire want, which had been and was keeping
them in a state of economic servitude, and creating for them
conditions under which they could break their fetters and rise
to the height of their stature. In 1929 this view emerged in a
concrete form in the resolution of All-India Congress Committee in which the opinion was clearly stated that "the great
poverty and misery of the Indian people are due not only to
foreign exploitation in India but also to the economic structure
of society which the alien rulers support in order that their
exploitation may continue. In order therefore to remove this
poverty and misery and to ameliorate the conditions of the
Indian masses, it is essential *to make revolutionary changes
in the present economic and social structure of society and
to remove the gross inequalities.*"[2] In the famous Karachi
resolution of the Congress it was even more clearly stated that

2. Emphasis added.

"in order to end the exploitation of the masses political freedom must include the real economic freedom of the starving
millions". In the resolution among twenty measures indicated
to enable the masses to appreciate what Swaraj would mean to
them was included payment of living wages to industrial
labourers and protection against the economic consequences of
old age, sickness and unemployment, freedom from serfdom or
conditions bordering on serfdom, reduction of agricultural rent
and exemption of rent of uneconomic holdings for such period
as may be necessary, a ceiling of Rs. 500 p.m. for salaries of
civil servants, control by the state of the key industries and
public ownership of mineral resources and imposition of progressive income tax on agriculture and of death duties. Later
at the Lucknow Congress in 1936 as a part of electioneering
programme it was felt necessary to state that poverty, unemployment and indebtedness of the peasantry was due to
antiquated and repressive land tenure and revenue systems. A
year later at Faizpur the need for a radical change in the
system was stressed and the need for unqualified exemption
from rent and land tax of uneconomic holdings and for effort
to introduce co-operative farming was clearly stated.

TRENDS SINCE INDEPENDENCE

These and similar trends have been further developed since
independence. The directive principles of the constitution, the
economic programmes of the Congress, Reports of the Planning
Commission and various policy statements and enactments of
important social laws have all made these social objectives and
their incorporation in theory and practice the avowed object of
policies and programmes.[3] Unfortunately however, perfor-

3. Apart from specific affirmation of socialist pattern of society as our goal
since 1954 by the Congress and the Government, objectives like establishment of a classless society, the reduction of inequalities, prevention of concentration of economic power or its material mitigation where it does exist,
social security against the risks of sickness, unemployment and death, payment of minimum and living wages, provision for institutions of national
life being informed by justice, social, political and economic, ceiling on

mance has fallen far short of the professions. If all these objects had been backed by earnestness of purpose and given their due priority in thought and practice at least by persons in key positions, the people at large would have apprehended them and made ten years of planned development a period of real advance towards socialism. That this has not happened in fact and outlook for socialism is, as explained in this book, not heartening is due, in spite of the general atmosphere being favourable for socialism, to these objects not having been pursued in all sincerity by most of the persons in power. The balance of social forces being against these pre-eminently desirable objects, from the socialist standpoint being taken as a cardinal part of the social mandate of the people and therefore the pressures from below not having been built up to an extent as to make their disregard in practice a liability for those who are in power or aspire to it. That these objects have revolutionary implications is conceded in words but denied in practice and their advocacy as a matter of expediency therefore has very often a hallow ring and produces, generally speaking, very cynical reactions. The last decade in India has not been lack-

personal income, land to the tiller and therefore abolition of all rentiers, i.e. all agricultural incomes derived from property without personal labour, public ownership of all key industries and increasing importance of public sector in all industries, promotion of decentralized industrial sector and its progressive co-operativization, occupation of all strategic points in the economy by the state and steering the latter through this control in the direction of a socialist society, building up a co-operative structure in rural economy from bottom upwards for credit, cultivation, marketing, crop-planning and essential services, making the good of the community the paramount consideration in the development, transformation and working of the economy and developing institutions through which this object can be achieved, taking measures to get private sector to accept the discipline of values and work in unison with public sector, changing man even more than the system and using economic development as much a means of enriching human personality as of increasing wealth and income, have all been repeatedly commended as objects to be pursued and realized. It is, of course, assumed that their realization has to be achieved in the framework of democracy and freedom, i.e. totalitarianism in any form has to be avoided and civil liberties have to be maintained.

ing in distinct social gains, but all the same even foundations of a socialist society have still to be laid and first steps towards making the revolutionary content of these objects a reality have yet to be taken. All that needs to be done is to "inform" these objects and measures with unity and intensity of social purpose and accept the commitments inherent in them a matter of extreme urgency. This sounds simple but is really baffling from practical standpoint, and has to be made the core of the search for key to the future of socialism in this country.

SPIRITUALITY AND SOCIALISM

There is one strand which has run through the thinking of Congress in the last three or four decades which has to be specifically pointed out, for it has even now practical significance. This strand of thought relates to the deep need for giving to all human efforts and achievements, aspirations and realizations a sense of "meaning of life" and not merely a social purpose, i.e. integrating individual with the community and achieving a high order of organic unity between them "a sense of purpose," in the words of Jawaharlal Nehru, "beyond the material and physical needs of our daily lives".[4] "The argument", to quote from another article of Jawaharlal Nehru, "led to the old Vedantic conception that everything, whether sentient or insentient, finds a place in the organic whole. . . . This very argument indicates how the mind searches for something underlying the physical." This conception is based upon what is a deeply spiritual view and implies a mystical sense which premises, to quote from the same article again, "ideal of the life force which is the inner base of everything that exists".[5] According to this view welfare state, democracy,

4. Jawaharlal Nehru, "The Basic Approach" A.I.C.C. *Economic Review*, 15 August 1959.

5. "This (view) is beautifully presented," in the words of Sampurnanand, "in the Indian concept of the Virat Purusha. Everything, sentient and insentient, finds a place in the organic whole which is the *Virat*. Every particle is bathed in those currents of life-force which pulsate through the whole and the weal or woe of the minutest cell is transmitted at once to

socialism, or communism are not enough because they leave something vital out, something without which a high standard of living, leisure, art and culture, non-acquisitive co-operative economy, political democracy and even an equalitarian society would be incomplete and fail to give an answer to the deepest longings of man "to find a place in the organic whole". According to this view this conception has to be an integral part of socialism in India. Its unique characteristic is in keeping with the genius of our people, our traditions, history and culture and social ethos, and our people can only respond to the call of socialism if it is based upon this philosophy. Both Jawaharlal Nehru and Sampurnanand are not in favour of dogmas of religion and social usages, which have been sanctified by the habits of ages but are today a hindrance even in the way of spiritual growth. The issues which are raised by this view are, both Nehru and Sampurnanand admit, really metaphysical but both point out that the line between science and metaphysics is very thin, and in India at any rate only this approach would move the people, evoke the best in them and provide a basis for enduring and satisfactory social change.

This view, in its present bearing, is what is known in India as Gandhian economics and is examined in the subsequent paragraphs. It has in practice been interwoven with socialism of the Congress and colours deeply thinking, reasoning and pattern of responses of not only Congressmen, but a large section of earnestly minded people. At first socialism was viewed with distrust because of its imputed materialistic or at least non-spiritual philosophy. But now that socialism, as a description for the prevailing social approach, is more commonly accepted, there is a widely shared feeling that socialism suited to the specific needs of our people should be in accordance with the age-old deep currents of their common life and true to the urges of their inmost spirit. This view is generally held and has

the most distant corners. In the good of all is the good of each; the good of each contributes to the good of all." A.I.C.C. *Economic Review*, 1 August 1958.

to be taken into account; but it is also used as a cover for reactionary resistance to the demands for rational social change and here, as in all countries, it is being posited that there is a deep contradiction between philosophy of socialism and the philosophy of life drawn from living communion with reality, i.e. truly religious philosophy. This view, in other words, is being pressed into service for maintaining status quo or at best for slowing the rate of social advance. It is not necessary to discuss the validity or otherwise of this view in the introductory chapters. Two points, however, need to be briefly mentioned. If this view, according to which life force as inner base of everything that exists, is the true view of life, it is true not only for India, but it is true everywhere and has to be its real meaning, and search for it has to be an essential part and climax of socialism whenever it becomes an inspiration for realizing a new vision. We have been long nurtured on the belief that our people are in a very special sense spiritually minded people, have therefore a historical destiny of their own, and our institutions, standards and conduct have, therefore, to express and embody this sense of mission. This is, however, pure national vanity and can, unless carefully guarded against, be exploited for sinister purpose. This does not amount to saying that all nations are similar and they are not capable of making their distinctive contributions. But in the deepest sense life has the same meaning for us as it has for the other peoples, and this meaning, from this point of view, has to be the basic approach of socialism everywhere. Our socialism cannot and should not be different and differentiated because of its spiritual content. The second point which also needs to be briefly mentioned is that it is complete misapprehension to assume that socialism is devoid of spiritual significance and it leaves out the deepest needs of man. Socialism, as a matter of fact, owes its appeal to its appraisal of the acquisitive society, and capitalism as a system under which extremes of wealth and poverty and social criteria by which men are judged and rated amount to negation of true humanity of man and impoverishes him spiritually. This applies not only to non-Marxist socialism but also Marxism. The realm of necessity under capitalism which man has to liberate himself from is, according to Marxian view, the realm in which man cannot express himself or live according to his own lights owing to the compulsions of the system being too much for him, and the realm of freedom, which man has after liberation to enter, has to be realm in which free will would come into its own and man grow according to the inner law of his being, i.e. according to the deepest urges within him and rise to his highest spiritual stature. These points have been briefly referred to here because of the misconceptions which are implicit in the assessment of socialism referred to above and would later be more fully considered. Here they have risen incidentally from the consideration of the commonly held view that socialism in India has to strike the spiritual keynote and its philosophy has to be true to the genius of its people. It has, however, to be repeated that socialism, as it has been conceived and developed, is not devoid of spiritual meaning. It is on the other hand an earnest plea and endeavour for ending the tyranny of things over the spirit of man, and creating the conditions under which the spirit can grow and express itself and soar to the heights unknown before so far as the overwhelming majority of men are concerned.

SARVODAYA

This point is also the cardinal point of the Gandhian approach and accounts for the view commonly held by those who are dedicated to it that "if the world were," in the words of Jai Prakash Narain, "ever to reach the port of peace and freedom and brotherhood, socialism must eventually merge into Sarvodaya."[6] Vinoba has expressed the same view in his statement, "as the Ganges becomes wider and moves on and finally merges into the ocean, I hope that Marxism will merge into

6. Jai Prakash Narain, Towards a New Society, p. 1.

Sarvodaya one day."7 As for Vinoba, "socialism and communism in substance are the same, in spite of their difference." What he says about Marxism also applies to socialism, i.e. it has to merge itself in sarvodaya if it is to fulfil itself—realize its dream of a world of equality, freedom and brotherhood. This implies not only that socialism and violence cannot go together but also that a socialist order must be charged with a all-pervasive sense of the unity of life at the deepest level and make it the source, the substance and the consummation of its thinking, feeling and action. This of course means that not only violence should be completely abjured as a means of achieving social ends but fellow-feeling and compassion arising from the experience of unity of life in its most inexpressible, timeless aspect become the fount of inspiration, enlightenment and sustenance of truly revolutionary social change. This has, according to this view, to be the rule everywhere and for all times, but in India with her own social heritage and the dispensation of a long chain of sages, seers and mystics going back to the time of the early Vedantic tradition and Buddha, the spiritual basis of the new social order has a very special meaning of its own and has to be its inmost core, its creative, regenerative and sustaining principle. This view can be clothed in conventional terms and used to support the traditional way of life and social structure and even the status quo; but rightly understood, it is meant to be a call to dive deep in order to lay the foundations of an entirely new social order on a sound and enduring basis. As stated above, the view that India has a special historic mission to conceive and develop socialism with this approach, and lead the way in evolving and applying a social philosophy based upon it, implies a somewhat inordinate faith in our capacity to make a unique contribution to the future of socialism. It is not easy to answer the question which this view raises: why is India specially cast for this role and why has she to assume it? All the same

7. New Age, October 1957, p. 41.

its clear implication is that socialism has to be instinct with this profound meaning if it be an answer to the urgent need of the world in general and India in particular in the context of today and tomorrow. That is why it is confidently forecast that socialism and communism have to be merged in sarvodaya[8] if they are to usher in a new epoch in human history— the epoch in which man will rise to his highest and profound social changes would be brought about by changes in spirit and social ethics.

This view, as stated above, commends a large measure of general assent in the ruling party though its implications are not clearly understood and it is not explicitly avowed even by most of its foremost leaders. Expediency rather than conviction accounts for wide formal allegiance that Vinoba commands among the congressmen, the general atmosphere of conformity to the approach which is created by them and large measure of government support which he receives. Its practical importance from the standpoint of the growth of socialism in this country is that it is not easy to distinguish the Congress creed of socialism from the sarvodaya approach, and though the former has not merged in the latter, it is, so to speak, largely enveloped by it. Empirically speaking, it has an important bearing on our policy decisions and programme, and a number of contradictions in policy and practice are due to the penumbra created by interpenetration of socialism and sarvodaya in theory and implementation of policies. On one point, however, it is safe to assume that the Congress has very largely accepted the sarvodaya approach even for practical purposes; and that the theory of class struggle as a force in human history, past and current,

8. Jai Prakash Narain has expressed this view even more pointedly in the same book cited earlier. He says, "socialism as we understand it today cannot take mankind to the sublime goals of freedom, equality, brotherhood and peace. Socialism no doubt gives promise to bring mankind closer to those goals than any other competing philosophy. But I am pursuaded that unless socialism is transformed into *sarvodaya*, these goals would remain beyond its reach; and just as we had to taste ashes of independence, so the future generations may have to taste the ashes of socialism." *Ibid.*, p. 21.

has no place in its article of faith and is really disavowed by it. "Even unto the last," Mahatma Gandhi's well-known adopted phrase, as the definition of sarvodaya, means that all individuals, groups and classes are objects of deep concern from the sarvodaya point of view and have to receive equal measure of consideration at all stages of social transformation. This does not mean that the existence and the decisive importance of dominant and exploiting classes is denied and the need for putting an end to exploitation as an essential object of social change is not fully conceded. Social justice and exploitation are, it is assumed, mutually exclusive and supremacy of the propertied classes in social relations and actual working of the economy has to be ended if the new social order of sarvodaya conception has to be introduced. But obligations of social change through absolutely peaceful means is that well-being of all should imply comprehensive social concern and no discrimination even in feelings, much less in action, be practised in regard to the classes now in position of power and authority. The underlying premise, of course, is that there is an essence of goodness in all persons, whatever be their class affiliations. Though a classless society has to be the goal of social change from the sarvodaya standpoint, class emphasis should not be the motive force of thought and action and certainly not fomented for creating or maintaining social momentum. The difficulty of making an omlette without breaking eggs is avoided by the assumption that the classes concerned can be brought to see the inequity of the present position and the need for altering it radically in the supreme interest of the community. This means that "change of heart" has to be the main instrument of social change and all other measures have to be auxiliary to it. Legislation, which obviously involves the use of state power as a sanction, is regarded as perfectly compatible with this approach, but main reliance for making basic changes in social structure has to be placed on the change of public mind through the change from within rather than imposition from without. The distinction between conversion and building up social pressures through satyagraha technique as a means of social transformation is not observed in theory, much less in practice; but renunciation of class antagonisms as an instrument of social change is clearly indicated by this approach and firmly advocated. As pointed out in the next chapter, the recent trend of opinion among the socialists in India and a number of other countries is also definitely against positing class struggle as a major moving force particularly in countries in which political democracy is a working proposition and can yield positive social results. This point is of special importance in relation to the strategy of social action and will have to be discussed in the general assessment of the present position and prospects of socialism in India, but here it is stated as a point which is of primary importance in the sarvodaya theory and owing to its practical bearing on thinking of even genuine socialists in the congress and the general trend of socialist opinion in the country. Significance of this point for theory and practice is clear and has to be given its due consideration.

Faith in non-violence, of which the disavowal in class antagonism as a force in shaping the future, is the direct outcome, is a negative word for love as the most dynamic factor in social transformation. It, besides implying the abjuring of force as a means of bringing about social changes, implies that no person or class is beyond the pale of true fellowship and a sense of community of feelings has to be an all-inclusive fact of experience and the way of life. This is to be not only the basis of the new society after it has been established but also during the process of its emergence. The view that class struggle is not a social theory but a positive fact in social life is from that standpoint not specifically denied, but it is held that development of fellow feeling is the right and the most effective way to end it and establishment of a society free from class conflict —a real classless society. Formation of peace brigades is the sarvodaya answer to the problems of the growing acute and chronic conflicts within the country, even conflicts arising out of the organised resistance to the process of social change. This means more than the use of parliamentary or constitutional methods to bring about revolutionary changes; it means reliance upon what Mahatma Gandhi called "soul force" for the introduction and development of the new social order —a true co-operative economy free from exploitation and strife in all forms. The view that this is a utopian approach, a real counsel of perfection which cannot be made the major factor in replacing the acquisitive society by a socialist one is countered by the view that any other method would create more problems than it will solve and in the last analysis involve exploitation and dominance of one class by another in a different form. This would mean change of masters, and not a society based upon freedom and equality. Its practical bearing on our problems is that even if perfection is not realized in adherence to this method, the extent to which it is relied upon or actually used for making basic social changes would reduce the need for alternatives, and if social strife is purposively avoided and electoral mechanism becomes the most important instrument of advance towards the goal of socialist society, those who have ardent faith in this approach and are working for it with devotion and fervour it is earnestly urged, can be counted upon to contribute positively to the emergence of the new society or at least create a favourable atmosphere in which it can emerge and be brought into operation.

DECENTRALIZATION

The importance which is attached to the development of village industries and decentralization for applying the sarvodaya principles to the actual problems of social transformation, is due to their having been made an important plank in our struggle for freedom and the increasing emphasis which was laid by Mahatma Gandhi in the last ten years of his life through what he called "penetential thinking" on the paramount need of a new social order. These, according to him, could "have permanent effect only when carried out as a part and parcel of the wider programme of non-violent village uplift

economic organization, social relations and norms of behaviour. Autonomy of the village 'as the basic unit of the national economy has to be provided in order that it may plan production, fully develop its resources and produce its own leaders who may work for the people and be accountable to them. This would lead to direct participation of the people in making policy and its execution in matters directly related to their well-being and thereby create real democracy at the basic level, throw the responsibility for its success on the people themselves and create the necessary interest in and enthusiasm for creative work for the village community and through it for the country. This object or complex of objects is expressed through village self-sufficiency—Mahatma Gandhi's prescription for new life in the villages—and Gramraj (village government as the foundation of the whole polity), which Vinoba is now putting before us as the goal of our national endeavour. This involves devolution of authority from the centre on the institutions, political and economic, i.e. Panchayet and co-operatives but a great deal more. Decentralization in this sense means making the basic units truly basic—the centre of the entire life of the community —the source and the seat for its strength, vitality and the processes of growth. People's power, as distinguished from state power, is to be its essence which amounts really to reliance upon peoples' own initiative and dynamic for building up and sustaining the economy based upon freedom and equality. In theory decentralization in this sense means changing the whole scheme of things and making stateless economy the goal of social change. It makes withering away of the state not a vision of the remote future but as the supreme object of immediate endeavour.

That in the context of our existing needs and conditions integration and not merely co-ordination, of our economy is an essential condition of its survival, health and growth is neither by implication nor explicitly denied from this point of view. The whole problem of achieving integration in combination with decentralization is the point on which difference in theory and practice between the sarvodayist and the other advocates of social change cannot but arise when the issue is discussed in concrete terms; and the sarvodayists yet have not shown clear awareness, much less understanding of the issue and the necessity of dealing with it adequately from a practical standpoint. The need for reliance upon intelligent consent, active co-operation and initiative of the people as prime requisites for introducing and developing social changes would be readily conceded by non-sarvodayist social revolutionaries, but it is when concerted action on a broad basis is called for and has to be realized that difference of degree almost becomes a difference of kind and the sarvodayists, in spite of their catholicity of outlook, are likely to find the gulf between them and the others most unbridgable. Their whole attitude towards organization as a factor in human affairs creates practical difficulties, reduces their effectiveness in practice and makes their emphasis on moral values merely a general exhortation for working for the establishment of a new kingdom of heaven on earth. Their moral earnestness, deep sense of unity of life, faith in the goodness of man and his ability to live up to the tenets of this faith and the belief in the capacity of the people to bring about and support fundamental change through their spontaneous action and drive generated from within are all qualities of inestimable value, and can be truly a social asset for total social transformation. All these can be put into the pool of common ideas and efforts and turned to a very good account.

SATYAGRAHA

Direct action has been given a place of its own in the sarvodaya approach and is known by the name of Satyagraha. Mahatma Gandhi on several crucial occasions resorted to fasts to evoke moral response from the opponents and build up social pressures. He also organized peaceful mass resistance to oppression and social inequities and, as is well known, achieved great success in South Africa and in the national struggle for freedom.

It is held that the same technique of direct action can be used against powerful vested interests and reactionary forces for removing or undermining barriers to social changes. Since independence, whenever civil resistance has been organized to redress public grievances, the propriety of doing so has been, on many occasions, questioned owing to its incompatibility with the basic assumptions of parliamentary democracy and the need for reliance on constitutional procedure for righting social wrongs or carrying out the necessary social changes. The whole issue turns upon the validity of extra-constitutional action on a mass scale in a parliamentary democracy when the balance of forces in the country makes parliamentary processes cumbersome and unresponsive to the needs or demands of the people. This is a fundamental issue. The parliamentary system in a society, in which, owing to the concentration of economic power and wealth, scales are heavily weighted against the masses being able to vote their masters out of existence even where adult suffrage exists, can be used to resist and prevent changes, the need for which may be widely recognized and admitted. Direct action can therefore not be ruled out under a parliamentary system and can, as a rule, be effective only when it is backed by mass organizations. The sarvodaya approach would, of course, be against mass resistance being inspired by passions or made an occasion to inflame them, but in itself it (mass resistance) has the sanction of hallowed precedents and can be built up to weaken the resistance of vested interests or countervail the effects of accumulated power. Social revolution by peaceful methods would, even from the sarvodaya standpoint, require that direct action be held in reserve for use under suitable conditions and with proper safeguards. From the practical standpoint it would create extra-constitutional pressures which would increase the social efficiency of parliamentary processes, assuming that formal rules of parliamentary game are being observed, elections are free and fair and opposition is not reduced to futility by recourse to illicit measures. The technique for direct action for bringing about social changes has to be thought out and developed, and so far this point has not received its due consideration. Even if violence as a measure of applying social sanctions is not permissible, alternative means of developing and applying social pressures have to be made a part of the technique of social change; and, as stated above, sarvodaya not only permits but also prescribes the development of this technique, for civil resistance to evil—including the evil of the use of organized power for the maintainance of the status-quo—is a cardinal doctrine of sarvodaya.

It has been stated above that a sarvodayist believes that socialism and communism have both to be merged in sarvodaya if they have to fulfil themselves. "Socialism and communism are," in the words of Vinoba Bhave, "reaction to Laissez-faire capitalism,—correctives to individualism and uncontrolled pursuit of profit motives, while sarvodaya is a complete philosophy and a way of life. It is not a re-action."[13] Practical bearing of this view is that sarvodaya is seeking a new unity—endeavours to establish harmony, and socialism and communism endeavour to redress wrongs and as a reaction have no inner integrity or force of their own and therefore cannot be a basis of a new social order. This is a profound mistake for socialism and communism are not merely negations and anti-thesis but are meant to be a real synthesis—a philosophy and a way of life. Vinoba has expressed two views on communism. One is that "it is with Gandhism with which communism will have real trial of strength" and "the fact of the matter is that these two ideologies are irreconcilable, differences between the two are fundamental" and "it is as clear as day that they are deadly opposed to each other."[14] "Capitalism under the mask of democracy led by U.S.A. has," according to Vinoba, "lost all vitality —though it might appear doughty on the strength of its military force"[15] and that is the reason why sarvodaya and communism are real rival ideologies and the contest between the

13. *Bhoodan*, August 21, 1957, p. 7.
14. *Introduction to Gandhi and Marx*, Mashruwala, pp. 16 and 17.
15. *Ibid.*, p. 15.

two is inevitable and will be settled by the course of events.
This view is likely to be widely endorsed in India and make it
difficult to find an area of agreement between the two ideologies. Vinoba expressed this view in November 1950, but seven
years later he spoke of sarvodaya and communism coming
close to each other and there being no permanent conflict between the two ideologies. "Two points at the end of a circle
are close to each other. The point at which the circle ends is
also the beginning of a circle. That which is the farthest is also
the nearest."[16] This point cannot be further examined here, but
it does indicate the possibility of a deadly contest between the
two approaches being avoided if not by the logic of thought,
at least by the logic of facts, and both being able to contribute
to a widening circle of common action because to quote
Vinoba again, "both regard the well being of the poor and the
oppressed with the intensity of loving regard of the mother."[17]
This is a very real bond and may become the basis of understanding and amity in action. Vinoba once attributed to the
communists the view that "there will be first rivers of blood,
then rivers of milk and then will follow those of fresh and
cool water flowing by each happy home assuaging the thirst of
all mankind".[18] The events, among them the impact of the
threat of total destruction of mankind owing to the nuclear
warfare, have brought home to the communists the paramount
need for peaceful co-existence, and it is clear that rivers of
blood cannot be a prelude to the flowing of fresh and cool
waters by each happy home. In fact therein lies the possibility
of at least avoiding mortal conflicts between social revolutionaries of different pursuations even on a wider scale, but in
India even more than elsewhere, the need for not only avoidance of conflict but of real concert between all "who regard the
well-being of the poor and the oppressed with the intensity of
loving regard of the mother" is a social imperative dictated by

16. *Sarvodaya,* May 1957.
17. *Ibid.,* p. 29.
18. *Ibid.,* p. 19.

the dire want and misery of our masses. "A society without vision is a decadent society. Vision gives vitality and strength and inspires a people to noble adventure—no society can survive or hold its head unless its members have a sense of purpose—in a poor country like India it is obvious that we need higher production urgently. Higher production would be a bye-product of national purpose. We need all-embracing national objectives. National purpose must mean a renewal and re-awakening of the spirit of man. We need the life-giving breath of Purpose."[19] This is a view which all sarvodayists, socialists and communists can and should fervently accept and act upon with the utmost sincerity and if they do, awakening of the spirit of man, which is so urgently needed but has as yet not been brought about, can give us a life-giving breath which would make much higher production not only inevitable but also profoundly beneficial. Prospects of a socialist society very largely depend upon this concert in action, and it may be in Vinoba's view that which is the farthest is also the nearest there is an element of real truth and can be turned to a good account from practical standpoint.

19. Vinoba Bhave, "Need of a Vision", *Bhoodan*, February 20, 1957, p. 1.

Chapter Two

SOCIAL HORIZONS II

DEMOCRATIC SOCIALISM

The trends of socialist thought and action referred to in the last chapter are closely, in some ways, indistinguishably related to democratic socialism—the approach which by historical association is specially espoused by the socialist parties in India.[1] These parties are anti-communist in their ideology and programme and as such stand for democratic socialism as distinguished from totalitarian communism. They are, however,

---

1. There are at present two political parties which are known to be identified with this approach, i.e. the Praja Socialist Party and the party which revolted against it, commonly known as Dr. Lohia's Socialist Party. Organized action to give a definite form to this approach was taken in 1934 by what is known as the Nasik group—a group of socially sensitive and earnest young men who having been drawn into the struggle of national freedom realized that this struggle has, though necessarily the prime concern of all political action in India, had to be given a social content which, after the attainment of independence, had to be made the basis of social revolution leading to an entirely different and, of course, far better social order. Since 1934 this group—really party—functioned within the Indian National Congress as it did not want to weaken the struggle for national independence and called itself the Congress Socialist Party. After independence it constituted itself into an independent party as it lost faith in the ability of the Congress to become an instrument and architect of social revolution and changed itself into the Socialist Party of India. Four years later it and the dissident party led by Acharya J. B. Kripalani—the Praja Mazdoor Party—were merged into Praja Socialist Party. In 1955 Dr Lohia revolted against it and formed the Socialist Party. There are a number of other minor parties which are also professedly working for democratic socialism, but, besides the Indian National Congress, which also avows faith in the same goal, the P.S.P. and S.P. are the two parties of any significance in theory and practice to advocate democratic socialism. They have gone through a process of fission and fusion, which can, given the necessary understanding, lead to beneficial results. The recent merger of these parties has created a new situation referred to later in this chapter.

owing to the impress of the different phases of their growth, an amalgam of Marxism, western socialism and Gandhism, and have, therefore, not been able to develop any clearly marked creed or theory of their own. Though some of their foremost theoreticians, like Ashoka Mehta and Ram Manohar Lohia, besides having a record of great devotion to the socialist ideal and selfless service, have in their writings and speeches, given unmistakable indication of insight into the essentials of social-ism, it is, however, a fact that "there are no straight issues of principles," in words of Guy Wint, a democratic socialist him-self, "on which the socialists occupy a clearly recognizable place".[2] Guy Wint also expresses astonishment at the lack of original thought among the Indian socialists[3] and though the judgement is somewhat harsh, it is undeniably true that socialist thinking in the country has not been an organic pro-cess, its premises have neither been clearly stated nor worked out with due care and thought and it has produced hardly any impact on the development of ideas or the course of events. Limitations of organization partly account for this state of things but inadequacy of thought process has been a much more important factor in producing this result.[4] A quarter of

2. Guy Wint, "What Hope for Asian Socialism", *Socialist Commentary*. September 1959, p. 32.

3. *Ibid.*, p. 33.

4. The leaders of Indian socialist parties have been greatly handicapped in this respect owing to practically having received no assistance from social scientists in the development of socialist theory in the country. Very few economists or sociologists in the country have ever given earnest thought to social issues which study of socialist problems raises, and there have been hardly any social scientists in India who have developed socialist convic-tions. Leaders of the socialist parties have been active politicians who have had to work against great odds. They were certainly entitled to a full mea-sure of assistance from the social scientists who had time, opportunities and resources to do earnest thinking on the problems of socialism. This assistance, as stated above, they have not received and the failure of socia-list thought is more a failure of social scientists than of active socialist lea-ders. As an economist, who has been a convinced socialist for at least thirty years, I have to plead guilty to the charge, which can well be levelled against economists with social convictions of having contributed

a century of socialist movement in the country leaves us without any tradition of earnest socialist thinking, much less of a body of ideas related to the problems of developing a socialist society in India, and the result is that—confronted as we are with the urgent need of not only propagating socialism, but building up a socialist economy—our thinking has mostly to be borrowed from the fund of ideas from other countries which have only an indirect bearing on the future of socialism in this country.

Taking these facts for granted we have all the same to make an attempt to examine the position of democratic socialism in India, representing as it does a point of view which is very widely accepted and is often tacitly assumed to be India's road to socialism. The first point which needs to be considered is the relation of democracy to socialism. In this point are implicit (a) the relation of parliamentary democracy to socialism and (b) freedom of the individual and respect for personality and its unhampered growth. In India parliamentary democracy has become a part of our history since the very start of the national movement in the country, and broadening from precedent to precedent, we have, after independence, become the biggest parliamentary democracy in the world. We have held three elections with adult suffrage and they have, by common consent, been free and fair. Parliamentary system with government responsible to legislature both at the centre and in the states and the procedure of other parliamentary democracies have been adopted with hardly any significant modifications and civil liberties, with occasional serious lapses, have been granted and preserved. These are distinct social gains and we are disposed to maintain that without parliamentary demo-

---

very little, if anything, to the development of authentic socialist thought in India. The number of social scientists with such convictions has been and is small, and from the present indications it appears that the number is not likely to grow in the near future. Most of the economists, with some notable exceptions, are concerned more with social statics rather than social dynamics and are, in most cases, involved in arid academic abstractions.

cracy or rather at the cost of the latter, it would not be desirable to realize socialism or rather that socialism, which involves serious departure from the political norms of parliamentary system, would not be socialism at all and therefore not
worth having. Socialism without democracy would, it is implied, be its negation as is, from this point of view, clearly
confirmed by the experience of the countries like the Soviet
Union, China and their associated countries. Apart from the
evaluation of the social and political systems of the communist
countries on which this view is based, it assumes that socialism
without parliamentary form of government would cease to be
socialism and has therefore to be discarded even as the destination of social endeavour. That this view does not take into
account the facts of the case and leaves out of account the
known serious faults and failures of parliamentary democracy
is fairly obvious. Full treatment of this aspect of the question
being ruled out for reasons of space only a few crucial points
needs to be considered. That if a perfect parliamentary democracy and perfect socialism could be combined, it would be a
real millenium goes without saying, but as millenial standards
cannot be applied, we have to take into account the parliamentary systems as they are and their prospects in discussing
their relation to socialism. Parliamentary system stands for
values which are and should be an essential part of socialism,
but if in practice these values cannot be realized, our faith in
the system has to be tempered by a vivid understanding of the
fact and a search for an alternative to parliamentary system
has to be made a necessary part of the faith.

Jai Prakash Narain who has been a fervent advocate of
democratic socialism[5] has lately developed a very critical atti-

5. Now after his full conversion to the Gandhian faith he holds that
"if the world were ever to reach the port of peace, freedom and brotherhood,
socialism must eventually merge into sarvodaya" (J. P. Narain, *Towards a
New Society*, p. 1). This change in the thinking is significant and has led
to his putting faith in small communities and partyless democracy but does
not really change his basic position or indicate a clearer comprehension of

tude towards parliamentary democracy. "Experience has
shown," to quote from his latest book, "that the present day
mass elections manipulated by powerful, centrally controlled
parties, with the aid of high finance and diabolically clever
methods and super-media of communications, represent far less
the electorate than the forces and interests behind the parties
and propaganda machines."[6] This almost amounts to stating
the view that powerful interests exploit elections and therefore
representative institutions for the promotion and realization of
their class ends, and this is the besetting sin of parliamentary
system which distorts and defeats the essential purpose of
democracy. This view, essentially speaking, is not different
from the Marxist view that "capitalism transforms democracy
into an illusion".[7] But it also implies that capitalism and democracy can co-exist, to use John Stratchey's words, "in a state of
antagonistic balance" and "pull in opposite direction".[8] This
co-existence in tensions in a country like India means that
"this young, vulnerable and experimental method of government" (parliamentary system), to cite from John Stratchey, is
in serious risk of being destroyed due to the encroachments of
"forces and interests behind parties and propaganda machines",
and is, in fact, being increasingly subjected to pressure through
encroachment. Jai Prakash Narain in his criticism of parliamentary democracy refers to other grave defects—among them
democracy merely as a device for catching votes, the rule of
small caucuses of politicians who exercise power in the name
of the people, heavy and for most persons prohibitive expenditure on elections, etc.—and points to the real danger of the
representative institutions being completely discredited and
replaced by dictatorships of the kind which have been estab-

the relation of democracy and socialism in the context of the world as a
whole or the extremely difficult and complex situation in this country. It,
however, does raise certain fundamental issues which need to be seriously
considered.

6. J. P. Narain, A Plea for Reconstruction of Indian Polity.
7. Lenin's Works, Volume 23, p. 13.
8. John Stratchey, Contemporary Capitalism, p. 253.

lished in so many countries of Asia and Africa. The values of democracy and socialism are cognate values—they are, as aspirations and purposes of living, rooted in the same basic human needs and draw their sustenance and strength from the same sources. That is the reason why the view, that democracy without socialism has no social context and socialism without democracy is devoid of intrinsic value, receives assent from all points of view though with varying intents.

SOCIALISM AND PARLIAMENTARY DEMOCRACY

Future of parliamentary democracy in India is far from assured. Democratic socialism, if it is taken to mean that without parliamentary democracy it cannot be realized, would in newly independent countries of Asia and Africa have a very uncertain future, for it is almost certain that in most of these countries model western democracies cannot yet be established; and unless the masses are made makers of history and have a decisive role in shaping their future, these countries cannot even maintain their independence, not to speak of solving their economic and political problems. But how this is to be done, what their constitutional framework will be and how the prime movers will be brought into action are questions to which no ready made answers are available. That does not mean that parliamentary democracy, in a country like India in which it is functioning, can or should be lightly discarded or the advantage which it undoubtedly offers should not evoke our organized action to defend it against encroachments or serious abuses. Despotism is not only an unmixed evil which has to be resisted, but willing consent and genuine co-operation have to be made the basis of both democracy and socialism and they have to be the prime concern of any institutional framework which is created for operating them. It is not at all easy to suggest an alternative to parliamentary system as a vehicle of general will, but an electorate consisting of aggregate of voters has been well compared to a sand-dune—a heap of atomized particles of sand —on which nothing can be built and which itself cannot func-

tion as an organ of the corporate life of the people.9 This is
true, and for development and operation of the creative life of
the people in an entirely new social context new organic process have to be brought into play and the masses—the people—
have to express their needs, urges and common efforts through
them and in an effective manner. That means that good of the
people has to be made paramount and they have to realize it
themselves. This is the essence of both democracy and socialism
and therefore of democractic socialism in the real sense. Parliamentary system is one way of realizing this object and its
experience is of great value; but its experience has also shown
that it can neither tame power nor ensure that it will be used
for common good. Exploratory and experimental process or
finding an alternative to it in India and elsewhere has to be
started and earnestly pursued; and though vistas, which can
be followed in this quest, are neither wide nor clear, the least
that we can do is to be aware of the fact that norms of parliamentary system as a working proposition cannot and should
not be taken as the limiting factors in what has to be a great
social adventure. "Temper required to make a success in this

9. Three constructive proposals have been made by Jai Prakash Narain to
replace the existing parliamentary system; political and economic decentralization of functions and powers to small communities, a system of indirect
elections and partyless democracy. These suggestions have been made by
others but are open to serious criticism. Decentralization, though very
desirable, has to function within the framework of central political and
economic institutions and of agreed major social premises. Indirect elections
are being pactised in communist countries, but Jai Prakash Narain regards
them as an instrument of tyranny and not of democracy. Non-party democracy is from his point of view an antithesis of one-party state, but though
in a small Quaker meeting the rule of unanimity can be practised in the
conduct of public affairs, a country of 450 millions with all its complexities
of transition and in the context of an unstable world in a state of real
crisis, cannot be run by formulating and executing all policy decisions on
the basis of unanimity, i.e. partyless state. These three constructive proposals,
in spite of their limitations, contain ideas of seminal significance and have
to be given their due consideration. Taken together, they are, however, not
a way out of the existing perplexities in this country or in any other
country.

great undertaking has to be," in the words of Bertrand Russel, "a half-way house between scepticism and dogmatism. Truth, it holds, is neither completely attainable nor completely un-attainable; it is attainable to a certain degree and that only with difficulty."[10] It has to be attained but with clear know-ledge of the extreme difficulty of attaining it. In India in the existing context of the fear of increasing political disintegration, unedifying struggle for power at all levels, falling political morals and non-existence of any centres from which counter-vailing processes can start, it is *real-politik* to know that in the house of democracy and socialism—the house which has to be built—there must be many mansions, and if we have to build that house, we have to transcend the parliamentary system and not be inhibited by it.[11]

10. Bertrand Russel, *Power—A New Social Analyses*, p. 313.

11. John Stratchey, who developed a fervent faith in political democracy before his death wrote, "The forms of democracy are various. It may be that one or two forms, which have so far been evolved in the West are by no means the last word. No one is in a position to say that one form is inherently better than any other" (*The Challenge to Democracy*, John Stratchey, p. 41). The truth of the matter is that one or two forms evolved in the West are not only not the last word but need to be radically reformed even in the countries in which they are taken to be successful. It is not necessary to recite all the known defects and shortcomings of these forms to state that they cannot, even in these countries, in their purest forms, meet the needs of today and tomorrow and radical changes in them will have to be made if they are not to create insurmountable difficulties in realizing the social objectives which, in one way or the other, have to be realized everywhere. It must be stated that, in spite of the considerable thought that has been given to the subject, no sure cures have been suggested for the evils of these "one or two forms". But the search has to continue, otherwise political processes will create deadlocks and, worse, political adventurism will have a free run. France, one of the oldest democracies, is a clear warning against putting undue faith in these forms. No one can say that Gaulism, though a short term answer for France, is the way out for France or any other country.

But the main point is that as long as consent is the basis of government, civic liberties are maintained and individuals are free to work their way up and live their own life, any institutional forms can express the purpose of democracy and serve its needs. Soviet democracy, as it was originally conceived by Lenin—democracy of representatives of factories, occupational

PERSONALITY AND FREEDOM

The other cardinal features of socialism from the democratic standpoint, i.e. respect for personality and individual freedom derives its basic importance from its philosophy and more so from the criticism of the communist states in which individual freedom and personality are, from this point of view, sacrificed

groups, agricultural and other co-operatives, etc.—was never given a fair trial and has not been revived. If the theory of the political system in communist countries in which the workers, peasants, etc. are taken to participate in the management of their productive units, can correspond to reality, participating democracy becomes a fact, the apparatus of repression completely dismantled and atmosphere of fear dispelled, this political system can become a real democracy even if it is completely unlike the "Westminister model" or any other model; and the fact that there is only "one party" in these countries need not—will not—make democracy an illusion or a deceptive fraud. The fact that property is no longer a power in these countries, equality of opportunities exist in a fair measure and social security has been almost fully provided would make democracy in these countries a model in itself and a very enriching political experience. "One Party" in that case would be, what it was meant to be, an organization of devoted, dedicated, selfless and enlightened workers with a very high level of internal discipline who will be a real elite and will not have recourse to what is called commandism in any shape or form. This concept is immanent in the working of the communist parties though in practice, it need not be added, it has been very seriously distorted. But in itself it is an authentic model, and if the communist countries wake up to the fact that they have gone a long way away from the model, they can still give to their people a truly dynamic living democracy and perhaps find in the Yugoslavian experience some very worthwhile lessons.

Taming of political power and using it only for public good is a problem which has still to be solved and any dogmatic insistence on particular practice or procedures only shows a lack of real understanding of the essentials of the problem. The fact that the Western system has already suffered an eclipse in a large number of independent countries should have a chastening effect on all democratic dogmatists and enable them to see the goodness that there is in "one party" African states, and the role of military dictators like Nasser, Ne Win in developing socialist societies from the standpoint of both democracy and socialism. With more than eighty independent states, which are muddling their way through to political stability and a new social order in spite of many evil legacies of the past, we should know that it is truly a miracle that all this is happening on a world scale and not make a fetish of parliamentary democracy as a necessary attribute of a socialist society.

at the alter of the state and the image of idyllic future. Socialism, with democracy as its substance, has to make man the
measure—the be-all and end-all of all social processes and social
change. That for historical and other reasons civil liberties have
been denied, coercive processes have been widely used and an
atmosphere of fear has been created in the communist countries
which has had a very repressive effect in the realm of mind and
spirit should not be denied—not after the "secret" speech of
Mr. Khrushchov at the 20th Congress of the Communist Party
of the Soviet Union, and national revolts in East Germany,
Poland and Hungary and recent manifestations of uneasy equilibrium in Rumania-Soviet relations. This makes it all the more
imperative that this history should not be recapitulated in the
national experiences of the countries which have still to travel
on the road to socialism, and it is essential that in India and
elsewhere this lesson should be made a guide to thought and
action. This is what all countries have to do to repay the debt
which the world owes to the socialist pioneers who, with faith
and daring, incurred all the hazards of going into the unknown
territories and uncharted seas, opened new vistas of hope and
achievement and in the process performed great deeds and also
committed equally great errors. "No political philosophy or any
scheme of social reconstruction can," in the words of Mr. M. N.
Roy, "have more than a very lmited significance if it dismisses
the concept of individual freedom as an empty abstraction."[12]
This affirmation by Mr. Roy is very relevent owing to his life-
long devotion to and work for the Marxian faith, and has a
special meaning on that account. That freedom matters and
human personality has to be cherished in order that man may
rise to the highest stature and unfold his possibilities and
develop the image of all that he aspires for has to be taken as a
cardinal tenet of socialism and made the basis of philosophy,
social vision, policy, programme, practice and day-to-day struggle for the future against inertia and resistance of the existing

12. M. N. Roy, *Reason, Romanticism and Revolution*, p. 291.

order. This is a point of profound importance and has to be given its due place in the aspirations and expectations of socialists in India and other countries which want to realize socialism.

This, however, does not contradict or negate the view that without society freedom has no meaning for man and he can realize and maintain it only if society so functions and is so organized as to provide a proper habitat for the growth of personality, and man learns the lesson that in order to fulfil life one has to lose it. That wide-spread hunger, economic servitude, exploitation of the many by the few and concentration of power and privilege are inimical to freedom and personality and even political freedom under these conditions loses its beneficent character, i.e. it is freedom in form but not in reality, is a view whose validity can hardly be questioned, and it is in fact very widely accepted. Removal of barriers to future opportunities for rising in the economic and social scale and a sense of fellowship, i.e. equality in social relations and vocational choice and advancement is, it is unnecessary to add, essential for individual freedom and growth of personality, and at present both are circumscribed and impoverished by all the disabilities and disadvantages under which most of the people have to live and work. Individual freedom is not an empty abstraction. It is a value of the highest importance and has, even after public ownership of the means of production, distribution and exchange—in some respects really because of it[13]—to be preserved and safeguarded; and in communist countries this need has to be emphasized and specifically provided for. It has also to be appreciated that by social security, health services and education without any social barriers, in which special provision has been

13. Combination of the monopoly of economic and political power, which occurs under public ownership of the means of production makes it specially imperative to provide built-in safeguards against abuse of the power. This can be done not only by jealously preserving "socialist legality" by preventing encroachment of the process of law, but also in the very concept and working of the mechanism of economic life.

made in the working of the economics of the communist countries, the scope for personality has been enlarged and placed on
a firm basis in these countries though full benefit of these
measures have still to manifest themselves, and in time they
will. In India and other countries, for whom socialism is still
a hope of the future, this issue should really not divide the
socialist parties. Freedom of thought, expression and association
has to be insured but a positive action to express individual
uniqueness in life, work and human relations and evoke the
best in man has to be taken, and socialist society has to be
charged with sentiment in favour of this view. Polemics apart,
the position is incontrovertible, and what is needed is that
growth of socialist society should be guided by keeping this
supreme object in view in the period of transition and thereafter.
Industrialization, modern technology and impact of world forces
all make community building in true sense a very uphill task
and call for the exercise of the highest creative powers. In
theory not only there is no contradiction between socialism and
deep social concern for the growth of personality, but without
the one, the other cannot be realized. In practice in a caste-
ridden country like India, in which most alarming economic
inequalities, class differences and social discriminations are
greatly intensified by allegiance to the hoary institution of
caste, dissolution of the existing barriers to the development of
freedom and personality rather than fear of their eclipse in a
highly centralized socialist society has to be our most powerful
incentive to earnest thinking and concerted action. In raising
controversies about this issue we are raising alarms which have
no relation to the existing facts and needs.

CLASS STRUGGLE

Socialist parties in India have, as Ashoka Mehta put it, "been
growing in reverse".[14] "The return of the rebel (Jai Prakash
Narain) after a prolonged tour of Communism, Marxism,

14. Ashoka Mehta, *Studies in Asian Socialism*, p. 96.

Democratic Socialism to the Utopianism of Gandhi," in the words of Ashoka Mehta, "symbolizes the transfiguring response from the individuals of Asia."[15] Jai Prakash Narain does symbolize in his person the trend which is significant and is, as indicated later, in keeping with the trends which are operating among the democratic socialists in the countries of Europe and elsewhere. This trend really amounts to retreat from Marxism and attenuation, if not abandonment, of one of its central doctrines—belief in class struggle as a motive force in human history and animating factor in dynamic social strategy. In the thinking of the Praja Socialist Party itself and in its public statements somewhat ambivalent attitude was being adopted in this regard and it is not clear that class struggle was a completely disowned social approach. But indications are clear that not only in the social thought of the Congress and Sarvodayist the class approach is being countered but Jai Prakash Narain in himself symbolizes a trend which is in the ascendant in the thinking of the socialist parties.[16] This point is of cardinal

15. *Ibid.*, p. 97.
16. The Congress Socialist Party was, when it was founded, a Marxist Party and the party members were exhorted "to fully understand the technique of revolution, theory and practice of class struggle, the nature of the state and processes leading to the socialist society". The party adhered to this approach. The tendency to live down Marxism started early and has been in operation all these years. Jai Prakash Narain made final break with Marxism during the three weeks' fast in Poona in 1954; but though under pressure it continued to be an important element in the official creed of the Party and in the policy statement of 1955 it was clearly stated that the Indian socialists still regarded "class struggle as inevitable in social revolution and never suffered from the delusion that moral appeals for justice will be so responded to by dominant classes that they would voluntarily agree to the liquidation of domination and exploitation" (Policy Statement adopted at the National Conference of the Praja Socialist Party held at Gaya in December 1955). This statement contained severe criticism of the policies of the Communist Party; it also contained Marxian concepts and analysed the national and international situation in terms of these concepts and stressed the basic importance of class sruggle in social revolution.
Since then formally the position remains unchanged, but the process of living down Marxism has gone on. Dr. Saul Rose of the Cambridge University, author of *Socialism in South East Asia*, has summed up the position

importance and needs to be clarified. The main point of this trend is that the class approach to the problems of social change is essentially an exclusive, discriminatory and antagonistic approach, it inflames class differences even when it does not create them and is based upon what is, from this point of view, a false assumption that co-operation between the upper and the lower classes—the exploiters and the exploited—has to be ruled out as a completely unattainable object. This approach, according to this line of criticism on its own underlying assumptions, is incompatible with the peaceful and democratic processes of social change. It lacks faith in human nature and believes in the futility of bringing about fundamental social transformation by appeal to goodness in the minds of men in dominant position, i.e. the class in power. The class approach is, it is further inferred, based upon hatred and has in it the seeds of violence which, as the history of the communist countries clearly shows, leads to resort to force not only before the capture of power but also after it—continued reliance upon it as an instrument of policy—and therefore the commission of all the acts of massive

in Asia in the following words: "It means decline and not just a temporary setback. The internal developments in these parties point to the same conclusion. At the end of the war they were broadly Marxist. Since then there has been a general trend away from Marxism in several directions.... The ideological ferment has caused the parties to crack and splinter. The consequence is that they are not only weaker in their organization but also less clear in their ideology than they were at the time of the Rangoon Conference", i.e. in 1958 (Saul Rose, "Socialist in Asia", Socialist Commentary, April 1959, p. 8).

According to Dr. Ram Manohar Lohia, the role has to be supplemented by recurrent awakening through invited suffering of civil resistance and "civil resistance and class struggle are but two names of the same exercise of power reduction of the evil and increase in the power of good" (Socialist Party Statement of Principles and Programme, 1956, p. 16). This is an attempted synthesis of Gandhism and Marxism but is really lacking in clarity and internal consistency.

The president of the United Party (Samyukt Socialist Party) has in his speech (delivered at Ramgarh at the National Conference on 17 May 1964) reaffirmed with some force his faith in class struggle as a moving force of history, but it is not certain how far the new party will make it a cardinal doctrine of its faith.

violence and callousness to pain, suffering and inhumanity which have been inflicted on a colossal scale in the communist countries. This is, according to this view, not the way of love and faith in all men—the way of Gandhi, the way of demo-cracy, the way of government and social change by discussion and pursuasion, the way of faith in fellowmen and their capa-city to respond to the call of compassion and self denial. History, it is admitted, records oppression of the many by the few and the use of violence in an acute form when the power of the few is challenged and threatened, but love, it is urged, is deeply implanted in the hearts of men, has been always a great sustain-ing and transforming force and can, if the power is rightly understood and utilized, enable men to transcend the limitations of historical experience and rise to ever greater heights of brotherhood as the fundamental fact of life and its upward self-fulfilment.

REACTION AGAINST CLASS CONCEPT

The reaction against the class approach has a philosophical—shall we say spiritual—basis, but its practical importance in India and other countries has been largely determined by the fruits of its application in practice in the communist countries and is now being used by the advocates of status quo or gradual-ism for resisting or undermining the revolutionary processes. The more ardent believers of the non-class point of view are aware of this fact and do not want that the forces of social change should be slowed down—much less thwarted—by abjur-ing class struggle as a driving force of revolution. They want in social revolution fundamental changes in social structure and relations, patterns of behaviour and social norms and know that time is the essence of the matter, i.e. the change must not be delayed, otherwise the consequnces will be catastrophic. This is true not so much of the socialists within the Congress or the socialist parties, but it is true of Vinoba and his foremost co-workers. The whole concept of class struggle conveys the risk of civil war, of setting different social strata against one another, of subversion by force of the existing order. If this happens, it will mean not only social strife but disruption of the existing order without any certainty of its being replaced by another and better order within a reasonable time. This is a grave risk for a country like India to take, for our national unity is still a fragile product and the forces which can bring order out of chaos if subversion means the end of all order, as it well may, are nowhere in sight, and there is every likelihood of chaos being mastered, if it can be mastered at all, by the forces of darkness. From the socialist standpoint this will put an end to both democracy and socialism and start a twilight period of indefinite duration in which these values and objectives would practically wither away. Class struggle, if it involves social strife on any considerable scale, in the context of existing conditions of India, would be so very risky as to make it highly undesirable to plan or carry out social strategy of change in these terms. From the practical standpoint these reasons are far more conclusive against making class struggle the motor of social change than the other reasons based upon high spiritual values referred to above.

This, however, does not settle the issue. Class struggle in the Marxian and socialist literature has not been understood to mean creation of social antagonisms, but understanding of their place in history and the working of economies as they are operating at present. In the Western democracies, owing to the high level of economic development and counter-vailing political and social pressures, class differences are not as sharp as they were; but even there class feeling is still strong and effective and has to be reckoned with in the working of the economies. In the rest of the world, social contradictions due to the class differences, are very clearly marked and their impact on policies and economies is not only unmistakable but also far-reaching. In India caste differences further accentuate and complicate class differences and make them a factor of great importance in our economic and political systems. These differences exist and are of real consequence. They generate antagonisms which plague our entire social and political life, express themselves clearly in the elections, choice of candidates, exercise of voting rights, making of cabinets and the response which they evoke to the various public measures and policies. These social antagonisms are there as integral part of our social structure, as of the social structures of other countries and are a, if not the, major motive force of events. The history of human society may or may not be the history of class struggle, as has been posited by Marx and Marxians since 1848, but the view is certainly, as Jawaharlal Nehru has stated, a profound social discovery and enables us to see "orderly process of history", to use the words of the Communist Manifesto, "in the seeming labyrinth and chaos". Capitalism in its early stages simplified these class antagonisms and accentuated them, but now in the countries in which political democracy is operating, they have become less sharp and class distinctions have to a certain extent been blurred. They, however, still matter and create, as John Stratchey has said, tendencies which need to be consciously counteracted. In India the caste and class factors have both to be taken into account and though they are interrelated, they are distinct up to a point and their combined working has to be objectively examined and assessed in social analysis and social strategy. The main point is that social stratification and the stresses inherent in it are an essential part of the existing situation and "an objective analysis of the situation of every class in modern society as well as the conditions of development of every class"[17] has to be a cardinal element in the theory and practice of our social engineering.

The basic point of practical importance, however, is that these stresses have to be intelligently understood and as far as possible mitigated. In India parliamentary system is at work, civil liberties are recognized and largely respected in practice and socialism is in the air, if not as yet a decisive force. It is necessary to know the advantages of the position and avoid the inflamation of antagonisms and the creation of an atmosphere of social strife.

17. Lenin, *The Teachings of Karl Marx*, p. 68.

The class differences have to be converted into democratic pro-cess to build up peoples' power and organizations and recourse to force has to be avoided to the utmost. Organizing the pea-sants, the workers, the lower middle classes who are fast being reduced to the position of white-collared proletariat and the intelligentsia is absolutely essential to support parliamentary processes and create the necessary driving power—social steam for revolutionary purposes. The risk of these processes being converted into acute social conflicts is there, but if we are vividly aware of the risk and people in power sincerely help and not impede these democratic processes being put into motion, this risk can largely, if not completely, be provided against. These peoples' organizations, at all levels, but particularly at the basic level, are, it is generally admitted, urgently needed in India to make democracy a reality and decentralization, political and economic, which is being given such high priority at present would, without them (the peoples' organizations) have no meaning and create oligarchies and not decentralized democratic units for the discharge of essential political and economic func-tions. This logic of the position can be accepted and acted upon even by those for whom class approach creates insurmountable ideological barriers, and initiating and strengthening of basic democratic social processes can be taken as an urgent necessity and a common undertaking of all earnest socialists and made the basis of broad-based unity in action so long as allegiance to class principles is used as a constructive factor in social strategy and not for promoting social strife. Class struggle in democratic context has been a central doctrine of the socialist creeds in all European countries for three quarters of a century, and its abandonment is not justified even in these countries after making due allowance for the developments which have taken place in capitalism since 1930. In countries like India where capitalism is more raw and ruthless, exploitation in rural areas is widespread and unabashed and the workers and the peasants —peasants even more than the workers—are in no position to defend themselves or use their organized strength for promoting socialist objectives, understanding of the necessity of building up social pressures by bringing the masses into action in support of socialist policies at all stages is all the more imperative and inescapable. Democracy in these countries has to be the core of socialism, but it has to be understood in comprehensive terms and has to be the operative principle of the whole social system in all its aspects. Parliamentary institutions not only do not exhaust the content of democracy, but their own validity depends upon the extent to which the whole society is shot through and through with an increasing social purpose derived from socialism as its very life breath.

MEANS AND ENDS

Relation of means to ends has also been given a preeminent place in discussion of socialism in recent years by the Congress, the socialist parties and of course the Sarvodayists. This has happened because communism, the communist parties and the communist countries are charged with having used what are called impure means for good ends. An order based on equality, freedom and fellowship cannot, it is earnestly affirmed, be built by violence, deceit and hatred, implication, of course, being that the communist countries and the communist parties have, in fact, largely relied upon these means for achieving their policies and programmes. That this charge is not baseless is a matter of common knowledge, but it is unfair to hold them (the communists) only responsible for the actual course of events, as, from their point of view, most of the measures they have had to adopt were forced upon them by wanton acts of terrorism by powerful reactionary forces in retreat and the need for self-defence and survival. That this does not explain fully all that has happened—particularly within the communist countries— is also borne out by the facts which have now been admitted by the communists themselves. Violation of what the communists call socialist morality is known to have occurred on a scale which extenuating circumstances of encirclement and counter-revolution cannot account for or justify. It is, however,

wrong to discuss the issue of the relations of means and ends
on the basis of the evaluation of the history of communist
parties and communist countries. This history of the valiant
struggle, heroic resistance against overwhelming odds, and positive achievements in the domain of economic development, pursuit of knowledge and social organization and growth of a new
social order with some very significant features is not a history
merely of violence, untruth and hatred. It is also the history of
a great social adventure whose results have, from unbiased
standpoint, been exhilarating in spite of all that can be rightly
set on their debit side. In our world of today no country can
afford to throw stones from its glass house—certainly not the
powerful countries of "the free world" whose cold-war strategy
has brought untold misery and suffering to millions and what
is much more important, serious retardation of the economic
and social development in so many "undeveloped" countries. It
is really not right, to repeat, to turn the whole issue of means
and ends on the moral judgement of the record of the communist countries and the communist parties or make it the
background of our thought and views on this fundamental
point.

RELATIVITY IN ETHICS

    This issue has to be considered more from the empirical rather
than philosophical standpoint. It is essentially speaking a spiritual issue and premises a certain conception of man, his nature
and destiny and a philosophy of history; and its more fundamental aspect is the problem of good and evil—rather the use
of evil means. In the widest consideration of the problem these
points have to be taken into account. Apart from the obvious
limits of space, it is not necessary in this short assessment of
this existing situation from the standpoint of socialism in India
and its prospects, to get involved in a discussion of points on
which conflicting views have been held throughout history and
there is no possibility of achieving any general agreement of
views. From practical standpoint, there is one point, however,

which is fundamental but is nevertheless relevant and has to be briefly considered; and that is as to whether in substance socialism is an ethical proposition and whether the ethical standards are relative, i.e. are related to time and circumstances. The latter point may first be considered. Its special relevance to this point arises from the fact that the Marxists speak of revolutionary ethics and its code, and many decisions and policies adopted by the communist countries, which have evoked wide disapproval, have been vindicated by them on the plea that revolutionary ethics has its own criteria and norms. As specific cases cannot be possibly considered here, it is necessary to confine attention to the general aspects of this question. Abuse of this approach has had and cannot but have appalling consequences. The worst crimes in history have been committed in the name of god, religion and the pursuit of spiritual salvation, and merely the fact that revolutionary ethics has been pressed into service in some cases by the communists to make out a case for what to many appears indefensible acts of inhumanity in the name of dialectic unity of the opposites does not settle the issue. There are in a sense eternal verities, but social ethics has always been changing and its relativity has, from practical standpoint, had to be assumed for passing moral judgement on individuals, communities and situations. A code of ethics which will hold good for all times and countries cannot exist; and in a revolution, when not only economic relations but all norms of behaviour, attitudes to life and its tasks and institutions and their forms, functions and their inner meaning are all being radically changed, this relativity of ethics acquires a crucial importance and a revolution cannot possibly be judged by the values which is its avowed object to repudiate, change and replace. This does not mean that inhumanity of man to man, wanton cruelty or rape of minds become right on that account. They do not, and yet it remains true that the context in which basic policies are framed and executed is of primary importance for their evaluation and cannot possibly be left out of consideration. Mystics, social rebels and social visionaries all defy conventional codes and pave the way for their necessary revision. They have to be judged relatively and not absolutely, otherwise life will become putrid and meaningless. What is true of individuals is also true of communities and countries intent upon and involved in social revolutions. They have to be judged by different codes and the chain of events which they start or carry out also call for different standards of inter- pretations and evolution. If customs change, lest one good custom should corrupt the world, so do social morals and their codes, lest one set of morals hold man as its captive and repress his aspirations. This is a pre-eminently practical conclusion and is based upon the experience of ages.

Moral Basis of Socialism

The other point, i.e. ethical content or substance of socialism, is also of fundamental importance. It is true that the founding socialists were deeply moved by ethical motives and worked with the hope that socialism would fulfil itself as a response to ethical needs of mankind, i.e. it would mean compassion, true fellowship and inspiration to live for the community. Wrong means can do immense harm because in the period of transition ultimate objects are sacrificed for immediate gains and the whole process of social growth and its mainsprings can thereby be badly twisted. That ethical considerations have also inspired Marxism and from Marx downwards they have hoped that pre-history will end and history will begin when man will become truly free and live a rich and creative com- munity life and realize the best in him through it, i.e. he will know from direct experience that all men are members of one another and no one can live unto himself which is only another way of saying that compassion, fellowship and crea- tive community life are the consummation of man and the scheme of things and the state which they signify is the end to which we have to move. The dialectic no less than idealistic socialism points to the same destiny and the same destination. That socialism is and has to be essentially ethical needs therefore cause no divergence of views. The fact that the democratic socialists find it necessary to stress the importance of social values is due to their assessment that in fact these ultimates have been completely lost sight of by the communists and in their pre-occupation with the capture and use of power they have thrown ethical considerations to the wind and lost contact with the original source of socialism of socialist movement. This again leads to a point of evaluation of the work and achievements of the communist parties and communist countries, and it is not possible to undertake this task here. All visions have been diluted and in different degrees vitiated in the process of realizing them and communism is no exception to this general rule. Dispensations spiritual, social or political, have always suffered in this manoeuvre and have had to pay the price of being mixed with the dross of mundane reality. The crucial point is not whether ethical aspects of socialism should have high priority in thought and action, but how ethical principles should be sustained while socialism is being developed and how they should be vivified after it has been developed. The later stage has not been reached anywhere as yet and it will take a long time before it is reached. But the danger of miscarriage of ethical values while the development is taking place has to be borne in mind and the ways and means of providing against it have to be devised. One of the ways in which this can be done is that the means by which socialistic objectives are realized have as far as possible to be in keeping with their inner spirit. In all cases relative standards have to be applied in assessing the developing socialist society and perfectionism in judgement has to be avoided. The emphasis on ethics of socialism is justified, for "a new world of freedom," in the words of M. N. Roy, "will not result automatically from an economic re-organization of society. Nor would freedom necessarily follow from the capture of political power by a political party claiming to represent the oppressed and the exploited classes."[18] Here is a prominent Marxist speaking again on the basis of intimate knowledge of "economic reorganization of society" and "capture of political power" in the name of the oppressed and exploited classes. This strain of thought is also, as stated later, very much to the fore in the recent discussions of the socialists in Europe. But there is no reason why the shift in emphasis should widen the gulf between the socialists and the communists as it is undoubtedly doing at present. If perfectionism in social assessment is, as stated above, avoided, it would be all to the good if faith in the essentials of socialism is kept alive in conceiving and executing socialist policies and the art of living it in work and personal relations is cultivated with care and practised with creative skill. It is, to repeat, very difficult to prevent completely adulteration of purposes and principles in practice, but with constant vigilance the evil can be reduced to the minimum and it should be, given the necessary understanding of why it has to be done.

ANTI-COMMUNISM

Fear of communism in India is not the kind of pathological state which exists, say, in U.S.A., but its distrust and even its dread is not confined merely to conservative sections. Politically conscious persons largely share this feeling and its undercurrent is fairly strong and can, as on the occasion of overthrow of the communist ministry in Kerala, be activated for political purposes. Our friendly relations with all communist countries, with the exception of China, are a check on this mass feeling, but generally speaking the spectre of communism haunts India as it does so many other countries of the world. Our uncommitted position in international affairs is a safeguard against seeing only in black and white and blatently hostile attitude towards the communist countries is adopted by only a small fringe of our population. But as is indicated

18. *Op. Cit.*, p. 278.

in the discussion of the various issues referred to above the
prevailing attitudes are, to a considerable extent, influenced by
common evaluation of the communist approach and the record
of the communist countries and show the impact of the communist theory and practice on thinking. Owing to the balanced view of Jawaharlal Nehru socialists in the Congress are, as
a rule, restrained in their dissent and criticism, and the
Sarvodayists also generally affirm their point of view without
entering into polemics on the subject. The socialist parties are,
however, more avidly hostile; their anti-communism, to an
increasing extent, assumes a militant form and they are in the
vanguard of all anti-communist thinking and forces in our
country. This leads to their forming political alliance with
anti-socialist parties and in their minds they are active participants in coldwar ideology rather than objective analysts and
discriminating critics. These facts make them, not unoften, uncompromising in their attitude to Nehru's foreign policy, and
even when they do not adopt an outright antagonistic attitude
in their veiled opposition, it is clearly indicated that they are
not uncommitted in thought just as they are definitely not uncommitted in action, on many important occasions. They have
been the most important rallying point of anti-communism in
India and this fact is an important factor in the over-all position so far as the future of socialism in this country is concerned. They have in the past been definitely to the right even
of the socialists in the Congress party and this fact affects the
balance of forces in the country.

Anti-communism is a world phenomenon and the socialists
in European countries and even more so in the Asian, with the
exception of left socialists in Japan, have been and are growing
more set in their attitude to communism, the communist party
and communist countries. Their retreat from Marxism, disavowal of class approach and therefore any special attachment
to the working classes, increasing support of mixed economy
and adoption of an unpliant attitude towards communist countries and their political achievements and even increasing

emphasis on values are all the result of this growing anti-communism; and the socialists in India are participating in a general trend at work all over the world and are in no way acting in a singular manner or in the context of specific conditions in India. Anti-communism of the Indian socialist parties has to be taken as a part of the world situation and understood in its historical setting, the most important part of which is bitter political strife between the socialists and the communists going back to the time of Lenin which, as is well known, was further intensified between the two wars. During the war their enstrangement became deeper and wider because of the change-over of the communists from anti-war to pro-war position after Soviet Union's entry into the war. In India even before the war the strain between them owing to the socialists' feeling that they had been badly let down in their joint efforts with the communists[19] to build up unity of the left forces became very severe, but after 1942 when the socialists were in the forefront of what is known as the August revolution and the communists were passing through their "peoples' war" phase, the tension between them mounted to a new height and has since then been kept up at a level which seems to rule out the

19. From 1936 to 1940 the communists were admitted to C.S.P. and allowed to function as members and office bearers. In 1940 they were expelled from the party, for according to C.S.P. this policy of collaboration all but finished the C.S.P. (*Silver Jubilee Conference Souveneer*, p. 28). "Only gain," in the words of the Chairman of P.S.P., "the C.S.P. derived from the experience was it learnt at last what the real nature of the Communist United Front was." Mr. Purshottam Tricumdas, the General Secretary of the C.S.P. in 1940 said in his report, "we are not sorry that the experiment was made, but because of harrowing experience we had to pass through we are sorry that it has ended".

This harrowing experience, more than any other event, means that as far as the P.S.P. was concerned Left Unity has become an unmentionable subject for them. The deep scars inflicted on the C.S.P. in this experience can easily be seen when the P.S.P. members discuss communism and the communist parties. They have made "anti-communism" a fixation for them. This point needs to be clearly understood by the Indian communists when they speak of the need for building up broad-based democratic unity.

possibility of the socialists co-operating with the communists in building up a socialist society in the country. "No truck with the communists" is their accepted guiding principle in their relations with the Communist Party, and in action they have clearly shown that all matters of theory and practice not only non-cooperation but initiative in taking and developing anti-communist position has been their special role in our national affairs.

THE PRESENT OUTLOOK

After the death of Nehru and owing to other developments an entirely new situation has arisen, and now the country needs urgently the greatest unity of purpose and action among the socialists. The task of building up a socialist society is so stupendous and the forces arrayed against socialism so formidable as to give Ashoka Mehta's appeal "to weld socialists into a single force entrenched inside the Congress" an imperativeness of its own in the present context. The merger of the two sections of the socialist parties and possibly of a number of other smaller parties can also be a contribution to socialist unity if thereby they can develop a new unity in essentials and social drive. All socialists including the communists have been invited to join the Congress and make it a mighty force of social change. Is it desirable for all socialists to join hands inside the Congress and forge it into an instrument of social revolution? The Congress is already in power and even if other socialists choose to keep out of it, it is likely to remain in power for a long time to come. Either it can be changed from within or fought and overthrown from without. It seems to be the line of the least resistance to pursue the former course, i.e. to change the Congress from within since it is already committed to democracy and socialism, and there is a considerable volume of growing articulate opinion in favour of socialism inside the Congress. This course is logical and seems to be obviously desirable on certain assumptions and there should be very weighty reasons why all socialists should not join the

Congress and consolidate socialist unity inside it. At the conclusion of the next chapter, in which the present position of
the communists in India has been reviewed, this crucial point
has been examined in its different aspects.

Chapter Three

SOCIAL HORIZONS III

NEW PHASE OF WORLD COMMUNISM

The Communist Party of India (the C.P.I.) as an organized social force has been and is an important factor in shaping, developing and, in some important respects, limiting the socialist thought and movement in this country. Its importance is due to its organization, the content of its policies and programmes and its being an integral part of international communism. From its very formation its affiliation with the world communist movement has given it its impetus and inspiration. It received active assistance and guidance from organized communist parties and Comintern, their international organization, and it is, as is well known, still in close and continuous contact with the communist movement all over the world. Proletarian internationalism—i.e. solidarity, real unity—of all working class (communist) parties is an article of faith of the C.P.I. as of all other national parties. "Workers of the World Unite" was the clarion call of the Communist Manifesto in 1848 and it has evoked positive response among the communists all over the world. The vision of a new world and one world which it conjures up has meant, in theory and practice, faith in man and his destiny and fervent hope of a world without exploitation, a world of abundance for the benefit of all and a world of fellowship and therefore enduring peace. The fact that C.P.I. and all other national communist parties have exposed themselves to the charge of being subservient to the Communist Party of the Soviet Union (the C.P.S.U.) and at times disloyal to their own countries is in real sense their liability which handicaps them seriously in playing their part in their national affairs and not unoften isolates them from the peoples of their own country. This is a handicap which, as pointed out later, the C.P.I. has, in the existing context of the national and even international situation, to overcome in the interest of becoming effective for building up socialism in India and counteracting the reactionary forces which are gaining strength particularly in the last five years. This is probably also true of most other communist parties in the non-communist countries and points to the urgent need of a "revisionist" approach in the best sense of the word.

It has, however, to be realized that unquestioning allegiance of the millions of the communists all over the world, which international communism has commanded and still commands, subject of course to reservation inherent in the split in international communism owing to Sino-Soviet conflict, is due to the fact that social revolution first in the Soviet Union and later in China[1] and other communist countries has meant for them that a great social vision has come true and holds out for mankind an inspiring hope of real liberation from age-old inhumanity of man to man and new vistas of limitless achievements and realization in the domain of economic growth, mind and spirit. Neither Moscow money, even if it has been liberally dispensed, nor any other kind of illicit pressure could have evoked or sustained this allegiance on a truly massive scale. Miscarriage of the social purpose of the revolution, recourse to gruesome methods and practices in some cases not at all justified by the need for self-defence against odds or for overcoming insensate resistance of the forces which had to be overthrown and the loss of sensitive understanding or moral sensibility are known to have occurred and in some cases assumed appalling dimensions by the admission of the communists themselves.

1. The present bitter controversy over ideological and political issues caused by Chinese intransigence obviously suggests a very serious qualification to the statement of the unquestioning allegiance of the communists to international communism. That, however, does not alter the fact that revolution in China is, taken as a whole, a beneficient factor, has changed the balance of world forces and, in spite of grave errors of policy and principles, is of great importance in the growth of socialism as a world force.

The world famous "secret" speech of Khrushchev at the 20th Congress of the C.P.S.U. is the most striking illustration of this admission, but not the only one. The communists all over the world, "dizzy with success" or under the pressure of adverse forces and circumstances, are known to have committed excesses which cannot be explained, much less justified, by the array of hostile forces against them. The 1956 was a big shake-up and disillusionment for the communists in all countries, but in spite of this phase and similar phases of the world communist movements the communist parties in most countries have recovered their internal balance, retained the support and confidence of rest of their members and are steadfast in their proletarian internationalism—in the solidarity of the communist parties. The stresses that have developed between the communist parties of the Soviet Union and China indicate "need for internal adjustments" in the communist movement of the world. The paramount position, which the C.P.S.U. has occupied in the counsels of the communist parties would now necessarily have to be radically modified in favour of a real, as distinguished from formal, equality among the communist parties. From the practical standpoint, due to China's rise to strength and power, her views are to be given their due consideration and the conclusive importance of those of the Soviet Union have, on that account, to be tempered by a touch of reality.[2] Peking has, in other words, to be considered as much a centre of the communist will in the making as Moscow. But the process of evolution from the monolithic unity of the communist parties has to go further. The parties of the other communist countries like Poland and Viet Nam and even in the non-communist countries like Italy and France can and have to exercise their autonomy in a

2. The position in the last few months has taken such a serious turn that a showdown with China seems to be inevitable. It is at the same time a great misfortune from the international standpoint. Solidarity without dominance has to be the keynote of the internationl relation of the communist parties. Even if China persists in the course which she has unfortunately adopted, Soviet Union has to and cannot help changing its approach and temper it by more than a "touch of reality".

more real manner and draw upon their own authentic experience for making a contribution to the common pool of ideas and
decisions. This has to apply in varying degrees to all the communist parties of the world and they have to keep in step with
one another not by the marching orders of a sergeant in command but to the symphony of notes played by a truly international band. Consummation of this process will take time and
the speed with which that happens would be determined partly
by the continuance or relaxation of international tensions and
partly by the level of maturity attained by the national parties
and their drawing their elan as much from being rooted in the
soil of their own countries as by the genuine response to the
needs of the one world in the making and their adaptation to
the requirements of the world community. Marxism or communism must be truly international if it has to be true to
initial and essential purpose of its being. National communism,
even more than national socialism, cannot but be begotten by
the rape of the hopes and the purpose which made communism
a call and vision of the future. This even more than a united
front against the common enemy has to be its *raison d'etre* of
proletarian internationalism—of a creative unity of purpose and
action for bringing a community of the equal and the free into
being and helping it grow from within by fidelity to the future
and concerted efforts to realize it.

COMMUNIST PARTY OF INDIA

This view has an important bearing on the position and
future of the C.P.I. because like all national communist parties
it has, as stated above, been seriously handicapped by its inability to assert and exercise its autonomy in a really convincing
manner. That this is so is a conclusion to which the C.P.I., like
every national communist party, reacts with great resentment
and even rancour. The facts of the case, however, make this
conclusion inescapable. There is a historical explanation and
even justification for it. The C.P.S.U. and all other communist
parties had to operate in an extremely hostile world, the Soviet

Union had from the very beginning to face international intervention and encirclement and is still, in spite of all the strength
that she has acquired, subjected partly to the pressure of an
economic seige, and her survival and growth are vital to communism and its future. That all the communist parties realized
the need of standing together and standing by the Soviet Union
and accepting her leadership can be easily understood and
allowed for. But even, within the limitations of this position, a
larger measure of autonomy could have been exercised by the
C.P.I. and the other national parties particularly in matters of
national concern, and they would have rendered great service
to the world communist movement if they had in their international counsels warned the Soviet Union against the restrictive and repressive policies which she and under her influence
the other communist countries had been practising with such
admittedly woeful consequences. Now the whole situation is
radically different. The communist countries which form one-
third of the world are strong from military, economic, political
and social standpoint. They are forging ahead and can more
than hold their own against the pressure of the U.S.A. and the
countries which follow her lead. Political emancipation of
Asian, African and now even Latin American countries is, it
is now fully realized, another favourable factor from the point
of view of the balance of world forces and has rendered it impossible for the West to maintain the attitude of supremacy
in international affairs. All this is common knowledge and is
posited with great clarity particularly in the joint statements
of the communist parties and countries. Unity of the communist
countries and parties does not cease to be important on this
account, but it has to have a different content and its operational technique has to be radically changed. The C.P.I., it
follows, has to attain and practise a higher degree of autonomy
in evolving and implementing its national policy and programme, and even its ideological approach has to be greatly
modified to suit the unique features of the Indian situation.
Revisionism is a dirty word in the communist parlance and

the way the socialist parties of the West and even of Asia are doing their "rethinking" and making it an instrument of a more sharply defined anti-communism shows a trend which cannot but intensify conflict and tension. This fact darkens the outlook for Left unity and makes the rapproachment between the communist and socialist parties even a more remote possibility. It does not, however, affect the vital point that re-orientation of thinking, policy and programme for the C.P.I. is urgently needed if it has to contribute to the consolidation of progressive forces, arrest the growing strength of reactionary elements and create conditions under which socialism can have a wide mass appeal and can be built up with the support of overwhelming majority of our people. This process has been actually at work and it appears that it is growing in strength in the counsels of the C.P.I. The process, however, has to go faster and farther and produce clarity in thought and practice and a sense of a new mission at this momentous hour. As it is, it is merely causing confusion and making it difficult for the C.P.I. to function with a new purpose or determination. It is, as a matter of fact, impairing its capacity for united effort; and even the appearances, which were being kept up for some years, have now been discarded and the C.P.I. has, it appears, been finally split. This is not only a matter for great regret from the standpoint of the future of the C.P.I., but even more from that of the country as a whole. At a time when Congress, the socialist parties and the other organized forces, which can be pressed into service for the growth of socialism in the country, are suffering from internal stresses and it looks as if they cannot acquire the badly needed unity of purpose and concerted action, the C.P.I., which is known to be better organized and more disciplined than the other parties, is also suffering from serious disunity and is in no position to pull its weight in realizing, what it calls, broad-based democratic unity. This is a matter, to repeat, for serious regret from the point of view of the nation as a whole and no effort should be spared to retrieve the situation.

ISOLATION OF THE COMMUNIST PARTY

The starting point of this improvement has to be for the
C.P.I. to realize clearly how much isolated it is and why its
isolation is not merely due to blind anti-communism, though
that is also an important element in the deplorable situation.
This fact has to be vividly understood, its causes have to be
clearly appreciated and every effort has to be made to undo the
past as far as possible and build new bridges for mutual understanding and co-operation. Jawaharlal Nehru often referred to
the C.P.I. as an alien party and its anti-national role in India.
He was not free from anti-communism, but was known to take
a more objective and balanced view of not only the C.P.I., but
of communism and the communist countries as one of the most
decisive factors in the world situation than most other persons
in power and authority, and in spite of some occasions on
which he departed from the implications of his approach, he,
generally speaking, threw his weight against blind anti-communism and contributd most to friendliness and understanding
between India and the communist countries. And yet he did
say that "the communist party leans or depends upon or looks
to foreign countries" and accuse them of "posing as if they
are Russians. Their body was in India but their mind was
somewhere else. The communists have no root in our soil."[3]
He expressed similar sentiments on numerous other occasions.
There are, as stated above, good reasons why the communists
have incurred this odium and how it is explained by the facts
of history. This view has, however, to be resolutely countered.
The communists in India, as in other countries, represent some
of the finest men and women who are moved by the highest
motives in their thought and action and do their work in a
spirit of real consecration. And yet it is idle to maintain that
their proletarian internationalism has not led them astray and
placed them often in a compromising position. In India their
attitude towards national struggle under Gandhi and the

3. *The Hindu*, 9 February 1954.

appraisal of his role, their part in the honest attempt made to achieve left unity in 1934-39, their role during the war and particularly after 9 August 1942, their assessment of India's independence and of Nehru's role in international affairs, their policy and programme in 1948 and 1951 and their attempt to overthrow the Government of India by force are some of the best known instances of what Nehru called disruptive approach. The C.P.I. on all these points has revised its views and in action admitted their grevious errors of the past and changed their approach and policies; and yet they have not really done enough to analyse the source of their errors and examined objectively why they have cut themselves off so completely from the mainstream of national life, and what needs to be done in order that they may strike deep "roots in the soil".

NEED FOR BROAD UNDERSTANDING

The crucial point is how to maintain unity of the communist parties and yet make autonomy of each national party a reality. Owing to the change in the situation a united front is not an overriding need of the world communist movement. It should be possible for the communist parties to carry on open debate without bringing in rancour now being imported into Sino-Soviet controversy, even on some of the major current issues without causing any fissures in their solidarity. The communist parties are already establishing friendly relations with the forces of national liberation and know that though non-communist, they are forces for good in the context of the existing world situation and in the struggle against colonialism they are allies and instruments of political and social advance. A similar understanding and discrimination has to be extended to the forces which, in capitalist countries, are working for the good of the people, international understanding and the relaxation of tensions. These forces are not in power yet, but they are exercising healthy pressure, and it is possible to enlist their support even though, basically speaking, the non-socialist countries have the same balance of forces, i.e. their economies are being dominated by the rich and those who carry out their bidding. Capitalism is still capitalism in spite of the considerable improvement that has taken place in the living conditions and social position of the working masses in the advanced capitalist countries. In the undeveloped countries of Asia, Africa and Latin America capitalism means very primitive exploitation of the workers and in alliance with the feudal classes it is exercising very sinister influence on their economies and also on their international relations. Capitalism will not transform itself into socialism as a matter of course. It is still an evil force and has to be combated and defeated by concerted action. But broad-based unity, on which so much emphasis is being laid in the national and international conferences of the communist parties, implies that there is a lot of good in non-communist and non-socialist communities which can be harnessed for making the most of peaceful co-existence and achieving a large measure of co-operation for the true well-being of the people. This broad understanding can provide a basis for a large measure of autonomy of the national communist parties and reduce the element of rigidity in proletarian solidarity. It has not only to be poly-centred but it has also to take within its ambit many diverse forces and give them their due place in the confluence of many channels and streams.

New Technique of Co-operation

The C.P.I. has to take part in a world movement of re-orientation and re-adjustment of the communist parties and get into the mainstream of our national life. In India the C.P.I. by itself cannot, it is admitted, bring about in the near future socialist transformation or build up the strength of the masses without which even a beginning cannot be made in the advance towards socialism. If it has to enlist the co-operation of like-minded persons, parties and organizations, it has to win their trust and confidence and create conditions under which real broad-based unity can be achieved. The C.P.I. has worked through many organizations, which though working for very worthy causes and movements, have really been facades behind which the C.P.I. has operated. It has to realize that this technique is now outdated, brings the few independent men with convictions, who work in these organizations, into disrepute and most of the persons who are given "front" position are really rank opportunists whose association with these organizations does no good to the movements or the causes for which they are supposed to be working. These "fronts" might have done some good, but are not the models for broad-based co-operation of what the communists call democratic forces. The C.P.I. has to learn to divest itself of exclusive initiative and power in co-operative efforts and has to be one of the factors in the formulation and execution of common policies. This means that the C.P.I. has to break the old habit of operating behind the scenes, work in the open for clearly avowed objects and learn the technique of straightforward creative co-operation. It would be unduly optimistic to assume that such conditions can easily be created. They do not exist at present, and unless the need for creating them is also realized by the other "democratic" forces and they are keen to contribute to this end, the C.P.I.'s oft repeated plea, howsoever earnest, for broad-based democratic unity can be of very little avail.

DICTATORSHIP OF THE PROLETARIAT

Dictatorship of the proletariat is a sacred tenet of the communist creed and has since 1848 been held to be of cardinal importance for the realization of socialist goal. "Only he is a Marxist," wrote Lenin, "who extends the recognition of class-struggle to the recognition of the dictatorship of the proletariat. This is what constitutes the most profound difference between the Marxist and the ordinary petty (as well as big) bourgeoisie. This is the touchstone on which the real understanding and recognition of Marxism is to be tested."[4] This view has been affirmed and reaffirmed in many statements of the international

4. Lenin, The State and Revolution, p. 24.

conferences of the communist parties and those of the national parties including the C.P.I. What is the bearing of this view on the C.P.I.'s role in the context of the existing conditions in India as that of the other national parties in the other non-communist countries? The real significance of the view has to be clearly understood in order to answer this question. Its underlying assumption is that all states have been and are under dictatorships of the ruling class whatever their political structure, and in bourgeoisie democracies, of the bourgeoisie minority on the majority of working people even under parliamentary system, and has to be replaced by proletarian democracy. In Lenin's words dictatorship of the proletariat "means just the following: Only a definite class, that of the industrial and urban workers in general is able to lead the whole mass of toilers and the exploited in the struggle for the overthrow of the yoke of capital, in the process of their overthrow, in the struggle to maintain and consolidate the victory in the work of creating the new, socialist social system, in the whole struggle of the complete abolition of classes."[5] This long quotation from Lenin is given in order that the vital concept be understood as it has been precisely expressed by Lenin whose authority is accepted without question by all communists. The revolutionary role of the working class is, on this assumption, assigned to it by history because it is engendered by capitalism, its only asset is its labour power, it is forced to unite against capital because without unity it cannot even mitigate its extreme exploitation, this unity becomes possible because the workers have to work in large numbers and thereby acquire and develop a sense of solidarity and social consciousness needed for understanding and utilizing the revolutionary processes at work and lastly because the salvation of mankind as a whole is linked with the salvation of the working class which cannot be realized without the abolition of all classes, i.e. the establishment of socialism, a classless society. Even when the work-

5. *Lenin's Works*, Vol. 29, p. 387.

ing class is a negligible fraction of the population it alone, according to this view, can assume the leadership of the working people, the peasants, petty bourgeoisie, the intelligentsia whose co-operation has to be enlisted in carrying out the revolution and who, without the leadership of the working class, vaccilate, are handicapped by the bourgeois and even counter-revolutionary concepts and ideas and can, therefore, not be depended upon to remain fully loyal to revolution and its tasks. The working class, the proletariat, has, therefore, a crucial role in Marxian approach and at all stages of revolutionary struggle, overthrow of the bourgeoisie, and the processes through which it is to be achieved, maintenance and consolidation of victory and the creation and building up of the socialist system.

THE COMMUNIST VANGUARD

The working class, however, it is also premised, cannot by itself, exercise this role. It needs a party of the working class, the communist party, to bring it into action, to guide it in different situations and at different stages and create and sustain the social consciousness without which revolution can neither be started nor developed. "Only a political party of the working class," in Lenin's words again, "is capable of uniting, organizing such a vanguard of the proletariat—can lead the proletariat and through it all the masses of the working people."[6] Marx and Engels were not in favour of the communists forming a political party of their own. They were in Communist Manifesto against forming "a separate party opposed to other working class parties"—they were not to set up any sectarian principles of their own by which to mould or shape the proletarian movement. "The communists were," according to the Manifesto, "to be distinguished from the other working class parties by pointing and bringing to the front the common interests of the entire proletariat and always

6. *Lenin's Works*, Vol. 32, p. 222.

and everywhere represent the interests of the movement as a whole." This was the intention of the founders of communism. "However critical Marx and Engels may be of the other socialist principles other than their own," in the words of Prof. Harold J. Laski, "their regard for unity among the working classes was paramount."7 The course which events have taken has made not the unity of the working class but its vanguard —the working class (communist party)—paramount in the development of communist movement, in carrying out revolution and in the fulfilment of their objectives in actual practice. This is what is called new type of political party—not an amorphous mass but a well-developed, thoroughly oriented and rigourously tried and tested monolithic political party. Such parties assumed decisive roles in the countries in which communists have already won victory and in those in which they are still struggling as advanced contingents of the working class, and as stated above, Lenin's view that without the communist parties, the working class by itself cannot play or fulfil its revolutionary role is now the working faith of the communists everywhere, and dictatorship of the proletariat, in effect, means in all countries, dictatorship of the communist parties.

That without the communist parties there would have been no revolution in Soviet Union, China, the countries of Eastern Europe and North Viet Nam is historically true; and it is also a fact that they (the communist parties), with all their shortcomings and lapses, have shown great courage, spirit of dedication, capacity for concerted action, qualities of leadership and ability to arouse and lead the masses, and ability to use revolutionary situation not only for overthrowing the obsolete regimes but also for social engineering of a high order. They have used force in winning and holding power and have committed excesses, in some cases revolting excesses, to which a reference has already been made; but the scale of their opera-

7. H. J. Laski, *Communist Manifesto—Socialist Landmark*, p. 40.

tions and the degree of success which they have already achieved shows that political parties of new types, their achievements and experience have been, from the point of view of opening new social vistas and bringing about fundamental social changes, of very great value and objective understanding of world history since 1917, clearly points to the need for assessing the role of the communist parties with due appreciation of what they have attempted and achieved.

SOCIAL STRATEGY IN INDIA

We, in India, however, have to assess the situation and also the position of the communist party in the light of our special requirements and circumstances and see how far readjustment in theory and practice is called for by our specific needs—particularly the need for achieving the largest measure of agreement and unity for advancing towards socialist goal, for pooling our human and material resources and utilizing them to the best advantage for progressively realizing our socialist objective. It has already been pointed out that the C.P.I. has to attain and exercise far greater autonomy in decision-making and implementation of policy than it has done so far, and international unity of communist parties has to be achieved within the framework of flexible national policies with due regard for the sentiments, needs and circumstances of the peoples of the different countries. It is necessary that the C.P.I. should retrieve the position by de-isolating itself and work in co-operation with all progressive forces in the country. "The communist parties," in the words of the statement issued by 81 Communist parties from Moscow in November 1961, "decide on the prospects and tasks of revolution according to the concrete historical and social conditions in their respective countries and with due regard to the international situation."[8] This may be taken as a declaration of the intention of the communist parties if not of actual practice, and it would be of

8. *World Marxist Review*, December 1960, p. 18.

enormous value if "concrete historical and social conditions" in India are given their due consideration in the formulation of policies and programmes. What does dictatorship of the proletariat mean in the context of these conditions? The C.P.I. has reviewed the situation, reappraised its former policies and conclusions, and in fact has admitted its error in the assessment of the national struggle for freedom, reality of independence, substance of Government's economic and political policies and the content of its foreign policy. They have realized that the struggle for freedom was a genuine struggle, Mahatma Gandhi won the confidence of the masses and brought them into action, the 1942 struggle was an authentic national rebellion, Indian independence won in 1947 was a real and no sham independence, the Government of India, with all its faults and limitations, has an independent status and position, the policy of overthrowing it by force attempted by the C.P.I. after 1948 in Telangana, Manipur, etc. was purely an adventurist policy, the foreign policy of the Government of India has not only been independent but also beneficial and it has very deservedly won for itself a place of great importance and honour in international affairs and lastly that India's road to socialism is through parliamentary system and full utilization of the opportunities that it offers.

All this means advance towards realistic understanding of the "concrete historical and social conditions" in India and a wholesome change in the right direction. The process has, however, to go farther and to be accelerated. We again turn to the question of dictatorship of the proletariat. The point of dictatorship of the proletariat has to be clarified in the context of concrete conditions of India. If this is the touchstone on which real understanding and recognition of Marxism is to be tested, what does it imply for the C.P.I. if it is not to, as it obviously cannot, deny or water-down Marxism? It cannot, it is clear, mean that the working class will become the ruling class and exercise its dominant power through its vanguard, the C.P.I. It cannot mean, as it does in the communist countries, suppres-

sion of civil liberties, freedom of press, association and expression. The C.P.I. is, as a matter of fact, committed to the preservation of democratic liberties and it is, as stated later, in its
interest that these should be preserved. What does it mean
then? Dictatorship of the proletariat, as has been stated and
restated in an authoritative manner, means democracy for the
vast majority of the working people and not only the proletariat—the industrial labourers—and dictatorship of the small
minority of the capitalists and other propertied classes and
vested interests who at present exercise dominant political
power because they have enormous economic power and are
likely to resist or sabotage all efforts and forces to establish
socialism—to transfer de facto power to the masses and use it
in their service, primarily for freeing them from their economic
bondage and making them the principle beneficiaries of the
economy and its growth. Is it possible to win majority in legis-
latures for the parties which are in dead earnest about the
introduction of socialism and are prepared to use fully constitutional authority to frustrate all efforts clearly directed
towards realization of a socialist society. Majority of the legis-
lators will have to be backed by organized strength of the
masses, the workers, peasants, agricultural labourers and all
employees in public services. This is implicit in the C.P.I.'s
acceptance of parliamentary road to socialism in India, and
would be readily agreed to by the Congress, the socialist
parties and all other independent socialists. It may be, nay it
is likely, that the reactionary interests would, when they
realize that they are on the eve of the transfer of political and
economic power from them to the people, make a powerful bid
for the overthrow of democracy and defeat of social revolution.
It is more likely that their resistance would be a continuous
process, class struggle will go on and at every step of socialist
advance resistance will have to be reckoned with, met and
overcome by the use of constitutional authority and what is
far more important, by the organized strength of the masses.
In building up and fully utilizing this resistance to counter-

revolution as a continuous process, all socialist parties, including the C.P.I., if they are united, can play a crucial role.

At present they are neither united, nor have a majority in the representative institutions, nor have they organized the masses or created democratic socialist consciousness among them. These essential conditions for countering, combating and quelling the resistance of reactionary interests in the process of building up socialism do not exist; and the present outlook is that the conditions cannot be created. This, however, is a basic problem which can be solved only if there is a real ground-swell from below and the whole nation can be moved to action for promoting, realizing and defending socialism. This touchstone of Marxism itself does not offer any inherent difficulty in realizing democracy for the vast majority of the toiling millions and negating the power of the bourgeoisie, capitalists and their allies, which in effect the dictatorship of the proletariat means, to frustrate democratic processes in the framework of representative institutions and their implicit obligations. The C.P.I. can, without abandoning its essential tenets or articles of creed, forge ahead providing it can build up or participate in a real united front of the socialist forces and contribute to rapid advance of the country towards socialism.

INDIA'S ROAD

"All nations will arrive at socialism," wrote Lenin, "but not all will do so in exactly the same way, each will contribute something of its own to a particular form of democracy a particular variety of the dictatorship of the proletariat, to the rate of socialist transformation in the various aspects of social life."[9] All are agreed that democracy in India should not be merely a replica of parliamentary system of the West. It should be based upon consent; there should be provision for peaceful transfer of power at all levels and it should not merely mean ballot box democracy—casting of votes

9. *Lenin's Works*, Vol. 23, p. 58.

say once in four years and otherwise bureaucratic administration. Democracy, even proletarian democracy, in theory
has to mean participating democracy, i.e. vigilant interest
of the people in democracy, decision-making by a very
large number of persons in factories, co-operatives public
organizations, cultural institutions and exercise of supervision
over the execution of the agreed policies. This is the kind of
democracy which *in theory* exists in Soviet Union, China and
other communist countries but is in practice severely circumscribed owing to the authoritarian trends which exclusive
power possessed by the communist parties has engendered or
not been able to check or counteract. This is the kind of democracy which is in the air in India at present—and the attempt
is being made to introduce it through what is called Panchayat
Raj and the net-work of the co-operatives, but the conditions
under which "democratic decentralization" can take root and
grow do not exist at present, are not being created or even the
need for providing them is not being seriously considered. But
India has "to contribute its own particular form of democracy"
—and its own particular variety of the strength of the people,
Lok Shakti—which will carry its own sanctions, have its own
compulsions based on the articulated will of the people and
sustained by the intelligent co-operation and enthusiasm of the
people, i.e. its own variety of the dictatorship of the proletariat. Dictatorship has implications of ruthless coercion, totalitarian power and disregard of human considerations owing to
its historical associations. The use of this word, in our democratic set-up and climate of public opinion, can and should be
avoided. But the need for counteracting the resistance of those
for whom fundamental social changes mean loss of wealth,
privileged social status, position and power is not the less real
and urgent on that account. Our democracy has to have its
built-in defences against wilful betrayal by the people and
classes now in authority. This is Marxism but also sound common sense and is borne out by everyday experience of the processes at work at all levels in our country at present. There is

no need to inflame class antagonisms or promote social antipathies. Democracy in India is a very young plant and cannot
thrive without providing the necessary protective shelters and
safeguards for it. Fortunately its best defences are also the most
favourable conditions for its growth, i.e. organization of the
masses for starting and sustaining democratic processes by
which they can exercise creative social functions and their
understanding and strength can grow from within. This kind
of democracy does not exist at present anywhere and it is one
of the most important tasks of social revolution to create,
develop and fortify it. In India we have to do it in our own
way and realize it in spite of fragmentation of our community
life not only through classes but much more so through our
innumerable castes and their heirarchy. It is a stupendous task
but socialism cannot be realized without undertaking or
accomplishing it.

IMPORTANCE OF DEMOCRATIC FREEDOMS

It is possible that before this task is accomplished, we will
come up against overwhelming odds and the dark forces of
reaction will rear their ugly heads and strike out at democracy
and socialism. Portents that this may happen are clearly visible
on the horizon and it would be highly imprudent to disregard
them. The dark forces must not be allowed to use democratic
procedures to defeat or negate democracy; but if democracy is
strengthened at the base and the people are organized and
mobolized to promote the interests of the community, i.e. their
own interests, they through their vigilance and prompt action
can nip any incipient counter-revolutionary trends in the bud,
and through positive, constructive measures not allow any
vacuum to develop which can be filled by the forces of darkness. This has to be done at all levels and, of course, before
democracy at the basic level can be built up, the top and the
near top levels, where power is now concentrated, need to be
watched and guarded with very special care. But the ultimate
bastion of democracy and social revolution has to be built up

with organized might of the people at the basic level—their awareness of their needs, tasks, responsibilities and resources. This awareness does not exist at present, and, as stated above, immensity of creating and developing it has to be known and provided for; but it has to be understood that political democracy, free and fair elections, civil liberties, due process of law and freedom of political action are, in spite of political power, the media of communication and, of course, wealth and property being in the hands of the rich and privileged classes and their control over all cultural and educational institutions, very favourable conditions for creating and developing vivid social awareness on a wide basis and they have to be preserved and guarded against all encroachments.

"The irony of world history," wrote Fredrick Engels in 1895 in his introduction to *Class struggle in France 1848-1850* by Karl Marx, "turns everything upside down. We, 'the revolutionaries' 'the overthrowers', we are thriving far better on legal methods than on illegal methods and revolt. The parties of Order, as they call themselves, are perishing under the legal conditions created by themselves. They cry despairingly— legality is the death of us; whereas we, under this legality, get firm muscles and rosy cheeks and look like life eternal. And if we are not as crazy as to let ourselves be driven to street fighting in order to please them, then in the end there is nothing left for them but themselves to break through this fatal legality."[10] "Its growth by voting strength of the communists," he also wrote, "proceeds as spontaneously, as steadily, as irresistibly and at the same time as tranquilly as a natural process. By the end of the century we shall become a decisive power in the land, before which all other powers will have to bend low whether they like it or not."[11] The communists did grow in strength and numbers, but nowhere did they become decisive power before which all other powers had to bow whe-

10. *Marx Engels Selected Works*, Vol. I, p. 125.
11. *Ibid.*, p. 124.

ther they liked it or not, but in India, if not the communist, the forces of social revolution are, it is almost certain, likely to thrive better on legal methods than on illegal methods and revolt, and they will be really crazy to let themselves be driven into street fighting or repeat anything like the performance of the communists in Telangana in 1949-51. The elections may be free and fair and yet it is true that the dice is likely to be loaded against the parties which genuinely believe in social revolution because of all the resources that the forces of reaction command; and yet it is in the interest of social revolution that democratic forms and processes be preserved and the opportunity be made available and fully utilized not only to win votes but what is far more important, build up mass organizations and use them for democracy and socialism. Political democracy and all that it stands for needs to be taken as a bulwark of revolution and not of reaction and defended by all revolutionary forces.

It may be that when the parties of reaction and even constitutionalists realize that legality, by the operation of the natural process, means the death of the old order, they will break through the fatal legality. It is likely that this will happen. This is a very good reason for making the most of the time when going is good and build up, not merely through ballot box but more by other democratic processes, the position of strength of the people's organizations. This needs to be done as much for constructive as defensive purposes, but the only way to fight counter-revolution is to make the organized strength of the people as irresistible as possible. Even their resort to arms may become unavoidable to defend revolution, but counter-revolution is likely to have a distinct advantage at least in initial stages and trials of armed struggle between revolution and counter-revolution has to be avoided as far as possible. Yes, as things are, in spite of many disadvantages, revolution is likely to thrive more on legality than on illegality, and the C.P.I. will do well not only to reaffirm their Amritsar thesis in which parliament's role as an instrument of socialism was accepted, but also to work out its implications to the full and make them an integral part of their working faith and strategy. They should, in good faith, project an image of theirs on public mind in which violence should have, if at all, a very secondary place and primarily they should stand out as a party which relies almost entirely on the peaceful strength of the masses. This has the virtue of being ethically a more desirable course. The communists, at least in theory, have always taken violence as a necessary evil, the recourse to which is forced upon them by counter-revolutionary interests. This attitude has to be maintained, for non-violence cannot, given their whole approach, become a matter of creed for the communists, but they should, in their tactics and strategy, mainly rely upon it and function as a democratic party—a party accepting conscientiously all the obligations of a parliamentary party with the intention of using all the democratic processes for accelerating the advent of a real social revolution. This is necessary for them to achieve the unity of all democratic forces on which they have rightly laid so much stress in their policy statement for a number of years, and also to gain confidence of the public and the support of non-party progressive persons and organizations.

TASK OF THE C.P.I.

The C.P.I., it is clear, cannot become the leading party of the country for a long time yet; and as it cannot capture power as a minority party in the country as the communist parties did with the assistance of the Soviet army in the countries of Eastern Europe; it has honestly to assume the role of one of the major parties in the country whose relative strength is likely to grow "tranquilly as a natural process" if they adhere to the rules of the game enjoined by parliamentary system and co-exist peacefully with the other major parties of the country and throw full weight for making democratic processes a means of rapid growth of the socialist forces. This is the task set for them by concrete historical and social conditions, and if creative Marxism—Marxism as an approach and not as a dogma—can mean anything as a force for good, it should mean that in the situation which exists in this country, and which is likely to last for many years to come, the C.P.I. has to apply itself to the task of building up socialism in the country in co-operation with the like-minded parties and persons and do all that is possible to make the use of force an unlikely contingency. "Broaden the front," according to an authoritative publication of the Soviet Union, "of the allies of the working class, i.e. broader the social basis of the revolution, narrower is the structure against which coercion is applied, the broader is the development of proletarian democracy."[12] This view is based on the assumption that "power passes into the hands of the working class peacefully", i.e. the communist party becomes the dominant party without encountering resistance or having to fight for gaining ascendency. This assumption is ruled out in India by the facts of the case; but nevertheless the C.P.I., not as the ruling party of the country, but a major party has to create as broad a social base of revolution as possible and develop a social momentum which will inspire respect and grow as a tidal wave of revolution. It is legitimate to be sceptical as to whether this can be done at all, and the prospect at present of a broad social base of revolution being created is, as pointed out later, really remote; but unless socialism is to be reduced to the position of merely a hope of some distant future, the prospect has to be realized as early as possible and early enough to make it the immediate task of the present generation. The C.P.I. has to apply its mind and energy to the task of creating this broad solid base and making the necessary readjustments in its theory and practice. In other words, it has to accept with real understanding and ardour the obligations and limitations of a revolutionary party which has to seek allies and co-operate with them in all sincerity and a sense of real fidelity—which would necessitate their acquiring a new habit of mind and an art of human

12. *Fundamentals of Marxism-Leninism Manual*, Moscow, Foreign Language Publishing House, p. 652.

relations which they have not practised so far. The conditions for creating this social base exist, political stability and its orderly growth require that this task be fulfilled and class forces of the country should be so directed as to make broad-based co-operation of diverse elements a practical, inescapable necessity. This is the task which has been placed on top of the agenda of current history and, as stated above, creative Marxism, if it means anything at all, means that it should be undertaken with a sense of historic mission. This is a historical necessity, but it is by no means decreed that its success in the near future is inevitable. That will depend upon the extent to which we can make our own history in the existing conditions and develop human resources for realizing this object. Being at the cross roads our going in the right direction with the necessary will and determination would depend upon our collective discrimination, unity of purpose and, of course, a sense of consecration. The C.P.I. can make a very significant contribution to the common pool of effort needed for achieving this result.

ABERRATION OF COMMUNISM

The avowed monolithic character of the communist parties is both an advantage and disadvantage. Its great disadvantage has been fully proved by the emergence of "the cult of personality" in Soviet Union—of Stalinism and all that it meant in terms of sacrifice of human values. That its own discipline has in it the serious risk of personal despotism of the leader who gets to the top and uses the power for consolidating his position and imposing his arbitrary will first on the party and through it on the nation was known and recognized long ago and has now been amply proved by the experience of the Soviet Union and later in the countries of Eastern Europe and China. The ascendency of pre-eminent leaders, some with strong autocratic strain, is not confined to the communist movements. All mass movements throw up leaders at different levels who exercise influence and authority and in different degrees become powerful, supreme and even irreplaceable. Nehru of India, Sokarno of

Indonesia and now Castro of Cuba are three of the most outstanding illustrations in the contemporary world scene, and they
only show the importance of the principles of "fuhrership" in
the best sense of the word. Without such personalities the movements lack drive, initiative and a focus of will and action; particularly at times when heroic qualities are needed for carrying
a people through dangers and difficulties. But concentration of
power in the communist parties, the habit of implicit obedience
to the orders transmitted from the top, cultivated and imposed
as a normal feature of the organization and a highly developed
sense of loyalty makes anything which looks like or can be
made to look like "anti-party" activity a cardinal sin—a crime
for which severe punishment is considered necessary and desirable. In the countries in which the communist parties are all-
powerful, it has in practice meant not always, but in cases of
aberration, denial of all freedom of expression and action and,
as is well known, personal despotism in its worst form. The
safeguards against that grievous risk are really inner-party
democracy, contact with the masses and learning from their
experiences and relying upon them and not the party bureaucracy and commandism from above for the necessary impetus
for achieving and fulfilling social revolution. Even in the communist countries after 1956 the need for the radical cure of the
evils, which have existed and taken serious form, has been
widely admitted and the process of democratization has been
at work; and there are clear indications that significant improvement in the situation in this respect has already taken place.
Now that the communist parties have to fear much less from
the enemies within and hostility without owing to their stability
and growing strength, the process of rectification can be carried
very much farther and the theory of democratic centralism,
which should mean as much democracy as centralism—really
more democracy than centralism—has to derive its legality and
authentic character from its being an expression of democratic
will—should be practised with the utmost attention to its inner
spirit. This is necessary for healthy development of the com-

munist countries, dissipation of the atmosphere of fear which, though very much reduced, still persists as a hang-over and creating conditions for mutual confidence and co-operation at the international level.

COMMUNIST PARTY AS A DEDICATED ORDER

The great advantage of the communist parties everywhere is that they are not political parties but as Webbs described the C.P.S.U., "they in their structure and in some of the leading features have a distinct resemblance to religious orders".[13] There is nothing religious about them in the ordinary sense; they are, as is well known, fanatically anti-religious, and yet their internal organization with rigorous selection of members, cohesion, self-discipline, code of conduct and ideology—in theory not a creed but an all-inclusive approach which is for them an illuminating account of how, whence and whither, a means of understanding the march of history and the direction of events and forces and what is even more important a guide to action which enables not only to know but also change the world. The communists attribute their achievements and contributions as revolutionaries to their being "armed with Marxism and Leninism", and the structure and organization of their parties. They have failed grievously and committed serious blunders in some important respects, but it is plain truth that in political, economic, social, cultural, scientific and human terms their record is a great chapter in human history, beginning of a new epoch of great achievements and even more a greater promise. Very heavy price in terms of human value has had to be paid for these gains—in some ways avoidable, in others unavoidable. It is the path of wisdom to learn both from their failures and achievements, but also to recognize that in the countries in which the communists are in power and also in those in which they are not, the communist parties have risen to great heights of creative action, given proofs of valour

13. Sydney and Beatrice Webb, *Soviet Communism*, Vol. I, 1935, p. 413.

and iron will against great odds, faced severe trials and sufferings with real heroism and among their members there are to be counted large number of some of the finest persons that the world has known. The communist parties are not political parties like other parties. They comprise a band of dedicated revolutionaries—men with a sense of vocation and a clear understanding of their role at this crucial hour. It is the tragedy of history that even in a crisis the worst in life gets mixed up with the best because "man", in Walt Whitman's words, "is immense, contains multitudes and therefore contradicts himself". The communist parties have to cleanse themselves thoroughly, recognize the serious distortions that have occurred in their structure and working and know that enormous changes have taken place and are taking place in the world situation. All this is necessary and it is also necessary that the best in them should be preserved and they should retain their solidarity, the sense of purpose and the selflessness for which their members are known all over the world.

LACK OF GROWTH FROM WITHIN OF C.P.I.

This also applies to the Communist Party of India. It is a small party, has been under ban for nearly half the period since it was formed and owing to its having isolated itself from the national movement most of the time, it has not been playing a very positive role in its development. And yet it is also a party of devoted revolutionaries, its members have been drawn from all parts and religious communities of the country, who have outgrown small loyalties, worked with devotion and self-effacement, have contributed to the development of socialist consciousness and in their work among the labourers, peasants, students and women they have, generally speaking, shown a comprehension of the essentials and promoted an interest in and understanding of socialism. With their pyramided structure, they have also been a disciplined party, a large majority of their members have maintained high standards of conduct and in some parts of the country like Kerala, Andhra and

West Bengal they have made strong bases for themselves. Their trade unions are also well organized, but owing to their partisan behaviour they have inspired distrust and provoked the other parties to have rival trade union organizations and thereby created splits among the working class. Their leaders are almost entirely drawn from the middle class intellectuals and they have hardly produced any leaders from among the workers and the peasants. Their thinking has been limited by orthodox interpretation of Marxism and the C.P.S.U. and the other important communist parties have had a cramping effect on the growth of independent thinking. It looked in 1956 that de-Stalinization would also mean democratization and liberization of the C.P.I., for it too, there were indications, was suffering from lack of internal democracy and struggle for power. The process of self-criticism was started in 1956 and in the various policy statements after that year it was clear that a true appreciation of the situation in India and her role in world affairs was being developed. But the process has not gone far and has now been arrested by the confusion caused by China's inroads into Indian territory and later by Sino-Soviet controversy. The Party, according to a report of the committee appointed by the Party itself, has been losing members, their standards of conduct are being undermined and a large proportion of members have become indifferent and inactive. The Party is now a house divided in itself and the Right and the Left of the Party are finding it difficult to find a common meeting ground.

Their great weakness is that among the peasants, their work is limited, ineffective and has failed to evoke any response. For the last eight years this serious deficiency has been noted and commented upon and resolutions have been passed for its removal but with practically no effect whatsoever. The various organizations— Indo-Soviet Association or Afro-Asian Association—have remained merely "fronts" and the need for finding broad basis for them is hardly understood. Their statements on world situation are merely a re-hash of the statements at their international conferences which, owing to the developing internal stresses, bear the mark of being a compromise between conflicting views. The Party, in one word, is not showing any signs of growth from within. With the exception of Communist rule in Kerala, which unfortunately was put an end to by an unholy alliance of diverse forces, the position of the C.P.I. has been static and it has not risen to the needs of the situation. All this is true and yet it is a fact that the C.P.I. is the best organized party in the country, its members still generally maintain a standard of behaviour which compares favourably with the prevailing standards in other parties and without it the outlook for socialism and socialist movement would be far more depressing than it is today. Self-criticism for it, even more than for the other communist parties, is urgently needed and it is essential that it should go through a process of severe re-examination and revaluation of values.

RELIGION AND SOCIALISM

There is one other point to which a brief reference is necessary if the need for revaluation is to be seriously conceded. Marxism has no place for religion in its approach, or rather it is avowedly anti-religious and it is militant in its denunciation of religion. All communist parties, including the C.P.I., are therefore anti-religious in theory and practice. All members of the C.P.I. presumably share this attitude towards religion, though they have not taken an aggressively anti-religious position in their policy statements and programmes because from the practical standpoint it was not necessary or expedient to do so. In India, as pointed out before, the Congress, the socialist parties and, of course, the Sarvodayists make religious outlook an essential part of their socialist approach and socialism in India. From the communist standpoint this is obscurantism, a wilful diversionist move to cloud the real revolutionary issues. The point is fundamental and it is not possible to deal with it at any length and yet it needs to be elucidated. Religious doctrine, rituals, observances, scriptural authority, theology, priestcraft and super-naturalism and esoteric lore are the entire content of religion from the practical standpoint, and they all have been and are being used to retard the process of scientific inquiry and defend status quo, the existing social order and therefore are, in effect, instruments of counter-revolution. This has been so in other countries, and it can be assumed that all the authority of established religion would be invoked and fully utilized to resist radical social changes when social revolution becomes a strong challenge to the existing social order.

And yet there is an element of truth in the statement that socialism has in essence to be a spiritual force and must express in its policy and programme the deepest yearnings of man for realizing the best in him in every day life, in work, economic and social relations and concerted efforts to end scarcity and produce a state of relative abundance in order that the spirit of man may be free from the necessity of want and toil and establish conditions for full creative life for self-realization. From this point of view both the means and end have to be spiritual—the effort has to be inspired by the longing for brotherhood of man and the goal has to be the fulfilment of this supreme object. "All men are brothers" is the cardinal doctrine of communism, and Marx and Engels and Lenin considered exploitation of man by man a deadly sin because it is outrageous from the point of view of what he essentially is and what he can become from the point of view of his potential and manifest destiny. Socialization of means of production and their utilization by and for the community is, from this point of view, essential because poverty, which the acquisitive society produces and perpetuates, means impoverishment of man's spirit and frustration of his appointed destiny. Vedantic vision, to which Jawaharlal Nehru used to refer, can be the basis of socialism, because it is based upon faith in unity of life, i.e. brotherhood of man. In this sense socialism has to be spiritual everywhere and not only in India. Communism posits emergence of a new man as its end-product and for its working—

man who lives for the community and fulfils himself in it. The new Man of communism is really the liberated man of Vedant, and in him the highest in man—call it God if you please, if the word must be used—is realized.

This is not a strained effort at reconciling the opposites but an inadequate indication of the view that the communists need not develop an allergy to the emphasis on spiritual content of socialism by Nehru, Sampurnanand, Jai Prakash Narain and Vinoba or regard it merely a diversionist tactic. They have, if they can, to go beyond words, at least to appreciate the validity of this view even if they do not accept it and certainly not dismiss it as a sinister move. Religion has been and is the cloak for reaction, a mask for counter-revolution, but there is a spirit of religion which has through the ages been in revolt against its form and formal observances. This spirit can be awakened and become the moving force of social revolution and not merely its ally. Understanding of this point can reduce, if not remove, mutual barriers and help in the realization of broad-based unity in thought and action for socialism.

SUMMING UP

These three chapters on "social horizons" can be concluded by bringing these arguments to a focal point. This country is passing through a very critical period of her history and there is a general agreement of vocal opinion that socialism is the answer to its own more urgent problems. The three leading parties in the country are officially committed to socialism. Socialism is in the air and open opposition to it, with one exception, is considered bad political tactic. It is being opposed and undermined in practice by inertia of the masses, silent but effective resistance of big business, bureaucracy and dishonest politicians. In the two plans, as the later chapter will show, in spite of the prominence given to it in political speeches and introductory chapters of the Planning Commission reports, it has not been at all a decisive factor and anti-socialist trends have made marked progress. Its future depends upon the earnestness, sincerity and strength of the political parties which profess socialism, balance of social forces and the compulsion of events in which is included the pressure of public opinion. At this point it is not necessary to assess the position in regard to the balance of social forces and the compulsion of events. The position with regard to both is changing all the time and it is not even possible to speculate about the course of events with regard to them. In the meanwhile disruptive trends in the country have gained strength and caste, communal antipathies and what is called linguism, strife caused by linguistic controversies, have assumed most disturbing dimensions. So far ad-hoc measures to deal with each trouble as it arises and exhortations to think and act in terms of the country as a whole and not narrow sectional interests have been our answer to these pressing problems; and it is obvious that it is no answer and the situation is fast deteriorating. Antagonisms are inherent in the size of the country, its diversities and social structure of which the caste system is the oldest and most intractible feature. These antagonisms cannot be removed even if the country is in a state of a real social revolution and forces of socialism are on the march. Socialism in India would not only have to reckon with them but its development would be shaped in a large measure by the strategy adopted to deal with these stresses and counter-stresses; but socialism would, it may be assumed, become an independent force in itself, its momentum would reduce the intensity of these antagonisms and a social infra-structure would be built up in which these contradictions would find a limiting and regulating factor. But the growing severity of these stresses and the way minor issues become major problems and expose to view our precarious position are an index of the social vacuum that has been developed in the country and of our inability to have engendered and brought into play any healthy or creative counter-vailing social forces. They, more than the statistical indices, clearly show that the balance of forces has been definitely unfavourable for socialism and the compulsion of events including the pressure of public

opinion has been diverting attention from the issues of socialism, the problem of building up a new social order and become
a very distracting factor. Nothing more need be said about
these antagonisms here except that a frontal attack on them
is likely to create more problems than it can solve. They can
be resolved only if the tasks set by socialism are undertaken
and fulfilled in all earnestness, and a climate of opinion is
created in which these antagonisms are cut to size and in the
perspective of an all-engrossing social endeavour they cease to
be the distracting problems that otherwise they are sure to
become and remain. The growth of these antagonisms, it may
be repeated, clearly reveals how superficial and uninspiring
have been our interest in and devotion to socialism.

OUTLOOK FOR SOCIALIST UNITY

As it is obviously impossible to have socialism in India without the devoted and effective work of the convinced, ardent
and capable socialists, the potential contribution of the Congress, the Sarvodayists, the socialist parties and the C.P.I. are
of vital importance for assessing the future of socialism in
India. It is, from what has been said in these chapters and what
is commonly known about them, clear that they cannot work
together for the common goal of socialism and the limitations
of each one of them make it very unlikely that their separate
contributions would add up to a socialist society or an appreciable advance towards it. Hope is sometimes expressed that the
rank and file can co-operate for socialist objectives even if co-
operation at the top cannot be realized. Though in some favourable circumstances co-operation at the local level may be
possible among all socialist sections, generally speaking the
gulf at the top would also mean gulf all the way down and it
is illusory to hope that a spontaneous movement from below
can develop and make co-operation for socialism a decisive factor in its development. It is a depressing conclusion but the
facts make it inescapable. Because of the deadweight of the
majority of congressmen who can either feel no concern for

socialism or are in fact against it, organizational and ideological weaknesses of the socialist parties and their blind anti-communism and isolation of the C.P.I. and its inability to counter-act the trends which prevent re-orientation of its policy and progress, in spite of the devotion and sincerity of its members, any hope of broad-based co-operation for socialism cannot be entertained at present. There is nothing in view which pro-vides a basis for the hope that through unity of action progress towards socialism can be accelerated. The Sarvodayists are men of piety, relatively free from the struggle for power and lately they have broadened and deepened their understanding of what a new social order for this country has to mean; but even their over-all comprehension of what this really should mean is limited and this fact comes in the way of their being effective and successful in their efforts. As the presumptive legatees of Mahatma Gandhi's heritage and as participants in the re-markable trek of the great Vinoba and also owing to their transparent sincerity and capacity for silent service their good-will is cultivated and their benevolent approval sought by Congressmen for political reasons. Owing to the standards which they are maintaining they are a force for good, but though their approach and programme are essentially socialist, it is unlikely that by their precept and example advance towards socialism would be materially speeded up.

It is a great pity because regarding the content of socialism, which we have to realize and work for, there is a great deal of general agreement about the essentials and a common pro-gramme to which all, who are virtually socialist in their basic approach, can easily be drawn up. It is, as a matter of fact, already contained in the programme of the different parties, and if the will for co-operation is there, its formulation should present no difficulties. On certain important points differences remain but are not fundamental and need not prevent practi-cal co-operation. What is really lacking is deep earnestness that socialism matters, the sense of urgency that time is against and not for socialism as a goal for the next five or ten years, whatever the ultimate outcome may be, and that anti-socialist forces are gaining strength and have to be combated and reduced to impotence. As a result of this lack, the masses are inert, unresponsive and greatly susceptible to the influence of sinister forces, devaluation of values is taking place, the standards of public morals are rapidly falling and general cynicism is growing and becoming dangerous.

These conclusions are realistic and yet in the post-Nehru era it may be possible, as it is necessary to re-assess the situation and indicate some lines of growth. Essentially the situation has not changed and yet the Congress after Bhuvaneshwar and through the declarations made by the new Prime Minister on the assumption of his office is firmly committed to socialism, and it will, it appears, not be possible to organize openly opposition to socialism within the Congress. The growing volume of opinion among Congressmen for socialism indicates that socialists in the Congress can, if they assert themselves, become powerful and effective. And yet the fact is that most of the Congressmen are interested only in power politics and not in socialism and the interests for whom the advance towards socialism means the end of their power and position are strongly entrenched in the Congress organization and wield great influence. It is likely that for some years to come the Congress will be subject to serious internal pulls of these interests and it will not be able to develop adequate drive from within for the realization of a socialist society. Assuming that the socialist forces within the Congress would be able to develop strength and impetus needed by increasing greater pressure in support of socialist policies, it seems to be fairly clear that the Congress as a whole would not be able to develop the necessary dynamism for a rapid advance towards socialism. The entry of Mr. Ashoka Mehta and his associates may be of use in developing internal socialist forces provided they can decondition their minds and behaviour and realize that socialism is not anti-communism and cannot grow through blind hatred of communists and communist countries. Similarly other small socialist groups can by joining the Congress radicalize it in some measure and reduce the resistance to socialism from within. But generally speaking, it has to be assumed that, given the necessary effort, reactionary trends within the Congress can be held in check and the development of socialist forces facilitated.

But radical movements all over the world are known to degenerate and use their position and prestige to defeat their avowed objects. The Congress has never been, from social standpoint, a very radical movement, and it has, largely speaking, been subject more and more to reactionary pressures in the last ten years. It can, given a favourable conjunction of circumstances, be radicalized, but not to the extent of becoming a vanguard of socialist transformation or carry out a programme of profound social changes. At best it can cure the abuses of factional politics in its gross forms and raise the standard of political morals within reasonable limits and implement measures of a welfare state bearing some semblance to socialist policies. But owing to its internal composition it cannot and will not set the pace in socialist advance or carry out basic socialist changes. If it has to face the competition of more determined socialist policies and has to reckon with strong social pressures, it will, in order to hold its own in electoral contests, have to respond to them and curb its more extreme reactionary trends. But competition and social pressures would have to come from outside the Congress. As it is likely to remain the strongest political organization in the country, it will be a service to it and the country if independent socialist parties and forces are strong and vigilant, exercise critical supervision over the Congress performance and reduce its inadequacies by presenting and promoting independent programmes of their own. Merger of all socialist parties with the Congress would, from this standpoint, be a disservice to the cause of socialism and undesirable from the standpoint of the working of the parliamentary system. This is a very weighty reason why the socialist parties outside the Congress should function with vigour and have faith in themselves. They should not only remain in advance of the Congress in their policies and programmes but also carry out political education of the people and, what is far more important, organize the masses for constructive work in selected spheres and develop social pressures to make more rapid tempo of advance towards socialism unavoidable from practical standpoint. These parties should, with discrimination, co-operate with the Congress in carrying out specific policies and measures. That would mean that party politics would be subordinated to the need for pooling energies for carrying out generally accepted policies and partisan struggle for its own sake will have to be avoided. That would improve the working of the parliamentary system itself and remove, within limits, some of its more serious evils.

The Samyukta Socialist Party has still to differentiate itself sharply from the Congress and develop a recognisably different programme of its own. In its statement of public policy two points have been emphasized. One is the importance of class struggle as an important factor in economic relations and the other is the necessity of organisation of the industrial labour, peasants and all other working classes as extra-parliamentary forces for giving dynamism to democracy. An effective organization of these classes is needed to develop their combative strength in case of need but more for exercising vigilance over the implementation of public policies, and what is of greater importance, for carrying out these policies through non-official, i.e. peoples' agencies. These are important points but not the only points which need special emphasis by the S.S.P. This party can elucidate by practice how class struggle can and should be conducted without inflaming passions or promoting antipathies, how respect for minority opinion can be made an essential part of the working of democracy and how the parliamentary system can transcend the limitations of "the Westminster Model" and through committee system and otherwise develop the technique of evolving agreements and pooling of ideas. In operating of the economy itself new modes of working have to be experimented with and developed and planning and freedom have to be combined in the formulation and execution of public policies. These points are illustrative of what can be done to make it clear how democracy and socialism are indispensible to each other or rather both are different aspects of the same basic approach. But the most important service which this party can render is to live down its anti-communism and without ceasing to be critical of the communists and their possible regressions in developing their new role, extend to them the understanding of their new problems and re-adjustment and be ready to co-operate with them, as with the Congress, in carrying out specific policies and programmes. Their relation with the socialist parties of other countries can be put to positive use by drawing upon the experience of the socialist countries and thinking out creative socialist policies. All socialist parties have to outgrow the phase of anti-communism, draw upon the theory and experience of communist countries for avoiding their mistakes and benefitting by their positive achievements. The S.S.P. has to grow, become a force for pointing the way to the future and developing democratic processes both for positive and dynamic purposes. It has to develop much wider appeal to attract socially adventurous youth and provide outlets for their minds, energy and the spirit of discovery. The immediate task of the S.S.P. is, of course, to consolidate its position and solve the organizational problems created by the secession of an important section of the P.S.P. and merger of the two socialist parties. In the last few years the socialist parties have been subjected to very severe internal stresses and found it very difficult to develop any initiative of their own. It requires new accession of ideas, strength and men with drive and clear purpose. It can and should play an important role if in thought and action it can take, what really amounts to, a new birth and go ahead with full knowledge of opportunities and needs which the existing situation has created and which have to be responded to adequately with understanding fervour and organizing capacity.

The Communist Party is passing through one of the most difficult ordeals and it is not known how it will emerge and how far it will be able to conserve its strength and resources for playing its new role in national and international affairs. It is a real misfortune from the point of view of each country and the world that the communist movement is, owing to Sino-Soviet differences, going through a process of conflict and disruption. As pointed out earlier in this chapter, the fact that the communist movement will cease to be monolithic and each national party will be able to have and exercise autonomy of judgement and action is a great advantage and can become a sources of strength and growth for the communist movement as a whole. But it will be a real misfortune if solidarity of the communist movement is lost thereby or what is far worse, internal strife takes the place of socialist unity. At present it is unpredictable how far China will succeed in disrupting the communist movement and sow discord on a world-wide basis. The C.P.I. has already been split and become a much weaker party on that account. When a drama of epic proportions is being enacted one has to wait upon events and see what the final shape of things is going to be. But assuming that the C.P.I. will not be irreparably damaged after the conflict has subsided, it should, as pointed out in this chapter, be able to play a very positive role in the development of a socialist society, retain its place in the international movement and become a truly national party. As a well-developed, disciplined and dedicated party it could set an example for the other political parties and make great contribution to the development of a socialist society. The ordeal, through which it is passing is, as stated above, a very difficult one; and if it and the world communist movement can go through the ordeal and still retain its vitality and power for good, they can participate with distinction in making new India and new world.

It is necessary to realize that the parliamentary system is the political system which we are operating and have to develop to suit our needs. All socialist parties have to do what they can to maintain this system, change and develop it to suit our needs and adopt and apply a code of political conduct by which the best in it can be preserved and its well-known limitations outgrown. Ceylon, India and Japan are the three countries of Asia in which the system has survived the post-war trials and tribulations. In India the system is being operated with great difficulty and it is far from certain that eclipse of this system can be fully guarded against. But we should know that it has to be guarded against by the combined efforts of all socialists and socialist parties. Purification and preservation of this system is our immediate obligation. It is a very difficult system to work; and even in countries like United Kingdom, U.S.A. and Sweden—the countries in which it is known to have achieved a large measure of success—it has glaring defects which are crying for removal. It is not the only system of political democracy and as pointed out in Chapter II, we should not think that our future and the future of socialism is indissolubly bound with it. But in our present historical context, this is the system which we have to operate with as much success as we can and do our best to go beyond its limitations. The Congress, the Socialist Party and the Communist Party have to combine together to make the most of it, cure its evils and, to repeat, transcend its limitations and remedy its inherent defects.

These are the anticipations which may or may not be realized. In the midst of great uncertainties it is necessary to indicate the possibly hopeful lines of development and the new paths which are opening up. We cannot write off our future. The world itself is passing through a period of great perplexities, and we have to know that our problems are a part of the problems of travail of a new world in the making. We have to face them with courage, faith and hope.

Chapter Four

THE AGRARIAN RELATIONS

GENESIS OF LAND REFORMS

"The wind is blowing in the villages and through the mud-huts, where dwell our poverty-stricken peasantry and it is likely to become a hurricane if relief does not come to them soon. All our political problems and discussions are but the background for the outstanding and overwhelming problems of India—the land system."[1] The wind was blowing; in the struggle for national freedom this "outstanding and overwhelming problem of India" received increasing attention partly to enlist the support of the peasantry for the political movement and partly because it was more and more realized that without significant betterment in the condition of the peasants, political freedom, in prospect and in fact, would have no meaning for the vast majority of our people, i.e. it would have no economic and social content. The wind was blowing; in certain phases of national movement, it became almost a hurricane, swept the rural masses into the vortex of the struggle, brought about a certain degree of political and social consciousness and largely generated the dynamic element in the onward advance of the struggle for national independence. The grievous evils of the old land system—the dominance of and oppression by the feudal classes in rural areas, the parlous state even of the protected tenants, the extremely precarious and deplorable state of the tenants-at-will and share-croppers, ruthless exploitation of the landless and the almost landless labourers, owing to their complete helplessness and the increasing pressure of population for

1. Jawaharlal Nehru—quoted by H. D. Malviya, *Land Reforms in India,* p. 55.

want of outlets for their labour and, of course, the growing burden of indebtedness of rural masses owing mainly to the insolvency of agriculture in general and the submerged position of three-fourths of the agriculturists in particular who constituted the small peasants and agricultural proletariat—was recognized and the programme of alleviation and amelioration was formulated on the basis of this social diagnosis. In places like Champaran and Bardoli, where the position was specially onerous and odius, the campaigns for getting immediate relief were started and acquired historical significance. In the country as a whole the peasantry was aroused to the dismalness of their condition and the need for nationwide action to bring about radical changes. In 1937-39, when the congress ministries were formed, in provinces such as Behar, U.P. and Madhya Pradesh, tenancy laws were passed, palliatives were introduced to mitigate rural indebtedness which, though not radical in themselves, in the context of conditions existing at that time had real political and social importance. During the War, the peasants participated in the political turmoils and were even further radicalized on that account. After independence in 1947 the social momentum, which had been created, was maintained and land reforms were given high priority by the Central and State Governments and the political parties. Land legislation, which has since then been enacted and implemented has made a considerable difference in the agrarian situation; and though the over-all position which has emerged is not, as indicated later, a solution of these outstanding and overwhelming problems, it is a real advance on the pre-war agrarian situation, and the changes which have been brought about have a greater significance than in the other independent Asian countries with the exception of China, Japan and perhaps even Burma.

BASIC APPROACH

The whole approach to agrarian changes has, however, necessarily undergone a basic change. They have to be conceived, formulated and carried out with full awareness of this revolutionary character. The old land system has to be replaced by a new land system, and though a period of transition from one to the other, has to be provided for the concepts, the norms, the operative principles and the criteria for social assessment have to be radically different and given definitely a revolutionary content. The balance of social forces existing and operating in the rural community has to acquire a crucial importance to be decisive for the emergence of a new social order. This is so not only from the point of view of rural but the entire national economy. The agrarian changes have, it is obvious, to be integrated with all basic economic changes in the national economy as a whole. They have, as a matter of necessity, to be their very core if dynamism of the economy has to be generated, developed and brought into action by a sustained upsurge at the basic level. In the villages and mud-huts, in which dwell our still extremely poverty-striken peasantry, the wind which did blow before independence and for a short while after independence, has subsided. The prospect of its becoming a destructive hurricane is at present rather dim. This is due partly to the inadequacy of the land reforms themselves but more to the centre of social gravity in the villages not having been changed, i.e. the pattern of power in the rural community having, if anything, been changed in favour of the privileged minority. This fact, as pointed out later, is largely admitted but its implication is not clearly and vividly appreciated, and consequential action for altering social alignments has not been taken and its need is not even clearly appreciated. This point is all-important and the extent to which land reforms can and will bring about the desired results which, in theory, are implicit in them, would almost entirely depend upon this basic shift in the balance of social forces in rural economy in particular and the national economy in general. Land reforms are not to be judged only by the extent to which they create and utilize the strength and force of the rural poor, and this can be done only if "all land" in the words of Mahatma Gandhi and Vinoba, "belongs to Gopal", i.e. again to use Mahatma Gandhi's words, "in modern language it means the state, i.e. the people".[2] And he added: "That today land does not belong to the people is too true." This was so in 1937 and this, in spite of our land reforms, is so in 1964, and this is the crux of the whole agrarian situation, and it determines, in a large measure, the substance of our rural economy. It is true that we are short of land, in some parts of the country desparately so. Even if land belongs to the people—the people in the villages cannot all have it—many will have to go without it, and therefore the only sense in which it can belong to the people is that it will have to be operated by the organs of the community and principally in its interests. We will have to utilize not only land, but also our enormous labour, now going to waste, in the interest of the community. These vital facts contain in themselves "the key to our future—they point to our fundamental needs",—to what needs to be done, why and how. This requires an all-inclusive action, and owing to their far-reaching significance call for thinking through all our major problems in relation to them and the entire economy. The point, however, which needs to be kept to the fore, is that thought and action on these lines require a social content in which the potential of the community can be brought into play and develop the required dynamics which will be generated in our mud-huts and even in the extremely poor urban dwellings which will become a mighty creative force.

MONEY POWER

The land system is, in other words, a problem in social dynamics and is interwoven with the whole economy in which, in the words of Lenin, "money has become the ruling power. All the goods produced by the labour of man can be exchanged for money."[3] This is so in spite of the relative importance of subsistence farming in our agriculture. This ruling power—

2. *Harijan*, 3.1.37.
3. Anna Rochester, *Lenin and Agrarian Question*, p. 181.

money—through the userer, the merchant and the rich peasant weaves a web in which all small farmers, landless labourers and artisans are caught, and though, as stated later, our land reforms have not made the tiller the owner of the land, but even if they had, they (the peasant proprietors) could not have broken the web of money-power. The trinity—the userer, the merchant and the rich peasant—in alliance with the money-power in towns and cities, remains the dominant element in the villages and can in effect control not only the exchange of commodities but also their production. Inadequacy of land reform combined with the dominance of money-power makes the former not illusory but deprive them of social significance as an instrument of the change of social relationship—as a means of altering radically the social structure without which land reform cannot change the land system in which money is the ruling power into a system in which the well-being of the community is supreme, i.e. a system which is the integral part of a socialist economy. In Chapter XXII of *The Rural Credit Survey Report* "Socio-Economic Context of Co-operation" has been explained at some length, and it has been very clearly pointed out how a combination of forces has worked to the grievous disadvantage of the weaker section that formed the bulk of rural population and "a mechanism of trade-finance, etc. has, by and large, been consciously or unconsciously against the interest of rural population generally and rural producers in particular. The new pattern was such that access to seats of power and source of finance was cut off from the weaker sections that formed the bulk of rural population."[4] The result, in the words of *The Rural Credit Survey* is, "that in India today there is aggregation of financial power which in point of location is largely urban, what is more important, in point of bias, that is to say, of the practices, attitudes, preferences and interests of the individuals and institutions, who share the power, is almost entirely urban-

4. *The Rural Credit Survey Report*, Vol. II, p. 296.

minded,"[5] i.e. it is working in the interest of trade and finance referred to above. Further "this affinity is not confined to private trader and money lender, it extends to the leadership of the village, but also to subordinate Government officials and the more powerful elements in the village". "The result," in the words of *The Rural Credit Survey*, "is that today there is aggregation of power located in urban areas but also extending to the village leader, trader, money lender and subordinate Government official and determining the contents of the attitudes, preferences, and interests of all who share and exercise power." There is on this account "a promotion of an impression of change around changelessness, of active obedience to behest around stolid resistance to instruction".[6] These are instances of what is clearly class solidarity which have defeated and are defeating the inner purpose of not only co-operation but all measures intended to change the socio-economic context of the social changes—including a change in the land system. Illusion of compliance round the reality of non-compliance and of change round changelessness applies even with greater force, as we shall see, to land reforms; but the main point is that the commercialization of agricultural production and the ascendency of the trader, the money lender and the rich peasants creates a context in which, in Lenin's words again, "money is ruling power". Production for market makes the land system an instrument of money-power, i.e. capitalistic forces, domination of capital in agriculture, what *The Rural Credit Survey Report* rather evasively calls urban-minded bias, and this bias cannot be changed merely by making the tiller the owner of the land.[7]

5. *Ibid.*, p. 225.
6. *The Rural Credit Survey Report*, p. 278.
7. An explanation is due as to why these long extracts from *The Rural Credit Survey Report* have been given; for, in spite of the fact that they state, in rather prolix and evasive manner, the pivotal fact of our village economy they bring out clearly what is the socio-economic context in our villages and who wields and exercises power in our rural economy. The conclusion of the survey which, as is well known, was conducted under official auspices are taken as authentic by our policy makers.

The conclusion to which these facts point out is that not only a change in the land system is essential for a socialist economy, but also a socialist economy in which the domination of capital in agriculture and in the whole system of production, distribution and exchange has been broken. This is also indispensible for health and strength of the land system. Revolutionary content of the agrarian changes, to which reference was made above, implies that a radical change in the balance of social forces not only in the village but in the economy as a whole, is of fundamental importance and must be brought about if the whole socio-economic context, in which agrarian changes, co-operation and the other new institutions have to operate and have their being, is to be sound, adequate and regenerative. This point is conclusive and is implicit in the long-term argument of *The Rural Credit Survey*.

ABOLITION OF INTERMEDIARIES

Abolition of the intermediaries has been given the highest priority in the agrarian programme in India and has almost been accomplished. The intermediaries were almost all functionless but powerful section of the rural community; they not only derived large incomes without in any way contributing to production but possessed immense power over the tenants and even more over agricultural labourers which they exercised, as a rule, in a very inhuman manner. They received rent both in cash and kind, were generally lacking in real culture and had all the vices of a degenerate landed aristocracy. A large majority of these landlords had small—in some cases ridiculously small—estates, generally lived beyond their means and the ruthless exercise of their power varied inversely to the size of their properties. They were mostly given the power, position and income which they enjoyed because it was convenient for the British to collect land revenue through them. In the process of collecting land revenue they exercised malign power over the countryside, enriched themselves and impoverished the peasantry. These reasons accounted for the great social odium which they incurred and the abolition of this parasitical class brought great relief to the countryside, and relieved the people of not only the heavy economic burdens but also of a great deal of suffering which was inflicted upon them by this class whose depravity was the greater because they had no social function and could not acquire any. These facts have been well known and have been very briefly cited here to indicate the achievements of the land reforms in India which, in spite of their serious limitations, has to be given its due place in the chronicle of events. This class has not been abolished altogether. They have been allowed to retain their home farms, *Bakashat* or *Sir* lands, in some cases up to a certain limit, in others without it, which they are expected to farm themselves without hired workers with personal labour, but in most cases they are still operating through tenants-at-will and share-croppers. These residual properties in a few cases have been converted into mechanized modern farms, but in vast majority of cases, they are still merely the source of unearned income and exploitation. These estates have been greatly enlarged through evictions and surrender of land under coercion though they are described as "voluntary" which is a well-known legal fiction. These estates are really survivals of a thoroughly discredited feudal class and in practice continue its evil traditions in the countryside. These facts have also to be stated in order to indicate serious reservation of the achievements of the new agrarian policy. In spite of this reservation it has, however, to be repeated that though the landlords have lost most of their property, position and power for evil, they are still a force to be reckoned with and together with the rich peasants, who generally belong to the same caste and have the same social outlook, they can be depended on to fight to the last ditch for the preservation of their privileged position. They are also a political power exercising a sinister influence in the villages. Loss of their feudal power and position is all the same a change for the better and has to be put on the credit side of the land reforms.

PRINCIPLE OF COMPENSATION

The principle of paying compensation for the estate of the intermediaries has been a part of the accepted approach to agrarian changes, and article 31 of the Constitution provided that compensation should be paid. The later amendment of this provision means that adequacy or otherwise of the amount awarded under the land laws should not be subject to adjudication. The Socialists and the Communists were for the abolition of the intermediaries without compensation, but even they were in favour of provision being made for grants in the case of small landlords. The market value of their estates and capitalized value of their net income at the current rate of interest—the two usual bases of assessing compensation for the acquired assets—were never accepted as valid and were not adopted. The view which had been held all along was that while payment of compensation at market value or its equivalent was impracticable and had to be ruled out, the payment of reasonable compensation was necessary and desirable. It was, however, not authoratatively laid down anywhere what the criteria of the reasonableness of compensation should be. Though in practice the amount of compensation paid has been inversely graduated to net revenue of property and in some cases additional rehabilitation grants have been provided for and paid—and therefore the needs test has in a vague manner been made the basis of assessment—there has been no rational policy in regard to the payment of compensation. In a country like India with all its diversities, rigidity in assessment of compensation had to be avoided and adjustment to specific conditions of each state provided for; but the range of differences among different states in this respect does not indicate any rational pattern or principle. The total amount of compensation, rehabilitation grants and interest according to a published authoritative document was estimated at Rs 641.42 crores out of which Rs 224.56 crores had been paid in cash and bonds up to March 1960.[8] It is re-

8. Of this amount the compensation due to landlords in Behar, U.P. and

ported that this represents the assessed compensation for the acquisition of 173 million acres of landed properties which includes about 20 million acres of forest lands and also about 20 million acres of cultivable waste which have been vested in state governments. Assuming that this estimate of 173 million acres is fairly correct the awarded compensation, even after an allowance is made for the fact that on most of these estates occupancy tenancy rights had already accrued and therefore property right in fact meant only the right to collect the authorized rent, payment of about Rs 37 per acre cannot be regarded excessive because the cash portion of the total amount is Rs 100.53 crores and the amount paid in 30 to 40 year bonds with an interest rate of 2½ per cent Rs 124.53 crores. The total area of land which the landlords have been allowed to retain for "self-cultivation", which they have enlarged by evictions and coercive transfers, is not known. But it is known to be considerable and is being let out generally on share-cropping basis. The landlords, it is reported, do not observe the statutory restrictions on the crop-share which they can take for themselves. This fact has also to be allowed for in the appraisal of the present position of the ex-landlords.

The main point, however, is that from social standpoint no rational criteria of the award of compensation have been adopted or applied and there is no upper limit to the amount which can be awarded. The permissible amount varies on the basis of inverse graduation, i.e. the lowest multiple being adopted in the case of the highest brackets and the highest in the case of the lowest. The award varies from 1 to 20 in U.P., 3 to 15 in Behar, 2 to 20 in West Bengal, 10 to 30 in old Hyderabad, 1 to 12 in Madhya Pradesh, 2 to 11 in Rajasthan,

West Bengal amounts to Rs 238.98 crores in Behar, Rs 198.31 crores in U.P. and Rs 70 crores in West Bengal, i.e. Rs 507.29 crores in these three states. This means that nearly four-fifths of the total compensation goes to these states (SOURCE: *Progress of Land Reform—Government of India,* Planning Commission, p. 4). But this, however, does not mean that feudalism was most powerful in these states. Feudalism in its worst form existed in States like Hyderabad, Rajasthan and other princely states.

3 to 15 in Orissa, and from 12½ to 30 in old Andhra and Madras. This means, for example, while a landlord with net income of Rs 1 lac is entitled to receive Rs 2 lacs in West Bengal, Rs 3 lacs in Behar, 5 lacs in Assam and Rs 12½ lacs in Madras and Andhra and in all these cases no upper limit has been put on the amount awarded, i.e. landed magnets with may be, income varying from 1 lac to 60 lacs are entitled to receive from 2 to 12½ times their net income. The highest multiples range from 11 per cent in Rajasthan to 15 in Orissa and Vindhya Pradesh, 20 in Behar, U.P. and West Bengal and 30 in Madras, Hyderabad and Andhra. The anamolies in the compensation provision of the different states are much greater than indicated by these illustrative cases if the provisions are analysed in greater detail but the facts cited above clearly show that reasonableness of compensation has had no definite meaning or principle in our land legislation and even the richest landlords have been paid 1 to 12½ times their net income by way of compensation. Abolition of landlordism to the extent to which it has taken place is, to repeat, a welcome development, but in spite of the fact that the assent of the President, i.e. approval of the Central Government, is needed and has to be obtained before land laws are implemented, these glaring anamolies have remained and cannot be explained in terms of differences of conditions and circumstances of different states and indicate a lack of national policy in this very important matter. Feudalism is not dead in this country, and though its relative importance varies from state to state, in states like Rajasthan, Orissa, Madhya Pradesh it is still a force which matters a lot. In all states, three-fourths of the rural population belongs to what are called the weakest sections and are still living in an atmosphere of fear and repression in which caste and feudal traditions combine to undermine their will to assert themselves for even getting their legitimate statutory rights respected, what to speak of developing the necessary awareness and strength for socialist transformation, which without their active support, cannot but remain a pious hope.

RENTIERS

Abolition of the intermediaries does not mean abolition of the rent-receiving classes, i.e. the classes living on income derived from landed property without making any contribution to production. Among the so-called Ryats who pay land revenue to the state, i.e. are in direct contact with it and are in law not intermediaries, there are large sections who are rentiers pure and simple, i.e. either have sub-tenants who pay rent in cash or kind or their land is cultivated by hired workers in some cases, but mostly by share-croppers. Leasing of land by owner-cultivator is also common at all levels from the lowest to the highest for various reasons, but leasing of land by owners, who are not cultivators and yet are not given the legal status of landlords, i.e. intermediaries, is an important factor in our rural economy. They are in fact landlords, and they have the attitude and bearing of that class. They represent concentration of economic power in the villages and generally exercise great influence also on account of their caste status. In parliamentary democracy now in operation in this country they are of growing importance in politics in the village and intermediate level. They are now less amenable to control from above than before and decentralization of political and economic authority now in progress is going to add to their strength and make politics not more democratic but subject to greater stresses owing to the pulls and counter-pulls at the basic level. The rentiers, who are legally not landlords, are the most important factors in this alliance of reactionary elements in rural areas, and owing to the virtual failure, as stated below, of the provision for ceilings, there is hardly any prospects of their power and position being diminished or their being assimilated in healthy democratic processes unless, as stated later, the village community in which its weakest sections, i.e. the majority of rural population count and have a decisive role.

FAILURE OF AGRARIAN POLICY

The agrarian policies of the state seek to realize the following objects: (a) all cultivators should be owners, (b) there should be no letting or sub-letting except in very special cases subject to effective regulations by the village community, (c) all transfers of land should be subject to public regulation and control, and take place according to well-defined priorities, and (d) cultivation should conform to the standard of good husbandry and schemes of crop-planning.9 There are other objectives besides the abolition of the intermediaries referred to above, but these four objectives are of fundamental importance. In the thirteen years of formulation and implementation of plans these objectives have been affirmed and reaffirmed in an authoritative manner, but have not been realized. In the Third Plan they have been reaffirmed perhaps even with greater emphasis, but so far the provisions made for their realization have almost been completely evaded owing to the state governments, administrative personnel particularly at the lowest level and political leaders being subject to forces and pressures antoganistic to the realization of these objectives. The failure to implement the provisions made for this purpose is admitted and it is also admitted, though not as clearly as it should be, that it is largely due to social forces and pressures arrayed against them being very powerful and no counter-vailing pressures having been engendered and built up. Whether the position in this respect will be materially improved would also depend upon this cardinal deficiency being removed or made up for by re-adjustment of social forces, i.e. by the forces being brought into play which will be more than a match for the forces which have so far made the provisions for the realization of these objectives practically nugatory.

Leased Land

The Congress Agrarian Reforms Committee was unable to give figures of the extent to which land is let and sublet in

9. Report of the Congress Agrarian Reforms Committee, p. 11, The First Five Year Plan, p. 17-100, Second Five Year Plan, p. 181-92.

India and described "various ramifications of complex relation-
ships" as "a weird zig-zag puzzle".[10] The position has been
rationalized and simplified to a certain extent since then, but
in spite of all that has been planned and achieved, complex
relationship is only a little, if at all, less weird puzzle than
before and the extent of tenancy and subtenancy and infringement of the various provisions of the laws is not known to any
degree of certainty. The one source which is being cited—a
source of information of the prevalence of tenancy even by the
committee of the Panel of Land Reforms (1961)—is the Eighth
Round of National Sample Survey (1954-55). It is better to
have this source of information than have none at all, but
limitations of the work done under National Sample Survey are
a matter of common knowledge and the validity of the conclusion based upon the results of these rounds is limited. According to this source about 24 per cent of the total area operated
by rural households was held on lease and the percentage of
the area thus held varied from 14 to 37 per cent in different
zones of the country.[11]

AREA LEASED AS PER CENT OF THE CULTIVATED AREA

Zone	Percentage
North Zone	14
Central Zone	20
South Zone	23
East Zone	25
West Zone	27
North West Zone	37
All India	24

These figures are based upon field survey carried out from
July 1954 to March 1955. Since then it can be safely assumed
that the area under tenancy has greatly increased, but no
authentic information is availble to the extent to which leasing
of land has increased. Mass eviction of tenants with secure

10. *The Congress Agrarian Reforms Committee Report*, p. 35.
11. The N.S.S. Report No. 10, p. 10, Panel on Land Reforms (1955) Table
VI.

rights, surrenders under coercion, and transfer by sales have gone on and occupancy and protected tenants (who for the purpose of the eighth round were treated as owners) have been replaced by tenants-at-will and share-croppers. The same result has been produced by the abuse of the provision for resumption of land for personal cultivation and tampering with records of right in collusion with the lower revenue officers—mostly village Patels or Patwaris. For example in old Hyderabad state the number of protected tenants decreased during 1951-55 by 59 per cent and in over 41 per cent of the area tenants were illegally evicted or lost their land by "voluntary" surrender and the area held by them was reduced by 59 per cent which is another way of saying that area cultivated by tenants-at-will or share-croppers had increased to that extent. According to another report the area under share-cropping increased by 90 per cent in U.P. and 50 per cent in the country as a whole. As stated above information as to the extent land is now being cultivated by tenants who are really tenants-at-will is not available. That the N.S.S. estimate of 24 per cent for 1954-55 is an underestimate admits of no doubt, and that in the last six years "land to the tiller" as a principle of our land policy has been operating in the reverse gear is also a known and established fact though it is not known how much suffering and depre-vation the process has inflicted on the poorest section of our peasantry. In the Second Five Year Plan it was clearly stated that action with retrospective effect should be taken to redress the wrong that had been done by mass evictions and "volun-tary" surrenders and the lands of the cultivators who had lost their lands should be restored to them.[12] Halting action has been taken in a few cases to give effect to the directive, but taking the country as a whole the position is that these wrongs have not been righted and the provisions of land laws have been successfully and finally defeated. Miscarriage of the pur-pose of the laws in the first instance and unwillingness and

12. *Second Five Year Plan*, p. 209.

inability to right the well-established grievous wrongs inflicted by this fact are entirely due to our policy makers and its executants having no genuine faith in its avowed purpose. It is a case of the governance and administration of the country being clearly in league against the honest formulation and execution of the policy of fundamental agrarian changes. The failure is an index of the resistance which is being in fact successfully offered to the latter and the spirit of radical measures of social policy. This is true not only of the provision of land laws, but it also applies to many other policy decisions which, as stated later, are being subverted and distorted in execution. This is due not only to the administrators but the policy makers being at heart against the change which for political reasons they have nominally to accept and legislate for. It is a case of the prime movers of the social system not working for but against the necessary and desired changes.

CAUSES OF FAILURE

The negative result of the implementation of our land policy is, of course, due to the failure of its major objects being put into effect in right manner and to the fullest extent. The prime object of this policy is to make the peasant owner of the land he cultivates and eliminate the rent-receiving class altogether. In the meanwhile it is obviously necessary to realize conditions under which the tenants can enjoy full security, pay only fair rents fixed by the state and increasingly acquire ownership of their land. Mass evictions, illicit surrenders and transfers, abuse of the right of resumption, tampering with records of rights and preventing the tenants claiming their statutory rights even when they know that they are all due to the cultivators being overawed by the might of the village oligarchy, bias of the administration at all levels being clearly against their interests, and, to repeat, policy makers themselves not being in earnest about the execution of the policies which they officially initiate and embody in land laws owing to the general climate of public opinion being very unmistakably in favour of the cultivators. On this point a quotation from *Ambassador's Report* of Mr. Chester Bowles is of interest. He writes: "In general tenancy legislations are unworkable because the landlord is still left in a powerful position. Often he is the only literate man in the village. In the Punjab, where tenants who have tilled a certain plot of land for five years, were finally given permanent tenure, I have seen in the villages where records show that no tenant has tilled the same plot of land for more than two or three years. The village head and his associates who own most of the land were able to juggle the books because he alone knew how to read them." Illiteracy of the cultivators is a handicap but is not the most important reason why the landlord and his associates juggle the books. The most important reason is that they are all powerful. They are acting in concert and can defy and violate the law with impunity because the cultivators are caste and class ridden, have weak bargaining power, are not organized and are in no position to assert themselves against "the landlord who may be money lender, who may also be a trader and the educated person, who may also be the subordinate official and all these in association with the outside urban world of finance and power".[13] This is really rephrasing what the Rural Credit Survey Committee has, as stated before, said about the urban-minded bias of the whole rural economy. Lenin's words, quoted already, that "capital dominates agriculture" accounts for juggling with books and the poor implementation of our land policy. Records of rights have been improved since independence. In Andhra Pradesh, Assam, Madras, Saurashtra, West Bengal, Behar and U.P., according to the Report of the Committee on Land-Reforms, considerable progress has been made in improving the Record of Rights, but even now no information is available about tenants, sub-tenants and crop-sharers in Andhra Pradesh, Assam, Kerala, Madras and Mysore and even in the states in which it is available, the juggling of books

13. B. Venkatapeah, *The Problem of Afro-Asian New States,* p. 30.

on a large scale has been and is being resorted to.

In U.P. and West Bengal all tenants and sub-tenants (not crop-sharers) have been brought into direct contact with the state, i.e. they are protected against eviction and even against resumption. In other states the right to resumption exists, but otherwise occupancy and protected tenants have the fixity of tenure, and other tenants need either security subject to the right of resumption or need qualification of continuous cultivation for 6 to 12 years to acquire the protected status. In Andhra and Behar bills have been introduced to increase the tenants' security and in several other states ejectment of tenants has been stayed and protective measures are under consideration. The position in this respect has improved but apart from the limitations inherent in the balance of social forces, further legislative and administrative action is called for to bring the new statutory position of the tenant into conformity with the avowed purpose of our land policy.

Fixation of fair rents has been attempted but by and large the attempt has not been successful. The First and Second Five Year Plans recommended that rent should not exceed 1/5 to 1/4 of the gross produce, but there are wide variations in the rates in the regulatory acts of various states. In Gujerat, Maharashtra and Rajasthan the mximum rent has been fixed at 1/6 of the gross produce, in Assam, Orissa, Delhi, Himachal, Manipur and Tripura 1/5 to 1/4, and in the bills of Andhra, Kerala and Mysore provision has been made to fix rent at 1/6 to 1/4, in the Punjab it is 1/3, in Madras it varies from 1/3 to 2/5, in Behar it is fixed at 35 per cent and in West Bengal at 50 per cent. In Madhya Pradesh the maximum is 2 to 4 times the land revenue. Share of the gross produce, even if it is a uniform rate, cannot but mean in real terms different rates for the cultivator; but as it is, even the rates vary and have no relation to productivity or equity. What is, however, more significant and disquieting is that fair rents as fixed by the law are in practice being disregarded and the tenants are being rack-rented without incurring the penalties of law, revulsion of public opinion or even the resistance or revolt of the tenants. Though this wide-spread practice is known to exist, action taken to enforce the law has, largely speaking, been ineffective and brought the very law itself into disrepute and contempt.[14]

14. The Research Programme Committee of the Planning Commission sponsored a number of studies for the evaluation of the progress of land reform. In the report submitted by the Gokhale School of Economics it was stated, "of the area which was tenant cultivated in the first year of the inquiry (1948-49) only 58.1 per cent continued to be held by the same tenant at the end of the inquiry (1952-53), 38.7 was resumed by the owner or the tenant changed. In over 80 per cent of the cases the landlord obtained voluntary surrenders from the tenants".

The Act (the Bombay Tenancy and Agricultural Land Act of 1948) provides for the purchase of ownership by tenant. However, tenants purchased ownership only over 3.2 per cent of the area. The Act before amendment regulated the rents by fixing one-fourth of the gross produce as maximum rent for irrigated and one-third for other land. In the Report it is also stated that "the third failure namely the failure to regulate rent is, however, the most distressing for it is entirely a failure of implementation". The share-rents have almost remained unchanged. The cash-rents also have shown no signs of lowering. "Even the landlords reported to us true rents and that they found no reasons to conceal the facts. For all practical purposes the Act did not exist' (*The Working of the Bombay Tenancy Act, 1948 Report of Investigation*, p. 187). The fact that no effort was made to conceal the facts has to be taken as an index of the helplessness of the tenants and complete ineptness and utter lack of concern of administration and obviously not of the truthfulness of the landlords. This was in 1951-52, but it is unlikely from what is known as the relative strength of different interests in the village and the country and owing to the known indifference, if not active complicity of administrative personnel, that the position is significantly different now. These restrictions are mostly needed for window dressing and have no bearing on the actual working of the agrarian economy. In Hyderabad similar inquiry showed that illegal acquisition by the landlords accounted for 55 per cent of the land lost by the tenants through evictions and surrenders. In the report of the same inquiry it was stated that "such surrenders have taken place even in cases when the tenant was aware of his right granted under the law. A majority of tenants did not want to estrange their relations with the landholders on whom they depend for many things in their day to day life. Most of them left the land immediately they were asked to."

The Poona and Hyderabad inquiries related the events which occurred more than a decade ago, but the position is practically the same even now, rents are paid at rates all over the country as if land laws did not exist and the tenants submit to the unlawful demand of the landholders owing to

There has been a provision in most of the states for the optional purchase by the tenants of the land which they cultivate from the landholders. This provision was made because in our land policy there is only place for cultivating owners in agriculture until they, as a matter of free will, join the farming co-operatives. In the last thirteen years, in spite of this provision[15] there has been practically no progress in the acquisition of the ownership rights by the tenants. This provision is a concession to strong bias in favour of peasant proprietorship, the relation of which to socialism will be considered in the next chapter. The point, however, which needs to be stressed, as stated above, is that this provision has remained with some exceptions, practically a dead letter and the tenants continue to pay rents above the statutory rates and their undoubted longing for owning land remains unfulfilled. In U.P., West Bengal and Delhi they have been brought into direct contact with the state and presumably are paying statutory rents. But

their dread of the consequences of non-compliance. The laws do not protect them and they cannot protect themselves. It is again a case of the poor masses being helpless against the system in which all who count are against them and they have not yet found the key to unlock the strength which they possess but cannot exercise. Either they themselves have to count for much more than they do at present or they have to learn to use the giant strength which they possess but are not aware of.

15. The right to purchase by tenants can be exercised by payment of compensation. In some states—Assam, Bombay, Madhya Pradesh, Rajasthan, Manipur and Tripura it is to be the multiple of land-revenue from 15-20 times, in Assam and Rajasthan 15 times and in Madhya Pradesh 30 times. In other states it is to be a multiple of rent 6-15 times in Andhra, 12 times in Bombay, 15 times of net rent minus revenue in Mysore and 10 times in U.P. In Behar Rs 90 to 1050 per acre have to be paid for exercising the right to purchase. These wide variations in the scheme of compensation again do not follow any national pattern in spite of the fact that these scales also have received central approval. As the right to purchase has been scarcely exercised these variations have hardly any practical importance. If the action indicated in the text is taken, this right can and preferably should be allowed to lapse so long as there is a rational scheme of fair rent, the option to exercise this right can be left to the tenant and he can be educated to waive this right in the interest of utilizing his available means for the development of agriculture.

in the other states in the words of the Committee of the Panel on Land Reforms (1961) "for several reasons optional rights of purchase have generally not been exercised". In some states like Assam, Jammu and Kashmir and Madras even the optional right of purchase has not been granted. The Committee has recommended that the government should take immediate action for bringing the tenants into direct contact with the state in all states. If this recommendation is acted upon, and the tenants are given the option of either to continue as tenants on payment of fair rent or acquire the right of ownership on payment of fair compensation, the system of landlordism will really end. They will have to be applied to all cultivators whether they have the status of occupancy or protected tenants or not. If the rents are standardized and are fair, the question of ownership will become a secondary question. A measure like this should have been adopted as part of the rational land policy immediately after independence and if this had been done, all the distortions of our land policy could have been avoided. This simple and bold step would have removed complications and made it possible to develop a rational land system as part of the socialist transformation of the country. The cultivators instead of using their resources to acquire ownership rights should now be encouraged to invest them in development of their holdings or better still pool them for carrying out the village community plans of the development of agriculture. The historical anamolies embedded in our land system would, if this is done, also be ended and the position changed for implementing a rational socialist land policy. Whether this will be done or not would, however, really depend upon the strength of social forces operating in the country. This fundamental change can be carried out only if the needed social steam can be generated and parasitical relation in agriculture terminated once and for ever. At present it is very unlikely that this will happen. The omens are all against it.

RESUMPTION OF RIGHT

The land owners have been given the right to resume land from tenants subject to certain conditions, for making farming their profession and developing agriculture. The intention of giving the right to resume was to convert rentiers into farmers and contribute to the development of agriculture. This right has in fact been abused, land has been resumed in most cases not for personal cultivation and agricultural development but to add to the leased agricultural properties, and the fact has been disguised by all sorts of artifices. This right has to be exercised within the ceiling limit, but as the ceiling can be and has been, as stated below, evaded in practice, the right of resumption has become an instrument of dispossessing the tenant for increasing exploitation. This right has really become a means for enforcing submission on the tenants, even if it is not exercised, and when it is, it generally means that the rentiers have more land which is cultivated by the tenants-at-will or share-croppers though nominally by the cultivating owner with the help of the hired labourers. The underlying principle of the right to resume is that interests of the small holders and tenants should be reconciled, and the latter should, as a rule, not be left destitute through the exercise of this right by the landlords. Hardship to small landholders has to be avoided, and when there is a real need for increasing land for self-cultivation the grant and exercise of this right serves a legitimate purpose. But such genuine cases are few and the resumption by more substantial landlords even nominally within the ceiling limit has been mostly used to enlarge their landed property. Even demarcation of holdings into resumable and non-resumable portions has not been made and the limit of five years for the exercise of this right recommended in the Second Five Year Plan has not been laid down. This whole scheme is based on the assumption that former rent-receiving land owners can be converted into progressive farmers within the ceiling limit and will be a leaven in the countryside. This is an unrealistic assumption. They, as a class, cannot by tradition and otherwise assume this role. These land holders, small and large, are, with a few exceptions, confirmed in their old habit of living on the labour of others and personal cultivation in their case can only mean exploitation in disguise. The condition that they should put in personal manual labour which has been laid down can be and has been evaded and, in the existing conditions, it cannot be enforced. The best that can be done is that the demarcation between resumable and non-resumable land should be expeditiously carried out and, say, within two years either the right should be honestly exercised or it should lapse. This right is a source of great insecurity in the country-side, and though a few genuine cases of bona fide exercise of the right should be provided for, generally speaking, it may be repeated, the grant and exercise of this right has done much more harm than good and been used to cow down the peasantry rather than develop new yeomanry in the villages. In the social context in which this right has been conceded and exercised it has fortified old prejudices, enabled a functionless class to prolong its existence and continue its exploitation and impeded the process of its change-over to a more productive role.

UNECONOMIC HOLDINGS

There is one aspect of the agrarian situation, which has now been lost sight of, but which for a long while was given a prominent place in our thinking on agrarian problems, i.e. the exemption of the owners of uneconomic holdings from the payment of rent and land-revenue. Pundit Jawaharlal Nehru, in his presidential address at the U.P. Political Conference in 1928, drew pointed attention to the need for exempting from taxation "the very poor holders of land who can barely make a living out of it". In the famous Karachi resolution of 1931 again the need for exemption from rent on all uneconomic holdings was specifically included (Article 5 of the Karachi Resolution). In 1935 at Kisan Conference at Allahabad, presided over by Sardar Vallabh Bhai Patel, it was urged "that those whose total income is insufficient to meet the necessary requirements of the family be exempted from the payment of revenue or rent". At the Faizpur Congress in 1936 again in clause 2 of the resolution on agrarian programme it was stated "that uneconomic holding be exempted from rent and land-tax". In the Congress Election Manifesto of 1936 also the need for exempting uneconomic holdings from the payment of rent and revenue was clearly reaffirmed. These quotations indicate that the exemption of uneconomic holdings of those "who can hardly make a living out of land from rent and revenue" features prominently in important pronouncements on the agrarian problem, but after independence this point has practically faded out of policy statements, programmes and agrarian legislation and even in our thinking the point has hardly any place. Dr. Lohia is probably the only public leader who considers this point of interest and importance and includes it in his programme of the party which he leads. This is a significant omission. Is there any case for the exemption of uneconomic holdings and those who cannot meet their minimum needs from not only revenue but also rent? If a ten-acre holding is taken as economic holding, nearly at least three-fourths of rural households and farms would have to be exempted from the payment of land revenue and rent. Those holdings and their owners are living in a state of chronic deficit not only from the standpoint of even subsistance minimum but also as operators of economic enterprises, for income from their productive units does not, on any system of account keeping, cover even the cost of the cultivation.

From the practical standpoint it may be that it is beyond our means to grant the exemption from land revenue even though there may be a strong case for it; but the same consideration does not apply to the exemption from rent of holdings which are so clearly below the line. They have paid rent in the past because their owners had no alternative; it was absolutely necessary for them to pay rent even for their tiny holdings because they could not have otherwise made even the kind of living they were making. It was absolute rent—a payment owing to the fact that the landlords had a monopoly of a very scarce instrument of production—land. Even marginal land had to pay rent. Should this continue even when all tenants are brought into direct contact with the state, i.e. assigned holdings by the state? At present the tenants who are in direct contact with the state pay the same rents which the landlords were charging them. If all the tenants are placed in the same position, they will follow the same practice, their liabilities to landlords would become liability to the state. For a while if the tenants exercise the option of remaining tenants, this liability will be accepted and met because of the old usage and habit. But before long the social ethics of this practice is likely to be questioned. They (the owners of these holdings) will have no surplus of income or differential surplus from which rent could be paid. Most likely these dwarf holdings will disappear and their owners cease to live below the margin of subsistence and in a state of constant deficit in a re-organized rural economy in which these holdings would be merged in joint cooperative farms and the surplus labour would be utilized in other productive channels. Unless this is done, inequity of the liability to pay rent will be so obvious as to call for immediate redress. The only way in which legitimate demand for exemption of such holdings from rent can be made is to abolish them and place their owners above want in a more diversified and developed socialist economy. In an economy of individual holdings and enterprise this contradiction cannot be resolved, "for rent in such an economy is a necessary tribute which even dire poverty must pay riches for their privelege of being allowed to subsist". It is absolute rent and is paid because land is monopoly. After independence demand for exemption of such holdings from revenue and rent was, as pointed out above, quietly dropped for it was realized almost unconsciously that there was no answer to this demand in the framework of an undeveloped private enterprise economy. This demand will be raised again, and in the context of the new economy, which may emerge, it will have a new meaning and a new answer. The demand itself is legitimate and carries in itself its own answer, for it really is a refusal on the part of the dispossessed to accept the poverty of an economy, which cannot find a way out of a blind alley, as an ultimate or irremovable difficulty. It is, however, not known whether revolutionary temper for such an act of non-acquiscence will be actually generated. The question which Jawaharlal Nehru raised in 1928 as a counter in political game is a fundamental question and requires fundamental changes in the economy. It cannot be evaded now. It is one of the fundamental questions which can be answered only if we can transcend the cramping limitations of the present economy, i.e. if we accept the necessity and logic of social revolution.

LAND CEILINGS

The question of having ceilings on land holdings has been in the air since the Congress Programme Committee in 1947-48 urged that in agriculture limit should be fixed for the maximum size of holdings. The Congress Agrarian Reform strongly endorsed the bill and laid down the general policy, the First Five Year Plan commended the principle, the Second again laid down the general lines on which the principle should be approached and left the formulation of the policy to the states and the Nagpur Congress resolution of 1959, owing to extremely slow progress in the states called for immediate action for the implementation of the policy. Now the acts have been passed in all states—in Behar, Gujrat, Maharashtra, Mysore, Madras recently —but even in Andhra Pradesh, Madhya Pradesh, Orissa and Rajasthan where ceiling legislation was passed earlier, governments are engaged in working out rules and procedures and only in two states some action in this regard has been taken. In West Bengal 2.5 lac acres have been taken and alloteed to share-croppers and 2.3 lac acres have been settled with tenants in Jammu and Kashmir. That this delay has been deliberate and due to the state governments' unwillingness to carry out the ceiling policy in right earnest admits of no doubt at all. As it is, loopholes in the Acts cannot but retard progress in the execution of this policy. Because of the built-in resistance to it at all levels, it would be unduly optimistic to expect that disparities in the villages would be significantly reduced by the execution of this policy, or surplus land would, on any scale, which matters, be made available for distribution among landless labourers or poor peasants. All this time the landed gentry in the countryside have taken full advantage of this delay in passing ceiling legislation and its implementation. There is evidence that it was intended that this should happen. Anticipatory action through nominal partitions, fictitious transfers and other dishonest devices has been taken on a large scale on a countrywide basis, and it is known that surplus land over ceilings would not make any real difference[16] to the general social structure in agriculture. Possibly in some cases with determined action in certain areas results of some importance could be achieved but the prospect of such action being taken is clearly negated by the experience of the last decade of bold resolutions which, it was known, were not even honestly conceived, much less executed.

There are, in this case, again very wide variations in the

16. The area which would be made available in the country as a whole if the proposed ceilings are enforced is not known. In West Bengal the state Government has already come into possession of 5.24 lac acres, in the U.P. 140,000 acres have already been declared surplus, in Maharashtra 90,000 acres and in Andhra Pradesh 50,000 acres. This information (Vide *Third Year Plan—Mid Term Appraisal*, p. 100) is not up to date and possibly the position now is slightly different but most likely not significantly so. In the 1st report of N.S.S. Report (8th Round), Prof. Mahalnobis indicated on the basis of the data in the Report, that if every household is to have two acres in agriculture and ceiling is fixed at 20 acres, the amount of land available for distribution would be 63 million or about 20 per cent of the cultivated area. This is also a very rough estimate, but the actual ceilings are between 12 to 324 acres, most of them about 30 acres, even if the rough estimate loses all meaning from practical standpoint. Dr Baljit Singh of Lucknow University, on the bases of the data published by N.S.S. has calculated that if in U.P. the ceiling is fixed at 25 acres, 1,544 thousand

states in the level of ceilings. In Andhra the limit has been set between 27 to 324 acres, in Assam at 50 acres, in Gujerat between 12 to 33 acres for wet land but 56 to 132 acres for dry land, in Jammu and Kashmir at 22 acres, in Kerala between 15 to 37½ acres, at 28 standard acres, in Madras at 30 standard acres, in Maharashtra from 18 to 126 acres, in Mysore 27 standard acres, in Orissa at 25 standard acres, in Punjab at 30 standard acres, in Rajasthan at 30 standard acres, in U.P. at 40 acres of fair quality land, in West Bengal at 25 acres, in Delhi, Himachal Pradesh at 30 standard acres and at Manipur and Tripura at 25 acres. These variations are accounted for partly—but only partly—by the variations of conditions; and in spite of central regulation and control, it can be stated that the family-holding rule prescribed by the Planning Commission for the imposition of ceiling has not been adhered to in practice. It is impossible to say what the final outcome of the implementation of the measures which have been taken will be. That the distortion of the ceiling policy will vary within wide limits is certain. The anticipatory action to defeat the ceiling laws has been effective in various degrees in different states. Resistance from within in the states would also depend upon conditions the effect of which cannot be estimated. And, of course, variations in the level of statutory ceilings being what they are, would make it impossible to say what emergent social structure in the villages as a result of the pressures of these distorting factors would be and how far it would diverge from the original

acres would be available for distribution and if at 40 acres, 4,308 thousand (Baljit Singh, *Next Step in Village India*, p. 90). In fact ceiling actually fixed for U.P. is 40 to 80 acres per person and not per family and Mr. Charan Singh's plea that at 40 acres very little surplus land would be available is more than valid. In the country as a whole "while the officials wrangled over schedules and catagories, the landlords hastened their steps to forestall the possible effects of ceilings" (D. Thorner, *The Agrarian Prospect in India*, p. 69). Dr Baljit Singh has made a good case for fixing the ceiling at 15 acres, but he knows that ceilings have largely been fixed for what he calls 'a show window effect' and the vested interests have already won the day.

policy. It goes, however, without saying that the range of inequalities in the villages would not be materially reduced by
the implementation of the ceiling legislation and the social
framework within which the rural economy will operate would
not be on that account favourable for the introduction or development of a socialist society.

LAND CEILINGS AND CEILINGS ON INCOMES

The ceiling policy has been taken exception to on the ground
that it is clearly discriminatory[17] against agricultural classes and
that it involves imposition of ceilings on agricultural incomes
without corresponding action being taken in relation to non-
agricultural classes. The counter-view that ceiling is, in the
words of Mr. C. D. Deshmukh, "in reality a way of ensuring

17. This view has been expressed very clearly by Prof. D. R. Gadgil. He
says, "I accept the concept of the ceilings on ownership holdings and
cultivation holdings in India. I accept the concept, however, as a part of
general programme of more equal distribution of income in society and as
counter-part of ceiling on non-agricultural incomes. If no ceiling on non-
agricultural income is contemplated, it it not only unjust to impose it on
agricultural income, but the measure is bound to create grave imbalance in
society. In this case in all the other sectors of economic activity increasing
acquisition of wealth and income will continue to be sought after by the
majority, and the prestige and power connected with riches will remain
unabated, in agriculture alone all will be condemned to a fixed permanent low
level, above which they will on no account be able to raise themselves" (The
Indian Journal of Agricultural Economics, Vol. XIV, No. 4, p. 33). Prof. Gadgil
is on very firm ground in the views which he has expressed except that the
implication that it is possible in agriculture to "condemn all to a fixed permanent low level" while "increasing acquisition of wealth and income continue
to be sought after by the majority" is not tenable. These two sets of values,
these two compartments of income and wealth, cannot exist together. The
attempt to achieve the separation cannot but recoil on the authors of this
policy. They can create a world of make-believe of "change round reality of
changelessness" and what is much worse, degradation of values and morals
owing to a widening gap between profession and performance but they cannot have power "connected with riches" in all other sectors and make
"agriculture a permanently depressed sector". Power connected with riches
will continue to dominate agriculture and all other sectors. In other words,
socialism will, if this happens, remain still-born in a world of decay and
disruption if it is sought to create or strengthen this contradiction.

that the scarce factor of production is not monopolized by few," and that "this is a special case of regulating land-ownership, tenure and land-utilization"[18] is valid up to a point. Land being all-important for rural economy it is necessary that it should be subject to special measures of regulation and control, specially in an old and thickly populated country. But it is vain to hope that rural economy can be subject to a set of regulatory basic principles which are not applicable to the economy as a whole and the economy can be half equalitarian and half non-equalitarian. As stated before, land system is now an integral part of the capitalistic economy in which money is the ruling power, and in spite of the importance of subsistance cultivation and other pre-modern factors, the system is largely being operated by moneyed interests. Not only this system cannot be isolated or its substitute function in an orbit of its own, but unless dominant moneyed classes are also in the main subjected to the same basic regulatory principles and function according to the same social norms, a land system, with floor and ceiling on holdings and with narrow range of disparities, cannot be established or developed. The high-ups in the rural economy are also traders, money-lenders and have, as stated before, social affiliations with the members of the hierarchy of moneyed interests. They not only exercise their power over the poor masses in the villages, but also derive their strength from their being a part of the economy which revolves round the money axis. The built-in resistance to ceilings and other radical features of land legislation, to which reference has been made, is a part of defense mechanism of the economy as a whole and can be counter-acted and overcome only by an all-round action against the forces with which the rich agriculturists are closely connected and from whom they receive active assistance. In regard to ceilings, the bearing of this point on the ceiling on land-holdings is that ceiling on non-agricultural incomes and wealth (for ceiling on holdings are first ceiling on wealth and incident-

18. Lok Sabha Debate, Vol. IV, No. 48, 21-4-56, p. 5900.

ally on income) have to be an essential part of national social policy, though this ceiling, to start with, cannot be as low as the ceilings on agriculture. The view which is put forward to defend ceilings that ceilings on holdings are not ceilings on incomes is not even ingenious, it is really very unconvincing. To the extent to which the ceilings are effective, they cannot but be a very important limiting factor in determining the level of agricultural incomes. Ceilings on all incomes and range of inequalities limited between the social minimum and maximum have been a part of our working faith[19] even before we made socialism the avowed goal of development and transformation. The more earnestly, however, we have professed our faith in socialism, the more unenthusiastic our government and political parties have become about ceilings and floors of income structure as a whole. The result is that we have got involved in a web of contradictions of which our difficulties in making effective ceilings in agricultural holdings is only one illustration. It may be repeated that unified action all along the line is called for if our ceilings on holdings are to be effective and a new socialist land system is to be brought into being and operation.

Apart from the illicit transfers, partitions and other devices

19. In the Congress Economic Programme of 1948 which was drawn up by a committee presided over by Pundit Jawaharlal Nehru, "a ceiling of income which should not exceed 100 times the national minimum, required for such primary needs as food, clothing etc. to be reduced by successive stages to 30 times the national income" was called for. The Taxation Commission a few years later suggested the ceiling of 30 times the national minimum. It is significant that one of the casualties of planning in India has been the ceiling on all incomes and even the opposition parties have never seriously raised the issue. Inequalities have, it is known, been increasing in the last ten years. It is not surprising that in this context ceiling on agricultural holdings has become an issue to be used as a garnish for policy statement and in practice has been evaded or disregarded. Ceiling on agricultural holdings, unless it is made a part of rational income structure of a socialist economy in the making, will remain a sore point with the uppermost section of the rural communities, and the climate of public opinion and administration will strongly favour its evasion.

for defeating the ceiling legislation exemptions from the ceiling laws provided in the acts themselves have been widely utilized to defeat their purpose. Among them the exemption provided for efficiently managed farms in compact blocks, it is known, has been most widely abused. The Mysore bill defines the compact block as a "farm which is so situated that no piece of land included in such farm is separated from another piece by a distance of more than ten miles". It is unbelievable that such a provision could be made in a ceiling bill, but it has been. In the Second Five Year Plan a list of factors is given for judging the quality of the management of farms, and though these factors are important in farm management, their judgement and evolution cannot be based upon well-defined criteria and they can and do provide scope for free play of subjective considerations, and our administrative personnel being what they are, it would not be surprising if the implementation of this provision is freely used more to defeat the real purpose of the ceiling laws rather than fulfil it. The fact is that in the Acts the size of the well-managed farm has not been laid down, small farmers can as easily claim exemption as large ones and thereby the ceilings can easily be made ineffective. Of the other exemptions plantations and co-operative farms, who need special consideration, the rest have implicit in them anomalies[20] which cannot

---

20. "Even the basic approach to agriculture," in the words of Prof. D. R. Gadgil, "is unfair to the agriculturists. This appears from several suggestions relating to the exclusions or exemptions from ceiling legislation, which are currently made. One set of suggestions relates to the type of activity in relation to land. Thus 'dairy farming' and 'breeding of live stock' are excluded from the defination of agriculture, and the growing fruits, flowers or vegetables or betal leaves is exempted from the operation of the reform measures. It is difficult to understand the logic behind these exclusions and exemptions. The growing of grass will be subject to ceilings but not the breeding of live-stock. What can make bananas exempt but not sugar-cane or betal leaves exempt but not tobacco? That most of the activities to which ceilings will not apply belong to the catagories in which urban and non-peasant elements are likely to engage makes them all the more objectionable" (D. R. Gadgil "A Ceiling on Holdings of Agricultural Land in India," *The Indian Journal of Agricultural Economics*, Vol. XIV, No. 4, p. 34).

but create serious difficulties in the implementations of these provisions. The ceilings even in the Third Five Year Plan have an important place in land reforms, but it is known that from practical standpoint the utility of the ceiling laws has been almost exhausted. These laws will remain on the statute book and their "shop-window" effect will be utilized, but it would be vain to expect that they will bring about changes of any consequence in our land system. They will neither contribute to the reduction of inequalities, nor provide land for the settlement of the landless labourers or development of farming co-operatives. Our agrarian structure will remain resistant to the advance of socialism in spite of these ceiling laws, and unless revolutionary forces begin to work in the villages we cannot expect that they will become nuclei of a socialist economy.

DISPARITIES IN AGRICULTURE

Disparities in agriculture are the root cause of the basic difficulties which we are up against in our villages. Abolition of the intermediaries has, within certain limits, reduced these disparities, but the big landed magnates were, relatively speaking, few and most of the land-holders were men of moderate, in many cases, very limited means. That they have had to hand over their properties under land legislation is of course a step in advance, but that is because rent-receiving classes have lost their pre-eminent position in agriculture and their worst malpractices have been curbed. But, as stated already, these classes have not been eliminated and the outlook and traditions for which they stood, are still an important part of the rural economy. Feudalism still lives not only in the minds of the agriculturists, both rich and poor, but also in the facts of our agrarian structure. Disparities are still very wide and make our political democracy in the villages devoid of economic and social content. Their significance for the transformation of our economy is a matter of analyses and interpretation. That there are great disparities in the distribution of holdings is a well-known fact and is borne out by the facts cited in the footnote.[21] Figures in these tables are not comparable, but both the National Sample Survey and the Labour Enquiry Tables bear out the extremes of disparities. According to the N.S.S. tables 1 per cent of the households own 16 per cent of area (above 50 acres), 3 per cent of households own 29 per cent of area (above 25 acres), 12 per cent

21. There is a very considerable amount of information available in the numerous village surveys which have been carried out in different parts of the country for the last four or five decades, and almost all of them support the view that in India, even in the area in which peasant proprietership has been the rule, holdings are very unequally distributed. This information is, however, widely dispersed and it cannot possibly be cited in a footnote. The results of three enquiries conducted more recently are tabulated. National Sample Survey conducted an enquiry into the distribution of holdings in 1953-54, the results of which are often cited. They are given in the following table:

CUMULATIVE PERCENTAGE BELOW SPECIFIED SIZE OF OWNERSHIP HOLDINGS

Specified size of ownership holding	Households	Area
0-1 acre (landless)	22	nil
1 acre	47	1
2.5 acres	61	6
5 acres	75	16
10 acres	88	35
15 acres	93	48
25 acres	97	63
30 acres	99	84
above 51 acres	100	100

DATA RELATING TO 1950-51 COLLECTED BY AGRICULTURAL LABOUR ENQUIRY IN CUMULATIVE PERCENTAGES

Size group of holdings	Percentage of holdings	Percentage area
up to 1 acre	16.8	1
up to 2.5 acres	38	5.6
up to 5 acres	59	15.5
up to 10 acres	78	33.1
up to 25 acres	94.5	65.6
All holdings	100	100

In the First Five Year Plan it was proposed that a census of land-holdings and cultivation be undertaken by the states, and the states were again asked in January 1954 to undertake such a census because a number of them had developed resistance to the proposal and a more preremptory central directive was called for. This was issued. After a lot of discussion action was taken.

of households own 65 per cent of area (above 10 acres), 75 per cent of households own only 16 per cent of area (under 5 acres), 47 per cent of households own only 1 per cent of area and 22 per cent households do not own any land at all. The Labour Enquiry figures for 5 acres or less are 59 per cent holdings and 15.5 of area, for 10 acres or less 78 per cent of holdings and 33 per cent of area, above 10 acres, 12 per cent holdings and 66 per cent of area and above 25 acres, 5.5 holdings and 34.4 per cent area. Making allowance for 22 per cent of households who are landless according to N.S.S. tables, these two tables point to the same broad conclusions. Nearly one-sixth to one-fourth of agriculturists own only 1 per cent of area, from 60 to 75 per cent own only 16 per cent of area, 65 or 66 per cent of area is in the hands of owners with holdings of 10 acres or more and 3 to 3.5 per cent of owned holdings account for an area of 35 to 37 per cent. There are two significant points which suggest themselves. The first is that three-fifths to three-fourths of holdings are below 5 acres and the second that nearly two-thirds of the area consists of farms above ten acres. The second point, it has been urged, indicates that peasant farming in India can be a viable proposition and the first that vast majority of holdings are uneconomic, i.e. they neither can be cultivated efficiently nor provide income to their owners to place them above poverty line even according to Indian standards. These points have obviously important bearing on issues which will be considered in the next chapter. Here the important

In three states the census was based upon complete enumeration of holdings. In seven states the census, though based upon complete enumeration, was restricted to holdings of ten acres and above; in the rest sample survey was undertaken. In the Second Five Year Plan results from 20 states mostly relating to 1953-54 were classified and given in an Annexure. The data was recompiled for the reorganized states and are now available. They too clearly indicate how wide are the disparities in the distribution of holdings (Vide *Second Five Year Plan Annexure II*, p. 213-20).

These enquiries relate to 1951-52 and 1953-54. It is necessary to conduct a thorough re-examination and re-assessment of the distribution of owned and operated holdings because since then it is known concentration and in-equalities have greatly increased.

consideration is that stratification of agriculturists in India is a decisive factor and three or four per cent of the agriculturists at the top are in a dominant position. Absolutely speaking they may not be—often are not—in a state of great affluence, but they are powerful and belonging as they often do to higher castes, they exercise an amount of power which in the villages is almost decisive and determines the framework within which rural economy functions. Power, it has to be added, is greatly increased—really multiplied—by the combination, as pointed out before, of money lending and trading with ownership concentrated in the hands of three to four per cent of the agricultural population. If the ceiling policy had been honestly and fully implemented, this power might, with the adequate provision of co-operative credit and marketing, have really been challenged and even greatly limited. But this has not happened and unless it does, oligarchy in the villages will rule supreme and make socialist democracy unattainable in the country-side and therefore in the country as a whole. That is why a socialist land system is incompatible with the concentration of economic power in agriculture, and social forces strong enough to countervail it have to be generated and brought into action. This power, to repeat, is power of capital—it is money power—and it can be displaced and replaced by power of the community—peoples' power—only if in the entire economy money-power ceases to run it, i.e. it is deprived of and excluded from all crucial positions in which major decisions are taken and from which the economy is directed and steered. In other words, a socialist land system can be built up and operated only within a socialist economy. These disparities referred to above are, from this standpoint, of great and far-reaching consequence and their real significance has to be fully appreciated.

Inequalities in the villages, which determine their power-pattern do not, it need not be stated again, merely depend upon the distribution of owned or operated holdings. Agricultural labourers and artisans, besides small peasants, represent the majority of the rural poor who not only do not participate in power but are its principle victims. Further combination of upper strata of the rural rich with money-lenders, traders and interests in urban area, as stated before, greatly increases the power of the privileged minority and make them even more formidable.

An observation of Mr. Kingsley Martin of *New Statesman* based upon an experience of recent visit to Indian villages illustrates how the power in our villages is distributed and exercised. "On one occasion," he writes, "I recall all the answers (to my questions) were given by apparently a rather insignificant personality. It was with difficulty that I could persuade any one else to talk. I learnt afterwards that he was the local money-lender, who in effect was the master of the village though he owned only two acres of land and kept a tiny shop."[22]

He further adds in the same article, "one of my conclusions was that with the best of will in the world—the government is unintentionally creating a new race of Kulaks." This is largely true and means, of course, the power-pattern of the villages has, if anything, changed for the worse.

The implementation and administration of land reforms has been the major factor, in determining the extent to which they have been disappointing and unsatisfactory. Land reform, being a means to the end of developing a land system, based upon sound and just social relations, will fit into an economy of increasing socialist content and, of course, contribute to the rapid rate of economic growth and will have to be administered through agencies, official and non-official, who will be animated by an all-permeating social purpose. At present our revenue agency, which is mainly responsible for implementation and administration, is known to be extremely corrupt and greatly biased in favour of and even influenced by the interests which want to maintain the status quo. There is at present no alternative to revenue agency and reform and replacement of the

22. Kingsley Martin, "India's Leap from Feudalism," *New Statesman*, July 28, 1961, p. 116.

agency is a part of the very much larger problem of creating the whole administrative apparatus needed for developing and administering a socialist economy. The essentials of this problem have still to be formulated before its solution is even conceived and attempted. This point will be fully considered in a later chapter. But the association of the organs of community life like Panchayats and co-operatives with the development and working of the land-policy has to be an essential part of the development and working of the new land system. The Panchayats and co-operatives, now in the process of formation, will have to be judged by the extent to which they actually become an important factor in the growth of the processes of socialist democracy. The function, which have to be assigned to them and which they have to perform with competence and success, will practically include all vital functions of a socialist village economy. They ought to be associated with improvement of land-records, leasing, regulation of rents, land-management, consolidation of holdings and co-operative farming even at the initial stages but it is not easy to refute the views of those who suggest caution in the assignment of these functions to representative bodies even on an associative basis. This is the index of how far removed we at present are from the goals which we have set ourselves, but in which real faith has still to be developed. It is, however, of fundamental importance that this fact should be widely and clearly understood, and it should be realized that without democratic processes, i.e. an active involvement of the people in a society in which class interests are being increasingly controlled and eliminated and an active social awareness is being developed, the grave defects of the existing land system cannot be corrected and it cannot be replaced by the kind of land system which has already projected itself in our concepts but has not yet acquired the quality of a social imperative.

In the Second Plan Report a rural economic structure was visualized. "In which agricultural production, village industries, processing industries, marketing and rural trade are all organized on a co-operative basis, distinction between those who have land and those who have not will lose much of its significance and the resources of the village community will be employed for maximum increase in production and employment through action in the village as well as co-operation in activities extending beyond the village."[23] This is a very good and adequate picture of what the village economy and its co-related land system have to change and grow into. It is, however, obvious that so far we have not made any perceptible advance towards this objective and the forces, which are at work and are being strengthened by such development as has taken place, are very unfavourable to its realization. What is called co-operative village management really amounts to a socialist village with a fully awakened and active social conscience functioning consciously and efficiently in an economy in which all citizens are workers, work is a social function and there are differences in skill, operational efficiency, responsibility and social authority but no social divisions. This is, to repeat, a good projection but is not the basis of actual policy and its execution. This is in fact a picture of Utopia, i.e. a state of things which has at present no relation to attainable goals. We have really been going in the opposite direction.

In conclusion it may be said that to achieve success it may be necessary to take co-ordinated action all along the line for improvement and maintenance of land records, consolidation of holdings, regulation of rents, grant of security to tenants to be followed by the state assuming direct relation with all cultivators, enforcement of ceilings and co-operativization of credit, marketing, service function and farming if new land system is to emerge and develop. The difficulties created by inaction and wrong action in the last decade are great, but they will have to be overcome if new land system is to be established. This will, however, mean also that all allied activities like husbandry, dairy-farming, afforestation, communication, conservation, re-

23. *The Second Five Year Plan*, p. 207.

clamation, irrigation, social service and rural industrialization will all have to be undertaken at the same time and their content and rate of development will all have to be co-related to the pogramme of the new land system. All this, however, is not enough. Development of a unified system has also to be integrated with the development of the economy as a whole, rational utilization of available man-power, rationalization of trade, price and income structure and similar action all along the line. Through all this has to run the thread of a common social purpose, i.e. an earnest desire to establish socialist economy in this country, with sincerity and determination. In other words, socialist planning has to be made a reality by our being dead earnest about socialism. This is plain common sense of planning and a point will be further developed in a later chapter, but is put in relief here to indicate the great contrast between full implications of land reforms and haphazard patch work development of the last decade. This contrast has to be kept in mind.[24]

24. Dr Baljit Singh of Lucknow University in his *Next Step to Village India* and Dr K. M. Khusro of Delhi in an unpublished paper have both put in a strong and convincing plea for integrated action in the implementation of land reforms. The logic of their argument requires that integrated action, relating to land-reforms should imply operating upon the whole economy with unity of purpose, drive and social momentum born of the resurgence of the people, i.e. a real social revolution in action. Inadequacy of land reforms rather stresses created by them are due to the fact that this fundamental need has not been understood.

Now it is officially admitted that land-reform has largely, speaking, fallen very short of targets and expectations and it has been decided to complete the land reforms in two years, i.e. before the end of the Third Five Year Plan. Very bold declarations are being made, the oft-repeated view has been reiterated that land-reform programme has an ultimate bearing on agricultural production; the Food and Agriculture Ministry is reported to be keen on changing the present obsolete and confusing pattern of land relation, a high level committee and special officer is to be appointed in each state to implement the land-reform programme according to a fixed schedule and will have to report to the Union Government every six months.

All this is meant to indicate a new determination and earnestness of purpose to replace the obsolete system of land-relation by a rational, modern and socialist system and complete the programme speedily. In the Second

Important as it is that all operations related to land reforms, like consolidation of holding, rectification of records, etc. be undertaken at the same time and on an inter-related basis, the transformation of the entire economy for making agrarian relations significant from the standpoint of socialism is far more important. Unless the thread of common social purpose, referred to above, runs through the entire economy and effective action is taken to alter radically the power-pattern, the imperative need for which has to be stressed again and again, we may get the shadow and rather the phantom of the new agrarian economy but its substance will remain for us an ever-elusive object.

Five Year Plan it was stated that retrospective effect had to be given to all corrective measures intended to implement land reforms in the spirit as well as the letter of the policy and lapses of the past had to be redressed by effective action. The declarations, which are, however, being made now make no reference to this need, and all the infringement of land-laws are, it appears, to be taken as settled facts. This is a very crucial point, and if nothing is or can be done about it, very little can be done to alter the position significantly or develop a system of new land relations. This means that all illicit transfers, evictions, ejectments, evasion of the ceiling limits, falsification of records and well-known failings of the implementing agency—the corrupt revenue administration—are to remain and the wrongs already committed cannot be righted. This is a realistic conclusion, but makes the outlook for completion of land-reforms very dark indeed. The Government, it appears, is going to compensate for the futility of its efforts in this sphere of fundamental importance by statements which sound daring in intention in spite of it being known that very little in fact will be done to put them into effect.

Chapter Five

PATTERNS OF AGRICULTURAL
DEVELOPMENT

NUTRITION DEFICIENCY

Indian agriculture is known to have very high development potential, and yet in spite of thirteen years of planning and agricultural development we have been staggering from one food crisis to another and are now passing through the worst food crisis since independence. These crises and the present crisis have nothing to do with the accelerated rate of the growth of our population. Growth of agricultural production and production of food grains has more than kept pace with the growth of population and the position is being well maintained.[1] Our targets of food production in the Third Five Year Plan, even in the revised plan, are nearly twice the estimated rate of growth of population of 12 to 14 per cent from 1960 to 1965. In our war against hunger we have invested Rs 2,380 crores from 1951 to 1964 on agricultural development including irrigation; our agricultural production has increased, as stated in the footnote, by 2.61 per cent per annum, of rice since 1949-50 by 4.27 per cent per annum and of wheat by 6.08 per cent per annum. In spite of this heavy investment and high rate of growth of our two principle food crops we have imported food grains to the extent of nearly 48 million tons since 1947 which have cost us Rs 2,168 crores in foreign exchange. In spite of large increase of production and heavy imports our food prices have increased by 40 per cent since

1. From 1952-53 to 1961-62 agricultural production has increased at compound rate by 2.91 per cent, food production by 2.61 per cent and population by 2.26 per cent (*Growth Rate of Agricultural Production*, issued by Ministry of Food and Agriculture).

1949 and by 13 per cent in 1963-64 and we are suffering from acute shortage of food, the distress of the people has become really appalling and as recent discussion at the highest level clearly shows, we do not know what short and long-term measures should be adopted to overcome the crisis and prevent its recurrence in future. The position to all appearances is really baffling and yet it is known that without unduly heavy investment of funds our production can be expanded rapidly to meet fully our present and prospective requirements of food. If our agricultural statistics are even reasonably reliable, all these crises that have arisen could and should have been avoided and we could face the future with confidence and not rely upon the bounty of U.S.A. for meeting our immediate or future needs. The fact that we are in the midst of a grave crisis and cannot do better than once more place our food production on a war footing and make bold declarations of our will to become self-supporting in the supply of food and all essential commodities shows the bankruptcy of our policy making. We have done that before a number of times since 1948 without any success, the ascending spiral of prices has continued and we have presumed that our people would endure the increasing pangs of hunger in silence and continue to repeat that production, more production is the only cure of our troubles. Our experience has not had any chasteneing effect on our policy makers, and searching self-criticism, the need for which is so clearly indicated, has not been and is not being undertaken.

The real fact of the matter is that we are not and should not be short of foodgrains if our agricultural statistics represent even approximately the actual situation. We should have been able to feed our population entirely from our own resources and not resorted to begging and borrowing for meeting our food deficit. Our real problem is not the shortage of food grains, as official statistics show that the availability of food grains per head per day in 1963 had increased[2] to 15.4 ozs from 13.5 ozs

2. Food Statistics, February 1964, Table XI.

in 1951 and is more than 14 ozs of food grains per head, which according to nutrition experts, are required for a balanced standard diet. This average means very little from the human and social standpoint, for owing to inequitable distribution of income, made much more so by continued inflation since 1947, the purchase of the grains in adequate quantity is beyond the means of a very large section of our people. But the average does mean that our pressing problem is not the production of more food grains but increase in the real purchasing power of the majority of our people and increase in the production and supply of vital protective foods in regard to which our deficiency is far more acute and which is really responsible for severe and large-scale under-nutrition and malnutrition of our people. This is the real crux of our food problem to which very little attention has been given.

Data on these shortages and their incidence are very scanty but such as we have show that our people are suffering from very serious deficiencies of these essential foods owing to the shortages and high prices of milk, vegetables, fruits, meat and eggs, i.e. protective foods which are the source of protein, calcium vitamins, minerals and salts, the irreducible minimum of which are beyond the means of three-fourths of our people and are in very short supply. In 1956-57, according to a survey, against the required minimum of 10 ozs of vegetables per day per head the estimated available quantity was 2.6 ozs, and of ghee and oil .39 ozs against the standard of 2 ozs, of milk and milk products 4.5 ozs against 10 ozs, of meat, eggs and fish .4 ozs against 4 ozs, and fruits and nuts 2 ozs against 3 ozs. Since 1956-57 the deficiency could hardly have been materially reduced due to the increase in the rate of population growth and reduced real income of the majority of our people owing to the inflationary pressure. These calculations are based upon estimates of supply of very limited value and actual shortage is likely to be greater. Moreover, the fact that the bulk of our population has no means to buy these essentials adds to the poignancy of these very critical shortages. We are now (June

1964) in a state of food crisis, which is more serious than ever, not because the food grains are in short supply seriously but because extreme economic disparities, which have, as stated in a later chapter, significantly increased in the last decade, and very low production of milk, vegetables, etc. Even though in the Third Plan revised targets of food grain production of 90 million tons are realized, our people, as a whole, will continue to suffer from these serious vital deficiencies acutely. That at the end of the Third Plan 16 to 17 ozs of food grains per head every day may be available will increase the imbalance of our food supplies without reducing to any degree our nutritional shortages. It was very clearly indicated by the Health Survey and Development Committee (popularly known as Bhore Committee) in 1946 in the concluding statement of its report in which it affirmed very clearly that, "Food planning should have as its ultimate objective the provision of an optimum diet for all, irrespective of income, and that plans should be laid to reach the objectives by forced marches, stage by stage and within a specific period of time".[3] The prime objective of a planned food policy could not be more plainly stated. That in theory and practice we have not even envisaged this goal, what to speak of advancing towards it, does not need to be specifically stated. The social minimum of any country which is conscious of the well-being of its people—much more so, of course, of a country which is committed to socialism as its social objective, has to be "provision of optimum diet for all irrespective of income" and plan "to reach the objective by forced marches, stage by stage and within a specified time". This, to repeat, we have not understood or appreciated, and the result is that under-nutrition and malnutrition have been, as stated below, increasing in our country and in our three plans we have not yet risen to the level of vivid awareness of the goal laid down by the Bhore Committee.

3. *Nutrition in India (1946-58)*, p. 5.

DISTRIBUTION OF INCOME AND FOOD PLANNING

Food planning in India, as anywhere, has to mean not production of food but also the distribution of income, i.e.,
purchasing power to guarantee the means to all to realize
freedom from primary want. We have not had any policy of
planned distribution of income in this country since we began
to plan and as stated in a later chapter, distribution of income
in the last decade of Planning, has become even more inequitable than before. Most of our people cannot have even the
minimum that they need even if production of food had
adequately expanded, but as it is even its production falls far
short of what is required to meet the physiological minimum
needs of our people. Our shortages acquire much more disturbing significance owing to extreme inequalities of income.
This conclusion needs to be supported by data which are
not available. In a publication of Indian Council of Medical
Research, which has been cited above, a table of comparitive
study of food situations since 1943 is given[4] in which percentage of deficit or surplus of food in 1943, 1951 and 1957 are
estimated. According to it the position in regard to cereals in
these years was that there was deficit of 10 per cent in 1943,
of 17 per cent in 1951 and surplus of 6 per cent in 1957. For
the other commodities there was deficit all through, of 30, 20
and 10 per cent for pulses, of 74 per cent for vegetables in
1943, figures for the other two years were not available, of
41, 51 and 55 per cent in milk, of 22, 21 and 13 per cent in
sugar, of 73, 82 and 78 per cent in vegetable oils and fats, of
90, 87 and 85 in fish and meat and 99 and 98 in eggs for 1957.
The limitations of these figures need to be borne in mind.
Figures for all "protective" foods are very rough estimate and
their limitations are implicit in them. And yet they reveal a
situation which is obviously disquieting. Shortage, according to
them, of milk, fats and fruits have increased since 1943 and
of the other essentials have remained high and serious. Probably

4. Ibid., Table I, p. 15.

actual shortages are greater, because the growth of population exceeds the presumed population of this table. These estimates are based on averages of availabilities and do not take into account the inequalities which price out most of these commodities for the bulk of our people. These surveys need to be much more extensive and intensive and have to assess the incidence of these shortages in different strata, areas and regions of the country if the true position is to be known. Disparities in intakes of diet in different classes and areas are known to vary within wide limits and the averages do not convey the acute shortages of different nutrients from which our people are suffering in different parts of the country. Owing to inflation, uneven development in different states and regions and accelerated and unequal growth of population in different parts of the country the patterns of incidence of these shortages is bound to have changed for the worse since 1957 and caused more widespread and greater distress in terms of general and specific hunger, i.e. serious inadequacy of food in general and special nutrients like proteins, vitamins, etc.

NEED FOR NUTRITION POLICY IN SPECIFIC TERMS

Food policy has, if it is not to be merely an essay in aggregates and averages, to be a nutrition policy and based on evaluation of actual supplies compared with minimum requirements of the people according to authentic diet standards in different parts of the country and among different sections of the people. We in India have had no nutrition policy since our planning started and our food policy has been formulated without due regard for production potentials and actual shortages in terms of needs of different regions, demographic facts and anticipations and nutrition deficiences of the peoples. The use of D.D.T., B.C.G., and anti-biotics have reduced our death rates, but they have not given us a nation of more healthy people in terms of real physical well-being. Regional disparities are known to be great and have, if anything, increased in the last decade. They have obviously a bearing on the assessment of the food situation and formulation of food policy. Owing to the non-availability of data, the regional disparities and changes in them can be indicated only by citing illustrative facts. The population data, its rate of growth, distribution and pressure have evidently a direct bearing on the relative potential and needs of the different states and therefore on regional disparities. In 1951-61 though the average rate of increase has been 21.49 per cent, in the major states the rate of growth varies from 9.44 in Jammu and Kashmir to 34.45 per cent in Assam and in the most densely populated states of Kerala and West Bengal the population in 1951-60 increased by 24.76 and 32.79 per cent respectively. In the three other densely populated states of Madras, Bihar and U.P. the rate of growth is below the average, 11.85 in Madras, 19.78 in Bihar and 16.66 in U.P. The densities of population varied from 1,127 in Kerala, 1,032 in West Bengal to 189 in Madhya Pradesh and 153 in Rajasthan. Uneven distribution of population is in India a well-known fact and is one of the important causes of regional diversities and has in regional planning of agriculture in particular and development in general to be duly taken into account. The cause of these differences in the rates of growth have not been studied and need to be carefully examined and production and supply of food have to be planned in relation to them. Vital shortages of food, due to this reason, are bound to vary from state to state and have to be counteracted by appropriate compensatory measures. It has been estimated that if 30 per cent increase in agricultural production in Third Plan is realized, availability of food would rise to 17 ozs per adult unit per day but this average has no significance from the point of view of demographic realities and other significant differences and is not really planning at all but an exercise in working out statistical averages.

These averages, it need not be said, cover a lot of diversities, but they are the other side of the pressure of population and are significant from the standpoint of regional differences. Data on regional differences of production, growth and income are, to repeat, very inadequate, and in our plans these differences have hardly been considered, much less provided for and no data have been collected to show the impact of development, particularly agricultural development, on these differences. It is, however, clear that our plans of development—particularly those of agricultural production—have not been formulated with reference to gaps between needs and production and investment and development have not been judged by assessed possibilities of growth in different regions. States in India are, in respect of population and areas, comparable to large countries and there are sub-regional differences in each state which are very relevant for planned development. All these differences —regional and sub-regional—and specific problems arising from them indicate the tasks which have to be undertaken in the formulation and implementation of all development policies— particularly food policies. That this aspect of planning has practically been lost sight of altogether speaks for itself and will be further considered in a later chapter. It is not only regional disparities but also diversities due to numerous causes which make it necessary to plan in terms of regions, sub-regions, districts, areas and even villages, but continuing and probably increasing disparities make it imperative that plans of agriculture and food production should be co-related to specific needs and potentials and not merely formulated and executed in terms of assumed aggregates and percentages of increase.

AGRICULTURAL DEVELOPMENT AND RURAL ECONOMY

The two plans of agricultural development have involved very large outlay, production of food grains and commercial crops has increased very considerably, there has been large addition to sown, irrigated double-cropped areas and areas under improved crop, use of fertilizers and organic manures have been extended and new implements, oil engines and pumps have been introduced in large number. The extension work has been undertaken under the community development programme, and with all its limitations can be taken as a contribution to the improvement of farming practices and plant protection. Agricultural production, as a result of all these measures, has been expanded, as stated before, by 35 per cent in 1951-60 and it was proposed to increase it by another 30 per cent in the Third Plan. This expansion really amounts to a break through of a long period of arrested growth, and in spite of the spurt in the rate of population growth, increase in the production of food grains and other crops has more than kept pace with the growth of population. From the point of technological development the achievements of the last decade can be taken as a source of real satisfaction, and in the next five or ten years the same measures have to be continued and greatly intensified; but the measures which have been taken are the measures which have to be adopted in this or any other country whatever the social system. During this period the agricultural prices have also risen in spite of all the increase in production and presumably the minority of agriculturists, who have marketing surplus, have been benefitted both in money and real terms. And yet it is well known that these developments have not even mitigated, what to speak of cured, the real ills from which agriculture is suffering, the agriculturists still do not cover their costs, relatively speaking the per capita average agricultural income is nearly half of national average, the pressure of population on land has increased, the proportion of national income accruing from agriculture has only been very slightly reduced. Under-nourishment and deficiency in the intake of essentials like proteins, probably more in rural than urban areas, has increased; and from the social standpoint owing to increasing disparities, inability of the small peasants and agricultural labourers (i.e. 75 per cent of the agriculturists) to protect and promote their interests and develop the necessary understanding and strength to contribute to and bring about social changes, on which the future of not only rural but national economy depends, has also increased, the social structure in the villages, in spite of adult suffrage and political decentralization now in progress, has not become more democratic both from political and social standpoints, i.e. the pattern of power in the villages remains unchanged and probably has, if anything, become less democratic—the upper strata are more dominant than before, and this fact owing to the four-fifths of our population being in rural areas determines and even accentuates concentration of power in our economy as a whole. The fact is that expansion of agricultural production in the last decade, very considerable as it is, has not made agriculture a sound industry, rural economy remains not a source of health, strength and vitality for the economy as a whole but a real massive built-in depressor. Technological changes are indispensable and have to be greatly accelerated but experience of the last decade, even more than that of earlier years, clearly points to the conclusion that they in themselves do not and cannot hold the key to the future. Their effect has been more than nullified by the social context in which they have been introduced and applied. They have really made the context more and not less unfavourable for solving the basic problems of our rural masses and therefore for the development of socialism not only in the villages but in the country as a whole. It is clear that not only the avowed object of relieving the chronic hunger of the people has not been realized, but conditions in which great production potentials of agriculture still remain in chains owing to the repressive social relations have, if anything, become much worse. This sounds like repetition of socialist cliches but, factually speaking, is true. This needs to be clearly understood and it, it alone, provides a clue to what needs to be done to break these chains and make agriculture not only adequately productive but also a healthy, self-propelled and expansive industry. Efforts are being made, as they have been made everywhere, to escape from this conclusion. But there is no escape from it. It has to be made an integral part of a proper understanding of our limitations and of our approach to the future

—to the third and all other subsequent plans.

One very significant indication of the state of our agriculture is that, in spite of heavy investment in agriculture and the adoption of the other measures referred to above, there has been no significant improvement in the yield per acre in agriculture not only in the last ten but the last thirty years. Our land, all these measures not withstanding, it is obvious, is not in good heart, and has not, to use the usual jargon, responded to the extra doses of capital and labour which have been applied to agriculture. Owing to reasons of space, the available facts in support of this view cannot be fully cited and analysed. A competent study of this issue has lately been made by Prof M. L. Dantwala, who is known for his increasing disposition to take an over-optimistic view of the trends now in operation and future possibilities. His conclusion, as based upon a careful analysis of the available data, is that "there was no increase in the yields per acre in any of the major crops during the period 1931-32 to 1958-59".[5] He spells out this conclusion in the following three propositions: (i) taking all crops together yields per acre appear to have increased only slightly and insignificantly during 1931-59, a period covering nearly three decades; (ii) individually some major crops, e.g. rice, show a slight decline per acre over the same period; (iii) both in war and post-war years (there is) a drop in the per-acre yields.[6] There has been increase in area under different crops since 1946-47—1948-49 of 4 per cent in the area under main crop varying from 6.2 to 11.4 per cent and most of the increase in production is presumably due to it, but though extension of cultivation to marginal land may have had depressing effect on the over-all averages, it should have been more than neutralized by irrigation, double cropping, the use of improved seeds, fertilizers and improvement of farming practices. This obviously has not happened and it

5. M. L. Dantwala in *Changing India*, p. 32.
6. *Op. cit.*, p. 36. *Essays in honour of Prof. D. R. Gadgil*, edited by V. V. Sovani and V. M. Dandeker.

means that agriculture is seriously handicapped by some drag which makes greater net output per acre an unobtainable object. The whole position needs to be more carefully investigated and the causes of this stagnation identified. The presumption, however, is that human factor has not been activated owing to the counter-vailing depressing conditions and application of labour, capital, technique and foreign aid in many forms have not been able to raise the yield from land. In India owing to the scarcity of land our main hope has been that both yield per acre and man will increase. As it is, yield per man, it is certain, has fallen after the war because labour force in agriculture has increased from 103 to 118 millions from 1951-52 to 1959-60, i.e. by nearly 15 per cent and net area sown has during the same period increased from 293.4 to 323 million acres, i.e. a little over 10 per cent and allowing for marginal land, it may be assumed that either agricultural unemployment has increased or larger labour force has been utilized on the land available for cultivation without any increase per acre of return from land, i.e. while there has been a slight fall in the yield per acre, fall in the yield per man has been even more significant.

POTENTIAL OF GROWTH AND HUMAN FACTOR

Yields per acre in India in the last thirty years and more have not only not improved significantly but compared with the other countries the position has, relatively speaking, become worse owing to the latter having greatly increased their yields. Yields in India are one half to one fifth of what they are in other countries and even in countries like Egypt, Italy, Japan yield of crop like wheat and rice is four to five times higher than in India. This is an old story. Elementary textbooks have for the last six decades contrasted the yields in India with those in other countries to indicate backwardness of the former. During this period while India has been standing still, the other countries have gone ahead and our backwardness has become the greater on that account. Even in the last decade the gap between India and other countries has been increasing, and without resolute action it is likely to become greater still. "The best in Indian agriculture is comparable," in the words of the Ford Foundation Team, "to the best in other countries, but the average is unduly low. The task before the country is to develop ways of raising the low average to the higher levels which many Indian cultivators have achieved."[7] Yields per acre in crop competition are 6 to 7 times higher than the average yields in the respective crops for the same year and in some cases the multiple is 9, 10, 14 and 26. Prize competition yields are the results of artificial stimulus, but it is not unreasonable to assume that average yields are capable of being raised much higher, and yields in India, given the organization and the drive, can be increased by 100 to 200 per cent within a reasonable time. We have placed agricultural production on "a war footing" a number of times since independence and yet with all this ado, we have not made any headway. The Ford Foundation Team has rightly pointed out that agricultural progress should be measured not by the increase in aggregate production but by the yield per acre. This is plain commonsense and judged by this standard there has hardly been any progress. Technological possibilities of agriculture, its production potential, are truly enormous. This was stated by Royal Agricultural Commission in 1929. It was restated by Sir John Russell in his report in 1937 and also in a publication of the Imperial Council of Agricultural Research in 1946. The Ford Foundation Team in its report in 1959 has only reaffirmed the same view after ten weeks stay in India, two-thirds to three-fourths of which was spent in travelling. What has been said by these and other distinguished men about land use, soil erosion, irrigation, bunding, drainage, manures and fertilizers, improved seeds, cultural practices, mixed farming, implements, plant protection and even milk, fish supply and marketing,

7. Report on India's Food Crisis and the Steps to Meet it.

etc. has been fully and adequately stated many times over before. Re-statement and re-affirmation neither adds to our knowledge nor conviction that India can meet her food requirements, and agricultural production in India can be very rapidly expanded. In all these statements is implicit the view that solution of this problem is more a matter of organization, administration, drive and what is called mass resurgence than of capital expenditure. What we need is not repetition that our production potential is very high, but an awareness that finance is only secondary aspect of agriculture —really of economic development. This is the lesson of why efforts to solve these problems have yielded such poor results. We need, as stated before, irrigation, fertilizers, improved seeds, better implements and higher standard of husbandry. If we realize that in agriculture, even more than in the economy as a whole, the intangibles, e.g. the real motive forces and social momentum, are far more important than capital expenditure and outlay, we will address ourselves to the task of bringing new levers into action which do not involve financial outlay but real social engineering and make it possible for us to make our money go very much farther in development. Provision of Rs 1,280 crores of outlay on agriculture in the Third Plan can give us a much higher return in real terms than is indicated by the anticipated rise of the index of agricultural production from 135 to 176. It can give us a new rural economy whose gains will be incalculable if we have a clear conception of what this economy should be and set about the task of building it in all earnestness. We need for this purpose not teams from outside who can only give us platitudes which carry no conviction but our own agronomists, agricultural engineers, social scientists, etc. and, of course, leaders of the people at all levels who have a common social purpose, i.e. believe in socialism and are prepared to work for it and can team up for realizing the production potential of agriculture by building up small communities which become nucleii of national economy and in fulfilling their own needs, they also promote and realize the social and economic objective of the country. That way not only production will be maximized because of agriculture being rationalized in a new social context, but human factor will acquire a decisive importance in the process and social values will be realized through it.

MISPLACED EMPHASIS ON PRODUCTION OF CEREALS

One main defect of our agricultural programme in the Third Plan is that it concentrates on production of food grains and commercial crops and gives to the problems of nutrition a secondary place in our agricultural policy. There is provision for increase in the production of milk, fruits and vegetables, fish, meat and eggs, but the provision has not been related to any budgets of deficits in its availability of these commodities, and any idea of going ahead by forced marches, stage by stage, and with a well-defined time limit for adequate production of these commodities has not even been considered. The assumption clearly is that it is impossible to increase their production to provide any balanced diet for all; and therefore within the limitations of our resources whatever is practicable should be done to reduce these shortages, it being assumed that majority of our people will have to go short of milk and vegetables for a good long while yet, and we should regard ourselves lucky if staple foods are provided for all and deficiency of other important nutrients is somewhat reduced. This view is essentially anti-democratic and not in keeping with our socialist objective. We have to provide balanced diet for all irrespective of incomes and make this object the first charge on the increase of our national income. The right course would, of course, be that under planned distribution of national income, it should be possible for all to buy the minimum of these essentials within a specific duration. This, of course, means not only that the rate of growth of our income has to be increased but there has to be a plan for its distribution. Corresponding to this plan, there has to be a programme of planned increase of production of protective foods and the plan has to be worked out in terms not on an aggregate basis but according to a budget of resources and needs of each village, area, town and city. This seems to be a very ambitious task, but when it is conceived and realized in specific terms and its accomplishment made a part of decentralized production, distribution and marketing and assigned to organs of planning at the basic level and a hierarchy of their federations referred to in a later chapter, it will not appear as formidable as it looks. There has to be a plan not only for production of all essential foods but also a planned income structure to go with it. There is no sense in increasing production of these foods if vast majority of our people have incomes which hardly give them even a bare subsistance. At present all increase in production of milk, vegetables, fruits, meats and eggs will be to the advantage of middle and higher classes and most of our people will have to do without them as they are doing at present for they will not have the means to buy them at current prices. For most of our people they will even then remain luxuries beyond their means and most of the calories will be derived from cereals and pulses with such meagre protein diet which the latter can provide. Plans for reducing surplus cattle, their segregation and sterilization, cattle breeding and improvement in their quality and increase of fodder and feed even then would be needed and orchards and truck gardening on a planned basis would have to be promoted and provided for even if production and income distribution plans are duly integrated; but the existing plans are in no way related to the framework of budget of needs and resources and on that account they are not plans at all, but merely isolated projects for the development of animal husbandry, poultry farms, milk dairies, orchards and vegetable farms and their benefits, whatever they may be, will accrue mostly to the more well-to-do classes. According to the report of Community Development Evaluation Mission in India appointed under the U.N. Programme of Technical Assistance "milk available per head of population has dropped since 1900 by perhaps one-third and village children, except in the richer families practically drink no milk".[8] The colonies of cattle at Aarey, Haringhat and Madhavran, and milk supply unions and dairying programme are good as far as they go, but they increase the supply of milk for towns at the cost of the villages and increase the disparity between towns and villages in respect of milk consumption. In the Third Plan the need for taking into account the vital interests of the agriculturists in the programme for dairy development,[9] has been indicated but that is merely piece of window-dressing and past experience clearly shows that it would be difficult to realize this object.

VITAL SHORTAGES OF PROTEIN FOODS

Shortages of vital foods according to a survey in 1956-57 have already been referred to. Some other estimates may also be cited. The shortage of milk, vegetables and fruits, fish, meat and eggs has been variously estimated. In 1944 the Imperial Council of Agricultural Research estimated that for undivided India the required quantity was 32 million tons and available supply only for meat, fish and eggs was one sixth to one fourth of required quantity—1.5 million tons against the requirements of 6 to 9 million tons, of fats and oils, 1.9 million tons against 4.6 million tons and of vegetables 9 million tons against 18 million tons.[10] According to the Indian Council of Medical Research in 1950 shortage of fruits was 55 per cent, of milk 55 per cent, of vegetable oil and fat 78 per cent, of fish and meat 85 per cent and of eggs 98 per cent.[11] According to an estimate of Food and Agricultural Ministry in 1958-59 our availability of vegetables, ghee and vegetable oil was 45 per cent and meat, fish and eggs 25 per cent of stan-

---

8. *Report of Community Development Evaluation Mission,* p. 30.
9. *Third Five Year Plan.* p. 356.
10. *Memorandum on Development of Agriculture and Animal Husbandry,* 1944, p. 17.
11. *Op. cit.,* p. 15.

dard requirements. All these estimates are very rough for the data on which they are based, are unreliable but they are nevertheless an indication of the extreme shortage of protective foods from which our people are suffering. Moreover, it has to be borne in mind they are based upon averages which means that the rich people can get all they need of these scarce essentials and the very poor ones have practically to go without them altogether. Incidence of these shortages falls mostly on the latter and undermines seriously the physical well-being of most of our people. Under the Third Plan it is proposed to increase our output of vegetables and fruits to 100,000 tons from 40,000 in 1960-61, and 20,000 in 1955-56;[12] the output of milk to 25.3 million tons in 1965-66 from 22 million in 1960-61 and 19.3 million in 1955; and the output of fish to 1.8 million tons from 1.4 million in 1960-61 and .7 in 1955. In percentages, if these targets are achieved, our vegetable and food supply will be five times of 1955-56 output, of milk 50 per cent higher and fish more than $2\frac{1}{2}$ times. Statistically it is satisfactory, but in fact it means that actual shortages of these essentials will continue and there will be practically no relief from them so far as most of our people are concerned. It also means that the pressing problem of increasing their supply has not been considered seriously even in the Third Plan and nutrition has not become a matter of real concern to our policy makers. Great as is the gravity of the problem, it cannot be solved by what are, as stated before, isolated projects and plans, and the only way even to make a serious attempt at planning for this purpose is, as pointed out by the U.N. Community Development Evaluation Mission, to have village land development plan.[13] Village production plans, including the programme for increasing the production of vegetables and fruit, milk and eggs, have in theory a place in our Third Plan,[14] but it is also admitted in the report on the Plan that

12. *Third Five Year Plan*, p. 320.
13. *Report of Community Development*, p. 31.
14. *Op. cit.*, p. 336-37.

progress has not gone beyond issuing instructions by the Community Development Ministry and their transmission by the State Governments.[15] In fact the very idea of village production plans, as emphasized later, has been practically abandoned. Serious implications of the fact, as stated below, are far-reaching, and one very serious fact is that our agricultural development will remain merely departmental programmes, evoke hardly any involvement of the people and their under and bad nutrition will continue until we realize the gravity of the problem and take appropriate measures to solve it. For next five years this problem is not even to be faced. Under village plan it should be possible by intensification of agriculture and significant increase of yields to reduce the area under food grains and release lands for dairy farming and fodder production, village forests and the production of vegetables and fruit, fish meat and eggs can be given the priority due to them. Our supplies were very near the requirement of cereals and pulses even in 1961. That is not a matter for concern as a production problem. The real problem is much larger than the production of these essentials, and it can be solved by stages on a planned basis if our available resources are fully and rationally utilized.

DEVELOPMENT AS A PROBLEM OF SOCIAL DYNAMICS

The importance of village production plans referred to above as a means of removing vital nutritional deficiencies is really related to the basic issue of organization of agriculture as the most important factor in development. Our large outlay on agriculture in the three plans and inadequacy of the achievements confirms the point that in agriculture finance and investment are really not the crux of the situation. The return from large outlay that has been incurred or provided for falls short of our needs because available resources have not been utilized wisely and well and, as stated before, the

15. *Op. cit.*, p. 337.

social context in which development has been taking place is not at all favourable for optimum results. In other words, in agriculture, as in economy as a whole, the existing social structure and the forces that operate and sustain it are the most important limiting factors in development. In most of the important activities in agricultural development programmes like soil conservation and reclamation, multiplication of seeds of improved variety, minor irrigation works and their maintenance, full utilization of irrigation potential and economy in the use of water, response to and acceptance of innovations, provision and use of organic manures, protection of plants and minimization of waste in storage and transport, improvement of cultural practices, marketing of produce and linking of credit to production, utilization of the enormous idle man-power, which can be an important factor in capital formation, and developing social drive and intensification of cultivation and re-orientation of administrative personnel and building up a new administrative apparatus animated by a social purpose and capable of initiating and developing new impulses in all these respects, which are very crucial from the point of view of production and development, the results admittedly have been very disappointing and this is so because of limitations which have no relation to finance, investment and expenditure; and a lot in future depends upon how far these limitations can and will be overcome. The chains, to use again the figures of speech used before, in which not only the immense production but also creative potential in the broadest sense of the agriculturists, has been held, have to be broken. We have to find an answer to what is a problem in social dynamics. This fact is generally admitted by men of all opinions, but its impact on our thought and action is negligible.

COMMUNITY DEVELOPMENT

The community development programme started in 1953 was meant to be an answer to this problem. It is admitted, however, that, in spite of the impressive scale on which this programme has been introduced and extended, it has not been an instrument for creating conditions under which agricultural development can be made adequate for the needs of the people and the social changes neecssary for the purpose can be introduced. The underlying assumption of the programme is that it should tap the latent spring of energy and enthusiasm of the people for working out their own salvation. In the words of Jawaharlal Nehru, "The community projects are of vital importance"—"to build up the community and the individual and to make of the latter the builder of his own village centres and of India in the larger sense".[16] And because "there is such a tremendous potential in the effectively mobilized man-power and ingenuity of the rural people of India that everything possible should be done to help them to become effective, confident, expecting community groups," and further "the method of doing so is technical know-how of community development".[17] Unfortunately the evidence is quite clear that this know-how has not yet been found and is provided by the seven reports of the Programme Evaluation Organization of the Planning Commission. The result is that "too little is being done to strengthen the foundation relatively to the resources spent on super structures",[18] and the people do not still consider it their own programme. It is not possible to present and analyse all the available data contained in the evaluation reports in support of this conclusion. In all important respects it is clear from these reports that the programme has not been able to achieve its avowed objects. Peoples' participation in the programme has neither been spontaneous, nor adequate and not even a fraction of the

16. Prime Minister's Inaugural Address at the Development Commissioners' Conference, May 1957.

17. Carl C. Taylor, Ford Foundation Consultant on Community Development, A Critical Analysis of Indian Community Development Programme, p. 15.

18. The Sixth Evaluation Report, 1959, p. 1.

immense man-power in the villages has been utilized for community development. Local leaders for assuming responsibility of the execution of the programme have not been found and village factions, which have disrupted the community life in the villages, are more rampant than ever. Very little, if anything, has been done to create a sense of social awareness, the weakest sections in the villages have not been benefitted by the programme and the gulf between them and the upper strata has been widened owing to the latter being the main beneficiaries of the development expenditure. The programme in its formulation and execution has been bureaucratically administered and bureaucracy has not developed any redeeming features by the coverage of the programme having been extended to almost the whole country. It still remains aloof, authoritarian, unimaginative and unresponsive to the essential needs of the people and its inefficiency and corruption, if anything, have increased by the rapid expansion of the programme. There is a lack of co-ordination at all levels between the various ministries of the Union, between the States and the Centre and between development officers at the district, block and village levels. Even in respect of simple functions like provision of drinking water, latrines, multiplication and distribution of improved seeds the programme has failed to achieve any significant results, and in respect of integration of all aspects of development, which was, and has to be, the prime purpose of the programme, it has not made any progress worth the name. Planning at the village, block and district level exists in name but not in fact, and as stated later the states have frankly accepted the position that this is an unattainable object. The new phase of the community development programme is the development of what is called Panchayat Raj—establishment of autonomous village communities having power, funds, resources, initiative and impetus developed from below—has meant that all over the country the new statutory institutions have already been established. This can be a development of profound importance and a great step in the right direction. It is meant to change the centre of social gravity of both our polity and economy and convert the country into an organism, in which small autonomous living communities become the most creative centres and the base for the whole federalized superstructure of the economic and political system. It is a revolutionary concept, and is in keeping with the most advanced contemporary political and economic thought. This concept, however, has not been realized anywhere, and though pre-eminently suited to our own needs, conditions and possibly even ancient heritage and potentially the most adequate vehicle of socialism and democracy, its realization is possible only in the context of social revolution in action. This condition does not exist at present. "It is," in the words of Jai Prakash Narain, the most ardent advocate of Panchayat Raj, "possible to construct the outward structure of Panchayat Raj and to give it no substance. That would be like a body without soul, dead from start, a still born child."[19] Make believe has been such an important factor in the community development programme so far, that misgivings as to whether the next phase of community development can be anything more than a still-born child are perfectly legitimate. The community development programme, the results make it abundantly clear, has been so far a body without soul. This assurance that soul can be inspired into this body cannot be generated by bold words of the community development ministers or administrators. Their words have to be discounted at a very high rate, for their bold words have in effect so far meant less than nothing. The unfortunate fact is that their profession and practice has been so far apart in the past, that the bolder their words, the greater is the mass cynicism that they produce, and this is not the least of the disservices which they have rendered by the grave shortfalls in the achievements of the community development administration. The scale on which community

19. Jai Prakash Narain's *Swaraj for the People*, p. 9.

development is being attempted is very impressive, but as, to use the words of Dr Taylor again, the know-how of community development has in itself been lacking, the scale itself becomes a disadvantage and not an advantage from the social standpoint. As it has been stated in the Seventh Evaluation Report, we have, so far as community development is concerned, to bank more upon hopes than the performance of the past. The hopes will be realized partly by the devolution of authority on the new institutions, but much more by our villages ceasing to be oligarchies that they are and becoming real democracies. Such surveys of the working of Panchayats as have been made in different parts of the country show that power politics are as important in Panchayats as in state and national politics, and particularly at the block level the Panchayats are being used as a means of increasing and consolidating power of parties, groups and individuals.

SIGNIFICANCE OF INTEGRATION

The community development programme was in theory intended to realize integration in agricultural development and the working of the rural community. Its failure is largely due to the fact that this object has not been even understood, much less implemented. Integration is a process of many aspects and implies unity of purpose and will in carrying out a programme of development and social transformation. In other words, it means that the increase of agricultural production depends upon co-relation of policy and practice, horizontally and vertically through simultaneous action in economic and social spheres in the framework of a changing rural economy in response to a social, i.e. socialist purpose, owing to socialism being the avowed objective of planning in India. This involves (a) formulation of village plans of production and development of social services; (b) all administrative departments working in unison and through agencies, e.g. village level workers, Panchayats and co-operatives for whom not only the village is one problem as a whole and its prospects, health and development are a matter of concern to the entire economy but the vital interests of the economy as a whole are promoted and preserved by the village and all its functionaries and institutions; (c) a new community built to replace the existing disrupted villages—disrupted by internal faction, the impact of the increasing power of moneyed interests and political, economic and administrative centralization; and (d) release of new dynamism, i.e. the power of a regenerate community expressing itself in economic, social and cultural spheres and in keeping with the general rhythm of the national economy and giving it a deeper meaning and purpose. These are the constituent elements of the process of integration, and this composite concept has been posited in our thoughts, theories and policies in all the three plans; and yet in practice it has been almost completely disregarded, and disintegration rather than integration has been the most outstanding feature of our common life at all levels—from the village to our metropolitan centres. This process can be arrested and reversed by integrated action at the village level—by making the village the starting point, the centre and the climax of all our plans of development and social change. This does not mean that village has to become a world in itself—a little republic of yore, but a focus of expanding life, Mahatma Gandhi's oceanic circle—life which by degrees becomes a part of and merges itself in one world which we all have to live in and work for. In our village—and therefore in our economy—what Tagore called "the threads of social communion" have been snapped. The rupture is the cause of our disintegration and the restoration of "social communion" is the substance of integration and also the essence of socialism. That is why integration is the key word of community development, its very life breath and that is why in our plans for the future we have to come back to it in spite of a record of unmitigated failure in this respect of thirteen years of planning.

INTEGRATION THROUGH PACKAGE PROGRAMME

This failure is being covered by making a show of realizing integration in practice without understanding its inner meaning and importance. The Ford Foundation has been able to make good use of the word from its point of view and "sell" an idea to our Government which is an old idea whose inadequacy has already been demonstrated conclusively by experience of its application a number of times and yet it is being put forward as a new panacea of the ills of rural economy; but it is, as pointed out below, already fairly clear that once again we are in for another serious disappointment. This concept is now being tried in the districts in which what is called the package programme is being implemented. This concept has really provided what is called "the philosophy of community development" and its inadequacy is fully proved by results. Now it is proposed to apply more intensely in sixteen pilot schemes in selected districts, according to the recommendation of the Ford Foundation Team which is generally speaking its sponsoring and guiding agency.

The essence of this programme is extension work on an integrated basis by combining *all* essential elements (for developing full food production potential) into one integrated food production programme. It has good features to which no exception can possibly be taken. It is to provide simultaneously adequate and timely supplies of products like fertilizers, implements, pesticides, etc. and also of credit of farmers, marketing arrangements, strengthening of the transport arrangement and increasing the number of godowns. This programme is to be worked in districts which have the maximum of irrigation facilities and minimum of natural hazards and is expected to set a pattern for extending such a programme to other similar areas. This intensive effort is to "reach all farmers through Panchayats and co-operatives and to formulate village and farm production plans which will progressively involve all farm families". The programme is to be co-ordinated at the central, state and district level, but is to be based upon the development effort at the village level by, as just stated, involving all farm families. The total production of food grains in the seven selected districts in which work was started first during the base year is about 2,100,000 tons and is expected to rise by 40 to 60 per cent at the end of the fifth year as compared with the estimated increase of 32 per cent for the whole country under the Third Five Year Plan. This programme also provides for utilizing all man power for local work programme. "It is not to be," in the words of the Foundation Team, "as the Community Development Programme in India is, a generalized statement of aspirations, but a real programme to be translated into plans for specific action in particular communities, have sufficient concern for human motivation, involve people in planning and pay due heed to social setting of the farmer."

All this is meant to be a great contribution to expansion of production and the resolution of our food crisis. That this has already been the perspective of our community development programme and it has in no way met or can meet the emergency which has arisen is left out of account. We are to traverse the same road again with the faith worthy of embarking upon a new social adventure, and find a new pattern of agricultural development for the country as a whole. This programme is to leave out all "ideological" considerations, i.e. assume that socialism as an issue is merely a distraction, social context, i.e. framework of social relation in which disparities and domination of the village economy by the trio of the powerful agrarian minority, the money lender and the merchant backed fully by the authority of bureaucracy, is an irrelevant consideration and the increasing deterioration in the position of the majority of the rural poor is of no specific concern. If as a result of adopting this line of development the gap between the minority and the majority, which has already increased, becomes still wider, it is from the point of view of this concept unfortunate, but it is the price which has to be paid by us for meeting the emergency created by the low rate of agricultural development in face of this menace of the "explosive" acceleration of the growth of population. The basic fact of the situation is that if this approach is adopted and this price is paid, the crisis will not be resolved but aggravated. That this is also the programme included in the Third Five Year Plan and is at complete variance with its social objectives and implications and also with the premises of other programmes included in the plan shows how plans and planning are lacking in integrity both in formulation and execution. In the first seven districts the total administrative expenditure on the programme is estimated at approximately Rs. 7.77 crores of which the Ford Foundation is providing Rs 4.40 crores, the Government of India .60 crores and the States Rs 2.77 crores. In these districts including the budget provision for 1963-64 the outlay of Rs 4.39 crores has already been incurred, and it looks as if at the end of the Third Plan financial targets of the programme would be fully realized. Whatever the shortfalls of the programme it looks as if there will be no shortfalls in expenditure. Further extension of the programme to more districts brings the total number to sixteen. Expenditure on these districts is to be entirely met by the Government of India and the State Governments and the same scale of expenditure is to be maintained in these districts. That means that in all about Rs 16 to 17 crores would be spent on this production-oriented programme. Even if the programme succeeds in realizing its object its extension to the country as a whole would involve on the same scale total expenditure of Rs 340 crores[20] and provision for loan expendi-

20. The gross area of the districts is seventeen lacs hectares which forms a little over 5 per cent of the total cultivated area of the country. It is proposed to "saturate" the first seven districts by 1965-66 by the coverage of the extension work. The total expenditure on the country if the whole country is to be "saturated"—say in the fourth plan—would be, as pointed out above, about Rs 340 crores in five years, i.e. by the end of 1970-71 and a provision of probably about Rs 1,200 crores on the basis of current estimates would have to be made for meeting credit requirements of the programme.

ture of the order of Rs 1,200 crores.

These amounts include expenditure only of short-term maturing items of the development. Expenditure on major and minor works of irrigation, soil conservation, etc. would have to be provided and would of course be much heavier. Moreover, the ordinary expenditure on community development would continue. All this expenditure may be worth while. That would depend upon the general approach of the programme and its results. An Export Committee on Assessment and Evaluation has already reported on the working and achievement of the programme in 1961-63. Its conclusion is that "even though the programme has not been in the field for experience to be fully crystallized the preliminary results seem to indicate positively in favour of the approach".[21] The facts cited by them, however, do not support this conclusion. Corp-cuttings experiments do not, according to the Report, show startling increase in production, and this, for a production-based programme must be reckoned as a serious failure. There is no clear indication that the problem of lack of co-ordination at the project level has been solved or its more serious bottle-necks reduced. Though crop plans for individual cultivators have been prepared and, in 1963-64, 753,000 of farm production plans were worked out, these plans are very elementary and it is not known how far they were actually implemented and with what results. What is even more important is that farm plans have no relation to village, block and district plans and the latter really did not exist and the need for preparing them has hardly been appreciated. "The new farm planning technique" has, in the words of the Report, "yet to break through tradition bound practice and get established in the farming routine of the mass of cultivators."[22] The co-operatives, again according to the Report, "cannot handle the programme of this order, they have yet to adjust their operation

21. *Intensive Agriculture Development Programme Report 1961-63*, p. 296.
22. *Ibid.*, p. 210.

in accordence with the working schedule of agriculture" and co-operation is at its weakest at present in respect of co-operative marketing. All these facts do not support the conclusion that results seem to indicate positively in favour of the approach. They, as a matter of fact, indicate clearly its inadequacy and that once again we have permitted ourselves to follow a path which, as pointed out above, has been trodden before and has led us repeatedly to disappointment after disappointment. The whole concept of the programme is based upon technological approach to agricultural development which, we should have known, cannot possibly resolve the current crisis or the more fundamental crisis of the rural economy.

The programme, the Report states, does not claim to initiate "anything startlingly new". It is, as a matter of fact, the old hackneyed approach of the agricultural department in the pre-independence period, of the Etawah Project of 1948, of the Community Development Programme, of Grow More Food Campaigns and their Intensive Programme and even in its diluted form of the Integrated Rural Credit Programme. All these programmes are known to have failed almost completely and yet, under high-powered salesmanship strategy of the Ford Foundation which with a contribution of Rs 4½ crores and the services of consultants who were, by no means indispensable, has led us to embark upon a programme which our new Prime Minister has recently stated openly has not been a success. The Report frankly admits that "socio-economic milieu" has been a hindrance in the way of the programme and that "the programme cannot stand outside the general socio-economic conditions in which everything has to function".[23] The conclusion should have been that a radical change in the general socio-economic conditions, i.e. in the whole social system—is an essential pre-condition of the success of this or any other comprehensive development programme. This is the reason why the whole approach is initially and

23. *Ibid.*, p. 115.

essentially wrong and cannot but lead us into a blind alley. As pointed out above, the experience of more than three years of the programme is already indicative of its inability to solve any problems of our rural economy. We should scrap the programme and make it the last time when we put our hopes in a purely "technological" solution of the problem of breaking through the stagnation of rural economy. It is a pure delusion that we can achieve this object through measures included in this programme. The whole rural economy needs to be basically and radically re-organized if we want to resolve this crisis and the fundamental crisis of the rural economy as a whole. In one word without a social revolution we cannot resolve the crisis and all attempts to keep clear of what are called ideological issues, i.e. issues relating to the norms, substance and objectives of our economy, are not and cannot be of any avail.

INTEGRATION THROUGH NEW RURAL ECONOMY AND NEW MAN

There is another concept of integration which has never been clearly stated but is implicit in the statements made in the plan reports and various programmes. This concept also implies combined application of all measures for expansion of agricultural production—fertilizers, implements, extension of irrigation, improved seeds, cultural practices, etc.—but in the context of the new economy in the making. The underlying assumption of this concept is that technological possibilities of agriculture can only be realized in the social framework of diminishing disparities, of developing counter-vailing forces against the powerful minority interests, planning in terms of a budget of specific socially assessed needs of the community and available local material and human resources, re-organization of village communities with a view to giving the submerged majority its due place in rural and national economy and making utilization of the idle man power as the most important task of planned development of the rural economy. This means that the programme of food production has primarily to be a programme of implementing an adequate nutrition policy to provide for irreducible minimum of nutrients for all people, of developing decentralized industries in order to employ man-power which is neither needed in agriculture nor in industry, commerce and services in non-agricultural occupations and for providing community overheads like soil conservation, reclamation, minor irrigation, afforestation, communications and local social services. This truly integrated programme can, it is assumed, be carried out in a healthy, progressive, expansive rural economy of which the real prime mover is new man to whom the community in all its inter-relationships is a living reality, i.e. he has his being in it, and from it he draws his physical, mental and spiritual sustenance and fulfils himself in it. It is also assumed that though small living communities are to be the foundation of new economic, social and political structure, they are and must remain an organic part of the whole nation and as a community, receive assistance from it on the highest priority basis and contribute to its prosperity and growth by well-directed and well-adjusted efforts at the basic level. This integration means that the local communities are not only autonomous but also self-sustaining and generate surplus which can be utilized both for local and national development. This concept of integration is socialist in content, has the best of what is contained in the other—i.e. extension—concept, but in its scope and social technique it has a much wider and deeper significance and it does not evade real issues as the other concept does on a calculated basis but makes their solution its prime object and purpose. This concept has, as stated above, not been clearly stated anywhere, but is nevertheless in theory a part of our planning approach, though it needs to be fully clarified and concretized and has to acquire its operative mechanism and implemented with clear sighted consistency. In the Panchayat Raj approach of decentralization, in the old Intensive Area of the Khadi and Village Industries Commission—a programme which has now been dropped, also *gram ekai* and *gram raj* programme, Integrated Rural Industrialization Projects of the Planning Commission and Integrated Rural Credit Scheme of the Reserve Bank, this concept is the working premises of planned development.[24] Integration, in the sense indicated above, is however the only sense in which integrated programmes of planned development of agriculture in particular and the economy in general can be formulated and implemented. It has also to be added that integration in this sense is not a mechanical but dynamic process. It cannot be realized merely through the mechanism of new institutional framework and technique of planning, but has to be common thread of a new social purpose—in Tagore's words again a real social communion based upon unified action of socially-conscious people.

VILLAGE PLANS

The starting point of integrated planning has to be the preparation of village and area plans by the organs of the community at the village and area levels like the Panchayat Samities. Delimitation of areas for planning is a matter which requires careful consideration and has to be made in relation to conditions of particular areas, but the view that basic units should plan for a population of say about 5,000 and the next step should be to have an institution which can plan for a population of 25,000 to 50,000 has been generally accepted. The main point for consideration is that these units should be organic entities, i.e. they should represent and express the working of real communities and function in the natural orbits of their common life. In the First Five Year Plan[25], in the Second Five Year Plan[26] and in the Third Five Year Plan Draft Report[27]

---

24. Unfortunately, as pointed out in a later chapter, the results of the implementation of these programmes have also been disappointing and this is again due to the fact that in carrying them out the vital importance of basic social changes has not been given its due consideration.

25. pp. 100-03.

26. pp. 305-07.

27. pp. 158-59.

and Final Report[28] the need for clearly defined village plans has been clearly indicated and stressed. It was also emphasized in the First and Second Five Year Plans that Co-operative Village Management, under which land and resources of the village should be organized so as to provide for maximum employment, was held as the broad aim of the State policy;[29] and it was also intended under it that all the land of the village was to be regarded as a single farm. In spite of this clear statement and reiteration of the policy, the position is that the possibility of realizing this object is remote, "what exists in each state is a plan for state and for agricultural production—prepared by the departments concerned,"[30] and its targets have been fixed in aggregate, which, in the words of the Ford Foundation Team, "may be reasonably accurate for the nation as a whole, but hide tremendous local variations—they (the targets) conceal inter-relationship among many practices that is the key to increased production".[31] These tremendous variations are also due to complex of inter-relationship and not only practices, and are mainly due to situations arising from diversities and disparities which have been referred to before. The programmes which leave them out are neither estimates of needs nor of potentials and are not, therefore, programmes for planned development at all. Planning has to mean specific quotas of production for every village and every family. This kind of planning in terms not of aggregate but specific quotas raises problems for which only solution is planning from below—planning by local peoples' committee. "Planning from below," in the words of the Sixth Programme Evaluation Report, i.e. "planning by the people in relation to their areas has still to take roots," and at present "plans are prepared at the higher and official level and handed down to lower bodies".[32] The Planning Commission has

28. pp. 335-36.
29. *The First Five Year Plan*, p. 100.
30. *Report of the Committee on Co-operative Credit*, p. 199.
31. *Op. cit.*, p. 108.
32. *The Sixth Evaluation Report*, p. 17.

itself admitted this fact and to quote from the Third Five Year Plan Report, "limitations persist and they (the targets) are not as yet firmly based on area plans as had been earlier hoped for".[33] This is a masterpiece not only of understatement but also of equivocation. The fact is that the area and village plans do not exist at present, and as things are, they cannot be framed. All that has been said about village and family plan, since the Five Year Plans were framed, has been sheer waste of words. It has no counterpart in reality and has only served the purpose of providing "frilling" for our planning documents.

SUBSTANCE OF INTEGRATED DEVELOPMENT

In spite of this conclusion it is of value to state even with extreme brevity what integrated planning should mean in concrete terms from the standpoint of what can be a big leap forward for our rural economy. The development potential of our agriculture is truly enormous, and the differences between our current yield and the yields which can be realized in agriculture can be taken to be a measure of our production potential; and though capital expenditure is needed for increasing agricultural production to the limit of its possibilities, that is not the primary or the most elementary need. Very low and non-increasing yields in agriculture, in spite of large investments, expansion of irrigation, etc. are due mainly to social inertia. This difficulty can be overcome and intensive development of agriculture can release a large area under production of food grains, which can be used for very significant increase of protective foods and also set up a high rate of expansion in non-food crops. This, however, can be done if individual rights on land do not remain barriers to rational utilization of land and resources and interests of the community become paramount in agricultural production. Without expropriation by force of proprietors of land it is possible to re-organize agriculture in order to create larger cultivated units, apply scientific methods

33. *Op. cit.*, p. 305.

in production, raise the standard of cultural practices and improve agricultural implements and *develop latent human forces*. These, however, can be done only if the community becomes the most important factor in production and its organs undertake what the Planning Commission has been calling Co-operative Village Management, i.e. all village lands become one estate, labour surplus to agriculture is utilized in development of local industries and other outlets mentioned before, and the purchasing power of the agriculturists is raised to a much higher level. Paramountcy of the community should mean not negation of democracy but its fuller realization by co-operativizing of the rural economy and the framework of the co-operatives is to be developed with a view to ending exploitation at all levels and in all forms. Marketing should become a social function and a means for directing rural economy and creating and channelizing its surpluses. Administration is not only to be decentralized and reoriented but concentration of economic power, particularly at the basic level, has to be combated and overcome by organized strength of the people. And lastly the state must truly become what the Rural Credit Survey calls "combination of the weakest at the top" and "rural orientation of all the forces that count in the country's governance and in the ordering of its economy".[34] This means, of course, that the highest well-being of the rural poor must become the prime concern of the men in authority, the state power has to be used for the protection and promotion of their interests and the latter, i.e. the masses in the villages themselves, must become the makers of their destiny. Major points of highly condensed statement on integrated planning in agriculture will have to be further elaborated and developed in the chapters on de-centralized industries, co-operatives, the role of labour, trades, finance, price mechanism, income structure and planning apparatus. The consideration of two important subjects of co-operative farming and price policy, which are of special interest

34. *All India Rural Credit Survey*, p. 519.

for integrated rural development, has also to be held over in order to deal with them later in a wider context. This statement, in spite of its utmost brevity, it may be hoped, does indicate how little the implications of the concept, which is so frequently cited, are even understood and how wide is the gap between what is being done in regard to integrated rural development and what needs to be done. Our inability to formulate and implement production plans for each village and each family, to which our planners have in theory been committed for the last decade, is one of our major failures which, due partly to our organizational and administrative limitations, stem mainly from our lack of power and courage to come into close grips with the issues implicit in them. Integration at a time of unavoidable profound social change means integrity in thought and action in terms of the latter (social change) and that is just which we do not possess and have not been able to acquire. We cannot plan from below and on an integrated basis because our economy is an inverted pyramid, the base is weighed down by the enormous burden that it has to carry.

PEASANT FARMING AND CO-OPERATIVE VILLAGE MOVEMENT

Leaving some of the major points related to rural organization and better development to later treatment in the book, this chapter can be closed with a brief discussion of two important points of interest which have a bearing upon the future of rural economy and can with advantage be dealt with briefly here. The place of independent peasants in rural economy is a matter of great importance, and has been exercising the minds of some very earnest-minded men vitally interested in the future of rural economy and socialism in India. Generally speaking, in India attitude towards peasants, as in most parts of the world, is one of solicitude and deep sympathy, and it is widely held that safeguarding and strengthening their position in rural economy is necessary and desirable for the future of socialism and democracy in India. Small land holders and family farms have evoked warm approval and support in many countries and legislative action has been taken in their favour and with a measure of success. This attitude is further fortified by the fact that the peasants are known to have had a very raw deal in countries, which are now under communism, and the fate that they have met with is taken as a serious warning against undermining their position in any country which seeks to avoid totalitarianism and is keen to make democracy an integral part of socialism—really its very essence. Power won with the support of the peasants with the slogan of "land to the peasant," was, it is rightly maintained, used in Soviet Union and East European countries to uproot the peasants with the utmost severity which was, as is well known, a major cause of upheaval in Poland and Hungary in 1956, and the absence of peasants' revolt in other communist countries is attributed to the odds being against them owing to the fear of the might of the state being able to crush ruthlessly all opposition. It is not possible to deal with these issues here. They involve questions of historical interpretation, value judgements and assessment of the situation for the discussion of which there can be no space in this chapter. It is necessary to consider the issue with as much detachment as possible and not cloud our judgement by controversies which are very remotely connected with it and without taking any rigid position.

The peasant, who makes an honest living on the land owned by him with his own and family labour does not, it is held, exploit anyone or create any problem from the standpoint of the growth and working of socialism. It is admitted that it is in their interest, and that of the country that the peasants with substandard holdings, who cannot under the most favourable conditions, provide even the social minimum for owners, i.e. income that can be considered even a living wage, should give up the effort to eke out independently a bare subsistence and develop co-operative organization for the cultivation of their land to enlarge the unit of cultivation and use the existing resources and technique fully and economically. Co-operative farming for cultivating their land is, therefore, conceded as a necessity and has to be developed for rational cultivation of land and maximizing its yields. The Congress Agrarian Reforms Committee proposed that owners of such midget holdings pool their land, resources and labour for cultivation and their surplus labour should be utilized in rural industries and other outlets should be provided for them. This view has been accepted by the Government and Planning Commission and even by the most uncompromising critics of joint cultivation, though hardly anything has been done to act upon it. The view, if implemented, would mean for the vast majority of our cultivating owners the issue of the peasants being left alone to cultivate their land, has no practical importance. They have to be either drawn out of agriculture and given opportunities to make a living in non-agricultural occupations or made into viable farmers through joint cultivation. This means that the whole village economy has to be re-organized for the small peasants and agricultural labourers cannot significantly improve their position or have a future worth living for in the existing conditions. The rapid growth of population, which is taking place, it need not be added, is adding to their number and increasing the odds against them. This makes it absolutely essential that serious effort should be made to introduce and develop co-operative village management and make mostly the small peasants and agricultural labourers its principle operators and beneficiaries. On this point, to repeat, there is a consensus of opinion in India which hardly any other basic question commands. The fact that, in spite of this agreement, the position of this multitude of our agriculturists remains unchanged or rather has become or is becoming worse, is very significant and also very revealing and shows that effective action in this respect requires the adoption of concerted measures with full support of "all the forces that count in the government of the country and the ordering of its economy". This support has not been and is not available and this challenge has not been and is not being met on that account.

PEASANTS WITH VIABLE HOLDINGS

The other point as to whether the peasant proprietors with viable holdings can and should be given an assured place in our new rural economy still needs to be considered and is of fundamental importance. Data about the agrarian structure and distribution of holdings are neither reliable nor up-to-date but taking the data of the N.S.S. Report on Land Holdings, to which reference was made in the last chapter, the position is that: (a) a little over one-fifth of households do not own any land; (b) about one-fourth of all rural households have holdings of one acre or less, i.e. nearly one-half of the agriculturists have either no land or less than one acre and they own a little more than one per cent of the cultivated area; (c) about three-fourths of the rural households had either no land or holding of less than 5 acres; (d) 83 per cent of the land is cultivated in holdings of 5 acres or more; (e) About 64 per cent of the total cultivated area is owned in holdings of 10 acres or more; and (f) less than one-sixth of the cultivated area is owned in holdings of more than 50 acres and less than 6 to 7 per cent in holdings of 100 acres or more. These data are not up to date and have to be used with reservations. But, as stated before, the picture of the agrarian structure, which they present, is more or less true and this general conclusion is supported by data derived from other sources. Two conclusions follow: (i) farms above ten acres, covering as they do about two-thirds of the cultivated area can be made into economic farm units, i.e. with the existing technique they can, given the necessary skill and equipment, be operated well and give reasonable return for acre and per man; and (ii) the area in possession of the large cultivators is less than one-sixth and does not therefore involve serious concentration of wealth and income in agriculture. This means that though three-fourths of our agriculturists need to be rehabilitated, more than two-thirds of the cultivated area can be made the basis, by Indian standards, of prosperous peasant farming and it is not necessary to develop co-operative farming so far as this area is concerned. If the holdings are consolidated,

Indian agriculture can with all other aids, be placed on a sound basis and with much higher attainable yields the general standard of income and living in agriculture can be raised well above the existing standard and a state of general competence, if not affluence, be realized.

The logic of this view is clear. Peasant farming can be an efficient method of agricultural organization. It represents values which are important for a democratic economy—values of respect for personality, dignity of the individual and a large measure of equality and decentralized initiative. It can also be made a bulwark against bureaucracy, concentration of economic power and all totalatarian trends. Since most of the cultivated area is owned by farmers who own units of ten acres or more, future of agriculture in India, according to this view, lies in making their operations viable and creating an assurance that property, investment, economic status and capacity to hold their own will be protected and they will have to be assigned a place in the economy which will entitle them to full appreciation of the community and be in no way in conflict with our socialist objective or rather it would be an important contributory factory in preserving democracy as the very substance of socialism.

This view is a reaction, as stated above, against the peasants having been ruthlessly liquidated in the communist countries and derives its appeal from the fact that the peasant all over the world has, with some reason, been idealized. The background of this attitude has to be understood, and yet the stubborn fact remains that nearly 87 per cent of the households who do not own any land at all or own less than ten acres and in all less than one-third of the total cultivated area, represent the most intractable problem not only of our rural but also national economy. The poverty, resourcelessness, incapacity to rise above their present level and exploitation may be due to our extermely unfavourable man-land ratio, pressure of population and the low level of industrialization and development, but they in their hundreds of million persons and more than 60 million families and together with artisans and other person in non-agricultural occupation, are nearly three-fourths of our total population. Co-operative farming is not the answer to the problem of these submerged masses but co-operative farming, by common consent, is unavoidable in the case of the farmers in this category, and as most of them cannot be absorbed in urban and large-scale industries and commerce, a planned co-operative agro-industrial economy in the villages is the only way in which even an attempt can be made to solve this massive problem. The proposed farming, service, marketing, credit, industrial and labour co-operatives, have to be built up primarily for their benefit but they are also essential for the rural economy as a whole.Peasant farming, even if it is continued, will need these co-operatives for its growth and stability but in any case these twelve or thirteen per cent of the peasants, who own two-thirds of the cultivated area, cannot be isolated as viable peasant farmers who can excercise all the values of peasant farming by themselves and create a stable basis of social democracy in the country-side. They will have necessarily to be integrated with the whole rural economy, operate within the new co-operative framework, be assimilated in its working and largely depend upon it for operative mechanism. They will buy their supplies from the co-operatives and sell their surplus to them, receive technical assistance and guidance from service co-operatives and personnel of the state and central government and their credit needs will, of course, be met by them and in crop-planning and utilization of land, they will have to be full participants in the preparation and execution of the village plans. If for all this the peasant farmer will be fully assimilated or integrated with the new rural economy, his independence and decentralized individual initiative would hardly have any economic or social significance, and experience will teach him that he gains nothing by remaining aloof only from joint cultivation if he in all other respects is active, contributing and benefitting member of the co-operative village community. In capitalist countries owing to the working of market economy production of the peasant farmer is fully socialized, i.e. he is enmeshed in the network of the economy as a whole and is largely dependent upon forces beyond his control. In a co-operative rural economy he cannot practise individual peasant farming with any advantage to himself or the economy. A village economy cannot be partly co-operative and partly a competitive private enterprise economy even if two-thirds of the cultivated area is owned by 13 per cent of the farmers. The co-operativization has to proceed by stages and by consent, but the view that because of two-thirds of the cultivated area being owned by 10 per cent of the farmers there is no problem of the small farms but only small farmers[35] shows an uncomprehending assessment of the present position and the future developments. The whole rural economy is derelict, farmers with holdings of all sizes and agricultural labourers are all its unconscious victims and they all have to be made aware of this fact and educated. Co-operative Village Management in which, as the Planning Commission has pointed out, the distinction between the owners and non-owners ceases to have any meaning, is the way out for the entire rural economy, including 13 per cent of the farmers on whom Prof M.L. Dantwala lays so much stress for saving Indian agriculture.

REARGUARD ACTION

This nostalgia for peasant farming is a phenomenon which has existed and exists all over the world, but in a situation like ours it really signifies a rearguard action for preventing an advance towards socialism in agriculture. It involves the support of the privileged minority against the bulk of agricultural population, creates the illusion that private property in land for small-scale farming is socially desirable and this property sense is no hindrance to realizing socialist objective. The most important need is not to strengthen the small minority but to

35. Vide M. L. Dantwala's note on "Small Farmers and Not Small Farmers," *Indian Journal of Agricultural Economics*, Vol. XIV, No. 3, July-September 1959, p. 51 and Presidential Address at the All-India Agricultural Economic Conference, December 1960.

get it to identify itself with the 87 per cent, who are without
land or whose grinding poverty and unremitting struggle to
eke out miserable pittance through almost super-human labour,
constitute the most depressing fact of our economy. The social
differentiation, which already exists and has been accentuated
by the effects of the development programme, is very significant.
The worst disservice that can be rendered to the future of agriculture is to foster the belief that minority can solve their
problems by developing their own small properties without
radically changing the rural economy and fully co-operating
with the efforts of the majority or those of the community to
solve the baffling problem of ending their misery. The slogan
that our problem is not "small farms but small farmers" is a
sure method of confusing the whole issue and accentuating
class differences. The only way in which this can be prevented
is to throw the weight of state authority in their favour (the
87 per cent) and do whatever is possible to make them a decisive force in the village economy. That primarily means that
they have to develop their own strength, to protect and promote their interests and make the minority realize that co-
operation on their part is not only desirable but that without
it they stand to lose rather than to gain. This has not happened
so far and will not happen unless the process of reorientation
and realignment, to which the Rural Credit Survey Report
referred, is duly carried out. Value of social democracy can be
realized not by investing our hope in peasant farming but in
transcending its obvious limitations. The inherent risk of co-
operative management becoming a coercive management has to
be duly considered, but it cannot be provided against by not
creating conditions for resolving the social differences and conflicts. The real risk is that ascendancy of the minority will be
greatly increased and the majority will suffer even from more
grievous disabilities. That is the way neither to demcoracy nor
socialism but to the negation of both. The ardent advocates of
peasant farming would be disagreeably surprised if that happens but this is inherent in their argument and the way of

thinking, and it has to be prevented.

BHOODAN AND GRAMDAN

In conclusion a few words may be said about the Bhoodan and Gramdan movements of Vinoba, i.e. donation of land and villages. Its impact so far has been more moral than economic and social, but it has in it several ideas with far-reaching implications and its appeal may have an abiding value. This great man of vision and piety has tried to awaken the social conscience of the nation to face some of the crucial issues of the country. In what is truly a pilgrimage of thousands of miles, he has spread ideas in the language of the people, which are of fundamental importance. The awakening which he has tried to bring about consists in: (a) questioning the social morality of private property in land and by implication of all private property not intended for use; (b) giving the highest priority to the forgotten man—the landless labourer in the scheme of development; (c) pointing out that fellowship or compassion has to be the substance of social change; and (d) stressing that peoples' democracy in the villages has to be the basis of democracy higher up and has to derive its sustenance and strength from the spirit and vitality of the people and not from electoral procedure or statutory sanctions. These fundamental ideas have been presented with dead social earnestness and in a manner which bears the impress of deep and direct experience. At present there is no way of evaluating the impact of these ideas or stating how far these ideas have actually moved the people or become a part of their being. They have been broadcast very widely and some of the seeds may have fallen on fertile soil and in fullness of time germinate and ripen into a harvest of thought and action.

In concrete terms the result has been that about 4.5 million acres of land has been donated for distribution among landless labourers and over 9 lakh acres have been actually distributed. Later donation of villages—*Gramdan*—was asked for and about 5,000 villages have been received. What each *gramdan* amounts to is not quite clear, but it implies that the property rights in village lands have been renounced and it has become the property of the village community and has to be utilized according to a plan formulated in the interest of the community and for the benefit of all. In some of the villages it appears that excellent work has been done for radical reorganization of their economy and full utilization of man power. Unfortunately an experiment with great promise in the beginning in Koraput, a district in Orissa, in which 1,500 *gramdans* were contributed, conducted by a band of devoted workers under the very capable leadership of Annasaheb Sahasrabudhe and with the support of the centre, has come to naught because of, in the words of the selfless leader, "open opposition from (Orissa) Government and an all-out offensive set into action against the movement".[36] This throws light on the way the forces within the country are frustrating development and change and the cross purposes at which the Centre and the States are working. In the *Gram ekai*—the integrated rural units—referred to earlier, the Khadi and Village Industries Commission under the same inspiration is proceeding experimentally for carrying out a five-year programme of integral rural development again under the leadership of Anna Saheb Sahasrabudhe. Credit for the rapidity with which Panchayats have been established all over the country and are expected to undertake a programme of all-round development is due at least partly to *gram-raj*, which Vinoba has made the key idea of his approach. Taken altogether all this does not sum up to an impressive record in tangible achievements for all the work of not only Vinoba but also of thousands of his devoted workers in whom he has evoked warm response. New donations of land are now not being invited, and in the words of Anna Saheb Sahasrabudhe, "The gramdan movement looks like being on the decline—and the flow of new gramdans is withering".[37] A movement which, it was hoped,

36. A. W. Sahasrabudhe, *Report on Koraput Gramdan*, p. 9.
37. *Op. cit.*, p. 15.

"would help in solving in some measure the most difficult land problem of our country" is facing a serious setback. This is disturbing and invites self-criticism on the part of Vinoba and his team. The donations of land and villages in quantitative terms mean more land given to the landless labourers and more nuclei of fundamental work than what has been achieved under land-reforms legislation and the work of the community development administration. That is, however, not saying much and is more a measure of failures of the state policy and not of the achievements of this movement.

This is so, and yet it may be repeated that the ideas propagated by the movement have seminal significance and they and the social earnestness which has gone with their propagation are assets of great value for the future of socialism in this country. What the movement needs now is a social analysis of its experience, and understanding of other approaches which it may differ from but which may all the same perhaps give it a fuller understanding of the social processes at work in our economy. Particularly it may point to the conclusion that though well-being of all has to be the object of social endeavour —the good of the lowliest and lost has to come first and be achieved largely by the democratic process of making them the chief motive power of the march forward. It will be a great pity if this movement is also lost in the morass of all-round frustration in the country. It has so far shown catholicity and receptiveness which may possibly save it from becoming a lost cause.[38]

---

38. "Gramdan is," in the opinion of Prof. D. R. Gadgil, "an unprecedented movement with many and complex implications of very great potentialities" (Indian Journal of Agricultural Economics, Vol. XII, October-December 1957, p. 10). This view is based upon the assumption that property rights in land will not only be extinguished but their re-accrual will be prevented in the Gramdan villages and the Gramdan authority will be able to divest the upper strata of cultivators, the traders and the money-lenders of the dominant power, assume responsibility of all economic activities and provide against all hazards. This is a correct assessment of the position and its possibilities, but Gramdan villages must, however, necessarily function in the whole complex

As this is being written at a time when crisis is in the air, it is necessary to say a few words about it specifically though it would involve repetition of earlier statements. What is this crisis due to? It is not due, to repeat, the growth of population. Increase in the production of agricultural commodities in general and food grains in particular has, as stated already, more than kept pace with the growth of population. It is not due to the setback in agricultural production or production of food grains in 1962-63. In 1963-64 we have more than retrieved the position. According to the provisional estimates our production of food grains in 1963-64 has again reached a peak level.39 All

of conditions existing today and cannot transcend the limitations imposed by the working of the economy as a whole. For this they need not only v ..t to change fundamentally on the part of the Gramdan authorities and the people but also active assistance of Government at all levels. "There is no prospect," in Prof. Gadgil's words, "of change in the countryside, and this is so because there is no desire for any such change among those who hold economic and political power" (f.n. please). Those who hold economic and political power not only do not desire change, but are ready to suppress it if and when there is a prospect of its being seriously introduced. The lesson of the Government hostility, which the Koraput experiment aroused and encountered, is clear on this point. Men in power are, in spite of lip service paid to Vinoba and all that he stands for, really against what he seeks to achieve; when there is any prospect of achieving it, they can be counted upon to use their authority to undo what has been done. This is one of the causes of the setback referred to in the text and the other is that Jan-Shakti (people's power) to which the organizers of the movement appeal and which they in theory depend upon, has neither been aroused nor utilized until now. This is due to the limitations implicit in the approach itself, the organizers not having understood the lesson of their experience and social intertia of the masses. All this makes the outlook what it is and the movement faces the prospect of being brought to a standstill. As stated in the text, re-thinking based upon a careful social analysis is clearly indicated by the facts of the case.

39. *Index of Agricultural Production with 1950 as base from 1950-51 to 1962-63.*

	1950-51	1955-56	1961-62	1962-63
All commodities	95.6	116.8	141.4	136.2
Foodgrains	90.5	115.3	137.5	131.87
Rice	87.9	114.9	140	133.0
Wheat	101.1	114.2	139	127.9

This decline in 1962-63 in the production of foodgrains, rice and wheat was

the same the prices of articles of food are rising with disturbing rapidity, shortages of food in some cases and even famine conditions, have arisen all over the country, long food ques are being formed and the people are in a state of real distress. As the discussion at the recent high level meeting clearly shows, the men in power are in a bewildered state. They have no answer to the problem of rising prices. They cannot bring themselves to take the necessary steps of introducing state trading in food grains and not even of implementing the decision for nationalization of processing mills. Belatedly they are realizing that inflationary pressures which have been built up in the past owing to very seriously mistaken monetary and financial policies are now producing their full impact on our price situation. But neither from the long-term nor from short-term standpoint any policies have been framed which can alleviate, much less redress, this situation. From the short-term standpoint the Government will have to take radical steps and prevent deterioration of the position. If they have not the strength and courage to undertake such measures, they will not be able to arrest—much less reverse—the process of serious deterioration which is well under way. But the real lesson of this crisis is that it exposes very sharply the lack of integrity in our basic thinking and formulation and excution of our policy. We have to know that the only way out for us is the way forward, i.e. introduction of

due to failure of rains, but according to provisional estimates the total production of foodgrains in 1963-64 was again 80 millions and of rice 36.4 million tons as compared with 78.75 millions and 32.2 millions in 1962-63. If this estimate is correct, production of rice in 1963-64 is the highest on record since 1950-51 and yet we are experiencing the most acute shortage in supply of this staple food. In 1962 we imported 4.56 million tons of food grains, total production was 67.10 million tons of cereals and 10.15 million of pulses which means that our total supply of foodgrains was 81.81 million tons even in the lean year of 1962-63. Since 1950-51 according to official figures increase in agricultural production has been continuous, and setback owing to the decline in agricultural production in 1962-63 of 3.3 per cent is, in this perspective, of no real consequence. Whatever may be the explanation of the crisis, it cannot be attributed to the shortage of production and supply of foodgrains.

government would have a crucial role in realizing this object. Mahatma Gandhi's criticism of modern industrialization induced reservations in our thinking in regard to it and created a political bias in favour of village and small industries which has made it practically necessary for the men in authority to avow belief in their beneficient role and make a liberal provision for them in our plans without giving a clear thought to the contradiction inherent in the co-existence of modern large-scale industry and crafts in various forms and shapes. Efforts made to resolve this contradiction have, as stated in the next chapter, been more or less ineffective. Limitations of our thinking, which are largely due to limitations of understanding of the context in which the two (modern industry and crafts) can co-exist and contribute to the health and strength of the economy, also still remain. We, the articulate section of our people, are still of divided mind as to how these two sectors of our economy are to be fostered and developed and be reciprocally helpful rather than obstructive, and the result is that our general approach in this regard is neither self-consistent nor can it provide a basis for an integrated policy and its clear-sighted implementation.

SOCIAL PURPOSE

There is all the same in practice a pronounced preference for modern industry and in the last decade we have not only invested very large funds in its development, but as a rule any conflict between it and the village industries has been resolved by action in its favour. There is a strong and hardly concealed feeling that modernization of Indian economy is indicated and measured by the extent to which large-scale power production is promoted and made a decisive factor in our economy. This is partly due to the fact that there is hardly any choice so far as heavy basic industries, generation of power except on a minor scale, and, of course, production of ships, aeroplanes and railway engines, coaches and wagons and of fuels of different kinds are concerned. There is not and cannot be any difference of opinion that India needs and must have these industries and they have as a matter of necessity, largely speaking, to be set up and organized on a massive basis and the presumption in favour of these industries being owned and operated by the state at different levels is almost conclusive. Already this is underlying premises of our industrial policy, though there have been, as indicated later, departures from it which cannot even be explained, much less justified. These industries comprise a very large sector of our economy, and in their scope and importance are bound to increase and not decrease as it reaches higher level of development. These are not only of strategic importance and can, with public ownership and management, be commanding heights from which the whole economy can be operated, steered and developed in the best interests of the community, but they also involve the acquisition of technical skills, knowledge and the capacity for making and applying innovations of basic importance which raises the whole level of technical potential and performance of the economy and creates conditions for higher cultural development and changing the ethos of the community in which scientific outlook becomes a clearly decisive factor. The necessity of developing those industries on a large-scale basis has to be utilized for the social purpose of regulating and controlling the entire economy and they have to be organized and operated with a clear understanding that this has to be done and they are of basic importance for the economy, not only because they are the foundations of economic development, but through them the whole economy can be animated by and respond to the central purpose of making it rapidly and increasingly a socialist economy. According to our Industrial Policy Resolution of 1956 it has been clearly stated that "this (industrial) policy *must be governed* (Italics ours) by the principles laid down in the Constitution, the objective of socialism and the experience gained during these years" (i.e. since 1948). The experience gained in the last decade shows that the objective of socialism has more often than not been disregarded in the administration even of public enterprises but much more so of private industrial undertakings. As in the words of the Resolution, "industrial undertakings in the private sector have necessarily to fit into the framework of the social and economic policy of the state", they have to be an integral part of, in the words of the directive principle of state policy laid down in the Constitution, "a social order in which justice, social, political and economic shall inform all the institutions of the national life". This, of course, means that private industrial undertakings as much as public enterprises have to be *governed* by socialist principles and cannot be granted or exercise exemption from the social imperatives implicit in them. The phrase mixed economy has been put into currency and is taken to mean as if public and private undertakings are of co-ordinate significance and our economy will be governed by one set of principles in the public sector and another set of principles in the private sector. The use of this phrase is to be avoided because it is very misleading. Indian economy is intended and has to be a socialist economy in the making and any elements not compatible with socialism have necessarily to be of vestigial significance and progressively eliminated until the whole economy becomes a homogeneous socialist economy. Private undertakings, to the extent to which they operate within the framework of public economic and social policy, are also to be instruments of a socialist policy and assigned specific obligations in the development of a socialist economic system.[1]

1. The writers like Dr. Loknathan and Mr. H. M. Patel, who are known for their connections with and pre-disposition for free private enterprise, justify the state undertaking obligations for developing heavy industries, transport, etc. because these are needed for the development of private enterprises (Loknathan, "The Public Sector in India", *The Indian Journal of Public Administration*, Vol. III, No. 1, Jan-March, 1957. H. M. Patel, "The Role of Private Sector in Indian Economy"). This view, though partly true, misses the most important point that the objective of socialism is and has to be all-embracing and public and co-operative sectors are intended to occupy a dominant position in our entire economy and private sectors have more and more to be given a subsidiary and secondary role in it as it moves towards the appointed destination—a fully developed socialist society.

To the extent to which they do discharge these obligations they become agents for the execution of a socialist policy, and it is an open question as to how far their private interests and public obligations can in fact be combined to the advantage of the community. In the transition period, however, socialization of economic enterprises has to proceed by stages and private sector has not only to be permitted to function but also to be utilized to realize objects of public policy. This can be done only if it operates within the framework of a socialist economy and social policy and those, who control all the levers of economic and political systems, believe in socialism and are intent upon using their authority and power for realizing its objectives. This condition unfortunately has not been fulfilled in the last decade and is not fulfilled now. In other words, balance of social forces has been and is against the realization of the social objectives of the industrial policy of the state, and this, as has been and will be stated again and again, militates very seriously against the advance of socialism in India. Rapid industrialization is essential not only for economic development but also for socialist transformation of the country, but it is and cannot be a neutral process. It can either accelerate or retard advance towards socialism, and all the vigilance that can be commanded is needed to ensure that industrialization becomes an instrument of socialism and not means for defeating its objectives.

For reasons indicated later in the text this process has not been fully brought into play, but that does not alter the fact that public enterprise has to set the norms which should apply also to private enterprises and replace the latter in the process of the country's economic growth. Private sector has to be assigned a role in national development on, in the words of the Draft Third Five Year Plan, "the assumption that the private sector accepts the broad discipline and values implied in the national plan and will function with public sector" (The Third Five Year Plan, p. 2). As it is, the public sector which is, as stated later, working in accord with the private sector and accepts the broad disciplines and values which the latter (private sector) identifies itself with. There is, however, no doubt that normative position has been clearly stated in the Draft Third Five Year Plan and is the right position from the standpoint of state policy.

PACE OF GROWTH

Industrial development of the country in the last decade has been very considerable and is really a matter for real satisfaction. There has been to repeat, in the words of the Third Five Year Plan,[2] "an upsurge of industrial activity" and more has been done for industrial development of the country in the last ten years than in the first half of this century, and a pace of

2. In assessing the relative importance of outlay on industrialization in our development it is, besides direct expenditure on factories and minerals, necessary to take into account outlay on power and transport and communications very large part of which is intended to contribute to the development of industries directly or indirectly. In this broad sense total expenditure on industrialization in the last decade was Rs. 857 crores or 44 per cent of the total of Rs 1,900 crores only in public sector in the first plan, Rs 3,460 crores or 51 per cent of the total of Rs 6,750 crores in the second plan and the provision in the third plan is Rs 5,368 crores or 53 per cent of the total of Rs 10,400 crores. Index of industrial production has increased from 100 in 1950-51 to 194 in 1960-61 of steel to 250, of aluminium to 500, of machine tools to 1,618, of iron-ore to 234, coal 169, of power 248, and of technical education to 239. In the Third Plan the index of general production is expected to go up to 329 or by 70 per cent, iron and steel to 637 or 168 per cent and very striking increase is contemplated in the production of the other items referred to above. These indices illustrate the progress achieved in the development of modern industry and in the allied fields. In this period in the words of the Third Plan, "three new steel works, each of one million tons capacity have been completed in the public sector and the two existing steel works in the private sector have been doubled so as to bring their output capacity to two and one million tons respectively. The foundations have been laid of heavy electric and heavy machine-tools industries, heavy machine building and other branches of heavy engineering and the production of machinery for the cement and paper industries has been started for the first time. In the field of chemical industries there has been advance on a wide front leading not only to larger units and greatly increased output of basic chemicals, e.g. nitrogenous fertilizers, caustic soda, soda ash and sulphuric acid and also to the manufacture of a number of new products, e.g. urea, amonium phosphates, penicillin, synthetic fibres, industrial explosives, polythelene, newsprint and dye stuffs. The output of many other industries has increased substantially, e.g. bicycles, sewing machines, telephones, electric goods, textiles and sugar machinery" (The Third Five Year Plan, p. 452). There has been "an upsurge in industrial activity" and though India is still, relatively speaking, a backward industrial country, the progress achieved in the last decade in industrial development and planned in the Third Plan are truly heartening; and if social content of the development is compatible with socialist objective,

development has been set up, which though by no means adequate in relation to our needs, has given to our industrial growth a certain measure of new dynamism, and can, if it is combined with a sense of social mission, carry the country forward on the crest of a wave. This is, however, a big if, and at present this sense of mission is very clearly lacking. The public undertakings in India are really units of state capitalism, as a rule are run as capitalistic enterprises and that very few, if any, seem to be concerned about striking new paths in the administration of these enterprises or using them to quicken the rate

it can mean not only industrial development but real advance towards socialism.

This is more so, because investment in the public sector and its strategic importance owing to public ownership and management in basic heavy industries, power production and development of communications is of crucial significance. Out of the total planned investment for industrialization of Rs 5,368 crores in the Third Plan private sector would account for Rs 1,350 crores or a little over 25 per cent. In the Second Plan out of the total investment of Rs 3,440 crores private sector contributed Rs 1,210 crores for the same purpose.

In 1960 out of the total paid-up capital of joint stock companies of Rs 1,593 crores the state enterprises accounted for Rs 477 crores—a little less than one third of the total, but if to this amount is added the total capital at charge on March 31, 1961, of Railways Rs 1,562 crores, of Post and Telegraphs Rs 228 crores, of Power Undertakings Rs 790 crores, of Shipping Companies Rs 71 crores and of Air Corporation Rs 72 crores, investment in the public sector in modern industry makes private sector really an adjunct of the public sector. The relative importance of private enterprise in our industrial economy has to be further reduced by nationalizing, as stated already, a number of industries, but even as it is the public sector is the leading sector in modern industry in India, and if the bearing of this fact is properly understood, it can become an instrument of real importance for the development of socialism. It is the public sector which has to develop new norms of management, industrial relations, social accounting, income differentials and what is most important, social awareness and private enterprise have to follow suit, i.e. keep in step with the public sector. This is just what has not happened and the result is, as stated in the text, that the objective of socialism is not taken seriously by those who are in power in public undertakings and the staff and the workers in them are neither imbued with a sense of working in socialized enterprises, nor are they aware of the social challenge or respond to it with intelligence or earnestness.

of advance towards socialism in the country as a whole.
Though a certain measure of dispersion of industries has been
brought about and new industrial centres have grown up in
relatively backward parts of the country and Bhilai, Rourkela,
Bhopal, Ranchi, Nieyvelli, Sindri, Cambay and Ankleshwar
are likely to serve as a means of diffusion of technical skill and
experience and produce, it may be hoped, a leaven which will
really cause a ferment among the peoples of the area in which
they have been located. This, however, has not been planned,
and the needs of the areas in which these enterprises are
located, have not been given their due consideration. This is
true of all regions, sub-regions and local areas, towns and
villages. There is no plan of integrated economic development
of the country, development and location of these industries
have been decided upon on an *ad hoc* basis, and their inter-
relation with the other schemes of development and their
impact on the economy of the region or sub-region have hardly
received any consideration. In other words, wider social aspects
of planned economic development of the country have practically been lost sight of in the development of new industries
or the expansion of old industries.

INDUSTRY AND ECONOMY

Though the rate of industrial growth in the country has been
greatly accelerated in the last decade modern industry still
occupies a secondary place in our economy. Factories, mining,
railways and communications taken together contribute, according to the revised estimates of national income by the
Central Statistical Office, 11.2 per cent of our national income
in 1959-60 and this proportion was 9.3 per cent in 1950-51.
Agriculture and its allied activities accounted for 51.8 of the
national income in 1950-51 and the ratio was reduced to 48.3
per cent in 1959-60 reduction of three per cent in the proportionate contribution of agriculture and increase of less than 2
per cent in that of modern industry sums up the major changes
that have taken place since 1950-51 in the distribution of our

national income by industrial origin and indicate how, in spite of rapid increase of our industrial growth, the structure of our national income has not changed materially and the relative importance of its different sources has not been significantly altered. Employment in those industries has since 1950-51 increased from 39.83 lacs to 51.60 lacs in 1959, i.e. by 11.77 lacs. During this period labour force in the country has been estimated to have increased by nearly 320 lacs, i.e. less than 3 per cent of this increase has been absorbed by modern industry. Rapid industrial growth is, to repeat, a matter for real satisfaction, particularly because foundations for the development of basic industries in India have been and are being laid. Impact of this fact is, however, not only small on our massive unemployment but it has not made any great difference to the distribution of national income according to its origin and India still remains predominently an agricultural country.3

Social Content: The main point, however, which is of vital interest from the standpoint of industrial growth is, as stated in the footnote, its social content. Public undertakings are from this point of view hardly any different from private enterprises, and the fact that they are owned and operated by the state does not impart to them any positive quality for the development of socialism or give them a leading role for the purpose.

3. By way of comparison the major facts of industrial development of China may be cited. From 1951 to 1959 the increased annual rate of growth of industrial output has been 28 per cent (5 per cent) index number of industrial output in 1959 was 949 (194) and share of industry in the overall product of agriculture and industry increased from 30.1 (20) to 67.6 (25) per cent from 1937-39 to 1958-59, the pre-war base being taken owing to industry and agriculture having been damaged seriously during the war and civil war years, i.e. until 1949 (Figures in brackets are corresponding figures for India). (Source of figures on China—"Economic Development of Socialist Countries"—*Supprement to World Marxist Review*, January 1961). It is well known and generally conceded that the rate of economic growth in China in the last decade has been much more rapid than in India and this difference is specially striking in respect of the rate of industrial development. This is true also of other socialist countries, but the bearing of the rate of growth in China, it need not be said. has for us a special significance.

Their administration has been further bureaucratized, but this is a negative quality inherent in all large-scale—particularly state—enterprises and has to be combated and overcome. Bureaucratization of economy under socialism is an old charge and the experience of economic administration in the Soviet Union and other socialist countries has unfortunately increased its validity. There the concentration of economic and political power has clearly indicated the need for bringing into action democratic processes to provide effective correctives against this distortion. This, however, is a danger inherent in all large-scale undertakings and private concentration of economic power which is also, as is well known, a serious problem, makes the risk all the greater and warps the growth and working of democracy. Social content of public enterprises has to be developed through social processes at work at many levels. The internal checks and balances have to be provided, new social norms have to be developed and applied, general awareness of the paramountcy of commonweal has to be promoted and fortified through training and vigilance of the workers. Moreover, through institutions specially designed for the purpose new patterns of behaviour have to be evolved and through clear understanding of implications of socialism in relation to the working of these enterprises, bureaucratic trends have to be inhibited and beneficient social impulses evoked and enlisted in the service of the community. It has to mean in the first place realization that the basic premises of administration in public enterprises are very different, and among them the most important is that market values, though of indicative importance, are not and should not be decisive in shaping policy decisions and therefore a system of social accounting based upon this view has to be developed and applied. The other major premise, of course, is that human factor is not only all important and has to be given precedence in the administration of productive undertakings and its potential, not only for efficiency but also for growth, but it has to be purposively tapped and made into an asset of increasing importance. All that is best in the experience of industrial management in any country or under any system in respect of technique, time and motion studies, layout of factories or working out of time schedule or other devices which have been known to contribute to the smooth and efficient working of enterprises, has to be drawn upon and fully utilized. Even this requires extensive knowledge and willingness to learn and assimilate. But replacement of market values by social values and application of the latter is a task of very different order, and it not only involves a different approach, but great alertness in social terms and capacity to understand and apply these values in relation to the day-to-day tasks of economic administration on an experimental basis. Public undertakings have to do this not only for the public sector but also for the private sector, for theirs is the responsibility for assuming a leading role in making the whole process of industrialization a social process in the best sense of the word and subject it to the discipline of values which are imperative for all industrial—really economic—undertakings in the country. The necessary compression of this basic point makes it impossible to elaborate it. It may, however, be repeated that its importance is hardly appreciated and even in thought and in practice there are no indications that it has any influence on policy or administration. Public undertakings in India, therefore, are not socialist enterprises and that they have to function as such, in a real sense, is not an essential part of our economic and social thinking. We have, of course, to bear the practical limitations in mind and realize that the accomplishment of this task requires changes which have still to take place and the men, who can carry it out, are simply not available. This makes it all the more necessary that social content of industrialization should receive very earnest consideration and be made its substance both in theory and practice.

Administration: The main point, on which so far attention has been focussed in discussing the question of public enterprises, is the relation of management to Government, i.e. the Secretariat and the Ministries and the extent of Parliamentary control and supervision to which they should be subjected. The general conclusion that they should be autonomous in their day-to-day administration and Government should give general directives but abstain from direct interference in administration, and Parliament should exercise general superintendence and vigilance through a special committee of its own is a sound conclusion, but in practice the line between directive superintendence and vigilance on the one hand and vexatious and annoying intervention on the other can not be sharply drawn and much has to be left to the good sense and discretion of the parties concerned and the right mean between undue interference and each enterprise being a law to itself can only be arrived at by mutual accommodation and experience, the lessons of which have to be built into the right operative conventions. Owing to lack of experience and disposition of the secretariat to occupy all key positions of authority, members of higher services have had more than proper share in formulation and administration of policies and have exercised authority which they could not wield with success and distinction, and the result has been that not only what is called "services mentality" has been carried into the administration of public enterprises, but tradition of prestige and power unsuited even to business enterprises and entirely incompatible with social purpose of public enterprises, have been imported into these undertakings in early and most formative period of their career, and a great deal of harm has been done to them. Members of the higher administrative services have been and are one of the closest trade unions and they have jealously and successfully guarded the service interest in administration, deplomatic positions and management of public undertakings.

The result of their monopoly of power and position of authority will have to be evaluated when all the facts of post-independence history are fully known; but enough is known to make it possible to posit the general view that these services by exercising their disposition to enlarge their power and be at the helm in the entire administration have defeated some of the most cherished objectives of the struggle for freedom. They have maintained and even widened the gulf between them and the people and by a working alliance with big business with a view to getting top positions in business and industry for themselves after retirement and placing their sons and relatives in well-paid positions during their incumbency of high positions of authority. They have thereby made a mockery of all high-sounding social objectives and created round themselves and the position of power which they have filled an atmosphere of make-believe and insincerity and grieviously prejudiced the chances of socialist policies of even being honestly formulated and much more so of their being executed with any degree of real drive or genuineness of purpose. One of the most cardinal sins which our public men, who have possessed and exercised political power after independence, i.e. our ministers, have committed is their having been a party to this aggrandizement of power by the services and done nothing to check it or miti-gate its consequences. That members of the services were, in a large number of cases, men of ability and not amenable to pres-sure in a small way, makes the processes that have been at work more and not less unjustifiable. So many men, who had greatly benefited by our struggle for freedom by being admitted to a share of the highest position by the British to meet the national demand for Indianization of services and have even benefited more after independence through accelerated promotion and otherwise, let down the people before independence and even much more so after independence by being untrue to the high-est purpose which the nation made its own or to which it solemnly dedicated itself. So much ability in the country has been not only lost but abused owing to this failure on the part of higher services. That there should be a proper devolution of authority in general administration and much more so in indus-trial administration goes without saying. A lot remains to be done even to realize administrative decentralization in the management of industries, but what is needed more is integrity in the highest sense—not merely resistance to the temptations of making money through use of public authority for private gains but fidelity to the supreme purpose of making India a socialist country and discharge in good faith all the obligations that it implies. This fidelity is non-existent at present in the highest places and without it administration of public enter-prises cannot but become a means for defeating instead of promoting socialism.

New Standards of Management: The task of finding the per-sonnel technically competent, imbued with social purpose and capable of initiative and drive not only for managing and deve-loping industries but also building up new traditions of eco-nomic administration—is difficult and bound to remain so for a long time. Apart from higher civil services having used their pre-eminent position to have as large a share as possible of the new prize posts, there was and still is scarcity not only of tech-nical staff and operatives but also of administrators of public enterprises whose social potential is of as great an importance as their production potential. Organizations of these under-takings and their relation to the economy as a whole have to be efficient in the sense of being suitable for maximizing phy-sical production. Norms of labour, raw material, utilization of machines, standardization of products and their accord with the specific needs of other enterprises and the consumers have to be framed and applied. Norms in the initial stages have to be based upon historical experience in our country and other coun-tries, but have to be rapidly modified in the light of experience and greatly improved by pooling the responses to a new and fast developing situation both in regard to particular indus-tries and the economy as a whole, specific and social costs have to be reduced and their return in financial and real terms maxi-mized. Moreover, norms of behaviour, relations and motives have to be conceived in terms of socialism and acquisitive trends transformed into drive in the interest of the community. Incen-tives of personal gains, achievements and opportunities have to be retained and utilized to obtain intensity and quality of work, but they have to operate in a new social framework and progressively the paramountcy of the good of the community has to be made an all-important factor, and it has to be the function and obligation of the executive officers of public enterprises that this happens not only definitely but also manifestly, i.e. all who are working in and for public enterprises are consciously aware of this need and work for it with intelligence and determination. The qualities, which an industrial administrator of public enterprises needs, are in some respects the same as the qualities which a builder and administrator of private enterprises has to possess in order to achieve success. He too has to be an enterpreneur— has to have foresight, capacity to organize and manage, an understanding of the complexities inherent in modern industrial undertakings, the will and ability to master them and develop a pattern of human relationship based upon gifts of real leadership. These qualities are general qualities which whatever be the social system, are needed for setting up and running modern industrial enterprises. But there are other qualities which are needed for building up and operating public enterprises of an economy which has to be increasingly transformed into a socialist economy and generate its own social motive power. Preeminent among them is a clear understanding of the fact and its full implication and willingness to grow and change to realize this fundamental objective. This means that each enterprise and industry has to be made an organ for the development of socialism and in its organization, working and results show how this can best be done. In an acquisitive economy the success puts premium upon qualities of drive, leadership, manipulation of men, materials and situations and mobilization and utilization of resources in which predatory elements are most important and moral and human insensibility becomes a practical necessity. These are, it need not be said, just the qualities which in a socialist society have to be first driven into the underworld of the economy and then eliminated. These are archetypal contrasts of two diametrically different societies; and like archetypes are based upon sharp distinctions which cannot be maintained in life; and though the extremes are clear and easily distinguishable, in practice transformation of one into the other has to be made through penumbra of different degrees and shades and even in the ultimate analysis allowance has to be made for imperfections which must remain, humanly speaking, even in the most perfect societies. These archetypes have, however, a real social significance which has to be clearly understood. In our circumstances when in public enterprises men have had to be drafted into service from wherever they were available in the hope that they would be equal to their tasks, it was inevitable that they would represent the old and not the new archetype and the gifts needed for developing these undertakings in the right direction would be hard to obtain. It is not only the members of the higher administrative services who have been found wanting in the new situations, but very few of the other men in higher technical and administrative posts have given any indication of being able to rise to the needs of the new tasks which have to be accomplished. Even in the new staff colleges, technological and other training institutes this need is hardly appreciated or provided for. It is, however, essential to realize that archetype needed for industrialization in a socialist society is very different and our thoughts, schemes of recruitment, training, promotion and organization have largely to be guided by it. This, however, has not happened and there is no indication whatsoever that even in the Third Five Year Plan any steps will be taken to develop the new type of industrial executive and standards will be set and applied for evaluating performance derived from this fundamental concept.

Existing Standards: The task of changing the type and standard of industrial leadership in an economy, which has been stagnant and even in a state of decay for a long time, is exceedingly difficult. Our public enterprises—railways, posts and telegraphs, power undertakings and new 125 public enterprises—are, as stated above, at present being run as capitalistic enterprises and there is very little distinction between them and the private enterprises except in regard to their ownership and the manner of constituting the boards of management. This change in type and standards calls for a new departure from the existing approach and practices, for the Indian industrialists are, with few exceptions, known to be lacking even in the accepted standards of probity and enterprise in the more advanced capitalistic countries and evasion or circumvention of the law is much more common than its honest observance and dishonest practices are known to be the rule in their dealings with the workers, the customers and the state. These industrialists are, as a rule, lacking in capacity to play the role of pioneers in development, are not even good immitators and in their behaviour represent some of the most undesirable practices of capitalism in the raw. What is, however, needed is not merely a change in business ethics according to the tenets of a well-regulated private enterprise economy but the assimilation of a developing social ethics according to the needs of a socialist economy in the making. There is no prospect of this happening if private enterprise is left to itself and goes on working in the ruts which it has made for itself. The atmosphere, which it has created and in which it functions, is inimical to the sense of social responsibility and understanding of the needs of socialism, and that it will, of its own accord, fit into the framework of national economic policy if the latter is to be a genuine and all-embracing socialist policy is a vain hope. Importance of private enterprise in the economy, relatively speaking, has to be reduced by more rapid expansion of the public sector and nationalization of banks, general insurance and internal and external trade. As it is, the state by using its political authority and strategic positions, can lay down and enforce a code of conduct more in keeping with the needs of a socialist economy. Private undertakings should, within limits set by socialist objectives, have reasonable freedom to exercise initiative and develop production, and bureaucratic interference in their working should be avoided; but that does not mean that they should continue to be guided by principles relevant only to capitalism in its early stages of development and not be alive to the social objectives of the country. By acquiring new strategic positions and deepening the significance of all regulatory measures, the community can and should bring home to private enterprise the need for playing the role of contributing to the development of socialist economy. This means that they have to be consciously utilized for this purpose and any serious deviation by them from the accepted socialist policy of the country is to be rendered risky and difficult. It is necessary to achieve this object and not to interpret or apply the provisions of the Indian Company Act or the Industries Development and Regulation Act without any reference to the social objectives of the economy. Mr C. D. Deshmukh, in his speech on the Indian Company Bill, clearly stressed the need of keeping in mind the social objectives of the country in its enactment and administration and the Industrial Development and Regulation Act is intended to give due importance to national objectives of economic policy in its application and implementation, and yet it is stated, "that the basic objectives under the reform of the Company Law, however, remains the same, viz. to encourage and safeguard private investment in fields which are not earmarked for the public sector and to regulate such investment for the common good, to maintain the confidence of the shareholders and to protect their legitimate interests".[4] This is an unduly restricted interpretation of the scope of the Act, but even if it is a correct interpretation, the Act should be amended to clarify the position and place it beyond doubt that private enterprise has to work in accord with the broad objectives of national policy and be subjected to the discipline of social, i.e. socialist values. This has been made plain on numerous occasions and yet in practice we speak as if public and private sector can co-exist in a mixed economy each with its own orbit and its own normative principles. As stated before, this is, in the nature of things, impossible and private sector in a socialist

4. A *Layman's Guide to Indian Company Law*, pp. 3-4.

economy can have a role—even an important role, if it functions as an instrument of socialist policy. In the interest of
rapid economic development in the words of the Indian Chamber of Industries and Commerce, "it is essential that the
Government rules and regulations are suitably streamlined".[5]
They have to be streamlined, not as desired by the Indian
Chamber, with a view to giving private sector scope for un-
regulated development not only in its own assigned sphere
under the Industrial Policy Statement but also in spheres
assigned to the public sector, with a view to fulfilling the
fundamental objectives of our economic policy, i.e. the realization of a socialist society. If this is to be done the spirit and
purpose of administration have to be changed and pressures
built up and made overwhelming which may make intentional
or unintentional backsliding from the position clearly adopted
by the state with full approval of the legislature an impossible
proposition. At present this condition is not at all fulfilled and
it is more often than not that it is the private sector which sets
the tune which has to be played by the Government and the
public sector. The theory of the matter is, however, clear. The
public sector has not only to be dominant, but it has to realize
socialism in its own operation and it has to call the tune which
the private sector has to play with sincerity and without
deviation.

Form and Organization: Forms and organization of public
and private undertakings are obviously a matter of great
importance from the point of view of the development of a
socialist economy. The four forms under which public undertakings have been organized in India, i.e. statutory corporations, Government Companies, Departmental Undertakings
and Committee, Boards and Commissions (Corporate bodies
with promotional, developmental and administrative economic
functions) are all more or less agents of state policy, are in
varying degrees under state direction and control and their

5. *Report on Seminar on Planning*, p. 13.

funds are largely, and in most cases entirely, drawn from the public exchequer. Of all these the Government companies are the most important. They are all registered under the Joint Stock Companies Law and governed by its provisions. The Government has come to the conclusion that of these the Company form has been the most fruitful, and on 31 March, 1960, there were operating 125 Government companies with total paid-up capital of Rs 465 crores, i.e. about 30 per cent of the total paid-up capital of all companies, and besides these very large sums, as stated before, have been invested in railways, communications, power, port trusts, Reserve Bank, State Bank and other statutory corporations of different types.[6] The amounts invested in non-company undertakings is nearly five times of that in the underakings organized as companies. Public investment, in industries, is very much larger than private industrial investments and are, qualitatively speaking, far more important. Diversity of forms, which the public industrial investment has taken, is accounted for largely by historical reasons, but the fact that the company form has become the rule for public enterprises is based upon presumption in favour of its suitability for economic undertakings in the public sector. The validity of this assumption has not been carefully examined before it was widely adopted nor has it been tested in the light of experience or results. Its validity is open to question, and it has been influenced by the bias in favour of the form which is so common in private economic undertakings. The adoption of this form has been seriously criticized from the standpoint of audit and parliamentary control, but is also open to criticism for other important reasons. Members of the board of directors and superior officers of these undertakings are mostly either members of the higher administrative service or industrial magnates with very important positions in the private sector. In the early stage it could not have been otherwise, but, as stated before, unsuitability of members of the

6. Vide Footnote, p. 197.

higher civil service for these positions could easily have been posited from the very outset and it could have also been easily assumed that the industrial magnates would be completely out of accord with the social purpose of the public sector. No critical evaluation of the actual position in regard to industrial management has been undertaken, from what is commonly known about the men drawn from the services or industry, it is not all an unwarranted presumption that the men, who have been at the helm of our nationalized undertakings, have neither the desire nor the capacity to organize and develop them as socialist undertakings. The actual and prospective interest of the high-ups in administration are, as stated before, closely interlaced with those of big business; and to most of the directors of public undertaking socialism, far from being the inspiring vision that it should be, is really, to say the least, a public nuisance if not a public danger. This is also true of public undertakings which have not been organized in company form and the general attitude and approach of the topmost men in railways, post and telegraph, power undertakings, the Reserve Bank, the State Bank, the various corporations and boards, etc. usually speaking, are no different from those of the tycoons in the private sector. The experience of organization and management in the private sector should, of course, be drawn upon for making the public enterprises a success, but the practices in vogue in the private sector have more often negative rather than positive lessons for the public enterprises. Though mechanics of management and organization both in the private and public sector is about the same, its dynamics from the social standpoint is entirely different and has far-reaching organizational and functional implications; and it is the dynamic and not the mechnaical aspects of industrial organization in the public sector which has to be given pre-eminence in our thinking, approach and policy decisions in regard to management and organization of public enterprises.

Preference for the company form of organization, which has developed in the country, has not even been rationalized. It is merely assumed that it is a good form, as stated above, and its evaluation in the light of experience and results has not even been attempted. The general view, that industrial management should be autonomous, flexible, non-bureaucratic within and free from bureaucratic or political intervention from without, and lines of communication between the government and the industrial undertakings and within the undertakings be kept clear of obstruction, is in theory a sound view, but it does not give clear indication as to where the line between autonomy and responsibility, flexibility and lack of clear policy, non-bureaucratic management and order, freedom from undue intervention and absence of direction and accountability is to be drawn and how the theoretical principles are to be applied in practice. In the nature of things it is not possible to have clear-cut demarcation between legitimate latitude for judgement, decision and administration and straight jacket of meticulous control imposed from above. It is necessary to do fresh thinking on these questions and formulate principles of economic administration which from empirical standpoint would enable public enterprises to work with due regard for the well-being of the workers, the standard of technical performance, the interest of the community and harmony and efficiency of organization. The public corporation concept, which has generally commended itself as a form of organization for nationalized undertakings, is intended to realize these advantages, though the solution of issues that are implicit in it has not been and is not easy. This concept has to be more clearly defined in the context of actual conditions of our country and developed from the practical standpoint. This, however, can be done only if a frame of reference is provided and thinking and action on this subject are guided by the social values inherent in the frame. At present this frame is lacking and avoidance of doctrinal rigidity is being interpreted as an argument for action without any reference to guiding principles. An earnest effort of the mind is needed if success is to be achieved in evolving suitable and adequate forms of management and organization. At present, formally speaking, different forms are being used and they are in some respects unlike one another, but in substance they all operate in the same manner and their basic assumptions are about the same. In other words, in spite of the distinction of forms, there is no real difference in their working from the standpoint of their impact on the economy and its future. When there is a wide variety of public undertakings like the railways with capital at charge of more than Rs 1,500 crores and over ten lac employees operating all over the country and, say, Nahan Foundry Ltd. with capital of Rs 40 lacs and 150-200 workers located in a small town of Himachal Pradesh, there has to be a wide diversity in the forms of organization to suite their functional and other differences. What is needed is not the common mould into which all public undertakings are to be put for organizational purposes, but similarity of normative considerations with reference to which their operative apparatus is to be developed and the unity of its animating spirit. This means that these undertakings have all to assume the obligations of functioning as organs of socialism and contribute towards its realization. This condition can be fulfilled only if socialism becomes the living purpose of the country as a whole and an atmosphere is created in which all economic units, including public industrial enterprises, express this purpose and work for it with real devotion. This condition being non-existent, at present our industrial undertakings in the public sector are drifting as best as they can and at best they are working, to repeat, as units, large and small, of state capitalism and not as socialist enterprises.

  Private Sector: Industrial enterprises in the private sector remain unaffected in their management and organization by the socialist objective, and labour laws and other measures intended to mitigate the rigour of the pursuit of private gain are either evaded by them or accepted with very bad grace. For them socialism is an unmixed evil and their avowed purpose is to impede its advance, enlarge their empire as much as possible and when they cannot prevent the adoption of socia-list policies, to do all that they can to negate or undermine them. The Indian private enterprises find in the foreign-owned or controlled enterprises powerful allies, who as a rule operate under cover, and through all kinds of schemes of collaboration and the appointment of dummy directors strengthen their hold and have become even more formidable bastions of private enterprise in this country. The Indian and foreign private enterprises are working in close alliance with those who have as administrators an important share in shaping and imple-menting policy decisions and count upon and in fact receive support in protecting and promoting their interests. They (the Indian administrators) are being duly rewarded by being appointed to high lucrative posts in industry after retirement and in some cases find it worth while to retire even before time and take important positions in private firms. Interlacing of big business and high bureaucracy is a fact of increasing importance in this country and has an ominous significance. Industrial development of the country has meant increasing power of private industrial interests, and their prominent representatives not only get appointed to the boards of direc-tors of public undertakings but otherwise exercise great power in the economy as a whole, by controlling the press, the banks and other financial institutions, and contributions to the elec-tion funds of the ruling and other political parties they are known to possess and exercise malign influence on men in high places in administration, politics and the entire economy. The economic growth of the country has greatly increased the strength and power of these interests. The basic assumption of the company law is that shareholders are the masters of the joint stock companies, and if their formal consent is obtained for the appointment or re-appointment of managing agents, terms of their agreement, appointment of the relations of direc-tors in the firm or selling or buying contracts and similar other important matters, democratic control of major decisions in industrial management is established. This assumption, not only in India, but all over the world, is completely at variance with the facts of the case, and 4½ to 5 lacs of shareholders of the corporate undertakings in India, it is very well known, have no power even to influence, much less determine, policy decisions of their administration. The directors are really self-appointed at the start and every time at the renewal of their tenures, and it is pure fiction to hold that they are responsible to shareholders and under their direction and control. All the regulatory measures of the Company Law are based upon the fiction and are, on that account, lacking in positive content. The boards of directors of the joint stock companies are oligar-chies everywhere and much more so in India owing to the operation of the Managing Agency System. The Managing Agencies in India exercise control of capital resources, produc-tion and assets which is largely based upon investments of shareholders who are, to repeat, in no position to exercise any control themselves, and the directors' power is derived from not their own private investments, which are, as is well known, a small fraction of the total investment, but those of the shareholders and of the accumulated reserve built from the earnings of the corporate concerns. If ownership of capital investments and the risk involved is the justification for pri-vate sector in corporate enterprise, the justification is not valid for those who own but do not control and those who control but do not own. The directors are in a fiduciary position from the legal standpoint but are virtually their own masters. The corporate form of private enterprise, to the extent to which it is a success, is an argument not for private ownership of industry but its socialization. The success is achieved not by the incentive of private gain, but presumably by a sense of public obligation. In fact, however, it means exercise of enor-mous economic power by the directors without rendering account to anyone except themselves and among the directors only a few really count and the rest are merely figure-heads. This fiduciary position is combined with complete allegiance to acquisitive values and power is exercised without owing responsibility to the community as a whole. In the Second Plan out of the investment of Rs 850 crores in the private corporate industrial sector only Rs 150 crores were derived from new issues, and the rest was supplied by the institutions, government, foreign capital and mostly with state guarantees and reserves, i.e. accumulated savings. In the Third Plan out of the prospective investment of Rs 1,250 crores in private industries all except Rs 300 crores from new issues are expected to come from the same sources.[7] As the new issues also represent shareholders' money, in the Second and Third Five Year Plans by 1965 the resources at the disposal of the few, who control the private corporate industrial sector, will increase by Rs 2,100 crores without their having themselves invested their own funds in industries to any significant extent. Increase in the resources of the private corporate sector[8] means increase in the power of industrial magnate without anything like corresponding increase in their stake in industrial production. Private corporate industrial sector means, it should be clear, concentration of enormous economic power in the hands of a very small section of men and this power has been and will be exercised for upholding and strengthening the values which are a negation of socialism and for defeating its realization. The corporate private industrial undertakings have either to accept honestly the obligations implied in our social objectives or they, from the compulsion of the laws of their being, will utilize the resource, power and widely ramifying influence to render it (the social objective) nugatory. This obligation they have not accepted and are in no disposition to accept, and therefore the fact that they are using all their resources and authority to frustrate the realization of socialism should not be a matter of any surprise. This is what "mixed economy" means and involves in practice. Private sector is not an ally of the public sector, but avowed

---

7. *The Third Five Year Plan*, p. 456, 464.
8. *The Corporate Sector in India*, Op. cit., p. 2.

opponent of the objects for which the latter stands and which it has to fulfil if it is to serve the purpose assigned to it in the development of our economy.

Concentration of Economic Power: There is a growing concentration of economic power in organized industry owing to, as stated above, vast resources, largely drawn from public sources, which it commands or controls and a few what are really family houses have acquired a dominant position in our economy.[9] This process has, as is well known, been greatly helped by our "unique" managing agency system. The Company Acts of 1936, 1951 and 1961 provided correctives for its gross abuses and restrictive measures are intended to "mend" the system because it is held, that it cannot be ended without creating "a dangerous vacuum". Under the Company Act of 1956 all agreements between the managing agents and the managed companies had to be terminated by August 15, 1961, and new applications had to be made for being appointed or re-appointed as managing agents. Before the due date 1,345 companies were granted permission to have their affairs administered by the managing agents. Of these 120 were placed under new managing agents and the rest under the old well-established managing agents. Most of the important concerns, which had been managing the major undertakings of the corporate sector, were re-appointed. This approval was granted because

(a) it was not against the public interest of the companies to have a managing agent;
(b) because the managing agents were considered fit and proper persons to be so appointed; and
(c) the conditions of the proposed managing agencies agreement were deemed fair and reasonable.

The number of managed companies in the process was reduced

9. In 1955 the total paid-up capital of the corporate sector was Rs 969 crores out of which the paid-up capital of managed companies amounted to Rs 465 crores (*Corporate Sector in India*, p. 18).

from 5,000 in 1955 to 1,345 in 1960 out of the total of 27,000 companies—or less than 5 per cent of the total number. "This," in the words of the Fourth Report of the Company Law Administration, "could be attributed to the provision of the Company Act of 1960." This has been largely achieved by reducing the number of managing agents having one managed company from 3,526 in 1955 to 776 in 1960 and 401 having two to nine companies in 1955 to 136 in 1960. The restriction that no managing agent should manage more than ten managed companies has been circumvented by securing their re-appointment as secretaries and treasurers in a large number of cases. The latter can not charge commission of more than $7\frac{1}{2}$ per cent as compared with the maximum of 10 per cent allowed to the managing agents and cannot nominate any directors, the latter being allowed to nominate two under the Act. The second restriction is hardly any disability for virtually all directors of the managed companies are nominees of the managing agents and know that their position depends upon being acceptable to them. Secretaries and treasurers in effect have all the power of the managing agents. It was expected that, "this new form of management would," in the words of Mr. C. D. Deshmukh, "fill up the void created by the disappearance of the managing agency system,"[10] and "preserve all that was good" in it. Management through "corporate managers", as Mr. Deshmukh called the substitutes of the managing agencies (secretaries and treasurers), is in no sense, as claimed by him, "managing agency system without its teeth". Teeth are all there, they have still long established "tie-ups with financial institutions like banks and insurance companies" and have, from practical standpoint, not been denuded of their powers "to dominate the affairs of the managed companies". It was a self-delusion to hold that they were so denuded. Secretaries and treasurers are still masters of the managed companies and the conversion of the managing agents

10. *Lok Sabha Debate*, Vol. I, No. 13.

does not mean "that they (companies) were", to quote again the words of Mr. Deshmukh, "out to hire the services of any willing persons". All that it does mean is that masters have changed the label and the managed companies are, as they always have been, the constituent units of their empires and as completely under their direction and control as ever. Though the latest figures are not available, the top managing agents are more and not less important in our economy than they were in 1955. Out of 5,000 managed companies in 1955, 60 were "giant" companies with paid-up capital of Rs 1 crore or more and 121 "big" companies of paid-up capital of Rs 50 lacs to one crore. These 181 companies, though only 3.6 per cent of the total of 5,000 of managed companies, were, from the point of size and otherwise by far the most important managed companies in the corporate sector. These companies are mostly being managed by the same giants either as managing agencies or secretaries and treasurers. The eleven top foreign managing agencies were managing, in 1955, 234 companies and, in 1960, 188 companies as managing agents and corporate managers, i.e. secretaries and treasurers.[11] The presumption that now they are as important as they were in 1955 has to be supported by figures which are not available, but nevertheless it is a fair presumption, and from what is known about them, they have strengthened their position and increased their powers. Importance of a managing agent is not to be measured by the number of companies but more by their size and what they produce. The Tatas in 1955, for example, were managing only 12 companies but the fact that their paid-up capital was Rs 32.75 crores and among them was the Tata Steel gave them a very pre-eminent position among the managing agents. "It is a fact", to quote Mr. Deshmukh once more, "that it is not axiomatic that all the concentration of power is solely the function of the managing agency system."[12] That is of course well known. The

11. *Managing Agency System in India* and *the Corporate Sector in India*, p. 150.
12. *Lok Sabha*, Vol. VII, No. 32.

massive concentration of economic power in U.S.A., Germany, U.K., France, Japan and even in a small country like Syria has been built by means other than managing agencies. But nevertheless this "unique" system is the most important source of great concentration of economic power that exists in this country and this concentration has, the pointers are unmistakably clear, increased in the last decade, even more in the last five years; and this in spite of the fact as stated by the late Mr. C. C. Shah, who was speaking for the government, said in his speech on September 5, 1955, in Lok Sabha that "the intention, I submit, is unmistakably clear that managing agencies system at a future date—not a very distant future—will be abolished."[13] The facts refute this view. As far as the most important managing agencies are concerned, it is clear that the intention is that it is in the public interest to let them keep their power intact; they are fit and proper persons to exercise it and their promotional activities and financial capacity are indispensable for the industrial development of the country. That in an economy which has, as soon as possible, to grow into a socialist economy, this great concentration is, apart from its abuses, itself a serious detriment to public good, is a view which is so obviously valid and yet has not become a part of the thinking of the men in public authority in India. Most of the important managing agents were re-appointed before August 15, 1960; and in the context of the conditions existing today, it is clear that they will be with us for a long time, promote Democratic Research and Forum discussions, masquerade as defenders of freedom and democracy, collaborate with big foreign cartels in various disguises and with their active encouragement and assistance fight rearguard action against the advance of socialism.

FOREIGN COMPANIES AND INVESTMENT

The managing agency system was an off-shoot of foreign

13. *Lok Sabha Debates*, Vol. VII, No. 31.

enterprise in India and was the means through which foreign investments in and control of Indian industries was promoted and still foreign managing agencies are playing a major role in the working of this system. In 1955 of the seventeen top managing agencies all except three, the Tatas, Birlas and Karamchand Thapar, were foreign concerns. The foreign managing agencies have maintained and even strengthened their position since 1955, the same firms which figured very prominently in the annals of such industrial development as took place in India before independence, and in crucial industries like tea, jute, coal, mica and manganese, held position of decisive importance, are still of great importance in our economy. Andrew Yule, Bird and Co., Macleod and Co., Jardine Hendersons, Shaw and Wallace and similar other names represent concerns which have made economic history of India in the 19th and 20th centuries and are still, as stated above, a great force in the country. They have now, by further investments, taking dummy directors in the managing agencies and in the managed companies, by tacit or explicit alliance with big Indian houses and subtle practice of the art of economic penetration, entrenched themselves more deeply in the economy of India, and with the growing solicitude of the Indian Government for increasing the inflow of private foreign capital into India, their position has become almost unassailable; and it has really become necessary to safeguard it with special care in order not to impair in any way the chances of fresh foreign private investments in the economy in general and the industries in particular. These concerns will, it need not be repeated, be a pillar of strength for anti-socialist forces in India and their resistance to any efforts for moving towards socialism can well be taken for granted. They are and will be strong links between forces within and outside the country which are wedded to the view that freedom in and future of India can be preserved only by making her a country which is safe for private investments and inflow of foreign capital. They, in alliance with powerful forces, can be counted upon to make India the "outpost of democracy" in this area—democracy of their conception in which private enterprise with free play of market forces would be the decisive factor in politics and economics. Their disavowal not withstanding, they are and will remain in politics and try their best to influence its course.

The number of foreign companies in India in 1959-60 was 565 and subsidiaries and their branches 132. The Reserve Bank of India has made special investigation in foreign investments in India and they show that they have increased from Rs 255.83 crores in 1948 to Rs 498.47 crores in 1958 and the loans of the Bank of International Reconstruction and Development to the private undertakings, which needed to be guaranteed by the state, amounted to Rs 72 crores. Of the amount of Rs 570 crores the U.K. contributed Rs 398 crores, U.S.A. Rs 59 crores and as stated already I.B.R.D. Rs 72 crores. In the total increase of their investment of Rs 319.7 crores, petroleum accounted for Rs 96 crores, manufacturing industries Rs 149 crores, tobacco Rs 19.7 crores, medicine and pharmaceuticals Rs 11.4 crores, iron and steel Rs 67.5 crores—world bank loan, and tea Rs 45 crores. The U.K. investments have increased by 19 crores, the U.S.A. by Rs 48.7 crores and the I.B.R.D. has invested, as stated above, Rs 72 crores. The I.B.R.D. loan is a loan to the private sector but not a private investment in any sense. It is granted on the basis of public benefit and has, to repeat, to be guaranteed by the state. Investment in tea, oil and the I.B.R.D. loan are the most important foreign investments in India and out of the total U.S.A. investments of Rs 59 crores, investment in petroleum amounts to Rs 41 crores and only Rs 14.9 crores were invested in manufacturing industries.

The whole question of foreign investments raises basic public issues which would be considered in a later chapter, but the figures given above point to the relative importance of private foreign investments in industrial development of the country. In the last decade nearly Rs 1,300 crores of foreign capital receipts have been used by the state to finance the first and second plans and Rs 2,200 crores are expected to be received from foreign sources in the third plan. Experience since the end of the war has borne out the conclusion that private investments are not likely to play any considerable role in the industrial development of the underdeveloped countries, and main reliance for the purpose has to be placed on the transfer of capital resources from governments or international development institutions to the governments of these countries. This aspect of foreign investment and aid would also be considered in a later chapter, but it is known that the countries, other than the socialist countries, have not unoften indicated their bias against the public sector and unorthodox economic policies and even the international institutions like the I.B.R.D. have made no secret of their clear preference in favour of the private sector and "conventional wisdom".[14] Our experience has shown that private foreign capital is not interested in planned industrial development of the country, and its priorities do not correspond with the priorities of our plans. In the context of the world

14. Mr Andrew Shonfield in his book, *The Attack on World Poverty*, a project of which the Ford Foundation was the patron, makes the following observation on strong bias of Mr Eugene Black, until lately Managing Director of the World Bank and Chairman of "the Aid India Club", in favour of private enterprise:

"Nevertheless he (Mr Black) is not one of the wholly liberated American spirits—the type of businessmen—who managed to slough off a whole lifetime of conventional ideas at a touch of fresh experience. His limitations appear most obviously in his attitude towards socialism and state enterprise. Black, at any rate, in certain moods, is inclined to talk as if he believed that his main task is, to defend only true economic faith throughout the world. It is no accident that the right wing opposition movement in India led by Mr Masani has adopted a slogan taken from Mr Black, 'People must accept private enterprise not as a necessary evil but an affirmative good'.

"All this goes back to a famous exchange of letters in 1956, with the Indian Finance Minister of the day, Mr Krishnamachari, in which Mr Black took him to task for putting too much emphasis on public enterprise in the Second Five Year Plan. The Indian Minister felt constrained to make the following point in his reply, 'I am aware that your views and ours about private and public enterprise do not altogether coincide'. We are, of course, not convinced that the motive of private profit is the only one which can ensure an efficient operation of industry; nor do we believe that private

situation it is idle to expect that inflow of private foreign capital would to any significant extent contribute to the planned industrial development of the country. All the concessions that we have already given in respect of nationalization, compensation, discrimination, repatriation of capital and transfer of income, etc. have had little effect on stimulating the inflow of foreign capital into the country, and it is unlikely, as stated above, that in the Third Plan, the position will be materially changed in this respect. If we want foreign capital to come into this country on any considerable scale that will have to be on terms, which may even compromise our independence but they will certainly not be compatible with our social objectives. Foreign business interests, as stated above, cannot but strengthen the anti-socialist trends and forces in the country. They are already, by various ways and means, on the move from this point of view and our increasing solicitude for securing private foreign capital has, as stated before, made them even bolder in the pursuit of their objects. Approval is being granted in in-

enterprise is inherently superior to state enterprise. Indeed the short experience we have had with state enterprises leads us to believe that they can often be more efficient than private units."

Mr Black, it can be well assumed, remained unconvinced, is still of the view that private enterprise is an "affirmative good" and the main task is to defend only true economic faith. He is defending the faith with all his might, and the fact that The Aid India Club of which he was for long the chairman, is faltering in the continuance of aid to India is, at least partly due to his fervent zeal. What is true of Mr Black is true of all men in authority and big business in the U.S.A. upon whom the continuance of aid to India depends. The U.S.A. government and financial institutions which it controls are committed to the view that "there is some kind of exclusive relationship between political freedom and private enterprise". This fact is so very well-known that no one should be surprised that the U.S.A. assistance to India is in fact being used to promote and strengthen private enterprise and against even co-operativization of production in agriculture and industry and much more against socialism. Mr Black is only an exponent of the dominant economic and social philosophy of the American government and people; the fact that he had been in a key position in relation to aid to India makes this bias of great consequence to us and shows what great risks we are incurring in being so largely dependent upon the U.S. assistance and inflow of foreign private capital.

creasing numbers to the proposals for the collaboration of foreign interests with the Indian industrialists.[15] The content and the extent of this collaboration in technical, financial and political terms are not known and it is not possible to evaluate their potential for good or ill from the national standpoint. Already international oil, chemical, steel and other cartels are operating in India in different forms and guises and these, as is well known, have operated and are operating in high politics, and not only in politics. From what is known of the forces which are working inside the government and in the country, there is reason to fear that in letting ourselves in for these schemes of collaboration, we will, perhaps unwarily, expose ourselves to various serious risks and give hostages to the future. There is hardly any awareness of this danger among the people, but the danger is real and should not be lost sight of. "The main conclusion", according to Prof. Gunar Myrdal, "is that for the time being—capital just does not flow to undeveloped countries in amounts that are in any reasonable proportion to the development needs of the world. Further, the little flow that

---

15. It is known how many projects of collaboration with Indian industrialists have been approved by the Ministry of Industry and Commerce since 1958. Their number of different years is given below:

1958—64	1960—231	1962—till March—123
1959—154	1961—403	

The real cost to us of the increasing number of projects of collaboration is not known, for the knowledge about the amount of foreign investment and terms of collaboration have been withheld even from parliament. Most of the enterprises relate to light engineering industries but also include transistors, frigidaires and other non-essential articles. The affiliation of foreign firms is not known, but it can be assumed that a large number of them are directly or indirectly connected with big business and monopolies in their home countries.

The Indian Investment Centre was established in February 1962 in New Delhi to promote collaboration, is being financed mainly by U.S.A. The I.C.A., the U.S. agent in India, has secured for the investment centre advisor, business analyst and investment promotion analyst. The total amount of aid from U.S. Government is $713,000 and Rs 25,18,250 including $659,000 for contract services. This centre has been sponsored and is largely guided by A.I.D. and through it, it can be assumed, are directed the efforts for defending "true economic faith" referred to below.

there is, usually trickles out in the most haphazard way without any relation to the real economic opportunities and real economic needs."[16] This conclusion is fully borne out by the post-war experience of India and should have a sobering effect on our zeal for going all out for securing an inflow of foreign capital for our industrial development. We have already incurred onerous commitments in our almost ill-advised eagerness to get private foreign capital to move into India. That has not helped us to realize our avowed object and we have to be on our guard against persisting in this course.

Public Ownership: We have, if we take into account our public investment in irrigation, railways, air-transport, communications, ports, road transport, power undertakings, banks, life insurance and industries in the public sector already brought under public ownership a very considerable sector of our economy[17] and the process will be carried further in the Third Plan. The extent of nationalization, which has already taken place, has placed the state in a position to steer the economy with success in the direction of socialism in spite of the limitations which we have imposed on our freedom of action. That we have not yet used our public investment fully as an instrument of a socialist policy is due to the limitation of our understanding and of the will to action and not to the lack of our capacity to move in the right direction. It is not necessary to define socialism in order to assume that the public sector has to be and should be used as a means for its full realization. The content of socialism has been indicated before and will be explained more fully in dealing with the problems of transformation of our economy on specific issues and all the basic points will be dealt with compendiously even though briefly in the concluding chapter. Here it is necessary to deal very briefly with the problem of public ownership of industries and its scope. We have gone far in replacing private by public

16. G. Myrdal, *International Economy*, p. 118.
17. Vide Foot note, p. 195.

ownership in important industries and built up a number of large new industries in the public sector. It is true that most of these industries could not have been established in the private sector owing to the magnitude of investment involved and the need for securing technical assistance for them from other states or through them. It is true that either these industries had to be established in the public sector or they would not have been established at all. This is the conclusive reason for their having been brought into the public sector. Moreover, there is sense in the view that the state should at this stage start new industries rather than acquire old ones, unless for some reason of public importance, it is necessary to do so in particular cases. But even then the question as to whether public ownership of large industries is needed for realizing socialism has to be faced and an answer to this question depends on whether public ownership should be extended within the limit of our capacity to find the resources and administrative ability. Among the socialist parties of a number of European countries the view is being favoured that, to use the words of Mr C.A.R. Crossland—a crusador for this view —"ownership of the means of production has ceased to be the key factor which imparts to society its essential character".[18] Mr Crossland speaks of "the growing irrelevance of the ownership of the means of production" and states that "ownership though important is not of crucial importance". He and others of his way of thinking—and this is the majority view among the socialists in France, Germany, Holland, Switzerland and strongly and widely supported by socialists in the United Kingdom—hold that "setting up of a large number of public monopolies in the most important industries is not socialism but its negation—i.e. it can become an instrument of imposing serfdom and ruthless state tyranny", and of course they cite the experience of Soviet Union and other communist countries in support of this view. That public

18. C.A.R. Crossland, *The Future of Socialism*, p. 74.

monopolies in a monistic state give immense power to those who wield ultimate political authority which can be grievously abused is self-evident and need not be questioned apart from the cold war issue of the evaluation of the Soviet and allied systems and their results.

This issue is fundamental—really doctrinal—but here it is not necessary to analyse it from this point of view. The grave risk which is posited by this view indicates clearly the imperative need for difussion of power, pluralistic organization of economy and polity, provision of built-in forces of counter-vailing influence and authority and, of course, ardent acceptance and implementation of values based upon compassion and absorbing concern for the needs and growth of personality. However, it does not follow that under public ownership of the means of production economy, in which all these social objectives are provided for, cannot be built or freedom of private enterprise is the essential condition for realizing them. These essentials have to be borne in mind, but private enterprise has everywhere frustrated and distorted these objects and not realized them, and to the extent to which they have been realized is due to the adoption of counteracting and corrective radical measures against it (private enterprise). The issue, though fundamental, however has to be considered on empirical grounds in the context of our actual conditions in India. Generally speaking, it is admitted that progressively not only in industry but also agriculture, trade, small industries and communications private enterprise is to be replaced by socialization of all these economic activities by state ownership, municipalization, villagization and building up of a framework of co-operatives from basic to the national level for all the important functions, and therefore ownership, as a rule of the means of production. All this would mean public ownership—socialization, ownership of the community through its different accredited organs with ascending or descending order of authority, preferably the former without creating concentration of power at any level, and with the necessary checks and

balances for preventing the misuse of power. Private ownership with the discipline of market mechanism and exercise of
individual judgment and decision without any reference to
any code required by the needs and the good of the community, i.e. the system of free private enterprise, under the
conditions existing today, cannot produce rapidly adequate
economic growth, which the country needs so urgently, materially mitigate and later abolish poverty and end the inequalities and inequities which make this country what it is today—
weak, miserable and stagnant. Whatever progress has been
achieved in the last decade is due to private enterprise having
been subjected to or replaced by social initiative and action.
Private enterprise is the cause of very serious shortfalls in the
last decade from the social standpoint, and it is necessary to go
ahead and socialize means of production as far as possible if
this country is to stand square to the grave dangers looming
ahead and make good in the highest and the deepest sense of
the word. There is hardly any country in which the question
of ownership of the means of production has become irrelevant
for socialism, and India certainly with her specific conditions,
problems and crying needs, is not such a country. It is quite
true that public ownership is not equivalent to socialism. No
one really ever said that it is, and the point does not need to
be laboured. Public ownership of the means of production is a
condition for realizing socialism in India but not its prime
mover or its substance; and the assumption that once this condition is fulfilled, all else will be added unto it is a false assumption. The provision of this condition is only the beginning of
the process of building up socialism, and very long and arduous
journey lies ahead after this beginning has been made. The
issue can be taken as doctrinal without taking a doctrinaire
attitude about it, i.e. even before complete public ownership of
the means of production has been established, the process of
making changes in outlook, approach, behaviour and social
relations has to be started and institutional changes made when
this process of replacing private ownership by public owner-

ship is getting under way and the balance of forces by organized effort is being purposively altered. Socialism requires and includes this fundamental change, but it has to transcend it completely and look beyond to the ultimate goal immanent in it.

It was convenient to raise and deal briefly with this basic point here owing to its bearing on the other point which is of special interest in this place, i.e. the extent and object of public ownership of large industrial undertakings. The present policy is governed by the Industrial Policy Resolution of 1956 but there is, it has been declared often by the government, no rigidity about it and it permits considerable scope for adjustments. According to this statement, basic and strategic industries, public utilities and other essential industries which require investment which only the state could provide in the existing circumstances are either "to be exclusive responsibility of the state" (Schedule A) or "to be progressively state-owned and in which therefore the state will generally take the initiative in establishing new undertakings" (Schedule B). This statement provides for the state securing the co-operation of private enterprises in the establishment of new units when national interests so require and "private enterprise in Schedule B industries is also to have opportunity to develop in the field either on its own or with state participation". These provisions have already been used, for example, to assign nearly half of the expanded planned production of coal which is in Schedule A, to private enterprise in both the second and the third plans and some aluminium and fertilizers undertakings which are in Schedule B, also to the private sector. No really convincing reason has been given as to why this has been done, though in the case of coal extension of the existing coalfields can be a valid reason for some extension of the private sector in coal production. The Federation of the Indian Chamber of Commerce and Industry is, as a matter of fact, of the opinion that the utmost encouragement should be given to the private sector for the establishment of the various industries such as mining and metallurgical, mechanical engineering, electric and electronic engineering. All these industries are scheduled industries, i.e. are of basic and strategic importance and industries in which the state is to take the initiative in establishing new undertakings. They also hold that co-operation of the private sector is to be invited even in the exploration of the oil resources of the country.[19] Most of the other industries have been placed under the third category and their development ordinarily is to be undertaken and has in the last decade been undertaken "through the initiative and enterprise of the private sector". It is open to the state, under this Resolution, to undertake any type of industrial production, but the state, apart from taking over some of the derelict private factories and contributing to the development of co-operative sugar, oil and spinning mills, has left this large field to the private sector. Their development has been regulated under the provisions of the Industries Regulation and Development Act, but this regulation has not served any basic social purpose and its provisions have been administered without due regard to the need for balanced industrial development or determining the location of these industries with reference to the employment situation in different parts of the country or the need for making up the lee-way in the more backward regions. Limitations of resources and administrative ability have, of course, to be allowed for, and public ownership of these industries has to be restricted on this account; but in principle and from practical standpoint there is a good case for socializing them by, say, investment of the funds of the Life Insurance Corporation and otherwise, and developing them to realize the objective of socialism. The managerial authorities of these industries are, to repeat, against advance of socialism in this country and are using their power and wealth to defeat it in the working of the economy as a whole, and in the internal administration of the undertakings. Several of these industries need to be publicly

19. *Report of the Seminar on Planning,* p. 15.

owned for practical reasons like the increase of investment funds, but the very principle of leaving the large field to the private sector needs to be reconsidered and revised. Expansion of private enterprise in industries has meant in practice increase in the concentration of economic power and this has to be prevented. This is another very good reason why their expansion should increasingly be taken over by the state. At present the trends are working in the opposite direction and, as stated above, even some of the industries in Schedules A and B are being assigned to the private sector and there is a distinct shift in emphasis on the industrial policy of the state in favour of the private sector. Whether this process will be arrested or reversed will depend upon the strength of the socialist forces in the country. At present the indications are not at all favourable from this standpoint, and it looks as if the private sector will gain ground at the cost of the public sector in spite of the fact that resources for development by private enterprise are being increasingly (as pointed out in a later chapter) provided by public institutions with active state assistance and by the banks whose investment policy should be directed by the state in the interest of the planned development. There is need for thorough re-orientation of the national industrial policy. The final goal has to be complete public ownership of the large industrial undertakings as a part of the socialization of the entire economy through co-operativization and other similar measures.

Higher Income: It is well known that the higher incomes in private Indian and more in foreign business undertakings are creating disparities in our income structure which are having disturbing effect and are against our social objective. The Pay Commission have clearly stated that "emoluments at the higher levels in the private sector has shown marked increase during the last twelve years—at the top even phenomenal increase".[20] The process has gone further since 1957, the year to which

20. *Report of the Pay Commission*, para 21, p. 25.

this observation relates, and the emoluments at the top continue to increase at what is truly a phenomenal rate. The emoluments are, as is known, greatly added to by expense accounts and other perquisites for which the employees at the higher levels are eligible. This is even truer of the employees of foreign firms, and yet the process, of what the Study Team on Democratic Decentralization has called "the day-light bribery of our elite by some extremely rich foreign and Indian firms"[21] is going on and undermining and defeating new social values. The Pay Commission has endorsed and recommended the principle of fair comparison with salaries in commerce and industry and its application with discrimination for fixing public salaries. As a matter of fact the phenomenal increase of salaries in the private sector is having a disturbing, in some respects, a demoralizing effect on public services; and the principle of fair comparison in practice is creating serious complications. It is a great pity that the Pay Commission have held the view that the fixation of public salaries should be determined by what they called "limited and proximate ends" and turned down the view that they should "subserve certain accepted social ends". This is obviously a very restricted interpretation of their obligation to "examine the principles which should govern the structure and the emoluments" of public employees, and really amounts to lack of appreciation of the real need for making a beginning for building up a new, rational and socially justifiable income structure of the country. Any way, it is evident that if higher incomes in the private sector are permitted to remain at the present level and increase at the phenomenal rate, the whole economy will be subjected to severe strains and stresses and make its integrated development impossible. The view which I stated before the Pay Commission appears to me the right basis of approach on this subject. "A purposive change in the entire income structure of the economy," to quote from my statement reproduced

21. *Report of the Study Team on Democratic Decentralization in Rajasthan*, p. 24.

by the Pay Commission, "being one of the prime objects of the social transformation, it is obvious that undesirable pulls of the private avenues of income... have to be consciously counter-acted by appropriate measures. . . . The conflicts, if any, have to be resolved by operating positively on private incomes."[22] The obligation of "operating positively on private income" has not been explicitly assumed in spite of the talk of need for ceiling on income. This obligation is, however, implicit in our social objective and has to be discharged if the latter is to be fulfilled. That it has not been and is not being assumed is due to the forces arrayed against it being on the move and being ascendent in the counsels of the Government and high politics. In 1957, 857 Indians were employed in certain foreign firms who were receiving salaries of more than Rs 2,000 per month and of whom 185 were in posts carrying salaries of more than Rs 2,000 and eight in more than Rs 4,000 income bracket[23] A large proportion of these highly placed men are well con-nected—sons and relatives of high bureaucrats and politicians and in some cases retired high bureaucrats themselves. Their number if complete count were taken of the men in such posts, is much larger and increasing. The open bribery, which the foreign firms which employ them are practising, has given them good berths which they are filling, but it has cost and is costing the country dear. Besides corrupting the men in high places, it is subversive of all social principles to which the coun-try is committed. The same, of course, applies to highly paid men in the Indian private firms. The only way to end this state is to have a socially justifiable income structure, which applies to all incomes, and we will have to adopt it when socialism becomes a matter of serious social concern.

22. *Statistical Supplement to the Report of the Pay Commission,* Table 2.3, p. 24.
23. Information available on the scales of salaries in the private sector is very meagre but it is known that nominal salaries are much lower than real salaries if all the perquisites, privileges, concessions, etc. are taken into account. *Ibid.*

Conclusion: The accelerated rate of industrialization, greater importance of the public sector and the development of basic industries can all be taken as welcome developments on which we can well congratulate ourselves. Industrialization is, however, a means to an end and not an end in itself. It has to be in the highest interest of the community, bring prosperity and strength to the people and promote and realize high social ends, i.e. contribute to the realization of socialism. These social objects have, it has been clearly brought out in this chapter, not been fulfilled by industrialization, which has taken place in the country and the manner in which it has taken place. It is still possible to remedy this situation, make the country duly aware of the importance of the social content of industrialization and its bearing on our approach, practice and operative mechanism of the industrial undertakings, both in the public and private sectors. The industrialists in India, and in every socialist economy have to assume the role which St. Simon in the first quarter of the 19th century assigned to the great entrepreneur of his social utopia—they have to become men of the highest technical attainments and combine them with social vision, consecrated work and capacity as social architects of the highest calibre. With all the technical progress that has taken place in the last 150 years and its direct relation to the happiness and well-being of the common man, the significance of this role has acquired immediate practical importance. The so-called managerial revolution can become a factor for public good only if it becomes an integral part of social revolution, i.e. if the great managers are awake to their social responsibilities and discharge them well with full understanding of the potential of industry and its relation to the new destiny of mankind. For our industrialists, both in the public and private sectors, St. Simon's vision, even if they know of it, would be an adventure still in social utopia and have no bearing on their immediate tasks. This is really a measure of our mental vacuity from the social standpoint and is no indicatiton of the irrelevance of St. Simon's projection into the future.

Chapter Seven

DECENTRALIZED INDUSTRIES

Two Techniques

Decentralized industries in India, for historical economic and social reasons, have been given a place of their own in our schemes of planned development, and in them are implicit issues of profound significance. Provision, actual and proposed, in the three plans for their development not only involve large outlay but also the choice of values, techniques and alternatives relating to economic organization, social structure and administrative and political relations. The fact that Mahatma Gandhi gave to decentralization a very high place in his economic and social philosophy and made it an integral part of the struggle for national freedom, has made it a part of our national legacy and created a strong bias in our thinking in its favour. This is one of the reasons why the development of village and small industries has, under a directive of the constitution, been made an obligation of the community and it is not easy in practice to separate the problems of their development from their emotional surcharges.

The result is that in the formulation and execution of the plans of decentralized industrialization there are contradictions which have been resolved neither in theory nor in practice; and an impression is created that we are making a vain attempt to live in two worlds at the same time—the new world of modern scientific industries and agriculture with a fast vanishing world of archaic handicrafts and subsistence farming on the assumption that both can and will co-exist indefinitely in our economy. This is exemplified, from this point of view, by our setting up some of the most modern steel and heavy machinery plants on the one hand and spinning, oil pressing and match making productive units with techniques which have and can have no future on the other. The two, it is held, simply cannot co-exist from the long term point of view; and our efforts to make them co-exist is a pure waste of very scarce precious resources of capital, the very scarcity of which is taken to be the reason for applying labour to inefficient technique for the production of goods. In a world of automation and atomic energy the old traditional techniques and instruments can have only vestigial significance and have to be replaced without undue delay by the most advanced techniques and machines. Industrialization, whether rural or urban, has to mean the use of power, the latest scientific knowledge and its application to production, otherwise our people will not only lag behind in a world of phenomenal advance in productive power but fail miserably in their efforts to raise themselves from the sub-human level, at which most of them are living today, to a level not of great affluence but of reasonable comfort and cultural life—the more so because our population is increasing very rapidly and we are in the midst of a great crisis of social and material expectations.

CONTRADICTION

There is a fundamental contradiction in Gandhian approach, which we have made our own and on which our policy of co-existence of the old and the new techniques is based. The contradiction is there, and yet our most crucial difficulty is as to how to find work and means of living for the multitude who can neither be absorbed in agriculture nor in modern large-scale organized industry. The estimates of "surplus" labour vary, but there is no doubt that it is enormous and is being added to very rapidly by the rate at which our population is increasing. If our agriculture is rationalized—i.e. if we use advanced farming practice without necessarily using the most advanced machines and promote intensive cultivation of land a vast number—say 30 to 40 million persons—would be thrown out of agriculture for whom work and living will have to be found in or near the villages in which they reside at present or in mobile units for carrying out works of public utility. Can this be done without landing ourselves in the ridiculous position of trying to find work for these enormous multitudes by methods that will not yield sufficient output even for meagre subsistance, what to speak of a minimum from a human standpoint to be raised by degrees according to the increase in production, which of course has to be the aim of a rational way of life. There is no question that work for work's sake cannot be the object of public policy under any condition —much less so in an economy which has set socialism as its goal. Work must mean worthwhile production—i.e. remuneration which is at least equal to the prevailing rate of wages in other comparable occupations and carries in itself the possibility of raising it (remuneration) to the level of human minimum referred to above as its full potential is realized. That is why the question of technique is all-important. The modes of production under which this object cannot be realized are not suited for any economic development—much more so for planned socialist economic development. The technique has, however, to be co-related to the available resources, and if advanced technique cannot be adopted owing to want of resources needed for obtaining the required equipment—capital goods—there is, reasonably speaking, no earthly reason why such equipment—tools of production—as is available should not be utilized until expansion of production and national income make it possible to acquire and press into service tools of ever-increasing efficiency and raise and keep on raising the level of production and therefore consumption provided in the process no economic or social obstruction is created to the adoption of the technique of greater and greater efficiency. Increasing output is the essential condition of increasing consumption, and it cannot be realized without continuous improvement in technique, which, as stated later, requires continuous increase of stock—capital formation. The contradiction arises because outputs of higher and lower techniques are both produced for the market and the former (goods produced with higher technique) undersell the latter and drive the producers out of the market, i.e. into destitution. From the social standpoint there is neither sense in using lower technique of production when the higher technique—the equipment in which it is embodied, is available, nor in not using lower technique when equipment needed for using higher technique is beyond the means of the community owing to the want of surplus—of capital resources. The essential condition for using both higher and lower techniques at the same time is that in their utilization the standpoint of the community should be supreme and the choice of technique should be governed by it; and that can only be done when production and distribution of goods is regulated by the community and in its interest and not in that of the individuals and their interest. The ultimate aim has, of course, to be the use of the highest technique for maximizing output and minimizing labour cost, i.e. labour input, and, as stated above, the level of technique has to keep on rising. This is the commonsense and right view for increasing aggregate production—per production unit and per worker. It can be taken exception to on the ground that production beyond a limit can only be made in response to insensate multiplication of wants and is neither desirable from the point of view of rational allocation of the resources nor rational way of life. This point is valid for a number of affluent countries in which private waste has assumed great dimensions; but in India, though steps have to be taken to reduce and prevent waste—particularly at very high levels, increase of production in aggregate and per worker is our paramount need both for freedom from want and provision of resources for economic growth, and the level of our technique has to be raised in our economy as a whole in all sectors.

MARKET MECHANISM

This, however, does not affect the necessity and desirability of using technique which in combination with our available surplus labour can contribute to the increase of production and consumption provided the forces of market can be brought under control, competitive underbidding by producers of goods produced within and from outside the country with higher technique, can be regulated and production at all levels is subject to the over-all control in the interests of the community as a whole. All this is also subject to the over-riding condition that available human resources must not be wasted and without creating a set bias in favour of lower technique, we have to use such tools of production as are within our means to satisfy the real needs of the people. The crucial point, to repeat, is that in planned production what is called free play of market forces must not be allowed and their distribution should be subject to public control within the country and in spite of varying costs, an integrated price structure to serve the interests of the community has to be built up and operated. This cannot be done in a free price and free enterprise economy, and our disappointing achievements in developing village and small industries are mainly due to our inability to appreciate the need for an integrated price structure and absence of an adequate organization to operate it. We have through subsidies and rebates tried to temper the working of market forces and provide a shelter for goods produced with lower technique with very limited success. The result is that, in spite of reservations and a partial ban on expansion of factory production, price differentials in favour of the latter have remained and subsidies and rebates have mainly protected inefficiency and not created conditions for rational utilization of available man power. In other words, lower and higher techniques can co-exist and be used beneficially when social purpose permeates and dominates the whole economy and private interests are subordinated to public good. This means that replacement of production for use and not free market according to a real effective plan for the existing almost truly blind production has to be achieved. The conclusion is obvious that we can neither utilize our economic idle manpower nor achieve purposive technical progress in the entire economy without incurring high social cost, without a framework of norms suited to a socialist economy. This, it should be clear, is not at all a backward-looking approach. It does not involve creation of arcadia and longing for a fast-vanishing world. It is definitely a forward-looking view and an argument for using to the utmost not only the scientific techniques but also social techniques of a high order. There is no question of relying upon obsolete or frozen techniques for development. These have, consciously and according to a planned programme, to be superseded and the development plans have to be so formulated and implemented as to assimilate most efficient techniques in the social context of rapid development and transformation from the very basic level. This assimilation is not possible unless, to repeat, market forces are brought well under control and the whole system of production—and not merely production of village and small industries—embodies social purpose and works according to its tenets, i.e. socialism becomes the all-embracing force of the entire economy. Our experience of the development of the village and small industries in the last decade and before fully confirms this conclusion. We have to follow with clear understanding and earnestness its logic and implications. Approximate parity of prices has to be one of the prime objects of the co-existence, when socially necessary, of higher and lower technique as a measure of decentralized industrialization.

DECENTRALIZATION AND INTEGRATION

The other social objects of decentralized industrialization have also basic importance of their own and need to be duly considered. Among them decentralization of personal initiative, planned dispersal of industries on a regional basis suited to local and regional resources and needs and developing the economy with a view to providing small units for planning, development and creative social effort on as wide and diversified basis as possible in order that social and economic pyramid may rest on its base and not on its apex are of profound significance and have to be duly provided for. This can be done only if decentralized industrialization is made an integral part of decentralized agricultural development and derives its strength and importance from it. This point has been dimly understood but not acted upon in the last decade. Now its importance has emerged more clearly and consequential action is being contemplated, but its far-reaching implications even now are not being fully appreciated. India has to be a country of small communities and the latter have to be consciously developed in order to give reality to our economic and political democracy. It has, however, to be understood that decentralization has to function within the framework of an integrated national economy, and the latter has to make efficient working of the organs of decentralized development of agriculture, industry and commerce one of its most engrossing concerns. Its policy decisions and their execution have to emanate from this prime object and framed for its full realization. India needs a strong and effective centre not only from political but also economic standpoint, and we cannot possibly underrate its importance; and all decentralized institutions have to function with a lively understanding of this all-important need, and any trends which undermine integration have to be countered and checked. But the central institutions have more and more to assume the responsibility for servicing the decentralized institutions and contribute as far as they can to their healthy growth. The balance between decentralization and integration can be contrived and achieved through building into the economy a working apparatus with internal initiating and counter-vailing devices and keeping clearly in view the need for continuous re-adjustment in the light of experience. The balance, however, has to be the balance of purposes and functions and can be realized if decentralization and integration are conceived as parts of the same social process and are informed by its socialist objective. Decentralization is needed because broad-based economy is essential for broad-based democracy, and it taps reserves of ability, energy and social interest, which otherwise remain dormant or unutilized.

SMALL PRODUCTION

Decentralized production would necessarily mean small production which according to the Marxist view, in the words of Lenin, "engenders capitalism and bourgeoisie daily, hourly, spontaneously and on a mass scale", and, "the force of habit, the strength of small production for those small commodity producers by their ordinary imperceptible, elusive activity engenders capitalism all the time". This view has widely influenced the minds of the communists and even socialists, they do not regard the development of village industries in particular and small production in general as welcome features of economic development or rather they are of the opinion that Charkha and all that it stands for are retrogressive in their effect, breed industrial romanticism, and divert attention from the real issues of poverty and exploitation of the masses and therefore blunt the edges of class struggle. The communists in India mostly share their views and are not at all enthusiastic about decentralized industrialization, they really fully share the capitalists' aversion to the use of lower technique for development, and what to them are purely utopian plans for developing village industries. This antipathy is intelligible for though the Sarvodayists, who are the most ardent advocates of village industries, have a great deal to their credit and their contributions to social thinking are not by any means negligible have not challenged the forces which are dominant in our economy and are therefore retarding the realization of the values on which they have laid so much stress. The real point is no violence versus non-violence—important as it undoubtedly is but generating of forces which can replace those who wield economic and political power and are upholding the values which are a negation of the values which they (the Gandhians stand for. A social revolution, even if it is non-violent, has to be a real revolution, i.e. it has to change the very basis of the economy and make the people masters of their own well-being and future. Their decentralization is meant to be a revolution from below—a manifestation of peoples' power—but in effect it has not created conditions under which this object can be achieved and a new social equilibrium brought about. The result has been that economic and social effects of the gospel of the spinning wheel and efforts made to propagate and support it have, in economic and social terms, been extremely disappointing. In all critical social situations the Gandhians have either been indifferent or at least neutral, and their strength, whatever it has been, has not been used for helping or promoting the forces of social change. This observation is prompted by the fact that industrial decentralization of the kind that has been attempted in India and its philosophy, have not refuted the view that in terms of social change they hardly make any difference so far as status quo is concerned and they cannot be a dynamic element in shaping the course of events.

That, however, does not explain why according to the Marxist small production engenders capitalism and bourgeoisie, and how the small commodity producer by his ordinary, imperceptible, elusive activity engenders capitalism all the time. Lenin also adds that "small commodity producers cannot be driven out or crushed and it is thousand times easier to vanquish the centralized big bourgeoisie than to vanquish the millions of small owners", and further, "they must be remoulded and re-educated by very, very, prolonged, slow, cautious organizational work". Decentralized production is small production and it is also small commodity production, i.e. production for the market and is governed by the principles embedded in the market economy. The small commodity production, again to quote Lenin, "the force of habit of millions and tons of millions is a most terrible force," and that is why the millions of small owners cannot be crushed, they have to be re-oriented. Among the small producers are included not only artisans but also peasants and they are all formidable because through them capitalism lives in the hearts of millions, and the process which creates bourgeoisie is at work all the time. Without attempting an analysis of capitalism—this obviously cannot be done—it is easy to posit that if millions are enmeshed in the working of market economy, they necessarily "by the force of habit" become acquisitive. In their calculus, human values have hardly any place and labour becomes merely a commodity and its human needs and social attributes are completely lost sight of. These are the results of commodity production, and if its scale is small, this force works in an imperceptible and elusive manner and the social milieu, which it creates, is completely unfavourable to the realization of socialist relations and values.

The question, however, arises as to whether it is possible to organize small production and reduce the impact of de-humanized market on it—or change it to subserve social values rather than work in opposition to them. The difficulties of organizing small production are, it is true, much greater than those of organizing large production from the socialist standpoint. In it is involved the slow and prolonged process of re-education and re-moulding. In India—really in all undeveloped countries with large, dense and rapidly growing population and with no empty spaces to fill—decentralized integrated production becomes an inescapable necessity, and with all its other social advantages, referred to earlier, acquires a special significance of its own. The main question is as to whether it can be given a real social content and become an instrument for the realization of the socialist objective. Answer to this question has to be evolved through elaboration of all the major issues of social transformation, but merely the smallness of production need not, *if other conditions are favourable*, itself be an insuperable hindrance in the way of realizing this object. There has to be inter-penetration and inter-dependence between large and small production, but if property relations are changed, accumulations of private fortunes for exploitation and self-aggrandisement is put an end to, all prime movers of the economy are controlled by the community and operated by it and the same social values govern all activities whether in small or large production, there is nothing in small production itself which can make it "a terrible force". If small producer ceases to be a small commodity producer and his activities are co-operativized in the context of a socialist economy, he too can become a contributing member of a socialist, i.e. truly co-operative, economy and be a constructive and not a terrible force. He can respond as well to the needs of a socialist economy as the large producer and contribute to its development and growth. The conditions indicated above are important and have to be realized. Decentralized production cannot be carried on in isolated islands of the economy, it has to be woven in its entire texture. That is why integration becomes a cardinal element of decentralized industrialization—its very sustaining principle.

CAPITAL FORMATION

There is another point, which has been urged against decentralized industries, and needs to be given a serious consideration; and that is the question of creating surplus for economic growth, i.e. the question of capital formation. The point is simple and can be easily stated though it is being unduly complicated by the models of economic growth which are now the vogue. We need heavy investment in the economy, including investment in human material, i.e. the development of social services, and the economy itself has to provide the resources for the purpose, i.e. ratio of savings to the total accrued national income has to be increased rapidly to accelerate the rate of growth. The first point, of course, is that the income itself has to be greatly enlarged if we are to find the capital needed for rapid development mainly from within the country. With our existing national income the margin for saving for vast majority of our people, it need not be said, is extremely limited. If we put an upper limit on higher incomes, as we should if we are really serious about socialism, and also on wealth, we will have to rely mainly on the community savings for capital accumulation. The extreme and growing inequalities in the distribution of income and wealth are at present a very limiting factor from the standpoint

of the community and have to be redressed. Decentralized development would mean greatly reduced concentration of income
and wealth and therefore the wealth and income of the rich
would be less and less available for capital accumulation. That
itself would make it necessary to bring compensatory factors
into play. Moreover, if in decentralized industries the output
per worker is so low as to make it impossible to accumulate
capital, even if work at low wages is provided by them for
most people, it would from the long term point, be a serious
disadvantage in as much as it would greatly slow down the rate
of development of the undeveloped countries. In the centralized
large industries output per worker being higher, they would
not only pay higher rates of wages, but also provide scope for
capital formation. The rate at which surplus would accrue and
be utilized for planned development would according to a
scheme of well-considered social priorities, of course, depend
upon adequate social control of the centralized large industries. But assuming that the control exists, they will be able
to contribute more to the accelerated development of the country than the decentralized industries. Their output, i.e. of the
decentralized industries, has to be large enough to pay reasonably good wages, or if self-employment is the rule, provide
reasonably good earnings and yet generate enough surplus to
finance its development from within. At present village and
even small industries are not in a position to enable the workers
or artisans to have earnings comparable with those of large
industries and create reasonably good surplus for economic
growth. Parity in earnings and capital accumulations can be
achieved, if at all, after a long time, but at present the gap
between the two is wide and has not been narrowed by such
development of small industries as has taken place in the last
decade.

Even output and surplus per worker is low in our large industries as compared with the developed countries, but output in
small industries is very much lower and they can neither
provide reasonable earnings nor surplus for development. If

decentralized industries are to have a more significant role in our development, this serious defect has to be remedied. Ther production not only in aggregate but also per worker has to increase very considerably if they are to develop on sound lines, i.e. in them the producer has to be much better paid than he, generally speaking, is today, and capital reserve for development have to be created and built up. At present the producer in Khadi and village industries particularly but also in other small industries have miserable earnings, they have not improved significantly under the two plans and they are being largely subsidized, what to speak of producing margin for capital formation. These industries have to be developed for the reason given above, but apart from raising greatly the level of their technical performance, they have to be re-organized, mostly co-operativized, in order that their marketing may become orderly, efficient and be related to the needs of the community, i.e. they too should produce for planned budget of needs and be able to dispense with subsidies and rebates. This can be done, as stated later, if these industries mostly centre round agriculture—rationalized and much more developed agriculture —and in the universe in which they function, the latter, agriculture and its allied activities, have to be the centre of their solar system. The scope for increase in production and reduction of cost in agriculture is so great that, given the necessary will and organization, the whole rural sector cannot only raise the production and income of the agriculturists but make developed decentralized industries an integral part of its development, raise the level of earnings in them very considerably and agriculture and industries together with local public works in which surplus manpower can be utilized can have enough surplus for their own development and contribute to the increase of capital resources of the country. *The most important condition for achieving this result is that technique specially designed for this type of development should be widely used and production should be planned and organized not primarily for the benefit of the producers but from the point of view of the community and its organs.* What is called propensity to consume is high among the agriculturists and producers in small industries, i.e. a large part of increase in their income is spent on increasing their consumption. This is neither regrettable nor undesirable. Their present standard of living being so sub-human, it is right that with the increase of their earnings, the rise in consumption should be assigned a very high priority in any rational scheme of planned expansion of production but if production and consumption are both planned, increase in consumption would be a regulated process and would not take place at the cost of capital formation. At present there is no scope for it in agriculture and small industries because their output is low owing to poor organization and inefficient technique. But if both are developed in the way they should be, they will become an important source of capital formation of the country. The technical potential of the increase in their production is so high that increase in the standard of living and investible surplus can both be achieved if production and the utilization of its increase are competently planned. The conclusion, of course, is that decentralized industrialization, instead of slowing down the rate of development, would greatly contribute to its acceleration, if it is integrated with agriculture and interests of the community receive the highest consideration in their development. This amounts to saying that with a socialist approach in the preparation and execution of the plans of development in agriculture and decentralized industries significant increase in consumption *and* capital formation can both be achieved through rapid increase in planned production.

EXPERIENCE OF TWO PLANS
    Khadi: The relevance of the observations becomes greater if the experience of the development of decentralized industries under the plans is briefly reviewed. Khadi and village industries have under them been placed in a prominent position. The expenditure on Khadi and village industries was Rs 15.20 crores out of the total expenditure of Rs 33.61 crores on village and

small industries under the first plan, Rs 82.4 crores out of the total of Rs 180 crores under the second and provision under the third plan for the same purpose is Rs 92 crores out of the total of Rs 264 crores.[1] Of the two plans Khadi and Village Industries, Khadi accounts for much larger proportion of expenditure. From 1953-54 to 1958-59, the expenditure on Khadi amounted to Rs 34.63 crores and on village industries Rs 1.27 crores.[2] In 1960 the total output of cotton, wool and silk, khadi was 64 million yards, including cloth in which Ambar yarn was mixed, out of the total production of cloth of all varieties of 6,750 million yards in 1959-60; and rise of Khadi output from 3 million yards in 1950-51 to 64 million yards in 1960 can, in a way, be taken as a rapid expansion, i.e. increase of more than 21 times, but if it is borne in mind that in all Khadi met less than one per cent of the total consumption of cloth in 1960 and in 1965-66, i.e. at the end of the Third Plan, khadi production, it is estimated, will be about 160 million yards out of the target of 9,300 million yards, which though an improvement upon the relative position of Khadi in 1960-61, will still be hardly of any consequence, and its value will have to be judged by its social content rather than its impact upon the supply of cloth in the country.

From the material presented in the Khadi Evaluation Committee Report it is disquietingly clear that social content of Khadi is very meagre and it has not been made any real difference to the economic and social conditions of the spinners, the weavers, the artizans and to the rural economy as a whole. The serious social deficiences have not been given their due consideration even in the Third Plan and with the exception of two very significant measures referred to below, both of which have so far produced very disappointing results, it appears that it is unlikely that any major change will be introduced in the production and distribution of khadi and also that any real change will take place in the social significance of Khadi to the com-

1. *The Khadi Evaluation Committee Report*, p. 22, 45.
2. *The Village Industries Commission Report*, pp. 298-99.

munity. Among the social deficiences which have been very clearly set forth on the Evaluation Committee Report are, (a) fall in the level of real wages as compared with the pre-war level, (b) development of khadi production without any reference to the incidence of unemployment and local demand and market, (c) complete non-participation of the producers in the plans for development of khadi and their execution, (d) growing resistance of the consumers to the prices of khadi and therefore embarrasing accumulation of unsold stocks,[3] (e) lack of any improvement in the technique of spinning in what is called traditional khadi and non-utilization and under-utilization of the improved spinning apparatus known as Ambar and consequent vast waste of capital resources, (f) failure of khadi to make any material impact on rural unemployment, the employment of all types in 1959-60 in terms of full days work provided by khadi being 2.77 lacs,[4] (g) hardly any evidence of social earnestness among bulk of the field workers and even among the newly appointed superior staff, (h) inability of the khadi workers to identify themselves with the village communities or assume any role in their development and, (i) most of the benefits of khadi work having accrued to the middle peasant and even non-agricultural middle class, the poor peasant and the landless labourers having been practically excluded from the range of khadi production.

Under the changes proposed to be made in khadi production under the Third Plan there is provision[5] of cotton cultivation

3. According to Shri Annasaheb Sahasrabudhe, Vice-Chairman of the Khadi and Village Industries Commission, "as the situation stood at present they had reached a saturation point. The production of Khadi stood at Rs 15 crores while the sale of khadi could reach the figure of only Rs 10 crores. Though intensive efforts were being made to push up the sales, it appeared doubtful if new avenues could be found out by following the present methods adopted for the propagation of khadi." *Jagriti* Vol. V No. 46, October 10, 1961, p. 6.

4. *The Village Industries Commission Report*, pp. 298-99.

5. The actual results of cotton cultivation, however, have been very meagre and Ambar still occupies a very secondary place in the total production programme of the Khadi and Village Industries Commission.

in all parts of the country, and what is even more important, the expansion of production of yarn on greatly improved six spindle Ambar, which is expected to yield an output of 16 hanks of yarn per day instead of 6 hanks of Ambar now in use. These are two measures of real importance, and if they are effective, reduction in cost and prices and reduction of differential between khadi and mill cloth can well be expected; but otherwise it is unlikely that any major change will be made in the organization of khadi work and its impact on employment, level of incomes or their distribution and rural economy as a whole cannot but continue to be limited. The important limiting factor in khadi work is the quality of new workers who are now being recruited for it. The contrast between members of the old guard, who in spite of their age, have not lost their zest for work and most of the new entrants is very striking. There is hardly anything in common between the two except their khadi dress. The main interest of the new entrants is their monetary reward; and as the latter is meagre and the prospects in this work are relatively poor, there is quick turn-over among these workers and they hardly show any spark of social understanding, interest and the spirit of devotion which is associated with khadi work. The appearance of austerity, which the khadi worker has to assume, is an obligation imposed upon him by the history of khadi and is no part of his real life. Still the old guards are at the helm, but their ranks are being fast depleted and even they, in spite of their fine spirit, do not, with a few exceptions, show much indication of being able to follow new trails and cross new social frontiers. Khadi needs new workers who can imbibe the spirit of the old veteran workers and yet not be conditioned by their nostalgia.

In 1962-63 out of the total disbursements by the Commission of nearly Rs 21 crores, Rs 19 crores were allocated for traditional khadi and less than Rs 2 crores for Ambar. Ambar had a serious set back and it seems very doubtful whether it will be able to make any significant contribution to the rehabilitation and development of khadi. It looks as if an innovation of real promise has had very disappointing results and now it has become a routine activity of the Commission without any real growth potential.

VILLAGE INDUSTRIES

The record of village industries under the two plans is even more disquieting than that of khadi and in the words of the Village Industries Evaluation Committee, (1) the actual work done so far has been small. The efforts of the last six years appear to be essentially exploratory, (2) many of the units were not located in proper places and the coverage of artisans is small even in the areas in which the work has been organized, (3) the quality of work generally done has been poor, (4) the impact of the development programmes on the problem of unemployment on those engaged in village industries has been at best very small, (5) and the organizational machinery at the headquarters and in the field lacks unity of purpose, clarity of approach and division of functions. These conclusions of the Evaluation Committee cited in their own words do not call for any comment, and in effect it means that the expenditure on the development of village industries has given practically no return and the work put into it amounts to a wasted effort. The Committee has also strongly recommended that these industries have a future only if they are made a part of integrated rural development programme and if they attain a much higher level of technical performance through improved tools and mechanization. Though the statistical information on employment and wages is extremely scanty, the earnings of the artisans are known to be exceedingly low and have, as a rule, not been raised owing to the development effort. Essentially speaking the development and income potential of these industries is very considerable and if proper organizational effort is available and suitable improvements are made in production technique, much better results can be achieved. What has been said about the implication of integrated development is also fully relevant for the development of these industries. Their integrated development involves pooling of all resources in the villages, planned allocations of available manpower according to a budget of needs and resources, regionalization of the plans of development and federalization and co-operativization of the agencies responsible for the development of these and other small industries. These are not new suggestions. They have been made before and are also contained in the report of the Evaluation Committee. Their implementation, however, requires that social structure, in which these recommendations can with advantage be implemented, has to be developed as an essential condition of their finding a place of growing importance in our economy. In the Third Plan a number of improvements in their working are contemplated, but their growth will be conditioned by the growth of the *ekais*; and if the latter do not come up to a level of performance by which they can make a real impression on the rural economy, stagnation or rather decay of these industries will continue to remain an enduring feature of our rural economy.[6]

6. Making village industries a part of the integrated development of the rural economy is the key to their future and has to include clear demarcation between the sphere of these and large centralized industries in production and prevention of competition between them which handicaps the former. At present whatever can be done to develop these industries in some respects is being neutralized by letting processing industries like rice hulling, oil expellers, spinning and sugar mills grow indiscriminately and without plan, in spite of, in some cases, like oil and rice, regulative legislation. Integrated development has to be related not only to agriculture and village industries but to all economic activities in the demarcated area or zone of planned development for regional purposes and the planning agencies have to take into account the impact of trade, large industries and the means of communication and regulate and control them with a view to real budgeting of means and resources on regional basis. In respect of trade, large industries and communications the regional planning agencies would, of course, have to secure the consent and active co-operation of the planning agencies at the state and national level. As a matter of fact, as explained more fully later, integrated regional planning can only be implemented in the framework of the planning of the economy as a whole with very clear and lively concern for the success of integrated development at the basic and area or regional levels. At present as stated above, one hand does not know what the other is doing and national resources are being wasted by the adoption and implementation of ill-co-ordinated and mutually harmful development policies.

The other implication of integrated development is the necessity of raising the technical level of agriculture and industries. The essence of integrated development is expansion of production through higher technique, greater productivity and much better organization for raising the income

OTHER SMALL INDUSTRIES

There are other small industries, handloom, handicrafts, and the standard of living of the poorest, majority of the rural masses, working from bottom upwards and generating surplus for capital formation for local and national requirements, and all this through the concerted and planned activities of the local communities' and the community as a whole with clear understanding of the socialist objective. This objective can be realized only by planned and regulated mechanization of agriculture and village industries. There can be no development with static technique. It has to be dynamic and planned in order that it may serve the best interest of the community rather than have a subversive effect on it. In theory this point is conceded even by the Sarvodayists and in industries like leather-tanning and paper-making partial mechanization of selected processes is being carried out. This has, however, to be done more systematically and with full realization that rural industrialization on a decentralized basis cannot be a sound and developing process unless it is carried out with the use of modern science and technique with full appreciation of its potential importance and beneficial character. There need be no mutual reservations on this point—and they at present do exist—so long as higher technique is made the means of realizing human and social values and is not indiscriminately applied without any regard for the social cost involved in the process. Integration has to mean also planned mechanization of production in rural areas and the process, as long as it is well in hand, has to be as rapid and adequate as possible. There is and should be nothing romantic about decentralized small production. It has to be, to repeat, a response to the call of the future and not a vestige of the past. The Khadi Evaluation Committee is of the view that khadi "through a succession of changes can be produced on a power-operated spinning and weaving appliance and yet remain khadi in the truest sense of the word. It is the social setting and social significance of the process that will give it (khadi) its meaning and not the mechanical and technical process used in production" (The Khadi Evaluation Committee Report, pp. 151-52). This is also true of village industries. "At a time of revolutionary technical advance," in the words of the Report, "decentralized textile industry has to fully participate in and derive the benefit of the changes that are taking place." This applies to all rural industries. Planned mechanization is an essential condition of their survival and planned development. Dr. M. Sadashiva Rao, Director of the village Industries Research Institute of the Khadi and Village Industries Commission, has put in a cogent and convincing plea for planned selective mechanization of village industries with a view to raising productivity, increasing earnings and creating surplus for capital formation without causing any technological unemployment. The Research Institute is reported to have devised a scheme of mechanization with these objects clearly in view (Khadi Gramodyog, Vol. 7, No. 5, pp. 19-30 and Vol. 7, No. 11, pp. 31-37). It may be earnestly hoped that results of this applied research would

small-scale, seri-culture and coir for which an allocation of Rs 174 crores has been provided in the Third Plan, as compared with the 98 crores in the Second. Of these the handloom industry, from the standpoint of employment and production is the most important. Production of handloom cloth has increased from 760 million yards in 1950-51 to 1,900 million yards in 1960-61 which, though less than the anticipated production, is 21 times greater than the expansion of production of khadi of 53 million yards during this period. The estimated increase in employment owing to this expansion of 394 million yards up to 1958-59 from 1955-56 is estimated at 6.20 lac persons[7] which is $2\frac{1}{2}$ times increase (2.7 lacs)[8] in employment in khadi production. The total expenditure on handloom cloth production including power looms was Rs 31.7 crores under the Second Plan as compared with that of Rs 70 crores on khadi development. In the Third Plan allocation of Rs 69 crores has been made for khadi as compared with Rs 34 crores for handloom, Khadi production is estimated to increase from 64 to 160 million yards, the handloom cloth to increase from 1,900 to 3,340 million yards, i.e. 1,440 million yards out of the total 2,300 million yards of cotton cloth from all sources or by 79 per cent and over 67 per cent of the total increase in cloth production. The total production of handloom cloth in 1955-56 was 1,411 million yards and increased by 429 million yards by 1960-61. If the Third Plan target is realized, it would mean

receive the earnest consideration that they deserve. As a matter of fact research in the technique of small industrial production has to become one of the most important functions of all technical institutes and laboratories in the country and a national scheme for the purpose has to be prepared and implemented. The Khadi Evaluation Committee in Chapter 13 of their Report made a strong recommendation on this point which practically has received no consideration. When integrated rural development acquires the urgency and importance, which it should have, it will become clear that undertaking of this research on a national basis has to be a very high priority assignment. The possibilities of modern technique for decentralized development have yet to be explored and realized.

7. *Report of the Survey Team for Handloom Industry*, p. 43.
8. *Khadi Evaluation Report*, p. 100.

more than 3½ times increase in the rate of production in the Third Plan as compared with the Second Plan and presumably with corresponding increase in employment. It is not unlikely that actual achievement will fall short of targets, if the experience of the Second Plan is any guide, but it is clear that in decentralized textile development in terms of production, employment and even the level of wages, invstment in handloom cloth production is giving much higher returns than khadi.

It is worth while considering why, in spite of this difference, Rs. 69 crores should be provided for khadi and only Rs. 34 crores for handloom.9 Originally the intention seems to have been that Ambar yarn should be extensively used in handloom production, but it was soon abandoned and in fact 3,952 million pounds of mill yarn was used in all handloom production except khadi and in the Third Plan also only mill yarn is to be used for its expansion, i.e. for 1,440 million yards anticipated increase of production in the Third Plan 320 million pounds of yarn would be required for its production (4 yards of cloth per pound of yarn). Expansion of production of handloom cloth of 1,440 million yards in the Third Plan would (if additional employment of 6.5 lakh of persons, say, for every 400 million yards increase in production in handloom cloth is assumed) increase in employment by about 22 lakh persons in terms of full-day work. To this of course has to be added the increase in production of spinning mills owing to the increase demand of 320 million pounds of yarn needed in handloom production. It would be possible to produce 160 million yards of cloth provided for under khadi programme by handloom with additional allocation of say Rs 4 crores while now provision has been made for expenditure of Rs 69 crores for realizing 94 million yards increase in khadi production.

9. It has, however, to be noted that Rs 34 crores is exclusive of the provision for working capital through institutional finance. The provision for Khadi includes the provision for working capital, but is also exclusive of outstanding loans granted to the institutions out of the previous allocations, which serve as revolving fund for the khadi operations.

The difference between the two modes of production and investment in them arises, it need not be added, owing to reliance on hand spinning, traditional and Ambar, for the production of khadi. At present there is very large unemployment and under-employment among the weavers. According to a recent report there were 26.75 lakhs of handloom weavers in the country[10] of whom 13 lakhs are reported to have been brought into co-operatives.[11] At present in spite of the improvement that has taken place, the idle potential capacity can be estimated at 2,780 million yards on about 15 lakhs of looms. This is a rough measure of increased employment which can be created if mill yarn is used for additional cloth production by handlooms. The weavers themselves, as *Khadi Evaluation Report* has stated, prefer mill yarn even to Ambar for weaving and as a rule receive higher rates of wages and earnings than they do in khadi production, and there is no doubt that left to themselves the handloom weavers would willingly change over completely to weaving mill yarn rather than hand-spun yarn. At present the rebate in handloom cloth is 5 Paise per yard while for khadi it is 19 Paise and price differential between handloom cloth and mill cloth is significantly lower than between khadi and mill cloth.[12] The cost of production of even handloom cloth is 11 per cent[13] higher than that of mill cloth and this handicap cannot be overcome; and this is so in spite of lower rates of wages and earnings in handloom industry as compared with those in the mill industry. From the standpoint of employment and production the case for giving precedence to handloom industry as distinguished from khadi pro-

10. *Fourth Report of All-India Handloom Board*, 1956-59, p. 59.
11. At the rate of the daily output of 6 yards per loom and 300 days per year, i.e. 1,800 yards per loom per year the potential capacity of 26 lac looms would be 4,680 million yards as compared with the target of 3,340 million yards in the Third Plan. This potential could, as is well known, be considerably increased by comparatively low-cost improvements in the technique of handloom production.
12. *Khadi Evaluation Report*, Table 3, p. 88.
13. *Ibid., Fourth Report*, p. 124.

duction in the development even of the decentralized textile sector is strong and more employment, greater production and higher level of earnings can be realized by concentrating on the development of the handloom industry.

This obvious contradiction[14] is due to the development of khadi and handloom industries being unrelated to each other. There is hardly any relation between the plan of development of the khadi and handloom industries. In fixing the target of production, selection of the development centres, preparation and implementation of the marketing schemes, location of service centres, fixation of the rates of wages and improvement of weaving techniques, these two sections in the decentralized textile sector move in different orbits, they compete with each other, produce largely coarse cloth and both, though in different degree, have to suffer from the competition of the textile mill industry. To these difficulties has been added the complication due to the installation of powerlooms in handloom industry, which according to a sub-committee of the Handloom Board "undermines the position of the handloom weaver",[15] and it was earnestly suggested by the sub-committee that, "a scheme for the introduction of power-looms in the handloom sector should be given up",[16] and yet in the Third Plan provision has

14. The only way this contradiction can be resolved is to improve the quality, reduce the cost and increase the acceptibility of Ambar yarn to the weavers. The whole Ambar programme originally was based upon the assumption that this could and would be brought about. Shri Annasaheb Sahasrabudhe, Vice-Chairman of the Khadi & Village Commission, is of the opinion that if Ambar yarn could be supplied to the weaver at a discount of 25 paise per rupee on the price of yarn and if the yarn produced by the spinner is of such quality that weavers would willingly accept it for weaving, the entire output of hand-spun yarn could be utilized by the handloom weaver (Jagriti, Vol. 5, No. 46, p. 6). This discount could be reduced and later removed and parity of prices between Ambar and mill yarn realized by raising productivity even to a higher level. The decentralized textile sector has to be one unified sector and has itself to attain the highest level of efficiency.

15. Sub-Committee Handloom Board, p. 129.

16. Ibid.

been made for installation of 9,000-9,500 power-looms[17] despite the view of the sub-committee that "competitive capacity of these power-looms will be even greater than mills as they will be located in handloom centres." Khadi is at a disadvantage compared with handloom, the handloom with the power-loom and the power-loom with the mills, and subsidies and rebates do not fully neutralize the disadvantageous position. The Planning Commission adds, "Effective steps have already been taken to check installation of power-looms except by the handloom weavers' co-operatives.[18] A power-loom is a power-loom whether it is operated by a co-operative or a private proprietor and competition to which a handloom weaver will be exposed will not be any the less because of its being operated by a co-operative—not unoften by a spurious one. This also applies to co-operative spinning, oil and sugar mills which are being started without any reference to the development plans in the decentralized sector and have an unfavourable impact on them. Owing to the lack of co-ordination in investment, production and marketing plans among the different sections of the textile industries there are persisting and even increasing differences in cost, price and wages among these sections, involve waste and misapplication of economic resources and create stresses among them which should and could be avoided in any planned development. If it is desired that these sections should co-exist, they have to be a part of an integrated plan and conflicts among them have to be reduced to the minimum, progressively these different sections have to approximate in social terms to a common cost, price and income structure and be governed by the same social principles. Without this co-existence can only mean continuing conflicts and stresses.

The Handloom Board, of all the agencies for the development of the decentralized industries, have been the most active in organizing production and marketing through the co-

17. *The Third Five Year Plan Report*, p. 439.
18. *Ibid*.

operatives. Since 1951 the number of industrial co-operatives have increased from 7,105 to 29,000 in 1959-60 and of these 11,200 are handloom weavers' societies. These societies have consisted of primary, federal and apex organizations and have large resources. This development is entirely due to the fact that all concessions, loans, grants, service facilities and institutional finance are made available only to the members of the co-operatives and non-members mostly are not eligible for them. Apart from this these co-operatives have hardly any other significance. They are organized by the officials, the weavers themselves have not developed any initiative or capacity, for them the co-operatives have no significance as organs of social democracy and they have not produced change of any real consequence in the areas in which they are operating. In this respect the Handloom Board has apparently scored over the other agencies in the decentralized section, but in fact, the Board and its officials have not broken any new ground from the standpoint of social change. There is no indication in their reports or in their operations that wider social objectives have any special meaning for them or members of the weavers' co-operatives are animated by what may in any real sense be called a new spirit. This point will be more fully dealt with in the next chapter. It is referred to here only to indicate that the fact that the Handloom Board has organized so, many co-operatives is only a measure of the extent to which public funds have been made available for the expansion of handloom cloth production. Production has increased, unemployment among the weavers has decreased and there has been some improvement in earnings, though not in wage rate. These are gains which should be given their due importance but importance of the handloom co-operatives should not be over-rated.

HANDICRAFTS

Development of handicrafts in India is more important for preserving and enriching our heritage than for their economic potential; and whatever has to be done to revive these crafts, most of which have a high artistic value, is commendable from that point of view. Rediscovery of old motifs and designs, assessment of their artistic quality, identification of their problems, development of their markets and scientific study of their techniques are all real gains and the expenditure of Rs 25.87 lakhs in the First Plan, of Rs 4.8 crores in the Second and the projected expenditure of Rs 8.6 crores in the Third are really worthwhile. Sales in cities through the emporia have been increasing, exports to foreign countries are considerable and training facilities have been provided for the artisans. No information is available about the total production of the handicrafts, as to how far it has increased and what is its regional distribution and development or the incidence of the benefits of public expenditure on their growth. They have no planned targets of development, all plans have been *ad hoc* and have little or no relation to other plans of development.

The most disquieting aspect of the handicrafts in India is the poor conditions of the artisans, who, one would think from the quality of the goods produced by them, must be artists in their own way and capable of expressing the sense of beauty in their own life and living conditions. They are in fact very poorly paid, are badly exploited by middlemen and the conditions under which they work or live give them no scope whatsoever for a life of dignity or culture. They are set in technique and artistic designs and they have no horizon to speak of for their work. It is fortunate that inherited skills are still there and these crafts, in spite of the damage done by the conditions under which they have been operating, have survived and can with right approach and organized effort be made strong and vigorous. The one essential condition for this object being realized is that the artisans should be paid well, freed completely from exploitation and the meaning and quality of their life should be radically changed. This aspect of the matter has hardly, if at all, received any attention, no serious effort has been made to break the hold of the middle-

men or organize co-operatives.[19] From the fragmentary information that is available, it appears that earnings of the artisans
have risen but not to any significant extent and rise has been
largely neutralized by rise in the cost of living. Under these
conditions they could not have been placed in a position to
develop any initiative or capacity to shape their own future.
They remain, as they always have been, members of the most
depressed sections of the community and in their poverty and
helplessness they present most depressing contrast between the
beauty of their products and abundance of those for whom
they are produced on the one hand and their own life without
meaning, beauty, and of means for even plain living on the
other. In this work that has been done since 1952, when the
Handicrafts Board was formed, there is a clear evidence that its
eyes have been set more upon the art of window-dressing and
salesmanship than upon the rehabilitation of the ignorant and
poverty-striken artisans or tapping their reserves of ability and
creative craftsmanship.

Another aspect of these crafts, which has to acquire increasing importance as the country advances towards socialism, is
that they have to become a part of the life of the community
and their products have to cease to be merely luxuries of the
rich or one of the obvious means for their conspicuous consumption. These crafts, not only in India but all over the
world, have thriven under the patronage of the princes, the
feudal classes and the commercial magnates and their aesthetic
values have been greatly warped by their dependence upon
them. These classes are now merging in the new rich—the
industrialists, the higher bureaucrats and the upper sections of
the professional classes. If socialism comes into this country,
the process will be arrested, there will be diffusion of income
and purchasing power and culture and its attributes will be

19. The working group has indicated that the co-operatives such as they
exist, have not been functioning satisfactorily and some of them are somewhat spurious organisations (*Report on the Working Group on Handicrafts*,
p. 13.)

widely shared. Utility and beauty as a result thereof will be completely combined in the products of these crafts, they will be meant not mostly for mantlepieces or decorations but have a meaning for the daily life of the producers and the consumers and express and promote the new forces at work in the community. This has not happened and could not have happened because the country has not even been set on the path to socialism, what of advancing towards it. To the Handicrafts Board these considerations do not matter, they are not oriented that way. Selling the products of these crafts in increasing value to the tourists or for export does help from the short-term standpoint, but their future cannot be saved by them.[20] All this has to be changed and handicrafts have also to be developed with reference to their employment potential, their ability to pay decent wages and their aesthetic qualities in terms of the changing life of the community. As stated above, we do not know to what extent their production has increased in the last decade and who has benefited by it. In other words, their development has not been planned in relation to the economy as a whole or to any social objectives. It is good that these crafts are receiving attention and organized effort is being made to put life into them. We have to make them a part of our new life because they are, to repeat, very precious from the point of view of our cultural inheritance. We have, however, if the object is to be achieved, to show that we know that their having been a part of the life of the rich and therefore symbols and means of a parasitical class society, is a historical disadvantage from the standpoint of the future and has to be purposely and consciously redressed. This, as stated above, can take place only if real social change becomes a fast developing process.

20. They, as our social heritage, can come into their own if they become an integral part of the emergent economy based upon the increasing well-being of the masses which has necessarily to mean fast decreasing importance of the classes, who in the past out of the surplus accruing to them. owing to their dominant position, have created demand for them. All this has to be changed.

As this process has not been under way, our handicrafts could not have been developed from this standpoint. But it should have been possible to have a clear awareness that this needs to be done and adopt standards of judgement, if not action, suited to it. This has not happened[21] and shows how dim is our understanding of the essentials of the development of our handicrafts.

SMALL-SCALE INDUSTRIES

Among the small industries small-scale industries have been

21. In the Report of the Working Group on Handicrafts it has been pointed out that in the Second Plan nirmal ware, ivory carving, jewellery, etc. which cater to foreign markets, tourists and the upper income groups have received by far the major attention during the first two plans and recommend that handicrafts which produce goods for middle and lower middle class consumers and crafts producing mostly for rural class, should receive greater attention in the Third Plan and suggested that at least Rs 10 crores would be needed for the purpose. In all about Rs 8.4 crores have, as stated above, been provided for handicrafts in the Third Plan and most of this amount would be needed for what they call "the present nature and tempo" of activities. That means that the Handicrafts' Board would give most of its attention to luxury articles which would be sold to foreign markets, tourists and upper income groups. As things are, that cannot be avoided, but it may be hoped that there would be greater concern for the conditions of the artisans and an earnest effort would be made to raise their wages, earnings and level of life. This aspect of the matter has been neglected so far and has to be seriously considered.

As producing goods for the lower income group and rural classes it would be necessary to change the existing division of functions among the different agencies to whom the work of developing decentralized industries has been entrusted. This will be best done, as stated later, by having one commission for integrated development of decentralized industries. But the real difficulty lies in the limited and even diminished purchasing power of the low income group and the rural classes. The Working Group assumes that these will be greatly benefitted by the development expenditure in the Third Plan. Experience of the first two plans does not justify this assumption and there is no indication that in the Third, the trends in operation and distribution of income will be materially changed. Moreover, the whole process of social thinking has to be radically altered if things of beauty are to become a part of the every day life of the masses. This requires a shift in the balance of social forces of which there is no evidence at present and which is not likely to occur in the Third Plan.

assigned a special place. In the Second Plan out of Rs 180 crores utilized for the development of small industries the outlay on these industries was Rs 56 crores (including the investment in industrial estate) or nearly 31 per cent and in the Third Plan allocation for them is Rs 124 crores out of the total of Rs 264 crores, i.e. about 43 per cent. According to the Planning Commission, "the growth of small-scale industries constitutes one of the most significant features of development during the Second Plan".[22] That it does. It is modern technology in small production and its underlying assumption, in the words of the International Planning Team of the Ford Foundation (whose recommendations were the basis of the "one of the most significant developments") is "that it is unsound to use hand-power, when machine power will enable industry to meet greater demand at greatly reduced cost and enable India's workers and craftsmen to produce according to their skills and capacities".[23] The International Team was also strongly of the opinion that, "for fast industrial growth private initiative should be encouraged to the fullest". And further, "as a rule no attempt should be made to have co-operators' association for production". They can and should, according to the Team, be organized for credit, marketing and servicing, but production, as stated above, in small industries should remain individual private enterprise. In other words, small industries were to remain nurseries for capitalists and main reliance was to be placed upon small enterpreneurs playing a decisive role in their growth and development.

Considerable increase in production has taken place in small-scale industries and, besides public expenditutre on service institutes, marketing organization, information service and credit, etc. considerable private resources for the development of these industries have been attracted, though the extent of their investment is not known and cannot be estimated. Ex-

22. *The Third Five Year Plan*, p. 448.
23. *Report on Small Industries in India*, the International Planning Team, the Ford Foundation, p. 2.

pansion of production in value and physical terms is also not known but the facts cited in the footnote[24] indicate that there has been considerable increase in production in light engineering industries like sewing machines and bicycles, machine tools and plastics and dye-stuff. The whole programme has however been, according to the Estimates Committee, "limited to certain specific activities such as construction of industrial estates, training, supply of plant and machinery on hire-purchase basis, etc. There is no co-ordinated industry-wise programme of development of small industries in the plan."[25] The *ad hoc* projects through which the programme has been implemented had no relation to the industry-wide development programme, development of the other small industries or that of the economy as a whole. There were targets of production only in two or three cases and even in those cases they were not fixed with reference to any economic criteria or guiding principles, comparative advantage or disadvantage of small-scale units in relation to costs, economies, markets and their competitive position were not assessed from the prospective or practical standpoint and the development has proceeded without taking an over-all view of the situation. Location of these industries has also not been planned and from the regional standpoint their distribution is uneven and benefits conferred have hardly any relation to the needs and possibilities of different parts of the country. Facts, which can adequately disclose relative importance of these industries and their contribution to healthy

24. "This is illustrated by such statistical data as are available for individual small industries. For instance between 1956-60 the number of small-scale units engaged in production of bicycles increased from 44 to 150, of sewing machines from 35 to 75, of machine tools from 344 to well over 500, of electric metres from 6 to 74, and of electric fans from 2 to 47. The production of bicycles in small-scale sector increased from about 25,000 in 1956 to 228,000 in 1960, of sewing machines from 23,000 to 52,000. The value of ungraded machine tools rose from 1.3 crores in 1956 to Rs 4 crores in 1960. Large number of new units also came into existence for the manufacture of dye-stuffs and plastics" (*Third Five Year Plan*, pp. 446-47).

25. *Seventy-Seventh Report of the Estimates Committee*, p. 16.

economic development of the country, are not available, and despite the growth that has occurred, in specific cases it is not at all clear that even in respect of production they have been placed on a stable basis and can grow through their intrinsic worth and vitality.

It is, however, from the point of view of their social significance that the whole position needs to be carefully examined and clarified. The Working Group on Small-scale Industries has stated that from the standpoint of decentralization and employment progress has been limited[26] and they have not contributed in any way to federalization of economic life on a

26. Messers P. N. Dhar and Lydall in their *The Role of Small Enterprises in Indian Economic Development* have prepared a table of average wages and salary payments per employee in different sizes of factories in four countries. In India taking the number of employees per factory of thousand and over as 100, the index for the small factories employing 10 to 19 persons is 47, for Japan it is 46, for Britain 84 and U.S.A. 79. (See P. N. Dhar and H. F. Lydall, *The Role of Small Enterprises in Indian Economic Development*, Table 6, p. 26).

It can almost be assumed that the rule is that lower the level of development of a country and lower the level of its wages, the greater are the disparities between the workers in large and small enterprises. The level of wages in the smaller factories employing less than 10 persons is known to be even lower and workers in these small units receive miserable wages, work long hours and under very difficult conditions. This also applies to self-employed artisans. Their earnings compare even more unfavourably with those of workers in large industries; and though slight improvement has taken place in the wages or earnings of workers in small industries under Government-sponsored schemes in the two plans, the improvement is hardly significant. Small industries if they are to have a permanent place in any healthy economy—much more so in a socialist economy must not pay the workers less than the average level of wages or in any way take advantage of their unorganized position—the level of wages of these workers must be high, their social security as complete and their other advantages as considerable as in large-scale enterprises in a socialist economy. This can only be done if the industries are well-managed, well-financed, well-organized, use efficient modern technique and their marketing arrangements do not leave any scope for workers being exploited by the middlemen. At present, it need not be said, there is not even a remote prospect of this essential condition being satisfied by our small enterprises. Workers, as is well known, even in large industries are very badly off and in the small ones much more so.

co-operative basis. Information on comparative wages in small-scale and large-scale wages in the same industries is not available, but it can be safely presumed that in the former the level of wages is much lower and the workers are unorganized, unprotected and in no position to hold their own against the employers. In Japan, in which small units predominate, it is well known that industrial growth has, to a very significant extent, been built up on the basic exploitation of the workers. Advantages of small units on lines in which the large firms are also operating have to be clearly indicated if they are to be developed on a planned basis, and if their main advantage consists in their being able to under-pay their workers or otherwise take advantage of their undefended position; this, it need be added, should be reckoned as a serious social disadvantage. This also applies to small units which are ancillary to large factories. In the Second Plan hardly any programme has been made in developing such units, and though in themselves such units may be desirable, experience of Japan, Italy and a number of other countries and of our own decentralized industries in which, as is well known, extreme sweating of workers is the rule, is a very clear warning against modern technology being used without due regard for the interests of the workers. This aspect of development of small-scale industries has received no consideration in the first two plans and has been also completely disregarded in the Third.

Modern technology has to be fully used in all small industries and not only "small-scale" industries, but its governing principles have to be the same in all units, small and large and in all small industries measures have to be taken to ensure that their development is planned and regulated with clear understanding of basic social principles. Social objectives of this country were not referred to by the International Team, and the Ford Foundation which is so closely associated with this programme, is, it can be assumed, not concerned about them. In the administration and evaluation of this very significant development scant attention has been paid to these objectives.

The International Team has, a number of times in their report, stated, "You cannot divide what you do not first produce." Implication of this statement, of course, is that it is production that matters and distribution is a matter of secondary importance. This is time-honoured principle of capitalism but can and should have no place in any pattern of socialist society. The whole programme of small-scale industries has been, to repeat, conceived and is being operated with a view to developing non-socialist forces in the country, and the bias which was so obvious when this programme was launched, persists and is being nursed with assiduous care. Mechanization and rationalization of small production are exceedingly necessary and desirable and have to be promoted in all possible ways, but their social content is of primary importance from our point of view and without it modern technology can do a lot of harm in spite of all the good that is implicit in technical change and progress. The significance of "small-scale" industries consists in their having been conceived and developed as dispersed outposts of capitalism and not in their being a means by which modern technology can be assimilated and utilized in our developing and changing economy.

CONCLUSION

Silk and coir industries are the two remaining constituents of the scheme of decentralized industrialization but they are, relatively speaking, of minor importance. As major decentralized industries and their development have already been broadly reviewed, it is possible to sum up the position in regard to decentralized industries as a whole. The first and most important point which this review leads to, from the economic and social points of view, is that this programme of decentralized industrialization taken as a whole has been a failure. It has not made any material difference to the mass of unemployment existing in the country—particularly rural unemployment or under-employment in rural areas. The level of wages in decentralized industries is low, whatever rise in earnings has taken place is marginal and artisans in these industries have not shared in the rise in national income that is reported to have taken place in the last decade· Their relative position has, as a matter of fact, become worse and their disadvantage is greater and not less after a decade of planned development in the country. It was expected that decentralized industries would, in production, marketing and in relation to prices, be better organized and be able through co-operatives and otherwise to protect and promote their interests and reduce the exploitation of their workers. There has been hardly any improvement in organization of these industries, their workers are as helpless and hopeless as ever and with a few exceptions, can neither help themselves nor contribute to the economy through their common and concerted efforts. And lastly, the two outstanding inadequacies of these industries are that their development has not been planned from the point of view of the industries themselves or from the regional or national standpoints. Inter-relations of the decentralized industries, the needs of their co-ordinated development and their relation to the economy as a whole on horizontal and vertical basis have not been duly considered in their entirety or in significant details and they (the small industries) in their working and development remain disjointed activities of an economy in which planning has still to acquire internal coherence in bringing about a balanced growth. The most important inadequacy of this programme has been its inability to achieve its social aim.

The Karve Committee has clearly stated that "a steady expanding federalization of economic life on a decentralized and wherever possible, on a co-operative basis is to be desired not only for maximizing the scope of efficient utilization of human and other resources but also making a democratic control of economic life possible".[27] The decentralized industries from this point of view, could not have been a greater failure.

27. *Report of the Village and Small Scale Industries*, (Second Five Year Plan Committee), p. 22.

They have not only to make democratic control of economic life possible but what is far more important, give it a democratic content, i.e. make socialism a force of increasing importance in the economy. The whole economy having drifted farther away from socialism in the last decade rather than advanced towards it, the small industries by themselves could not have countered the trends that have otherwise been at work. But as it is the same trends have been operating in small industries as in the whole economy and their development, such development as has occurred has been bereft of any social meaning. They have not been able to reduce inequalities, increase self-government in small production, diminish concentration of economic power or bring about any change for the better in the centre of social specific gravity.

Decentralized industrialization in the existing condition of India has been and is an inescapable necessity. Without it we cannot find productive work for our fast growing population or make it possible for the people to rise above their present dismal conditions. Decentralization is an organizational problem, i.e. powers, functions and agencies of planning and implementations have to be decentralized. But more than organizational, it is a fundamental social problem, it is a problem of waking up the people to their urgent needs in every day life and using such resources as they have or can command for satisfying them in their order of social importance, by their own concerted efforts. The problem of decentralized industrialization is therefore a problem of developing decentralized economy. The whole process of growth and change has to be decentralized and social prime movers have to be brought into action at all levels—social relations have to be changed and also their governing operative principles. In concrete terms it means that we have to give them such tools and techniques as they can readily use and develop and conflicts in production and distribution have to be resolved by comprehensive control evolved from below in a framework of social objects and purposes to which allegiance is given spontaneously and sincerely.

This is the meaning of integrated development of the economy as a whole. Decentralized industries are to be developed in both urban and rural areas and have to be brought into some working relation with the principle economic activities of towns and villages. Integration, as stated before, implies diversification and ascending levels of social importance in the economy. It also means that unity of purpose and operation has to be maintained and the whole economy has to be steered with a purpose in the desired direction. That means further that central direction and guidance are not to be abrogated because of decentralization and have to be so used as to make decentralization a reality and a means by which creative powers of the people are fully developed. This is another way of saying what has been said already that the national and state government have to use their power, functions, resources and levers of economy for ensuring the success of all decentralized economic activities and develop centres round which they revolve in an orderly manner.

In rural areas this has to mean that agriculture has to be the pivot for the development of the economy and round it industries and trade have to be developed first in the interests of the village community and with full realization that now no village community or group of such communities can live unto themselves. They have not only to depend upon technical and economic guidance and help from the centre, but it is also essential for their health and growth that the economy as a whole should work efficiently and harmoniously. Rational utilization of enormous manpower being the most important and pressing problem, allocation of resources, use of technique and distribution of the produce have to be governed by imperatives inherent in the problems. This point has been explained before, but it is again referred to in conclusion in order to indicate how the failure of the decentralized industries can be redressed if conditions favourable for the integrated development of agriculture, industries and trade can be realized. Agriculture is and has to be not only the most important activity of the village but its unutilized production potential is so great that its realization, with outlay of resources well within our means, can, besides reducing and, given the necessary effort, removing shortages of food at the basic level, bring about the necessary expansion of purchasing power and therefore local market for products of decentralized industries, provide food in increasing quantities for urban areas and growing non-agricultural population and last but not the least, create surplus for development of local areas and the economy as a whole, it being assumed that first charge on this surplus has to be the development of the villages themselves. But as the number of persons in agriculture has to be reduced realization of its unutilized production potential of agriculture has also to involve the concurrent process of development of efficient decentralized industries as an essential part of the expanding rural economy. All this of course needs to be planned and at the basic level by the village communities but as stated before, conditions for integrated development of agriculture and industries have still to be created and the necessary will for carrying it out developed. Panchayats and co-operatives, which are our chosen instruments for this purpose, have not only to have autonomy through devolution of power but have also to be developed from within and can do so only if village communities become truly democratic, i.e. monopoly of power by the few is broken and real power is transferred to the rural masses. There is no indication at present that this can or will be achieved, but without it neither decentralization nor integrated development of rural economy can be achieved.

GRAM EKAIS

Integration is a blessed word, but in practice it means all things to all men. It has already been stated and re-stated that its full implications are neither understood nor acted upon. There is a great deal of confusion of ideas in thought and practice, and the result is that a number of programmes of integrated development unrelated to one another and bereft of any unity of purpose, have been introduced and dropped and are being implemented with the avowed purpose of integrated development of rural economy; but these programmes have in effect failed, involved great waste of resources and dissipation of efforts. Of the programmes which have been dropped the abandonment of the Intensive Area Schemes of the Khadi and Village Industries Commission and the Pilot Industrial Projects of Community Development Administration is specially to be regretted. This applies with even greater force to the Intensive Area Schemes for they were essentially sound, had the right objects and approach and yet it produced no results whatsoever and after being carried on for seven years at very considerable expenditure decision to drop them has been taken in January 1964 without any analysis of the causes of this really regrettable failure. All these failures, however, have not produced any real self-criticism and we remain caught in a web of contradictions and seem to be incapable of breaking it.

Besides the Package Programme, which has been commented upon already, there are two other programmes, which are being experimented with on a large scale, but the experience which has been acquired so far clearly points to the fact that they cannot lead to the realization of the object of decentralized integrated development from economic and social standpoint and are suffering from serious inner contradictions. It is necessary to explain the intent, purpose and the manner of execution of these programmes as briefly as possible to indicate how these two very well-meant and well-conceived social endeavours have again produced such disillusioning results.

First of these programmes for decentralized rural industrialization is the adoption of the programme of starting new centres of integrated production—*gram ekais* as they are called. Three thousand such centres have to be started in the Third Plan and 600 in 1961-62. The Community Development Administration is also to co-operate in this undertaking by assuming responsibility for another 250 similar units. "This," according to the Khadi and Village Industries Commission, is "the

Integrated Development Programme for rural reorganization which will include schemes pertaining to agriculture, animal husbandry, health and education and other social and cultural activities besides those of khadi and village industries."[28] This is to be the main expansion programme of the Commission in the Third Plan. The Commission itself is to restrict its active participation to its own schemes of khadi and village industries though it will be fully associated with co-ordinated functioning of all other agencies responsible for the other development activities included in the programme. The Panchayat Samities and Zilla Parishad are expected to co-ordinate these activities and at the state level an *ad hoc* committee is to perform this function. The State Development Commissioners and the State Ministers have warmly approved of this programme and declared their intention of making efforts to implement it.[29]

The Commission and the Development Commissioners have stated that concurrence of the Panchayat Samities and Parishads is to be given after 80 per cent of the families in the Ekai areas have taken a decision to constitute an Ekai. This decision, according to the Commission, is to mean that the members of the Ekai are to make a Sankalpa (a solemn declaration of dedication to the purpose of this programme) for, (a) building up a homogeneous co-operative community, (b) assigning to the primary community the responsibility for taking the initiative for providing the members of the community with the basic necessities of life and enabling them to have a feeling of security within the community, (c) planning to secure land for the landless and provide work through the rural industries, (d) assessing and utilizing the available resources of the village for achieving maximum output primarily for the satisfaction of the basic needs of the community without losing sight of the obligation to contribute to the resources of the nation, i.e. the larger community of which every primary community is a part and,

28. *Gram Ekai Scope and Operation*, Khadi and Village Industries Commission, p. 10.

29. *Ibid.*, Appendix A, pp. 68-69.

(e) diversifying the economy of each community for better living conditions of the people and finding opportunities within it for its most gifted youth for full creative life. Khadi, according to this declaration, is to be taken as a symbol of non-violent social order and used as an instrument of integrated development of village community and make khadi and village industries a means of building up agro-industrial community and ushering in "an era of liberty, fraternity and equality for all". This is the import of the decision which is to precede the selection of an area for creating the new unit under the Khadi and Village Industries Programme, but it also implies that the programmes of all other agencies with which this programme is to be co-ordinated will keep the same social objects in view and work, otherwise co-ordination cannot but mean discord rather than concord.

The preparation of the programme in selected villages is intended to be based upon the data collected through surveys for framing estimates of the unutilized labour force, condition of the village industries, requirement of cloth and products of village industries, the irrigated and unirrigated cultivated area and under different crops suplying raw materials for village industries and the wage rates of artisans and agricultural labourers. These surveys under the Commission's programme would, it is assumed, be directly related to its work, it being assumed that the other agencies would collect data on the same lines to make them adequate for integrated development for rural organization, i.e. establishing a rural economy through which, in the words of the Khadi and Village Industries Commission, "an era of liberty, fraternity and equality for all" to be ushered in.

This is a great dream but if it is to be realized not only the Khadi and Village Industries Commission has to attain a much higher level of performance than it has attained so far, but all other agencies, most of all the Community Development Administration, have to function at the same level and realize as completely as possible unity of purpose and action. These are obviously essential conditions of the success of the undertaking and on the basis of the past experience it is quite legitimate to feel serious misgiving as to whether these conditions can or will be[30] fulfilled.

EXTENSIVE DEVELOPMENT OF SMALL INDUSTRIES IN RURAL AREAS

The disappointing results of the Gram Ekai Programme have not given rise to any re-examination or criticism of the programme. A year later another programme, which has practically the same object and sponsored by the same men, has been launched on a much larger scale and is being proceeded with. There is really no connection with the previous programme of rural industrialization directly undertaken by the Khadi and Village Industries. But prominent members of the latter are closely associated with it and the chairmen of the Rural Industries Planning Committee is also the well-known outstanding

30. These misgivings have unfortunately been more than amply confirmed by experience of three years of the working of this programme. It was introduced on April I, 1961 and on March 31, 1964, its results, it is apparently clear, could not have been more disappointing. The total expenditure on the programme from 1961-64 was Rs 39.52 lakhs and it is proposed to spend Rs 45.26 lakhs on it in 1964-65. During this period 1,646 Gram Ekais were approved and concrete results of their working and heavy financial outlay (from April to September 1963) was 5,533 traditional 'charkhas' and 7,600 'Ambar' were working in the Ekais, 9.27 lakhs sq. metres of khadi valued at Rs 19.29 lakh was produced and the value of products of village industries was Rs 14.33 lacs.

These are the only available figures of production in the Ekais. The other information about the programme which is available is that 55 per cent of Gram Ekais do not send any report, co-ordination even within the Commission has not been realized and co-ordination with the other agencies and the other departments simply does not exist. The brave new world, which was to be created by the programmes according to its original object, does not remain even as a dream and the programme is being continued with the certainty that "an era of liberty, fraternity and equality for all" cannot be created by Gram Ekais and any other measures which have been and are being taken by the planning authorities.

The lesson of the complete failure of the intrinsically sound scheme is that even our well-conceived schemes are becoming a travesty of what

Sarvodaya leader, Shri Annasaheb Sahasrabudhe, who is vice-president of the Khadi and Village Industries Commission and was also responsible for the introduction and implementation of the Gram Ekai Programme.

"The primary object" of this programme, in the words of the Planning Commission, "is to bring about a co-operative agro-industrial economy. This involves all-round development of agriculture, irrigation, communications, industries, social services."[31] Development of rural industries is necessarily the most important aspect of the programme, but the underlying assumption is that their development is to be an integrated part of the entire development programme of the selected areas and the initiative and effort of local communities will have to be stimulated and mobilized to the fullest extent for carrying out the programme. It is intended to "provide larger opportunities to the landless and weaker sections of the village communities" and "contribute to the solution of the unemployment problem". It is also clearly stated that "for drawing up the programme of rural industries and for securing adequate results from those undertaken, such over-all area or regional plans are essential".

Essentially speaking, there is no difference between this programme, its intent and purpose, and the Gram Ekai Programme. The local communities are not to make any solemn declaration

they were meant to be because our efforts are feeble and fragmentary, are lacking in integrity of purpose and are being carried out under extremely unfavourable conditions owing to the entire social system being dominated by the forces which are against social change.

The other programme of the Khadi and Village Industries Commission which still remains its main pre-occupation, in spite of its announcement that it would make Gram Ekais its most important activity, is still suffering from all the evils to which attention was pointedly drawn by the Khadi Evaluation Committee, and no action was being taken to mitigate these evils, what to speak of remedying them.

It is very painful to have to record this conclusion because Khadi and all that goes with it, stand for great nobility of purpose, disinterested and dedicated endeavour and affirmation of values which have to be embodied in the ends and the means of a socialist society.

31. Pamphlet issued by the Rural Industries Planning Committee, para II, p. 1.

(*sankalpa*)of their dedication to the "new order of liberty, fraternity and equality" and determination to build it up but presumably they are to work in the same spirit and produce the same results. The programme was introduced in April 1962 and has been in operation for over two years and by the end of the Third Plan its first phase is to be fully implemented. Provision has been made for the expenditure of Rs 8 crores for 40 projects and Rs 7 crores for a contingent fund up to the end of 1965-66. Allocation of funds from the states plans and from the all-India Boards according to their respective programmes for selected area are to supplement this specific provision and additional funds are to be provided by loans and credits from financial institutions. In order to carry out this programme a high level Rural Industries Planning Committee, a Standing Committee, State Committees and Project Committees have been constituted and the Projetc Staff has been appointed. Forty areas have been selected from all over the country, each area consisting of several community development blocks, the areas have been surveyed and their reports have been prepared and submitted. Hardly any information is available as to whether any project plans have been prepared and are being implemented and what is their relation, if any, to the area and regional development plans. As it is known that the area and regional development plans practically do not exist, it can be assumed that the project plans are not related to the development programmes of the country as a whole. As it is a far-flung programme and is intended to contribute to the building up a co-operative agro-industrial economy based upon the initiative and effort of local committees, its success has to be measured by the extent to which the people are involved in this programme, i.e. they participate intelligently, actively and fully in its preparation and execution.

On the basis of the available information results of the programme cannot be evaluated. This programme, it was meant, should be given the very highest priority, really made the core of the entire development effort of the country. "It is most saddening," in the words of Jai Prakash Narain, who is the inspirer, the author and the guide of this programme that, "the state governments have failed to give top priority to this programme" and "have not found it necessary to apply to this programme the attention and the energy it deserves". At the project level, according to him, there was no integration between the Project staff and the other development agencies, the departmental control of and interference in these projects continues. It was stated pointedly by Jai Prakash Narain that the organizations like Khadi and Village Industries Commission, the Handloom Board, Handicraft Board should all cease to function separately if substantial results were to be achieved, and he, as a matter of fact, suggested the formation of a Rural Industrialization Commission which should replace all these separate agencies. This view was endorsed by some other prominent members of the Rural Industries Planning Committee. As its acceptance as a basis for action would have necessarily involved dissolution of a number of agencies, which have acquired a vested interest in the existing frustrating state of things, this step could not be taken and was not given any serious consideration. These agencies continue to function separately and their programmes are prepared and carried out without any inter-relation or coordination, and as pointed out above, they are not planned in the real sense and the need for integration is no part of approach or application of effort. Surveys of forty project areas have been prepared, but according to Prof. D. R. Gadgil, "They appeared to have lacked a definite objective. The result is that the reports of the surveys are like the usual compilation of data—and contain nothing which can be considered helpful for evaluation."

These conclusions relate to the situation as it existed about a year ago (July 1963) and though the facts about the present position are not known, it would be more than surprising if the over-all position, taking into account the original object of the programme, has materially improved. A sense of frustration, to which authentic expression was given a year ago, is a part of the all-round frustration of the economy as a whole which continues to exist and has really been greatly accentuated. In all the discussions which have taken place on rural industrialization the urgent need for a national research and action programme of what is called "intermediate technology", i.e. research into technical programme suited to dispersed country-wide production of manufactured goods in accordance with the specific needs, resources and man-power situation of each area, has been duly and appropriately emphasized. Rural industrialization cannot and should not rest on primitive technique, and a national programme of intensive research as a basis for development is absolutely essential. A great deal of clear thinking has been done on this subject, issues have been stated with understanding of essentials and their different aspects set forth with clarity. On the basis of available information it appears, however, that no positive results of any kind have been achieved so far and a start has not been made even in framing the programme.

In view of these facts it should not be necessary to add that complete prospective disillusionment stares us in this face. This programme can be a success only if an earnest beginning is made in re-organizing, rationalizing and socializing our agriculture, full utilization of unused man-power on a planned basis is aimed at, rural industrialization becomes an integral part of an all-out effort to re-organize rural economy basically and make the people and their organized effort with a social purpose its motive force. There has to be one and not many programmes of industrialization including large-scale, small-scale, traditional and non-traditional small industries, and modern technique adapted in a creative way to the economic and social context of the different industries, regional and functional needs, with clearly demarcated spheres for each industry and type of technique has to be evolved and applied in the same social framework to realize optimum social well-being.

It is really more than inexplicable why men of outstanding sincerity, ability and devotion with real social vision, who have been associated with Khadi and Village Industries and its rural Intensive Area Programme, are not applying themselves in a consistent and a continuous manner to the carrying out of well-conceived integrated development programmes which they have undertaken and are virtually responsible for the large waste of resources, energy and earnest endeavour. The work of the Khadi and Village Industries Commission continues to be as moribund as ever, the Intensive Area Development Programme has been abandoned, the Gram Ekais have produced most disappointing results and now the Rural Industrialization Programme has also, it appears, run into a blind alley. That men of such high calibre and probity should allow themselves to be caught, as stated before, in a web of contradictions and not be able to break it is very saddening indeed and cannot but produce deep pessimism.

The moral is clear and need not be spelt out. We have to change our direction and bring into action forces which at present are being thwarted and repressed. Decentralized rural industrialization as a part not only of the new rural but also national economy moved forward by a real revolutionary purpose is a task of the very highest importance but at present, it cannot be accomplished.

Chapter Eight

THE CO-OPERATIVE SECTOR

ROLE OF CO-OPERATION

In India the co-operatives have existed for nearly sixty years, but now they have been assigned a new role in our economy —the role of being the most important means of establishing a socialist society in small, i.e. small-scale production in agriculture, small industry, retail and even wholesale trade in countryside—i.e. over more than 90 per cent of our economy. They are, according to the avowed objects of our plans, to be the most important vehicle and embodiment of the spirit of socialism— they are in reality, very largely to be socialism itself. This is a truly revolutionary role—the role of changing the very foundations of our economy, its social norms and relations, distribution of power, property and income and substance of every-day life of our people. "The socialist pattern of society implies the creation of a large number of decentralized units," in the words of the *Third Five Year Plan*, "in agriculture, industry and services. . . . The influence of co-operation extends far beyond the particular activities based on co-operative basis and gives to the social structure and the external economy balance, direction and a sense of values."[1] This view has been implicit in the enunciation of the objects of co-operation since 1951, but in the various pronouncements since the famous Nagpur Resolution in 1958, the role of the co-operatives has been brought very much to the fore and, in theory, the standards by which the policy and performance has to be assessed is the extent to which it can and will fulfil this object of altering radically the very basis of our national economy, and the latter in action can

1. *The Third Five Year Plan*, p. 200.

advance towards and progressively realize socialism. Co-operation has, the experience of the last sixty years has made it abundantly clear, failed to bring even succour to our poverty-stricken peasants, artisans and small traders—has not materially reduced the burden of their debts and the dependence on the money-lender or improved their productivity, income and position and increased their self-reliance, resourcefulness or capacity for concerted action.

This did not happen before independence and has not happened since. Now it is imperative that not only the lot of these extremely unfortunate masses should be very significantly changed, but this should—really only can—be done in the context of the new economy in which power-pattern has been changed and from base upwards those whom co-operation has been and is intended to serve become the most decisive factor in the working of the economy. From what has been said so far, it is clear that we have been moving away from and not in that direction,and the co-operatives cannot possibly fulfil their new role unless this shift is brought about in a manner which does not admit of any doubt. The co-operatives, which also does not admit of any doubt, cannot perform this role which has now been assigned to them unless those who wield economic and political power at all levels and to whom this new role is and cannot but be repugnant from the point of view of their interests, way of thinking and exercise of authority, have inevitability of this shift brought home to them and know that resistance to it is of no avail. Co-operation, even as a palliative, has, to repeat, definately failed; but it is no longer possible to use and develop it as such. It has to be a radical cure—both means and end of revolutionary social endeavour. Jawaharlal Nehru for some time before his death spoke with great fervour of co-operative sector as being the third sector. In the wider sense the latter has to be the all-embracing sector of our economy, i.e. both the state and the shrinking private sector—and relatively shrink it must, if we are to have socialism—have, in their essence, to acquire the essential qualities of the co-operative sector, i.e. draw their strength, momentum and resources from within themselves, from the organized will of the real producers, the workers with brawn and brain, who can see and realize that their own well-being and that of the community are inextricably inter-woven. The co-operative sector has a specific meaning in the present context, but if it is to give "to the social structure and the national economy balance, direction and a sense of value", its spirit has to permeate both the state and the private sectors, they have to become integral parts of an all-embracing co-operative sector. But it is all-important that the co-operatives in their sphere should be true to their inner purpose and draw their life breath from an economy in which power is an incident of social function and is exercised subject to social direction and control. A shift in power-pattern referred to above means and has to mean replacement of power derived from property and privilege by combination of social function and authority and of course, as just stated, subject to social direction and control.

CONVERGENT VIEWS

This approach is, with all its implications, not completely or entirely accepted by all planners or co-operators in India but there is a very large measure of convergence of views on the more vital points in regard to the development of co-operation. It is now generally realized that its failure is largely due to co-operation having been conceived and applied in a fragmentary way in its relation to the economy in general and rural economy in particular. Rural credit marketing, small industries, better farming, production and distribution of milk, animal husbandry, irrigation, processing, village sanitation, etc. are all activities in which organization on a co-operative basis has been attempted and in a number of cases good results have been achieved; but the co-operative agencies, which have assumed and discharged these functions, have not understood or kept in mind the organic inter-relations of these activities or their bearing on one another or the rural economy as a whole. Generally speaking the outcome has been disappointing and frustrating, and in spite of considerable advance in quantitative terms in the last decade co-operation has contributed very little to the development or transformation of the economy. Apart from the basic importance of power-pattern, which has been and still is a serious limiting factor in the growth of co-operation from within, the isolation in which the various activities referred to above have been co-operativized has been self-defeating and these activities have been gravely hampered in the realization of their potential. Now it is very clearly realized that this fragmentation has to be ended and co-operation has to be expressed and developed as an organic whole and find not only a unifying purpose but also organizational unity and a living centre around which the whole movement revolves and from which it draws its sustenance and impulse for growth. This means integration in practice of all co-operative activities without losing the advantage of functional specialization, but it has also to mean a system in which there is a central gravitational pull and diverse activities with their own orbits are all directed towards the consummation of the same cardinal objective. This objective, owing to the compelling necessity of our entire situation, can be no other than revivification of village communities in the new context of increasingly integrated but not centralized national economy as a part of the progressive emergence of a world community. In concrete terms it has to mean the utmost development of agriculture through full realization of its productive potential with the application of modern knowledge and technique and rational utilization of the entire man-power. The enormous waste which is taking place today, owing to the under-utilization of this great productive asset has to be prevented and that can be done only if through its rational utilization it (unutilized labour) can become the most important instrumnt of increase in income, the means for raising the standard of not only living but also life of our people much above the present sub-human level and a source of accumulation of capital which is rightly considered as one of our most cramping deficiencies. This potential productive asset can be converted into larger income, nutrition, comfort and culture at a much higher level for our people in the villages, and surplus for rapid development not only of the countryside but also the country as a whole. This, however, can be done only if a sense of community is created and maintained and concerted efforts are made to use our land, other natural resources and human assets primarily and mainly for the well-being of the village community as a whole which means, of course, that of the lowliest who are a vast majority of our people in the villages. This means greatly intensified and diversified agriculture, production for use mostly for the village community, decentralized industries producing for local and wider market at continuously rising level of technique, development of all ancillary activities and amenities needed for a developing village community and planned outflow from and inflow into the villages of goods and services. All this implies that co-operation has to be widely used for realizing these objects and its whole super-structure going right up to national level has to be erected on the basis of a fully awakened and growing village community with co-operation as its very life-force and means and end of its all-round development. This does not mean a self-contained autarchic village in any sense of the word, but a self-reliant village-community which can, with knowledge and confidence, overcome its stupendous difficulties, receive material aid and technical assistance from the country as a whole and the working of the entire economy is articulated for the great task of building from below in the best sense of the phrase; it has to be clearly understood and vividly realized that this regenerated village community has to be an organ of national economy and cannot and will not live unto itself.

This is a good and adequate conception of co-operation about which there is hardly any difference of opinion. It is the underlying conception of the important policy statements of co-operation and the arguments and conclusions on the working groups which have reported on the programme of co-operation under the Third Plan. This conception, if adhered to in practice in letter and spirit, can be very fruitful provided the pre-conditions of its realization receive their due consideration and the forces, which in effect are working for negation of co-operation, are held in check and are not permitted to defeat its object. This is a very serious qualification of the programme of co-operative development. In the villages there are forces at work which have succeeded very largely in reducing co-operation to an empty form and taken away most of its social significance. It is not the framework of co-operatives or the theoretical ap-proach which can determine or change the substance of co-operation, but the network of social relations, and the spirit in which the policy makers or the administrators formulate and execute the programme of development to be implemented through the co-operatives. The fact, however, that there is a large measure of agreement in regard to the content and measures of co-operation has a significance of its own. It shows that futility of fragmentary efforts so clearly demonstrated by experience is duly appreciated and it is realized that co-opera-tion is and has to be an attribute of the economy as a whole and its beneficience depends entirely upon motive forces of the economy and the direction in which it is moving. Co-operation has not only to be the means but also the substance of socialism and that necessarily implies that essentials of socialism are ardently desired and made an object of conti-nuous pursuit. In other words, co-operation has to be the inner life of the economy if it is to be co-operation at all. It cannot fulfil itself merely through the framework of co-operation and its avowed objects.

GROWTH OF CO-OPERATIVES FROM 1939-40 TO 1959-60

	1939-40	1949-50	1959-60
No. of co-operatives	1,17,000 (100)	1,64,000 (140)	3,13,499 (268)
No. of Members (thousands)	5,077 (100)	14,605 (287.5)	31,313 (617)
Working Capital (Rs Lakhs)	10,468 (100)	21,940 (209)	1,08,347 (1,035)
Loan Transactions of Primary Societies (Rs Lakhs)	2,170 (100)	5,438 (251)	16,901 (779)

The primary agricultural societies are, as is well known, the most important constituent of all co-operative societies and it is planned that by 1965-66 the number of their members will rise from 17.49 to 37.22 millions and advances to them from Rs 204.55 crores to Rs 529.17 crores, i.e. both in respect of members and advances there will be very great acceleration in the rate of growth and, if the plan targets are realized, the number of members of the primary agricultural credit societies will increase by 112 and of advances by 158 per cent. According to the mid-term appraisal of the Plan it has been estimated that co-operative credit in the last year of the plan is not likely to exceed Rs 400 crores. It was intended, as stated below, that advances should be linked to production and marketing, but the object has not been and most likely will not be realized to any considerable extent. These estimates are, therefore, not related to the anticipated rate of growth in agricultural production and marketing surplus and are therefore to be taken merely as the departmental estimates and not the budget of credit requirements of the rural economy. The fact, however, that from 1950-51 to 1955-56 the number of members of these societies increased from 4.4 to 7.5 millions, and from 1956-57 from 9.1 to 17 millions, and advance from Rs 22.9 crores in 1950-51 to Rs 49.6 crores in 1955-56 and Rs 61.3 crores in 1956-57 to Rs 200 crores in 1959-60, shows that in quantitative terms these targets may possibly be attained, though the assumption on which these targets have been framed are not known, and it cannot be stated to what extent these and other targets of the development of co-operation in the Third Plan are warranted by a firm estimate of the potential of growth. But even making allowance for this vital fact, it is undeniable that in regard to a number of societies, number of members, working capital and advances a degree of optimism based on experience of the growth of co-operatives in the first two plans is justified.

Under the Second Plan the following targets were fixed for primary agricultural credit societies: Members 15 millions, advances Rs 225 crores—short term Rs 150 crores, medium terms Rs 50 crores, long term Rs 25 crores. As stated above the number of members in 1959-60 was 17.1 million and short and medium term advances amounted to Rs 200 crores. The outstandings on June 30, 1960 of the Land-Mortgage Banks were Rs 28.50 crores. The target for long term advances under the Third Plan is Rs 150 crores. This is a very big leap and would require in the words of the Planning Commission, "a very large measure of assistance from the national institutions like the Reserve Bank of India, the State Bank of India and Life Insurance Corporation". It would, besides this assistance, require great expansion of the owned resources of the co-operative institutions themselves which can take place only if there is great expansion of agricultural production and channelization of the accrued surplus for planned investment in the development of rural economy is brought about. The channelization can take place if the whole rural economy is re-organized and the co-operatives assume a decisive role in production and distribution of commodities. The significance of these figures, however, lies more in the economic and social impacts of these developments than in the figures themselves. Statistics themselves do not reveal their real meaning from the point of view of economy as a whole or social change and it is necessary to probe deeper into the bearing of these statistics on our basic needs to make an evaluation of the position and prospects.

RATING OF THE CREDIT CO-OPERATIVES

The primary agricultural credit societies are graded according to the quality of their performance, the proportion of owned funds, deposits, overdues, etc. and the standard of management. In 1958-59, 17 per cent of the audited and classified societies were classified under categories A and B (Excellent and Good) 68 per cent under C (just Fair) and the rest under D and E. Of 186,507 societies in 1958-59, 152,211 were audited and classified—the rest were neither audited nor

classified or were audited but not classified. The latest figures
of classification are not available but indications are that there
has not been any material improvement from the qualitative
standpoint and generally speaking the proportion of poorly
managed societies continue to be very high, and though there is
a provision for what is called revitalization of 52,000 poor
societies under the Third Plan, the facts do not justify the
expectation that the standard of performance by the co-
operatives would come anywhere near the level needed to
make them a real dynamic feature of the economy. In 1956-57
nearly three-fifths of the societies were placed under Category
C and in some provinces the proportion was much higher. In
Behar, for example, the proportion in 1956-57 was 68.99 per
cent, in Madhya Pradesh 79.05, in Madras 74.44 per cent, in
Orissa 70.44 per cent and in Uttar Pradesh 75.89 per cent. If
all societies had been audited and rated, it is a safe presumption that the proportion of just fair and very poor societies
would, instead of being less, have been probably higher. Even
strong societies are rated as such (i.e. A and B) because of the
observance of rules and regulations, more efficient collection of
dues and similar other administrative tests and not because
they have given an evidence of possessing the capacity for
breaking new ground, enlisting the interest and enthusiasm of
the people in taking a wide view of their functions and responsibilities and broadening their base, i.e. increasing the proportion of members drawn from the poorer and depressed section of the village community. All co-operatives, including the
good ones, take only hum-drum view of their role and the
ordinary and poor co-operatives, nearly six-seventh of the co-
operatives, were, by standards of administrative performance of
their duties, just passable or very much sub-standard. Consolidation or re-vitalization has to be, as the Planning Commission
has pointed out, the first step in implementing the programme
in a large number of states, but further expansion of the movement (presumably on the lines laid down in the Plan) has to,
as the Planning Commission has also pointed out, depend

largely on the extent to which primary agricultural credit societies succeed in mobilizing local savings, improving management and linking credit with marketing and with production.[2] These conditions, specially the last, i.e. linking credit with marketing and production, are not, on the existing indications, likely to be realized. It is really necessary, if the prime purpose of the programme is to be carried out, to go much farther and expect the co-operatives to develop a new dynamism which so far they have not acquired or possessed. This has to be done if co-operation is to become the principle instrument and the very essence of socialism. If the standard of rating of the co-operatives is applied with reference to this supreme object, even the societies placed under the categories A and B would not measure to the needs of the programme. Real significance of the increase in the number of societies, their members, working capital and advance is to be judged from this standpoint, and judged as such, the position is truly depressing. This point is also relevant in regard to the other co-operatives and has to be given its due consideration. Increase in expenditure, which in quantitative terms appears so impressive but has mostly taken place at a low level of performance, does not carry in itself the promise of advance at high or even rising level. Merely multiplication of co-operatives in C class is hardly any contribution to the building up of a co-operative sector.

UNEVEN DEVELOPMENT

Development of co-operation has been very unevenly distributed even at the existing level among the different states and inter-state disparities among them have not been reduced as a result thereof. Andhra, Madras, Maharashtra in respect of members and working capital have been more highly developed, their percentage of dormant societies has been, relatively speaking, low and proportion of overdue dues has also

2. *Third Five Year Plan*, p. 204.

been not high, while in Behar, Assam, West Bengal and Orissa development in proportion to population has been, from both quantitative and qualitative standpoint, unsatisfactory and number of dormant societies has been high, working capital more inadequate and overdue much higher; and this gap has continued over a long period and hardly anything has been done to reduce it. In the other states development is also uneven and in each state the areas of low development have continued to be depressed areas for a long time.

These disparities are due to deep-seated causes and can be removed only if in planned development the need for balanced development of the different parts of the country is given much higher priority than it has been so far, and in the more under-developed areas not merely organizational but also basic changes are brought about. Co-operation being of such fundamental importance for realizing the social objectives of our economy, it cannot be the great leveller that it should be unless, in the areas which have been and are handicapped, new social forces are brought into play and the built-in depressors in them are replaced by the built-in raisers and sustainers. Co-operation all over the country cannot play its due role, to repeat, unless the balance of forces is changed and new atmosphere of social endeavour is created in which building up the new economy of the country becomes a great social adventure. In the areas in which co-operation has failed to come up to the average level of the country and the level attained in the less undeveloped areas, adverse social forces were stronger and the entire social structure was more unfavourable than in the other parts of the country. Co-operation, generally speaking, has not made headway in the states in which feudal elements were comparatively strong and the people more poverty-stricken and without any will or strength of their own owing to the conditions under which they had to work and live. This means, of course, co-operation can only come into its own when the country is well on its way to socialism and in the states in which the need of social transformation is the greatest, the wind of basic change will have to blow with greater force and keep on blowing for a longer period.

BENEFITS OF CO-OPERATION

It is now an admitted fact that benefits of co-operative development, as of developments in general, have largely accrued to the well-off sections of the community and the poorer sections are, relatively speaking, the worse off on that account and the benefits which they have derived from co-operative development are in most cases very meagre and in others almost negligible. It is possible to cite figures derived from various sources in support of this statement, but a comparison based upon the available data in Rural Credit Survey and the two follow-up Surveys issued by the Reserve Bank of India can be taken as an adequate testimony to show that co-operation, in spite of its absolute inadequacy, has been and is a factor very much to the advantage of the upper section of the rural community and has increased the gap between them and the lowest strata.

In the words of the Rural Credit Survey, "class-wise distribution of co-operative finance is pre-ponderately in favour of the large cultivators compared with medium and small cultivators—and among large cultivators themselves, preponderately in favour of the big cultivators".[3] This statement was borne out by the fact that of the amount borrowed from co-operative cultivators per family, Rs 210 were borrowed by the cultivators with an average holding of 26 acres, Rs 139.5 by large cultivators with an average holding of 16.9 acres, Rs 4.7 by medium cultivator with an average holding of 6.8 acres and Rs 3.0 by small cultivators with an average holding of 1.9 acres.

In the years 1956-58 two follow-up surveys were conducted in the selected eleven districts in ten states in the first case and selected twelve districts from twelve states in the second

3. *Rural Credit Survey*, p. 231.

with a view to collecting statistical data relating to outstanding debts and borrowings and assessing the performance of the
co-operatives for supplying credit. These follow-up surveys
have very clearly confirmed markedly inequalitarian trends at
work in the country since planning was introduced and their
growing strength. Among other data bearing upon the working of the rural economy as a whole, these surveys have also
given "class-wise" distribution of co-operative finance—utilization of co-operative credit by the same sections in rural
areas referred to above. The proportion of the borrowings of
this class in various districts are given in the table in the foot-
note4 and clearly shows the continued preponderance of the

4. Borrowing of Different Classes of Cultivators from Co-operatives as
percentage of the Total Borrowings from co-operatives by all cultivators.

	Big		Large		Medium		Small	
	1951-52	1956-57	1951-52	1956-57	1951-52	1956-57	1951-52	1956-57
Broach	26	32	58	61	37	34	5	4
Coimbatore	18	10	45	48	38	14	17	38
West Godavari	46	34	73	75	20	16	7	9
Jaipur	—	20	—	48	—	36	—	16
Jullundur	26	23	55	47	31	36	14	17
Monghyr	—	16	—	46	—	26	—	28
Quilon	20	73	74	100	19	—	7	—
Sagar	3	21	48	65	52	28	—	6
Sorath	—	21	—	47	—	36	—	16
Nizamabad	26	39	51	88	38	11	11	2
Akola	36	43	60	71	34	23	6	6
Bangalore	—	33	—	72	—	28	—	—
Burdwan	15	58	30	91	40	9	30	—
Chingleput	21	54	43	87	57	10	—	3
Deoria	30	28	62	60	26	27	12	13

Big 10 per cent; Large 30 per cent (including Big); Medium 40 per cent;
Small 30 per cent. In a speech delivered by Mr. S. K. Dey, Union Minister
for Community Development and Co-operation, delivered at the Annual
Conference of the Registrars of the Co-operative Societies and the State
Ministers of Co-operation in February 1963 said, "Even today co-operative
credit is largely confined to the richer sections who need it less than the
weaker sections of the community." Report of the Annual Conference held
at Lucknow, p. 33.

large cultivators as compared with medium and small cultivators (the upper Ten) among the large cultivators (including
the big cultivators). The tabulated information relates to 15
out of 23 selected districts but can be taken as an indication
of the actual position in the country. The proportion of utilization of co-operative funds varies from, for example, 100 per
cent by the large cultivator in Quilon district, 91 in Burdwan,
88 in Nizamabad and 87 in Chingulput—four districts with
the highest percentage—to 46 in Monghyr, 47 in Jullundur,
48 in Jaipur and Sorath and Coimbatore. The portion of
utilization by big cultivators among the large cultivators was
73 per cent in Quilon, 52 per cent in Broach, 45 per cent in
West Godavari and 45 per cent in Sorath. Expansion of working capital from Rs 276 crores in 1950-51 to Rs 1,083 crores
in 1959-60 has really meant that funds to which the state and
institutions like the Reserve Bank and the State Bank have
contributed so liberally[5] have very largely been made available
for adding to the resources, power and position of a highly
privileged minority in the country; and whatever else it may
have done, it has certainly not in any sense made credit co-
operation the peoples' movement. It has probably to a certain
extent assisted in the expansion of agricultural production, but
at the cost of increasing the preponderance of the rich cultivators most of whom are also rentiers, merchants and money-
lenders. It will be seen also from this table that position in this
respect has become worse, i.e. preponderance of this class has
become even relatively greater as a result of expansion of the
resources of the co-operative, i.e. it is drawing a large portion
of the loanable funds in 1956-57 than it did in 1951-52 and
in some cases the rise in the proportion is very marked indeed,
e.g. from 20 to 73 per cent in the case of big cultivators in
Quilon, of large cultivators 53 to 88 in Nizamabad, from 43 to
87 in Chingalput and from 30 to 90 in Burdwan. There is no
doubt that in the utilization of agricultural credit societies the

5. Of Rs 1,083 crores working capital in 1959-60, Rs 85 crores were
contributed by the Reserve Bank of India and Rs 54 crores by Government.

co-operatives have been from the socialist standpoint moving in reverse gear. In 1951-52, of the total credit requirements of agriculture the state and co-operatives were contributing nearly 6 per cent (3 per cent each). Since 1950-51 the working capital of the co-operatives has, as stated above, risen to Rs 1,083 crores in 1959-60; in a decade it has risen by nearly four times. It is quite obvious that co-operative finance was in 1959-60 a far more important factor in rural economy than it was in 1950, a decade earlier, and yet its social content, it is also obvious, not only has not changed, really it has had a more regressive impact on the rural economy, i.e. the extent to which it has increased is also a measure of the increasing strength and power of richer agriculturists who, to repeat, with the merchant and the money-lender—often being three in one and one in three—exercise a detrimental influence on the village economy and have most of the levers of power in their hands.

INTEGRATED DEVELOPMENT PROGRAMME

The convergence of views referred to above has found expression, ever since the Rural Credit Survey formulated its integrated scheme, in, as stated already, all discussions, official statements, reports of the committees and groups, general directives issued by the Central Government and what is more, in the Second and Third Five Year Plans. And yet in the Second Plan period the integrated scheme was not given even a fair trial and achievements in this respect could not have been more disappointing. In the Third Plan after truly voluminous discussions the need for and basic importance of integrated development as a means of rebuilding and radically changing the entire rural economy has been re-affirmed with clarity and force; and yet it does not look as if we are going to get a real move on in the right direction and proceed towards the accepted goal with speed and determination. That is so because the conditions for realizing this object do not exist, have not been and are not being created and because advance is necessarily being conditioned by, in the words of the Rural Credit Survey, "the social background, social structure and social attitudes" which "in spite of the locale of all three in the villages, the background is a part of the economic background of the country" and "attunement of the Government and its more important financial and economic institutions to the more important social, economic and political groups who share between themselves all the real power in the country."6 This attunement also exists in the villages and it is there that it has to be altered both in the villages and at all other levels right to the top, if integrated development of rural economy is to be seriously undertaken and accomplished through the primary co-operatives and their federations at all levels. "Rural Credit," to quote again from the Rural Credit Survey, "is—a part of the larger and living context of India"7 and an essential condition of integrated development is that this context should not only be understood but changed fundamentally and the beginning must be made in the village itself and the impulse of forces generated therein has to be transmitted to the group "which share between themselves all real power in the country". Co-operation, so far has meant "attempt to combine the weak against the strong in conditions in which the weak had no chance",8 but the shift in power has first to take place in the villages and become a part of the enveloping process in the country as a whole. This has not happened and is not happening; and the extremely poor results of the attempt to introduce and develop the integrated scheme are due to this fundamental failure. Integration requires and presupposes unity of purpose and will, and as these have been lacking—as a matter of fact their dissipation and disruption has been the rule—we have not got anywhere in realising the objects on which the Rural Credit Survey, the National Deve-

6. *Rural Credit Survey*, p. 375.
7. *Ibid.*
8. *Ibid.*, p. 376.

lopment Council and the Planning Commission have laid so
much stress.

In its schematic part the most important features of integrated programme was to be linking of rural credit with marketing, production and processing, bringing about a divorce
between grant of credit and possession and value of property
and formulation of production plans centring round the expansion of agricultural production but also comprising milk
supply, animal husbandry, cottage industry, local works like
soil conservation, minor irrigation, afforestation and communications and all that was to be done as a part of one and the
same project. This approach has been avowed at the top, but
been completely lost sight of in practice, and barring abortive
schemes like the Intensive Area Schemes of the Khadi and
Village Industries Commission, the Pilot Projects of the C.D.A.
Gram Ekais and Rural Industry Project to which reference has
been made already, and which in intention were meant to
realize integration in the real sense have record of successive
miscarriage of the inner purpose of co-operation and integrated
development. We have, as suggested by the Rural Credit
Survey, various Development Stabilization and Guarantee
Funds, liberal assistance of the Reserve Bank and the State
Banks to the co-operatives and enlargement of their resources
by Government participation in their share capital, the Warehouse and Development Co-operation and State Warehouse
Companies, also the Central, the State and the local warehouses and godowns. We have the whole skeleton of the
integrated scheme, but without any life or substance in it.
We have, to repeat, no production plans for each village and
though individual marketing societies and federation have
been established, their operation and their share in marketing
of produce or distribution of goods required in the villages for
production or use has been negligible, and there is no co-relation between production and credit and no reduction in overdues—the increase in the latter has more than kept pace with
increase of co-operative finance and co-operative processing

and integration of credit and production though not non-existent and in few cases really significant, has not assumed the dimension of a real change or made any difference to the economic landscape of our rural economy. "The problems," to quote the Rural Credit Survey once more, "is not one of re-organization of co-operative credit as one of the creation of new conditions in which it can operate effectively and for the benefit of the weak." It is, as it has had to be repeatedly pointed out, really more than that, it is the problem of bringing forces into play which will bring in a new equilibrium in social relations and impart to the economy an integrity of purpose and produce capacity for coherent action and advance, i.e. make socialism the real moving force of minds, concerted effort and community life. The co-operatives are not merely to operate for the benefit of the weak but give the weak faith to work for themselves and the strength to know that the future belongs to them and they can shape it in a way as to make mass strength of the weak the strength of the community as a whole and its saviour. This is the only way in which integrated development of the economy can be achieved and a structure built up in which the new "larger and living context of India" can come into being and the co-operatives and their federation can at the village level and above make the ancient co-operative principle of "each for all and all for each" a real life force.

In the Rural Credit Survey integrated approach implied (a) linking credit to marketing and production, (b) liberal assistance by and support of Government and national financial institutions for the primary co-operatives, (c) grant of crop loans on the likely value of the produce, (d) preparation of plans for development, sale and purchase, cottage industries and allied industries like milk supply, local works and, (e) provision of storage facilities. If action had been taken on these lines and earnest effort made to make it fruitful, it would have meant considerable improvement in the position of the village and a federal structure of co-operatives could have been built up, which, assuming the necessary corresponding changes in the institutional framework of the economy as a whole, would have brought about profound and beneficial changes in its social content and working. This approach, however, did not provide for a focal point of reference or a clear conceptual projection for the future. The result was, even theoretically speaking, it lacked some essential ingredients of effective planned action and had to include nebulous devices like "chit funds" for making total provision for credit requirements. The fact that the necessity of linking credit not to production but production plan which is very different and of making a budget of needs and resources for rational and full utilizaation of man-power was not understood or appreciated, made the approach deficient and inadequate for really integrated development. As it is in spite of the scheme having been authoritatively accepted at the highest level and its underlying principles repeatedly endorsed, nothing much has come out of it, and we are where we were before the scheme was presented and accepted, except that quantitative expansion of co-operation has taken place and created an illusion of development. As stated before, integration as an approach has caught on but in its implementation the attempts made so far, have been untrue to its real purpose and only produced disillusionment. It is necessary to do fresh thinking on this subject and resist the temptation of starting new hares. A focal point of reference for this purpose has to be the universally acknowledged and the need for rational and as far as possible complete utilization of available and increasing man-power given the primacy to which it is entitled. This is the most urgent and baffling problem of our economy. It is not at all easy to solve it, but with all its magnitude and complexity, it is an inescapable problem and must be squarely faced. The problem was pressing even in 1921 when "Charkha" was conceived as an immediate answer to its call as a part of our national struggle for freedom. Since then the problem has acquired much greater gravity and urgency because its explosive possibilities have greatly increased. This situation has created its own social imperative and makes it essential for us to face the problem with all its implications.

SERVICE CO-OPERATIVES

The view that because of the increasing urgency of this problem we must control the growth of population by limiting the size of families is a measure of foresight which, as it can be easily demonstrated, has no bearing on the immediate issue. The persons who are going to increase our labour force in the current and following two plans have already been born, and the family limitation, however vigorous, is not going to make any difference to it. We have to find work for the labour force by all ways and means—in large industries, trade, communications and services of all sorts—and yet it is clear that most of this labour force has to live in the villages and utilized in its present habitat. The rate at which our population is growing has to be "slowed down", but the process will take time and for the next fifteen years it is likely that either this rate will go up or be maintained or at best after five to ten years a slight falling trend. It is likely that up to 1970 our labour force in the rural areas will increase at least by about the rate of three millions a year and will have to be utilized in or near the villages. Redistribution of population in the country is possible, but it cannot relieve the existing pressure satisfactorily. As population in India is, as is well known, very unevenly distributed, the problem of utilization of the existing and additional labour force creates, as pointed out already, a strong presumption in favour of local, sub-regional planning. Regioning concept needs to be defined in India in physical, geographical, economic and social terms for the purpose of planned development, but the criterion of the pressure of actual and potential unutilized or under-utilized labour has to be, from practical standpoint, a very basic consideration for planning and must be given its due weight. This very clearly indicates why it is necessary to have village plans which in an ascending order will coalesce in and with sub-regional, state and national plans. There is no question of creating any economic cordons or coming in the way of free mobility of labour. As a matter of fact outflow of labour from the centres of high pressures will have to be planned and provided for, and the country and its parts will have to increasingly become a single market for the entire labour force. But the fact that labour will be free to go anywhere does not mean that its inflow and outflow will in fact become a factor of any great consequence. Most likely movements of population will, though important, not materially change the existing distribution of population, not for many years and a large majority of people will continue to live and work in and around the place of their birth and the development plans will have to be adjusted to this somewhat stubborn fact. Presumption in favour of planning in concentric circles with each village as a centre becomes all the stronger on that account.

The need for village production plan was posited in the Second Plan and was restated in the Draft Third Plan; but in the final Plan it is stated somewhat evasively that "it cannot, however, be said that village production plans are yet established as a normal method of work in agricultural development or the various practical problems involved have been resolved". This is truly a masterpiece of understatement. The truth is, as stated by the Committee on Rural Credit that "what exists at present is a plan of state aid for agricultural development drawn up by the state under various heads. . . . With rare exception there is no agricultural plan for each village, much less for each family."[9] The significance of the above statement is that it cannot be said that village production plans are yet established as a normal method of work in agricultural development. The staff for preparing such plans does not exist and the co-operatives and Panchayats cannot prepare these plans themselves, and therefore, there is no question of the development

9. *Third Five Year Plan*, p. 337.

programme in agriculture and all the allied and related activities like cottage industries, dairies, etc. being anything more
than a programme of state aid for development. This is a frank
but honest statement of the position. It is true, as stated by
the Committee on Rural Credit, that each farmer has a plan
of his own, and programme including credit can be linked to
it, though as stated before, even that is not being done; but if
that becomes the normal method of work in agricultural development, it virtually amounts to going back to pre-planning
development. It may be that this is all that is feasible and to
ask for village production plans and individual family plans
and area and district plans as an integral part of state and
national plans is a purely utopian proposition and does not
take into account the stern realities of the situation. In the
present context it is so, and yet that does not mean that no
planned agricultural development is possible and reversion to
pre-planning processes has to be accepted as unavoidable.

Given this situation, the discussion of an integrated programme envisaged by the Rural Credit Survey of credit linked
to agricultural production of programme of development of
dairy farming, cottage industries and local works like irrigation,
etc. become purely speculative[10] and much more so the dis-

10. The Integrated Development Scheme of Rural Credit Survey was
intended to achieve (a) state partnered co-operative credit to be promoted
by the State Governments with the active assistance of the Reserve Bank;
(b) promotion of activities such as marketing, processing and development,
of storage and warehousing of agricultural commodities together with distribution of goods of importance to the cultivator as producer and consumer, and (c) provision of trained personnel for the task of re-organization
and development.

To realize these objectives it recommends that Reserve Bank should create
the National Agricultural Credit (Long Term Operation Fund) and National
Agricultural Credit (Stabilization Fund). The Long Term Operation Fund
was created in February 1955 with initial contribution of Rs 10 crores and
annual contribution of Rs 5 crores; and for the year ending 30 June 1960, a
provision of Rs 1 crore was made for the Stabilization Fund by introducing a
new section of the Reserve Bank of India Act.

Government contribution towards the share capital of co-operative societies up to 1959-60 was Rs 32.71 crores and loans advanced by the Reserve

cussion of an integrated programme based on budget of man-power and other resources on the one hand and socially assessed needs on the other focussed on the paramount need for rational and full utilization of available actual and potential man-power. And yet without this co-relation, integrated development loses most of its practical importance and significance. In spite of

Bank in 1959-60 to all co-operative societies amounted to Rs 76.86 crores and by Government to Rs 74.32 crores.

It was also recommended by the Rural Credit Survey that Imperial Bank of India should be nationalized and the State Bank of India should open new branches in semi-urban centres, should stimulate the development and growth of co-operative banking, assist in the financing of co-operative marketing and processing societies and provide for remittance facilities. The State Bank has carried out the statutory programme of opening 400 new branches in 5 years, by opening 416 branches since 1955, the total remittance issued by the State Bank on behalf of the co-operative institutions has, under the Reserve Bank Remittance Facilities Scheme, increased from Rs 54.4 crores in 1957-58 to Rs 90 crores in 1959-60 and under its own supplementary scheme from Rs 29.9 crores in 1958-59 to Rs 65.9 crores in 1959-60. The Bank has assisted the Land Mortgage Bank by increasing its holdings of their debentures from Rs 5 lakhs at the end of 1955 to Rs 1.34 crores at the end of May 1961. The Bank introduced schemes of financing, marketing and processing societies in 1958 and at the end of May 1961 had sanctioned limits of Rs 251 lakhs to 173 marketing societies and processing factories other than sugar factories and the outstandings stood at Rs 49.2 lakhs. This is not a large amount and is an index of the slow growth of these societies. Besides these co-operatives sugar factories have been granted interim accommodation of Rs 115 lakhs pending receipt of loans from the Industrial Finance Corporation, they have also been granted loans of Rs 4.50 crores for working capital and a number of sugar factories have been assisted by providing letters of credit facilities and deferred payment guarantees to cover the import of machinery.

For increasing storage and warehousing facilities, as recommended by the Rural Credit Survey Committee, National Co-operative Development and Warehousing Co-operative Development, Central Warehousing Corporation and State Warehousing Corporations in all the States have been established. The Board has set up the National Co-operative Development Fund and the National Warehousing Development Fund. The former fund is meant for making long-term loans to state governments to enable them to subscribe to share capital of the co-operative processing and marketing societies and for giving recurring and non-recurring subsidies to state government. The second fund is meant for subscribing to the share capital of the Central Warehousing Corporation, the State Warehousing Corporations and to deve-

the position being what it is, the idea of having village production plans by service co-operatives, and where these do not
exist, by the Panchayats, being pursued by the Ministry for
Community Development and co-operation and detailed instructions have been issued by it to the states for the preparation
of village production plans containing directions as to the agency
for preparation and implementation of village production plan,

lop warehousing through the co-operatives. The Central Warehousing Corporation builds warehouses in centres of all-India importance, the State
Warehousing Corporations in centres of regional importance and warehouses
below the sub-divisional level are constructed by the various co-operative
societies. By 1960-61 the Central Warehouse Corporation provided 36 warehouses, the State Warehousing Corporations 223 and the co-operatives 4,480.
The Central Co-operative Development and Warehousing Board granted loans
of Rs 371.4 lakhs and subsidies of Rs 82 lakhs by the end of 1959-60 to the
co-operative institutions for warehouses of local importance. As a result of
all these activities approximate storing capacity of 73,000 tons is to be
provided by the Central Warehousing Corporation and 1.39 lakhs by the
State Warehousing Corporations. Even this capacity is unfortunately
under-utilized.

As compared with these achievements, the progress of co-operative marketing and processing makes a depressing story. The number of co-operative
marketing societies in 1959-60 was 2,501 and purchases by them were of
the value of Rs 30.27 crores and sales both by owners and agents of Rs 45.64
crores—nowhere near the target of 10 per cent set by the Second Five Year
Plan. Programme of the Third Plan was to realize 20 per cent of agricultural
sales through the co-operatives—not an ambitious target by any means and
yet its realization cannot be taken as an act of a firm estimate. In 1962-63
the agricultural produce marketed by co-operatives was estimated at Rs 183
crores. The sugarcane supply societies in 1959-60 marketed cane of the value
of Rs 16.37 lakhs in 1959-60; at the end of June 1963, 91 sugar co-operative
factories were working and crushed 26.03 lakh tons sugarcane and produced
sugar weighing 4.7 lakh tons. In all in 1962-63 there were 6,021.50 primary
agricultural marketing societies, and 657.57 central marketing societies.
In the production of sugar co-operative processing has made not very
rapid but satisfactory progress and produced 21.4 per cent of national
production in 1962-63. Among the other agricultural processing co-operatives sales of cotton ginning and pressing societies amounted to Rs 7.24
crores in 1959-60 and of the rest—paddy husking, groundnut decortifi-
cating, coffee curing, etc.—to Rs 2.98 lakhs.

The most disquieting feature of the position, from the point of view of
the Integrated Development Scheme, however, is that loans are still being
granted mostly on the security of land and crop loans based upon production

pre-requisites of drawing the village plan such as collection of data, measures for strengthening the co-operatives, categorization of the draft plans, its publicity, follow-up work and action programme.[11] This is a valiant effort to redeem the situation, but does not thereby create conditions under which integrated village production plans can be prepared and implemented.

Service co-operatives have been given a special place in the

and repaying capacity are hardly of any importance. In the words of the Committee on Rural Credit, "it is clear that by and large the grant of loans to individuals follows landed property rather than the productive purpose for which loan is taken" (*Report on the Committee for Rural Credit*, p. 85). The view of the Rural Credit Survey was that for rural credit crop loans should become the rule and loans based upon the value of owned land should cease, which though endorsed in high places and authoritative quarters, has in practice been completely disregarded. In some states, e.g. the Punjab and U.P., in fixing the quantum of loan for an individual member even extraneous factors like income from sources other than agriculture are also taken into account for assessing credit worthiness. The principle that what is most important for sound credit is personal trustworthiness of the borrower and the purpose for which he borrows has never received its due consideration in co-operative rural credit; and even after the changes introduced since 1956, which were meant to change the whole basis of rural credit, the old practice of fixing credit limits according to the value of property remains unaltered. "To those who have, more will be given" this still remains the basis of rural credit, and fourfold expansion of rural credit has further accentuated this discrimination in favour of the propertied classes. This conclusion is fully confirmed by the results of the Follow-up Surveys 1956-57 and 1957-58 of the Reserve Bank of India (vide Section 20.2, *Report* for 1956-57, Section 14-3, 1957-58 *Report*).

If to these facts is added the inherent limitation of the concept of Integrated Development in the Rural Credit Survey Scheme, i.e. lack of co-relation between credit and production plan and of understanding of the need for the production plan being centred round a focal point comprehending all activities with a view to utilizing fully available man-power, the inadequacy of co-operation as it is conceived and practised becomes all the greater. The latter conception is being, as stated in the text, vaguely apprehended, but as yet has no practical bearing or importance. As it is, loans policy has not been linked even to production and marketing and Integrated Development Scheme, even in the limited sense, has practically not been implemented.

11: Letter No. 1/23/61—Agr., dated July 22, 1961 issued by the Ministry of Community Development (Department of Co-operation) to all State Governments and Union Territories.

programme of development and yet their functions and relation to the other co-operatives still remain to be clearly defined. Village Panchayats have, as stated below, to assume the responsibility for development and promotion where the co-operatives do not exist, but it has been admitted that all functions related to economic development have to be assigned to these co-operatives and they have to assume a variety of forms. Among them there has to be a general purposes co-operative, which in consultation with the Panchayats, has to undertake the over-all responsibility of preparing an all-inclusive production plan, implement it through the specialized or functional co-operatives and through continuous contact, ensure that they function within the general framework of the plan and do not get out of step with one another. "It is in this context", to quote from Report of the Working Group on Panchayats and Co-operatives, "that the service co-operative assumes such overwhelming importance and has to be treated as the mother co-operative in the village".[12] Service co-operatives are not to be merely multiple purpose societies combining credit with purchase and sale but the very core of the co-operative movement—a central organ in the village which should cover all families and be the centre round which all other functional societies will revolve and from which they receive guidance and through which they will be integrated with the entire programme of co-operative development. They will allocate the available man-power according to a well-framed budget to the various functional uses and in cases in which there cannot be a viable unit of a specific economic activity, in collaboration with other villages and a federation of functional societies operating over larger area and for wider markets. Service co-operatives may have to discharge special functions before co-operatives for them are formed and can efficiently operate, but as a rule credit, farming, industrial, dairying, irrigation, labour and construction co-operatives, etc. should undertake these specialized duties and service co-opera-

12. Report on Panchayats and Co-operatives, para V. I.

tives should be the general-purpose co-operatives and as stated above, prepare and implement over-all plan in co-operation with the functional co-operatives, and in consultation with the Panchayats, undertake such duties which relate to over-all economic development, realization of essential social objectives and maintenance of balance among different co-operatives and through their federation and among different regions. For the assumption of these responsibilities the service co-operatives have to develop strong community sense, comprehension of the essentials, drive and of course technical competence and the assistance of a well-qualified staff.[13] At present these conditions are non-existent and taking the existing state of the co-opera-

13. In Yugoslavia, Poland and Hungary what are really "service co-operatives" in our sense have assumed increased importance since it was realized that farming co-operaitves have to be developed with the consent of the farmers and the pace of their development could not and should not be forced. The general co-operatives in Yugoslavia, the agricultural circles in Poland and other similar institutions in Hungary have performed the functions of "service co-operatives", i.e. have assisted and guided the farmers in crop-planning, helped them in maintaining stable agricultural prices, carried out economic and technical education of farmers, have given tractors, reapers and harvesters, etc. on hire, marketed agricultural surplus and supplied consumption of goods and commodities like fertilizers, agricultural implements, etc. and even taken the holdings of the farmers and cultivated them for them, for a charge for their services. In Yugoslavia particularly the general co-operatives have achieved a large measure of success, won the confidence of the farmers and led the way in infusing the spirit of co-operation among them, socializing agricultural production and raising the level of agricultural production and productivity. Suspicion of co-operative farming, due to the use of coercive processes in the earlier phases, has not yet been fully dispelled; but experience and achievements, particularly of Yugoslavia in realizing the benefits of co-operation, short of pooling land, labour and resources, is of great interest and value to us and indicates, how if we religiously avoid the use of force in promoting farming co-operatives, we can by creating the right atmosphere, starting the necessary social process and making the economy as a whole socialistically oriented, expect that farming co-operatives, to repeat, will become the coping stone of the co-operative structure by a process of natural growth. The preconditions of such a transformation—the necessary self-generated drive from within—has still to be created in India and the fact makes the outlook for them, as for all other basic changes, what is today, really dark and depressing.

tives, radical change has to be brought about before they can be created. An estimate of unutilized and under-utilized man-power has to be, as pointed out above, the starting point of this undertaking. The concept, if it is to be elaborated, would make it necessary to prepare a model of the whole new co-operative structure, indicate inter-relations, specific functions and *modus operandi* of realizing the integrated purpose. Apart from the limitations of space, this elaboration at present would be an essay in the domain of fancy. Realistically speaking, it is true that village production plans with all their implications in the way of integrated development are not feasible; and yet to admit this is sheer defeatism and abandonment of planning itself. We cannot accept that we have come to a dead end and this basic objective of planned development from below through the mass effort of the people themselves has to be given up. We have to know the essentials and refuse to take make-believe plans as a substitute for real plans, but we cannot and should not write off the end of integrated development itself. All are agreed that without it we can neither rehabilitate our rural economy nor make any headway towards the chosen goal. If we set our face against the spurious, we will, as a matter of necessity, develop the right understanding and the necessary capacity for right action.

Co-operative Farming

In regard to the co-operatives in general and the need for making them integrated parts of a common structure, whatever the failings in performance, there is hardly any difference of opinion in the country; but, as is well known, about the farming co-operatives there is a real divergence of view and their deve-lopment or its prospect arouses suspicion and fear. This is, as is also well known, due to the co-operative farming being specially associated with communism and experience of its growth in Soviet Union, China and the other communist countries. In this country the proponents of anti-communism—including its agents of foreign countries—openly and in disguise, are making co-operative farming a highly controversial issue and raising a lot of dust which affects the clarity of thought on the subject. Co-operative farming, really joint farming and management in which, as pointed out by the Planning Commission, all agriculturists become agricultural workers and distinction between previous owners and non-owners of land loses its meaning and importance, has to be the destination of agricultural policy and development. This view has been officially accepted as the perspective of agricultural development in India, and though there is a great deal of hidden resistance to it even in the Congress party and in high places in Government, it has now become an important maxim of the economic policy of the country and cannot be branded as a communist or even pseudo-communist view.

· The logic of this view is simple and clear. It has been stated already but may be reiterated that in India because of the extreme sub-division of holdings most of the cultivators are below the very basic standards of cultivation, i.e. most of them even with the knowledge and application of advanced technique cannot, generally speaking, develop the productive potential of land and from agriculture make a living anywhere near the social minimum. For them, from their and national standpoint, creation of much larger units is an absolute necessity, and as they constitute 70 to 80 per cent and in some cases more, of the agricultural population, for them pooling of holdings, cattle, implements and other resources is an essential condition and has, with their consent and co-operation, to be brought about in the interest of maximizing the yield of land and raising the earnings of the cultivators to the level needed for healthy and cultured living. If four-fifths of the cultivators have, as a matter of necessity, to pool their land and resources, it must necessarily involve a fundamental change in the rural economy itself and bring about an economic and social revolution. Most common and from the point of view of the co-operatives and joint farming, the strongest objection to this change is the attachment of the peasants to land and their unwillingness to put their best into it unless the right of ownership is vested in them. This objection is valid as far as it goes. Land-hunger of peasants and their tenacious attachment to land have existed and exist everywhere, including India and has to be taken account of and allowed for. But property sense and accumulation are a strong motive force in all privately owned and operated economies— and the peasants' attachment to land is only a more sharp manifestation of this psychological disposition. It is rooted in history and represents the innate desire for continuity, security and self-impelled activity. Now it has become a strongly ingrained habit and implies fear of the unknown. In any well-conceived and well-operated socialist society this innate desire has to be duly considered and provided for. It, without its acquisitive aspect, is an essentially wholesome and beneficient, motivating force, but in the new context has only a vestigial value in a country like ours. In all countries in which market forces are strong, continuity, security and autonomy of all farmers and not only the small peasants are seriously impaired by the impact of market forces and make action on the part of the community for their protection and defence unavoidable. The peasant proprietor, who lived a self-sufficient life, called no one his master and had a sturdy independence of mind and spirit in most countries has either vanished or is vanishing. Merely individual cultivation when his other needs of farming, credit, marketing, processing and guidance in technique and farm management are provided for by the co-operatives, the community agents or official agencies lose most of their significance as an independent activity and makes them (the peasant proprietors) client, subject to servere pressures from which they cannot protect themselves and have to be protected, and illusory character of their independence has to be brought home to them. In India the preponderance of dwarf holdings is a conclusive reason for making co-operative farming the most effective measure for expansion of production, improvement of technique, rational utilization of land and most desirable allocation of man-power. Without it these necessary gains cannot be realized and this has to be done also in case of large and big landowners. This is so because they are in themselves generally rentiers rather than farmers and combine trading and money-lending with farming, such as it is, and are resistant to change; but much more so because sixty to seventy per cent of the cultivable land which they own has also to be merged into the village estates if the benefits of crop planning, reclamation, conservation and all-round technical development have to be fully realized. Agriculture cannot be developed partly by and for the community, i.e. partly on co-operative and partly on acquisitive basis. The village economy, even more than the economy as a whole, has to have the same purpose, norms and moving spirit, and that cannot happen if owners of most cultivable land keep out of co-operative farming. They, like the small peasants, have also to be won over to this change and not be coerced into it; and this process in their case will take longer and meet with greater resistance. It has first to be introduced and applied among the small peasants, but by demonstration effect, change in the climate of opinion and the pressure of the growing socialist transformation, it has also to be extended to the upper strata of the rural economy and become comprehensive and complete. Individual farming with all that it implies is, it has to be realized, incompatible with a really developed and fully operative socialist economy. It is not, as it is often claimed, a foundation of village democracy. Owing to the forces which it creates and the trends which it fosters, it produces oligarchy, breeds acquisitiveness and poisons the community life at its very base. In the existing context a real socialist community cannot be built on the basis of individual farming.

It has however, to be realized that introduction of co-operative farming, apart from the all-important need for making consent as its basis in our country, has to be preceded by long and careful preparation. That means that economic and social education of the prospective co-operative farmers, understanding on their part of the organizational difficulties and problems and implications of democratic farm management, but more than that it means the spirit of co-operation and capacity for co-operative action has to be developed as far as possible through the formation and functioning of a framework of inter-related co-operatives like the service, credit, marketing, industrial and allied co-operatives for milk supply, dairy farming, organized rural labour and the assumption of many other developments activities, and a big co-operative sector from the village to national level has to be built up of which farming co-operative has to be only one though very essential constituent. It does not mean that all these co-operatives have to be developed before farming co-operatives are introduced or attain importance, but it does mean that the full development of these co-operatives is a very necessary and desirable condition for facilitating the formation of farming co-operatives and ensuring their effective and successful operation. In India our serious handicap is not that unwarranted distrust of co-operative farming is being created and developed for ulterior purposes but that growth of all the other co-operatives, in regard to the necessity and desirability of which all are agreed, is being retarded and distorted because the masses, i.e. disinherited and oppressed sections, for whom the current phrase is the weaker sections of the community, are not aware of their need and importance, are not organized to use them for the well-being of the community which, of course, means primarily their well-being and the motive power needed for their rapid development and operation, owing to the existing power-pattern, has still to be generated. This is the preparation which is needed for the introduction and development of co-operative farming in this country. The latter has to take root in a favourable co-operative soil—really to repeat, be the coping stone of a well-built co-operative structure. It has been made abundantly clear that in this respect the present position[14] is very unsatis-

14. *Co-operative Farming*. There are 1,440 co-operative joint and collective farming societies in the country as on 30-6-1958 out of which 1,098 were

factory and the portents for its being changed for the better are far from favourable. A more detailed consideration of co-operative farming would require that the problems of organization, farm management, apportionment of the value of the produce between owners and workers, finance and capital formation, its relation to the other co-operatives, to local bodies and state and central governments, and also of the steps needed to complete the process of transition from co-operative farming with recognition of and reward for property rights to community farming in which only permissible differential in incomes would be due to differences in the quantity and quality of work and complete equality of status would be attained—all these problems have to be given their due attention and carefully discussed. Working Group on Farming Co-operatives has submitted a report in which most of these problems have been discussed and made recommendations which, largely speaking, can stand the test of scrutiny and careful examination. Action in the pilot projects and the other farming co-operative is

reported to be actually working. The membership of these societies was 39,075 but only 24,687 persons worked on the farms. The rest were sympathizers, absentees or non-working members. The area held by these societies was 3 lakh acres, i.e. less than 0.1 per cent of the total, cultivated area; of this, 2.12 lakh acres of land was under cultivation during 1957-58.

Taking state-wise position of these societies, Punjab accounted for 541 or 37 per cent; Bombay 223 or 15 per cent; Uttar Pradesh 161 or 11 per cent and so on. Madras and Jammu and Kashmir had the lowest number of societies, i.e. 4 each. The total of these socities in the Union territories numbered only 22 out of which Delhi accounted for 13, Manipur 8 and Himachal Pradesh 1. There were no societies in Tripura, Andaman and Nicobar, Laccadive and Minicoy and Pondicherry (*Report of the Working Group on Co-operative Farming*).

In December 1963 the number of co-operative farming societies was 2,298, number of members 45,814 and the area was 293,587 acres. A large number of these co-operatives are spurious and have been formed to evade the provisions of land-legislation, and take advantage of the concessions for which only the co-operatives are eligible.

The programme for the Third Plan is that 3,200 pilot co-operative farms are to be started, roughly ten in each district — "as the first phase in the development programme of co-operative farming". The Study Group's proposal for organization and administration of co-operatives provides a good basis

mostly based upon these recommendations. If the difficulties due to bureaucratic procedure, social inertia and lack of genuine faith of the men in power can be resolved, farming co-operatives can be formed in large numbers and made to work well on the basis of these recommendations. We have extensive experience of many countries to draw upon and a considerable amount of thinking has been done in our country on the vital points of co-operative farming; and all the important issues implicit in co-operative farming can be dealt with with confidence and success. Flexible action on an empirical basis is clearly indicated by the facts of the case, can easily be taken and co-operative farming can move forward on its own power provided our economy as a whole—and rural economy in particular—gets into and begins to move in a socialist orbit· This is a very big proviso, and it is not necessary to repeat, that at present it does not look as if it can and will be fulfilled.

for developing co-operative farming. Co-operative farming has, as stated in the text, to be the highest stage in the development of co-operative structure and if the latter has strength, vigour and momentum, the problem of farming co-operatives would, it can well be anticipated, solve itself and lead to the pooling of land, resources and labour and all the fears of those, even when they are not created by political motives, would be dispelled by the natural course of development. The opposition to it, which is now being worked up is inspired by a set purpose of preserving the power and privileges of interests now in command to arrest the advance of socialism, i.e. put the clock back. Future of co-operative farming, therefore, depends upon the extent to which these interests not only in agriculture but in the economy as a whole, can be neutralized and deprived of their power to block the course of development and change. "The contribution of co-operative farming," in the words of the Planning Commission, "will be significant in the measure in which it develops a voluntary mass movement *under genuine local leadership and as a logical growth of community development and co-operation at village level*" (emphasis added) (*Third Five Year Plan*, P. 209). Co-operative farming has to be an integral part of transformation as a whole, at the village level of course, but not only at the village level. It has to be an all-inclusive transformation and be realized at all levels. The whole economy has to be moved and changed by the spirit needed for making co-operative farming a success—an irresistible development from within.

PANCHAYAT RAJ

Introduction of what is known as democratic decentralization has brought institutions into the field which are intended
to make all the difference to the future of the village and to
its role in the rural and national economy.[75] Panchayats in their
modern form had existed in the country even long before
the end of the British rule, and were assigned more or less the
same functions which under recent legislation have been
assigned to them. There were taluq boards and district boards
and they too had not only self-government but also some developmental functions. These institutions produced, however,

15. The following table gives the figures of Panchayats and their growth
since 1957.

	30 Mar. '61	30 Sept. '57	1 Dec. '61
1. No. of Panchayats	1,60,396	1,93,527	2,05,452
2. No. of villages covered (thousand)	410	502	520
3. Rural Population (Lakhs)	1,973	2,701	3,395
4. Percentage of Rural Population (covered)	74	92	96
5. Average No. of Villages per Panchayat	2.5	2.6	—
6. Average population per Panchayat	1,299	1,396	—
7. Percentage of Villages covered	75	89	97

In 3½ years increase in the number of Panchayats, their coverage and
percentage of villages covered by them showed considerable expansion, but
more important than this is the fact that real significance of their role in
the working of our political system and economy is meant to be changed,
and they are to become an instrument by which system of government
which is, in the words of Mr. Jai Prakash Narain, "an inverted pyramid or
Swaraj from above, has to be changed into Swaraj from below" or "a participating democracy"; and in which there is to be not only decentralization
but also diffusion of authority. They and the co-operatives can, if they
fulfil the purpose which is inherent in the whole scheme, transform our
government, parliamentary democracy and the economy and give them a
truly pluralistic federal and socialist content. That this scheme, with primary area, regional, state and national institutions can make a fundamental
change and alter radically the very basis of our political life is undoubtedly
true. But the essential conditions of realizing this object, as stated in the
text, are sincerity of purpose, shift in the distribution of power and a widely-
shared concern for the future of our people. These conditions are at present
non-existent and there is no indication that they are likely to be created.
A political facade of Panchayats and co-operatives, without any real substance can only breed cynicism and give rise to a revulsion of feelings, and
at best it can mean decentralization without democratization.

negligible results both in self-government and development in their history of 90 years; though there were exceptions but mainly speaking these institutions, it is well-known, had hardly any place in our political and economic development in spite of universal professions in their favour. Now another brave effort is being made and practically the whole country has been covered by what are held to be new institutions, and it is held that they have already created great stir in the countryside in many parts of the country and they will rapidly acquire a decisive importance in self-government, planned development and social change. These institutions have so far been dominated by the well-to-do sections of the village community and like the co-operatives are mostly being used to promote their interests and consolidate their power. There are again exceptions; and though these institutions have not functioned long enough to provide a firm basis for appraisal of their working and result, but from whatever information is avaliable, the conclusion that they can and will redress the balance in favour of weakest section of the community, to use the phrase of the Sarvodayists, the lowliest and the lost, is not borne out by the facts of the case. Most nearly all representatives in these institutions still belong to higher castes and classes and devolution of authority and function on the new institutions have brought about political and administrative decentralization, but they have not meant greater democratization of administration or government to any significant extent. These institutions have wider power and functions, but that means that propertied classes are even in a stronger position and power derived from wealth and economic status has been further increased by the devolution of authority; and as in the case of expansion of co-operative finance, enlargements of resources at their disposal through new taxation, grants and implementation of schemes through them invests them with greater authority which they, as things are, are likely to exercise with a view to entrenching themselves deeper in all key positions in the village economy.

This is not surprising, though, as stated above, it is too early to assess the present position and prospects. What is, however, of interest is that the Panchayats, the Panchayat Samities and the Zila Parishads have been charged with the duty to make over-all planning, formulation of production programme, its implementation, assessment and supervision. From the reports of the two study teams in Panchayat Raj in Andhra Pradesh and Rajasthan it is clear that these institutions are more interested in amenities rather than production and they have neither interest nor ability to undertake over-all planning and execution of plans and generally speaking, they are indifferent to the discharge of the obligation—really hardly appreciate its need. As the main object of decentralization is to 'involve' the people in the development programme of carrying it out with their intelligent co-operation and initiative, the prevailing apathy is obviously a serious hindrance in the way of realizing this object. Another point of vital interest is the question of demarcation of responsibilities between the Panchayats and the co-operatives and provision against the risk of conflict between the two. A working group has examined the question and reported on it. That these institutions have to function in a manner so as to avoid any conflict of jurisdictions or functions due to divergence of views and policies goes without saying. Whatever the line of demarcation and however carefully they adhere to it, they have not only to co-exist in harmony but from the nature of things, reciprocally help each other. It is also fairly clear as has been suggested, that planning in which all general and functional activities can be articulated with reference to economic units of operation is of crucial importance and either Panchayat Samiti or federation of general and functional co-operatives at block level have to perform this cardinal role. Preparation and execution of plan of development, including marketing, price regulation and planned movement of goods and labour, when different co-operatives from primary to national level have been formed and are functioning efficiently and in proper co-relation and co-ordination are the functions which logically belong to and have to be performed by them. But the net-work of co-operatives has not been as yet even conceptually worked out, what to speak of its having been created and brought into an efficient working order. As these co-operatives in their variety of forms are constituted and begin to function as parts of an integral whole, preparation and implementation of over-all plans can, as a process of natural growth, become their responsibility and be discharged with due consideration for efficiency and the needed sustained progress. For the time being, however, Panchayats can assume this responsibility as and when they can and transfer it to the co-operatives when they are in a position to undertake it adequately and well. As it is, from the point of view of integrated development neither of these institutions is equipped to perform these functions and even the state and central government have still to grasp its implication fully or make the consequential changes in their approach, policy and programme. The view that the Panchayats and the co-operatives are the two institutions on which we have to mainly rely for development and socialization of the larger part of our economy, is essentially a sound view; but the social context in which, it may be repeated, they are to have their being and function, is of far greater importance than structural arrangement and relations. Importance of this new living context is not yet realized and the fact that the existing context is a distorting factor is not even clearly understood. Lack of this understanding is the source of our confusion and frustration.

CO-OPERATION MUST SUCCEED

The oft-quoted lines of the Rural Credit Survey—"Co-operation has failed but co-operation must succeed"—imply that there is no alternative to co-operation in India if derelict rural economy of India is to be set on the path to recovery and regeneration. As stated above, in spite of expansion of credit and working capital etc. of the co-operatives, co-operation still has remained a failure; and unless causes, which inhibit its recovery and prevent its potential strength from being tapped, are removed, there is no possibility of co-operation becoming a sound proposition or realizing its capacity for developing a dynamics of its own. It has been stated already that co-operation is both the means and end of socialism, i.e. a truly co-operative economy is socialism and the co-operatives are the most effective instruments of advancing towards and realizing it. "Society as a whole should," as Lenin pointed out, "represent a universal co-operative when socialism becomes not only its destination but also when it is its driving force and its guiding principle." This can be done only if forces which are favourable for its growth are increasingly gaining ascendancy and those which are unfavourable are clearly in retreat. This is just what has not happened and the former, i.e. the forces which can create favourable conditions for socialism, are in retreat in this country and the adverse forces are increasingly gaining ascendancy. Dr. Daniel Thorner, who undertook a country-wide study of agricultural co-operatives at the instance of the Indian Co-operative Union and submitted a valuable report has stated, "People like to think that a comprehensive, well-supported, well thought-out Government programme of setting up co-operatives will change the pattern of village power. The evidence suggests that the structure of village power has imposed and will continue to impose its own pattern on the co-operatives."[16] The evidence which Dr. Daniel Thorner has collected and cited fully supports this statement. He further adds, "Firmly lodged in chief position of village power today, the dominant families stand ready to seize the lion's share of the vast programme of co-operative development."[17] Rural Credit Survey had also practically stated the same views, and pointed out that, "the state is or ought to be a combination of the weak at the top" to assist and promote, "the combination of the weak at the bottom".[18] That it ought to be a combination for the weak is obviously needed but since

16. *Prospects of Co-operation in Indian Agriculture,* Para 83.
17. *Ibid.,* p. 89.
18. *Rural Credit Survey,* p. 177.

the Rural Credit Survey was published in 1954 it has more and more become a combination of the strong not for the weak but against them; and the result is that the dominant families have seized "the lion's share of the vast programme of co-operative development". This is the root cause of the continued failure of co-operation in India. It must succeed; but it will only if and when those in power really believe in it, do what they can to help what is generally called a "mass upsurge from below" and throw their weight in its favour.

Chapter Nine

ROLE OF LABOUR

SHIFT IN POWER

A socialist economy is by definition an economy which is managed by and for the workers—by those who earn their living and whose earnings are determined by their contributions to national income measured by the amount and quality of work. That means that it is an economy in which there are no social parasites, power is an incident of function, only permissible differentials of income are those which are needed as incentives for harder and better work, social security, common services and social assistance for the needy and the unfortunate are provided and paid for by the community and it is known and realized that at the highest level, work cannot be measured in terms of money and has to be performed more and more as a way of life rather than as a means of making a living. The state in such a society has to be a workers' state because otherwise it cannot be established, developed and maintained, i.e. all the objects referred to above cannot be realized and the community, which means the workers taken together, cannot make the state an instrument of its will and well-being.

The essentials of a socialist society have been very briefly restated above to bring out the point that the very discussion of the role of labour implies that the worker has not yet come to his own and the economy has to strive, if it is to be truly more and more a socialist economy, to make his increasing ascendency a matter of paramount importance and therefore give it the highest priority. The extent to which this is consciously aimed at and realized has to be the criterion of the process of the establishment of a socialist economy having been started in earnest. Labour, in this context, of course, does not mean merely industrial labour. In India, the latter category, i.e. industrial labour being less than 2 per cent of the labour force, included all who have to work for their living and privilege and property do not in any way determine their income or position. In a class society it is not easy to define or delimit this category with any degree of precision; and yet practically speaking those who belong to it are either allied with it or subservient to the propertied, and privileged classes can be differentiated from those who are not in this category. Caste being such an important factor in Indian life, class divisions are further complicated by its operation. But nevertheless it is not difficult to frame or execute our policy in a manner as to make advance towards the workers' state and society an end and the measure of social progress. Increasing ascendency of the workers in the first place, of course, has to mean that all the disadvantages from which he suffers and disabilities under which he labours, have to be neutralized, and this itself is obviously a gigantic task. But it is not enough to lessen or redress these discriminations. It is necessary to realize that the workers' rehabilitation necessarily means not only that they have to share the highest benefits of the community life but also to replace the privileged classes in the positions of importance and authority and do all that is necessary to make this transfer as complete as possible. This sounds anti-democratic but is really the essence of democracy. Social mobility, about the necessity of which in democracy, there can be no difference of opinion, implies not only that all, however lowly their birth and whatever the means of their parents, can go to any position right to the top if they have the necessary ability but also that dice are not loaded in anyone's favour and rules of the game require that no one can attain or retain positions of power or authority who has not risen to it only by dint of sheer merit. The state has to use all its means, resources and measures, if socialism is its goal and informs its decisions and actions, to introduce and accelerate the process of transfer as much as possible and bring forces into play which reduce greatly the need for the state itself directly intervening in this transformation. It can and should back these forces; but mostly within the right framework the transformation has to be a natural process and proceed from within.

The Congress party, Sarvodayists and the political leaders who are running the government of this country, are for collaboration, mutual understanding and agreed action for resolving the difficulties in industrial relations and promoting industrial peace, for they believe in safeguarding and promoting the interests of labour through negotiations, mutual trust and concord and not by militancy in approach and action. In this they, according to them, are following in the footsteps of Mahatma Gandhi, for he saw nothing but harm in making conflict an instrument of advance in the position and conditions of labour. Replacement of the propertied classes, who wield economic and political power at present, by concerted efforts and organized action by the workers can, from this standpoint, be viewed as a policy of social antagonism and therefore not in keeping with the approach of goodwill and peace. The issue is important—really fundamental—for with it is connected the whole concept of class struggle as a means of establishing and maintaining socialism. It cannot be fully discussed here, but if it is conceded, as it has to be, that socialism must involve the transfer of power and authority from the minority which in the existing circumstances, is all-powerful and is in fact exercising decisive control over all political, economic and social institutions and using it to preserve its highly privileged position, to the workers in the widest sense, it is necessary to devise measures and frame programme of action by which this end can be achieved. It has, on this premise, to be the role of industrial labour to act in unison, realize the necessity of bringing about this shift of power and regard it as a pre-eminently desirable object of social endeavour. Government's faith in socialism and its ability to realize it can be measured by the extent to which it is aware of this need and its power to promote policies and measures by which it can be fulfilled. There is no need to inflame passions, accentuate social tensions or make social hatred the basis for the formulation or execution of social policies if labour organizations— all such organizations and not only trade unions—are strong, socially conscious and aware of the need for building up their mass power and can count upon the support and approbation of the Government at all levels to back them to change the balance of forces in their favour and know that this change is needed in the interests of the community. The Government can really adopt a positive role in this respect and guide the non-state organizations to look ahead, practise self-denial for capital accumulation, and guard against infantalism of all sorts and perform a constructive role in introducing and developing socialist society. Real democratic processes imply that a change in the minds and behaviour of men can be brought about by pursuasion and habit of co-operative endeavour with a social purpose. Socialism has to mean a new social equilibrium and a new poise in the minds and conduct of men, but it has to be understood that the existing disequilibrium is the result of contradictions which cannot be resolved merely by pious intentions and wishes. A plea for building up organized strength of the workers as a necessity for bringing about fundamental social change is not and need not be a plea for violence. There is a risk of organization of labour being used for social strife, but this risk is very much greater if the present pattern of power is continued and consolidated, creative democratic processes are frustrated and the workers are either unorganized or badly organized or rendered ineffective by the designs of those in power or apathy or even antipathy of the Government avowedly committed to socialism. Unfortunately the trends at work show that the possibility of new balance of power being attained with active support and guidance of the Government is rather remote. Organization of industrial workers, though capable of giving a fight in some cases on disputed issues, are not yet a force for building up the economy and being divided, among themselves, are in no position to develop or use their own united strength even for self-defence. Non-industrial labour is, as is well known, practically not organized at all and peasants and agricultural workers are particularly in a defenceless position. Attitude of the Government, though in theory sympathetic, has in effect not promoted the development of labour organizations and not contributed to their strength or growth. Labour has to be organized and become an autonomous force in the economy and its organized strength has to be used to provide first counter-vailing power to check and later to reduce the growing might of the interests now accupying the centres of authority and eventually to bring about transfer of power from them to the workers. So far the workers have lost than gained ground since planning began in this country; and the chances are that the position will get worse before a change for the better gets under way.

Labour Policy

The whole economic policy of the Government of India, broadly speaking, has to be taken as labour policy, for its content has,. from the social standpoint, to be beneficial for the workers and it has to be so formulated as to promote their well-being and importance in the working of the economy. In a limited sense labour policy is taken to mean the policy relating to industrial labour. As the whole book is intended to analyse and assess our economic policy in theory and practice from the socialist point of view, in this chapter it is necessary to confine attention to labour policy from the limited standpoint but including in its scope a brief appraisal of the impact of economic policy on the position and prospects of agricultural labour owing to its over-shadowing importance in the working and development of the economy.

Labour policy in relation to industrial labour—labour employed in large-scale organized industries—has been framed and applied on the assumption that while welfare of the workers has to be promoted and they have to be placed in a less unfavourable position to negotiate with the employers, main reliance has to be placed on the processes of conciliation, arbitration and adjudication for resolving or reducing differences and area of agreement has to be widened by bringing the workers and employers together at conference table and the Government can, by holding the scales even, achieve a reasonable settlement of disputes and provide a basis for agreed action in all matters affecting the welfare of the workers. This approach is taken to be in keeping with the essentials of a policy of general good-will (the Gandhian approach) for all and realization of the good of the workers by relying mainly upon peaceful methods for improving industrial relations and placing them on a sound and stable basis. It is not necessary to examine and evaluate this approach in the context of the existing situation in India or in general terms. That conflict between the employers and employees should be reduced to the minimum if this can be done without sacrificing the interest of the employees and redressing the balance in their favour for the development of the economy owing to the odds being against them in the existing distribution of resources and power is a point which can be readily admitted; but if it is not to mean merely an empty platitude, political authority of the state has definitely to be used to support the worker and it has to be assumed that the balance cannot be redressed in his favour unless it is known and realized that the Government cannot be neutral between the employers and employees and within the limits set by the good of the community as a whole, it has, if socialism is to be the objective of its policy, to do all that it can to give the workers a growing share of the national income and increasingly make them a decisive factor in shaping the future. This, of course, assumes that the Government itself is not only above suspicion but it declares its policy in unambiguous terms of throwing its entire weight in favour of the workers and acts upon it resolutely with full understanding of its implications. This can happen only if it is not exposed to the pressure from within and without of the employers and their allies; and can, if such pressure is exercised, resist it with confidence and success and bring it home to those who exercise it the futility of their endeavours. This has not happened and is not happening, and explains why, in spite of some real gains in the position of the worker since independence, he has lost more than he has gained[1] and cannot count upon the government using its power to safeguard and promote his well-being or make him more and more master of the future. Militancy in industrial relations becomes unnecessary and undesirable when the worker himself can more than hold his own against the forces arrayed against him and the state becomes a bulwark of strength in his favour. Militant action has to be avoided and the necessity of recourse to it minimized; but essential condition for this is obviously that industrial peace should mean that the weak, the worker, can have faith in the bona fide of the state, full assistance from it for retrieving his position is freely and fully available and the chronic and continuous pressure to which he is subjected owing to the very nature of economic structure is counter-balanced by the pressures which the worker can build for himself through mass organization and mass strength and, as stated above, the state can muster its forces to re-inforce that pressure. This is the only way in which there can be equality between the employers and the employees and they can face each other with assurance and collaboration in their own interests and that of the community. This is the condition under which fruitful class collaboration can be realized and class conflict in industrial relations avoided, it being, of course, assumed that the latter, i.e. industrial relations, have to be so changed and developed as to eliminate altogether the class of employers who owe their position to private property and accumulated wealth, and replace it by organs of the community who will be a party to negotiated settlements with the workers but will not assume the role of the employers standing apart from and above them. That

1. Report at the 26th Session of the All-India Trade Union Congress, January 6-12, 1961. p. 33.

means, of course, that true co-operation between management and labour is only possible in a classless society. As things are, all that is possible is that the cause of conflict, be removed as far as possible by making the state a custodian of the interests of the workers and those of the community and ensuring that this position of trust is adhered to in letter and spirit. It is necessary to add that in India this condition has not been created so far, and the framework within which real industrial peace can be realized has not been provided.

It is not necessary to examine and analyse the whole labour policy in India in all its aspects. There have, as stated already, been improvements in some respects and labour has been able to make use of statutory gains to make advance towards a position in which its weakness has to a certain extent been definitely reduced. We are, as stated above, nowhere near the position in which the state itself becomes the guardian of the interests of the workers and protects and promotes them with all its resources and strength. But nevertheless there have been distinct gains. "Those who have seen, worked and lived in 1939," in the words of Mr. S. A. Dange, the well-known communist labour leader, "and see things today, definitely see a change, an advance in the life and demeanour of the working class in India."[2] This is so and yet it is not true that labour either in public or private sector has become an object of serious concern and paramountcy of the need for making its well-being the most important goal of social policy is recognized in theory and granted in practice. The gains, which have

2. Mr. Dange enumerates seven "vital counts" in his report on which the workers since the end of the war, have made advance. They, according to him, are (1) Substitution of 8 hour for 9 hour day in the prevailing practice; (2) bonus gratuity with provident fund have become common; (3) contributory health insurance for industrial worker has been introduced; (4) holidays with pay become a right; (5) laws and conventions govern service conditions; (6) right of the worker to demand neutralization of rise in the cost of living has been conceded; and (7) the case for standard rates for the job, gradations and minima has been conceded even though standardization of wages and their differentials has yet to be achieved.

been realized, are really more in keeping with the needs of a welfare, rather than a socialist society, and even at that, they do not compare at all favourably with the gains of labour even in most of the capitalist countries like the U.S.A., Germany, France and Japan since the end of the war.

WAGE POLICY

It was stated in the Second Five Year Plan that "a wage policy which aims at a structure at rising real wages requires to be evolved".[3] It is pointed out a little later that real wages in India have mostly been stagnant and in some important industries have fallen since 1951, and that in spite of the fact that according to official estimates, our national income has risen by 42 per cent and per capita income by 16 per cent from 1950-51 to 1960-61. Even industrial labour, it is clear, has not derived any material benefit from development and increase of 94 per cent in industrial production since 1950-51 has not to any significant extent contributed to "the rising level of real wages". This is a fact which needs to be explained, and a thorough examination of the entire position needs to be undertaken in order to disclose the causes of the stagnation of real wages of industrial labour. It was expected that the Committee appointed by the Government of India to inquire into the distribution of wealth and income in the country would be able to give an answer to this fundamental question. But in the report of the Committee (The Mahalnobis Committee) the position has not been analysed to disclose the causes of the stagnation of real wages of industrial labour; and the presumption that bulk of increase in the value of industrial production in the last decade has been appropriated by the owners of industries, can be taken to be perfectly legitimate and valid unless it is convincingly contradicted by statistical evidence. There is hardly any chance of the contradiction being provided by objective investigation of the position; and it, therefore,

3. *Second Five Year Plan*, p. 578.

can be assumed that appropriation of the material gains of industrial expansion mostly by the owners of large-scale organized industries is an index and a measure of their dominant position in the economy in general and in the industrial structure in particular.

A wage policy in a planned economy has necessarily to aim at a structure of wages which expresses and embodies principles of national wage-fixation in accordance with its basic social objectives which in India has to be taken to mean realization of a socialist society. "In spite of the best efforts," according to the Second Five Year Plan, "have been unable to evolve a consistent formula"4 for condification of fair wages. The tribunals, industrial courts, arbitrators, adjudicators, wage boards and various committees and commissions, including the two Pay Commissions, have failed to evolve any general principles or even a body of case laws with reference to which a structure of wages can be built up or developed, and all important recommendations with regard to wages have been formulated and discussions taken on more or less an *ad hoc* basis. Experience of all countries, including the socialist countries, shows how difficult it is to rationalize a wage-structure, and a fully integrated wage-structure with its lower and upper limits and its differentials in each industry and between different industries — i.e. its vertical and horizontal relativities — rationally determined and standardized does not exist anywhere. It is a task of bewildering complexity to build such a structure and much more so when it has to be evolved out of a position which has developed in a completely haphazard and accidental manner. The task is difficult and its accomplishment must necessarily be a matter of major adjustments spread over time. Difficult as the task is, it has to be faced, and earnest efforts made to formulate its principles and implement them with determination and clarity of purpose. This is just what has not even been attempted so far, and it is clear from the Third

4. *Ibid.*

Five Year Plan that there is hardly any prospect of the attempt being made in earnest in the current plan period to advance towards this accomplishment.

In spite of the position being ill-defined and vague, there has been a shift in approach towards wage-determination which is, to use the words of Lord Amulree, in accord with "current mood and ethical opinions, not right according to law, but right according to prevailing ideas". The tribunals etc. have generally assumed that the worker is entitled to minimum wage, the amount of which should be fixed with reference to nutritional and other minimum requirements, reasonable differentials have been permitted and the concept of paying capacity of industry has been stated, though not clearly defined. The view that wages are more a problem of social ethics rather than pure economics has been very largely accepted, and the implication of the Declaration of Peace Conference in which it was stated that "in right and in fact labourer or a human being should not be treated as a merchandize or an article of commerce" has received a large measure of assent. This has not altered radically the basis or practice of wage determination in India, but it has changed the current moral and ethical opinion, i.e. prevailing idea of what is right in the domain of wages.

The Planning Commission in the Second Five Year Plan clearly indicated the need of appointing a commission to enquire into 'the role of wages, profits and prices taking into account the declared social objective of the community,' but though wage census which was to precede this inquiry has been taken in hand and a number of wage boards for various industries have been appointed, a comprehensive examination and revision not only of wages but also of wage-structure has still to be undertaken. It is not yet realized that wage policy in relation to industrial labour must necessarily be a part of the policy on which the entire income structure of the country has to be based. The wage structure has, in its wide sense, to be an integral part of the whole income structure of trade, professions, services and employment in administration and service enterprises. New economic inter-relationships have to be created among the different economic sectors and pursuits, old relativities have to be replaced by new relativities, payment by results has to be maintained and extended and it has to be clearly understood that in a socialist society or in a society which is advancing towards it, the qualities needed for filling the topmost position in the economy with success and distinction cannot be evoked or evaluated in terms of monetary awards and more and more reliance has to be placed on a growing sense of social obligation, insight into social processes and creative urge of men who are called upon to discharge the highest social functions in a socialist economy in the making. In other words, income structure has to be integrated, has to express and realize new social values and the existing anomalies and contradictions have to be resolved in the light of new basic concepts and the emergence of new contradictions has to be provided against. The Pay Commission has, as stated before, chosen to disregard the need for a comprehensive approach, but it nevertheless remains imperative and without it, a rational wage structure even for industrial labour, which is less than 2 per cent of the total working force of the country, cannot be evolved. One has to be vividly aware of the fact that the replacement of an income structure based upon heirarchical, inequaliatarian and acquisitive social assumptions by another based upon new social values is a task of immense difficulty, and yet it has to be faced and accomplished within the limitations of the past and its legacies. Without this integrated approach there can be no rational and adequate wage policy in the country and without it we will not be able to develop a new system of social relationship, new social norms and new social forces, i.e. we will not be able to realize a socialist society. This is the reason why a new wage policy is such an urgent practical necessity. The essential purpose of this policy has to be a change of the whole macrocosm of the economy. There can and should be no question of making the existing macrocosm the basis of the new wage policy.

This approach does not find a place in the labour and wage policies of the country and the result has been that in matters of wage determination we have as yet no guiding general principles and all the irrational diversities, anomalies and contradictions of even the existing wage-structures of industrial labour remain unresolved. This is an admitted fact and it is not necessary to dwell upon it at any length. The fact of the matter is that owing to disregard of the interests of labour the wage-fixation and the impact of inflationary pressures, real wages of industrial labour have been almost stagnant in the last fourteen years and in the last nine years they have actually fallen.[5] Research in the problems of a new wage-structure

5. Two index numbers of Real Wages of factory employees one with 1939 as base (1) and the other with 1947 as base (2) are given below:

Index Number of Real Wages

	I	II		I	II		I	II
1947	78.4	107.4	1951	92.2	116.6	1956	105.4	134.5
1948	84.4	107.4	1952	101.6	127.6	1957	104.5	133.5
1949	91.7	116.9	1953		131.1	1958	103.4	125.6
1950	90.1	114.0	1955	113.5	144.9	1959		123.9

These indices show that in 1952 real wages rose nearly to pre-war level; and after reaching the highest in 1955, they practically fell again in 1959 to the pre-war level. These indices are a rough measure of the movement of real wages, but they do indicate that the worker has practically gained nothing in real earnings since 1939, and all the gains of development, so far as he is concerned, have been appropriated by his employers. In the meanwhile the index of profits in all industries with 1950 as base went up to 158.7 in 1958. A recent inquiry confirms this conclusion and shows that since 1955 industrial wages have been stagnant. (*The Reserve Bank of India Bulletin*, April 1964).

There are wide variations in the movement of real wages between industries, states and zones and the general indices therefore have significance only within broad limits. There are large pockets in which real wages were below pre-war level in 1959.

This conclusion is further supported by results of an official inquiry on *Movement of Minimum Wages during the Plan Period*. The conclusion of this inquiry has been summarized by a writer in *Economic Weekly* in the following words, "The industrial worker has thus at best held on to the pre-war level of wages. The workers in the unorganized section are worse off as increase in their earnings has not kept pace with the rise of prices. The actual position may be worse than it appears from a comparison of

as a part of a new income structure has not been undertaken and even its need and importance is hardly appreciated. The theory of wages which generally provides the premises on which the problems of wages are formulated and discussed have hardly any relation to our actual problems and in this respect, as in many others, we are at sea without any rudder or compass. Industrial labour is really in a more fortunate position in this regard. There has been at least a profession of interest in its welfare, a lot of industrial legislation has been undertaken, and through agreements and conventions,6 the

wages and price level since the working class cost of living index is out-dated and does not take into account new wants of the workers" (*Economic Weekly*, Vol. XIV No. 7 p. 302).

This conclusion carries its own moral. The industrial worker, in spite of all the advantages he has, has hardly been able just to maintain the pre-war position while the non-industria' worker, without any organization and protection, finds forces against him too strong for him and with rising cost of living has to acquiesce in the falling level of real wages. It is obvious that under these conditions the object of having a new wage structure with a rising level of wages cannot be realized. The whole position needs to be re-examined in this context and measures devised for safeguarding the position of the worker. Development, in which vast majority of the people in the country have either stagnant or falling real incomes, is obviously for them development in reverse, whatever the general indications of economic growth statistically may be taken to imply or point to.

6. Among other conventions, the one adopted at the 15th Indian Labour Conference which met in July 1957 has acquired a special importance. The Conference is a tripartite body consisting of the representatives of central and state governments, employers and employees. The 15th Conference adopted unanimously a resolution indicating the criteria for minimum wage determination as a guide for all wage-fixing authorities. According to it minimum wage was to be fixed to provide for a family of three consumption units nutrition according to a standard prescribed by experts and also clothing, housing, fuel, lighting and other miscellaneous items of expenditure according to standards indicated in the Resolution. This is the famous need-based formula which became the basis of demand of Central Government employees in a short general strike to which they resorted and which ended in failure and also in the reports of the various wage-boards and other wage-fixing authorities. The Second Pay Commission considered this resolution in their discussion of minimum remuneration and came to the conclusion that it was not feasible to make this formula the basis of wage-fixation. The wage-boards, which have considered this question have also,

work of wage-fixing authorities, a shift in the prevailing ideas and, of course, work of the unions, the matter has at least received some consideration. This does not apply to workers in unorganized small industries, agricultural labour and many other categories of workers who are unorganized, unprotected and undefended and have even no nuisance value, who have suffered much more in the matter of earnings and provision of amenities and services. And yet the earnings of even industrial

while conceding the fairness of the demand for fixing wages on the basis of needs, not based their recommendations according to the formulation of the 15th Indian Labour Conference. The question is very complex and it is not possible to discuss it here in its various aspects. But the point of the argument against it that, in spite of 42 per cent increase in material income from 1951-52 to 1960-61 the country cannot afford to grant minimum wages based upon an authentic estimate of minimum requirements of nutrition etc. needs to be understood for it means that now and for a fairly long time to come the country is not in a position to grant wages based upon what is really an estimate of physiological minimum. This implies a severe criticism of food policy of the country since 1951 and inadequate appreciation of social priorities in planning. Provision of this minimum has to be the highest priority in our planning, and the gap between it and what the economy, with its present economic and financial structure, can afford is really the measure not only of our poverty but also of inverted understanding of our real problems. Speedy reduction and early elimination of the gap has to be, if we know the implications of planning, our task no 1 and its accomplishment our real social imperative. This aspect of the matter has received no consideration so far; and after having demonstrated to its satisfaction that provision of the minimum is beyond its and country's means at present, the Government seems to have taken the position that nothing needs to be and can be done about it. If decentralized formulation and execution of plans from below, however, becomes a reality, need-based formula for an estimate of requirements and income on the one hand and an estimate of the available resources on the other—i.e. the budget of needs and means—would become the very basis of planning in real terms, i.e. real planning. For this, however, it is necessary not only to provide a framework of democratic decentralization but create conditions under which it can acquire substance and develop its own drive and momentum. These conditions are at present non-existent. All that central government employees asked for was that increase in their cost of living since 1947 should be neutralized. That the Government of India could not even accept the legitimacy of this demand, even if they could not meet it, is a good index of the poverty of our social thinking on our basic issues.

labour have in real terms fallen in the decade of planning, development and expansion of national income; and this
is, to repeat, clearly indicative of the fact that those who are
at the helm of the economy and otherwise count in directing
and controlling its course are concerned much more about the
interest, income and position of the social class to which they
belong rather than about the earnings and welfare of labour,
including industrial labour.

INDUSTRIAL DEMOCRACY

Industrial democracy, according to the Second Five Year
Plan, "is a pre-requisite for the establishment of a socialist
society". It is really more, it is in its wide sense, its very substance for it means that the worker is the moving spirit of
society, its most important object of concern and real instrument for the realization of socialism—i.e. he is both the end
and the means of a socialist society—it is run by and for him.
Among the objects mentioned for achieving this object are
increase of productivity, making the worker fully conscious of
his role in the economy and satisfying his urge for self-expression. This view was clearly stated in the Second Five Year Plan
and has been re-affirmed in the Third. The content of this concept is not and should not be merely industrial paternalism,
introduction of welfare schemes and patronizing the workers.
Industrial democracy which has to be the basis for establishment of a socialist society cannot merely be a lubricant of
industrial relations to minimize conflict and friction but a
means through which every undertaking can be developed into
a real co-operative guild which can through a vertical and
horizontal federation at different levels right to the apex,
become the very appartus of a socialist society and its animating spirit. Yugoslavia is perhaps the only country in which an
earnest effort is being made to implement industrial democracy of this conception. There is association of labour with
management in a number of capitalist countries and good
results have been achieved through it; but it is not intended

to make any radical social change in society through it and they have in fact strengthened conservative rather than radical trends. In the communist countries in theory and practice good of the workers is the most important consideration and they have very impressive and significant achievements to their credit; and yet industrial democracy in these countries has in fact not been realized because conditions for its development were not favourable and repression of the spirit of democracy was the rule. Now conscious efforts are being made in these countries to introduce and apply correctives, and movement in the right direction is under way even though its development is not at all even. It should, if the present trends gain strength and operate on a deeper and wider basis, make industrial democracy the most important governing principle of the economy of these countries, its very life-force. That is what it has to become if it has to be a success and fulfil itself. Industrial democracy, or rather the form which it takes in a particular context and meaning, experience shows clearly, depends upon the social milieu in which it takes shape and functions. Association of labour with management can be of use even if it is the result of benevolent paternalism on the part of the employers, but all such association is not industrial democracy— certainly not industrial democracy which has to be a pre-requisite of a socialist society. Industrial democracy can operate in the real sense only if basic social premise of society is that functional differences do not and should not involve social divisions and all social barriers in the way of upward vertical movements of individuals and groups would be progressively reduced and finally removed. Without this operative principle industrial democracy cannot even be introduced, much less realized.

In India active association of labour with management has been introduced more as a concession to socialist tradition and as a frill of policy statement than as a principle of basic social change in spite of the professed object of building a socialist society through it. Urge to self-expression has figured in the statement of the measure but there is no indication at all that there has been any earnest thinking on this fundamental point or its implications are even understood. The measures taken to bring about participation of labour in management are lacking in earnestness of purpose and determination and actual results, as pointed out in the footnote,7 could not have been

7. Association of labour with management has been provided by creating Management Councils. The function of these councils, on which the employers and employees are equally represented, are grouped under four categories:

(a) the general objectives;

(b) matters in respect of which they have the right to discuss and in respect of which they have the right to receive information and offer suggestions;

(c) matters in respect of which they have the right to be consulted;

(d) and those in respect of which they are to be entrusted with responsibility which can be taken to mean, those in relation to which they exercise administrative power.

Under (a) Councils are under the obligation to improve working and living conditions, increase productivity, encourage suggestions from employees, assist in the administration of laws and agreement, serve as authentic channels of communications and create among the employees a live sense of participation. Under (b) are covered such matters as general economic situation of the concern, the state of markets, annual balance sheets and long-term expansion, etc. Under (c) matters on which the councils have to be consulted are included general administration of Standing Orders, introduction of new methods of production and reduction and cessation of operation. And under (d) are matters of welfare schemes, safety measures, vocational training, schedules of working hours and payment of rewards for suggestions. The Joint Management Councils do not exercise any administrative authority over matters other than covered by (d), and though they are not unimportant, they do not affect the economic administration of the enterprise or the exercise of authority. The workers' representatives are nominated by Trade Unions and management, and the collective bargaining is excluded from purview of the Councils. This is the keeping with the practice in all other countries, as it is important that the Trade Unions should not be bye-passed if their co-operation is to be obtained for working the schemes of association.

In 1962 this scheme was being tried in 16 undertakings in public sector and 37 in private sector. This means that we have experience of 53 undertakings in both private and public sector which have given this scheme even a trial. None of the big undertakings in public or private sector have shown interest in this scheme; Hindustan Steel, Hindustan Chemicals, Hindu-

more meagre or disappointing. Industrial democracy, to repeat, is an instrument and integral part of a socialist economy in the making; and it can be established and grow only if there is a shift in the distribution of power, the orbit of the whole economy is changed and forces, which make it inevitable and create their own compulsions because they are backed by the

stan Aircraft, Neivelli Lignite, Heavy Electrics, Bharat Electronics, Hindustan Shipyard, the Reserve Bank of India, the State Bank of India, Air India, Indian Air Corporation and Life Insurance Corporation have all kept themselves out of it and shown no inclination to introduce the schemes even on an experimental basis. Among the big units in public sector Hindustan Machine is the only exception and it is reported that a Joint Management Council will soon start functioning in it. Among the big industrial undertakings in the private sector Tata Iron and Steel is the only concern, which is reported to have introduced this scheme but it is also one of the seven undertakings in the private sector which have not furnished information about its working. The Tatas as a whole, the Birlas, the Associated Cement, the Wimco, the other giant concerns and monopolies, which, as is well known, represent massive concentration of power in this country, are not even disposed to consult their employees, give them information or invite their suggestions or even let them administer their welfare schemes or supervise safety measures. This is the net result of all the talk of labour participation in management which has figured so prominently in the discussion of the problems of industrial relations and industrial management. "The Third Five Year Plan has," according to the Planning Commission, "to make its own contribution to the evolution of labour policy and the realisation of its basic aims" (*The Third Five Year Plan*, p. 253). In the exposition of approach and outlook we are told on the basis of labour policy and realization of its basic aims "a new type of community is being created in which indivduals and groups are moved more by a sense of mutual obligation than the spirit of acquisitiveness or making of private gains at the expense of the general well-being" (*Ibid*). The facts make it unnecessary to make any comments on these statements or the present position or prospects. On this basis it will be impossible even for a most incorrigible optimist to feel anything remotely like a glow of hope about the spirit of acquisitiveness passing away or even materially abating in the country. The Planning Commission speaks of the Second Five Year Plan having evolved a scheme of labour participation in management to give the workers a sense of belonging and stimulate their interest in higher productivity. These facts are known to the Planning Commission and yet in complete disregard of facts they postulate that a new type of community is being created in which a sense of mutual obligation will govern the economy. Words lose their meaning when they are used in a manner so unrelated to the actual

masses, are brought into play. In an economy in which in the last fourteen years disparities have increased, income and wealth, according to all available evidence, have been more inequitably distributed and at all levels greater concentration of economic power is taking place, industrial democracy, not merely as a prelude to socialism but its essential part cannot but have odds all against it. The spirit of industrial democracy cannot prevail in India by merely active association of labour with management. In an economy in which large industries employ about 2 per cent of the total working force and contri-

---

facts. Gap between professions and performance is very wide in most spheres of our social policy, but perhaps in respect of industrial democracy it is about the widest.

No independent assessment of the working of the scheme in the under-takings about which information is available has been made. According to an authoritative assessment not much has been achieved in regard to the delegation of administrative responsibility, on very few occassions consulta-tion has been made on matters on which consultations have been prescribed in the agreement and neither the workers seek information on economic position of the undertaking, its finances, its marketing problems nor do the undertakings offer such information voluntarily. The gains of the scheme are reported to be improvement in production and productivity, a better understanding between the workers and the management, and stabilization of labour force in spite of increase in absenteeism. These gains, such as they are, are something to be thankful for, but they themselves are neither a portent nor a promise for the future. The fact is that scrappy information about the working of the schemes in some relatively small undertakings provide very slender basis for judgement. In all major respects, even this assessment points to the results being anything but re-assuring. They are not even a beginning of a new chapter in "industrial relations" from the conservative standpoint, what to speak of creating a new community with a newly awakened sense or mutual obligations.

Mr. S. S. Khera has given the evaluation of the present position in regard to industrial democracy and says, "I would evaluate the results so far achieved rather in terms of association without involvement in managerial responsibility which falls far short of the concept of what workers' participa-tion in management really connotes." S. S. Khera, *Government in Business*, p. 186.

This is really another masterly understatement by a senior member of the Indian Civil Service, who has had very special opportunities of knowing the inner working of public industrial undertakings. The scheme in terms of real industrial democracy has been, in fact, a complete farce:

bute 8 or 9 per cent to national income, worker in agriculture, small industries, trade and services has to become a decisive factor through co-operatives and otherwise because it develops self-government in the more-important economic institutions of the economy before industrial democracy begins to take shape and become its most important feature. As this has not happened and is not happening even remotely, outlook for industrial democracy in the country cannot but be extremely depressing.

TRADE UNIONS

Trade unions have necessarily to play a very important role in development and social transformation. They have to perform their conventional role by increasing the bargaining power of labour, promoting and safeguarding interest in respect of wages, conditions and hours of work, being vigilant against the violation of its statutory rights, generally speaking working for its welfare, if necessary, organizing and leading strikes and assuming and discharging the obligation on behalf of the workers for fulfilling the terms of contracts and guarding against their breach by the employers. These functions have been assigned to them all over the world by the course of economic evolution, and they have to perform them as best as they can. In their performance thay have, as a matter of necessity, to build up their organizational strength and solidarity, educate their members, foster and develop habit of concerted action and create a sense of belonging to a new social class. All this is necessary if they have to create a unity of thought, purpose and action among the workers and use it in their interest. Even to perform their conventional role members of the unions have to acquire an intelligent understanding of their problems, to know the place of their industry in the economy and of their union in the industry, to have and throw up leaders of ability and integrity and to learn to think and act in very wide terms.

In all countries experience has brought home to the unions the necessity of going beyond the limits of the conventional role and undertaking wider responsibilities. They have—really have had to — become an important and more and more a decisive political factor, organize themselves for political action to protect themselves and promote their interests and much more to bring about fundamental changes in the economic and political systems and align themselves with all forces working for this object on a national and international scale. According to the Marxian view it is the historic destiny of organized industrial labour, in their own interest and that of mankind, to organize, lead and bring about social revolution, abolish all classes including its own and start a new epoch in human history. Their relation to the other classes in the performance of the role is a matter in regard to which there is a difference of opinion, but that the unions are and have to be a political factor of great importance in shaping the affairs and future of man and cannot, therefore, avoid assuming wide responsibilities is a matter on which, experience has made it abundantly clear, there can be no difference of opinions. From practical standpoint bringing party politics into the affairs of the unions under a parliamentary system is a source of confusion and distraction and it is necessary to provide against it as far as possible. But politics as such cannot be excluded from the organization and working of the unions and they have to be an instrument by which a shift in power can be and has to be brought about. In a country like India the peasants and the agricultural labourers are necessarily of greater importance for developing a new power pattern, but that does not alter the fact that the the unions as organs of organized industrial labour have to perform a crucial role for this purpose and perform it consciously and consistently. Wider issue of "the dictatorship of the proletariat," which is linked with this point, has already been considered and must be viewed in the context of our own conditions and problems. But organized industrial labour has to acquire awareness of its special role in the process of social change and it can only disown it at the grave risk of delaying and distorting it. Trade unions, which deal with and are interested only in the problems of wages, hours and conditions of work to the exclusion of wider and basic social issues are turning their backs upon the course of history and disregarding the clear lessons of experience. The unions, to repeat, have to go beyond the limits of their conventional role and undertake wider responsibilities. Primary functions of the unions can be neglected only at the cost of support and allegiance of their members without which they must lose all their strength and capacity for action; but the inner meaning of this allegiance is that it should be a source of strength for the union and a focus of countervailing power. In this sense separation of politics and unions is neither desirable nor practicable. They can only abjure the former by sapping their own strength and prolonging the servitude of their members and the community to those for whom socialism must be the end of their supremacy and power.

In India the trade unions are weak, their members are ignorant and not politically conscious, they have very limited resources, their leaders are drawn from non-working classes and roots of most of the industrial workers are still in the villages. In the last decades they have improved their position, proportionate strength and even sense of responsibility.[8] Their

8. From 1950-59 the number of workers in factories, mines, plantations, railways and post and telegraph increased from 53.27 to 78.72 lakhs and number of members of trade unions from 17.50 to 36.47 lakhs which show that the proportion of organized worker increased roughly from 32 in 1950 to 46 per cent in 1959.

Number of members affiliated to the Federations of Trade Union in 1949 and 1959 was as follows (in thousands):

	1949	1959
Indian National Trade Union Congress	1,023	1,050
All-India Trade Union Congress	741	670
Hind Mazdoor Sabha	679	241
United Trade Union Congress	331	91

The I.N.T.U.C. is a labour counterpart of the National Congress, A.I.T.U.C. of the Communist Party and Hind Mazdoor Sabha of the Praja Socialist Party. In a decade practically the relative positions of the I.N.T.U.C. and A.I.T.U.C. have not materially changed, but H.M.S. has definately lost

greatest weakness is the lack of working-class unity—their rivalries which are entirely due to their federal organizations and therefore the affiliated unions being pawns in the game of narrow party politics and unable to appraise the situation and problems objectively and with due regard for the interests of the workers and good of the community. It is easy to bewail this lack of unity, point out its grievous consequences and ask why it should not be ended and replaced by solid, unassailable working class solidarity. But rivalries between the communists, the socialists, Christian democrats and Catholics in the field of organized labour are a world-wide phenomenon and have not been overcome even in countries like Germany, France and Italy in which they have had dire consequences and are even now their besetting weakness. This is, as is well-known, due to deep-rooted differences of views, approaches and interests which cannot be reconciled. The unions are or can be a power and every political party with or without the support of churches or other organizations to which its members belong, want to use it for its policies and purposes. The communists, owing to the logic of ideologies, attach the greatest importance to organizing trade unions of their own, and in the countries like France, Italy and Indonesia, the position of their parties is

ground among organized labour. "The stream of trade union unity" in the words of Mr. S. A. Dange, "was taking a zig-zag course." Really speaking there has been hardly any improvement in trade union unity in spite of the co-operation on local issues on occasions as in the case of the strike of Government employees in July 1961. Number of members of these big Trade Union Federation has decreased from 27.74 lakhs to 20.5 lakhs. There are however, other federations like railway federations, etc. which are independent and which do not owe allegiance to any of these federations. The relative position of the four big federations controlled by the big political parties has definitely become weaker in organized labour and there is no compensatory development in the healthy growth of the other unions. The position on the whole from the point of view of trade union unity is really worse than it was in 1949.

Differences among the All-India federations with different political complexion remain as sharp as ever and reflect the persistent divisions among the political parties; and there is no chance of working class unity being realised in practice.

determined almost entirely by the strength of the unions under their control. They (the unions) have in all countries in which they have power, as is well known, been greatly instrumental in determining their political fortunes. This point need not be laboured. The unions are and are meant to be the most effective weapons in the struggle for power and the communist and the other political parties in India, as elsewhere, do not want to and cannot abjure power politics in the pursuit of their industrial labour policies. All central trade union federations in India have, therefore, been formed and are being developed and operated more as bastions of power than as institutions for the protection or promotion of the working class interests. The fact is in many ways a source of annoyance and vexatious to the administrators of labour laws and industrialists and it does mean that on many occasions direct interests of labour become secondary and the strategy and tactics of political struggle between different parties acquire primary importance. Casteism in India, in the unions as is other mass organizations, further complicates the position, adds to and intensifies the union rivalries.

There is no way out of this truly disconcerting situation except that socialism and the need for joining forces by all parties, which believe in it, should become the most compelling consideration for them and prevent or greatly reduce the dissipation of precious but limited energy which is taking place at present. If this does not happen—it looks as if it will not—the trade unions must remain what they are today, instruments of partisan political policies from which the workers derive not inconsiderable benefit but which weaken the unions and their federation in the struggle against the employers and in pursuit of the more basic objectives. In these circumstances the possibility of the unions becoming a force for changing the pattern of power and quickening the pace of social change by themselves or in alliance with other mass organisations is somewhat remote. In India in any case 3.6 million members of the unions can, by themselves, not change the course of events though on occasions some of them can use their strategic position to cause a great deal of embarrassment and even disturbance. They need the massive assistance of the organizations of the peasants and agricultural labourers if labour as a whole is to become a counter-balancing force and create an atmosphere favourable for social transformation in ordinary times and in times of crisis give a revolutionary content to the alignment and movement of social forces in the country. The peasants and agricultural labourers being almost completely unorganized and afflicted by inertia and apathy, so far as the advance of socialism is concerned, and the unions being as divided and as largely ineffective in matters relating to the basic issues as they are, labour in India cannot become, objectively speaking, a revolutionary force in the march of events or by the use of its strength greatly affect the balance of social power. This is again a depressing conclusion like most other conclusions of this book, but one which is inescapable owing to the facts being what they are.

In India industrial labour working in large enterprises and factories being a small proportion of the working population of the country, industrial workers in small, decentralized enterprises and agricultural labourers are a vast majority of the workers in this country, and the role which they can play in the future of our economy depends upon their relative position, strength and earnings. The workers in decentralized industries—mostly household enterprises—are, as is well-known, far more numerous than the workers in large manufacturing establishments and other large undertakings. The proportion is probably 4 : 1 if not higher, and their earnings when compared with even industrial workers in large industries are very much lower. During the planning period, their real wages have, as stated already, fallen, and being almost completely unorganized, they are in a very vulnerable position and rise in the cost of living has eroded their incomes even more than those of the organized industrial workers.9 Special measures taken to develop small and household industries, as stated in an earlier chapter, have not made a significant difference to their position, bargaining power and earnings; and they are, as they have always been, among the most low-paid and vulnerable sections of the community. The co-operatives, excepting a few, have not, as pointed out before, placed them in a position to resist and reduce severe exploitation which is their lot and a large proportion of them is really ekeing out a miserable pittance and development of our economy has passed them by altogether. These industries have to be given a place of great importance in our plans for the workers in them cannot be expected to acquire and muster strength, resources and drive needed for making them also architects of their own and country's future. The unhappy and helpless position in which they are placed, specially in rural areas, makes it impossible for them to lift themselves out of it and take their place in the development of a healthy and progressive economy. In spite of all the plans that have been made for these industries and special boards which have been constituted for their development, their workers, to repeat, remain in a precarious state and can do little or nothing to change the

9. The number of workers in small and household enterprises is a matter of some uncertainty. According to the best available estimates their total number in 1959-60 was 9.2 millions and their net output amounted to Rs 78 crores which gives an average net output per capita of nearly Rs 873 per annum. Average earnings of workers in these industries are not known. In factories in 1959-60 number of workers was 3.6 millions and their total net output was estimated at Rs 936 crores which give per capita output of Rs 2,600 per annum. Average net earning of a factory worker in India in 1959 was Rs 1,342 per annum. Roughly speaking the average earnings of the worker in small enterprises would be about Rs 450 per year and in a large number of cases significantly less (SOURCE: National Income Statistics —Revised Series and Indian Labour Statistics, 1961).

The co-operatives, except among handloom weavers, do not play any significant role in production. They are practically unorganized, are, as is well known, in an exceedingly weak bargaining position and at the mercy of the middlemen and moneylenders.

distribution of power or accelerate the pace of economic growth and social change.

AGRICULTURAL LABOURER

Agricultural labourers, some of whom own land and others do not, almost, according to available information—equally divided in these two categories, are, it is universally admitted the most baffling problem of our economy. Not only are they numerically of far greater importance than the other classes of workers, but they are also most poorly paid, belong very largely to the depressed classes, suffer most from unemployment and destitution, are badly under-nourished, have benefited least from development and their relative economic and social position has in last decade become worse. Statistical evidence on these points is available but not conclusive in some cases; but owing to the lack of capacity of their class to resist the extreme pressure to which they are being subjected because of having little or no land, the growth of population and increase in their numbers not only from among themselves but also from members of the classes above them who are being reduced to the lowest position in large numbers by the pressure of population and lack of employment opportunities and their inferior social and economic position as the most despised and badly treated members of the rural community, the general statement that the agricultural labourer has lost ground during the last decade and the outlook for him is very unpromising is fully supported by facts.[10] That the position calls for immediate

10. Number of agricultural labourers is also a matter of great uncertainty, but the total estimated working force, according to revised National Income Estimate of 118.35 millions in agriculture in 1959-60 on a cautious basis their number could not be less than 40 million, i.e. about one-third of the total. The proportion of agricultural worker varies from state to state. The proportion, for example, is estimated to be 50 per cent for South India, 36 per cent for Central India, 32 per cent for North West India and 30.4 per cent for the country as a whole according to a publication of the Labour Ministry (Rural Man-Power and Occupational Structure, 1954, p. 13). These are also rough estimates but they do not indicate the order of

attention and action to give him relief and place him on the
road to advancement and equality has become so very commonplace to have acquired a strong flavour of a demagogic proposition. The fact, however, neither makes the situation any the
less serious nor makes the future of 100 to 120 million persons
belonging to this class any better.

They are our proletariat who can make or unmake our

magnitude and the range of variations. There is no doubt that proportion of agricultural worker varies widely and creates regional diversity of
great significance. As regional and local planning in India has not even
been attempted, there is no relation between agricultural and village and
small industries development plans and the incidence of agricultural unemployment and working force in different states and parts of the state.
One of the most conclusive arguments for preparing and implementing
village plans on an integrated basis is this important basic fact of our
economy. These plans, though very much in the air, have yet a very uncertain prospect, and it may be assumed that the position in this respect, is
not likely to be materially changed in the near future. Agricultural labour
is still only a statistical concept and not a problem of serious concern or
importance for practical purposes. Its magnitude and significance being
what it is, it is not likely to remain under the surface for a long time, and
when it does come to the surface, it is, it need not be added, likely to have
an explosive effect.

According to The Agricultural Labour Enquiry, 1956-57 annual per capita
income of agricultural labour was Rs. 99.4 in 1956-57 as compared with
Rs 104 in 1950. The Study Group on the Welfare of the Weaker Section of
the Community has stated that about 50 per cent of the rural households
have an income of less than Rs 500 per year (Report of the Study Group,
p. 13) and all agricultural labour belongs to this section and their average
income is well below this limit. The fact that the position of agricultural
labour has not significantly changed even if it has not actually worsened
since 1951 does not admit of any doubt whatsoever. According to an
enquiry conducted by the Ministry of Labour, it has been found that there
has been hardly any improvement in employment in the community development area and wage employment both for casual and women labourers
was relatively little less in C.D. areas. In the report of this enquiry a view
has also been expressed that the scope of hired labour in agriculture is
being reduced due to the growing pressure of population, sub-division of
holdings and more intensive utilization of family labour. It is clear that
agricultural labourer has not benefited from the execution of development
plans so far and any improvement in his position can take place only if
permanent employment is created in the rural area in which he lives and is
adequate to his need for work.

future in spite of the present pitiable position and inability to make the weight of their numbers and potential importance from the point of production and development felt in the higher counsels, economic policies and administration of the country. They are, as stated above, completely unorganized except in a few places; and though all political parties profess to be aware of the urgent need of organizing them for their own sake and for democratic process of creating new dynamism through them, yet in fact have achieved very little to satisfy it (urgent need) and in this regard are completely at a loss as to how to awaken them to their own plight and the necessity of bringing them into action for ending their appalling misery and opening a new chapter in their and the country's history. Without raising the question of agricultural versus industrial proletariat as carriers of revolution, it has to be posited that if a shift in power is necessary for establishing and maintaining a socialist society, the rural poor with their stupendous number and potential strength have to be a very important, if not decisive, factor in shaping our future. Industrial labour, if it has to be in the van of the forces of social revolution, must win the confidence, support and active allegiance of agricultural labour and industrial labour in unorganized industries for social revolution, and work out a really indissoluble alliance with them. The intelligentsia, who can be effective as makers of the future only if their guidance and lead is accepted and followed by all these classes and they draw freely upon them for adding to their strength, understanding and experience, are a factor of great importance and at present matter most in our public affairs. But they are, it is clear, losing their grip and are being increasingly involved in wasteful and distracting game of power politics at a low level. They are really being submerged by the rising tide of rank opportunism and unscrupulous struggle for power; and unless they realize the gravity of the situation and go through the regenerating experience of genuine mass contact with all workers, but particularly with agricultural workers and know how to move, organize and bring to the fore this growing class, growing numerically and as the most deprived and distressed section of the community, they will be overwhelmed by the rising tide referred to above. The portents are clear. Forces not only of reaction but also of anarchy are gaining strength and it may not be long before they gain the upper hand and in the short, if not the long, run ruin our future, i.e. make any advance towards socialism impossible. The form of unholy alliance, through which this may happen, cannot yet be predicted. Possibly some political adventurers with active assistance, if not at their instance, can make a common cause with big business, high bureaucrats and surviving feudal and princely elements, within the steel framework provided by senior military officers can and perhaps will stage what they will call a revolution and overawe the inert and apathetic but truly, distracted masses of the country in general and the countryside in particular. That this is not an idle speculation is more than indicated by recent happenings in the country and the trends that are at work. In this possible milieu of forces the agricultural proletariat with full assistance and even guidance of the other forward-looking classes, can be a great counter-weight and eventually even redeem the situation and make socialism a reality. For this, however, this class must be moved and activated first before they throw their entire weight behind the struggle for the future. At present the agricultural labourer represents a void—a mass being dragged itself and serving as a drag on the advance of the economy as a whole. But key to the future of socialism in this country and to accelerated adequate economic growth is what can be done for and through the agricultural labourer. So far, to repeat, we have done next to nothing, and that is why we have to run as fast as we can, not to stand still but not to be left far behind at this highly critical time in our history and that of the world when things are moving so fast as to make it unavoidable for all—particularly for a country like India—to keep pace with the course of events. If the point of this chapter has not been lost owing to the inadequacy of presentation, the role of labour in this country is to gather strength, make a future which will truly belong to it and become its chief beneficiary, maker and sustainer. This is what has to happen—if we are to have socialism—really any future at all. Cold unemotional assessment of the present position and of the forces that are at work clearly point to the conclusion that this cannot happen. And yet our major premise is that socialism is our future and without it we will be lost.

PRODUCTIVITY

It must be assumed that the main purpose of organizing labour and arousing it to the need for defensive and positive action is to change or redress the balance of forces and protect themselves against exploitation. This is an object of basic importance and has to be realized if radical social change has to be brought about, democracy must necessarily mean continuous vigilance on the part of the people and sustained interest in public issues. Labour organizations can and should obviously play a vital part in realizing this object. But even more important purpose of organized labour is the need for bringing the best out of the worker for production and raise the standard of his efficiency to the highest level. An acquisitive society is and cannot but be an extremely wasteful society for in it the most precious productive asset is used very badly or not used at all. All the latent gifts of millions, who do not get a fair chance in life, are neither discovered nor utilized, they have to lead mostly a barren life and suffer from frustration and worse because they do not get an opportunity to develop or express themselves and contribute to the development and enrichment of the economy. In India the enormous man-power which goes to waste because of the existing non-utilization or under-utilization has to be and can be turned to a very good account, as clearly indicated before, by a radical reorganization of the rural economy. It can thereby be given a new hope and purpose in life and contribute greatly to the increase in production. But it can do more. It can awaken them to the new possibilities in themselves and in the economy and create what is more important than capital formation, a

new fund of energy, initiative and enterprise from the social
point of view which can be drawn upon for creating a new
momentum and carrying the productive processes forward to
what may now appear as unbelievable level of achievement.
This fund can be immense value for tapping hidden source of
strength and efficiency. Extremely rapid growth, which the
countries like Soviet Union, have realized is, in spite of their
undue reliance upon the use of force, largely due to their having created this fund and drawn freely upon it. This has been
done not by driving people but inspiring them to a new sense
of purpose and achievement, and from all available evidence is
clear that this fund is growing in volume and significance and
is their most valuable capital asset. In this country we can, if
we move the minds and hearts of agricultural workers, do like-
wise, and if we believe that in India we will use democratic
processes for development and carry the country forward on
the swelling tide of voluntary and spontaneous efforts of our
people, we have to organize agricultural workers and tap the
best in them for development and rapid growth. According to
all accounts this is just the line in which we have failed most
miserably and the result is that most of our plans for co-operation and participation of the masses have been lost in the bog
of frustration and cynicism. This is an index and measure of
our inability to bring truly democratic processes into play and
made democracy at all levels, but particularly at the basic level,
a word without any meaning and message for our people and
has therefore made its future a depressing prospect. This applies
to industrial workers, craftsmen and the intelligentsia as much
as it does to the agricultural worker, and the general lack of
buoyancy and will to action on a mass basis, from which the
country has been and is grievously suffering, is almost entirely
due to it.

"Their gains (the workers') arise only out of strength and
dynamism of the economy, the only enduring basis of which is
rising level of productivity."[11] This is profoundly true and also

11. *Third Five Year Plan.*

profoundly platitudinous. Exhortations to higher productivity have become so commonplace, and the view that we must produce first before we can distribute is propounded with such an air of new discovery as to disclose clearly its misplaced emphasis and vacuity of statements from the standpoint of their social content. In India productivity is low, about the lowest in the world[12] and very great rise in productivity has to be our most important means of raising the standard of living of the people, accumulation of capital and development of our social services, i.e. investment in human capital. All this goes without saying but as in spite of increase of 42 per cent in national income, 35 per cent in agricultural production, 94 per cent in industrial production and 22 per cent in productivity from 1951-1961, real wages of industrial labourers, craftsmen, agricultural labourers and most of our intellectuals have either been just maintained or in a very large majority of cases actually fallen. Merely increase in production and productivity cannot lead to the realization of all the objects referred to above. It is obvious that if exhortation to rise to a higher level of productivity is not to fall on deaf ears and what is worse, produce a revulsion of feeling; this exhortation has to be backed by convincing evidence that "gains which arise out of the strength

12. Productivity is an elusive concept and its measurement raises difficult problems which become much more so if international comparisons are to be made. According to one estimate productivity in India is 1/15 of the U.S.A., 1/13 of Canada, 1/7 of U.K., 1/6 of Australia, 1/5 of the Union of South Africa and 1/3 of France. (Productivity, Vol. III, No. 1, p. 59).

According to another estimate productivity has, from 1951 to 1958, increased by 31 per cent in vegetable oil, 25 per cent in soap, 21 per cent in cement, 51 per cent in paper, 62 per cent in chemicals, 35 per cent in jute, 57 per cent in aluminium, 19 per cent in iron and steel, 59 per cent in engineering and 22 per cent in all industries. In sugar there has been decrease of 6 per cent and in cotton textiles of 17 per cent in productivity. (Ibid., p. 75).

These estimates are also subject to very serious reservations; but if they have any relation to facts, they make the present position of industrial labour even more poignant. With 22 per cent increase in industrial productivity and much greater increase in a number of sectors of the economy industrial wages as indicated already present a very sorry picture.

and dynamism of the economy and the enduring basis of which is and has to be the rising level of productivity" will not remain illusory gains so far as the majority of our people is concerned and they will have to be tangible proofs that the rising level of productivity will be entirely used for the good of the community. This is so very simple and obvious that it seems to be uncalled for to lay so much stress upon it; and yet the simple and obvious point is almost completely overlooked in our theory and practice of planning. Reiteration of the need for rising productivity is our only stand by when we find that these exhortations fail to touch any cord in the minds of the bulk of our producers, i.e. the workers.

In India we have a National Productivity Council which, according to the Planning Commission, has created a realization of the importance of productivity movement and industry is being increasingly involved in the drive to raise productivity. There are 43 local Productivity Councils and a very large number of seminars have been organized and many groups have been taken abroad to study productivity methods in foreign countries, mostly Germany, U.K. and U.S.A. The emphasis upon standardization, quality control, time and motion studies and similar other practices is in order, but only if it is realized that productivity depends as much, if not really more, upon organization of industry and what is far more important, of the economy as a whole, sense of loyalty of management to the worker, the community and its social objectives and the motivation of the worker and social ethos and the network of social relations in which he has to work. Techniques and capital equipment are of very great importance, but there are what a Polish writer calls "non-investment factors of the growth (of industrial production)".[13] In a country like ours in which there is acute shortage of investible resources, the greatest attention has to be paid to non-investment factors in growth and make them, as far as we can, our most important source of acquiring momentum

13. Zymagint Kvyzisk, "Investment and Non-investment Factors of Growth of Industrial Production in Poland 1950-60", *Economista*, p. 1.

for development. This has largely to be the motive force of the strength and dynamism of the economy. We need standardization, rationalization, quality control and all other devices which are the stock in trade of our productivity evangelists, and also of course wide application of higher techniques and larger investment of capital resources. But our National Productivity Council, due to its foreign inspiration and very clear bias for status quo, does not realize that resort to "non-investment factors" must have much higher priority in our schemes of expanding production and raising the level of productivity than the traditional methods by which it lays so much store; and this cannot be done without disturbing status quo and setting the economy on the path of a real social revolution. Even with it we will need all the methods which the Productivity Council is propagating, but they cannot be a substitute for it so far as rising productivity is concerned, and without it, they will only become a delusion and a snare. The National Productivity Council is one of the agencies which are playing a diversionary role and are trying to turn our minds away from real issues.[14]

In our context the most efficacious method of raising productivity and making the worker productivity conscious is to organise him, give him a real understanding of our position and problems and produce a realization that he has to rise to a higher level of social consciousness and make it the most important driving force of our economy. In other words, it has to be realized that the worker has, by changing the very basis of the economy through his understanding and organized strength, to use the common phrase, release new productive forces which

14. The Planning Commission, to be fair to it, has stated that "a nationwide effort to lift levels of productivity involves not only more efficient methods and organization and a scientific approach, but also changes in human and personal relationship, recognition of the worth of each man, team work and within each work, a continuous sense of common interest and obligation." This is good as far as it goes, but in practice this aspect of the matter is completely lost sight of and the so-called "productivity movement" has become a movement, to repeat, for diverting peoples' minds from the basic issues.

will make all the difference to our future. If we have to know
the facts of the case, we should know that treasures of energy,
drive and higher productivity lie hidden in our workers in
agriculture, industry, large and small and all other economic
activities, which can be discovered and drawn upon by the
worker himself becoming aware of this fact and developing the
will to use it fully and with a purpose. This aspect of the
worker's potential importance needs to be understood and also
the fact that great inadequacy of our planned effort is largely
due to the lack of understanding of the worker's role in it.[15]

15. Substantially speaking, this Chapter has been included in "Labour
and Planning" as the author's contribution to *Essays in Honour of Sri V. V.
Giri.*

Chapter Ten

PLANNED TRADE

NEED FOR PLANNED TRADE

In a planned economy it is obviously necessary that trade should also be planned, and in a socialist economy it has not only to be planned but also socialized, i.e. its flow has to conform to the needs of the community and its pattern respond to an increasing social purpose. In a private enterprise economy trade follows the incentive of difference between prices in different places, areas and countries and the movement of commodities is directed by the quest for profits. The profits accruing from taking advantage of price differentials, according to the underlying assumptions of the conventional approach, are taken to be the reward for reduction of these differences by trading, i.e. transfer of goods in time and space in pursuit of private gain. This is the time-honoured explanation and justification of the gains of trade; and though it does contain an element of real truth, it is also well known that social odium which has clung to trading all through the ages is due to the widespread awareness of the anti-social role of the trader who harms the consumer and the producer by mulcting both by the anti-social operations like hoarding, cornering, speculation, etc. and charging, 'unjust,' prices. In a socialist society, however, not only such ill-gotten gains have to be eliminated, but the distribution of goods has to become a social function because production has to be undertaken according to the assessed needs and resources of the community, and distribution of goods has necessarily to reflect the production plan. This is the plain and simple reason why trade has to be both planned and socialized. Vital importance of trading—distribution of goods—lies in the fact that on it depends specialization and location of production and transfer of goods according to the needs of social production and consumption, and a socialist society cannot possible leave the discharge of this basic function to the profit making propensities of the private traders.

What is more, one of the necessary steps which a country, which sets out on the path to socialism has to take even before production is socialized, is to occupy the "commanding heights" of trading in order to direct and steer the economy as a whole and its price structure in the desired direction, even when production cannot, in the transitional phase, owing to the limitations of resources and old institutional framework, become a social function. The fact that in all socialist countries this step was in fact taken, before they embarked upon public and co-operative ownership of the instrument of production, was due more to the logic of necessity than any doctrinaire prepossession. This has to be an essential part of their economic strategy, for trading is a strategic position of such fundamental importance that if a society, which wants to realize socialism in all earnestness, does not occupy it, even if it knows it has to reach its goal in stages, it cannot but create for itself immense avoidable difficulties. A network of commercial organizations has necessarily to be established and brought into a working order before this take-over can be brought about, but in a country of dispersed production it is relatively speaking easier to build up a distributive than a productive organization in the initial stages, though in itself it is a task the performance of which requires very high level of organizing capacity. Socialization of distribution carries with it the possibility of socialization of price structure even though the latter is a task of much greater complexity. A change in price structure, once distribution is socialized, becomes unavoidable even though formulation and application of principles of a socialized price structure in their entirety in a specfic context takes time and calls for adjustments of a far-reaching character. The strategic importance of distribution in the development of a socialist society is, however, undeniable and has to be conceded and acted upon in the strategy of economic development and social transformation when a country sets itself the goal of socialism and wants to reach it without avoidable delay.

In India the view that "commanding heights" of the economy have to be occupied by the state has been affirmed and re-affirmed on a number of occasions and even the importance of state trading as a measure of realizing socialism, has been recognized; and yet in actual practice trade, external and internal, has been left mostly to private enterprise and measures of regulation and control, which have been and are being exercised, are inadequate, halting and subject to sudden and from the standpoint of public policy, unaccountable, changes. The essential point that for a planned economy, planned distribution of commodities is necessary and unavoidable has hardly received its due consideration; and decisions have been largely shaped by hidden pressures of private interests and firm commitments of policy and practice have in effect been undermined by adoption of subtle and insidious measures of retreat without open disavowal of the accepted objectives. It is, of course, necessary to repeat that a public distribution organization should be built up to replace the organization of private trade before this function is socialized. This obvious need has in practice been deliberately neglected and at present lack of public organization to undertake the distributive function on a country-wide basis is a serious hindrance in the way of realizing this object. Brave decisions in the past in favour of socialization of trade have been easily defeated by their not having been backed by a will to meet the challenge of private interests in trade, general inertia of administration and absence of any effective pressures of the people and organized political action in favour of public trading. Commerce accounts for 8 per cent of the total working force in the country and eleven million people make their living by it.[1] For most of them life

---

1. *National Income Statistics* (Revised Series), Central Statistical Organization, p. 6.

is a hard struggle of existence at a low level and in trade disguised unemployment is, relatively speaking, as important as
in agriculture though in aggregate it, of course, does not
assume the same proportion. Rationalization and socialization
of trade in India, therefore, cannot but involve major structural
changes and would affect millions who at present make a precarious living from it. They, however, occupy a position of key
importance and use it to the serious detriment of the interests
of the people, particularly in the rural areas. The merchants
at the higher level, i.e. mostly wholesale merchants, are playing a crucial role in the movement of goods and perform it
without any concern for the interest of the community. The
decision which was taken a few years ago to replace them by
public trading in food grains was well-conceived but badly executed and was practically reversed owing to the determined
opposition of the commercial interests which was supported by
the men in high places in the central and state governments. In
June 1964 history has repeated itself and powerful commercial interests have again thwarted the attempt to socialize
wholesale trade in food grains in spite of the country being in
a state of grave crisis. Co-operative marketing having, as stated
already, failed to make any real headway, it is likely that at
this stage the co-operatives will not make any real difference
to the organization of trade within the country or with other
countries. The state's part in the distribution of commodities
like coal, steel, cement is of regulatory significance within
certain limits, but it does not and is not meant to replace private by public trading and does not reduce the importance of
the private trade in the distribution of these important commodities. Private trading remains the rule at all levels and has
not been subjected to planned regulation and control to any
significant extent. Under the conditions existing in India occupation of "the commanding height" of trading at all levels is of
fundamental importance for formulation and execution of plans,
enunciation and implementation of a rational price policy
and checking and remedying all the serious abuses which private

trading is known to give rise to. If need for taking the important step had been duly appreciated at the initial stages of our planning, we would have by now gone a long way in creating the necessary organization for replacing private by public trading. As it is, we find the difficulty of bringing about this change overwhelming and have again and again been daunted by them in our efforts to promote state or co-operative trading. The result is, of course, that this pre-eminently strategic position has remained in the hands of those who are against both planning and socialism and use it to realize anti-social ends and throw the whole weight of their position and resources against any advance towards socialism. In India mercantile capitalism is of much greater importance than industrial capitalism. We have a public sector in the industrial sphere and it may, given the right conditions, assume a crucial role in the country's industrialization. In commerce, however, the public sector, though not non-existent, hardly matters and there is for the time being no prospect of its assuming any role whatsoever, what to speak of a crucial or decisive role.

FOREIGN TRADE

Importance of foreign trade in our economy has greatly increased owing to our increasing need for import of capital and intermediate goods for industrialization. Our imports have been increasing on that account while our exports have been stagnant for a number of years. We have to expand our exports in order to earn enough foreign exchange to buy even our 'maintenance' imports. We have through export councils, commercial diplomacy and delegations, etc. been trying to develop an export drive which so far has not yielded significant results. In export trade we can, by reducing cost, standardization and improvement of quality, grant of fiscal and other concessions to our exporters and market research, etc. take measures to promote our exports. These measures have been recommended by our export promotion committees between 1951 and 1962 but these measures taken together have not solved any of our major export problems, and there is no assurance at all that we will be able to realize our Third Plan targets in exports and meet our much larger requirements in the Fourth Plan, i.e. double the value of existing exports.

The world trade situation is the most important limiting factor in the development of our exports. The highly advanced countries of the world are now trading more among themselves than with the undeveloped countries and with the increasing use of synthetic products their need for natural raw materials has been decreasing. Our traditional major exports—tea, jute, textiles—have not been able to keep pace with the growing world trade, and they are being subjected to pressures arising from adverse conditions of markets, relative costs and increasingly severe competition. We have to develop new exports and increase in the exports of ores, light engineering goods such as cycles, fans and sewing machines, handicrafts, etc. can relieve the pressure and has in fact been of some help. But as yet they are of minor importance, and though all that is possible to develop them further has to be done, we cannot count upon them to counteract the shrinkage or at best stagnation or slow growth of our major exports. The discussions at the meetings of the export and import councils or official reports clearly show how we are merely repeating old formulas and not facing squarely the difficulties which we are really up against. World trade is taking its own course, our proportionate share in it is decreasing and its trends are, from our point of view, largely unfavourable. Though we should improve our competitive position, and through commercial agreements and otherwise find new markets and expand old ones and participate fully in the reduction or removal of trade barriers, we should realise that our relative position is getting weaker and not stronger, we have not got strong bargaining counters, and commerce is increasingly becoming less a matter of business and more of politics.[2] Through non-alignment in commerce as

2. This view is fully borne out by what Prof Halstein, who was Dr Adeneur's Foreign Minister before he became President of the Common

in politics, we will probably serve our national interests best; we have also to realize that as yet we have done very little to reduce our dependence upon our traditional markets, i.e. Commonwealth and Western Europe and our balance of payment problem is not, to an inconsiderable extent, due to it. Our foreign reserves are near the irreducible minimum and they are not enough even for meeting one month's requirements of imports. We may be lucky and continue for a while to receive foreign aid when we get into an extremely tight corner. But

Market Commission, said in a speech which he made at Harvard on May 22, 1960. He said: "We are not in business to promote tariff preferences or to establish a discriminatory club, to force a large market to make us richer or a trading block to further our commercial interests. We are not in business at all; we are in politics." (Quoted by Konni Zillocus in the article on "Britain and the Common Market", *Monthly Review*, Vol. 13, No. 9, p. 400.)

This is a frank and true statement. Common Market, from which Great Britain lately has been kept out, in the words of an Economic Correspondent of *New Statesman*, "provides a framework for an ever closer economic integration" (*New Statesman*, Vol. LXIII, No. 1620, p. 439). The object of the Economic Market is not merely to build one politically integrated union of Europe but as pointed out by Mrs Barbara Castle in the same issue of the well-known weekly, an "Anti-Socialist Community" (*Ibid.*, p. 442). It is intended to be a community to block the advance of socialism and create economic counterpart of NATO.

We in India at present are concerned about protecting our exports against discriminatory tariffs of Common Market; but we have to know that Common Market is meant to be "an anti-socialist community" which will make access to this important market very difficult for countries like India in accordance with its "politics". The Six being in politics and not in business will be arrayed against the objects to which we owe allegiance and the realization of which is of fundamental importance to us. Common Market, according to Article, (a) of the Treaty of Rome has to eliminate any legislative or administrative provisions which distort the conditions of competition. This in effect really means building up giant international cartels which will use their immense strength to prevent the emergence of socialist societies and promote what Marx called "cosmopolitan exploitation". As pointed out by President Nkrumah, Common Market is really an attempt to build collective imperialism of the West European countries.

These are the trends of world trade today and if we want to steer our course through these shoals and whirlpools with care, we have to make trade, internal and external, a function of the community as a whole. This is another conclusive reason for socializing the entire trade of the country

"Aid to India" Club has politics of its own, and though exigencies of world situation may relieve us when we are in straits again, they cannot be depended upon to mitigate the stresses of a chronic adverse exchange position or meet the deficits of our development finance indefinitely. The exchange and development deficits can easily become instruments for exercising pressure on our international policies or decisions on, e.g. choice between the private and public sectors. As a matter of fact pressure has already been exercised to influence or alter decisions of public policy; and knowing as we do the high politics of the countries like the U.S.A., Germany, Britain, France and Japan, which have come to our rescue, it would be more than naive to expect that we would continue to adhere to our international or national policies without being confronted with pressures in some form or other from these countries for altering them to their advantage or in keeping with their own ideological approach.3 It is not easy to suggest an alternative to the aid from these countries for meeting trade and development

3. This danger was very clearly demonstrated by unwillingness of 'Aid to India Club" to commit itself at its meeting held in May 1962 and the whole position from the point of view of foreign aid became extremely uncertain and incalculable on that account. This point has become even clearer owing to the pressure exercised on Government of India because of our even entertaining a proposal for the sale of M.I.G. planes by the Soviet Union for our defence services.

As Jawaharlal Nehru pointed out in his speech on Foreign Affairs in the Rajya Sabha on June 23, 1962, "So in effect as someone said that although there are no strings attached, somethings happen, that is in its very nature some kind of threat which has and which may have a certain psychological effect."

This is also a masterly understatement of the real position. In a world in which cold war is the most dominant fact, independence of foreign policy and dependence upon one of the blocks for a large measure of assistance for development cannot be combined. As stated in a later chapter, if the U.S.A. is going to contribute a major portion of foreign assistance she, from the nature of things, as the most important antagonist in cold-war, cannot but use it as an instrument of its foreign policy. This position should have been known to us even without any sharp reminder; but now that it has been so clearly brought home to us, we have to know fully how precarious and vulnerable our position really is.

deficits. But the risk in receiving this aid is obvious—the more so because the aid is given on *ad hoc* basis for specific projects and is not generally untied—i.e. open aid both in regard to the object for and the country in which it is to be utilized. Every time that the aid is granted, India exposes itself to the risk of being subjected to such pressure (as pointed out at greater length in a later chapter) even when it is not made conditional on open change of policy or purposes. This pressure strengthens similar pressures at home which are known to be growing— pressures from big business, opposition parties, high bureaucracy and from within the Congress party itself emanating in a number of cases from political leaders in high places. These continuous chronic trade deficits are, from this standpoint, a source of real danger.

The position needs to be reviewed and measures devised by which this embarrassing dependence upon clearly aligned countries for foreign exchange can be reduced. One obvious method by which this object can be achieved is a careful scrutiny of our development projects and reduction of their exchange component as far as possible. Projects like development of rayon industries, producing small cars, refrigeration, even scooters should be postponed and even cut to reduce the extreme shortage of foreign exchange. The development projects—both public and private, but more private than public—have to be reexamined and their need reassessed from this point of view. We cannot slow down the industrial development of the country in essential respects and have to incur some risk for this purpose. But we must not give hostages to fortune in doing so, and at any rate rigorous scrutiny of all development projects with a view to evaluating their exchange components is urgently called for and has to be undertaken. This is not being undertaken and a lack of concern about the continuance and even increase of these trade deficits is very much in evidence. Reduction of our imports to a real austerity level is urgently needed. The value of imports which had been reduced from Rs 1,035 crores in 1957-58 to Rs 859 crores in 1958-59 again rose to Rs 1,070 crores in 1960-61, to

Rs 1,001.6 in 1961-62 and Rs 1,089.4 in 1962-63. Value of imports of consumers' goods which fell from Rs 201 crores in 1952-53 to Rs 83 crores in 1956-57, has from 1958-59 to 1960-61, been again round about Rs 200 crores. Without a careful examination of imports it is not possible to indicate the scope for their reduction, but the figures cited above do show that considerable reduction in imports can be effected. Intermediate goods account for nearly 46 to 47 per cent of the value of imports, and though in theory they are assumed to be goods needed for maintaining production, this category is known to hide many non-essentials which the country can, given the will, well do without. In 1960-61 we imported food to the value of Rs 213.2 crores, in 1961-62 Rs 117.0 crores and in 1962-63 Rs 117 crores. If we exert ourselves to the limit of our capacity and undertake integrated development of our rural economy, mobilize our own surplus instead of drawing up the "burdensome" surplus of U.S.A., we can in a large measure spare ourselves the humiliation of having to rely upon P.L. 480 as our saviour in our recurring ordeals. Our battle at the food front has to be won not in our negotiation for P.L. 480 imports but in the fields of our villages by adoption of "non-investment" measures for expansion of agricultural production.

It is not possible to go into greater details; but the view that our imports can be considerably reduced if we really pursue the object of reducing them to an austerity level with greater vigour is a valid view and our import policy should be modified on its basis. Great increase in our "defence" imports since 1962-63 alters the position radically but also increases the urgency of reducing our normal imports. To rely upon external assistance for easing the situation is the line of least resistance but is fraught with serious dangers for our future. It is being too readily assumed that industrialization of the country necessarily involves high level of imports. It does within certain limits, but it does not follow that we must import about Rs 78 crores worth of mineral fuels, etc. every year on that account and their consumption must keep growing even if for these and similar imports we have to mortgage our future and acquiesce in the disquieting prospect of meetings of "Aid India Club" having to be convened for an indefinite period. We need foreign aid for development and should take it from all sources without incurring onerous obligations. Our exchange shortage will remain with us for a long while yet and is a part of the process of accelerating development; but if we are to retain unfettered freedom of choice in our internal affairs and external relations, we have to reduce the problem to manageable proportions and exercise extreme vigilance against being forced to place ourselves in a position in which we have to expose ourselves to unwelcome and undesirable pressures from powerful countries. It may be hoped that foreign aid would in course of time develop into truly international aid and we and other underdeveloped countries would be able to avail ourselves of it without any cost to ourselves in terms of independence of policy and action. At present it does not at all look as if this will happen soon, and we have, therefore, to curtail our requirements of foreign exchange to the very minimum without arresting the process of economic growth of the country. At present this aspect of the matter is not being given its due consideration and our imports are being allowed to grow without reckoning carefully their cost. The position is obviously a matter for serious concern and should not be allowed to drift. The estimated level of average annual imports of Rs 1,270 crores in the Third Plan has to be reviewed and revised by the exercise of rigorous scrutiny.

For the Third Plan it has also been assumed that the value of our exports would increase by Rs 250 crores, i.e. to Rs 3,700 crores by 1965. This is not an ambitious target, but in view of the conditions of trade and demand for our staple exports it cannot be assumed that even this target will be realized. The Planning Commission has pointed out that primary object of carrying out the export programme is "to create the necessary climate in the country for the necessary export effort". This climate, it should be clear, cannot be created for export effort only. It has to be a part of the climate of all effort for quickening the pace of development and giving it a social content. As stated already the world trade situation is the most important limiting factor in the growth of our export trade; and though we should improve our competitive position by reducing cost and adjusting production to the requirements of export markets, our foreign trade from regional and commodity standpoints has been and is still unbalanced and in fact limits our capacity to expand our exports quickly. We are largely dependent upon Western Europe, including the U.K. and North America, for our imports and exports and since 1952 our foreign trade with them has proportionately been increasing. From 1952 to 1962 our imports from these areas have increased from 50 to 67 per cent and our exports, from 56 to 65 per cent. Tea, jute, textiles have been and still are our most important exports and outlook for them, it is a matter of common knowledge, in the world market does not hold out hope of any significant expansion. As a matter of fact maintenance of relative position would require an all-out effort on our part. The tea and jute industries are the most important foreign exchange earners and their production and export are mostly controlled by foreign interests; and in the creation of climate for export their contribution has obviously to be of great importance. These interests have also foreign affiliations and it would be more than generous to assume that they would give to our national interests the primacy which they should have in the development of our export trade. New exports like ores and light engineering goods can be further developed but they will not affect the dominance of our staple exports in the overall position of foreign trade for a good while yet. This makes the modest target of the increase of Rs 250 crores in the value of exports by 1965-66 an unrealistic target,4 and as stated above,

4. The latest available figures of foreign trade for 1964 show that during this year while our exports increased by Rs. 52 crores, our imports increased faster by Rs. 72 crores, and our exchange reserves fell by Rs. 18 crores. The increase of our imports from Rs. 1178 crores in 1963 to Rs. 1250 crores

it is not likely that even the maintenance of the existing position would need all the export drive that we can develop. Reduction of our imports is really the most important method open to us in reducing our trade deficit and our undue dependence on foreign aid for meeting it.

Diversification of our foreign trade is obviously of great importance and has to be brought about by conscious regulation and exploring all possible avenues for trade promotion in new directions. In 1961 Asian countries accounted for 17 per cent of our exports and 13 per cent of our imports, the communist countries 8 and 3.7 per cent, Latin America 2.5 and .1 per cent and Africa 2.5 and 4.4 per cent. India should expand her foreign trade with Asia, Africa and Latin America but economies of these areas and their foreign trade in particular are dominated by foreign interests and these countries themselves have to achieve economic independence to a much greater extent before adopting any measure of co-operation for developing closer and broader trade relations with India and other emergent countries. Though growing sense of independence would, in these areas, in due course, lead to co-operative action, the prospect of achieving material results in this respect in the near future at present does not exist. The Asian Planners at their conference held at Delhi in November 1961 expressed the view that "in a dynamic context, if the various economies of this region expand steadily and simultaneously towards high level of development, progressively greater possibilities or mutual co-operation in industrial and agricultural production and in trade and transport, as in other fields, could be realized".

—of which nearly one-sixth were cereal imports, which increased by Rs 56 crores to Rs. 213 crores in spite of our bumper cereal harvests in 1963 and 1964—has been the major cause of worsening trade position. The imports of cereals, if we had fully utilized our own resources, could have been almost eliminated. Why we have had to import heavily cereals on this scale is a very sad commentary on our economic policy and its administration. Sharply rising food prices make the position even much worse and our inability to implement an adequate food policy, more pathetic.

This is more an expression of a pious wish than a sober estimate of actual potential for as things are the difficulties, political and economic, in the way of creating and realizing such
possibilities are truly insuperable. All that can be done should
be done to promote this object, but it is not right to count
upon them to any extent for diversification of our foreign trade
and reducing our dependence upon traditional markets and
commodities.

Our trade with communist countries is, however, a case by
itself and needs to be seriously considered. Our imports from
the communist countries of Europe including Yugoslavia have
increased from Rs 8.38 crores in 1955 to Rs 36.60 crores in
1960 and our export to them from Rs 4.36 crores to Rs 49.03
crores. Our exports to these countries and China have increased from 1.3 per cent in 1952 to 3 per cent in 1960.5 This is the
one development in which state trading has been of decisive
importance and exchange of goods has been mainly determined
by considerations of the promotion of development of our economy rather than by ordinary commercial considerations. All
these countries are keen not only to export, but export capital
goods for the development of our industries of strategic importance. They already have made valuable contributions, not
only to our economic development, but also economic independence and are capable of carrying the process very much far-

5. Trade with China owing to the aggression by that country has now
unfortunately come to an end but the trade with the other communist
countries has a distinctive feature which is very advantageous to us. Trade
agreements with these countries mean a firm commitment on their part to
sell and deliver according to a time-schedule, the commodities which they
undertake to export and their prices are not subject to change or fluctuations.
That also applies to imports from India, i.e. flow of commodities from India
takes place on a planned basis and *at stipulated prices.* This is the only
part of our foreign trade which is really planned, i.e. interchange of goods
takes place with firm commitments on both sides and fits into the development plans of the trading partners.

The position in 1963 improved further very greatly and our imports from
U.S.S.R. rose to Rs 58.16 crores from Rs 24.66 crores in 1960 and our exports
to Rs 48.57 crores from 29.27 crores.

ther. Moreover they do not create any exchange problem for us. Besides the fact that these transactions are largely covered by long-term credits on very liberal terms, payment for them has to be made, when necessary, in our currency and the amounts so paid are utilized for larger stipulated imports from us. This is not only good trade but also very good aid and goes with a large measure of technical assistance. We have to avail ourselves of opportunities which are placed at our disposal for reciprocal trade and such new opportunities for enlarging the scope of these transactions. We have to and should trade with the West, but development of trade with these countries is very good business for us. We should, to repeat, do our best to promote trade between India and these countries and realize its great value and importance. The fact that thereby these countries become not only our partners in trade but also in the development of key industries like steel, oil, heavy machinery and pharmaceuticals invests these transactions of inter-national exchange with special significance in the development of our economy. In accelerating the rate of growth of trade with them we really plan our trade in specific terms and for specific purposes and in keeping with our planned targets.

STATE TRADING

These considerations clearly indicate that foreign trade policy has to be formulated and executed with a view to satisfying the needs of our economy as a whole and steering its course towards socialism. At present there is very considerable amount of state trading in India and co-operative marketing which, however, has only a minor significance in the economy as a whole. Of the total imports of Rs 1,089.4 crores in 1962-63 Government imports amounted to Rs 463.5 crores and private imports to Rs 625.9 crores. From 1957-58 to 1962-63 the total value of private imports was Rs 3,629.8 crores and of Government imports Rs 2,729.7 crores, i.e. they were in the ratio of nearly 4:3. During this period value of imports of food was Rs 917.7 crores. State trading is a controversial subject in India, but these figures clearly show that Government has already a very significant position in foreign trade and is presumably handling its foreign trade business successfully. The view, therefore, that the state has no experience in the field and has no personnel to conduct business in foreign trade is, factually speaking, not correct. The state can, if it wants to, draw upon its very considerable experience and organization in import trade and nationalization of the whole import trade therefore, need not present any insuperable difficulties.

Exports, however, are almost entirely in the hands of private merchants and in 1962-63 their value was Rs 682.2 crores. The State Trading Corporation, which was established in 1956-57, has acquired an important position in export trade and had monopoly in the export of iron, manganese and chromium and trade with the communist countries was largely handled by it. Trade with these countries has increased rapidly and, as pointed out already, is the only section of our external trade which has been planned and contributed in a large measure to the development of some of our key industries.

The State Trading Corporation, however, is still an organization of very secondary importance in our external trade and is subject to severe pressure of private interests. It is conceded that in trading with the countries in which foreign trade is a public monopoly, the S.T.C. is needed and has served a good purpose. But as the Government has not formed a clear policy in regard to state trading, the S.T.C. is under constant attack of private commercial interests and they jealously guard against an extension of the field of its activities. It is a bureaucratically managed organization, and though it has broken new ground but is always on the defensive and is in no sense an instrument of advancing socialism. Nationalization of foreign trade is, to repeat, essential from empirical and fundamental standpoint. In our export trade tea and jute—two most important exchange earners—are dominated by foreign interests and the exchange banks with affiliations with very powerful financial institutions have the monopoly of financing foreign trade.

There is a very good case for nationalization of foreign trade in the special circumstances existing in India but no country which is committed to a socialist goal, should allow such strategic positions to be retained in the hands of private enterprise. This applies with very special force to our export trade which is so completely dominated by powerful foreign interests. As stated above, state trading in India has already assumed large dimension, experience of conducting foreign trade by public agencies is already available and the establishment of an organization which could take care of our entire foreign trade need not present any formidable difficulties. Licensed regulation can, within limits, be an alleviating factor, but experience since independence has clearly shown its inadequacy and in any case it is no substitute for a fully developed, rightly oriented and properly organized state trading organization. In foreign trade of India foreign interests occupy, to repeat, a dominant position and their replacement by public agencies is urgently required both from the national and socialist standpoint.

In India state trading in food grains was organized during and after the war, and even now food grains are being imported from foreign countries and distributed through what is virtually a public trading organization. All purchases of capital goods and stores for railways, ordinance factories, large undertakings like river-valley projects, state transport, air corporation, and post and telegraph, etc. and of course all industries in the public sector have their own purchasing organizations and they undertake public trading on a very large scale. And in the case of commodities like steel, coal, cement, soda ash, sugar, their distribution is subject to public control and their prices are fixed by the authorities concerned in accordance with principles of public importance. There is, of course, state trading corporation, which was constituted in 1950 primarily to negotiate agreements and conduct trade with the communist countries in which foreign trade is a monopoly, and it has mostly confined itself to trade with these countries.

But it has also struck deals, for example, with Japan for export of iron ore and even import of certain commodities.

Public trading in a socialist society or for its realization is more than an act of substitution. It does not merely mean a replacement of private traders by agents of the state or co-operative trading organization. It means a change in the trading functions—its object, purpose and the manner of its operation. It means, as in private trading, exchange of commodities but with a view to maximizing social well-being through specialization in production on the basis of true relative social advantage and purposive utilization of human and material resources in the interest of the community, fixing prices in such a way as to provide at least social minimum and incentive differentials to the producers and to supply goods to the consumer which he really needs and wants at prices which either mostly cover cost or in some cases are above and below cost according to the social judgment of the price-fixing authorities and making distributive function not merely a means of transfering goods between places, groups and individuals but also a positive instrument of relating it to the objects of social policy. Private trader merely indulges in the age-old propensity to truck and barter and take advantage of the price differences for making a living or amassing fortunes. His successor in a socialist society becomes a creative conscious link between different phases or stages of social production, an instrument for maintaining the rythm of goods in production and has to ensure consciously their sustained flow in order to attain equilibrium between production and consumption of commodities in general and specific commodities to make their inter-relation an expression of balanced operation of exchange mechanism in a socialist society. An agent of public trading, essentially speaking, does not merely buy cheap and sell dear; but performs the distributive function of a differentiated socialist economy in order that it may operate as an integrated whole and through an efficient discharge of this function bring the processes of social valuation into play and assign to commodities and service their relativities in the entire scheme of socialist exchange economy. This somewhat abstract and highly condensed statement of fundamental differences between public and private trading has been given to indicate how public trading is, as stated above, not merely an act of substitution but a fundamental change in intent, content and effect of trading, i.e. distributive function of exchange economy under socialism. This statement also re-inforces the point that public trading is an inescapable necessity even in the initial stages of advance towards socialism not merely from standpoint of economic strategy but also from an all-inclusive functional standpoint. Private trading is, as stated before, incompatible with a socialist society in action or in prospect because it is the quintessence of acquisitiveness which of course from the socialist standpoint is the cardinal sin. But private trading has to be replaced by public trading also because only through it a new social calculus needed for a socialist society can be developed and applied to its new exchange apparatus and become the normative force of economic life as a whole.

In India we are, in a fragmentary way, practising public trading without co-relating it with a central social purpose or making it an instrument of organic activity of the economy as a whole. We are practising in this respect, as in many others, a frustrating short-sighted empiricism and are not prepared to think through the issues which it raises and the consequential action which is so clearly implicit in them. Decision with regard to public trading in food grains was strongly recommended by the Food Grain Inquiry Committee 1957[6] and was

6. "We would like to emphasize here that until there is social control over the wholesale trade, we shall not be in a position to bring about a stabilization of food grain prices. Our policy should therefore be progressive and planned socialization wholesale trade" (*Food Grains Enquiry Committee Report*, p. 86).

This recommendation, though not as unambiguous as it should have been, does provide for purchasing of surpluses, limited compulsory procurement, fixation of prices and long-term agreement with Burma and U.S.A. It does envisage a very large measure of effective public trading.

endorsed by the famous Nagpur Resolution of the Congress Party, was again affirmed by the National Development Council (of which all the Chief Ministers of the States and important Ministers of the Central Cabinet are members and which is presided over by the Prime Minister of India) and became the formal decision of the Government of India. For a time it appeared as if state-trading in food grains was in fact going to be introduced on a national scale and would, with the marketing co-operatives at the village and market level, change the whole face of rural economy and all surpluses of food grains would be mobilized and made available for meeting food requirements and "holding the price line"—the new slogan for price stabilization. No preparation was made for implementing this decision and soon most of the Chief Ministers and some of the Central Ministers started working actively against the decision being implemented. The Ex-Food Minister of the Government of India consistently used his position and authority to make this decision a dead letter and now (August 1964) again in the midst of grave food crisis were hopelessly wobbling about it and are frightened of establishing a state monopoly in wholesale trade in food grains. It shows how bold decisions are taken in this country and how easily they can be set aside or relegated to the background by underground pressures.

SOCIAL ALIGNMENTS

The fact of the matter is that powerful mercantile interests at all levels, whom introduction of public trading on any significant scale would naturally supersede, are all dead against it and they are deeply entrenched in our economy and are a great force in our political life. If their opposition has to be overcome, organized will of the community has to assert itself and prevail through the exercise of authority and with the mass support of the people. This has not happened and as far as one can see, cannot happen because the mercantile interests can count upon the support of most of the men in authority and organized will of the community is used by them and cannot be used against them. This is another instance of distribution of power in India being unfavourable for any real radical changes and a shift in it, being an essential pre-requisite of any big move forward in the direction of socialism. Public trading will really be a big move in this direction, and yet it can be made and maintained only if the shift referred to above in fact takes place. Essential differences between public and private trading, indicated in the preceding paragraphs, can be enunciated and used for conceptual clarification but they are purely of academic interest and will acquire practical importance only if the balance of forces within the country is really altered and the people come into their own. When they do, mercantile interests will not be able to impede the introduction of public trading or sabotage it when it is decided to introduce it as they have done in regard to state trading in food grains. These interests particularly sense danger to themselves in the trends that are at work and are the backbone of most of the reactionary forces in the country.

Public trading or socialization of commerce would need many organizational forms, but the co-operatives and their federations for small independent producers and state corporation at the state and central levels are the two main forms which are likely to be needed for replacing the private trader by public agents. In foreign trade the State Trading Corporation and, within the limits set for it by legislative and administrative provisions, has been a success in spite of its bureaucratic operation and lack of well-defined policy. If foreign trade is to be socialized entirely a number of state corporations will be needed for specialized functions on regional and commodity basis. In extending the scope of public trading in foreign trade we have to take into account the fact that in important commodities like tea and jute foreign interests can and do exercise semi-monopolistic control and they have long-standing contacts with commercial interests in all important foreign markets which give them strong strategic position in foreign trade in these commodities. Their resistance to the introduction and development of public trading in what has been their close preserve will, it may be assumed, be formidable and will have to be counteracted by a well-conceived and carefully administered plan of advance towards socialization backed by knowledge, resources and strength. Foreign interests are, as a matter of fact, very strong in the entire foreign trade of India and the fact that foreign exchange banks have, as pointed out above, virtual monopoly of financing our international trade and close relations with the big financial institutions of foreign countries, makes their position even stronger and their obstruction to any scheme of nationalization or socialization can well be assumed; and this assumption has to be the basis of counter-strategy and tactics. All these reasons make it necessary to acquire positions of strength before a challenge is thrown to the powerful private interests through schemes of public trading in external trade. But the same reasons also clearly point to the necessity of bold decisions on this all-important subject and with due preparation its execution on an extensive and comprehensive basis. Assuming that there is no lack of firmness on our part and all the hesitations have been set at rest before this decision is taken, organizationally speaking the implementation of such a decision need, to repeat, present no insuperable difficulties. A firm decision on this point is urgently called for, for external trade is a commanding height of great importance, and export and import control, even much more honestly and efficiently administered than they are today, are, it may be re-stated, no substitute for all-out public trading in international commerce from the national and socialist standpoints. The assumption referred to above is a big assumption and as stated above, factually speaking, is not warranted; but this reservation, as has been made abundantly clear, applies to the whole question of developing a socialist society in the existing situation, and does not weaken the case for socialization of foreign trade in India. Without taking over this strategic height for the country and the community the development of socialist society in India will be greatly hindered, and we should know this vital fact and act upon this knowledge.

Foreign trade, in spite of its great importance represents only 5 per cent of gross national product and is less than 4 per cent of world trade. Foreign trade can be fully planned only and adequately if internal trade is co-operativized and when necessary nationalized and its flow is placed on a rationalized basis by avoiding all unnecessary movement of goods and planning it in terms of village, area, district, state and national production plans. Decentralization of planning and development on an integrated basis, which has been duly stressed already, and the need and importance of which is universally admitted is urgently needed in the context in which mobilization of all surplus can be achieved and their distribution and allocation according to a budget of needs on a social priority basis brought about. A network of marketing co-operatives from the basic to national level has to be built up and linked to production, credit and development plans. As stated already socialization of internal trade on this basis together with a state trading organization at the state and national levels was the substance of the decision of the Government of India a few years ago which was sabotaged; but the formal position is that this major decision is still in the field and can, if the necessary conditions be created, become the basis of nation-wide action. This is a non-controversial proposition and could be implemented if the enormous problem of fitting millions of traders, big and small, into a national plan of public trading, can be solved. Progress of marketing co-operatives has, as pointed out already, been disappointingly slow so far, and it is unlikely that even the very modest target of the Third Plan will in fact be realized. But there is no doubt that this development is of fundamental importance, and, if the crisis of will[7] with which we are griev-

7. That we are very seriously afflicted by the crisis of will has been very clearly indicated by the poverty of thinking and futility of action in the current decisions on food policy and anti-inflationary measures at the highest level. The mercantile interests have once more, with the silent but effective

ously afflicted, can be resolved, socialization of internal trade is not only imperative but also practicable and can take us a long way on our road to socialism.

Besides the necessity of public trading for the reasons discussed above, it is also of great potential importance as a means of enlarging our internal capital resources for development, stabilizing prices and developing a national price structure needed for an emerging socialist economy. As pointed out in the next chapter, our failure to prevent the rise of prices and even formulate a socialist price-policy is largely due to our internal and external trade being almost entirely in the hands of private merchants who not only are indifferent to the needs of socialism but are, so far as they are operating consciously, checking its development and are aligned, in politics and otherwise, with anti-socialist forces. Public trading is both business and politics. The whole mentality of the merchants is, to repeat, quintessence of acquisitiveness; and by force of tradition, habit and personal interest they are not only a drag on the advance of socialism but among its most persistent and uncompromising opponents. They have to be dislodged from their present important position and their capacity to obstruct and defeat socialist policies and measures has to be resolutely neutralized. Resolutely? Yes. But how has the strength necessary for the purpose to be mustered is a part of the fundamental problem of developing the required steam for socialist advance and answer to it has to be a part of the complete answer to the wider question. In a sense the answer is simple. The necessary social momentum has to be generated and made the propelling force of the socialist advance. This is, however, not the answer

support of the men in high places, sabotaged all proposals for nationalization of wholesale trade in foodgrains and rice mills and control and reversal of the trend of rapidly rising prices. Augeries for real and adequate action in this respect could not be more gloomy and yet the case for planned trade through public trading organizations remain as strong as ever—is really stronger because experience makes it clear that socialization of distributive apparatus of the country has to be one of the highest priorities of our public policy.

but repetition of the same question in other words. This is the question of all questions and answer to it has yet to be found from the national standpoint.

International setting of trade has been made clear by the discussions and conclusions of the World Conference on Trade and Development recently held at Geneva. For the expansion of trade of the underdeveloped countries it is necessary for them not only to consolidate the solidarity which they realized at the Conference but plan their trade with a view to developing markets independent, as far as possible, of the markets of the developed countries and also realize as large a measure as possible of harmony in their development plans and rely more and more upon mutual assistance. They have to develop and exercise pressure through which they can secure better terms of trade, stabilization of commodity prices, markets for their manufactured and semi-manufactured commodities, reduction of discriminatory tariffs and allocation of a large measure of international assistance on a fair basis without their having to compromise their independence of policy and action. These countries have very largely a socialist approach and goal, and have to re-orient their trade policies in new terms. This means that the emergent countries have to change the very basis of their trade policies and link them closely with their social objectives and policies. India, in this new setting, can play an active role and will be able to do so if her own internal and external trade is planned in relation to the need for realizing a socialist society with the utmost speed and earnestness.

ment of the developments that have taken place and in the various projections into the future there is no indication that the fact that the country is formally and finally committed to the realization of a socialist society has had any impact on the thinking of the policy-makers and those who are managing our monetary institutions; and their practice has, it need not be added, hardly been affected by it. Not only has the country been in the grip of continuous and increasing inflation in this period, but it has run its course without any effective measures being taken to arrest its course and even the fact that it could not but involve more inequitable distribution of income and wealth has not even been appreciated, and no attempt has been made or is even now being contemplated by which its disturbing effects can be counter-acted or neutralized. The severity of the strains that it involves has not been even admitted and very misleading comparisons have been made between inflation in India and other countries to posit its inevitability in a developing country and the gravity of the evils from which the country is suffering on that account have been greatly underrated. Currency, credit and prices have almost been entirely unplanned, and in the sphere of rural credit, in which the need for integrated credit programme and therefore for introduction of some element of planning was recognized and made the basis of action, quantitative expansion of credit owing to the expansion of advances by the Reserve Bank to the co-operative institutions has only strengthened, as stated in an earlier chapter, the hold of the upper strata in rural economy and linking of credit to production and marketing, which was the prime object of these measures, has not taken place. Our currency and credit system has, to repeat, been operated on principles entirely unsuited to a planned economy, and fragmentary efforts to contribute to the country's development by changes in credit policy have mostly defeated themselves. As stated above, it is a matter of the utmost importance that currency and credit system of the country should, in principle and working, be in accord with its social objective.

Even in a socialist economy in the making it cannot and should not be autonomous, it must increasingly fulfil the purposes for which the economy is being developed and use its authority to introduce and accelerate the process of social change. It has to be an instrument of an integrated social policy, but as an instrument it is of great importance and has to be designed and used as such.

THE RESERVE BANK

The Central bank even in unplanned capitalistic economies is meant to regulate and direct the entire currency and credit systems, promote stability of prices, increase supervision and control over the banking system and as banker of the state and custodian of currency and international reserves, keep a vigilant watch over the economy as a whole and either take action itself if it can or indicate to the Government the need for taking action when the economy shows signs of getting out of gear and calls for remedial measures for removing the cause of its developing stresses. It, in other words, is meant to be an organ of directing and steering the economy and planned purposive action in order to keep it on an even keel. In almost all countries the central banks have been nationalized because experience has made it abundantly clear that private institutions could not possibly discharge the important public functions which have to be undertaken by it. The fact that the Reserve Bank of India, as our Central Bank, was nationalized after independence, has assumed supervisory and regulatory functions over the banks and generally speaking has taken an over-all view of the economy does not mean that it has become plan-oriented in its approach or its avowed social objectives have had any real impact on its policy and administration. The governor, deputy governors and largely speaking directors of the Reserve Bank have, by training, experience and associations, been men of pronounced conservative leanings, if not actually wedded to the maintenance of status-quo; and could not possibly be expected to think in terms of bold departures or radical innovations. All available material already shows that their minds, policies and practices were tradition-bound, the range of their thinking was limited by the views and experience of the institutions like the Federal Reserve System or the Bank of England and that it was not realized at all that tasks, which have been set us by special conditions and problems of our economy, adoption of socialism as the goal of economic development and inflationary pressure created by forces released during and after the war and greatly aggravated in the period of planning, called for a courageous path-finding effort and could not possibly be performed on assumptions the inadequacy, if not falsity, of which was demonstrated even by experience of the countries whom we looked up to for inspiration and guidance.

Issue of currency by the Reserve Bank requires no initiative or policy decision on its part. It issues notes either because the banks convert balances maintained by them in excess of the statutory requirements into cash or take advances from the Reserve Bank against securities. And further it also issues notes to make short-term ways and means advances to the Central and State Governments or against *ad hoc* treasury bills when expansion of currency takes place to meet capital needs of the plan, i.e. for deficit financing. The rate of interest which the banks have to pay for their advance against securities also makes it possible for the Reserve Bank to charge for the expansion of currency, but as the banks charge higher rates of interest from their clients, receive interest from the Government on the securities and also use the cash which they acquire to increase their credit which is a multiple of their cash reserve, this rate in itself does not make this acquisition of currency an onerous transaction for them. Issue of currency is more a passive than positive act for the Reserve Bank and, as stated above, does not require or involve initiative or policy decision on its part. During the war, as is well known, the Reserve Bank issued currency for financing war purchases against sterling balances, i.e. the securities of the British Government. It had no say in the matter, its role was purely mechanical. Expansion of currency against *ad hoc* treasury bills is also purely mechanical and against securities deposited or pledged it is almost, though not quite, the same. In both cases notes are issued without any assessment · of over-all situation by the Reserve Bank and there is no planned expansion of currency.

There are five instruments of credit control which are being used by the Reserve Bank for regulating the credit operations of the banks. The rate of interest, the use of variable reserve and open market operations are methods for quantitative regulation of credit and have no relation to the implementation of the plan. But even as such they have not been found effective in practice and even from traditional standpoint have not fulfilled their avowed object. Rate of interest, the rate charged by the Reserve Bank for its short-term advance to the banks— our Bank Rate, was maintained at 3 per cent from 1938-39 to 1951, was raised to 3½ per cent in 1951 and 4 per cent in 1957. In 1951 India, to keep company with the advanced countries changed its 'cheap money' policy and raised the rate from 3 to 3½ per cent and six years later it was, as stated, raised by another ½ per cent. The bank rate in India has a psychological effect and the rates charged by the banks move in sympathy with it, but as an instrument of credit control, particularly in a highly inflationary situation, which has existed in this country, it has practically no effect and expansion of currency and credit and even seasonal variations in money supply were not significantly affected by the changes in the bank-rate. There is hardly, it is well known, any relation between the rate of interest, which the agriculturists have to pay for more than 80 per cent of their credit requirements even now, in spite of the considerable extension of assistance by the Reserve Bank since 1955 for expansion of rural credit, and the bank rate and the rates charged by the banks and the rates charged by the indigenous bankers, though not unrelated to these rates, follow as a rule their independent course and are not amenable to the credit control measures of the Reserve Bank. Even in countries like the U.K. effectiveness of the bank-rate as an instrument of credit control has been authoritatively questioned[2] and in most other countries reliance upon it for the same purpose is being diminished. In India for reasons

2. The Radcliffe Committee, which enquired into the working of the British Currency System, very clearly indicated how the Bank Rate had ceased to be an effective instrument of currency and credit control. But in spite of the *Radcliffe Committee Report* the Bank Rate myth in Great Britain is still alive. The anti-inflationary measures taken by the Chancellor in Great Britain in the first half of 1962, when, according to the financial correspondent of the *Observer*, the British economy was *not* overloaded, invited the following observation from him: "For the urgent need is to debunk the whole ridiculous myth, the whole psychological symbolism that has been built round the Bank-Rate. In no other country in Europe does the central bank's lending rate attract much public attention.... The main guardians of the Bank-Rate mythology are the politicians and some treasury officials who have built up a fantastic world of green, amber and red lights. It is high time to start treating the Bank-Rate as a useful technical instrument to be changed whenever necessary by the Bank of England on their own initiative without any portentious implications for the national policy" (*The Observer*, London, March 11, 1962).

The British worship their precedents and keep up their rituals like "change of guards" or the change of the Bank Rate when both have become obsolete. But why should we refuse to debunk this myth even after having committed ourselves to socialism and planned economy. When the Reserve Bank was formed, we introduced this "ridiculous myth, the whole psychological symbolism" when it had no relation to the facts of our economy because in the country of our rulers it had a tremendous prestige or rather our rulers introduced it themselves because they knew no better. Now after independence and when the whole position has been radically changed by our planning programme and socialist objective, we still persist in living in "this fantastic world of green, amber and red lights" even when the traffic has long by-passed the crossing on which these lights are being operated. As stated above, in the matter of credit and finance we are still even more hide-bound than in other matters. The fact that the Reserve Bank has had three I.C.S. Governors, all the more hide-bound because of belonging to the most hide-bound "the Superior Service", explains, besides of course other reasons why this myth is not being debunked in India. It is high time that not only we should debunk "the Bank Rate myth" but also other myths which are entirely irrelevant to the kind of economy which we have to build and which, according to our professions, we want to build in this country.

given above this rate has, it is clear, only a symbolic value and as an instrument of credit control it is hardly of any importance.

Moreover reliance upon bank-rate and unplanned interest rate structure in a planned economy with socialist objective is wrong in principle. Rates of interest should be used for planning for accounting purpose and even to direct and regulate investment, but such rates have to be specific rates and related to specific purposes and used to promote economy in the use of capital goods. Keynes's view, that interest is a monopoly charge, is not needed for regulating savings or investments and only strengthens the position of the rentier class, is as valid now as it was twenty-five years ago, though its content and implications are being forgotten even by the most ardent Keynesians. Under socialism or in an economy in transition towards socialism in which savings and investments have largely, though not entirely, to become functions of the community, interest, as an important category of income and determinant of costs and prices, has to be reduced to a secondary position and assigned a new functional role in the economy. Anyway, apart from the fact that the rate of interest has been and is largely ineffective in India, money-supply in general and particular regions and areas should not depend upon and be regulated by it. The bank-rate in India, even as a symbol, has only a vestigial significance and should not have any place in the armoury of credit control, which as stated below, should be determined by a budget of planned credit requirements of all economic units in agriculture, trade, transport and industries—large and small. This budget can be prepared and executed only if the whole economy is re-organized on a co-operative or corporate basis and individual producers, traders, etc. can be contacted and receive credit assistance through some form of association, which is amenable to public guidance, supervision and regulation. This condition, it need not be added, does not exist at present and has to be provided.

The other methods of quantitative control, i.e. open-market

operations and use of variable reserves, are also of little importance and have no relation to our actual conditions and problems. Sale and purchase of public securities by the Reserve
Bank in order to replenish or reduce the reserves of the banks
with a view to bringing about expansion or contraction of
credit—i.e. open-market operations—have been resorted to in
the post-war period but more for the purpose for credit expansion than its contraction—i.e. to provide a large base for credit
structure. Now the Reserve Bank does not buy Securities but
gives advances with securities as collateral and purchase of
securities is generally speaking more an operation in carrying
out the borrowing programme of the central and state governments than an instrument of credit control. The banks hold
large stocks of public securities which they use freely as collateral for strengthening their reserves. They continue to receive
interest on them and can, even if the bank rate is raised to
increase their cost of borrowing, use their credit advances for
advancing loans to their clients, as stated above, at higher rate
of interest and, of course, their credit deposits as multiple of
the additional reserve, if the Reserve Bank advances are retained as a base for credit expansion, increase their lending and
income-earning capacity. The open market operations have an
expansary rather than regulating function, and in practice the
Reserve Bank has not been able to utilize them for curbing any
undesirable growth of money-supply. Even in the countries like
U.S.A. and U.K. open-market operations are of limited value
when eligible securities can be used as collaterals by outright
sales for monetizing their investments—i.e. adding to their
monetary resources either by selling or pledging the securities.
In India, as indicated above, "they are guided," in the words
of a Reserve Bank Publication, "also by the exigencies of
Government borrowing."[3] These exigencies have been growing
in importance and practically eclipsed the credit control functions of the open-market operations.

3. *The Reserve Bank of India—Functions and Working*, p. 40.

By the amendment Act of 1956 the Reserve Bank can vary the statutory reserve of the banks from 5 to 20 per cent in respect of demand liabilities and 2 to 8 per cent in respect of time liabilities. The object of this provision, which also exists in the U.S.A. and a number of other countries, is to exercise a restrictive effect on the expansion of credit when the banks are in a state of excessive liquidity and can bring about undesirable credit inflation. This provision was used in 1961 by requiring each schedule bank to maintain additional reserve of 25 per cent of the amount by which its total liabilities on May 6, 1962 exceeded the total liabilities on March 11, 1960 and 50 per cent of the increase in total liabilities since May 6, 1960. This did not have the desired effect and had to be followed up by a system of graded lending rates and graduated rates were charged for amounts exceeding certain quotas. This restriction brought about decline in scheduled bank credit and was later relaxed. The significance of these measures lies in the facts that these restraints, while limiting credit for less urgent needs and generally discouraging recourse to the Reserve Bank, placed no restrictions on the volume of credit. These provisions are, however, of minor importance and do not make any change of principle in the working of the credit system.

The Reserve Bank has since 1956 used the power which it has acquired under the Banking Companies Act, to restrict their advances against certain selected commodities and also against selected securities. These restrictions have been imposed from time to time and withdrawn when their need was assumed to be over and their object was to check unhealthy speculation in commodities and securities. They were partly circumvented by obtaining unsecured advances and raising credit by other ways. The selective controls are now a general feature of the credit system of a number of countries and imply that credit institutions need to be restrained in specific terms and not merely by quantitative restrictions. This is indirectly a step in the direction of planned allocation of credit, but does not go far enough. It prevents abuse of credit but does not involve its planned distribution. In a socialist economy credit has to be granted, as stated before, according to a credit plan for the economy as a whole. It is not enough to take preventive measures. Positive steps have to be taken to ensure that credit is made available and utilized according to a schedule of social priorities, and no one gets credit against collaterals. The whole concept of collateral securities is contrary to the purpose of planning. All credit, including co-operative credit, should be granted according to credit worthiness of persons and purposes and not according to the possessions of material assets. This means that new premises have to be adopted for the working of the credit system.

Credit itself has to be provided and utilized—selective according to the objects for which it is granted and their relative importance in the scheme of planned production. Selective credit controls are, if they are effective, a safeguard against lapses in an unplanned economy, and not a measure for channelizing credit in specific uses.

The Reserve Bank has, in the last seven years, acquired a positive interest in economic development by participating actively in co-operative credit and industrial finance. In co-operative credit, as stated in an earlier chapter, it has granted long, medium and short-term credit for agricultural development on an extensive scale. Financial accommodation provided by the Reserve Bank to the state co-operative banks rose to Rs 89 crores in 1960-61 from 13.20 crores in 1955-56. For short-term finance for seasonal agricultural operations limits sanctioned to the State Co-operative Banks amounted to Rs 115.04 crores in 1960-61 as compared with Rs 28.79 crores in 1955-56. The Reserve Bank also granted loans for periods between 3 to 5 years for reclamation of land, building and improvements etc. and the outstanding credit for the purpose in 1960-61 amounted to Rs 8.63 crores. It also contributed Rs 33.17 crores to the debentures issued by four Central Land Mortgage Banks—53 per cent of the total issued in 1960-61. Loans were also provided for working capital, purchase of shares and block capital of co-operative sugar factories and it also contributed largely to the finance of the National Co-operative Development and Warehousing programme and 37 warehouses were set up by the Central Warehousing Corporation and 85 by the State Warehousing Corporations. These are important developments and have made the Reserve Bank an active participant in rural development. It has, however, been already pointed out in an earlier chapter that this programme has mostly benefited the richer sections of the rural community, credit, largely speaking, has not been linked to production and no changes of any importance have taken place in the basic facts of rural economy. This means that expansion of rural credit has strengthened status quo, i.e. the relative position of the minority in power has greatly improved and that of the majority of dispossessed classes has become definitely worse. The Reserve Bank, in other words, has by active participation in rural development, used its large resources and authority to make the rural economy even more oligarchic than before and widened the gulf between the small privileged minority and very large disprivileged majority. The fact of its active participation is significant, it has ceased to be merely a custodian of central reserves and lender of last resort. It has initiated important developments and made much larger funds available for rural finance. That has, however, accentuated social divisions and made the task of the new social forces, which are working for a classless society, more and not less difficult.

In the sphere of industrial finance also the Reserve Bank has initiated measures which have largely expanded funds available for industrial developments and contributed, it may be presumed, to the increasing industrialization of the country. Through Industrial Finance Corporation, the State Finance Corporations and Industrial Credit and Investment Corporation, the Re-finance Corporation, National Industrial Development Corporation, the Small Scale Industries Corporations and the State Bank Schemes for financing small industries the

Reserve Bank has also become an active participant in industrial development, contributed large funds for the purpose and enlisted the co-operation of commercial banks, the Life Insurance Corporation and other financial institutions. Since its (Industrial Finance Corporation's) inception up to March 1961 sanctioned loans of Rs 99.67 crores and disbursed Rs 54.90 crores, the State Finance Corporations sanctioned loans and advances of Rs 36.17 crores of which Rs 22.16 crores were disbursed, the Industrial Credit and Investment Corporation's total financial assistance sanctioned by it up to the end of 1960 amounted to Rs 34.41 crores. The National Industrial Development Corporation provided Rs 19.59 crores up to March 1960 for modernization and rehabilitation of jute and cotton mills. The Government of India provided assistance to the state to the extent of Rs 19.59 crores for loans to small-scale industries from 1958-59 to 1961-62, the State Finance Corporations in first four years of the 2nd Plan advanced Rs 10.07 crores for the same purpose and the amount of credit by assistance by the State Bank of India for co-ordinated provision of assistance to small-scale industries amounted to Rs 8.85 crores in 1960-61. Assistance in the sphere of industrial finance was granted not only by the Reserve Bank, but it played a very active role in its extension and its own contribution was very considerable. Large as the financial assistance granted from public sources to industries in the private sector from the published reports of the various financing agencies is, it is not clear how far their operations are co-ordinated, how the prospects and performance of the units applying for assistance are assessed and to what extent social content of industrial development receives its due consideration. Some attempts have been made to promote coordination, but the spheres and functions of these agencies are neither clearly demarcated nor defined. But from the available information it is quite clear that resources of their financial

4. "It is also evident that the working of the planned economy has contributed to this growth of big companies in Indian industry. The growth of the private sector in industry and especially of the big companies has

agencies have been largely used4 for promoting the growth of very large business concerns. It is a fair presumption that these agencies are mostly prompted by orthodox considerations in the grant of financial assistance. In the private sector there has not existed and does not exist any plan of development. Rough targets of development for particular industries are fixed, but actual investment in and development of industries, in spite of the licensing procedure and capital issues control, do not proceed on a planned basis and location and regional distribution of industries are determined by considerations of private gain rather than public good. Private industries have received a large measure of public assistance but their development has taken place without giving any heed to the needs for regional balance or social objectives of the economy. Information regard-

been facilitated by the financial assistance rendered by public institutions like the Industrial Finance Corporation (IFC), the National Industrial Development Corporation (NIDC) etc. Thus, as on 30th June, 1963, loans had been approved by the IFC for a total sum of Rs 127.7 crores. The number of concerns to which loans had been sanctioned was 244; 143 of these concerns were given loans of less than Rs 50 lakhs each, the total amounting to Rs 32.7 crores, while 101 concerns were given loans exceeding Rs 50 lakhs, the total being Rs 94.9 crores. Loans exceeding Rs 1 crore each were given to 22 concerns and accounted for Rs 34.8 crores, while loans below Rs 10 lakhs were given to 32 concerns, the total amounting to Rs 1.8 crores. Lending by NIDC which totalled Rs 3 crores up to March 1963 would also generally be to bigger companies."

This also applies specially to the loans advanced by the Industrial Finance Corporation. The Committee has indicated the process by which the loan assistance given by the IFC becomes more concentrated with time. It says, "Thus, as on 30 June 1963, in respect of the total amount of loans extended of Rs 127.7 crores, the number of individual loans for amounts not exceeding Rs 50 lakhs was 350 (60 being to co-operatives) and the total of such loans amounted to Rs 68.7 crores (of which Rs 14.5 crores was to co-operatives) while only 69 loans for amount in excess of Rs 50 lakhs had been given for a total amount of Rs 58.9 crores (including Rs 22.3 crores for co-operative societies). As the number of concerns receiving more than one loan increases, the proportion of concerns in the lower size category of loan recipients declines and that in the higher size category increases. The fact, therefore, remains that the loan assistance given by the IFC has assisted the growth of bigger companies more than that of the smaller companies." (*The Mahalnobis Committee Report*, p. 30-31.)

ing the working of these financial agencies is limited and a general independent review and critical examination of their operation is called for. The Reserve Bank has been closely associated with the inception and working of these corporations, but its own horizon being limited by orthodox canons of financial propriety, it has not and could not have used its position and authority to develop the assisted industries to apply and express new social values. Public financial assistance has, there is reason to believe, largely made big business bigger and even small industrial units which have been assisted, have not acquired any sense of social obligation and in respect of wages, labour relations and general business ethics their standards are even lower than those of the larger industries. It has not been appreciated at all that these financing agencies could and should, in granting assistance, have been guided broadly by the social objectives of the economy and applied criteria of wider social import in granting applications for assistance to and appraising the performance of the assisted undertakings. The result, of course, has been that liberal financial assistance has been granted to private industrial undertakings, but they have not assumed any obligations to the community or the country's future on that account and are mainly functioning purely and entirely as agents of a capitalistic society.

Assumption of the new duties by the Reserve Bank in the sphere of co-operative credit and industrial finance, in spite of the limitations (the nature and importance of which it is hardly aware) under which these duties have been discharged, is indicative of a trend which needs to be consciously promoted and quickened. The Reserve Bank has to retain the responsibility as : —

(a) the bankers of the state, other public and semi-public authorities, all important financial institutions,

(b) fiscal agent for receipt and disbursement of public funds,

(c) custodian of international and other liquid reserves,

(d) administration of foreign exchange control and,

(e) managers of public debt.

These functions are almost obligatory for an institution like the Reserve Bank and their performance by it is inherent in the needs of the economy and much more so in the needs of a planned economy. But the Reserve Bank has more and more to function consciously and creatively as an organ of planned economy and make socialism its motivating force. Certain changes which have already taken place have to be carried out consistently and in the perspective of the future of the economy. International reserves have to be separated from the internal reserves necessary for maintaining the liquidity of the economy and regulated mainly with reference to fluctuations in the balance of payments. Issue of notes has to be regulated with reference to estimates of the cash requirements of the community and it is not necessary to maintain any backing or 'cover' for it. Inclusion of the Government securities, short, long-term and *ad hoc* in the currency reserves adds nothing to the security of note issues and creates an illusion of the currency being backed by assets which are also obligations of the Government. There is no sense in supporting one I.O.U. by another I.O.U. and only rational method of note-issue is to ensure that it does not exceed the cash requirements of the country and does not fall short of it. As the economy becomes more and more a planned economy and distribution of goods is carried out through public agencies, cash will be mainly required for purchase of consumption goods from retail stores and payment of wages. For all other transactions credit and debit in entries in bank accounts would do, and through off-setting of payments would make the banking system a clearing agency and keeper of national accounts which would maintain its own liquidity and elaborate provisions for the purpose would not be needed. Every productive and marketing undertaking would do what all public offices and undertakings have to do, i.e. make all payments to one another by drawing upon its balances, send all cash receipts to the central pool and meet their cash requirements by converting their credit balances into cash.

This is the logical line of evolution for our currency and credit system and the Reserve Bank can and should become the central clearing house of the whole exchange mechanism of the country. But even now the Reserve Bank should issue notes without any cover, evolve criteria and methods of planned injection of currency into circulation according to genuine cash requirements and not merely be giving advances against eligible securities and bills and the limits of issue of notes should be raised from time to time according to the estimated cash requirements of the economy. The fact that at present government securities of all sorts, some issued in the past, others acquired as a part of floatation of new loans, others provided for meeting fluctuations in revenue receipts and lastly *ad hoc* treasury bills to cover the issue of currency for deficit financing, i.e. mostly for investment needs of the planned development, are made cover for currency issues, creates unnecessary complications and confusion and provides only an imaginary backing for it. Public debt office should be under the Reserve Bank but its operations should be regulated by principles applicable to public borrowing and not by the needs of the currency. The strength of the note issue should lie in balance between it and the value of transactions for which cash must be used and of course in the general soundness of the economy and the economic policy of the state. If the note issue is strong in this respect, it does not and will not need any backing for maintaining public confidence in it. These changes, as stated already, have taken place or are in progress. What is needed is that their implications should be clearly set forth and their logic followed consistently in theory and practice. If this is done, the Reserve Bank, given the social premises of our overall policy and the imperatives inherent in them, can acquire a positive role in the planned development and transformation of the economy—really become one of its most important organs. If this is to happen, it will have to cease to adopt and act upon the tenets of the currency and credit management of the advanced unplanned capitalistic economies, do its own creative thinking and proceed empirically in the fulfilment of its new role in the light of the experience and working of a planned economy advancing steadily towards the goal of social-ism. This is a paramount need of the Reserve Bank and the economy—a need which has been woefully neglected because it has been, as stated before, bound by convention and tradi-tions of countries like U.K. and U.S.A. and its policy makers and principal administrators have been men without any social horizon and even without any sincere obligation to the avowed policy of the country. That is why the Reserve Bank has been a break on the country's economic and social progress instead of being what it should have been a lever for raising it to a different and higher plane of thought and action. It has, on that account shared even to a greater degree social inertia, myopia and pronounced bias for status-quo which have afflict-ed most men in power in our economy. This state of things has to be altered radically if we are really to go ahead in the direc-tion which the country is taken to have formally set itself as its orienting point of reference.

COMMERCIAL BANKS

The Commercial Banks are, with the exception of the State Bank of India, privately owned and the view once widely held and voiced that they should be nationalized, until 1963 was expressed somewhat casually in the election manifesto of the leftist parties and was not pressed with any perseverence or fervour even by them. The position has changed since the mid-dle of 1963 and now demand for nationalization of these insti-tutions even within the Congress has become insistent though it is being resisted by mainly silent but effective opposition of the conservative forces. These institutions have in the last ten years enlarged their operations, resources and hold over our economy and the fact has involved greater concentration of power, interpenetration of finance and industry and, in spite of the wide powers acquired and exercised by the Reserve Bank to inspect their accounts and working, what happens in the innermost recesses of these institutions in regard to the utilization of credit cannot be known as industrial and financial magnates are such a small and close-knit fraternity that they can by well-known manoeuvres and manipulations, convert the short-term advances and loans by renewal virtually into long-term accommodations, evade restrictions on the banks granting advances to concerns in which the directors are interested and otherwise defeat the purpose of banking legislation. Liquidity has been and still is highly prized as a great source of strength for the commercial banks and maintenance of a high reserve ratio, i.e. ratio between the deposits and cash in hand and balance with the Reserve Bank, in call and short-term loans and investment in Government securities are taken as an index of wise management and sound credit position. A very large but unknown proportion of the current deposits are credit deposits, i.e. they are created by loans granted by the banks themselves and yet it is assumed that cash and ability to convert these assets into cash to meet the possible depositors' demand for it is the essence of good banking and protection of the interest of the depositors is held to be the prime consideration. The proportion of time to total deposits is nearly 60 per cent of the total deposits,5 has been at that level since 1959-60 and yet more than 60 per cent of the funds of the resource of the banks are, as a rule, invested in advances and bills purchased and discounted. Short-term loans can, as stated above, virtually become long-term accommodations by renewals, but the assumption is that mostly banks should lend only for short periods and against bills, merchandize etc. in order to ensure safety of deposits and liquidity of their resources. All this shows how our banking theory and practice in India are still dominated by ideas prevailing in U.K. and other Western countries—particularly the former. Liquidity is measured by the ready marketability of assets, and though it is known that

5. On March 31, 1963 the total deposits of the commercial banks were Rs 2,053.39 crores, savings deposits were Rs 1,187.30 crores and current deposits Rs 866.08 crores.

if selling pressure develops, i.e. there is a general demand to convert assets into cash even the liquid assets like the Government securities cease to be liquid and their market values are bound to collapse unless the Reserve Bank is prepared to support them by liberal assistance, i.e. make cash freely available by using its power to issue notes. In other words, liquidity is really a function of availability of currency to meet the fairly genuine demand for cash; and if it can be established that the demand is genuine either because of the ability of a bank or banks to meet it is in doubt or the economy itself, owing to the expansion or otherwise, has developed the need for more cash, the Reserve Bank can easily make the required amount of currency available as it can expand it (currency) at will without being under an obligation to provide any cover or backing for it and that need not involve any cash to the community. What is necessary is that panics should be allayed as soon as they arise and stringency of cash not be allowed to develop. The Reserve Bank as the lender of last resort already has assumed and can discharge this responsibility as there is no problem of liquidity if the genuineness of the need for cash can be tested and measured. The banks will need some currency in hand as till money to meet their day to day requirements of cash, but they should be able to receive as much of it as they require on their producing evidence of their need for being bona-fide i.e. it having arisen by increase in the number and value of exchange transaction for which credit cannot be used. Their investment in Government securities or discounting of usance bills in themselves are not an index of the cash needs of the community, but it is necessary to frame economic criteria for the purpose which can be objectively applied for the issue of notes to meet their need for cash. They can and should use their real savings for investing in development loans—they should lend them for medium and long periods. They should also invest in private industrial securities if they are issued within the framework of the plan and according to approved priorities. But such investments should be independent of the issue of currency and not become a basis or security for it. Current deposits, assuming they are mostly credit deposits, should be mainly used for providing credit for the period during which economic inputs are 'ripening' into outputs—the duration of gestation of producing process. Investment and credit operations of banks should be clearly distinguished and separated from each other. Credit should be used for current purposes and to the extent to which currency is required for this purpose, it should be made freely available. Investments cannot, without creating inflationary pressures, be financed from credit deposits, and the latter, as stated above, should not be used for the former. For current purposes the need for currency should, to repeat, be independently and objectively measured and met by the Reserve Bank —the note issuing authority.

LIQUIDITY OF ASSETS

At present investments are distinguished from bank credits, but the fiction is maintained that government and other securities against which credit is granted can be made the basis for current loans because they, being easily marketable, are liquid assets. From the point of view of individual banks they are liquid, but from the point of view of banking system they are not and cannot be and represent assets which are either fixed investments or no investments at all as in the case of securities issued by Government for unproductive purposes. Issue of credit and currency against such securities means their "monetization"—converting them into circulating media as a part of the exchange mechanism of the country. In an economy in which market-values determine its workings, this may be the process and may be taken as a rough index of the requirement for currency and credit; and even as that it has, as is well known, a disturbing effect on it. But the process should have no place in a planned economy for in the first place it has no relation to current exchange transactions for which currency and credit are required or for carrying on production during the period of ripening of inputs into outputs. Conclusion, which follows from this line of argument, is that issue of credit and currency in India follows this practice in vogue in unplanned economies and has no relation to the objects, processes and priorities of planning. To the extent to which credit is granted against merchandise or inventories of industrial concerns, it is related to current transactions, but there is no way of differentiating it (credit) from advance needed for "pipeline" requirements from credit for stocking commodities, for hoarding and speculation purposes and selective credit controls, which limits credit by fixing margins or ceilings, are a very rough and ready but not effective means of inhibiting undesirable trends. As stated already, what is needed is truly selective credit—a credit plan with priorities with objective criteria— and not selective credit controls. This credit plan for all purposes and at all levels can be prepared when all production and distribution of goods is planned and is subject to public regulation and control through institutions which can plan for farms, village, area, zone, state and the country—including all industrial and commercial units and without sacrificing flexibility can introduce order and purpose in production and distribution at all levels. The Reserve Bank, the commercial banks and other financial institutions have to assume the responsibility for preparing and implementing currency and credit plan and the need for doing so should have been realized when planning was started in 1951.

The Reserve Bank and the Commercial Banks have, to repeat, yet to understand the implication of planning in the sphere of credit and currency and realize that the social objectives and priorities must determine their policy and operations. They are being run as institutions of an unplanned economy, their top men are, when they are qualified for the positions they hold, drawing salaries which can be justified only in an avowed acquisitive society and are exercising great power and authority without allegiance to the country's goal of socialism. This is also true of the Reserve Bank and the State Banks which have been nationalized, and is, of course, very much truer of the commercial banks which are in the hands of men for whom, as pointed out before, socialism is an object to be frustrated and defeated and not to be promoted or realized. These banks and big business trusts are, in this country, as much if not more than in other capitalist countries, practically being run by the same tycoons. Their financial stake in the banks and even industrial concerns which they are operating and controlling is very small—almost a negligible-proportion, and yet they control the enormous deposits and corporate resources of the business undertakings over which they exercise well-nigh monopolistic power, they have acquired even greater concentration of power since 1951 and the most that one can expect from them is that their operations will not fall short of reasonable standards of an undeveloped capitalistic economy. Even this expectation can in fact not be realized, a very large proportion of them, even judged by these standards, it is a matter of common knowledge, is found wanting and they live and operate largely in an underworld of manoeuveres, manipulations, shady transactions and doubtful deals. They have been and are using their opportunities for aggrandisement of their own powers and many of them are deliberately working for thwarting and defeating the forces of social change. Through inspection, directives and moral suasion crude malpractices of banks can be and have been checked by the Reserve Bank; but that, it ought to be clear, is not the approach which is called for if effective planning is to be introduced in this sphere and the men in authority accept the obligations of socialist planning and work purposefully to make it a reality. To ask for this is to ask for the impossible under the existing conditions. The increasing power and its concentration which the banks stand for in our economy is being used to make a mockery of its socialist aims. This fact is well-known, and yet, even the need for taking action against this abuse of what is an entirely fiduciary position and authority is not understood—much less provided for.

NATIONALIZATION OF BANKS

As stated above the demand for nationalization of commercial banks, which before and after independence was put forward earnestly by articulate sections of the community, faded away until 1963 and is now being thwarted. Even in academic circles it was generally assumed that commercial banking should remain a private enterprize and no appreciable intellectual effort was made even to work out the implications of planning in the sphere of currency and credit. The Planning Commission, the Government of India and of course, the Reserve Bank and the State Bank of India assumed that nationalization of the Reserve and State Banks being an accomplished fact, nationalization of the commercial banks was neither necessary nor desirable; and they could, subject to the exercise of the authority to license, inspect and regulate them, which is vested in the Reserve Bank, be free to grant advances, discount bills and invest in government and other securities as and when they like. It has been clearly indicated above that this is, from the standpoint of planning and socialism, a completely inadequate conception, the very premises of banking in India are traditional and incompatible with the essentials of planning and the general attitude of our top bankers and the way they are conducting affairs of banks are a very serious hindrance in the way of the growth of a socialist economy. This state of things cannot be mended merely by nationalization. The State Bank, which accounts for 25 to 30 per cent of the banking operations in India, has been nationalized and yet the only significant result of this change has been that 400 new branches have been opened in smaller towns. This is a gain, but it does not alter the purpose and scope of operations of this important institution; and the Reserve Bank itself has, as stated before, been operated on principles which practically means continuance of the traditional central banking theory and practice and has hardly assumed any role in the sphere of currency and credit planning. This is subject to reservation regarding the role which Reserve Bank and the State Bank are playing in respect of rural and industrial finance since 1955-56; and it is from the point of view being urged here, not a significant reservation because rural credit expansion has had no relation to production and marketing plans, and industrial finance also has not been linked to any plans, functional or regional, and the cannons of credit advances have practically remained unchanged. Yes, merely nationalization of commercial banks is not enough for changing India's currency and credit structure in the right direction, and yet this has to be first step if India is to have a credit system suited to the requirements of the planned economy. Banking is of such strategic importance for growth and social change that unless it is publicly owned, operated and its working is completely free from the taint of the pursuit of private interest and gain, it cannot be fitted in the framework of a planned economy or function with due regard to its primary needs. Currency and credit differ in form but not in substance so far as the provisions of the media of exchange is concerned and it is necessary that they should be administered on an integrated basis and be subject to the same operative principles. These are very convincing reasons why commercial banks should be nationalized and even much more so is the need for putting an end to the massive concentration of power which commercial banking in India stands for and actively promotes.[6] It is abso-

6. It is well known that the largest industrial complexes controls and operate the big commercial banks and their resources can be drawn upon for consolidating and extending their economic power. Of the eight most important commercial banks 77 per cent of the directors are also the directors of the big industrial houses and exercise a decisive voice in their policy and administration. Over twelve per cent of their total advances in 1962 were given to the companies in which the directors were directly interested, but this is not the limit of the accommodation received by them from the banks which they were controlling. There were other methods by which the resources of the banks were utilized by them for their own concerns. It is significant that proportion of such advances by the nationaliz-ed State Bank of India in 1962 amounted to 26 per cent of the total such advances by 15 largest banks. The State Bank advances to its directors for the undertakings in which they were interested amounted to Rs 72.8 crores. This shows how true is the statement that nationalization of the State Bank

lutely wrong that there should be a private quasi-monopoly in the control and allocation of the capital resources of the community and it should also exercise the crucial function of creating credit. That this quasi-monopoly in India is opposed to and incompatible with socialism makes it all the more imperative that it should be terminated by public ownership of the commercial banks. The fact that public pressure in favour of this change, has been greatly weakened in spite of the climate of vocal public opinion having changed since 1963 for the better is due to the balance of forces, to repeat for the nth time, not been in favour of socialism. It does not, however, make it any the less essential that this change should be brought about and the demand for it pressed home with full vigour of the organized public opinion.

Nationalization of commercial banks will raise very important issues of organization, norms of credit policy and the technique of credit planning and control which cannot be discussed here. As stated above, credit and currency functions have to be clearly differentiated from investment functions. Currency and credit are, to repeat, needed as circulating media and are a means by which the need for working capital can be met. The cost of supplying credit and currency is negligible. But for investment, surplus has to be produced, mobilized, pooled and allocated on a planned basis and though it involves a choice between immediate and deferred consumption, incentive of a

---

of India has made practically no difference so far as its relation to the powerful private economic interests are concerned. There is no doubt whatsoever that the increasing resources, power and strength which the big industrial houses have acquired, are, not to an inconsiderable extent, due to the fact that they have been able to use the rapidly expanding resources of the commercial banks for building up their economic empires. "The presumption seems," in the words of the Mahalnobis Committee, "to be strongly in favour of the thesis that there is an intimate relation between the growth of the big banks and the growth of big business in the country during the Plan periods" (Op. Cit., 48, para 51). The only way in which this relation can be put to an end is to put an end to the private ownership of the commercial banks.

high rate of interest is not required in order to increase the supply of surplus. In all countries public and corporate savings are increasing in importance and relative importance of personal savings is decreasing. In all planned economies including ours, provision for credit and currency for current transactions and of surpluses for capital formation, i.e. provision of fixed material assets for development, are functions which have to be assigned to separate institutions and their working has to be co-ordinated. A complete re-organization of our current credit and investment institutions will have to be undertaken if it is decided, as it should be, that private enterprize, both for the provision of credit and capital resources for investment, is irrelevent if these functions are to be discharged in the highest interests of the community. The country will need for planned development currency and credit plans on the one hand and investment plan on the other. They have to be inter-related, but specialization of functions and institutions is inherent in the very conception of these plans and will have to be provided for. It may be repeated that nationalization of commercial banks should not mean that, apart from the change of ownership, banking system will continue to operate as it is being operated today. The operative principles, techniques and objectives will be very different. These will have to be worked out with care and put into effect with clear understanding of the significance of the differences. And, of course, the men, who will develop and operate the new system, will have to educate themselves in its essentials and create a cadre of officers who will, besides having integrity and capacity for hard work, have social daring and due understanding of the credit needs of a socialist planned economy. A banker of the latter will have to develop and project a very different image of himself than what is associated with the banker of today. He, like all other key men of this economy, will first and foremost have to be a social architect, i.e. he will have to make banking an instrument of socialism and himself be its devoted votary. A statement like this brings into bold relief the gap between what we have or are likely to get and our manifest needs in banking as in other fields. The width of this gap, however, should not cloud our understanding of the essentials, lead us to our taking anti-thesis as a substitute for the thesis or nurse the hope that banking of today contains even the germs of banking of a socialist economy.

PRICE POLICY

Experience since 1951 has made it abundantly clear that fluctuations of prices in India have been wide and violent, and it has also demonstrated our complete inability to regulate or control them with any degree of success or express and implement any coherent, consistent policy through prices and their movements. And this has happened in spite of the fact that prices of a large number of essential commodities like steel, cement, fertilizers, coal, oil, soda-ash, sugar etc. have been fixed by the State and their distribution has also been subject to public control; and in spite of our oscillating between controls and de-controls, prices of food grains have not, as it was inevitable, been left to follow their own course and pattern of these movements, as of the movements of all prices, does not indicate any relation between them and, as stated above, any coherent and consistent policy. The general upward trend of prices has also been the result of forces beyond our control, all attempts to check or stabilize them, in spite of the repeated declarations of the Government's determination 'to hold the price line' have failed, and this trend has caused economic distress to a vast majority of our people and been one of the most important factors in having made the distribution of increasing income and wealth in the country even more inequitable than before. The severe hardships involved in this process have been superimposed on the hardships caused by the rise of prices in the war and post-war years, which in themselves had a most disturbing effect on the relative positions of the different social classes, increased greatly social disparities and caused widespread distress. Now once again it is being declared with a show of great firmness that the upward course of prices has

to and must be arrested, every effort should be directed
'towards preventing a rise of prices of essential commodities,'[7]
and it is intended, as it was under the first two plans that a
price structure should be maintained which should encourage
a pattern of production which accords with the requirements
of the plan. So far prices and their movements, broadly speaking, have had hardly anything to do with accord between
them and the requirements or achievements of the plans, the
course which the prices have followed and their inter-relations
have not conformed to pre-designed pattern or relativities and
their impact on the economy has also been not the result of
any conscious purpose or action on the part of the planning
authorities and really speaking there has been no price-structure as such but merely an incidental combination of unplanned price movements each of which was brought about by
factors unrelated to any policy or programme. This has happened in spite of the fact that prices of a number of important
commodities have been fixed by public authorities and their
movements have been determined by policy decisions. But even
among these prices there has been no planned inter-relation
and *ad hoc* decisions have determined their course. In other
words, all price movements in this country have been, since
1951, as before largely the result of fortituous conjunction of
conditions and circumstances and most of the measures taken
to control or regulate them have "been of *ad hoc* nature—
more or less administrative improvisations intended to meet
particular problems regarding individual commodities from
time to time" and "it has not been found possible to weave
these *ad hoc* measures into a concrete programme of action
covering all important commodities".[8] There has been in fact
no comprehensive price policy and given the existing planning
and institutional set-up and the structure and premises of the
present currency and credit system such a policy could not

7. *Third Five Year Plan*, p. 127.
8. *Changing India*, edited by M. B. Sovani and V. M. Dandeker, S. R. Sen,
'Price Policy in India', p. 262.

have been formulated and implemented.

MONEY-SUPPLY

Money supply is not the only determinant of prices and price level; but it is of fundamental importance in shaping the course of prices, and money supply in India has from 1950 to 1963 increased rapidly but without any planned relation beween it and the needs of the economy. From 1950-51 total money supply increased from Rs 1,971 crores to Rs 2,184 crores in 1955-56 and Rs 2,793 crores in 1961-62 and Rs 3,322 crores on March 31, 1963; currency increased for the same years from Rs 1,331 to Rs 1,505 crores and Rs 2,027 crores and Rs 2,386 crores and current deposits from Rs 640 crores to Rs 679 and 784 crores and Rs 906.89 crores.[9] This expansion of money-supply has been largely determined by the government expenditure on development and otherwise, but has not been planned in any sense of the word. In the table in the footnote[10] indicators are given of expansion of money supply, increase in national income, in agricultural and industrial production. These are rough indicators, and as relation between

9. Basic Statistics relating to Indian Economy Table 55, and Economic Survey 1963-64, Table 4.1.

It has, however, to be borne in mind that savings deposits are now nearly two-thirds of the total deposits of the commercial banks, They are, generally not included in money supply; but the distinction between the current and savings deposits is increasingly becoming less clear owing to the facilities being granted to the depositors for drawing upon their savings bank account for making payments.

10. Comparative Indices of Increase of Prices, Money Supply, National Income, Agricultural Production & Industrial Production

	Prices (Base 1951-53)	Money Supply	National Income (Base 1948-49)	Agricultural Production (Base 1949-51)	Industrial Production (Base 1950-51)
1950-51	102.3	(100)	102.3	96	100
1955-56	92.5	(105)	116.0	117	139
1960-61	124.9	(140)	137.1	135	184
1962-63	127.9	(—)	154.33	141.6	—
1963-64	139.1	(165)	—	—	—

money supply and the number and value of exchange trans-action is a matter which requires very careful analysis and appraisal, it is not possible to explain the movement of prices in terms of this relation merely in quantitative terms. Besides the changes in the turnover of money, it is necessary to take into account the extent to which market factors are increasing in importance in our economy, i.e. the extent to which the latter is being increasingly monetized and how far investment is increasing incomes without at the same time increasing pro-portionately the supply of consumption goods according to the changing pattern of demand. Moreover, distribution of national income about which we know next to nothing at present, has necessarily powerful impact on general prices and relative prices of different commodities, and owing to our ignorance of the effects of this important factor, we cannot explain or indicate how the prices, general and specific, are related to national income. Statistically these indices may have some very rough indicative value, but they have no significance from the stand-point of causal relations and our ignorance, to repeat, of the working of the forces which determine price levels and price relations is so great that it is not possible to indicate even broadly the inter-relations of money-supply, national income, exchange transactions, prices and their relativities. That also shows the great complexity of the problems, how difficult is the task of developing a planned price-structure, in relation to a planned developing economy; but the point, which needs to be understood, is that we have not even given serious con-sideration to the essentials of the problem and even if we had evolved a policy, which would necessarily have to be con-ceived in tentative terms and implemented empirically, we would not have been able to carry it out owing to our currency and credit mechanism being inadequate for the performance of the task. Really speaking our production, agricultural and industrial, has not been planned in specific terms and even the need for the production of the different commodities and their prices being co-related as an integral whole has not been even clearly and fully understood or appreciated. We have had really so far no price policy at all and, as stated below, there is no indication that even now the fact is grasped and the need for making up for the lack of purposive action in the sphere of currency, credit and price since the inception of our planning is realized. It is imperative that this urgent need must be vividly realized if we have to have an accord between planned pattern of prices and pattern of production. Price mechanism in an avowedly planned economy like ours which, it is intended, should rely as little as possible on administrative measures for carrying out its self-assigned tasks, has to be forged into a reliable and effective tool of policy and must fulfil it, within the limits of its capacity, its main economic and social objectives.

INFLATION

Inflation in the country is and has been a serious problem. The fact that in spite of the increase in national income, agricultural and industrial production, increase which was much higher than the increase of 21 per cent in our population from 1951 to 1961, our prices between 1951-61 rose by 30 per cent, of foodgrains by 26 per cent, of manufactures by 24 per cent, and an essential commodity like oil seeds by 50 per cent which clearly points to the growth of inflationary pressure which is and cannot be explained by shortage of goods or excessive increase of population. Attempts are being made to under-rate the gravity of the situation by comparing the rise of prices in India with their rise in unplanned economies of countries like U.S.A., U.K., Germany and France and point to the conclusion that rise in the other countries has been much greater and therefore there is no need to get unduly concerned about upward movement of prices in this country. Such attempts fail to take into account vital differences between the conditions of this country and those of the countries with which comparison is made. Inflation in India during the war and post-war years was much greater, as stated in the footnote than in countries like U.S.A., U.K., Germany etc. and inflation since 1951, has, as pointed out before, been superimposed[11] on the inflation of the war and post-war years. If the pre-plan inflation had worked itself off by the income levels of all classes—particularly the vast majority of our peoples—poor peasants, agricultural and industrial workers, small traders and middle class employees with fixed incomes—having adjusted themselves to the changes in the prices, i.e. of rise of the cost of living of these classes had been neutralized by rise in their money earnings, the comparison would have some validity. As a matter of fact it is known that this has not happened and the classes referred to above, had suffered severely by the erosion of their incomes. In the richer capitalistic countries the corresponding classes owing to democratic pressures, the action of

---

11. Index number of cost of living in 1945-46 was with 1939 as base 225 in India (which really indicated rise in the cost of living much below the actual rise), 128.4 in U.S.A. and 131 in U.K. Index number of wholesale prices in 1945-56 in India was 245, while in U.S.A., Canada, Australia and Germany the prices had risen by less than 50 per cent. In 1964 index number of prices in India was 532 with 1939 as base and in 1963-64 prices have risen by 13 per cent in one year. From 1950-51 to 1955-56 our prices rose by 7.8 per cent and in the 2nd Plan period 21.7 per cent. Our prices have not only been rising since 1950-51, but the rate at which they have been rising has been accelerating continuously and the rate at which they are rising currently has assumed almost alarming proportions. We are, it appears, in the grip of a continuing serious inflation and the authorities seem to be practically unable to arrest its course. The economy has not yet come to the stage of frenzied hyper-inflation—a run-away inflation— but it is well cantering ahead, if not galloping already. The position at the time of seeing this book through the press (February 1965) is shown by the indices of the latest price. On November 14, 1964 the indices with 1952-53 as base were: Food Article 166.2, Industrial Raw Material 165.5, Manufacture 138.6 and All Commodities 156.8. On the 16th November, 1963 the All-Commodities Index was 134.4, i.e. in 1964 the prices have risen further by 16.6 per cent in one year. The index of general prices on November 14, 1964 with 1939 as base was 596. For practical purposes the 1939 base seems to be per-historic to most people and even to the professional economists, but for measuring the distortion of the economy and its income structure, this base has not ceased to be relevant—is really more significant for understanding the position in its perspective. There are countries like Indonesia, Chile and Brazil, which are in the grip of galloping inflation and

organized labour and the general economic development, had
in most cases not only redressed the position but in a large
number of cases actually improved it. The cumulative effect of
further inflation in India under the two plans, has carried the
process of the erosion of exceedingly limited incomes of these
classes further and heightened the contrast between their increasing penury and conspicuous waste and extravagance in
which the richer classes, to whom has accrued a large proportion of increase in national income, indulge freely and even
flamboyantly. The masses of our people have not participated in
the benefits of whatever economic growth has taken place in our
country, while the real cost of growth has largely been borne by
them. This fact is a pathetic commentary on social results of

have learnt to live with it; but it is clear that unless effective action is
taken not to stabilize but reduce materially prices in India, the consequences will be really dangerous. Nationalization of banking and whole-sale
trade in food grains, which are being so widely urged, are the measures to
which political resistance is being offered at the very highest level and is
due to the pressures exercised by the richest classes, and if the latter can
continue to have their way, the outlook cannot but remain very gloomy
for our people.

As regards the inevitability of a price rise in developing economies, it
has been stated in the text that inflation is not and need not be an inevitable consequence of development—even rapid development. The following
quotation from an economist, who is dead against both planning and socialism, is relevant on this point and is factually sound.

"Recent experience of a number of countries, Canada, West Germany,
Italy and Japan among them, and, to some extent, our own experience
demonstrates that the official thesis has no empirical support whatsoever.
From 1953 to 1959, West German national income rose at an annual rate of
over 12 per cent. And yet, prices in Germany rose only by about 1 per cent
per year during the same period. The Japanese record is even more striking.
During the same period, the Japanese national income rose at an annual
rate of 12.3 per cent, probably, a world record for a sustained rise at this
high rate. But the Japanese price index showed a rise of only 2 per cent
over the whole period. The Italian experience is no less impressive. Though
the Italian national income over the six-year period went up by 49 per cent
prices fell, instead of rising, by 1 per cent. So far from generating inflation,
in the post-war world generally, rapidity of development has been in proportion to the achievements of monetary and fiscal stability." B. R. Shenoy,
Indian Planning and Economic Development, p. 121.

the planned development of our economy. Price relations have created income-relations which have made the position more and not less inequitable. The contrast between stability of prices in planned economies like those of Soviet Union and China since 1950 in which investment rate of 18 to 25 per cent and the rate of yearly growth of 8 to 12 per cent have been achieved and the situation in India makes our position in the context of changes in other countries even more unfavourable for us. The attempt to under-rate real burden of inflation on our people is extremely ill-advised because evidence, to show that the strain caused by the growing inflationary pressure is creating a seriously imbalanced situation which can and will have very dangerous and social consequences, is cumulatively growing more and more conclusive and has to receive very earnest consideration. Inflation in all countries always has increased disparities and made the lot of the poor an object of concern. If income relations are not distorted by changes in price-relations, i.e. if changes in income and price relations keep in step, inflation ceases to be inflation. It merely means a new unit of account is being established. Inflation is a problem just because its severity is measured by the severity of the distortion of income-relations and of social equity. It is, it follows, a grave disservice to our people and their future to underrate the gravity of the inflationary situation or explain away the failings of policy and administration which have given rise to it.

INFLATION AND DEVELOPMENT

A brief reference to another argument has also been pressed into service for finding an alibi for inflation in India is necessary. The argument is that in developing economy inflation is inevitable. The only point of substance involved in this argument is that large investment in an economy in which pace of economic growth is being consciously accelerated, particularly in the development of 'heavy' industries—i.e. production of commodities like steel, machine tools, machinery, cement, chemicals etc.—creates the imbalance between disposable income of the people and the value of the articles of every-day use available for consumption. This imbalance arises because investment in capital goods generates incomes but does not lead to equivalent production of consumers' goods; and that because there is a long interval between the production of capital goods and the increase in the supply of consumers' goods which they inevitably lead to. In this period of 'gestation' supply of consumers' goods falls short and cannot but fall short of effective demand for them. This is true of all economies, capitalistic or socialistic, and their lack of balance creates a problem of redressing this disequilibrium. In a planned economy this problem can be foreseen, gap between the anticipated income and value of consumers' goods measured in advance as far as possible and what is very important, planned action taken to fill up this gap by deliberate counter-measures like higher taxation on selected goods or on incomes, encouragement of private savings and planning of public or corporate savings, planned profits of industries, both public and private, control over all investments and their planned allocation, planned prices and imposition of a general and selective levy like turnover tax in Soviet Union to 'mop up' the purchasing power in excess of the value of consumers' goods. This gap can arise in spite of all care and foresight and extreme vigilance is needed to prevent or counter-act this imbalance as and when it arises. But as a major problem in economic equilibrium it should be dealt with by anticipatory action to cover this 'inflationary gap'; and if in spite, as stated above, of all care and foresight the gap in the economy or in its certain sectors or regions does arise, the technique of removing it after the event has to be evolved and utilized. Planned economies of the socialist countries have not fully but largely succeeded in preventing inflation or keeping it within manageable proportion, the lessons of their experience can be adapted to the specific conditions of our country. But planned anticipatory action can and should be taken to remove the disequilibrium or deal with it with competence and confidence. The need for taking such action has not even been realized in this country and of changing of the currency and credit system—its structure and mechanism—to perform this role in co-operation with financial and industrial institutions has not been even understood. Errors in phasing and timing of the development programme present another aspect of the same problem and calls for similar corrective action. Perfection cannot be attained in any economy in maintaining this equilibrium; and even in the socialist countries it is known that a more adequate technique has to be evolved for this purpose. But given the will to action and understanding of the essentials of planning, there is nothing inevitable about inflation being a part of the process of accelerated development. To the extent to which it does occur, it is the result of faulty or inadequate planning and inability to adopt measures to correct imbalances when these do arise. In India there is no doubt that inflation is the result of bad planning and inept implementation of plans. The view that all countries which embark upon the adventure of planned development must be prepared for income relations and price relations not being in accord with each other that is, as pointed out above, what inflation means in practice—is really an alibi —a cover for our sins of omission and commission which our planning authorities are neither prepared to confess nor provide safeguards against their repetitions in future.

ESSENTIALS OF PRICE POLICY

Assuming that a price policy for the country has still to be formulated and implemented, it is worth while to indicate very briefly the general lines of this policy without even attempting to deal with the major problems which are inherent in this formulation. Price policy has to achieve the following broad objectives:

(1) A stable price level without frequent or sharp fluctuations has to be established.

(2) Prices of specific commodities have to be so determined that, within the desired limits, they should exercise incentive

or disincentive effect on production and yet contingent scarcities and surpluses of economy should not be permitted to upset the balance of price structure or involve undue hardships for the producers and the consumers.

(3) Buffer stocks in all essential commodities should be maintained and operated with a view to safeguarding against the balance of price-structure being upset by scarcities and surpluses.

(4) For a planned price-structure it is necessary to plan costs, and as all costs in the last analysis are incomes, it would be essential to plan income structure and its differentials in order to provide a rational basis for planned price structure.

(5) With given level of technique costs will have to be standardized and all high costs due to inefficiency, poor management or bad location of economic units would, as far as possible, have to be eliminated.

(6) When costs vary between different units, areas and regions, and such variations are necessary and unavoidable from social standpoint, the practice of pooling of costs and prices should be adopted and provided unnecessary and avoidable movements of commodities are prevented, i.e. their distribution is planned on a rational basis and according to the genuine needs of the community, even transport costs should be merged into pooled costs and all staple commodities should, as a rule, be sold at uniform prices all over the country, making provision of course, for the necessity of selling perishable commodities locally in order to avoid waste.

(7) Structure of the distribution of commodities should be built up from the village to the national level, and without losing the advantage of specialization, the utmost care should be taken to provide for full utilization of local human and material resources.

(8) Special measures should be taken to match surpluses and deficits of the economy and movements of commodities should be governed by the needs of village, area, region, state and national plans.

(9) Corresponding to production and distribution plans there

should be prepared and executed investment and credit plans and, assuming the change in inventories had to be included in investment plans, provision of credit should be almost a costless process from the standpoint of the community and the price charged for it, i.e. rate of interest for the supply of credit should be determined by social considerations.

(10) Creation of credit should depend upon credit plan and be independent of international reserves or the so-called 'liquid' resources of the credit institutions.

(11) A planned income structure as a basis of planned cost structure would have to be built within the socially determined maximum and minimum limits, i.e. ceilings and floor, and relativities between different grades of skills, and efficiencies in each industry and between different industries and areas, i.e. vertical and horizontal relativities, will have to be worked out with care and any alteration in them would be permitted within the framework of planned income structure.

(12) Money supply itself has no relation to the variations of prices i.e. any excess or deficiency of the former would be ruled out by integrating the currency and credit structure with the economic structure and requirement for currency and credit would be fully but no more than fully met on a planned basis.

These broad objectives of the price policy at present cannot be realized owing to our economic, currency and credit system not being designed for the purpose. The fact that most of our producers are small, resourceless and unorganized and independent in the sense of not being amenable to guidance, regulation and control, and their response to price changes are merely reflex actions unrelated to any trends, short or long-term, and to any planned targets and the needs of the community, makes it almost impossible to plan a price-policy as a part of the economic policy of the country. "Given the structure of Indian economy," in the words of Dr Gunar Myrdal, "with the enormous number of small economic units in agriculture, trade, crafts and industry the more comprehensive control of the whole economy implied in the idea of state planning cannot be easily realized." What applies to planning in general applies even with greater force to price-planning, and this is the reason after the attempted planning in this country since 1951, there has been no price-planning at all. It is, therefore, necessary, for formulating and carrying out a planned price-policy that the existing structure of Indian economy should be radically altered. This means that currency and credit system will have to be integrated with a new economic and social system and both will have to fulfil the same purpose. The latter has to be based upon decentralized planned production in agriculture, trade and industry from the basic to national level mainly on a federated co-operative basis through the formation of the service, credit, farming, industrial and distributive co-operatives drawing their sap from the tap-root of concerted common effort of the producers in particular and the community in general at the basic level. The structure will be erected and operate as an integral part of the national system in which private sector to the extent to which it exists, will work, as stated already, in accord with and carry out the socialist objective of the economy as a whole. In a fragmentary way this conception has been adopted in our approach to planning, but it has been neither clearly thought out nor consistently or adequately carried out. Without it, however, there can be neither general nor price planning. All these broad objectives of a price policy stated above can be realised only if the task of developing a socialist society is undertaken in all honesty, seriousness of purpose and with determination. Realization of these objectives has necessarily to be a long term process, but transition to the goal has to be real, it must create and gather momentum as it proceeds apace and carry its authentic character manifestly on its face. Lack of price-policy in the country, to repeat, has its roots in the conditions and motives of socialist planning being largely absent in the country.

Chapter Twelve

RESOURCE OPERATION

Role of Finance in Socialist Economy

Finance, as an instrument of socialist policy, has necessarily very different functions from those which it is expected to perform in an unplanned private economy. Even from the conventional standpoint it has now acquired a broader content and it has been and is being used to achieve stability, prevent and mitigate fluctuations in economic activity and reduce economic disparities. In a planned economy with socialist objective these broader objects become even more important, but the fact that the economy is intended not only to be rapidly developed but also radically changed, makes it essential to take an integrated view of the economy as a whole and think and plan more in real than in financial terms and use the latter as a means for realizing social ends of planned development. This is in the first instance means that more and more firm control of the entire resources of the economy has to be established, their allocation for production, investment and consumption has to correspond to a scale of social priorities and a system of social accounting under which all flows and interflows are not only known and measured but also subjected to regulative processes from social standpoint, has to be introduced and made effective. All important indicators for this purpose have to be fully used, but it should be possible to use the indications as the basis of purposive action all along the line and in accord with the aims of socialist policy. Full realization of this object has to be a part of the process of social growth, but all the key points of the economy have increasingly to be brought under public control and inter-related in order that understanding, assessment and planned operations of the economy as a whole may become a continuous and growing process.

This does not imply that administrative directives have to replace financial measures and continuous re-adjustment needed for flexible working of the economy has to be made more difficult. All that it does imply is that conscious choice has to be substituted for reflex, uncorelated reactions of the different parts of the economy and has to be made in the context of the working of the economy as a whole, social purposes which it has set itself and the new institutional framework which has necessarily to be built up. Planning in real rather than financial terms, i.e. making finance an instrument rather than prime object of policy, does not dispense with the need for having a calculus for framing and implementing the policy and using it for quantitative measurement and qualitative evaluation. In the sphere of finance as that of money in a planned economy, what used to be known as spontaneity and automaticity of the monetary and financial mechanism, can have no place, and primacy of radical decisions in regard to the object, the rate and the methods of development has to be recognized. Within this limit finance still retains its importance as an instrument of policy and a means of its implementation on a flexible basis in all stages of realization of a socialist society.

The conclusion implicit in this view is that resource operations of a planned economy have to be placed on an integral basis and economic surveys, which have in the post-war years become a common feature of the budgetary system of most countries, including our own, have to be not only merely a narrative but also have normative significance. The facts and trends have not merely to be presented in their entirety, but resource operations, their generation, distribution and utilization, have to be organically related to the objects and working of the economy and made as comprehensive as possible. The limitations of these resources in aggregate cannot be overcome without their expansion. The real advantage of socialism is that it can make this expansion a process of community action, accelerate its rate by bringing into play new social motive forces and their rational utilization in the interest of the community as a whole on the basis of its socially appraised needs. There is no question of distributing poverty or achieving any economic and social miracles. The fact that in a country like ours resources are limited and we cannot on that account, embark upon courses for which resources are lacking, cannot be lost sight of in theory and practice. But this fact makes it all the more necessary that waste, due to the existence of economic extremes—waste of material resources owing to a small minority at the top indulging in display and dissipation and that of the human resources owing to the majority of the people having to live under sub-human conditions, has to be reduced as fast as possible. The primary object of our resource operations must be their rapid enlargement by realizing our economic potential mainly by removing the existing hindrances due to social rigidities and inequalities and tapping fully our natural and human resources and modern knowledge and technique to the utmost for this purpose. Enlargement of resources has to be accompanied by judicious utilization and success of these operations can be measured by the extent to which both are in keeping with socialist objectives.

In India this role of finance has neither been understood nor appreciated as an essential part of planning process; on that account it has not been and could not be used purposively to promote and realize socialist policies. According to the general analysis of the additional income generated from 1951-1961 as given by the Mahalnobis Committee,[1] 73 per cent of the increase in real incomes has been utilized for increase in consumption, 13.4 per cent for increase in Government expenditure and 13.3 per cent for saving. This analysis though of interest, can become really meaningful, if from the point of view of the economy as a whole when its relation to the

1. *The Mahalnobis Committee Report*, Statement 2, p. 7.

broader processes at work is indicated and understood. As no information is available about the distribution of national income and the increase among different classes and regions and data about the amount and utilization of the investment resources are also very inadequate and fragmentary, some of the most vital questions relating to the generation and utilization of national income during the Plans periods cannot be answered and therefore real significance of the increase and allocation of the additional resources generated during this period cannot be known or explained from the over-all standpoint. Analysis of the financial operation of the State and their relation to the economy as a whole can, however, be undertaken with a view to the understanding their bearing on the problems of development and transformation.

ADDITIONAL TAXATION

The manner in which the requirements of development have been met has to be examined with care to know the relative importance of different sources from which the funds have been drawn and their impact on our economy. Excluding external assistance of the total outlay on development in 1951-61 of Rs 6,560 crores in the public sector, taxation accounts for Rs 1,802 crores or 28 per cent, loans Rs 986 crores or 16 per cent, small savings and provident funds Rs 870 crores or 14 per cent and deficit financing Rs 1,238 crores or 18 per cent. These four sources among themselves provided 76 per cent of the total outlay on development. Tax revenue increased during the decade and additional taxation by the Centre and the States yielded Rs 1,301 crores—Centre Rs 930 crores and States Rs 323 crores. The point of interest in the yield of additional taxation is that Union excises have contributed Rs 712 crores to the increase of the central tax revenue and sales tax of Rs 194 crores to that of the states. This means that of the total increase of tax revenue these two taxes together account for Rs 903 crores or nearly 69 per cent of the increase, central direct taxes Rs 197 crores or nearly 69 per cent of the increase, central direct taxes Rs 197 crores or nearly 15 per cent and customs Rs 64 crores or less than 5 per cent. The yield of excise duties has increased from Rs 407.9 crores in 1961-62 to 769.59 in 1964-65 (budget estimates). According to the Mid-Term Appraisal of Third Plan by the end of the plan period Rs 2,400 crores of additional tax revenue will be realized as compared with the Plan target of Rs 1,710 crores. This increase has been made necessary by the heavy increase in defence expenditure and the union excises are the most important source through which this expansion has been achieved. Regressive character of the excise duties and sales taxes cannot be questioned and the increase of the tax-revenues, however unavoidable owing to the national emergency, has not only made the incidence of tax burden even more unfair but has, it may be assumed, contributed to the rise of prices which has taken place since 1962-63. As the people know from experience that the benefits of development expenditure have not accrued to them, the prevailing conditions are intensifying a sense of frustration. Given the state of public mind, reliance upon the Union excises and sales tax for major expansion of tax-revenues is really risky

The States, as a matter of fact, have been and are unresponsive to the need for expansion of the revenue and from 1961-62 to 1963-64 the yield of additional state taxation amounts only to Rs 323 crores and in the whole plan period it is expected, in spite of the emergency, to yield Rs 501 crores as against the provision of Rs 610 crores which the states were to realize through additional taxation. The yield of income-tax, corporation tax and other central direct taxes was 207 crores in 1951-52 and Rs 252 crores in 1960-61 which shows an increase of 25 per cent. The yield of customs, the third important central source, decreased from Rs 232 crores in 1951-52 to Rs 162.50 crores in 1960-61, a decrease of nearly 30 per cent. There has been significant increase in the yield of central direct taxes, and customs since 1961-62 as shown in the footnote,[2] but this was rendered inevitable by the emergency. These sources, relatively speaking, have again become inelastic. Even now there is much greater reliance on excises than the other important central taxes for increasing the tax revenue. Of the other important state taxes excise revenue has decreased from Rs 51.44 crores in 1951-52 to Rs 48.46 crores in 1960-61, agricultural income tax has increased from Rs 4.37 crores to only Rs 8.20 crores, entertainment tax from Rs 9.32 crores to Rs 12.77 crores, registration and stamps from Rs 27.89 to Rs 41.58 crores and tax on motor vehicles from Rs 10.12 to Rs 27.11 crores. The only state tax, other than the sales-tax, whose yield has increased materially is land-revenue—from Rs 50.66 crores in 1951-52 to Rs 100.55 crores in 1960-61—but this increase is, as is well known, mostly due to the impact of agrarian changes and the payment by the tenants of rent to the state instead of private landlords. Land-revenue is really one of the most inexpansive sources of public revenues in India and though the

2. Yield of Central Direct Taxes and Customs from 1961-62 to 1964-65 (In crores).

	Customs	Income Tax	Corpora-tion Tax	Wealth Tax	Estate Duty	Expendi-ture Tax	Gifts Tax	Central Total Direct Taxes
	(1)	(2)	(3)	(4)	(5)	(6)	(7)	(8)
1961-62	189	160	160	8	4	—	—	332
1962-63	240	185	222	9	3.94	.20	.97	421.11
1963-64 (Revised)	301	235	275	10	4.35	.17	1.11	625.63
1964-65 (Budget estimate)	330	250	295	10	4.40	.7	3.10	563.2

Inelasticity of the new direct taxes (3, 4, 5 and 6) is very clear. In a period of inflated capital values the inability of the state to realize more revenues from capital taxes like Wealth Tax and Estate Duty is clearly indicative of the lack of earnestness on the part of the tax-collecting authorities and of course resistance of the powerful tax payers.

is a growing menace, it is extremely unwise to cause seriously disturbing stresses by continuing to depend mainly upon such taxes for expansion of tax-revenue. Under the first two plans only 28 per cent of our development outlay has been met from enlargement of tax-revenue. Under the Third Plan there is a provision for defraying the plan outlay from taxation only to the extent of 23 per cent. The additional tax-revenue of Rs 600 crores referred to above is needed for meeting heavy and increasing defence expenditure in 1962-63 and 1963-64, it is estimated that there is to be a deficit of Rs 442 crores in the balance of revenue for financing the Third Plan. Equity of the tax system depends as much upon the purpose for which tax-revenue is used as the incidence of taxation; but in the context of the existing situation and pre-disposing factors which make it difficult to redress the lack of balance in the tax system, it would be desirable to think less in terms of additional taxation and more in that of its alternatives for ampler provision of resources for accelerated development.

Borrowing Operations

Borrowing in theory is a programme of diverting personal income of individuals from private consumption, saving or investment to public exchequer, and to the extent to which the loans are used for development it is assumed that individuals through their savings contribute to the development finance. Under the two plans loans receipts of the Centre and States are taken to amount to Rs 986 crores or 16 per cent of the total development outlay. On this assumption the private savings have been used to this extent for financing planned development. From 1951 to 1961 the outstanding medium and long-term loans, i.e. internal permanent or funded debt of the Government increased from Rs 1,438 crores to Rs 2,572 crores and of the States from Rs 69.11 crores to Rs 442 crores, i.e. the total debt increased by Rs 1,508 crores.[5] Of the amount accord-

5. The 1951-52 figures for the States relates only to Class A States.

ing to the Planning Commission, Rs 986 crores, as stated above, were utilized for development.[6] During this period, however, Government securities held by the Reserve Bank increased from Rs 508 crores to Rs 1,627 crores and by the commercial banks from Rs 346 crores to Rs 558 crores, i.e. the Reserve Bank and commercial banks together lent to the Government Rs 1,252 crores. In other words 83 per cent of what are called market loans were subscribed by these institutions. The other 17 per cent were mostly taken by the Life Insurance Corporation, Provident Funds, public trusts, local bodies, etc. Those institutions use the genuine savings of the community for investment in Government securities, but that does not apply to the Reserve Bank and the commercial banks. They invest in these loans largely by the creation of currency or credit. In effect these investments involve currency and credit creation for investment in state loans and therefore have expansionary effect on our money supply and have, unless countered by other factors, an inflationary impact on our economy.[7] The factors which affect and determine money supply, have complicated interactions and it cannot be assumed that all investments

6. From 1961-62 to 1963-64 net public borrowing by the Government of India amounted to Rs 548.96 crores but it is not known what proportion of it was financed by the Reserve Bank and commercial banks.

7. Under the Second Plan it is stated by the Planning Commission that while market borrowing amounted to Rs 780 crores, the net absorption of market loans, including commercial banks was less than Rs 300 crores (Third Five Year Plan, Para 8, p. 19). Total outstanding investment of all commercial banks in state securities in March 1956 was Rs 408.60 crores and in March 1961, as stated above, rose to Rs 558 crores, i.e. market borrowing by the state from the commercial banks under the Second Plan was nearly Rs 150 crores. On this basis borrowing from non-bank sources amounted to Rs 150 crores. In the 1st Plan according to a valid estimate 90 per cent of non-bank investment in state securities was made by Life Insurance Corporation and Provident Funds and 10 per cent mainly by public trusts, local bodies, etc. (I. S. Gulati, Resources Prospects of the Third Five Year Plan, p. 41). In the Second Plan investment by the Reserve Bank and commercial banks, according to the above estimate, amounted to Rs 630 crores out of the total of Rs 780 crores or nearly 89 per cent of the total. That this cannot but have exercised inflationary pressure on the economy, admits of no doubt or denial.

by the Reserve Bank and commercial banks in Government securities are inflationary in effect, but it is a fact that currency and credit creation is largely involved in such investment. The main point is that assumption that "market" loans of the state represent savings is only partly true but not mainly valid, and to the extent to which the banking institutions subscribe to these loans and retain them, and their proceeds are used for the execution of planned projects, currency and credit are created for development finance. This is also 'deficit financing' and should be taken into account as such in the analyses of the provisions for and actuals of the ways and means programme of the planned development expenditure.

Contribution of small savings and provident funds to development finance need not be commented upon. They are very desirable but have marginal significance in our development finance. There are, however, indications that expectations of raising funds from this source have been pitched high and have not been and may not be realized.[8] The best use of small savings is their utilization for local projects. If development of the economy on decentralized basis and in relation to the assessed needs of each small community but within the framework of national plan, referred to a number of times in this book, can be earnestly undertaken, savings of small communities through the Panchayats and co-operatives can in aggregate become a factor of significant importance in development finance and success of these institutions should mean great expansion both in planned production and accumulation of the capital through community action. This can, however, be a part of a process of community action at a high level the conditions for which are still to be created.

8. Small savings in the 2nd plan were initially estimated at Rs 500 crores but actually yielded Rs 400 crores. Savings in 1961-62 or net collections of small savings amounted to Rs 87 crores and in 1962-63 only Rs 70 crores. In 1963-64 they improved and the collections rose to Rs 115 crores, i.e. the total collection in the first three years of the Third Plan amounted to Rs 275 crores. It is obvious that it is unlikely that the target of Rs 600 for the Plan period will be realized.

Deficit financing in the limited sense has been given a place in our resource operations and, as stated above, accounted for 18 per cent or Rs 1,238 crores of our financial resources under the first two plans. From 1961-62 to 1964-65 deficit financing is estimated to amount to Rs 606 crores as compared with the Plan provision of Rs 550 crores. Planned outlay from 1961-62 to 1963-64 amounts to Rs 4,198 crores, i.e. nearly 12 per cent of the total outlay has been covered by deficit financing as against the provision of 5 per cent in the whole plan period under the Plan. Deficit financing in this sense means straight-forward creation of currency to cover the deficiancy in receipts —revenue and capital—to meet the entire planned expenditure. What are called *ad hoc* treasury bills are made the basis of note issue for this purpose, and the creation of these *ad hocs* is merely a ritual for which there is a historical explanation, but which in fact, has no functional significance and could easily be dispensed with. That inflationary risk is inherent in this process has been recognized by all, and various estimates have been made by our financial experts, economists, foreign consultants and international missions,[9] of the extent to which

9. The panel of economists in their memorandum prepared for the Second Plan committed themselves to the view that, if vigilant watch is kept over the implementation of the Plan, deficit financing of Rs 1,000 crores, i.e. the issue of currency notes against *ad hoc* treasury bills, would be well within the limit of safety. This view based upon the assumption that as expenditure on planned development would be reflected in increase in current production, "addition to money supply will not have an inflationary effect, but may be required to prevent a decline in prices which may lead to distress or distortion of economy."

The economists, however, failed to distinguish between provision for investment and the need for increase in money supply to keep pace with increase in current production, and to analyse the proposed investment expenditure from the standpoint of its impact on current production.

Without any basis to go upon, they stated that they did not recommend deficit financing of larger amount than that indicated by the figure of Rs 1,000 crores, i.e. if deficit financing did not exceed that limit, the position could, with due care, be kept well in hand. The events have clearly shown that this was an erroneous view, and based upon unwarranted assumptions.

A delegation of the International Monetary Fund visited India in 1953 and expressed the view that in the First Plan period credit creation to the

notes can be issued against *ad hoc* treasury bills to finance our development investment programme without creating undesirable inflationary pressures, i.e. within the limit of safety, but all these statements have given no reasons for the "safety limit" indicated by them. No criteria were and really could be laid down for measuring the degree to which deliberate expansion of currency could be resorted to for development without having a seriously disturbing effect on the economy. Now the Planning Commission admits that this method has in fact generated inflationary pressures and that "there is no precise way of estimating the limits of safe deficit financing."[10] This obvious fact was disregarded under the two plans and with assurance born of make-believe it was asserted that the projected deficit financing could be resorted to without causing disturbing inflation. Now that prices and cost of living under three plans have risen by 56 per cent and this has, as stated before, been super-imposed on rise of prices during the war and post-war years up to 1952-53 and accentuated the distortions of income relations. Now (July 1964), the cumulative effect of the currency and credit expansion, deficit financing and regressive taxation is expressing itself in severe inflationary pres-

extent of Rs 500 crores could be safely resorted to. This view again was not based upon any well-reasoned argument and represented an estimate based upon subjective considerations. (*Report of the Mission of the International Monetary Fund on Economic Development and Stability*, p. 48).

In 1956 Mr. Kaldor in his Report of Indian Tax Reform stated, "In my view, (and this I think will be shared by most economists) deficit expenditure, which economy can absorb is not likely to exceed Rs 150 crores per year or say Rs 800 crores in the five year period." (Kaldor, *Indian Tax Reform*, p. 1).

It is not clear whether in 'deficit expenditure' Mr. Kaldor includes only expenditure financed by the issue of currency notes against *ad hoc* treasury bills or also credit creation by the commercial banks. In any case whatever the meaning neither the Mission of the international Monetary Fund nor Mr Kaldor supports these views with cogent reasons. As stated in the text, all these estimates are highly subjective and have no relation to any objective criteria.

10. *The Third Five Year Plan*, para 23, p. 90.

sure. The prices are continuously rising at an accelerating rate, public discontent has taken a very disturbing form and created a serious law and order problem. All the arguments put forward so far to explain away or minimize the gravity of inflation, the events have clearly shown, could not be more invaild in retrospect. Deficit financing, though only one of the causes of regressive financial policies, is an important factor in the situation, and its impact on the economy has to be known and understood. We are not suffering from serious deficiency of production or even over-investment, but from the rigidity of the social structure and resistance to all radical remedial policies by the dominant powerful economic interests and the wooden administration. Short-term measures to master the situation have to be taken with firmness and courage, but the root causes of inflation go deep and can be removed by operating upon the evils of the economy as a whole, i.e. by remedying the fundamental disequilibrium of the economy, i.e. removing the imbalance between our pressing needs and means which are inadequate because the men in power are afraid of the powerful interests upon whose political backing they depend and have to depend.

In spite of the conclusion being fully borne out by facts and experience, it is necessary to examine the main arguments for inflation on which the inflationary policy has been based. That currency and credit expansion are needed for a developing economy is so obvious that it does not need to be specifically stated. Even in unplanned economies this expansion has to be provided for and it is the function of the banking system to meet this requirement empirically and through short-term advances, discounts and purchase of bills and securities to bring about the needed expansion of currency and credit according to the needs of the economy or an overall prospect of development. The assumption that so long these loans are secured and are repayable in the course of the year, credit inflation can be avoided is contradicted by the facts of experience, and inflation and deflation occur and cause serious dislocation of economy.

That adoption of the Keynsian technique of compensatory public expenditure and counter-fiscal measures introduces an element of induced and, therefore, partially planned, precesses,
which are effective within limits, indicates, how currency and
credit should not be left to "autonomous" or free play of economic force. The Keynsian approach and technique are, however,
very inadequate if planned development and transformation
of the economy is to be aimed at. The point, which matters
for the purpose under consideration here, is that expansion of
currency and credit as a part of a planned economic growth is
necessary, desirable and unavoidable and has to be planned
as a constituent of the whole process of development and social change. This expansion does not require any savings or
involve social costs and can, if a broad correspondence is established between the rate and kind of growth and planned supply
of currency and credit, be brought about and vigilance exercised to insure that both keep in step with each other and the
balance of the economy is not disturbed by ill-considered, and
poorly adjusted action. For this it is essential that credit should
be linked to production plan of the economy as a whole and
credit plan prepared for each economic unit and on territorial,
state and country-wide basis. This can be done only if planning becomes a comprehensive and effective process and in-
stituational agencies are provided from the basic to the apex
levels of the economy for the prepartion and implementation
of the plans, and banking institutions are socialized and re-
organized with a view to achieving a large measure of social
accounting and social control over the entire monetary and resource operation of the economy. The whole conception of
what finance and banking can do in a planned economy in
the process of rapid growth and transformation has to be
changed and complete re-orientation of ideas and efforts has to
be brought about. From this point of view expansion of currency and credit would not be for investment in fixed assets
but for carrying over the necessary stocks of the economy and
requirements of expanding exchange transactionts. That

would not be "deficit financing" at all in the sense the phrase is understood now and would not be required for meeting the deficit in real resources for investment.[11] This

11. It has been earnestly urged that in "India minimum amount of pressure must be exerted to get development started; and also a country with a growing population must achieve a rate of development which outdistances population growth. In these circumstances the strategy of a development plan has to be to attempt the largest initial effort that a counry's economy can stand. In this sense the development effort is like waging a war. There is a complusion about certain efforts and certain expenditures being undertaken within certain periods. This explains why planned development invites efforts larger than the resources in sight and is financed initially by the creation of mony." (D. R. Gadigil, *Planning and Economic Policy in Inda*, 114).

This view has been subjected to reservations. (1) That it is imperative that prices are kept well in check and (2) there must be effective curbs on spending. "The moral, in short," to quote from Prof. D. R. Gadgil, "is, deficit financing only if you are sure of successfully checking inflation." In India the events show that deficit financing has been attempted, inflation has not been checked, prices have risen rapidly and effective curbs on spending have not been applied. Prof. Gadgil made the observations referred to above, in a radio talk on September 7, 1957, when it was known that the imperatives to which he refers, had been wholly disregarded in practice. It should have been easy to foresee that, given the conditions in India, the approach of the people in power and the pressures to which they are subjected, this was inevitable. This "strategy of development" was initially wrong in conception and has in fact defeated itself.

This argument has, however, a wide appeal. For example, Mr. W. T. Newlyn of Leeds University has expressed the view that productive credit creation has important role to play in producing "take off". Productive credit for investment which in creation, according to him, consists in expanding credit for investment which increases production sufficiently quickly to avoid inflation." "If human barriers in development," he adds, "are removed, credit creation will have an important role in deploying resources in the take off." (*Federalism—Economic Growth in Under-developed Countries*, pp. 94-95). It is virtually the same argument. Minimum amount of pressure must be exerted to get the development started. There is a compulsion about certain efforts and certain efforts being undertaken within certain periods.

The argument is plausible, but it overlooks that rigidity of barriers inherent in the situation referred to in it cannot be removed merely by currency or credit creation. They can be removed only by a social endeavour involving profound social change which creates its own compulsions to meet the compulsion of "a truly challenging situation." What is needed

deficit, if it exists, cannot be met by creation of currency and credit. The latter can, as it does, reduce the real resources of the people who are in no position to defend themselves against the inflationary pressure which it inevitably generates—vast majority of those who live on the earnings of labour—and enables the propertied classes in key privileged positions to receive large unearned increment in their incomes and wealth. This is the essence of deficit financing and if its clear implications are understood, it will be realized that it should have no place in the development finance of any economy—much less in a planned economy like ours which has to reduce the economic distress of the masses whose life is a continuous struggle against odds and not create greater stresses for them by what one writer has called financial sleight of hand—

is strategy of development based not upon the creation of money but on the social impetus of the people themselves. Money can be created but it cannot create social forces needed for the strategy of development. If the necessary social endeavour can be made available, development can be started and gains momentum, creation of currency and credit can be used as an effective instrument of social policy, prices can be held in check, curbs on spending can be applied and inflation can be prevented. But in a situation which is otherwise static and political and social conditions are unfavourable for dynamic advance, creation of currency and credit by itself extracts resources from those who are already living in a state of semi-starvation and brings about redistribution of income and wealth to their grievous disadvantage. Inflationary finance in underdeveloped countries in the initial stage of development is specially dangerous because it weakens those for whose benefit development should primarily be undertaken and who have to be its prime movers, and brings new accession of strength to those who are clearly entrenched in the economy and are exercising their power to the serious detriment of the interests of the community. Take off, it must be realized, is not what Mr. Newlyn calls an 'Indian rope trick'; it is essentially a social process the consumation of which requires a real basic change, to use the metaphor drawn from the well-known Indian myth, a real churning of the sea by the tussle between the forces of good and evil out of which the the 'the nector of new life' has to come. In a situation like this what is called 'magic of money' simply does not work. "Illusion of money" accounts for the belief that this magic can get development started in a big way to achieve a rate of development which outdistances population growth or play an important role in producing the "take off".

reducing their extremely meagre real resources without their consent and even their knowledge.

As a token of making amends for the wrongs of inflation under the first two plans it is proposed to limit deficit financing to Rs 550 crores in the Third Plan—to 5 per cent of the total outlay instead of 18 per cent under the first two plans, and it is expected that the reduction would make it possible to attain the stability of prices and cost of living. The fact,[12] however, would not in itself set a limit to the increase in money supply. Mr G. D. Birla has stated that in the Third Plan currency is likely to increase by Rs 1,000 crores and credit by another Rs 1,000 crores.[13] Money supply in March 1961 was Rs 2,902 crores; and if it is increased by Rs 2,000 crores in the Third Plan period it will mean an increase of nearly 70 per cent. From 1951 to 1961 money supply increased from Rs 1,804 to Rs 2,902 crores, i.e. by about 71 per cent and in January 1964 it was Rs 3,679.07 crores, i.e. it meant a further increase of 27 per cent in money supply or increase of more than 100 per cent since 1951 and all this involved increases in prices of over 56 per cent since 1952-53. Money supply depends upon interaction of a number of factors and is not the only determinant of prices. 'Deficit financing', i.e. expansion of currency against ad hoc treasury bills in the first four years of the Third Plan, i.e. up to 1964-65, as stated above, is estimated to have increased by Rs 606 crores. But taking into account the resistance to additional taxation, and the undue reliance upon indirect taxes, financing of state loans by credit creation, grant of credit to the private sector, and uncertainty about the amount and timing of external assistance, there is a clear risk of expansion of currency and credit creating excessive inflationary pressure and producing a

12. As stated above, this proportion has already been largely exceeded in the first three years of the Third Plan and deficit financing has been 12 per cent of the total development outlay.

13. Presidential speech of Mr G. D. Birla at the 19th Annual Meeting of the United Commercial Banks.

situation of extreme gravity which, as a matter of fact, has
already arisen. The present position is due to the cumulative
effects of the extremely erroneous monetary and financial
policies which have been followed since 1951 and cannot be
redressed without long-term remedial measures. The existing
spiralling of prices, it is now officially admitted, is not due to
deficit in production or shortage of supply. Hoarding, which is
attracting so much attention, is the result and not the cause of
rapidly rising prices. Dishoarding has to be brought about, but
this is only an immediate palliative and not a real radical cure.
The target of Rs 550 crores for deficit financing is not the result
of any careful calculation of Government receipts from other
sources. The latter has again been estimated on assumptions
which have not been stated and cannot be evaluated on the
basis of probabilities. The amount of Rs 550 crores was merely a
residual figure after the estimates of receipts from other sources
were given a definite content, and as pointed out above, was
based upon unstated and uncheckable assumptions. This amount
is not related to any estimate of currency or cash requirements.
It is an arbitrary figure and cannot be, to repeat, explained or
analysed on any rational basis. It is certain already that this
limit would in fact be greatly exceeded; and it is very likely
that even greater creation of currency and credit in 1964-65
and 1965-66 would not be avoided. Our currency, credit and
prices, as indicated in the last chapter, have not been and are
not being planned. The essentials of planning in this field are
not understood or appreciated and conceptual and operational
requirements of such planning are yet not within the ken of
our planning theory and practice. Reduction of provision for
deficit financing from 18 per cent to yet unknown rate of
planned outlay in the Third plan may have the value of a
gesture—an admission that all the premises on which deficit
financing was resorted to under the two plans were invalid and
untenable, but it does not mean that lessons of experience have
been learnt and that currency, credit and prices are to be
planned and rationalized in relation to our needs and social

objectives. The Finance Minister in concluding his speech on budget of 1964-65 pointed out that over-all gap between the total receipts and expenditure, both revenue and capital would be Rs 86 crores and added, "This order of deficit, I think, should serve the best requirements of growth as well as reasonable stability." It is impossible to believe that a Finance Minister, right in the midst of a grave crisis, could make a more meaningless statement. It is quite clear that the lesson of our sorry experience has not yet been learnt.

DIRECT RECEIPTS

In a socialist economy the state should derive most of its revenue by intercepting its share of the national income before it is distributed among the individuals as their disposable personal income. Taxation as such must, relatively speaking, have a subsidiary place and the need for using it as a redistributive agent should not arise if the income structure is reasonably free from anomalies and unjustified inequalities. This is what is actually happening more and more in socialist countries and shows that in this respect they are going in the right direction.[14] India has to maximize its revenue from public economic undertakings, increase their number and extend the range of their operations in order to make up for the deficiency of other sources. The prospect of the revenue from these sources expanding to the extent and in the manner clearly indicated by our

14. The budgetary receipts in percentage in Socialist countries from economic undertakings and taxation in 1950 and 1959 were:

Country	Receipts from economic undertakings		Taxation Revenue	
	1950	1959	1950	1959
U.S.S.R.	83.7	90	16.3	10
Poland	—	72.2	—	7.2
Czechoslovakia	57	85	16	11.7
Rumania	—	91.6	—	8.4
Hungary	—	88.4	—	10.6
Bulgaria	66.7	90.3	13.9	9.6

(SOURCE: *Economic Development of Socialist Countries*, p. 14, Supplement to *World Marxist Review*, January 1960)

pressing needs, is definitely disquieting; and if we know the bearings of this fact on the future of our plans, we should strive to the utmost to expand our surplus from public enterprises; and yet in the first two plans railways' revenue contribution to the exchequer amounted to Rs 62.21 crores[15] and that of posts and telegraphs Rs 34.86 crores. In the States both irrigation and power undertakings operations resulted from 1951 to 1961 in loss of Rs 34.86 crores and Rs 8.23 crores respectively but road transport yielded net surplus of Rs 23.84 crores. In Central public undertakings up to the end of 1960-61 investments amounted to Rs 720 crores and net profits in 1960-61 and 1961-62 to Rs 1.63 and Rs 3.22 crores respectively, .3 and .4 per cent of the total investment. A large number of these undertakings have not yet gone into full production and some of those, which have, have produced good financial results. Outlook in this respect continues to be very unpromising in central undertakings. Total investments in 1964-65 (including the budget provisions for 1964-65) amounted to Rs 1,184 crores. In 1962-63 operation of these undertakings resulted in loss of Rs 9.34 crores and in 1963-64 the estimated profit was Rs 2.16 crores and in 1964-65 Rs 2.32 crores. In the Third Plan provision has been made for Rs 100 crores from railways and Rs 450 crores from other public undertakings as contribution to total outlay in the public sector which is nearly 5 per cent of total development expenditure. According to the available information the Railways are estimated to contribute Rs 192 crores in the first four years of the Plan and it looks as if their contribution would be nearly Rs 240 crores, but according to the mid-Term appraisal of the Plan, receipts from the Central undertakings is likely to fall considerably short of the target of Rs 300 crores but those of the public undertakings of the States would reach close to the target of Rs 150 crores. For the heavy

---

15. Investments in public undertakings have assumed large proportion. Investment, for example, in three major undertakings—railways, posts and telegraphs, and the commercial departments and industrial undertakings of the Government of India amounted to Rs 2,243.95 crores in 1961.

investment in public undertakings this is not at all a good return. With our defence expenditure at about Rs 800 crores and mounting liabilities on account of development if an adequate effort is to be made to meet our minimum national requirements, rapid expansion of receipts from the existing and new public industries, nationalization of trade, banking and other specifically fiscal monopolies, referred to below, is an absolute necessity. We will otherwise continue to make external assistance our permanent stand by—a position which is neither consistent with our self-respect nor, owing to the undependability of the source, with our safety.

And yet there is no doubt that unless these undertakings produce much greater surplus for development and more undertakings are socialized as much for fiscal as for social reasons, the position of our development finance will continue to remain a matter for very serious concern and give rise to real difficulties. Among the new undertakings which have large revenue potentials, if they are socialized, are state trading both in internal and external trade, banking, production and distribution of salt and fiscal monopolies like matches, tobacco and sugar. Extension of socialization to these and other undertakings is necessary in the interest of right social strategy for development and change, but it is also very necessary to bring about this extension for enlargement of our development resources. Moreover, development of decentralized undertakings if properly developed and operated from the village to the national level in agriculture, trade, industry and credit cannot only democratize our development process but also become a source of capital formation of very great importance. All this is not only essential in the interest of advance towards socialism, but is the most effective method of creating and utilizing surpluses for rapid development. Other sources of revenue will remain important, but if we want to avoid the pressures referred to above and develop economy, which will really get to the stage of take-off and become self-sustaining at a rising level, we have to generate these surpluses through public undertakings and use them for raising the standard of living of our people, development of social services and accumulation of capital for investment. Increasing income investment rates to 20 to 25 per cent of our national income is taken by many to be the key to the future of our economy and of the economies of other under-developed countries. Proportion of investment to income is important, but much more so is the social context in which investment is made and the sources from which the funds for it are derived. Not only the ratio of investment but the aggregate of national income has to be rapidly raised and apportioned among consumption, social services and economic development in a balanced manner and with due regard for social priorities. Problem of resources is not merely a financial problem but more the problem of getting the whole economy into a high gear of performance and acquiring complete control of its rapidly increasing dynamism in the best interests of the community. This is implicit in reliance upon increasing surpluses from public undertakings for resource mobilization.

Socialization of economic undertaking for this and other purposes, however, pre-eminently desirable it may be, cannot be brought about merely by stating the case for it. However convincing the case may be, this object cannot, it has to be reiterated here, be achieved without oberwhelming support of crucial social forces. At present these forces are weak, badly organized and in no position to exert the pressures urgently needed for carrying through a change of this kind and order. As a matter of fact resistance to this process, to repeat, is on the increase, and it has not been and as things are, it cannot be reduced, much less overcome, by bringing the countervailing forces into operation. This is, objectively speaking, the position as it is and is developing. And yet the fact remains that without bringing about the change of these dimensions, we cannot make any headway against our stupendous financial and other difficulties, i.e. our resource operations cannot be made adequate and equal to our manifest social tasks.

UTILIZATION OF LABOUR

A very brief reference to the enormous idle man-power of the country as a potential source of revenue and capital is necessary in relation to our resource operations. Idle man-power of the country is known to be enormous though no really dependable estimates of its size have been made. In the Third Five Year Plan Report it was stated that there was a backlog of unemployment of 9 millions at the end of the Second Plan, and there was to be addition to labour force of 17 millions in the Third Plan period and addition to employment of 14 millions which of course means that backlog unemployment in 1965-66 was estimated at 12 millions. All these estimates are very rough indeed and actual unemployment cannot be known with any degree of precision. Under-employment, which is known to be very widespread and large, cannot be measured even very roughly. The estimate of under-employment given in the Third Plan Report of 15-18 million has no known factual basis. The estimated addition of 17 millions to the census 1961 figure of 188 millions of labour force, if even approximately correct, would bring the total labour force to 205 million in 1965-66 of which labour force of 30 millions, according to these rough estimates, would not be employed. The actual unemployment is more likely to be nearer 50 than 30 million, though no estimate of real value can be framed on the basis of the existing knowledge. But the most important fact of the matter is that this enormous unutilized man-power is very unevenly distributed in the country owing to the variations of demographic, economic and social conditions and can be known and utilized only on the basis of the preparation and execution of village, area, district and regional plans, the importance of which has been repeatedly referred to already but which at present are non-existent. The need for preparing such plans has been stressed in all the Plans but has been persistently disregarded in practice, and the result is that we do not know at all the real position in regard to unemployment and underemployment in the country, and whatever

efforts have been made to deal with the problem have, as
pointed out with some degree of earnestness, been ineffective
and ill-directed.

Failure, almost complete, of our programmes for the utilization of this enormous man-power does not, however, affect the
basic point, about the validity of which there is no disagreement of view, in India and elsewhere, that the unutilized man-
power is a potential productive asset of great importance which
can and should be utilized in all underdeveloped countries to
start and develop their production processes and bring all the
wheels of their economies into action. Realization of this
object is more a problem of radical reorganization of the entire
economy than of investment; and the fact that it has not been
achieved in this country and most other non-socialist undeveloped countries is due to what is called macrocosm of the
economy being inimical to the realization of this object. From
the point of resource mobilization this enormous source is
lying untapped as the men in power have not got the insight
and, what is even more important, the courage to act upon the
implications of this challenge. From what has been said about
integrated development in the previous chapters, it should be
clear that the problem of drawing upon the potential resources
can and will be solved when we are willing to learn the lessons
of our own experience, cease merely talking about this great
potential and take the consequential action to draw upon it in
a truly creative manner with dead earnestness. It is not possible
to evaluate in money terms what the full utilization of the
productive asset would mean from the point of growth of
income and well-being of our people. But that it will make all
the difference to our rural economy in particular and national
economy in general admits of no doubt whatever. It is because
we pay only lip service to Gandhi and his message that we
have failed to produce any worth-while results in the way of
utilization of this source. When his spirit really animates our
planned development, we will be able to realize this great
potential for rapid growth and transformation of our economy

with confidence and success.

INVESTMENT IN PRIVATE SECTOR

Of the total estimated investment of Rs 10,110 crores under the first two plans, Rs 4,900 crores are taken to have been invested in the private sector. These estimates are, according to the Planning Commission, 'exceedingly rough'.[16] Most of the estimated investment is self-financed and its sources and distribution are more a matter of guess work than any planned mobilization or allocation of resources. "The data in respect of investment and savings over a considerable part of the economy", to quote again from the Planning Commission, "are inadequate and it is not possible to attempt any very precise estimate regarding the sources and uses of funds for private investment."[17] As dependable estimates cannot even be attempted, what to speak of being framed, their undependability necessarily impairs seriously the authenticity of the estimates of:

(a) total outlay on development,

(b) the ratios of output to investments,

(c) ratio of investment to the national income and,

(d) its distribution.

What is true of the first two plans is equally true of the third and the estimated proposed private investment of Rs 4,100 crores out of the total investment of Rs 10,400 crores is also purely speculative; and with the possible exception of the estimates of investment of Rs 895 crores from 1951-61 and projected investment of Rs 1,020 crores under the Third Plan in organized industry and mining, the rest of the estimated and planned investment of Rs 4,205 crores in the first two plans and Rs 3,080 crores in the Third, i.e. Rs 7,085 crores in the private sector of the total actual and projected investment of Rs. 20,510 or nearly 30 per cent has hardly any validity as planned actual

16. *Third Five Year Plan*, p. 105.
17. *Third Five Year Plan*, p. 105.

or proposed expenditure. Really speaking, it represents an exercise in statistical legerdemain and has no meaning in real terms from the point of view of planned development. Even in regard to investment in organized industry and mining planning as conceived and practised in this country is no planning at all; but in the other sphere of private investment there is not even shadowy planning in the provision and use of resources, and to speak of planned outlay and investment in respect of these spheres is, to repeat, going against the very elementary concepts of planning. It is not necessary to add that there is hardly any planning in this sphere, which accounts for nearly 90 per cent of our national output, that no effort of any significance has been made to make socialism as the objective or operative principles in nine-tenths of our economy and in the remaining one-tenth the net result, as pointed out again and again, has been not realization of socialism, but in effect its defeat or frustration. In the development of the private sector as a whole this country has not only failed to bring about any accord between the public and private sectors, but in the latter forces have been at work and are gaining strength for whom socialism is an object to be set at naught rather than realized. This is due as much to make-believe in planning as to inability to muster and use the pro-socialist forces. The Government is, of course, mainly responsible for this sorry state of things, but responsibility for it has also to be shared by all other political parties which are avowedly working for the realization of a socialist society. They have, in this respect, let down the country as badly as the Government and the Congress Party.

The total investment under the plans in the private sector, including the provision in the Third Plan for investment in organized industry and mining, is estimated at Rs 2,415 crores[18] of which Rs 579 crores have been and are to be derived from financing institutions like Indian Finance Corporation, Indian

18. *Third Five Year Plan—a Draft Outline*, India 1960, Publications Division.

Credit and Investment Corporation, State Finance Corporation and direct participation by the State, Rs 454 crores from foreign capital, Rs 1,160 crores from internal sources, i.e. accumulated reserves, built from undistributed profits and the rest from new issues, etc. This means that for investments in industrial and mining in the private sector under the three plans, funds derived from public funds or funds provided under public guarantee amounted to nearly 45 per cent of the total, accumulated reserves to 46 per cent and the rest from new issues, etc. The accumulated reserves are, rather should be, regarded as corporate funds the investment of which in a planned economy should be under the control of the community. In any case, public and corporate contributions are the main source of funds for investments in industries and mining in the private sector and are therefore not private investments in the real sense. Power exercised in the private industrial sector by a small more or less closed group is not based upon their personal contributions to the industrialization of the country. Since 1951 only 9 per cent of investments has been financed by personal savings and the industrial and financial magnates, who are all powerful, have contributed only a portion of the 9 per cent. These powerful men are abusing the fiduciary position, which enables them to control the resources of the private industrial sector, for personal enrichment and, of course, the frustration of the socialist objective of the country. The private sector of organized industries has been greatly expanded since 1951 and the control of small coteries greatly widened by funds placed, as stated above, at their disposal by the public financial institutions, utilization of the accumulated reserves and to a much smaller extent by fresh issues to which the directors have made, relatively speaking, an insignificant[19] contribution.

19. Based upon a study of the Company Law Administration the Mahalnobis Committee found that of "the 883 directors of 121 companies held among themselves directly only in their own names 6 per cent of the total paid up capital of the companies of which they were directors. The percentage of the directors in the companies managed by their managing

EXTERNAL ASSISTANCE

We have been and are relying very heavily upon external assistance for financing development; and the proportion of the amount drawn from this source has increased from 10 per cent of the total outlay on development in the first plan, to 29 per cent in the second plan and will rise to 36 per cent in the third if the target of Rs 3,200 under this head is actually realized and it is likely that this amount will in fact be exceeded. Our increasing dependence upon external assistance is a very marked feature of our resource operations and its likely impact upon the course of events needs to be clearly understood.

Largely speaking this assistance has come from the U.S.A. and her allies, but the U.S.S.R. and her allies have also contributed to it liberally. This fact is in one sense a compliment to the non-aligned foreign policy of our country—the policy of goodwill toward all countries. It can be taken as a measure of our success in having steered our course with skill in the intricate maze of world events and without losing our own integrity, it shows how we have won the confidence of the major countries in the two grand alliances, commonly known as the American and Soviet blocs. India had attained a high position, thanks to Jawaharlal Nehru, in international councils owing to independence of her foreign policy and imaginative understanding of the meaning of measures and events from the long-term standpoint. Within the limit set by the magnitude of the great tasks undertaken by her due to her pressing needs

agencies worked out around 3 per cent whereas those of the directors of the companies which are managed directly by the boards of directors work out to around 9 per cent" (*The Mahalnobis Committee Report*, Para 4-7-, p. 45). "Due to dispersal of shareholding over a large number of people, a majority of whom do not take any interest in corporate decision, it is not necessary to have a majority of voting rights to get or retain control of a company, even a block of 10 to 20 per cent of the voting rights being enough some times to acquire control" (*Ibid*). This is true of corporate undertakings all over the world. As stated before, there is generally almost complete divorce between ownership and control and the controllers in most cases are self-appointed and can perpetuate their hold over the corporate undertakings which they acquire control of by manoeuvres and manipulations.

in changing world relations and her own internal weaknesses and difficulties, she has been able to attain and maintain her independent position by her positive policy and constructive statesmanship. In a sense, therefore, external assistance received by India from the protagonist of rival policies and interests is the fruit of this constructive policy, and it is not illegitimate to regard it as an index of its success.

But we have also to realize that today the world is being moved by the struggle for power in a shifting balance of world forces and a sense of world solidarity is at a low ebb. The donor and recipient countries have both been involved in this struggle and international aid has neither been granted nor received as a measure of redistribution of world resources according to capacity and needs. International altruism has been of some but very limited importance in the dispensation of resources and very largely international aid has been determined by exigencies of the struggle for power and its changing amounts, rate and allocations have been determined by them. Assistance which India has received and is likely to receive is due more to India's strategic importance in this uneasy equilibrium than to the success of her constructive policy. The latter, to repeat, has been and is successful as far as it goes; but it is not of decisive importance in determining the flow of funds and technical assistance to India from the advanced countries, and the latter are mainly guided by their own assessment of the international situation and their judgement of what is truly beneficial from the standpoint of their own national interests. The fact that military aid has been of far greater importance in the grant of international assistance than economic aid speaks for itself and shows the relative importance of their interest in and the desire for accelerating the rate of development of the undeveloped countries; but even in the grant of economic aid objective assessment of needs has played a very inconsequential role and the contributions of the rich to the poor countries have been largely, though not entirely, determined by the importance which the former attach to the latter as actual or potential pawns in the game of power politics.

The U.S.A., the chief donor country, has been guided mainly by her global policy of fighting communism and allocation of her aid has been mostly determined by this supreme object. It is not necessary to cite facts in support of this view. Its validity does not admit of any doubt or difference of opinion. What is true of the U.S.A. is also true of the U.K., France, Germany, Italy, Japan, Australia and New Zealand and though not to the same extent, of Norway, Sweden, Denmark and Holland. The U.S.S.R., Poland, Czechoslovakia and Rumania are, on the other hand, guided by the new assessment of the role of the movement of "democratic national liberation" in world affairs and therefore of the countries like India, Indonesia, Burma, Egypt and African countries which have won recently their national independence. India's role, from this point of view, is of the highest importance in checking the forces of colonialism and intensifying the sense of independence and nationalism in these countries; and investment in her development is for the Soviet Union and her allies, investment in the development of forces which in the last analysis will change the world-balance against what, according to the U.S.S.R., U.S.A. and her allies stand for, i.e. colonialism and neo-colonialism. For the U.S.A., on the other hand, India is the most important bastion against the advance of communism and is of great importance because as a parliamentary democracy and a country committed to a non-communist social philosophy the weight of her position and influence is likely to be thrown against communism internally and externally. Moreover, since India's own internal position is in a fluid state and there are forces at work which are not only against communism but also against socialism, assistance to India can be used insiduously to strengthen these forces and, it would be unrealistic to say, that it is not being actually used for this purpose.

In a way external assistance to India does not involve any interference in her internal affairs and legalistically speaking, this is so; but in fact American aid is largely motivated by an earnest and even avowed desire to win the battle for 'the soul of India', i.e. to roll back the forces of communism and even arrest the growth of socialism which, by its own inner logic leads to negation of freedom from the American standpoint. The purpose of assistance to India and other countries which need it badly, is veiled in professions of disinterested help, but, it is very thinly veiled and the amount, the form, the rate and time of assistance are largely determined by the exigencies of cold war. The obvious conclusion is that though India is not a participant in the cold war, she is one of its principal bene-ficiaries and the grant and continuance of assistance largely depends upon the place which she occupies from the point of view of world strategy of the major powers. In other words, aid to India, both from the American and the Soviet standpoints, is strategic aid, and the extent to which she continues to get this aid, would largely depend upon the strategy and counter-strategy of the donor countries in their struggle for power. India can remain true to her own policy, receive and use the aid without incurring any commitments, do her best to promote a world without tension and with largest degree of international co-operation. But integrity of this approach is exposed to serious danger owing to the internal forces which are against the preservation of this integrity being propped up through this assistance, and what is more, through world pressures which are being built up and exercised through the programme of external assistance against the continuance of this policy by India and other countries. From the Soviet point of view, it would be to her advantage if India does not deviate from the path of non-alignment and realizes the avowed object of building up a socialist society with the consent of the people and without recourse to force to any extent; India's own road to socialism will also, from the Soviet standpoint, be a road to a world in which peaceful competition between communism and capitalism according to this view, can remain operative with a certain prospect of the victory of the former. From the American stand-point India's remaining outside the Soviet camp would itself be a great gain, but social premises of her working faith by implication and in fact makes America an instrument of a policy largely opposed to socialism. In the assistance which U.S.A. or America Foundations have given to, for example, community development, small-scale industries and intensive agricultural development even co-operative production has been, as pointed out before, specifically discountenanced and the consultants have propagated the gospel of private enterprise and individualism. Through the pressure excercised by the U.S.A. financial institutions and even the I.B.R.D., which, as stated before, is virtually an American Agency, the interests of the private sector in India have been clearly protected and promoted with special solicitude. It would have been really surprising if it has been otherwise. The U.S.A. is not only actively interested in securing through pressures modifications of our foreign policy of non-alignment but also in weakening, diluting and even undermining our socialist objective. This does not need to be even specifically pointed out. This is and has to be the inevitable result of the U.S.A.'s own foreign and domestic policies.

India's internal position is itself unstable from the point of view of socialism and the forces working for it are weak and ineffective in action. Foreign assistance and the forces emanating from it cannot but have a bearing upon the currents and cross-currents in the Indian economy itself and the outcome of all these complicated inter-actions cannot but be uncertain and un-predictable. It is, however, clear that external assistance, upon which we are relying to an increasing extent for financing our plans, is for us an incalculable risk, and there is no assurance at all that we will get it into the extent and in the form suited to our needs and its timing would fit into the priorities and time-schedules of our plan. Real international assistance should be a planned allocation of pooled surplus resources of all relatively affluent countries by a world authority or a number of regional authorities according to a scale of assessed needs of the countries in need of assistance in order that the gulf between the rich and the poor countries, which is known to be widening at present, may be narrowed, the people of all countries raised to a certain minimum level and placed in a position to achieve a rate of sustained growth at an ever rising level. This is, however, at present an unattainable object, and the "ultimate reason", in the words of Dr Gunar Myrdal, "for this difficulty is, of course, that we are not living and, in our time, shall not be living under a world Government which due to political processes, would decide upon sharing of burden and redistribution of income and wealth."[20] International agencies, which are at present charged with the function of allocating funds for development, are exposed, and not without factual basis, to the charge of being partisans in cold war and not impartial dispensers of world's surplus resources. The world has at present the means and the technique by which in a comparatively short time of a decade or two poverty can be abolished as a painful fact of the world situation. Even if $20 billions out of $120 billions now spent on potentially disastrous war preparations can be made available for peaceful development of the two-thirds of world population now living in a state of misery and deprivation, the whole face of the world can be changed out of recognition and the world started on the path to an immeasurably happy future. At present, however, this is only a pipe dream and only visionaries can feel its need and importance.

In India, as in other countries in similar position, we have to reckon with the situation as it is and with the risks inherent in assistance granted largely on bilateral basis, with very mixed motives and primarily with the conscious endeavour on the part of each major donor country to project a particular image of its own on the minds of the peoples of the recipient countries and promote the objects of its foreign policy. Most of the international assistance at present is being granted in this context and apart from its complete inadequacy, it is tainted because

20. Gunar Myrdal, *An International Economy;* p. 121.

it is a part of, to repeat, the strategy of struggle for power on a world scale. This is inevitable at present, and the degree to which a developing country can receive and utilize assistance without becoming an instrument of the policies of the donor countries partly depends upon the balance of forces and counter-forces but mainly upon its internal strength, generation and development of its own resources and the degree to which it can understand and provide against the risks inherent in any pro-gramme of international assistance. The world may, with luck, move towards a state without war, tensions may be materially relaxed and large measures of international co-operation achiev-ed in practice. This being the condition of survival of mankind, it may be hoped that a significant advance towards it will in fact be made; but any progress in this direction cannot but be a zig-zag course and serious setbacks are unavoidable. For India owing to the crucial position which she occupies because of the conjunction of forces and events, the need for continuous vigi-lance and alertness is all the greater. Increasing dependence upon external assistance is for us a matter for concern because our own resources have neither increased nor been channelized adequately, but, what is far more important from this point of view, politically and socially, we have not been able to throw up defences against these and similar other dangers and our internal position is precarious and very vulnerable. The motives of the richer countries for granting assistance to the poor coun-tries cannot be radically changed. They are to be taken as given facts, and in negotiating agreements on a bilateral basis and even with international agencies, we have to be on our guard against risky commitments and reduce, as far as we can, the vulnerability of our internal position.

Assistance can and does mean penetration and infiltration, and great as is our need for it, we must not accept it merely because it is offered. We have to take it when we really cannot do without it, but, as far as we can, we must guard adequately against the serious risks inherent in largely depending upon it. It is not possible to analyse the assistance which has so far been accepted by us from this point of view, but cases can be easily cited to show how the clear need for caution and vigilance has been largely disregarded in practice and a considerable proportion of the assistance offered to and received by us, could with proper scanning and scrutiny have been dispensed with or very materially reduced. This is specially true of the multitude of technical experts[21] and consultants whom we have imported. Some of them are highly competent and their services have been of inestimable value; many more, particularly in non-technical fields, are men whose ability, not to say anything about good faith, to play constructive role in development is very much in doubt. The cost of their inflated salaries and of luxurious living, which is charged to our assistance account, really adds to our existing inflationary pressures. Taking the conditions under which external assistance is being made available as they are, we have to be keenly aware of the need for reducing our dependence on external assistance. We cannot and should not slow down the rate of growth or industrialization in the country but with due care, caution and vigilance we can build up our defences against the dangers of such assistance and agree to receive and utilize it when, as stated above, we cannot do without it.

The total external assistance for India authorized up to the end of 1961 amounted to Rs 4,000 crores[22] and out of which

21. The extent of the provision for technical experts can be gauged by the fact that under Indo-U.S. Technical Co-operation Programme up to the 30th September 1961 amounts up to Rs 201.41 crores were spent for this purpose and this is exclusive of the provision for technicians by the Ford and Rockefeller Foundations whose number is known to be large and who, besides being persons of mixed quality, are even more in politics than the other experts in the U.S. programme. Burma's action in closing down Ford Foundation in that country is significant and points to this danger from the international standpoint.

22. External loans have to be repaid and of course interest has to be paid on them as long as they are outstanding. The repayment and interest obligation of these loans create heavy liabilities for us and a provision of Rs 500 crores has been made in the 3rd Plan to meet these liabilities. Owing to our balance of payment and revenue deficit these capital obligations can

the U.S.A. loans and grants amounted to Rs 2,511 crores or nearly 62 per cent. The loans authorized by the U.N. special fund and the International Bank of Rehabilitation and Development up to 1961 amounted to Rs 416 crores.[23] These International Agencies derived a large proportion of their funds from the U.S.A. and are very largely amenable to its guidance and control, and therefore nearly three-fourths of the total external assistance can be taken as having been contributed by the U.S.A. or the institutions which function for practical purposes more as American than international institutions.[24] The U.S.S.R., which is the next important donor country made available assistance to the extent of Rs 499 crores or 12.5 per

only be met from fresh loans. These loans carry rates of interest varying from one to $5\frac{1}{2}$ per cent but generally speaking the rates are high on loans from the U.S.A., her allies and World Bank while the loans of the U.S.S.R., as a rule, as a rule, carry interest rates of $2\frac{1}{2}$ per cent and are repayable generally in 12 years. Some of these obligations can be discharged by payment in rupees but most of them involve foreign exchange payments. Unless we can create surplus in our balance of payments these obligations will have to be met from the proceeds of new loans. Interest on our foreign debt increased from Rs 1.6 crores in 1951-52 to Rs 3.3 crores in 1955-56 and since then it rose to Rs 36.1 crores in 1961-62.

23. "The International Bank" to quote from Gunar Myrdal again, "has rightly been characterized as an American lending agency." He adds, "But it has been able to carry on its activity with considerable degree of independence and objectivity" (op. cit., p. 131)—really an ambivalent statement. The view that the Bank has been functioning with independence and objectivity is just not supported by facts. It has been really working, as stated in the text, as an American institution. There are no internationally decided and fixed norms for its operations. It is in fact guided by the norms and directives of the national foreign economic policy of the U.S.A.

24. The total external assistance received in the first four years of the Third Plan including the budget estimates of 1964-65, amounts to Rs 2,346.58 crores. This amount is made up of:

1961-62	414.95 crores
1962-63	511.94 ,,
1963-64	575.16 ,,
1964-65	844.54 ,,

2,346.59 crores

The U.S.A. continues to occupy a pre-dominant position in our external assistance programme and the conclusion of the analysis remains valid.

cent of the total. Czechoslovakia, Poland and Rumania contributed Rs 44 crores for the establishment or development of some of our key industries or about 1.4 per cent of the total. Of the remaining 11 per cent Yugoslavia granted .5 and Switzerland .25 per cent and the remaining 10 per cent was made available by U.K., Canada, Western Germany, Italy, Australia, New Zealand, Norway and Holland—all countries in the American grand alliance. These figures very clearly show the extent to which the U.S.A. has acquired a dominant position in financing the programme of external assistance to India and how necessary it is to realize that this is a very risky position for us.

To what extent the U.S.A. by her enormous contribution can call the tune and shape our policy is a matter of speculation. The decisions of the Senate Committee to reduce assistance to India in 1962-63 to censure India for Goa and Kashmir policy is an overt act which speaks for itself. Withdrawal of the offer of assistance for the Bokaro steel plant is again a clear indicator of what the real position of the U.S.A. is in this regard; but even if overt interference in our affairs is avoided to spare our national susceptibility, it has to be realized that politics cannot possibly be taken out of external assistance programme of any country—much less that of the U.S.A. with its well known cold war obligations. The U.S.A. can, without inviting the charge of open interference, through its active participation in our far-flung programmes like community development, intensive agricultural development and development of small-scale industries the programmes which were initiated and are being carried on under her aegis and that of the Ford Fundation, import her own philosophy and policy into the implementation of many projects all over the length and breadth of the country. The U.S.A. has specially interested herself in our private sector by contributing to the funds of the institutions like Indian Credit and Investment Corporation, Indian Finance Corporation and Re-finance Corporation—the three important financing agencies for private investment, through the World Bank loans to private enterprises like Indian Iron and Steel Company, Tata Iron and Steel Company and Trombay Thermal Station, etc. and by utilizing the rupee funds accruing from the sale of surplus agricultural commodities for financing development of private firms under what is known as the Cooley Amendment. The U.S.A. is using the counterpart funds, from the sale of these commodities, for a great variety of projects and in each case the U.S.A.'s approval is necessary for the allocation of funds. The necessity of obtaining her approval is and can become an occasion for its having a voice in the development of these projects even when there is no question of special technical assistance being required for their execution. The U.S.A. assistance is not only a means through which, behind the scene, pressures are exercised over major decisions but it has become also means for having a determining share in the undertaking and execution of numerous specific projects. That provision of the three-fourths of the external assistance by the U.S.A. carried with it, as stated already, incalculable risk of its being used as an instrument of undermining the independence of our internal and external policy is undeniably true, and the amount, form and allocation of this assistance have given her an opportunity to participate extensively and intensively in our development programme without being able to contribute in most cases significantly to the successful execution of the numerous projects for which allocations are made. The whole situation needs to be reviewed from the point of our real needs and their priorities and we have, to repeat, to do what we can to limit foreign active participation in our development programme to our assessed need for resources and real technical assistance. Through assistance which we are getting from the U.S.A., it has become a senior partner on a country-wide basis in our numerous development projects.

P.L. 480

A word may be said about what is called P.L. 480 programme under which we purchase agricultural commodities from the

U.S.A. which are for the Americans what they call 'burdensome surpluses'. Under the five agreements under which we have signed these since August 1956 Rs 1,103 crores worth of commodities under the first four agreements were purchased, and, under the fifth signed in May 1960 we were to purchase 16 million tons of wheat, one million ton of rice at the cost of $1,276 million and under supplements to this agreement we were to purchase cotton, tobacco, corn and soroghum at an additional cost of $93.80 millions. Of Rs 2,511 crores American grants and loans referred to above since the inception the purchase under the previous and the five P.L. 480 agreements the cost of surplus agricultural commodities received or to be received by us amounts to Rs 1,830 crores or 72 per cent. It is really pathetic the way we have become dependent upon the import of surplus agricultural commodities for meeting our current requirements of food. From 1951 to 1962 our production of cereals has gone up by 55 per cent, of rice by 58 per cent, of wheat by 76 per cent and of pulses 30 per cent and our population during this period has increased by 26 per cent. And yet we have imported food worth Rs 1,830 crores since 1956—mostly wheat—and have entered into another agreement with the U.S.A. to import more surplus commodities after 1964. It is true that consumption of food increases with increases in the income of low income groups owing to development expenditures and possibly the tendency to hoard also becomes stronger. It is not and cannot be known how far what are called 'propensities to consume' and propensity to hoard have increased since 1951; but that cannot explain why in spite of considerable increase in production of food grains from 1951 to 1962 we cannot provide even cereals for our growing population and must import mainly wheat from U.S.A. in order to have confidence in our capacity to get over the shortage of our food. Wheat is, roughly speaking, 16 per cent of production of cereals in this country and yet we are mainly relying upon the import of this food grain under these agreements in order to overcome our shortages, if our agricultural statistics are even approximately correct, we require more than three times as much rice as wheat, two times as much coarse grains and yet with this pattern of normal consumption, under P.L. 480 under the total imports of $2,031 million of agricultural commodities from 1956 to 1962 we imported $165.3 million worth of rice and wheat valued at $1,630.6 millions.[25] Rice is a minor crop in U.S.A. and she does not have much surplus of rice or inferior grains. Our shortage of rice, if there is shortage at all, must be much greater than that of wheat and our import of rice under these agreements is less than one eighth of the import of wheat. Our whole policy and programme in regard to these imports does not seem to have any rational basis or explanation.

We could have, if we had really control over our economy, procured our own surplus—easily more than 3 to 4 million tons of food grains—the quantity which we have on the average been importing from U.S.A. under these agreements since 1956, built our buffer stocks of 5 million tons and used it to reduce rise in and fluctuations of agricultural—particularly food—prices. And if we had gone further, nationalized our wholesale trade in food grains and also processing industries —rice mills, flour mills and oil mills—we would have not only been independent of the import from U.S.A. surplus commodities, but acquired a mastery of the market, stabilized agricultural prices and prevented greater malnutrition of the masses in the country. But these steps we did not and could not take because of the pressure of the mercantile interests in particular and that of the propertied classes in general. We have preferred to rely upon P.L. 480 instead, acquired a false sense of security, increased our foreign debt by Rs 508 crores and found ourselves in the existing crisis of spiralling prices. We have not learnt the lesson of this experience still and are hoping that by further imports under P.L. 480 we would be able to retrieve the situation.

25. Food Aid, Its Role in Economic Development (a Publication for the Organization For Economic Development and Co-operation, Table II, p. 25).

The fact of the matter is that if we cultivate self-reliance, make the most of our agricultural resources, rationalize, modernize our agriculture and use fully our own agricultural potential through a programme of integrated agricultural development in the sense explained clearly before, we cannot only surmount the present crisis, but also lay the foundation of a healthy, strong and vigorous rural economy. We already know that this is the way out for us and that is why again and again are falling back upon schemes of integrated agricultural development. We have introduced them, carried them less than half way and abandoned them one after another because we cannot muster the courage needed for basic structural changes without which any scheme of integration is bound to fail. It is much easier to lull ourselves into a sense of false security and enter into further agreements under P.L. 480 in spite of the clear evidence of our experience in regard to their futility.

The question of the use of counter-part funds, i.e. the rupee equivalent of the cost in dollars of these imports which are acquired when these commodities are sold to the consumers, has acquired great practical importance. The U.S.A. is following a set pattern of allocation of these counter-part funds. Out of the total of $8,179 million which she acquired up to 1961-62, since this programme was introduced in 1954, the global average allocation has been 43 per cent loans for projects, 20 per cent grants, 6 per cent loan for private enterprise, 24 per cent for U.S. requirements and 7 per cent for common defence.[26] In India there can be no allocation for common defence. Under the first four agreements out of the counterpart funds of Rs 1,103 crores loans accounted for Rs 537.10 crores (48 per cent), grants Rs 375.33 crores (33 per cent), Rs 143.25 crores were retained by the American Embassy (12 per cent) and Rs 77.23 crores (7 per cent) for capital advances to private enterprizes under what is called Cooley amendment. The proportions may be somewhat differ-

26. Op. cit., Table IV, p. 33.

ent, but the pattern of utilization of these funds is about the same. Grants and loans for development constitute the bulk of these allocations, and the use of the U.S.A. Government and the provision of capital funds for private enterprize are the other important objects of these allocations. Provision for private firms are for private American firms and their Indian collaborators and is intended to promote the investment of private American capital in Indian industries. As regards the provision for U.S. uses, the amount is at free disposal of the American embassy and according to one estimate was large enough in 1959 to cover its needs for eighteen years.[27] The loans and grants for economic development have been given largely for purposes like community development, agricultural research, engineering education, farmers' association, river valley projects, productivity council and particularly for financial institutions like Refinance Corporation, Industrial Finance Corporation and Indian Credit and Investment Corporations intended for making funds available for investment by big industrial undertakings. These financial institutions have contributed largely to the growth of big business in India in the last thirteen years and assisted them to acquire even a more dominant position, as pointed out already, in the Indian economy. Interest in and solicitude for the private sector are matters of special concern to the dispensors of the counter-part

27. H. J. P. Arnold, *Aid for Developing Countries*, p. 59. This large amount at the disposal of the U.S.A. embassy is presumably being utilized by it in accordance with political strategy implicit in U.S. policy. Nothing authentic is or can be known about the utilization of these large resources. But it would not be wrong to assume that the pursuit of the objects of cold war is and cannot but be an important factor in the allocation of these large funds. They are, on this assumption, being allocated for U.S.I.S., Education Foundation and other similar agencies, but particularly for C.I.A. (the wellknown Intelligence Organization) which in countries like Congo, Cuba and South Viet-nam has played and is playing such a sinister role. This organization, it is known, has assumed a quasi-independent position and is not even subject to the control of the State Department and the American embassies. In countries like India, C.I.A. naturally occupies a less obtrusive position but is not the less dangerous on that account.

funds and are in keeping with the economic faith of U.S.A.[28] That this, as a matter of course, means frustration of socialist objectives of the Government of India should be fairly obvious, but is hardly taken into account. Through large-scale assistance to big business and collaborationist industrial undertakings everything is being done to make the country as safe as possible for private capital in general and private foreign capital in particular and to build counter-pressures against the advance of socialism in India.

Even more important aspect of the matter, however, is that though loans and grants for development, for which the bulk of counter-part funds are set apart, U.S.A. becomes an active participant in the formulation and execution of numerous projects of development all over the country, imports into them, as stated before, her own social philosophy and has a decisive voice in policy and programme relating to these projects. She has, generally speaking, no special role to play in framing and carrying out such programmes, the experts who are brought for initiating and administering these projects have, as a rule, no special competence in regard to them and are ignorant of the essential characteristics and needs of the Indian economy. Through the allocation of these large funds for developments U.S.A. is not only becoming a senior partner in the country-wide development projects but bringing into our development a social philosophy opposed to the accepted social philosophy of the country.

As this is being written (July 1964) the Minister for Food and Agriculture is reported to have stated that there is no alternative to the import of wheat under P.L. 480 from U.S.A. until 1970-71 even if India has good crops this year and the

28. Though counter-part funds and the other assistance by U.S.A. and the international financial institutions have been used in a few cases for assisting the private industrial undertaking like Tata Iron and Steel and Indian Iron and also thermal and hydal power projects, they have been mostly used for projects which do not promote industrialization and enable U.S.A. to participate actively, as pointed out before, in the formulation and execution of numerous development projects.

years to come. No reason has been given in support of this statement and none is available. But the real fact of the matter is that there is no alternative to these imports and has not been all these years because the Government of India's unwillingness and inability to take the necessary action to utilize our own agricultural resources effectively and to the greatest advantage. From short term point of view vigorous administrative action, as stated before, is called for to deal with the present crisis, but from long term point of view the way out is full utilization of our agricultural production potential and enormous idle man-power on an integrated basis to build up a new rural economy. Given the right social framework and drive there is an alternative to the defeatist policy of relying upon P.L. 480 for the solution of our food problem. There should not have been and need not be any food shortages in the country. If we cannot deal with the organizational and social problems involved in the utilization of our own agricultural resources, we will continue to stagger under chronic deficits of food, unstable and rising prices and possibly suffer a serious collapse. The policy of dependence upon 'the burdensome surpluses' of U.S.A. is no policy at all, it is an open invitation to the believers in the gospel of private enterprize and free competition to join hands with our big business and reactionary interests to promote and strengthen monopoly interests in this country in the name of food aid. In their own country they have succeeded in cartelization of their economy with full profession of faith in free competition. They are seeking to do the same in this country and we, through our weakness and lack of understanding, are playing in their hands and refusing to be fully self-reliant as we can and should be. This is what aid under P.L. 480 means for us and we are not aware of this meaning.

AID BY CONSORTIUM

It has now become a regular practice for the most important non-socialist countries, which are giving assistance to India, to review the progress of the Indian economy and the development in industrial sectors collectively as members of the Aid India Consortium sponsored by the World Bank.[29] At these meetings the progress of Indian economy is reviewed, the country's development and requirements are assessed and each member pledges a certain quota of assistance in principle, and on the basis of these pledges, bilateral agreements with each member of the Consortium are concluded. In the review of Indian economy and the assessment of her needs, it is known that ideological considerations and the question of high politics play an important role and the aid is granted on the assessment of not only the economic but also political aspects of the aid programme.[30] The first meeting of the Consortium was held when India was confronted with serious difficulties on account of

29. Originally the consortium consisted of Canada, Japan, United Kingdom and the United States of America. In May-June 1961 France and International Development Corporation also joined the Consortium and Austria, Denmark, Norway, Sweden and International Monetary Fund sent observers to this meeting. The sum of $2,225 millions was made available for aid to India and consisted of the following contributions for 1st two years of the Third Plan—U.S.A. $1,045 millions, West Germany $364 and $67 million for the remaining period, U.K. $250 millions, Canada $56 million and France $30 million.

30. A knowledgable contributor in a recent issue of Economic Weekly (The Economic Weekly, Volume XVI, No. 14) draws pointed attention to the increasing habit of the World Bank as leader of Consortium, not only to offer criticism and advice but also interfere actively in the policy making processes of our country. He sums up the position in the following words, 'India welcomes constructive criticism but it is equally for the Bank to realise that there is a line which divides criticism and advice from interference. It would be better in the interests of fruitful and constructive Indo-Bank relations if we tell the Bank right now before it becomes embarrasingly late to do so, that while we will take note of their views, the Fourth Plan will be a truly Indian document." This is very mildly put. As stated elsewhere the Bank is taking upon itself the responsibility of sitting in judgement upon not only individual projects but also our approach and objectives of economic planning in the country; and as pointed out above, the imminent scrutiny of the working of our economy and the new plan under preparation by the Bank, indications are clear, not only would amount to criticism and advice but active interference. We have to be aware of this danger before, as pointed out by this contributor, it is too

shortage of foreign exchange in the middle of the Second Plan. At the meeting held in May-June 1961 the Consortium undertook the commitment of aid to India totalling $2,225 million. Since then the meetings have been held at intervals. The latest review, which the World Bank is undertaking on behalf of the Consortium, is intended to be a more intensive examination of the economic outlook and position in India and would, it may be assumed, involve consideration of some of the very basic issues of the economic development in this country. Experience of the meetings of the Consortium indicates clearly the pressures that are developed and applied at its meetings.

The Consortium, for example, met in May 1962 but its meeting was adjourned without coming to any decision, because in the words of The Times, London, "one or two members were unwilling to extend their commitments at this stage." This fact made us clearly aware of the processes at work at the meeting of the Consortium. Goa, Kashmir, V. K. Krishna Menon and the purchase of M.I.G. planes from the Soviet Union,

late. We have already, as shown by the last budget speech of the Finance Minister, gone too far in submitting to this pressure. We have to know how we are sliding down, otherwise the Consortium and the Bank will virtually take over the plan for development of this country. That, apart from the surrender of economic sovereignty, will mean turning our back completely on socialism and all that it implies. That is why we must beware before, to repeat, it is too late.

Another sharp reminder of the growing habit of the World Bank to assume a posture of authority over our economic policy has been given by the World Bank's reported strong criticism of an amendment to the Company Act. In its unusually forthright adverse comment on this ammendment the World Bank is said to have reminded the Government of India that the move will have "deleterious repercussions on the flow of foreign capital." We should know what we are in for if we continue to rely upon the World Bank, i.e. the U.S.A. and its associates to such an extent for external assistence. This action has been taken mainly in support of the Tata Iron and Steel Company and Indian Iron and Steel, for whose interests the World Bank has always shown special solicitude, and presumably with their active consent if not at their instance. The World Bank, even now is largely guided by the spirit of Eugene Black, its ex-president, whose economic faith in the primacy of private enterprize has been referred to elsewhere in this book.

general foreign policy of India and perhaps some other unknown factors accounted for that meeting of the Consortium
having been inconclusive. The Times frankly called for a
change in our policy and approach. "India," in the words of
this oracle, "seems to be unaware of how much she continues
to strain the generosity of her friends. Western Aid needs a
matching Indian realism."[31] No one could have any doubt
as to what this 'matching realism' has to mean if India is not
to strain the generosity of her friends. It implies that we
should undertake a complete re-orientation of our policy of
non-alignment and our whole development programme. Since
then a lot has happened. We have been invaded by China,
Sino-Soviet differences have acquired an acute form and Nehru
has passed away. The Consortium, however, is still at work,
its internal processes have not been altered and the imminent
scrutiny of our economy by the World Bank indicates clearly
what the programme of external assistance by the U.S.A. and
her allies means for us. Our non-alignment, socialism and other
basic issues are evidently at issue in the review and re-assessment of our economic policy and programme. We have to bear
this vital point in mind and base our action on it.

APPROACHES SOVIET ASSISTANCE

The assistance extended by U.S.S.R. and her allies to India
is only one-ninth of the total assistance received by us from
the U.S.A. and her allies, but its significance to us lies in the
fact that this assistance is being given for the establishment of
undertakings like the Steel Plants, Heavy Machinery Plant,
Mining Machinery Plant, Oil Refineries, Heavy Electric Equipment Plant, Oil and Gas Exploration, Thermal Power Stations,
Institute for Machine Tool Technology and Design, Foundry
Forge Plant and Coal Mining and Coal Washery Projects. The
Soviet assistance is also, as stated before, a part of world strategy
and through it world balance of power is sought to be changed.

31. *The Times*, London, July 6, 1962, Editorial "Helping India", p. 13

This, however, fits in admirably into the priority pattern of our development programme and helps us to strengthen the very foundation of our economy. The Soviet Union can hardly make any direct contribution to the growth of a socialist economy in India. The development of heavy industries can create conditions for its growth, but cannot by itself bring socialism in this country. Moreover, it is to the advantage of the Soviet strategy if India finds and goes ahead on its own road to socialism, the assumption of Soviet approach now being that there are many roads to socialism. The Soviet Union cannot, to repeat, take any positive action to help us to advance towards socialism, but she, it may well be assumed, will not want to create any barriers in our way, or attempt to distort the processes, that may be brought into operation, to bring about socialist changes. The one contribution which she perhaps can, through the Communist Party of the Soviet Union, make to the growth of a socialist economy in this country is to pursuade, as far as it can, the Communist Party in India to complete the reorientation of its policy which is taking place at present as fast as possible, to think creatively in terms of Indian conditions and problems and to come fully into the mainstream of our national life. This, of course, applies, in the present context, only to one section of the Communist Party. This is how international proletarian solidarity should express itself now and the extent to which the Soviet Union attains success in this respect, will also be a measure of its success in giving assistance to India in the realization of socialism. The Soviet technologists are mostly confined to and engaged in building the plants which they are helping to establish and have no opportunity to participate in the formulation or execution of any other projects. They are not spread all over the country or trying to take part in the growth of processes which, in the very nature of things, must be left to Indians and in which foreigners should have no place. The Americans are out of sympathy with the socialist objectives of our programme and the expansion of the public sector, while the Soviet are, it need not be said, predisposed by their philosophy and experience, to favour and support both. They are keeping out and should keep out of the planning and implementation of overall programme of development, but there can be no doubt as to where their sympathies lie and what their reactions will be to any advance towards socialism, which by our unaided effort we may be able to achieve. This is a distinct advantage from our point of view. We, on our part, have to know that the Soviet aid is also a part of their world strategy and excercise due measure of care and caution in utilizing it. In regard to them also we have to be on our guard; but according to all reports, the patterns of human relations, which have been established in the undertaking to the development of which they are contributing equipment and technological assistance, is good, and they, unlike other foreign technicians, find no difficulty in adjusting themselves to our people and conditions. Vigilance with discretion is necessary in all undertakings, for which we are receiving external assistance; but in respect of the Soviet aid we should know that the chances of our co-operation with them on terms of equality and non-interference are definitely better and we can feel a sense of reassurance on that account.[32]

32. While the main field of economic co-operation between the Soviet Union and India has been heavy industries in the public sector, in agriculture Soviet Union has made a very significant contribution which has, according to all accounts, been a real success. Financially the Soviet aided mechanized farm of 30,000 acres at Suratgarh (Rajasthan) has yielded a gross profit of Rs 12.65 for total investment of Rs 228 lakhs; but that is, however, the less significant part of this development. The average yield of wheat in this area is 20 maunds per acre though higher yields of 39 maunds per acre for wheat, 43 maunds for paddy, 24 maunds for jawar and gram, 15 maunds for mustard and 1,400 maunds for sugar have been registered. The Government of India on the basis of the report of a Committee presided over by Mr. Damle, has started another 20,000 acre farm at Jetsar very near Suratgarh, to carry this development farther and establish another large state mechanized farm. Jawaharlal Nehru is reported to have said that he would like to see established 100 such large mechanized farms all over the country to increase materially the supply of agricultural commodities in general and food grains in particular. It has been estimated

Foreign private investment in our development is now being assidiously solicited and promoted in this country and the acceleration of the rate of the increase more is a major premise of the American policy of foreign aid.[33] The collaboration of foreign with Indian interests in the development of Indian industries is not only being permitted but positively promoted. Big foreign cartels like General Electric, Imperial Chemical, the Oil Companies, Krupp and many others are not only operating in this country but inter-lacing of foreign monopolies with the big business in India is proceeding apace at a rate and on a scale which should be a cause of serious concern but is being viewed with complacency, if not with growing satisfaction. Our pre-independence misgivings about the nature and intent of foreign assistance are no longer

that if 100 such farms are actually established they would probably provide besides fruit, milk and eggs, 4 to 5 million tons of cereals. One hundred such farms, at the rate of Rs 2.5 crores per farm, would involve the total outlay of Rs 250 crores. India imported cereals of nearly 4.5 million tons in 1962-63. The total expenditure on import of food on Government account alone amounted to Rs 283.4 crores in 1961-62 and 1962-63. It is obvious that investment of Rs 250 crores, provided it increases our supply of cereals by 4 to 5 million tons, would be very much worth while and relieve the strain on our foreign exchange resources and our dependence upon P.L. 480 with all its undesirable implications. The whole question needs to be examined with care and of course in this land-short country it will require special effort to make 3 million acres of extra land available for this purpose. The problem will not be insoluble given the will. In Rajasthan, U.P. Terai, Dandakaranya, Assam and through reclamation of soil in eroded areas it would probably be possible to provide 3 million acres of land for putting an end to our need for importing food grains under these onerous conditions. This is not the only way in which this object can be achieved. Intensification of agriculture and reduction of waste which is taking place at present through storage and pests and of course effective control of marketing operations would more easily enable us to terminate the present position in which for want of understanding and will we have got badly involved and with such truly onerous consequences.

33. In 1961 the Senate Foreign Relations Committee after declaring "that security and general welfare of United States" was to be the general aim of assistance, made the following declaration: The Congress declares it to be the purpose of this title (i.e. the Foreign Assistance Act of 1961), to strengthen friendly foreign countries by encouraging the development of their

widely shared and have given place to the increasing interest in and support of joint ventures in industrial developments in the name of Indo-foreign co-operation. Very scanty information is available of the extent to which such joint ventures are involving onerous commitments on our part and the terms on which they are being promoted. Foreign interests in this country are already well entrenched, they occupy dominant position in the key sectors of our economy like foreign exchange, banking, foreign trade, coal industry and tea and jute industries, chemicals and oil industry, etc. and though the inflow of foreign capital into this country since independence has been on a moderate scale, foreign interests through investment of their reserves, inter-lacing of business connections and joint ventures have occupied position of even greater importance, are exercising ever-widening influence over our economy and by offering relatively junior but well-paid posts to very well-connected Indians in increasing numbers are enlisting the support of men in high places in politics and administration. Assurances that have been given regarding remittances, repatriation and safeguards against confiscation without compensation are, relatively speaking, not onerous obligations. What, however, does matter and seriously is that these powerful combinations are throwing their entire weight against

economies through a competitive free enterprise system; to minimise or eliminate barriers to the flow of private investment capital and international trade; to facilitate the creation of a climate favourable to the investment of private capital" (Quoted in V. I. Pavlov's *India—Economic Freedom versus Imperialism*, p. 185).

A very powerful Committee presided over by General Clay in its Report submitted in March 1963 barred U.S. aid to Government owned enterprises in foreign countries which compete with the existing private endeavours. Recommendations of this report were accepted as basis of foreign policy by the Kennedy Administration and are now the basis of Foreign Aid Policy. U.S. foreign aid to India has been, with one or two exceptions, given almost entirely for schemes of agricultural development and private undertakings. The U.S. economic aid and that of institutions like The World Bank under its control is, it should be evident, avowedly meant for not only not supporting or strengthening socialism but actually defeating its realization.

socialism, are bringing high international politics into the
working of our economic and political system and doing so in
a very insidious and far-reaching manner. The fact that significance and the risk of this position are not even understood,
what to speak of being provided against, makes the position all
the more dangerous. Diminishing awareness of these dangers
is even of greater consequence than the dangers themselves,
and we have good reasons, as stated above, to be seriously concerned about the position but are not. The men in power are
not only being won over to the view that these developments
are necessary and desirable, but are getting entangled in
devious ways in the operations of foreign interests. We are
thus giving hostages to fortune and may have to pay dearly
for it.

This brief review of external assistance, its needs and
increasing importance, may be concluded with one or two
general observations. For development of the country we cannot
but depend upon external assistance in a large measure. If it
were possible to get it on our terms and as a part of world-wide
effort to redistribute world resources in the interest of world
community and therefore its more necessitious members, it
would signify a measure of advance towards realization of the
ideal of one world which could be a matter of great jubilation.
But it is neither possible for us nor for any other country in a
similar position to receive international aid on this basis. We
have to make the best of a really bad situation. We cannot do
without international aid and we cannot get it on terms which
would involve no threat to our future.[34] It is, therefore, necessary to thread our way in the present tanglewood of world

34. "Giving and taking aid", in the words of Dr Gunar Myrdal, "is an
extremely delicate matter, the psychology of which should be studied with
the utmost care before a position is taken. *This is particularly needed when
the giving country is a world power involved in a violent world conflict*
(emphasis added). In the interest of international harmony and understanding I would warn off any country from giving or receiving unilateral
international aid except when there are no other means available. If this
is the situation and unilateral aid becomes necessary, I would advise the

affairs with extreme care and circumspection. The world situation as it is developing makes it likely that international aid will grow in volume and importance, and it may be hoped that increasing proportion of it will be used to promote true international co-operation, but most of it will be unilateral and

most circumspect consideration of the political and social form in which it is going to be awarded and received" (op. cit., p. 127).

We have "in this exceedingly delicate matter" acted with great disregard of the care needed in accepting unilateral aid not from one but two world powers "involved in violent world conflict". The fact that we have received aid from both may be taken to have an element of safety in it by intro-ducing reciprocal neutralization of risks; but as three-fourths of the aid received by us has come from one of these powers (U.S.A.) and its Allies and involve, by the amount of aid and the form in which it is given, as stated in the text, participating extensively and intensively in our deve-lopment programme and this participation is hardly distinguishable from subtle but effective intervention in our economy, reciprocal neutralization of risks can hardly be achieved in practice. It is not possible to undertake a more detailed analysis of the facts bearing upon this point. The aid is being granted, as stated above, for projects in agriculture, community develop-ment, small industries, health, education, training of personnel, productivity studies and particularly in the field of private industry and private foreign investment. This is a subject which needs to be investigated fully and with care. What is happening in the negotiation of the numerous agree-ments in all these fields, how the pressures are being developed and applied and how our internal weaknesses are being utilized to create a web of difficulties almost unknown to us are matters about which very little is known. The assumption, however, that the opportunities which have thus been created by the dominant position acquired by one of these world powers through the grant of assistance, are being used fully to our dis-advantage is not at all unwarranted. The other world power (Soviet Union) has granted us assistance for developing key industries, but apart from the scale of its assistance being more limited, its assistance is confined to highly specialized fields and in that it is making contributions of great value. The Soviet Union has its own politics in this programme, but it hap-pens to fit into, as pointed out in the text, the pattern of our national priorities and India's economic independence and strong foundations of the economy are desirable from the Soviet standpoint. The assets, which we are creating through Soviet aid, are real assets, but are incidental to the pursuit of the broad objects of Soviet strategy and the fact indicates that vigilance in this case is also called for. The whole question of external assistance needs to be reviewed from our national standpoint and its implications and effects set forth in proper perspectives.

not multilateral in character, and a recipient country like ours will not be able to avoid entering into bilateral agreements with the donor countries. We will have to negotiate these agreements with the utmost care and not incur any commitments incompatible with the preservation of our independence and realization of our social objectives. External assistance is needed, but if we have to compromise our future on that account, we should know that this is not inevitable. Our own resources fully utilized and in the right social context can carry us a long way towards our goal. This will undoubtedly mean slower rate of economic growth than we would otherwise be able to achieve, but that would be any day better than exposing ourselves to serious dangers referred to above. The real point is that we have to build up our internal strength if we are to practise greater self-reliance in development, and face the dangers inherent in depending upon and receiving external assistance. Our real problem is the problem of developing our own strength by unremitting efforts for bringing a sound socialist economy into operation and arousing our people to full awareness of the fact that this can be done without any external assistance whatsoever. For this we not only can be but must be self-sufficient. Our own reserves have to be drawn upon for this purpose. That we do not know the importance of this fact and are doing so little to live up to it is our real lack. We have to know that we can make our future with external assistance if possible *but even without it if necessary. In the last analysis it is we who matter and not external assistance.*

FEDERAL FINANCE

From the constitutional standpoint it is not clear that Democratic Republic of India is a federation. Answer to the question whether it is or it is not depends upon how we define federation and its essentials. But in any real sense that matters India has to be a federal state, and we have really to go very much further and make federalism the basic principle of not only our polity but also our entire society. Fuller elaboration of this point cannot even be attempted here, but federalism as it has grown and is increasingly understood implies combination of the increasing autonomy of the constituent units with solidarity and integrity of the state as a whole. Whether it is formed by disaggregation of a unitary state or aggregation of independent political units is a matter of historical interest and importance, but it is not a vital point in the incorporation and application of federal principle in modern societies. The principle is really a new principle altogether and has very little in common with the principles of historical federations like those of the U.S.A., Switzerland and even Canada and Australia. The substance of even these federations has been profoundly altered in practice and the content of the old forms has been radically changed. But federation of today, as conceived and developed by contemporary theorists and constitution makers, is an all-embracing principle of social organization and not merely of relations between the states and the central government. In its fullness it has not been made operative as yet anywhere and has to be incorporated in the working of new societies as they develop on the basis of "from each according to capacity and to each according to needs". Integration, as distinguished from centralization, is its keynote and implies that the whole and the parts are organically related and functionally their roles are of co-ordinate importance and do not involve a hierarchical relation based upon division of powers. Societies are, from this standpoint, to be decentralized and yet integrated and "all for each and each for all" has to be the spirit of their laws. Modern societies are, imperfectly but nevertheless very really, moving towards this goal. The bearing of this principle on practice is not clearly understood, but "one in many and many in one" is the meaning of the process of unfoldment and growth from within of modern societies, and that is the sense in which federalism is increasingly becoming an operative principle of movement and change in political and social relations. It can be fully realized only in a completely developed socialist society in which all

political, social and economic relations express this principle
and are governed by it.

In the Indian constitution there is no rigid division of powers,
functions and resources, and as our society grows and is changed by the application of new social principles, the flexibility
of the provisions of the constitution can be used to promote
integration without centralization. Its bearing upon the
resource operation of the country is that though for administrative purposes there has to be a division and allocation of
resources between the Centre and the states, and some have to
be assigned to the former and others to the latter, in practice
all receipts have to be parts of the common pool and distributed according to a scale of priorities applicable to the economy as a whole. From practical standpoint it is necessary that
regional units and constituent states should not only enjoy a
large and increasing measure of autonomy, but also fully
assume its obligations, the most important of which is that
they should help themselves to the limit of their capacity by
developing their own resources. But it also means that national
minimum of the level of resources and services should be laid
down, and that if the regional units and the states even in
spite of their utmost exertions, cannot attain this minimum,
the deficiency should be made up by contributions from common pool. This is the principle of "each for all and all for each"
in action in resource operations and has to be the basis of
allocation of receipts. In all countries, as a result of the application of this principle, grants are assuming increasing importance; and as common pool has to be created and administered
by the centre, it means that the transfer of receipts from the
centre to the constituent units has to be a factor of increasing
importance in financial relations. This has in various ways
happened in almost all countries and not only countries in
which constitutions are expressly framed on federal principles,
but in the latter it has greater significance because of demarcation of powers, functions and revenues provided for in them.
Owing to the size of India and its great diversities, centraliza-

tion of authority is not only undesirable and also impracticable; and the necessity of increasing measure of decentralization has been felt and acted upon for the last ninety years, in initial stages in a very shadowy form. In successive stages its importance and scope have increased; and after independence the constituent units have on the one hand acquired a large measure of autonomy, on the other increasing proportion of their receipts have been derived from transfers from the Centre to the states. With the reorganization of states on linguistic basis, all states have, more than before, become organic entities; and though linguism has at times become a disruptive factor, linguistic states as such are based on right principles and can give to federalism new scope and meaning. The process has to be carried further by democratic decentralization; and though the latter can acquire reality only when spirit of democracy and unity can grow from below, in conception the new measure is an extension of the principle of federalism; and if corresponding social changes, which reduce inequalities and end oligarchies, are brought about, a real beginning can be made not only for establishing a federal state but also a federal society which in effect means a socialist society. But if this is to be achieved social changes have to give reality to new constitutional arrangement, and in resource the principle of each authority doing its utmost to develop its own resources and drawing upon the common pool to remove their inadequacies has to be carried right down to the basic level. In other words, full development of federalism in India has still to be achieved and will be only when new spirit referred to above becomes all pervading principle of society. But increasing importance of transfers from the Centre to the states is significant for increasing the application of this federal principle and has to be analysed from that standpoint.

TRANSFER TO STATES

Transfers of the four main varieties — tax receipts, revenue grants, capital grants and loans — have increased from Rs 160.1

crores in 1951 to Rs 741.67 crores in 1960-61, and total expenditure of the states both on revenue and capital account, from Rs 544 crores to Rs 1,278 crores and the ratio of the transfers to the expenditure from 22.2 to 58 per cent. The total transfers in the First Plan period were Rs 1,412.97 crores and in the Second Rs 2,867.92 crores and total expenditure again both on revenue and capital account was Rs 2,835.64 and Rs 5,283 crores, ratio between the two being 49 per cent and 55 per cent respectively for the two periods. Transfer from the centre to the states from 1961-62 to 1964-65 (including budget estimates) have increased from Rs 2,867.92 crores to Rs 4,133.56 crores — increase of 44 per cent in four years — a measure of the extent to which the dependence of the states on the Centre has increased and made it more necessary to rationalize the increasing process of transfer of resources to the states. Though tax-receipts, grants and loans are transfers of different types and are assessed on assumptions which differ in kind, but really speaking the estimated needs of all states and each state are taken to be the most important major consideration in the determination of their amount and distribution and are assumed to vary directly according to needs and inversely according to means. If estimates of means and needs were made according to certain objective and accepted norms, the rising proportions of the transfers to the expenditures would be a matter of great satisfaction, for it would imply that pooled resources of the country were being increasingly allocated and used for reducing regional disparities after making due allowance for the revenue potential of the states as a whole and each state. Though in theory it has been postulated that broadly this principle has been acted upon in practice, really no norms for measuring needs and actual efforts to enlarge revenues have been adopted or adhered to, and the rapid increase in transfers from the Centre to the states in fact have taken place without valid norms and they have not served the purpose of building up the standards of development in the states, or reducing the gap between more and less developed states or rather between less and more backward states, for the whole country, being under-developed, it is more appropriate to speak of the differences in the degrees of backwardness rather than development. Neither the Finance Commission nor the Planning Commission has, in spite of having accepted the criterion of varying the transfers directly according to needs and inversely according to means, been able to give a positive content to this criterion or in practice act upon it for assessment of needs and allocation of resources. Experience all over the world shows that while validity of the criterion has been and is widely accepted, its application creates serious problems of theory and practice, and there are great difficulties in the way of making it a guide to action in the allocation of the available resources of the economy as a whole. The criterion is realy the basic principle of family life, and its application to the community as a whole pre-supposes that its members and parts feel and act as one family which is not true of any country, much less of the countries in which acquisitive impulses are taken to be the basic motive forces of society. In spite of cardinal difficulties, the growth of redistributive revenue and expenditure in social welfare states does indicate that the position is getting significantly better and the improvement is a continuing process. In India also we are proceeding in the same direction, but the true community sense, or what is now commonly called emotional integration, has not grown perceptibly in the country. In fact, it is now recognized that the country in this respect is moving in the reverse gear. Futility of stopping this deterioration merely by exhortations has been very clearly demonstrated in the past two or three years, and what is needed is effective action in regard to every day life of the people, basic changes in social relations and in the working of the community life, i.e. real advance towards socialism in positive and concrete terms. But the failure to apply this principle, though primarily due to this lack of true community feeling, is also accounted for by the whole process of the preparation and implementation of plans being very seriously defective and inadequate to our requirements, and the failure of the

Finance and Planning Commissions is really a failure of our entire apparatus and process of planning.

The point just referred to above is a little out of proper sequence. It is somewhat anticipatory and its supporting facts need to be examined and analysed in some detail. The table[35] in the footnote gives the relative importance of transfers to the states from the Centre through tax receipts, grants and loans and shows how great is the importance of loans and grants in these transfers. The yield of the two taxes, income tax and excise duties are shared between the Centre and the States and three other taxes, i.e. estate duty and tax on railway passengers[36] and the additional excise duties are transferred to the states after deduction of collection costs and the share of the union territories. By far the greater proportion of these receipts was assigned to the States on population basis—population being taken, broadly speaking, as a measure of needs.

The receipts of the estate duty, the additional excise duties and the compensatory amount for the merger of railway passenger tax have to be distributed on different bases. The first two are to be distributed partly on population basis and partly according to criteria which recognize the principle of derivation, while the third, the amount which is to be paid by railways in lieu of the tax on railway passengers, has to be shared among the States in a manner as to place them broadly on the same footing as before. The main point, however, is that in the apportionment of the tax-receipts largely speaking, the decisive consideration has been the relative needs of the states and not their contribution to the total yield of these

35. *Transfer from the Centre to the states, 1951-61.* Percentage of the total Tax-receipts, grants and loans.

	Tax receipts	Grants	Loans
1951-52 to 1955-56	25	17	58
1956-57 to 1960-61	25	24	51

36. Tax on railways has now been merged in railway fares and Rs 12.5 crores are distributed among the states according to the recommendations of the Third Finance Commission.

taxes where the criterion of population as a measure of needs
has been modified, as in the case of the excise duties, it has
been done to make needs even a more important factor in
distribution, transfer of tax receipts from the Centre to the
States has therefore not been determined mainly or primarily
according to the incidence of these taxes or contribution of the
residents of the States to their total yield. In other words,
States' share of transferred receipts has not meant that they
have received what was rightly theirs but according to the
broad objective of national policy.

The transferred tax receipts were, however, 25 per cent of
the total transfer both in the First and Second Plan periods
and 75 per cent of the transfers consist of loans and grants
and the proportion of the latter has increased from 17 per cent
in the First period to 34 per cent in the Second. The grants are
of different kinds and of these two are important from the
practical standpoint—first grants under Article 275 of the
Constitution and the second under Article 282. The first are
general grants intended for balancing prospective revenue
receipts and expenditure—including the plan expenditure on
revenue account. This grant is made on the recommendations
of the Finance Commission and is in effect an equalizing grant
—its amount varies according to assessed requirements of the
states for central assistance owing to their actual and potential
revenues falling short of the development expenditure charge-
able to revenue account under the plan. They are intended to
fill the revenue gap and correspond, as stated above, to the
revenue deficit due to the assessed requirements being in excess
of the anticipated revenue receipts including the transfer from
the Centre to the states. The other major grants under Article
282 of the Constitution are *ad hoc* grants sanctioned by the
ministries of the Government of India for specific purposes and
are intended to be matched by budget provisions of the States
themselves from their own revenue. Total general grants in the
First Plan period amounted to Rs 23 crores and in the Second
Rs 33.89 crores, while the specific grants out of central reve-

nues for the same periods were Rs 248.01 crores and Rs 667.67 crores respectively, grants from road fund to Rs 15.93 crores and Rs 18.96 crores and other specific grants to Rs 23.71 crores and Rs 59.00 crores. These figures show how relatively small general grants have been as compared with *ad hoc* specific grants in the two plan periods. The general grants have from the First Plan increased from Rs 27 crores in the First Plan to Rs 153 crores in the Second while specific grants—revenue, road funds and capital grants—have increased during the same period from Rs 288 crores to Rs 746 crores. Though the general grants have increased more rapidly but even in the Second Plan they were nearly only one-fifth of the *ad hoc* specific grants.

DISTRIBUTION OF GENERAL GRANTS

A great deal of thought has been given to the need for having general principles for the distribution of general grants but it is also essential to distribute specific grants according to a pattern of assistance based upon a comprehensive assessment of the resources and needs of the community as a whole. The three Finance Commissions have stated principles according to which "the need of assistance" referred to in Article 275 of the Constitution should be assessed. These principles in theory are unexceptionable. In any assessment the relative level of administration and social services, the structure and incidence of taxation, the scope for the expansion of tax revenue and the efforts made to realize the potential, provisions and priorities of the plan, the devolved revenue through transfer of tax receipts and special conditions and problems of the states are all to be taken into account and grants have to be given to make the position of the States broadly comparable. These grants, in other words, are equalizing grants, i.e. are meant to promote and realize equality in broad terms among the different States in respect of services, administration, economic growth and development of resources. This has been the object of allocation and distribution of these grants and though the

same principles have been affirmed and reaffirmed by the three
Finance Commissions and have in effect been endorsed by the
Planning Commission, but no effort has been made to appraise
the relative position of the states to know how far this object
has been achieved. In three respects the failure of these grants
admits of no doubt.

(1) "The States, secure in the knowledge that annual budgetary gaps would be fully covered by devolution of these
resources and grants in aid, have not developed their
resources or exercised reasonable economy in expenditure."[37]

(2) The grants instead of promoting a solidarity of interests
and endeavour between the states and the Union have
made the former indifferent to the needs of the latter
and they have shown no concern for and interest in the
state of the country as a whole.

(3) There has been a widening gap between the resources
and functions of the states brought about mainly by the

37. The Third Finance Commission has laid great stress on this point in the
following words: "Secure in the knowledge that annual budgetary gap
would be fully covered by devolution of Union resources and grants in
aid, the states are tending to develop, as we have noticed, an allergy to tap
resources in rural sector on many considerations and also a disinclination
to make up the lee-way in others. They do not attach the same importance
to a proper and adequate context of expenditure in the matter of services
and supplies as before. Cadres expand, pay scales get revised upwards,
negligence develops in the procurement of supplies and execution of projects in the absence of proper cost control. While there is a close scrutiny
of, and consultations on, the content of the plan, there is hardly any on
the content of the annual estimates, there is no counterpart at the national
level in regard to non-plan expenditure which is progressively increasing
as a result of planning itself." (The Third Finance Commission, p. 38,
Para 89.)

The view that the contents of the plan receive their due consideration
has to be considered in relation to the planning process itself; and if the
latter is open to criticism, the content of the plan itself needs to be examined from a different standpoint. But the point that examination of non-plan
expenditure is as important as of Plan expenditure is sound and has to be
given its due weight.

planning process. This shows that the true spirit of federation has been entirely lacking in this country and financial arrangements for the distribution of resources between the Centre and the states have not fulfilled their constitutional purpose.

SPECIFIC GRANTS AND LOANS

But the most outstanding defect of the whole system of devolution of resources, the distribution of grants and the large-scale lending to the States by the Centre, in spite of the three Finance Commissions and the continuing examination of resources and expenditure position by the Planning Commissions, as stated before, is that norms of means and needs have not been developed or applied, and whatever other disadvantages of the increasing dependence of the states on the Centre may or may not have, it has not given us a calculus with reference to which all the states and Union can "be brought into a state of comparable balance" or the processes at work can be subjected to the discipline of common purpose and common goal. This fact has been frankly admitted by the Third Finance Commission. It points out that for want of time and data it has not been able to avaluate the extent to which efficiency or economy in administration has been observed by the states or their tax efforts been even approximately equal to their potential. These two vital considerations have, according to its own admission, been left out of its own assessment of the existing position and prospects and that of its two predecessors. The present undesirable system of affording assistance by covering revenue gaps, in the words of the Third Finance Commission, "howsoever they have arisen or been caused" has to be put a stop to by the appointment of an independent high powered Commission. The urgent need for taking effective action to retrieve the existing unsatisfactory position is obvious. But whether an independent Commission will be able to undertake this review and set up enforceable norms of means and needs, is a different question. It suggests that "the state government should develop a compact efficient machinery for the formulation, execution and evaluation of the programme".[38] This amounts to saying that in planning at all the state levels an apparatus for the purpose has still to be created.[39] Inadequacy of planning at the central level is also responsible for our whole planning apparatus having created an increasingly difficult situation in this and other respects. The task of evolving order out of the existing confusion is exceedingly complex, but the fact that in the last ten years even essentials of the problem have not been understood, much less faced, has made it much more so.

The general grants have at least been reviewed and as stated above, their underlying principles thought about. The specific grants, which are, to repeat, five times the size of the general grants have not been reviewed and the need for bringing them within the scope of integrated view of the whole position has not been even conceded, and no attempt has been made to know what their impact has been on the relative position of different states or the economy as a whole. The twenty-seven broad heads under which these specific revenues or eight heads under specific capital grants, have been allocated have not been considered in relation to needs for specific development, for the country as a whole or individual states. These grants are sanctioned on an *ad hoc* basis and though the objects for which they are given are, in most cases, important and desirable, they do not form part of an integral whole and

38. *Op. cit.*, p. 31, Para 70.

39. The Finance Commission has at another place in their Report emphasized this point in very clear words: "We consider that it would be useful if the states were to set up a machinery to draw up their own development plans and also to undertake a review at suitable intervals, of the progress of the execution of projects and also their non-Plan programme. In other words it should be a planning apparatus with added functions of audit of performance" (*Op. cit.*, p. 41, Para 99).

The States have, it is clear, so far been planning without a planning apparatus and it ought to be added without understanding the essentials of planning.

therefore do not express a planning process. The Central loans to the States have been more than 50 per cent of the total transfer from the Centre to them; they are either interest free or carry a rate of interest varying from 1 to 5 per cent, their terms of repayment also are determined on an *ad hoc* basis and the mounting interest and repayment liabilities[40] are one of the most important causes of the widening gaps between the resources and expenditure of the States.[41] If the purpose for which these loans are granted were not what they are, i.e. mostly beneficial, one could well call it a rake's progress. But in the first place growth in the repaying capacity of the States is not keeping pace with the growth of these liabilities, and, as stated above, interest and repayment obligations are causing serious strain for state finances.[42] A detailed analysis of these loans cannot be attempted for want of data, but it is known that investments in the public sectors have not so far given sufficient return for meeting these obligations. What is, however, even more important is that constituting as the loans do more than 50 per cent of the total transfer to the States which accounted for 55 per cent of the total revenue and capital expenditure, in the next Plan it is essential that these loans should be included in an overall view of the distribution of resources. The Finance Commission is precluded from making

40. Interest liabilities of the states, which are largely due to central loans, increased from Rs 64 lacs in 1951-52 to Rs 45.79 crores in 1960-61. Provision for reduction of debt during the same period has increased from Rs 9.01 crores to Rs 33.3 crores. As the states have had deficit budgets in the last decade and there were no surpluses from which these liabilities could be met, they have been really covered by receipts from new loans.

41. In the 1st Five Year Plan liabilities of the states increased at the rate of Rs 159 crores a year, in the Second at the rate of Rs 282 crores and in 1961-62 they amounted to Rs 468 crores and in the budget of 1962-63 there was a provision for lending of Rs 453 crores by the Centre to the states.

42. The total permanent debt of the states in 1960-61 amounted to Rs 490.65 crores while the loans advanced from the Centre to the States from 1951-52 to 1960-61 amounted to Rs 2,209 crores. It is estimated that from 1961-62 to 1964-65 (including budget provisions) loans of the Centre to the States would increase by Rs 2,207.85 crores.

any recommendations on the specific grants and loans. The Planning Commission presumably takes them into account in determining the total planned expenditure of the States and its annual review from the integrated and relative standpoints; but knowing the limitations of the planning processes, particularly in the states, they are to be treated more as *ad hoc* allocations than a part of a well coordinated effort to mobilize resources or utilize them with due regard for all needs and their relative importance.

Transfers from the Centre to the states have assumed large dimensions, increased their dependence upon the former and weakened their sense of responsibility. Increasing deterioration of the position can be stopped only by changing the planning processes, and providing conditions under which the local communities can become more and more responsible for their development, create their own resources and imbibe true federal spirit in their relations among themselves and with the central authorities. These transfers are necessary, but in a different social context they will have a different content and import. Without a federal society, federal finance cannot really become a means by which the entire resources of the community are pooled and utilized according to a well considered and well coordinated scheme of social priorities. This should be the essence of federal finance, and at present this object is not being realized.

REGIONAL DISPARITIES

If the devolved revenues, grants and loans had largely been allocated according to needs, it would have secured regional balance in developments or at least reduced the regional and other imbalances existing before the planning started. The Planning Commission and the Finance Commission have, as stated above, made no effort to assess the position from the point of view of balanced regional growth. Though there are a few fragmentary studies on the rate of growth in different states most of them are of doubtful value. The question of relative development of different states during the last fourteen years has still to be examined and answered. The data for a careful evaluation of the whole position are not available and special effort needs to be made to collect the data and analyse them from this point of view. There has been a certain degree of diffusion of industries, power projects, etc. and possibly the imbalances have been reduced to some extent. How far the reduction is significant is not known. There are no reliable and comparable estimates of national and per capita income in each state, and it is not possible to know whether inter-state disparities have or have not decreased. In evaluating the general impact of development on the well-being of the people the distribution of additional income has also to be known and taken into account and though the presumptive evidence in support of the view that inequalities have increased is strong, the rates at which inequalities have increased during this period in different States are also not known. Unfortunately therefore, we have come to the conclusion that we cannot evaluate the impact of development on the relative position of the different states. The overall position probably is that the gap between the different States has, if anything, increased; but this again is a presumptive conclusion and cannot be supported by statistical evidence. The way that the Centre has distributed large amounts, i.e. the process of transfer of large resources to the states being what it has been, it would be really surprising if it had been otherwise. The whole planning process has been so seriously at fault that it would have been a miracle if the weaker states had improved their relative position as a result of uncoordinated distribution of large resources among the States.

UTILIZATION OF RESOURCES

Resource operations include and should include their utilization. It is well known and widely admitted that implementation of plans is even more seriously open to criticism than their formulation; and inefficiency, waste, lack of coordination and rank corruption are widely prevalent and no progress has been made in remedying these evils. Reports of the Estimates Committee and Public Accounts Committees of the Centre and the states are full of adverse comments on the way the funds have been utilized and plans implemented. It is unfortunately true, that return that we are getting for our outlay is very poor in real terms and moral deterioration of the people and administration have greatly increased owing to the enormous expenditure that has been incurred on development. Moreover, the administrative and financial apparatus of the country is not suited to the needs of rapid development and radical changes. Our budgetary system, the method of financial control and audit and accounts rules and organization all need to be completely revised if they are to serve the ends of building a socialist economy in this country. A large-scale clearance operation has to be undertaken if this jungle and its undergrowth have to be replaced by a rational system of allotment and disbursement of funds. Of course a bureaucracy and all that it means in terms of vexatious delay and perversion and frustration of the purpose of development has to be mastered and converted into a civil service in the real sense of the word. These points can only be mentioned but their relation to our resource operations cannot, for obvious reasons, be discussed. The obvious conclusion is that the social forces at work are favourable to their continuance and aggravation of these evils, and only replacement of these forces by others which are equal to the new tasks of complete social renovation and reorganization can materially improve the situation. As the unfavourable forces are strong and getting stronger, we have to reckon with the fact that these serious evils cannot be remedied unless stronger counter-forces are brought into play.

This analysis of receipts of the Central and State Governments from taxes, investments, loans, currency and credit expansion, external assistance and their apportionment between the Centre and the State shows how ill-planned have been our resource operations and how ill-suited are the present methods to the need for their planned utilization. Our whole budgetary system originally designed for ensuring parliamentary control of receipts and expenditure needs to be changed to suit the requirements of a planned economy which must necessarily provide not only for orderly allocation and expenditure of public funds, but also the development and transformation of the entire economy with clearly defined and understood social objectives. A new calculus of needs and means has to be devised and the total resources of the economy have to be operated upon in order to maximize the advantages from the utilization of resources. The role of finance in a planned economy has not been understood and we have not begun to think in real terms and know that it is the reality behind the financial transactions which, through planning, has to be changed and made more fruitful and meaningful from the social standpoint. The result is that very great increase in public outlay has given us poor return, allocation of resources has not been related to a rational schedule of social priorities and disparities from the personal, social and regional standpoint have increased and we have not even established a system of comprehensive investment control without which planning can have very little significance. In a planned socialist economy the entire resources of the community and their utilization have, as pointed out at the beginning of this chapter, to be planned and made the means for the realization of socialism. Even the utilization of resources in the public sector in India has not followed any rational pattern. The extent to which taxation, borrowing, currency and credit expansion and external assistance have been drawn upon for raising the required resources has not been guided by any well-framed criteria or rational principles. Our resource operations, to repeat, have not been conceived or carried out in terms suited to the needs of a planned economy and have not acquired or expressed any coherent purpose.

Chapter Thirteen

OPERATIVE ORGANIZATION

ORGANIZATIONAL FAILURE

It is generally agreed that in the last decade organizationally our difficulties have been greater than those which we have come up against in formulating our objectives, preparing our plans and imparting to them the necessary qualities of coherence and balance. As pointed out again and again our most besetting weakness has been our inability to evoke and master the will of our people and find an effective expression for it. "Our people" is and has to be an all-inclusive concept and eventually all have to be the beneficieries of the new society that we have to establish and develop; but those, who have so far been excluded from the major advantages of the existing society and have suffered grievously on that account, have first to come into their own and become the most important instruments of change from the old to the new society. Our inability to move the excluded majority to the realization of their needs and their future is also an organizational failure, but it is primarily a failure of understanding, of meeting the challenge of the excluded masses and awakening in them a sense of deprivation and urgency, i.e. creating real social consciousness. This is primarily due to the elite, the leaders, the policy-makers, whatever word we may like to use for those, who have been in authority or in key position in political parties and other mass organizations, being without a widely shared genuine and deep concern for the people and in a real living contact with them. This is and has been our main deficiency, and cannot be made up by the efficiency and adequacy of organization.

And yet it is true that even understanding, concern and response to social imperatives, such as we have had — and these

have not been entirely lacking — have not been turned to
good account because our public administration, the organization of our institutions like the universities, cultural societies
and other corporate units, or political parties like Indian
National Congress, the Socialist Parties and the Communist
Party have been seriously at fault, and in the last decade
the attempts to change them for the better have yielded very
poor results. It is not easy to explain why this has happened.
Again it can be maintained that the quality of men and the
spirit, which moves them, makes the organizations what they
are, i.e. inadequacy of organizations is in reality due to
inadequacy of the human factor. Fundamentally speaking this
is so; and yet organizations as such have a place of their own
in the affairs of men, and it is their function to transcend
limitations of the individuals, build up new traditions and
change or break the old ones which are dead or have lost
their soul and help men to acquire new ways, habits, reflexes
and therefore become more effective in thought and action.
In India owing to historical reasons, we have been so conditioned that organization is not one of our strong points; and
from running of homes to the running of government we
have not been able to conduct our affairs in an ordely, business-
like and efficient manner and use our human and material
resources to real advantage.

SOCIALISM AND ORGANIZATION

This is a part of our heritage and we have suffered seriously
on that account. Owing to our people, like all other peoples,
having been thrown into the vortex of the new world, we,
as a matter of necessity, have to surpass this limitation and
know how to organize our affairs better — from the organizing
of our private lives to the organizing of public affairs in all
spheres and at all levels. This is all the more essential if we
want to introduce and build up socialism in this country and
with our exceedingly limited material and human resources
we simply cannot afford to defeat or frustrate our ends by

our organizational failures. We have to make the most of what we have and even convert the dross into gold. But in fact we have not done well at all in organization and our failure is writ large, as stated above, on public administration, organization of all common efforts in political life, our educational and cultural institutions and, of course, our development programme. Socialism, being the great undertaking as it is, calls for "capital formation" at the highest level —creation and utilization of intangible but nevertheless the most important assets of *modus operandi* on the assumption that whatever is worth doing is worth doing well. We need men of outstanding ability and drive at all levels and in all fields; if the country is stirred to its very depth by the adventure of building up a socialist society, these men would be thrown up. Intrinsically speaking our men have it in them to rise to this great occasion in these momentous times; but what is even more necessary is that through organization our common men should be able to do uncommon things.[1] We have not realized the importance of this consideration. This has to be done on a comprehensive basis, i.e. organization has to be good in all our undertakings and to be built with fidelity to the goal of socialism. The norms of organization in a socialist society have to be, it need not be added, necessarily different from the norms of a non-socialist society. The qualities of industry, honesty, conscientiousness, harmony in human relations, discipline and skill are qualities which are common to all organizations. Socialism, owing to its embarking upon the great en-

1. This view has been well expressed by Peter F. Drucker. He writes, "It is the purpose of an organization to make common men do uncommon things. No organization can depend upon genius, the supply is always scarce and always unpredictable. But it is the test of an organization that it makes ordinary human beings perform better than they are capable of, that it brings whatever strength there is in its members and uses it to make all other members perform more and better. It is the test of an organization that it neutralizes the weakness of its members." Peter F. Drucker in the *Practice of Management* quoted by E. N. Gladder in *Civil Service and Bureaucracy,*' v.

deavour of creating and developing a new social order, needs them even in a larger measure but it also needs in all organizations a sense of real democracy, i.e. men of all grades and abilities have to be knit together by a sense of belonging to the same community, having a common purpose, work in an atmosphere of true equality and make self-discipline a substitute for discipline and authority to the greatest possible degree.

These are common place considerations but are nevertheless of fundamental importance and the working apparatus of a socialist society has to be based upon them. A socialist society cannot expect to have perfect men or geniuses to run it and for work-a-day purpose human frailties and limitations have to be duly allowed for; and yet by organization they can do better than they otherwise would, and the fact that it is an organization in or at least for a socialist society can and will make a real difference. If organizations are built empirically and with knowledge that all men have lapses and failings, good results can and should be achieved. Organizations even in socialist societies can become incubuses instead of being good instruments. Contemporary experiences, it need not be added, are full of warnings on this score, but it also illustrates very fully what organization operating with a genuine and abiding social purpose can and do accomplish. We in India have to change and develop organizations in the context of our own conditions and requirements; but knowing its faults and failings in the past, we have to know that it has been the most important limiting factor so far and success of socialism would also greatly depend upon the extent to which we can change and develop it to suit its purpose.

Public Administration

It is not possible to indicate how operative organizations as a whole can and should be changed to meet the requirements of socialism. Public administration is one of the most important aspects of organization and it is necessary to consider briefly some of its major points in relation to the future of socialism in this country. One of the results of the peaceful transfer of power to Indian hands has been that the pre-independence system of public administration remained intact, we have had to carry on Government of this country through it and it has not been possible to adapt the system easily to our changing requirements. Defects of the pre-independence system were serious; but it had, as is well known, some very good points which have stood us in good stead after independence. The repatriation of most of the senior British officers left a void which could have been very dislocating, but the Indian members of the Indian Civil Service and other higher services, largely speaking, took over responsible positions with confidence and kept the administration going in the ordeal of the immediate post-independence years. What is true of the civil services is also true of defence services. Senior officers of our defence forces and defence forces as a whole also acquitted themselves very well in the first few years after independence; and since then they have distinguished themselves in what are called missions of peace in Korea, Suez and Congo and generally speaking their performance in Kashmir and on Sino-Indian border has been creditable. That the record of our Government in respect of stability and development compares favourably with that of Governments of countries like Burma, Indonesia and Ceylon is, in no small measure, due to the level at which our civil and defence services have operated and used their training and experience under the British to good advantage from the national point of view. Under socialism these services will have to change and acquire new norms of thinking and behaviour; but it is a matter of real satisfaction that in the post-independence years in the important tasks of maintaining law and order and carrying on the administration of the country these services have not been found wanting. That the members of the Indian Civil Service asked for and received guarantees for the preservation of their privileged position after independence is a matter for regret and the fact has produced harmful results; but it is undeniable that the fact that India has been able, in spite of the post-independence stresses, to face and overcome many crises, is partly due to our higher civil and defence services having brought to bear some excellent qualities on the performance of their duties. Members of the Indian Civil Services have had opportunities of very quick promotions owing to large number of vacancies and great expansion of new opportunities; and they have used the positions which they have occupied in our administration, to keep for themselves many high posts for which they were not fitted by experience or training. As all-purpose men of the whole administration they assumed that they could also perform the role of all-purpose men even under the changed conditions and do equally well. The results have proved that this was an unwarranted assumption, and virtual monopoly of power in high places, which they have acquired, has done a considerable amount of harm to the best interests of the country. All the same it is also true that members of this service have shown their high calibre in many new positions; and won laurels which have brought credit to them and the country. This only shows that in ability, resourcefulness and mastery of new situations, our best men can prove themselves equal to very arduous tasks; and in a socialist society with the necessary fundamental changes in approach, motivation and pattern of behaviour, men drawn from all parts of India and a fair diversity of social origins, provided the selection is on merit and reasonably fair, can and will be able to run a socialist system with success and distinction.

Besides civil and defence services there are other higher services also whose members have done well and assumed wider responsibilities with confidence and success; Members of the Indian Civil Service and Indian Administrative Service and their cognate service—Indian Police Service—serving under the Government of India in 1957 were 330 while members of Railways, Posts and Telegraphs, Defence Civil Service and other higher services, which accounted for 60 per cent of the total, numbered over ten thousand.[2] In the States there were working in 1957, 28,651 (excluding Mysore and Rajasthan) in the higher grades and positions.[3] Roughly speaking excluding defence forces there were about 40,000 officers in India in all services who held responsible positions, which for a population of 440 million gives a proportion of one for 11,000 persons. This is, it need not be added, a low proportion when we take into account the total requirements of the country in which the tasks, which the state has been performing and has to perform, are growing in magnitude, complexity and importance. In spite of the over-shadowing position of higher public services in India it is clear that the number of their members is far from excessive, and they have, under difficult conditions, been able to give the country, to use rather a discredited word, a "steel frame" which it could not have done without. Though they have not been and are not above suspicion, their record compares well with the record of services in most of the other countries (excluding China) which have become independent after the war and generally speaking, it has been an advantage for the country to have drawn upon their training and experience. This is an advantage which should receive its due appreciation and not be lightly thrown away.

DISQUIETING POSITION

This is so and yet the position from the long-term standpoint is unsatisfactory and even disturbing. A comparative view of our services is reassuring and indicates that we have, in a way, fared better than the other countries in similar position. But that is far from enough. It is known that the standards of morals, discipline and performance of our services have been corroded in the last ten years; and the fact that in the other countries the position is worse is a cold comfort when we take into account what has been happening in this country as a

2. "The Pay Commission Table", 32.13, *Statistical Supplement.*
3. *Ibid.,* Table 2.20.

whole in the domain of public administration. But even at the higher level there has been deterioration in standards of honesty and devotion to duty, but in the lower ranks the position, it is generally conceded, has become much worse. The total public employees in Central and State services in 1957, excluding defence forces, numbered 3.72 millions[4] of which the number of higher services were about 40,000, i.e. for every officer there were about 93 public employees in the lower grades. They were not only far more numerous, but as they come into far closer contact with the people, their conduct and morals are of much greater importance in determining the tone and impact of administration. For people generally they are the Government, and the latter is judged by the standards and performance of public employees in the lower grades. Even if the members of the higher services had been able to maintain and even improve these standards, increasing rot among the vast majority of the public employees would have set at naught the good which they could have done; but as it is, even their standards and performance have been and are open to criticism and they have been able to do little, if anything, to stop the rot below them; and the net result has been that among the people at large their faith in the Government's capacity to perform well even the ordinary duties of administration has been greatly undermined, and, of course, all bold and oft-repeated declarations for changing the foundations and face of the whole economy have been and are very heavily discounted. That these great tasks cannot be carried out only by the state employees is taken to be axiomatic, but the poor response to the appeals for public co-operation and participation in the work of reconstruction and development is, among other reasons, due to the diminishing confidence of the people even in the sincerity and much more in the integrity and ability of the state to realize its avowed aims and objects. This is not due only to the members of the higher services having been unable,

4. *Op. cit.*, Tables 2.11 and 2.20.

by precept, example and excercise of their authority, to take the necessary corrective measures, but also to the general decline of standards in conduct and performance in politics, i.e. among the political leaders in the Central and State cabinets — much more in the latter than in the former — and in responsible positions in political parties and organizations. The rate at which this deterioration has been and is taking place is truly disquieting, and its impact on the services, senior and junior, has been and could not but be far-reaching. Members of these services have, in self-protection, to adjust themselves to the prevailing stresses and pressures and as they cannot as a rule, be expected to run the risk of losing their jobs or being demoted, they could not possibly develop resistance to the political pressures to which they have been and are continuously being subjected. They have had to compromise their independence, dignity, rectitude and even self-respect and are being demoralized on that account. The fact that, in spite of these falling standards, our administration has remained and is a going concern shows that our pre-independence legacy and the general quality of our administration have enabled us to withstand the effects of these corroding factors. Our reserves have been drawn upon in meeting our growing difficulties, but how near they are to the point of exhaustion is not and cannot be known. There have been clear indications that our administration is not far from the brink, and unless early action is taken to redress the position, it will be a piece of good fortune if we can and do keep the evil day off indefinitely or for long.

ADMINISTRATION IN A SOCIALIST SOCIETY

Our higher services would be of crucial importance even if we did not have to introduce socialism in the country. For building even a welfare state without any radical change in our social objective and structure, these services must necessarily play a decisive role, which, the conditions being what they are, they cannot owing to the distortions

which have been and are taking place. That all our higher
services and not only Indian Civil and Administrative
Service, are capable, under trying circumstances, of doing
well, has, as stated above, been fully demonstrated by our
experience after independence. Owing to the extreme poverty
of our people and the increasing pressure of our population,
even according to the standards applicable to a liberal state,
we have to attain and maintain a much higher rate of economic
growth than we have achieved so far, and its benefits have
to be shared much more widely. Even on this assumption our
services have to be greatly expanded, assigned far more important roles in development and excercise qualities of different
and higher order if the objects of a welfare state have to be
realized. This is a task of truly gigantic proportion and our
administraters have to rise equal to it. But if the conception
of a welfare state is a limited conception and it cannot provide
an answer to our urgent and enormous problems (and this is
the underlying assumption of this book) all the working premises of our administration has to be radically altered, our
frame of reference, values and methods completely changed
and the role, which our administrators have to play in building a socialist society, has to be conceived and concretized in
much wider, deeper and different terms. They, according to
this conception, will cease to be merely executive agents of
a policy determined for them and have to assume the responsibility of becoming architects of a new social order. Administration, from this point of view, becomes social engineering
and those, who are given key position in carrying out this
task, have not only to put their very best into it, but also
have to do so with knowledge and conviction that any hum-
drum approach to it is entirely irrelevant and the qualities
of head and heart which they require for performing this
task are the qualities of explorers, innovators, designers and
builders. This task cannot be accomplished only by them. The
whole nation has to embark upon it with practical insight,
ability and, of course, ardour and an adequate comprehensive

operative orgainzation for the purpose has to be created. But that increases and not diminishes the importance of the role of public administrators in carrying out their tasks. The administrators have to know that they have to work in co-operation not only with the people but also with social builders in all fields and this art has to be practised under conditions in which they have to participate and even initiate new social processes. They have, in other words, to become creative collaborators in a big adventure and cease to think in terms of power and authority. They will have to be given the authority necessary for the performance of their tasks, but as such it (authority) will lose its meaning and its functional aspect will have to be kept to the fore and give it the context in which it will have to be exercised. Hierarchical conception of status, power and positions would necessarily lose its validity, and it will have to be realized that differences of function need not and should not involve social divisions, i.e. stratification. All-purpose men, as a class apart from and above members of all other services, would have no place in this organization The men who understand social principles, intricacies and inter-relations of policies, forces and events and can steer administration in the right direction and with skill, competence and insight will, under socialism, be of greater and not less importance; but they will not constitute a service by itself. All men at the top, whatever their specialization or qualifi-cations, will have to possess and excercise the qualities referred to above. The whole system of education on the job or in-service training, and interchange of views, experience and specialized understanding will have to be suited to the need of discovering, fostering and developing the vital qualities without which socialism can neither be established nor deve-loped. These qualities will be needed more and more at the initial than the later stages of socialism, and it is essential that the need for acquiring and exercising them should be duly understood and provided for.

ADMINISTRATIVE NEUTRALITY

If the implications of the view briefly stated above are understood, it will become clear that neutrality of services as a necessary adjunct of parliamentary democracy is a matter which can have no place in a socialist society. The British Civil Service, it has been assumed, owed its success and efficiency to the selection of members through competitive examination, it being completely free from politics in the sense of its rendering loyal service to all governments, whatever their political complexion, giving them advice without fear or favour and carrying out faithfully the policy of the state as enunciated by the party in power. It has also been assumed that parliamentary democracy can work only if permanent public services have no politics of their own, and the cabinet's decisions on all policy matters are put into effect by the services without reservation or hesitation — much less resistance; and in all countries in which parliamentary systems are at work relations between the Government and services are taken to rest on this basis. As a maxim of practical conduct neutrality of administrative services is of real utility when politics is a game of 'ins' and 'outs' and there is no fundamental difference between the major articulate and inarticulate premises of the policy and programme of the principal political parties. Under these conditions independence and non-partisan role of the services becomes a great advantage when their career is not affected by the electorial fortune of political parties and they can perform their duties, enjoy security of tenure and succeed in their career without incurring any hazards owing to swings in the verdict of the ballot box. This, however, works and can work only if there are, as stated above, no real differences between the major premises of political parties and the services themselves accept the same premises as the basis of their working faith.5 Public servants in responsible positions

5. The British Civil Service, which was supposed to have been neutral in politics, could maintain this position because political parties in Great Britain were of the same mind generally on basic issues. "No Government

connot and should not be merely automatons for the execution of policies. They should keep out of the foam and froth of electioneering politics and should not get involved in the strategy and tactics of party warfare. This they can and should do; but it cannot be a matter of indifference to them whether the policies, which they are executing, command or do not command their ready assent and warm allegiance; and though the parliamentary system necessitates adjustment on the part of the services within broad limits, the latter cannot function well if they are at heart opposed to the very basic tenets of the policies which they are implementing. For most public servants the necessity to choose between their social conscience and official duties does not arise. It is, for example, a matter of no concern to public servants even in high position as to what is definition of assessable income for income tax purposes, how the tariff valuation is calculated or who are or are not eligible for public scholarships. In such cases the policy decision can be carried out without putting any strain on

in a period of modern Civil Service has embarked upon measures," in the words of Harold J. Laski, "which called into question the foundations of the State. Succeeding Governments have differed in degrees. They have not differed in kind. The neutrality of the Civil Service has not yet been tested by the need to support policy, which like that of the Socialist Party, might well challenge the traditional ideas for which it stood." The coming into power of the Labour Party in England after the war, however, was taken as a test of the British Civil Services' neutrality and it was held that it stood the test well. The challenge however was not severe and the Labour Party did not call into question "the foundations of the State" and later developments have shown that gulf between the Labour Party under Gaitskell and the Conservative Party had been further narrowed. (H. J. Laski, *Parliamentary Government in England*, p. 319, quoted by S. Lall in his "Civil Service Neutrality", *The Indian Journal of Public Administration*, Vol. IV No. I, p. 2).

In India the issue is that a Socialist Party needs not the passive support but active and intelligent allegiance of the men, who must necessarily occupy key position in the execution of the policies through which socialism is to be developed. Not only the Civil Service should fully support these policies but carry them out with conviction, fervour, intelligence and devotion to their purpose.

one's sense of right or wrong or creating unresolvable inner contraditions for the administrators. But in other cases, which need not be ullustrated by citing instances, acute conflict of principles and purposes can arise and unless the administrators are insensitive to basic issues and the well-being of the people which depends upon them, their efficiency and integrity cannot but be seriously affected by the continued persistence of divergence between their convictions and the objects of the policies which they are called upon to implement. These conflicts, however, in practice do not arise because the policy makers and high-ups in public services are, through family upbringing, education and class relations, conditioned alike and there is, as a rule, no serious variance between what public servants are called upon to do and what they would like to do if they follow the dictates of their own social conscience. The principle of neutrality can, under these conditions, become a worth while principle and its observance contribute to the success and smooth working of the parliamentary system. It in effect means that dust of politics and not politics itself is kept out of administration.

But this principle cannot be valid when what is at issue is the very constitution of society, its social foundations and its values. Dedication of a country to an objective like socialism is not like choice between high or low tariffs, long or short haul rates in railways or even age limit of 15 or 16 for free and compulsory education. The objective, being fundamental, all-embracing and involving as it does change in social relations, transfer of power from one class to other classes or the community as a whole and a complete change in the complex of values and replacement of one complex by another with all that goes with the change in terms of social loyalties, the meaning of life and its animating spirit and consecration to this object, political fortune of a party or its commitment in elections have hardly any bearing on this issue. This implies that the working of the parliamentary system itself has to be adjusted to the needs of socialism and for realization of this objective and it is essential that whole community should participate actively and consciously in its formulation and implementation and it should have the will and ability to overcome all resistance to it. Assuming that these conditions are fulfilled, all policy decisions taken in pursuance of this objective have to be carried out by all public servants not only faithfully but also with courage and conviction and the best in them has to be enlisted for the realization of this objective. Neutrality of public servants under these conditions can be likened to their neutrality when a country is at war. It is unthinkable and impermissible. Socialism, if it has to be realized, must command complete allegiance of public services of all levels and in all spheres; and as this undertaking cannot be carried out without expansion and increasing importance of public services, it has to mean that they have to be one of the most important instruments for not only the execution of socialist policies but for developing their full potential. Socialism is a process of growth and realization, and public services have to participate in it intelligently and creatively. They have to contribute to its growth and grow with and through it. There can be no question of public service assuming the position of neutrality in regard to socialism. If they do, they really condemn themselves and virtually declare that they have to be and must be replaced.

This applies to all public services and not only so-called administrative service. Engineers, doctors, agronomists, scientists, educationists, in one word all functionaries, have to participate in this process and do so with conviction and with knowledge, and it is a calling to which they have to respond fully and with their entire being. Through education, reorientation and refresher courses in their best sense their cooperation in spirit has to be enlisted for realizing socialism in their special field and in the life of the community as a whole. Creative participation in the performance of this task cannot mean regimentation, superficial conformity or lip service to new slogans or formulas. It has to mean that not only right spirit has to be created and made freely available for the realization of this objective, but also that public servants themselves have to evolve and apply the know-how of fulfilling it in their own particular sphere and there has to be complete accord between the means and ends. There is or should be real difference between an engineer who is working in and for a socialist society and one who is not, and that must be true of every functionary of a socialist society. This difference cannot be imposed or commandeered. It has to be generated, fostered and developed and one of the most important means of realizing socialism has to be that this significant difference should be produced by evoking full response of mind and spirit on the part of all who are living under and for socialism, i.e. all members of the community whether they are public employees, self-employed or employed by some economic or cultural organization even if it is a private organization. But public servants have, of course, very special responsibility in carrying out these tasks particularly in the initial stages. Eventually there will be no difference between public servants and others. Under socialism all will have to work for the community and their income and position will be the measure of the extent to which they work in this spirit. But in early stages of socialism public administration in its widest sense will have to be streamlined for the realization of socialism. This will have to be its all-engrossing objective—the purpose of its very existence.

EXISTING POSITION

What has been said above is meant to put into bold relief the essentials of administration under socialism, and show how little has been achieved so far to change our public administration for development and socialism. Even if it is granted, as it should be, that from comparative standpoint our administration has done well, the fact that it has not been able to maintain its old level of performance and the growing inefficiency and dishonesty at the lower levels has presented an insoluble problem is a matter of great concern. But what is,

however, more important is that even if this problem could
be solved and higher services had maintained their standards,
that would not answer the needs of a society avowedly in
transition towards socialism. The need for finding this answer
has not been admitted even in theory and of course no steps
have been taken to start the process of change. Public servants
even at the highest level are mostly devoid of any interest in
and earnestness for socialism. Their thinking, their reactions
and behaviour clearly show that socialism hardly matters to
them. They do not take it into account in the preparation or
execution of development plans, and the fact that in the economy anti-socialist forces has been growing is no problem for
them. Big business and higher services have, as a matter of
fact, been, as stated before, developing close ties and after
retirement from government service use their old relations and
contacts to promote the interest particularly of the firms which
employ them and also big business in general. This inter-
lacing of our higher services with industrial and commercial
giants, Indian and foreign, is truly an ominous development, of
the seriosuness of which our Government and the people are
hardly aware. By natural inclination our senior public servants
are conservative in their interests and outlook, and a number of
them have actually joined the Rightist parties after retirement.
What is, however, more significant is that, even without these
ties and interests, our higher services cannot adapt themselves
to the requirements of a socialist society. Their innate inclination and acquired pre-disposition make it very difficult for
them to participate in or promote the process of change. They
are a vested interest and with all other vested interests, they
are for hastening slowly, if not for *status quo*; and they are
mainly interested in their own future and not that of the
country. They possess and exercise enormous power and they
not merely carry out policies but also shape them. The new
entrants in the higher services are being largely moulded in
the image of their seniors, and it is almost certain that they
too will acquire the same interests, habits of thought and

code of conduct. They are highly status conscious, and among the services, and different divisions of the same service there are strong 'caste' feelings. The Indian Civil and Administrative Services are, as is well known, the highest caste, but the same feelings in different degrees exist among other services also and makes team work among them very difficult. They generally move in the grooves which have been made for them and they have made for themselves. At a time when new trails have to be blazed and followed, our higher services remain in their old ruts and are so conditioned as to make it difficult for them to see the new vistas which are so clearly coming into view. Members of these services are men of ability. There are some outstanding men among them and the general level is good. But these are not the men who can and should occupy key positions if the country has to go ahead towards socialism. For the latter, as pointed out in the above paragraphs, very different types of men are needed. These men also can be changed into builders of socialism. That has to be done because new socialist cadre cannot be created overnight. If this has to be done, a process of deconditioning has to be undertaken; but no one knows and cares what has to be done or how this object has to be achieved. Below the higher services are a mass of junior public servants to whom socialism matters even less than to their superiors. Their life is a hard struggle and they have been hit severely by inflationary pressures. Their performance is open to serious criticism, their standard of honesty pitifully low and they know from experience that even public good, what to say of socialism, receives scant consideration in the minds of the men in authority, and, of course, they have neither the ability nor the inclination to do better in this respect than their superiors. Being in direct contact with the people their failings are of greater consequence from the point of view of the confidence of the people in administration. But that does not worry them at all. It is none of their business to safeguard the reputation of administration. Being taken and taking themselves as worms under the feet, it is not for them to feel concerned about it. They need not be worms and in a socialist society they too will be active participants in creative processes of the community. This, however, is at present an irrelevant consideration.

RESULTS OF ENQUIRIES

Problems of administration have been made the subjects of enquiry on the part of foreign experts, several committees and Organization and Method Divisions. These enquiries have been mainly interested in issues like procedure, delegation of authority, reduction of control from above, of communication and the need for cutting out red tape as far as possible. These are all objects of great interest and importance, but there is nothing to show that some of the admirable, though platitudinous, observations and maxims put forward in a pontifical manner have had any effect on the principles or practices of our administration. Machinery of administration remains as slow, dilatory and ineffective as ever. Political pressures on administration are growing in volume and intensity. Files still go round and round and up and below in their wearisome course. Men on the spot or in general administration and public enterprises are still subjected to excessive control and they themselves have not realized that public enterprises have to be not only technically efficient but also acquire new standards in human relations and a sense of responsibility to the community and its social objectives.

The Organization and Method Divisions have been functioning and proliferated, and though they may have given attention to subjects such as work measurement, work flow, office management, filing system, space arrangement and the like—all problems of mechanics of management—they have not been "giving extensive and intensive leadership in respect to structure and management and procedure".[6] They have not given any leadership at all, and from what is known

6. Paul H. Appleby, *Report of a Survey*, p. 59.

about them, they could not have done so. Fundamentals of the problem—the problem of the striking at the root of the great evils of administration, from which the country is suffering, and the bearing of socialism on the structure, functions and working of the administration as a whole have not been even understood, much less duly considered. We were told by Dr. Appleby in 1953 that "India is ready for flowering of special interest and advancement in public administration and that of some special opportunities rather unique in India make it likely that the movement may be of world-wide significance." Such statements have also been repeated later, but the events clearly show that they have no relation to facts. "Flowering of special interest and advancement in public administration", whatever it may mean, has not occurred and the strains, which have developed owing to the misdirection of our attention and effort in administration, are of "world-wide significance" owing to our position having become even more weak and vulnerable on this account and created a truly disturbing outlook.

BUREAUCRACY

Bureaucracy[7] all the world over has a bad flavour[8], socialism has, by its critics, been condemned because it must, according

---

7. A summary of the more important attributes of bureaucracy may be given in the words of a British report, "The faults (of bureaucracy) most frequently enunciated are: over devotion to precedent, remoteness from the rest of the community, inaccessibility and faulty handling of the general public, lack of initiative and imagination, ineffective organizaton and waste of man-power, procastination and unwillingness to take responsibility or to give decisions." "Report of the Committee on the Training of Civil Servants" (May 1944) quoted by E. Straus in his *The Ruling Servants*, p. 43.

These are faults of all bureaucracies, but to these have to be added, exclusiveness born of a special type of snobbery, love of power for its own sake and special pleasure in exercising it to demonstrate the might of position and authority. These are also faults of bureaucracy everywhere but have a special meaning in the context of our conditions.

8. "However ill-defined in daily usage, the term is normally employed as an unflattering description of a badly functioning and otherwise reprehensible administrative system." *Ibid.*, p. 40.

to them, inevitably mean mandarinate—rule by bureaucracy at all levels. In Soviet Union, China and other communist countries bureaucracy is admitted to have entrenched itself in the economies of these countries and persistent struggle has been carried on against it, and from all reports, not with conspicuous success. Bureaucracy, even in countries where planning is neither favoured nor practised, is a factor of growing importance—not only in public administration but also industrial and business organizations, in organization of political parties, trade unions and other organizations. In India the hold of bureaucracy has greatly increased and not decreased after independence, and what has been called "permit" and "license" *raj* by Mr. C. Rajagopalachari, is only one though very conspicuous aspect of an all-pervading phenomenon. The fact that bureaucracy is everywhere, does not know any ideological barriers or curtains of any kind and is growing in importance in developed and undeveloped countries clearly shows that there are forces at work everywhere which make bureaucracy so very powerful; and it is clear that this Leviathan cannot be killed and has to be tamed—has to cease to be a Leviathan and change its very inner nature.

Increasing importance of bureaucracy is really one of the most serious diseconomies of scale and has to be provided against by bringing new inner processes into action. As it basically stands for the letter that kills and not the spirit that vivifies, it can be successfully combated and overcome only by effective action in the domain of mind. Built-in safeguards against it are necessary and can, up to a point, produce results; but that generally means strengthening the system of checks and balances and not unoften aggravates the position. Decentralization is necessary and should be carried out as far as possible. Small self-governing communities should be organized and acquire vitality. Small-scale productive and distributive co-operatives and a federalized co-operative organization has also to be built up as a part of a national community of small self-governing communities. But even then in administration, industry, trade and communications, in currency, credit and finance and in, of course, international organizations of growing importance, which are needed for the survival of mankind, large-scale organization is necessary and unavoidable and inevitably creates the problems of bureaucracy. Socialism should mean a wide measure of decentralization, but it also means integration—unity of purpose, a frame of agreed major decisions, co-ordinated concerted action and a spirit of increasing harmony, not in spite of but because of decentralization. Pluralism is necessary, it has to negate centralism but not integration. It has to mean widely distributed focii of functions, authority and co-operation; but at a time when a world community has to be created and developed, large national communities cannot be weakened, though their sovereignty has to be circumscribed and partly surrendered. This is a fundamental point and it has to be realized that large-scale organizations are needed and cannot be dispensed with. One writer has suggested that large-scale organization being inevitable, we have to learn to live with Leviathan which is its legitimate child. It is not easy to understand what that would mean in actual practice. It is better, however, to work on the premise that large-scale organization without bureaucracy and all its evils is an attainable object—an object which is not at all easy to realize, but we cannot on that account commit ourselves to the view that it is an unattainable object. By empirical process we have to define the problem, seek ways of solving it by stages and keep up the effort in investigation, discovery and innovation in this field. Socialist democracy in all spheres of activity, industrial democracy in the working of the economy and spirit of equality everywhere would provide the conditions under which success can be achieved progressively in exorcising the spirit of bureaucracy. As common men can do uncommon things through organization, they also, on that account, can be denied the opportunities of doing common things and rise to their own stature in their everyday life. It all depends whether organization has a soul or is soulless. A soulless organization must necessarily mean Bureaucracy with capital B. But all organizations are not soulless, and we have to proceed on the assumption that large organizations, which are unavoidable, can also have souls. This needs to be spelt out in concrete terms, and it is the task of social discoverers and craftsmen to know and work out what this can and should mean in actual practice. This is one of the new social priorities everywhere, but particularly in socialist countries and countries which are advancing towards it.

Under socialism India will need many more men to operate the economy, resolve its conflicts, promote its efficiency and realize its unity in conception and action. It has to be an order in which there will have to be regulation, control and public operation of all important levers of economy, and these will have functional significance, i.e. they will have to promote and realize the ends of a socialist society. The point to be realized is that even without socialism large-scale organizations have become the rule everywhere and cannot be avoided. In the most advanced capitalist countries that has meant giant enterprises, concentration of economic and therefore political power, all strategic positions under control of business magnates, trustified press, bureaucratized trade unions, political caucuses and machines and elections manipulated by sinister forces behind the scenes. In India also similar situation is being increasingly created and is assuming dangerous proportions; and our bureaucracy, i.e. higher services, is being more and more drawn into the net of private controls and manoeuvres. Bureaucracy, it has to be reaffirmed, is not specifically a problem of socialism in India or anywhere. It is a problem of large-scale, widely ramifying organizations everywhere and, as stated above, in so-called "free" countries, it is taking sinister forms and producing sinister results. That the countries with planned socialist economies, have yet to solve the problem and show how the problem can only be solved by the effective operation of creative socialist processes, the working of which has, as is well known, been greatly impeded partly by the enormous difficulties of the task itself and also by the cold war waged against them not since 1948, when the Truman doctrine was propounded, but since 1917 when the "ten days that shook the world" became one of the most important episodes of world history. Since then the Soviet Union has risen to its present position, new China has also shaken the world and the ascendancy of the self-styled "forces of freedom" is being challenged and undermined everywhere. Solution of the problem of bureaucracy has to be an integral part of the new trends and its forces have to come into close grips with the problems inherent in large-scale organizations everywhere and solve them successfully. The problems can be solved if they can be solved at all, by making the spirit of socialism an all-permeating force. That is the only way in which this Leviathan9 can be tamed— really acquire an entirely new personality.

9. E. Straus in the last chapter of his *Ruling Servant*, in the first section entitled "Coming to Terms with Leviathan" makes the following observation:

"Bureaucratic rule is an evil which once established, is almost ineradicable. It distorts the play of social forces, suppressing its enemies and supporting its sycophants. Either way it makes gradual reform difficult or even impossible and invites violent revolution, as a rule at high cost in human lives and material resources. But its overthrow by hostile forces rarely disposes of its historical consequences. Although discredited and defeated, it has created an ineluctable pattern for the succeeding regimes, which may at first try to adapt the organs and methods of the old system to its own purposes, only to end by re-establishing its substance while denouncing its forms."

"If bigness itself," he goes on to say, "were sufficient to cause bureaucracy and bureaucratic governments, the battle would be lost before it is joined, for the giant state—mass organizations in party politics—has come to stay and may well continue to grow. But although the enormous size of modern organization is the source of some of the serious bureaucratic defects, it does not necessarily produce bureaucratic degeneration." E. Straus, *Ruling Servants*, pp. 281-82.

Later in this chapter he suggests various ways by which bureaucratic degeneration can be prevented under the British parliamentary system and concludes with the observation that as owing to Labour movement being a problematic factor in the political life, the prospect of realizing freedom from bureaucratic tendency and machine rule is by no means encouraging.

Now that the Labour Party is in office in Great Britain and Harold

In the meanwhile bureaucracy in India is gaining strength, our planned development programme is adding to its power and insensibility, putting a premium not on its qualities but its faults, heightening the trends which make it a repository of power without responsibility, making it more and not less stratified and, of course, greatly increasing the opportunities of graft and grab which members of bureaucracy are utilizing to the full. Its illicit alliances with big business and foreign monopolies, to which reference has been made above, make it even more dangerous and create, as stated already, very ominous possibilities. Accelerated development under the Third Plan would only strengthen these trends and therefore make the advance of socialism more and more difficult. That so many very capable young men are, for want of other opportunities and owing to the glittering prizes which it holds out, being drawn into this bureaucracy, is inevitable; but it is obvious that the store of ability of high order for starting and developing creative processes in the country is being depleted on that account. India is, at this time, suffering severely owing to not being able to throw up new leaders with ability and drive in politics, public administration, education, technical and other services and in all fields of social endeavour. This is due to the complex of forces operating in the country, but in it the lure of higher services has to be given an important place of its own. We need our very best men in administration, but in

Wilson is trying to deal with this problem in characteristically British way, future developments have to be awaited with interest and even some hope. The record of Harold Wilson, however, since he became the Prime Minister, does not provide much basis for optimism. On crucial issues like British Guiana, M.L.F. Congo and South Viet-Nam the policy of Labour Party in office has been lacking in real daring and constructive ability. It may be that the Labour Party is in office but, owing to its extremely narrow majority, not yet in power and lacks the necessary strength and courage on that account. And yet it may be that the compulsion of events would make it necessary for the British Government to attempt to cure what Straus calls "bureaucratic degeneration", and even the famous British Civil Service may be modernized and therefore at last partially debureaucratized.

order to provide creative leadership and not to be assimilated
into an unimaginative, wooden and deadening bureaucracy.
This is what unfortunately is happening today and has to be
reckoned as our misfortune—a drain on our available human
capital resources, a real disinvestment which has to be stopped
not by slowing down the recruitment of the "cream of the
nation" for higher services but transforming their (of the
higher services) inner purpose, functional interrelations and
animating spirit as an essential part of the total social transformation of the country. India, intrinsically speaking, is as
well endowed with ability of high order as any other country.
But the stock of such ability, in the nature of things, is limited everywhere. So it is in India and at this critical time we
cannot afford that it should be depleted—we cannot afford the
disinvestment which is taking place at present.

SALARY SCALES

Reduction in the salaries of higher services in India has had
an important place in our national movement from its very
beginning, and the demand for it influenced our political
thinking for a long time. The view that the scale of public
salaries should bear some relation to the level of our national
income, the prevailing standard of living and with the need
of reducing the gap between the rulers and the people in general has been widely shared, and is still a part of the prevailing
public opinion on the subject. The main factor, which determined the scales of higher public salaries in India, was the fact
that most of the members of these services were British and
their salaries in India had to be fixed with a view to making
careers in this country attractive for them, i.e. they had to be
higher than salaries in home service if the British young men
were to have an incentive to work under Indian conditions.
The salaries were probably higher than were necessary to provide this incentive because in effect the Government of India
was government by higher civil servants and they used their
power and position to give high priority to the protection and

promotion of their own interests.

After the admission, first small, and later increasing, proportion of Indians in these services, we, in the name of equal pay for equal work and false sense of national dignity, demanded that Indian entrants into the higher services should receive the same scales of salaries as the British were receiving. Apparently it was a fair demand and had to be conceded by the British; but in fact it meant that Indian entrants to these services were to receive in their homeland the salaries which the expatriates had to be given, and the fact that their admission into these was the result of the growing strength of the national movement and had to be in keeping with its basic impulses was lost sight of altogether. The British wanted complete assimilation of the new entrants into the ways and social codes of the British members of the Indian Civil Services—really it was intimated that they should be brown bureaucrats who identified themselves with their rulers and not their people. In this they succeeded pre-eminently and as Indian members of the Indian Civil Service acquired some of their virtues and qualities but more their vices—sense of aloofness, complete preoccupation 'with power and authority, caste feelings and careerism in really bad sense of the word. As stated above, these qualities were brought to bear on our post-independence tasks and up to a point proved to be a great advantage from the point of view of the country, but as a vested interest they asked for and received a highly differential treatment, they have occupied most of the highest positions in administration, for a number of which they were and are obviously unsuited, and the I.C.S. and its successor services the Indian Administrative and Foreign Services, have carried into the post-independence period the ways of thinking and action which have created a great contradiction between our needs and objectives and the motivation and conduct of these services. This is partly due to the demand for equality of pay and terms of service having been conceded when the Indians were admitted into the higher services. After independence if we had the necessary insight and courage, we would have made a clean break with the past in this respect and begun a new chapter not only in public administration but in our general approach to the problems of the future. This we completely failed to do, and now have to carry the dead weight of outworn and obsolete mores in our administration and organization and suffer from frustration owing to the outdated ideas and practices of our senior administrators. Financial aspect of this question was and is not of fundamental importance. What we could have and can save by the revision of the higher salaries, was a small, almost negligible, proportion of our public expenditure; but with this false step we created prescriptive rights and very harmful fixed ideas which are a serious hindrance to making the necessary adjustments in administration and the ways of thinking.

Now the position has changed owing to the erosion of higher incomes by inflation, reduction of 25 per cent of higher salaries, raising the lower salaries mainly by the grant of dearness allowance and therefore narrowing of gaps between[10] the higher and lower salaries, and what is even more important, rise of incomes and salaries in the private sectors,[11] particularly in foreign owned and controlled industries, and appointment of high-placed public servants to top-posts in business and industries after retirement. Most of the public servants are drawing incomes below Rs 2,000[12] and a vast

10. According to the Pay Commission the proportion of the income drawn by the peons (Class IV officials) to the post-tax salaries drawn by the members of I.C.S. and the I.A.S. from 1939-40 to 1957-58 was:

	1939-40	1947-48	1951-52	1957
I.C.S.	329	46	37	34
I.A.S.	257	38	31	28.5

(Report of the Pay Commission 1957-58), p. 79.

11. In 1957 according to the Pay Commission only 357 posts carried salaries of Rs 2,000 under the Government of India and the number of those who carried salary of Rs 3,000 or more was 57. (Ibid., p. 78)

12. In 1956-57 out of the purely salary earners assessed to income between Rs 40,000-70,000 a year only 270 were in Government service out

majority[13] of them have been severely hit by inflation and the Government has been able to neutralize rise in the cost of living only very partially and their real incomes have fallen seriously since 1947. Real incomes of members of high services have also fallen, but even now, relatively speaking, they are well off and with new opportunities of quick promotion, they have made up to a considerable extent for shrinkage of real purchasing power of their incomes. The lower salaries really need to be raised and by stabilization of prices their purchasing power has to be stabilized. The whole system of dearness allowance and sliding scales, even if the rise of the cost of living could be fully offset, amounts to an admission that inflation cannot be stopped and its palliatives have to be provided — an admission which is due to the price policy of the country being fundamentally at fault and the Government having fully demonstrated its inability to hold the price line. The main point, however, is that incomes in the private sector have been and are rising and in the context of the new income-structure, which is growing in the country, reduction of higher public salaries has become an exceedingly difficult proposition. Under socialism maximum and mini-

of the total of 2,240. The total number of assesses in the private sector in this bracket increased from 321 in 1948-49 to 1977 in 1956-57.

In the highest bracket the average post-tax income in the private sector has increased from Rs 77,750 in 1948-49 to Rs 2,86,929 in 1956-57.

Disparities in the private sectors between the comparatively well-paid factory operatives in textile industry in Bombay to average post-tax salary incomes in the private sector have increased from 77 in 1948-49 to 242 in 1956-57. (Ibid., pp. 86-87)

These figures relate only to the salary earners. If the allowance is made for pre-requisites which the salary-earners in the private sector receive, e.g. expense account, etc. the disparities are really greater than are indicated by the above figures.

13. On 30th June 1956 only 0.1 per cent of the Central Government employees were receiving Rs 1,000 or more basic monthly salary, 2.4 per cent between Rs 250-1,000 and 41.3 per cent per cent between Rs 51 and 250 and 56.2 per cent up to Rs 50.

(Table 2.12, Statistical Supplement to the Report of the Pay Commission)

mum limits will have to be fixed and all differentials fitted into them on a rational basis according to well-understood principles. But this has to be done in relation to the income structure as a whole and not only salaries in public administration. In an economy like ours the principle of fair comparison on which the Pay Commission has laid so much stress — the principles of making scales of public salaries comparable with scales in the non-government services — is obviously an inescapable necessity, otherwise the pull of private salaries and incomes cannot but have a very deleterious effect on the recruitment, morale and working of the public services. That is what is already happening. The prize posts and positions in the private sector carry incomparably higher incomes; and though the higher public services are still attracting men of ability, the general prevailing standard of private expenditure at higher levels is rising, is incompatible with our professed equalitarian principles and is creating expectations and habits which are making a mockery of our socialist professions. Problems of higher public salaries, though more important than before, cannot possibly be considered, much less solved, without an integrated policy in regard to the income-structure as a whole. If we are living in a society in which inequalities are increasing, as we actually are, premium is being put on conspicuous consumption among higher classes and the rich are finding the latest luxuries of the rich countries an irresistible attraction and class differentiation, instead of diminishing, is becoming more pronounced, the higher public salaries cannot possibly be reduced. The highest salary in public administration, leaving out the salaries of posts like those of judges, Governor of the Reserve Bank and of course, Central ministers, state governors, President and Vice-president is Rs 3,000p.m. which, by existing standards, is not high salary at all. From the socialist standpoint the salary is not defensible, but as no one is adopting or applying this standard, it cannot and should not be held applicable only in the case of higher public services. They can, given the necessary conditions, combine simple living with high standard of devotion to social objectives; but when these conditions do not exist and cannot be created, it is truly impracticable to expect the public servants, particularly our public servants, who have been conditioned according to traditions of Indian Civil Service, should practise austerity and live for the future. It is when the whole income-structure of the country embodies and expresses the values of socialism, that even the range of variations[14] in public services which is common in so many capitalist countries, can be adopted in India.

Unfortunately the example set by our public leaders, the President, the Vice-President, the Governors, the Prime and Chief Ministers, the Central and State Ministers after independence have created an atmosphere which is very unfavourable for the growth of the standards of simplicity in public administration.[15] The houses in which these great dignitories live, the entourage and liveried servants with whom they surround themselves, the style of living, travelling and entertainment which they adopt, have no relation to the requirements and income of our people and our avowed values. These are the men who have been known to have been inspired by Gandhi and still use his name all the time. That the standard of simplicity, which he stood for, is being betrayed by most men who wield political power at the highest level is so manifestly obvious that it calls for hardly any comments. The problem of salaries of higher public servants, it should be clear, is a part of the problem of organization, standards, income-structure and values of the country as a whole. It cannot be isolated from the latter and can be solved only if the whole economy is on the move towards socialism and makes it its goal.

Organization is and has been after independence important

14. According to the Pay Commission, in the United Kingdom the disparity ratio is 1:15, in the U.S. Federal Service 1:5, in Canada 1:6, in Australia 1:13.6 and in Japan 1:13.6
15. Op. Cit., p. 80.

bottlenecks of development and realization of social objectives. As stated above, our failure in this regard is not confined to our public administration. The latter is an aspect — though a very important aspect — of our organizational problem as a whole. When organization in political, social, economic and cultural spheres is in a state of decay and degeneration, our public administration cannot possibly rise to new standards, level of performance or height of creative activity. The malaise from which it is suffering is the malaise of the community as a whole.

The problem of building up a new organization for developing a socialist society, involving as it does, and entirely new approach and changes in the scope and method of training has, it is clear, not yet received serious consideration — really any consideration. The National Academy of Alministration, the Staff College at Hyderabad, the Institute of Public Administration, National Institute of Community Devedopment and Panchayat Raj and the various specialized Training Institutes have provided training, and through Foundation Course, refresher course, educational tours, etc. and deputation of administrative officers to foreign countries attempt has been made to broaden the scope of training of higher services. These measures indicate that it is realized that public services for New India have to be very different from the old services, and have to be equipped for the new tasks which they have to undertake and accomplish. Though Gandhian philosophy and socialism have been given a minor place in the courses of one or two of the training institutes, fundamental importance of an entirely new outlook and equipment for building up socialism in this country has neither been recognized nor made the basis of action. In a socialist society the distinction between the generalist and the specialist loses its practical significance, and the view that the generalists have to be on top and the specialists on tap ceases to have any validity. Technical competence has to be acquired by all public servants including the administrators; but there cannot be, as pointed

out already, any all-purposes men with assumed omnicompe
tance for all tasks. The breadth of outlook and perceptiveness
when faced with new problems and situations, which th
generalists were assumed to possess, would be needed even i
greater degree in a socialist society. What will be needed
however, even more urgently by the men in authority, part
cularly in key position, will be:

(a) insight into relation between purpose and function,
(b) grasp of inter-relation among different spheres of th
    economy,
(c) knowledge of the bearing of socialism — in its substanc
    and application on the working and the concrete task
    of the economy and more than all these,
(d) cultivation and practice of the true values of socialis
    in the performance of duties, development of team wor
    and social craftsmanship.

These qualities will be needed in varying degrees by me
in all positions and at all levels. This also applies to th
managerial, engineering, technical and commercial staff of a
economic undertakings *in the public and private sectors*, scie
tists, educationists, journalists, writers and artists, i.e. all elit
under socialism. The inner purpose of socialism has to
all-embracing and express itself in multitude of forms. Buil
ing up an organization which will be adequate for the pu
pose will take time and have to be created by stages. B
when we really embark upon the introduction and develo
ment of a socialist society, we will have to know that orga
zation for this purpose in the widest sense, has to be giv
the highest importance in development with a clear-sight
purpose.

As already stated, failure of planning in India is due to
conceptual inadequacy but more, to the organizational set-
being completely unequal to the new task. The attempts ma
so far to remove this basic deficiency have been based up

piece-meal and patchy understanding of this need and have lacked the focus of insight. That our administration needs to be radically altered and streamlined has become a commonplace and is a part of the pep talk of public leaders. But nothing has been done about it and no constructive thinking of any sort has been undertaken as to how this pre-eminently desirable object is to be achieved. Organization of our political parties, educational and cultural institutions, various voluntary bodies and associations, as stated above, are suffering greviously from the same deficiency and the result is serious falling of the standards of political life, educational and cultural institutions and voluntary public work. Organization means public administration, but it means a lot more; and an all-out stupendous effort in all directions will be needed and have to be carried out with set purpose and determination if we are to produce any worth while results and make even a beginning in building up socialism. This again is an indication of what needs to be achieved and is also a measure of the extent to which our achievements in respect of organization so far have actually fallen short of our needs.

Chapter Fourteen

POPULATION PLANNING

ACCELERATED RATE OF GROWTH

The accelerated rate of growth of population in India has given rise to earnest thinking on the subject, and the need for population planning is now generally accepted as imperative. This is, as is well known, a part of world movement — really what a U.N. publication calls a unique phase in human history.[1] In 1860 world population was 1,250 million, in 1950, in 90 years, it rose to 2,500 million and by 1975, according to this publication, a further 1,250 million will certainly be added and probably more. The world population increased by 23 per cent in 1900-25, by 31 per cent in 1926-50 and is estimated to increase by 53 per cent in 1950-75. The corresponding rates for Asia are 19, 35 and 60, for Latin America 57, 65 and 85 and for Africa 22, 35 and 52. These figures are fairly reliable and show the rate of acceleration of population growth which has already occurred and is likely to occur and give general picture of the world demographic situation.

In India the total population was 235 millions in 1901, 248 in 1921, 356 in 1951 and 438 in 1961; and the rate of increase in six decades was 0.2, 5.7, 6.4, 11.0, 13.5, 14.4. In the first two decades our population increased by 13 millions, in the next two decades by 64 millions and in the last two decades by 126 millions. Since 1901 our population rose from 235 to 438 millions, i.e. by 190 millions or by about 80 per cent. According to the Planning Commission estimates our population in 1966 will be 492 millions, in 1971 558 millions, in 1976 625 millions.[2] These forecasts have been made on

---

1. *The future Growth of World Population*, p.21.
2. *The Third Five Year Plan*, p. 22.

certain assumptions, which may not be borne out by facts, but they are, in the existing circumstances, warranted assumptions. In the third quarter of the century population of India will, on this basis, increase by 269 millions, i.e. nearly 70 per cent as compared with the anticipated increase of 50 per cent in the same period in world population. The U.N. forecast of increase in the population of Asia, as stated above, is 60 per cent for the third quarter. This is a unique phase not only of human history, but also of Indian history and no one can or should suggest that it does not call for the most earnest consideration and action.

FALL IN DEATH RATE

This, what is called "demographic explosion", is due mainly to the rapid decline in the death rates all over the world, but particularly in the undeveloped countries. The birth rates in these countries have practically not changed at all in the recent period, but their death rates have fallen very rapidly in the course of a decade and the excess of births over deaths, i.e. the rate of growth of population, has been very greately increased.[3] The rate in India has fallen from 42.6 per thousand in 1901-11 to 31.2 in 1931-41, 27.4 in 1941-51 and 21.2 in 1951-61. The death rate in countries like Ceylon, Puerto Rico, Formosa and Phillipines — all undeveloped countries — was between 9 to 12 per thousand and was not much higher than that of the advanced countries in 1960, e.g. U.S.A. (8.2), U.K. (11.5), U.S.S.R. (7.2), Switzerland (9.2), Germany (11.4), France (11.1) and Canada (7.2). Reduction of the death rate in the undeveloped countries is due to measures like the application of D.D.T. for fighting malaria, B.C.G. injections for fighting tuberculosis, wide use of antibiotic, and adoption of other relatively inexpensive preventive measures which can, and most likely will, be more widely adopted probably with the help of international agencies and by the governments of

3. Op. Cit., p. 32.

these countries. The death rate of the world in 1950 was 25 according to the U.N. estimates, of Asia 33, Africa 33 and Latin America 19 and North America 9, Europe 9 and U.S.S.R. 7.4 The mortality rates in the undeveloped continents can be reduced to the 9 to 15 level with more vigorous application of measures which have already proved so effective in saving life. It has already been demonstrated that this can be done even in countries with limited budgetary resources. That our existing death rates too can be materially reduced within even five years can be safely assumed. Our birth rate for the last 20 years has been about 40 per thousand since 1941, even if it can be brought down it is very unlikely that this reduction will keep peace with reduction in the death rate. According to the same U.N. estimates the rate of natural increase of the world will increase from 14 per thousand in 1950 to 16 in 1960 and 20 in 1975, of Asia from 13 to 17 to 23, of Africa from 14 to 16 to 17, and of Latin America from 21 to 24 to28.5 There are number of countries in which the rates of increase from 2.5 to 3 per cent per annum have alrealy been realized. That the population of the world and the countries which must, in their own interest and that of the world as a whole, attain a much higher rate of development, will expand rapidly until 1975 has to be taken as a given fact of the situation. What will actually happen, no one can foretell; but if wholesale destruction by nuclear warfare can be prevented, we have to take it that rapid expansion of population in the world and in large areas is inevitable.

CONTINUED DEVELOPMENT OF HEALTH SERVICES

Population planning under these conditions, has in the first place to mean that all available measures to save life have in India, as everywhere, to be fully utilized. There are men

4. Op. Cit., p. 32.
5. Op. Cit., p. 32.

in high positions, who have seriously suggested that it is dangerous to adopt this course in the undeveloped countries; and from their point of view, balance between life and death can be maintained only if serious efforts to reduce the death rates in underdeveloped countries are slackened. This callous and inhuman course, besides being impracticable, is a counsel of despair. No self-respecting country in the world can even consider such a course, what to speak of adopting it; and there is no power in the world, which can impose it on the undeveloped countries. In India our health services, we know, compare very unfavourably with those of the advanced countries and preventable loss of life on a vast scale is taking place. Preventive more than curative measures have to be given high priority. Education of the people in matters relating to health, sanitation, nutrition and art of living can and will produce very beneficial results; of course all the prophylactic measures have to be fully applied and housing conditions and municipal services greatly improved. Provision of Rs 341.9 crores for health in the Third Plan is very inadequate. This is about 4.25 per cent of the total planned outlay, and the Health Survey and Planning Committee has expressed the view that the proportion should be ten per cent.[6] Our financial limitations are due to the poverty of our resources; and poverty of the people is the root cause of their being disease-ridden and in such a vulnerable physical condition. Conquest of hunger and poverty is the greatest health service that can be developed; and this is a question not of institutional care, but of developing the economy for and through the masses, i.e. of developing socialism. The vital point, however, is that everything possible has to be done to fight disease and press into service all the most recent advances in medical science for the purpose. Malaria has to be eradicated, all epidemics eliminated, mother and child care services developed, hospital training and medical research facilities expanded as much as

6. *Report of the Health Survey and Planning Committee*, p. 477.

we can. This is the beginning of population planning in this country and also its ultimate goal.

FAMILY LIMITATIONS THROUGH CONTRACEPTION

The other essential step which has to be given the priority, which it is receiving in this country, is propagation and adoption of measures for family limitation through purposive use of contraceptives on a wide scale. This is not family planning; but family limitation, in the existing conditions, is a very urgent necessity, and all that can be done has to be done to promote it to the greatest possible extent. Contraception now is not as controversial as it was two or three decades ago. Contraception has been practised to an increasing degree in the Western countries and is now an essential part of their culture. Prejudices against it do still exist, but they are of diminishing importance and now no crusades for it are necessary. What is, however, even more significant is that in all communist countries, including China, in which contraception was disfavoured and discouraged on ideological grounds, the battle for contraception has, for all practical purposes, been won, instruction in and appliances of contraception are being made freely available, and the practice of contraception is growing, birth rates are falling and small families are becoming the rule. Progress is uneven; but it is being maintained. With rising level of education and remarkable improvement in the position of women in the communist countries, no barriers can be successfully set up against the increasing use of contraception. It is realized now that this tide cannot be stemmed and all the powers of authoritarian regimes cannot restore the large-family system. Even more significant is the fact, that generally speaking, Governments in all newly independent countries of Asia and Africa and Governments also in Latin America are keen on introduction and wide adoption of contraception, are sponsoring and developing programmes for the purpose and generally speaking the men in authority and public opinion are favourably disposed towards this fundamental change. The battle for population control has not been won as yet, the difficulties in the way of implementing official and non-official contraception programmes are serious, the birth rates in the undeveloped countries are high and have not even begun to fall. These are the countries in which explosion of population growth is the greatest and in the next phase rapid growth of population, as stated above, is bound to take place. But these countries are ready for the great change. What is needed in that organization for the purpose should be built up, suitable contraceptives at low prices made freely available and social intertia of the people overcome by a mass drive as an integral part of a comprehensive social drive for development and change. It has to be realized that contraception, though it has its mechanics and chemistry, is primarily a social process and its adoption is a matter of motivation, change in intimate social relations and a completely new attitude towards one of the deepest facts of human life. In the Western countries this practice was widely adopted, in spite of open or tacit opposition of Governments, churches and upper classes, social taboos and the whole weight of social inheritance because the whole social fabric was being changed by industrialization, growth of radical outlook, silent revolt against clericism and what used to be called "revolt of youth" against conventional repressions and authority of traditions. A few clinics, which were organized by pioneers like Marie Stopes and Margaret Sanger, brought this revolt into the open, provided focus for its expression and removed fear. But it is wrong to isolate contraception from the whole social context and assume that it spreads quickly and without any social ferment. All laws against contraception and contraceptives, silent sonspiracy of those who controlled media of mass communication against the diffusion of interest in and knowledge of contraception and insincerity of the men in power, who practised contraception themselves and yet assumed the pose of indifference, if not opposition, to contraception could not stop the spread of the knowledge and practice of contraception because society in the West was going through a process of profound change from within and it (contraception) was a part thereof.

In India and all other countries in which the problem of growing pressure of population has acquired such great urgency owing to the rapid fall in the death rate in a decade, there is an immediate necessity for making contraception a part of the mores of the people and in as short a time as possible. What was accomplished in the West in seven to eight decades has to be accomplished in India and other countries in one fourth that time if not less, and as stated above, a mass drive as part of an all-round social drive for creating a new social ferment and moving people to face what are called "the facts of life" has to be started. Family limitation is necessary for individuals because they have to know that without it they and their children cannot in most case escape serious privations. This provides a very good case for it; but if a social movement in favour of contraception on a country-wide basis has to be organized and given an authentic character of its own, it has to be made a part of general movement of social aspirations and endeavours and directly linked with social stirrings of the people. Contraception is a simple act, but its implications are wide and far-reaching and its effects extend to the deepest recesses of the sub-conscious. It can add to the family stability and security, it can give relief from economic pressure and it can enrich intimacies and give them a new content free from fear; but it can also create stresses, give rise to problems which as Kingsey's six volumes show that society in U.S.A. is up against and requires a new code of personal and social ethics of its own. These aspects need to be considered and taken into account in developing a social movement for contraception. An awakening in the country for socialism and socialist values is needed if socialist economy is to be realized. These will and should include deep and active interest in contraception. This movement has to be a mass movement for "selling" this idea to the people by technique of mass suggestion and mass propaganda. Those who organize and develop it have to be persons of great sensitivity, deep understanding and knowledge not only of technique of contraception, but more of its psychological and social aspects. They have to build up the movement through close contact with the people and special conditions and circumstances of the different areas in this vast land of great diversities.

Conditions for the success of the movement for contraception[7] are favourable in the country. The Government has

7. One of the most serious difficulties in the way of the success of contraception, however, is that the question making available a suitable, appropriate and inexpensive contraceptive to our people still remains an unsolved problem. We started with popularization of 'safe period method' and found from experience that it was neither acceptable nor effective. Since then foam tablets, condumn and jelly and diaphragm are the three methods which are being largely recommended and adopted, but all the three, in practice, are unsuitable under conditions existing in India. Jelly and diaphram in combination are taken to be in India, as elsewhere, the most effective method of contraception. But they together cost Rs 10/- in the market and the conditions under which they can be used do not exist in most homes in India. Foam tablets are being popularized in rural areas and the use of condumns is also increasing. But their limitations are known to the specialists in contraception and greatly limit their utility and effectiveness.

Oral tablets are the methods on which 'planned parenthood' workers all over the world have been basing their hopes. The discovery and availability has been round the corner for over a decade now. The Health Minister of India very recently announced that research in this method has already been fruitful and these tablets would soon be available. If this is so, the problem of making suitable contraceptives available may solve itself if they are produced on a mass scale and their cost is low and is reduced to the minimum. Sale of these tablets can and should be heavily subsidized and the results carefully watched.

But before this mass operation starts, extreme care has to be taken to make sure that these tablets are not harmful. Warnings have already been issued by men who are in a position to speak with knowledge that indiscriminate use of these tablets can be very risky and the utmost vigilance is needed in their use on a mass scale. This warning has to be heeded.

There are two other methods which have been recommended and are being used. Of these sterlization is the method which offers the greatest hope. As already stated, in some states earnest effort is being made to offer

sponsored it. There is no organized opposition to it except

facilities for the extensive use of this method and a measure of success has already been achieved. Even money inducements are being provided to induce men and women to avail themselves of these facilities. This is a hopeful develpoment. It is reported that 'vasectomy' i.e. sterlization of males, is being resorted to on a voluntary basis with certain amount of readiness which is really surprising and gratifying. This method seems to provide ground for optimism which, however, has as pointed out in the text, to be restrained owing to our health services being, relatively speaking, in an undeveloped state.

Japan has become, after the war, a classic case of family planning through abortion and still a million abortions are taking place in that country every year. In our country non-availability of health services in large rural areas, apart from other reasons, makes if impracticable to use the method extensively for family limitations. But the method itself is open to serious objection, and it has to be used within very narrow limits.

The conclusion is obvious that in India, as in most countries, in which population has 'exploded', conditions under which the people are living, the state of their education and knowledge and unavailability of suitable contraceptives make it necessary not to be unduly optimistic about adoption of contraception on a wide scale. All the same it is essential that the utmost efforts should be made to provide contraceptives and instruction in their use with a real sense of urgency and earnestness. This will not solve our population problem, but this does not make it any the less necessary that an organization for making contraception a part of our development programme and 'way of life' should be built up intelligently and with zest. At present our general organizational weakness also impairs the efficiency and adequancy of 'family planning' organization. A constructive attitude towards this commendable national effort is called for, and the general agreement on the need of making this effort should make it possible to secure a large measure of co-operation for it of all parties, persons and classes. It has, as pointed out in the text, however, to be realized that a movement in favour of contraception has to be a part of the general peoples' movement for carrying the country forward on the road to its future. This is an essential condition for the success of 'family planning' as a national undertaking.

This, however, in spite of being very encouraging does not even touch the fringe of the problem. Mr R. A. Gopalswami, ex-Registrar General of Census and now Director of Institute of Man-Power Research, has great faith in sterilization, particularly vasectomy for reducing our birth-rate. According to him 1,200 surgeries working whole time on vasectomy alone can carry out 3 million sterlization operations in a year and growth of population from 1967 to 1981 can be decreased from uncontrolled increase of 16 crores to under 7 crores by 1981 by halving the birth rate (R. A. Gopalswami, *Planned Development and Population Growth*, p. 40).

perhaps in Kerala where the Catholic Church is creating difficulties in its way. All political parties seem to be agreed that it is necessary and desirable.[8] The educated middle classes, who are all-important in the political and other social spheres, have adopted contraception with conviction and are practising it successfully. Contraception has been made a part

Mr Gopalswami has great faith and drive and he produced significant results in Madras, which is now ahead of all other states in carrying out sterlization operations. The possibility of reducing the birth-rate by a nation-wide programme of extensive sterlization needs to be given most earnest consideration. If results of this magnitude have to be achieved, we will have to develop a social momentum which we have as yet not developed in any other field of national endeavour. General Sokhey's point, referred to in the text, is valid. Even if Mr. Gopalswami's estimates are correct, 1,200 surgeries to which he refers will have to cover our entire population of which more than four fifths is rural. These surgeries will have to be very mobile and conditions for their effective functioning will have to be created. All this can be done only if the country is going through a process of mass awakening and endeavour. Our latest experience so far provides us a basis for optimism. Through sterlization, oral contraceptives or any other method which is inexpensive, effective and acceptable to our people we should make our family limitation programme fully fruitful within as short a time as possible. So far, in spite of all the publicity, we have, as stated above, achieved very meagre results.

8. In spite of this fact the need for production of contraceptives in India has been completely lost sight of. "Service and supplies" according to the Health Survey and Planning Committee, "are not often available to meet the demand for family planning advice and appliances.... The indigenous production, barring that of foam tablets, is practically insignificant, and difficulties in regard to import licenses and availability of foreign exchange are understood to have come in the way of adequate imported supplies being available.... Indigenous production of contraceptive appliances should, in our view, have been simultanously taken in hand when the family planning programme was launched on a national scale, and we consider, therefore, a priority no less high than for any other major projects should be given to this project for setting up the plants for production of contraceptives within the next two or three years." (Report of the Health Survey and Planning Committee, pp 402-403)

The Health Survey and Development Committee 1946 (Bhore Committee) had made a similar recommendation for the production of contraceptives in the country, but in spite of 'family planning' programme having been launched on a national scale, the need for production of contraceptives in India has been almost completely neglected. It is almost incredible

of health services, its knowledge and technique have been made a part of medical and nursing training, three demographic research centres have been set up, research in contraception is being carried on in three medical institutes of national importance and many clinics in rural and urben areas9 have been started. Provision for "family planning" in the Third Plan has been increased from actual expenditure of Rs 3 crores in the Second Plan to the provision of Rs 27 crores in the Third. In the Fourth Plan, according to available information, provision of Rs 97 crores is being made for this purpose. Actual expenditure for this purpose, upto 1964, is expected to be only Rs 12 crores. But short-fall, in terms of achieve-

that with all the publicity which has been given to family planning programme, this obvious need received no consideration whatsoever, and shows that behind the scenes some powerful interests have been operating to prevent the undertaking of the manufacture of contraceptives in the country.

It is absolutely essential that plants for the production of contraceptives in the public sector should be set up without any delay and their supply should be ahead of the demand and not lag behind it. Prices of contraceptives, it is known, can be very greatly reduced if their mass production is started and they are sold even below cost if necessary. Increase in the demand for contraceptives is shown by the fact that the import of rubber contraceptives has increased from 7 million pieces in 1957 to 30 million pieces in 1962. Demands for condumns in India constitute the bulk of demand for rubber contraceptives and it should not be at all difficult to meet this demand from indigenous sources.

In 1960 position was that production of even a simple appliance like condumns was 159,000 while their demand was estimated to be 8 millions (S. N. Aggarwal, *Ten Years of Population Planning in India* in A Decade of Economic Development and Planning in India p. 132). Precious foreign exchange should never have been wasted on the import of contraceptives. Investment in setting up a few plants in the public sector could have made it possible to meet the demand by domestic supplies and reduce very considerably the prices of contraceptives.

9. In 1955-56 there were 147 centres in which instruction in contraception was given. In 1960-61 their number increased to 1797 and in 1965-66 it is expected that their number will rise to 8,147. This increase should make a difference provided lines of communication with the people are created and contraceptives suited to their needs are made available. With a few exceptions, however, according to the available information impact of the programme on the birth-rate has not been significant.

ments, is even higher than that in financial terms. Whatever may be the explanation for meagre achievements, lack of adequate financial provision is not responsible for these results. In the training centres of the workers, wider aspects of the problem have not been lost sight of. It is, however, known that the practice of contraception is limited mostly to educated classes in urban areas. In rural areas there are clinics but from all reports it appears that they have achieved a very limited measure of success. The fact that in Maharastra, Madras and some other states sterilization camps have been organized and a large number of operations been performed is a heartening sign.[10] But as General Sokhey has rightly pointed out, "When we utterly lack the facilities to render ordinary surgical aid to the people to attend even to their boils, it is not sensible to think of millions of operations to make them sterile."[11] Apart from the important fact referred to below, that the available contraceptives are unsuited to our needs and conditions, the present organization, experience makes it clear, cannot produce easily any significant results in reducing the birth rate. In the last ten years this programme has had hardly any effect on it and our birth rate still what it has been for the last twenty years, i.e. about 40 per thousand. It may be assumed that in the next ten if not five years, our death-rate can be reduced from 21.2 to 15 per thousand and if our birth rate cannot be reduced even to 35, the excess of births over deaths will increase and the rate of growth of our population would be further increased. We have to develop our programme as fast as we can, but owing

10. According to official figures total number of sterilizations in Maharastra was 862 in 1957, 4,557 in 1958, 10,843 in 1959, 12,009 in 1960 and 18,094 in 1961. In 1960 and 1961 number of 'male' sterilizations was 17,361 and 12,525 respectively which again is a very significant change and indicates a real change in the mentality of men. In other states also the number of sterilizations have been increasing. Up to March 1963, 3,85,870 sterilization operations had been performed of which 2,42,371 were 'vasectomy' operations, i.e. operations on males.

11. S. G. Sokkey, A *Balanced View*, Semminar No. 33, May 1962, p. 23.

to our health services being what they are and also our inability to touch or move the masses, it is idle to expect that
the lag between the fall in the birth and death rates in India
can be materially reduced. The programme, it is to be stated
again, has to be a part of general social ferment in the
country if it can make a real difference to our population.
Of this there are no indications at present and those who
are expecting that it will carry the country forward on the
road to population planning, are building false hopes.

FAMILY AND POPULATION PLANNING

The whole concept of population planning needs much
greater consideration than it has received so far. Family limitation through contraception is very necessary in the countries referred to above, and, nationally and internationally,
every effort has to be made to examine the position objectively
and devise measures by which voluntary limitation of families
can be promoted to the greatest extent. That, however, means
neither family planning nor population planning. Family
planning is a genteel word for contraception or birth control;
and as it has become widely current, no exception need be
taken to it. But the family, being the basic unit of society,
its size is only one of its aspects; and it as a whole has to
be planned, its other aspects have to be duly considered and
changed if society itself is undergoing a change. With development of social services and social insurance, with increasing
responsibility of the community for the well-being of children,
with growing participation of the woman in political, economic
and cultural life, her equality at home and as a member of
the community and the necessity of taking into account
eugenic considerations in marriage and the exercise of reproductive function; it has to be recognized that changing family in
a changing society requires earnest consideration in any planned
economy. In a country in which caste is still the most important factor in marriages and customary obligations determine family duties and behaviour, family planning in the

wider sense referred to above can have hardly any practical interest or importance; but India has adopted the goal of a casteless society and experience is making it more and more clear that the caste as an institution is incompatible even with parliamentary democracy and much more so with socia- ism, the changing role of the family in new society has to be thought about as a whole and consciously provided for. The small family system has to be adopted owing to the impending pressure of population; but even if this pressure were not here, the size of family has in a rational society to be deter- mined by choice and each family, in the light of its own needs and conditions, has to determine what this size should be, even a large family needs to be planned as much as a small one; and timing and spacing of children has to be consciously regulated. In an economy in which the future of the children is completely independent of the means of parents, i.e. there is complete equality of opportunity, women too earn their living as a matter of course, risks of illness, age and death are socially provided for and marriage becomes a partnership based upon freedom and ceases to be a bondage, family planning means conscious choice in the excercise of reproductive func- tions, but it also means a great deal more. It means a new relation in personal intimacies and making them truly crea- tive both from personal and social standpoint, it means econo- mic equality of men and women, it means combination of home and work and it means a new sense of responsibility towards children in spite of the community assuming greater obligation towards them. In a socialist society the family has to acquire these attributes. In India we have already introduced divorce in Hindu marriage, woman's economic equality is being promoted, the state is, to a small extent, off-setting the disadvantages of children of poor families and it is being assumed that inter- caste marriages are desirable and will become more and more common. These changes have to go very much farther before the role of the family becomes different and is brought into accord with our new social objectives. All these changes are

or should be implicit in the concept of family-planning and
have to be correlated to the realization of our social objectives.
These have been referred to here to indicate what family
planning in a real sense should mean, how in an unplanned
way the family in India is already changing and will, as
planning becomes more effective, acquire a different role and
make other institutional changes unavoidable.

POPULATION POLICY

Family planning is, however, not and cannot be an end
in itself. It has to be a basis for and instrument of population
planning, i.e. planning of the population of the country as
a whole, its composition and its distribution. The concept
of optimum population, in the sense of fixing its maximum for
maximizing per capita national income, which was in vogue
for a while, is now realized not to be a valid conception. But it
is necessary that the question of a limit to the growth of population should receive serious consideration and population and
its distribution in different areas of the country should, as far
as possible, be regulated according to an estimate of their
carrying capacity — their capacity to maintain the population
in the desired state of comfort. There can be no simple criteria for estimating the carrying capacity of the country and
each area. It requires an over-all view of all the factors and
their inter-relations which have a bearing on the growth of
population; and for practical purposes it means that family
limitation through wide use of contraception has to be promoted, as stated above, with the utmost earnestness. Population planning, however, has to mean:

(a) the development of health services as fully as possible,
(b) increasing attention to the health, nutrition and bring-
    ing up of children,
(c) studying and dealing with specific features of the demo-
    graphic situation in each region, state and area,
(d) examining the position in each state and part of the

state from the eugenic standpoint and taking corrective
measures against the dysgenic factors which may be at
work,

(e) promoting distribution of population in each state and
the country as a whole in a planned manner to reduce
the existing uneven distribution of population.

(f) research in reproduction and contraception,

(g) and what is most important, planning economic development of the country in terms of specific needs and
resources of each state and area and with special reference to the varying incidence of the pressures of population and its results like the incidence of unemployment, proportion of landless labourers, age structure of
each area, the difference in the number and proportion
added to its labour force from year to year and the
difference in the standards of undernutrition and
malnutrition.

The last point is of paramount importance, and as pointed
out before, has in fact been woefully neglected. But if planning itself and population planning is to mean anything at
all, it has to mean formulation and implementation of development programme in specific terms for each region, state and
area and full utilization of its human resources. A national
policy of population planning with these major constituent
elements must be worked out and put into effect as a part
of the whole planning programme of the country. Population
planning has to mean family limitation programme, but unless
it includes a comprehensive policy of dealing with the aspects
referred to above and as an integral part of the realization
of a socialist society, it will not be population planning. These
aspects have received and are receiving consideration in a
fragmentary and disjointed manner, but an integrated view
of population planning as a whole has still to be adopted.
Family planning, as explained above, has to be a necessary part
of population planning, and role of the family has to be

consciously changed in our changing economy. In the last analysis it is the family which has to play a decisive role in shaping and executing population policy; and every effort has to be made to make it a conscious agent in framing and carrying out this policy.

POPULATION PLANNING AND SOCIAL ISSUES

It is well known that population has been and still is a very controversial issue in terms of basic approach and policies, and the consideration of its problems is greatly vitiated by political pre-conceptions and prejudices. Unfortunately it has now become a part of the cold war strategy and family planning evangelists are largely actuated by their zeal to fight and anticipate communism in their advocacy of and reliance upon family limitation as an important weapon in their armoury. There is, as it has already been made clear, a very good case for contraception even apart from the acceleration of the rate of growth of population that has taken place. All families, large and small, have to be planned, and it is due to every child that its parent should want it and eagerly welcome its birth. For other reasons also it is essential that sex and reproduction should be delinked and they should remain distinct though closely allied functions, and in a socialist society contraception has to be accorded an important place in its working as a method of social regulation and change. Ardent advocates of contraception are, however, rendering a great disservice to its introduction and acceptance by bringing anti-communism into their campaigns for contraception. They are haunted by the fear of communism and act on the assumption that, unless misery due to over-population is prevented by wide use of contraceptives by the people in poor countries, communism will find in their misery a very fertile ground and all these countries will go over to communism. This is a most short-sighted view for there is already so much misery and poverty in these countries, that communism, if it thrives on misery and nothing but misery, has a field clear to itself and can go ahead, contraception or no contraception. It is the next ten or twenty years that matter so far as the relation of communism to the future of these countries is concerned. It is more important that through international co-operation and resurgence of the people of these countries that their misery and poverty should be reduced in a short time than a holy war against communism should be waged and among other things, contraception should become one of its most important weapons. The issue will be settled otherwise and it is exteremely unwise to prejudice the future of the programme of family limitation by making it a part of world-wide struggle against communism. As pointed out above, the need for contraception is now widely accepted and in the communist countries the battle has been already won. In poor countries the need for it is conceded and all that needs to be done is to take effective action to organize intelligently and constructively a movement for the adoption of contraception as a part of the social movement for conquering poverty in a new social framework. Birth control enthusiasts in the Western countries would do well if they will not intervene in these countries in promoting the use of contraception and confine such assistance as they can give for introducing research in contraception and make its results available for the government and the people of the countries under heavy population pressure and that also under international auspices. Most of them are so deeply involved in ideological controversies that they cannot even consider the population situation of the underdeveloped countries objectively and in a balanced manner. They are mostly committed not only against communism but also against socialism, and are out of accord with the prevailing social objectives of these countries, the future of which they are so very concerned about. Anti-communism is a bad plank to work for contraception. This work has to be mainly done by the people of these countries themselves and experts from the U.S.A. and other Western countries, generally speaking, needlessly complicate the problem by importing considerations into it which are more or less irrelevent.

POPULATION AND CHANGE IN DEMOGRAPHIC BALANCE

It is certain that in next forty years the relative proportion of the population of Asia, Africa and Latin America, in the total world population is going to increase. Even in 1925 their proportion was 66.4 per cent, and in 1950 it rose to 70.6 per cent. In 1975, according to the same U.N. publication, it is going to be 72.6 per cent and in 2,000 to 79.4 per cent.[12] And this is going to happen when the peoples of these countries, it can well be expected, will be able to consolidate and greatly improve their relative position in world affairs, and, let us hope, rise to a much higher level of economic development and social well being. The powerful nations of today will not only numerically have a lower weight but their economic ascendency will be greatly weakened if not completely counter-balanced. This is the prospect which the West has to learn to live with and make the most of. Its significance in terms of the future of mankind is truly heartening, and it will also mean that racialism of today will in four decades largely pass away and the world will be made a better place to live in. Besides anti-communism, the fear of lower breeds multiplying and inheriting the earth is also an important factor in the greatly revived enthusiasm for family planning in the Western countries. The position, as it is developing being irreversible, the dominant countries of today have to accept the prospect with good grace, and if they know what is really good for them and the world, even with genuine enthusiasm. They will be twenty per cent of world population in forty years, but they will not be swamped on that account. What they will lose is their dominance, but not their capacity to maintain and even greatly improve their existing standards of living and not their capacity to enrich and deve-

12. *Op. Cit.*, Table 7, p. 24.

lop their culture and contribute greatly to the development of world culture.

The bearing of this point on our population planning is that if this change is demographic balance can be constructively used, it among other things, will mean that planned redistribution of world population on a co-operative basis will become a practical proposition, and India can give the directed international migration a place in her own population planning. This she cannot do at present for racial barriers against it are at present strong and irremovable. It is, however, too much to expect that this development will be actually brought about. India has to plan in terms of her own resources to maintain the growing population, and if she can develop, and utilize them fully, lack of scope for international emigration need not be a matter of serious concern to her.

POPULATION AND POVERTY

Family limitation and regulation being conceded as a necessity in order to mitigate the increasing pressure of population when even the existing pressure of population makes the task of adequate economic growth such a stupendous proposition, it is, however, necessary to state clearly that population is not the major cause of poverty in India or anywhere and it is wrong to posit that contraception is badly needed in order to remove this cause of poverty. It has been duly stressed that since 1951 nearly 70 per cent[13] increase of population in India by 1975 is almost inevitable even if the movement for contraception can go ahead as fast as it is humanly possible. We have also to live with this fact and develop rapidly the resources

13. This statement is, of course, based upon certain assumptions which can be upset by radical changes. Our present death rate may be reduced to 10 per thousand as it has been in a number of undeveloped countries and we may be able to reduce our birth rate to, say, 30 if the country can develop a big drive as a part of social drive in changing the entire economy. But in the next ten years a growth rate of at least 2 per cent, really more, has to be postulated from a realistic standpoint and has to be made a working premise of our plans of economic development and social transformation.

of the country on the assumption that standard of living of our people and their general condition can be changed out of recognition if we use our potential to the full. Our population, just as the population of the world, will have to be stabilized before the century is closed; but at present we know that 70 per cent increase in population by the end of the next decade has to be and can be provided for and our people can raise themselves to a high level of development and prosperity, the accelerated growth of population notwithstanding. This is so because population, though a very important factor in world history, is at present not the root cause of poverty in India; and two-thirds of world population, who are at present living in dire want and hunger, do not owe their position primarily to their excessive population. The 70 per cent increase in our population by 1975, 60 per cent in Asia and 50 per cent in the world being inevitable, it is, from the practical standpoint, inexpedient to keep on harping on the point that excessive population is our major problem or of the world as a whole. It is much more fruitful to explore and realize the possibilities of accelerating as much as possible the rate of economic growth to meet successfully this "demographic challenge". If the challenge cannot be met this way, it cannot be met at all. The view that poverty of our people is largely due to our unjust social system—the evils of an acquisitive society —and can be conquered only if we use the existing knowledge, technique and the latent productive capacity of the people to the full by making fundamental changes in its very basis is, from empirical standpoint, the right view; and if it can be supported by facts, as it can be, it becomes a conclusive point and has to be made the basis for constructive action.

Africa and Latin America are not over-populated continents and poverty of their people is certainly not due to excessive population pressures. Their poverty clearly supports the view that countries and continents can be underpopulated and yet extremely poor. In India there is heavy population pressure and yet in 1921 when her population was 190 millions her people were still living in extreme misery and dying in millions of famine and epidemics even in the last quarter of the 19th century and their lot was, as is well known, bewailed by Dadabhai Naoroji and Digby who in their books showed vividly how appalling it had been and was. Since then India has more than doubled her population and yet poverty remains a pathetic but not a more pathetic fact, and bears out the fact that major changes in population have not changed this aweful reality. This does not mean that population does not matter but that there are other factors which matter much more and account for the general position of Indian people having remained as sad as it still is. As it is, enormous increase in population is inevitable; and yet if we act on the assumption that basic social changes combined with adequate investment of resources would definitely make a lot of difference in the condition of our people, we can adopt it as a valid assumption and provide a rational basis for future policy. The issue referred to here is the old issue between the Malthusians and Marxians and it is not necessary to discuss it in its different aspects. It should, however, be realized that as immediate necessity for large-scale planned effective action for family limitation is posited, this is not a dogmatic position and is based largely on the logic of facts arising out of the unavoidable large increase in population in India in spite of vigorous effort to start a movement for family limitation on a nation-wide basis. There is no contradiction between large-scale family limitation and the premise that without fundamental social changes the potential of our productive capacity cannot be realized. Both are really part of the same process of taking bold action to face a compelling social imperative; large increase of population, which has taken place and is in view, reinforces the need for complete social overhaul—of harnessing new social forces to modern knowledge, technique and organization to produce results which cannot be produced otherwise. For socialists it means reaffirmation of their faith that socialism not only means social equity but also much higher level of productivity and man himself has to be the most important agent of production and master of his future. This faith is fully supported by experience and can be made the basis of social policy. This also means that without socialism population can neither be planned nor raised to a plane of living which makes the future worth working and living for.

RATE OF ECONOMIC GROWTH IN RELATION TO POPULATION GROWTH

The crucial point which emerges out of this discussion is whether the rate of our economic growth in India can be raised to a level which exceeds the rate of population growth of more than 2 per cent to an extent as to make doubling of our per capita national income, say in ten years or less, feasible and distribute it in such away as to confer the main benefit of the increase on vast majority of our people. Our per capita national income has increased from Rs 284 in 1950-51 to Rs 330 in 1960-61 or by 16 per cent, and in the next three plans it is estimated to increase to Rs 385 in 1965, Rs 450 in 1971 and Rs 530 in 1976 which means in twenty five years per capita income would increase by 86 per cent if the forecasts of the Planning Commission are realized.[14] Their estimates for 1966, 1971 and 1976 are largely speculative and those for earlier years have serious inherent limitations; but taking them as they are, they show a rate of economic growth which cannot but damp our hopes and enthusiasm for the future. Sixteen per cent increase in the first ten years has meant little or nothing so far as vast majority of our people is concerned, and the forecast increase of 38 per cent in the next fifteen years, even if it is actually realized, would also not significantly add to their well-being unless there is a plan for the distribution of additional income, i.e. most of it is either distributed to raise the standard of living of the people to the social minimum or invested according to a carefully worked-out scheme of social

14. *The Third Five Year Plan,* p. 28.

priorities. This has not happened so far and a complete change has to be brought about in methods and mechanism of planning, of the implementation and administration of plans and the degree and manner of enlisting the co-operation of the people. National income per capita estimates remain statistical abstractions unless their meaning is known and understood in terms of what they signify for the welfare of the people, the relation of different classes and working of the social system as a whole. It is this significance which makes these averages meaningful for understanding the development and operation of the economy as a whole. At present whatever we do know of the economy and its impact on the life of the people shows that those averages are no index of the changes in the well-being of the people or healthy growth of the economy.

The point, however, which matters even more than the rate of growth which these figures show is that it is not at all sufficient for placing the nation well on its way to working off the evil legacies of the past and realizing its future. In 1960 per capita national income of India was 53 per cent of Ceylon, 57 per cent of Afghanistan, 26 per cent of Ghana and 13 per cent of Yugoslavia. These statistical abstractions again do not mean anything unless the substance and working of the economies of these countries are known and analysed. They are no index of the relative development of these countries or economic position and achievement of their people. They, however, show that even if our per capita income in one generation is doubled, that will not in itself signify any material advance towards a state of real economic well-being. In 1976 our per capita income will still be one-eighteenth of the income of U.S.A. in 1960, one-ninth of U.K., one-ninth of Western Germany, one-seventh of France and two-fifths of Japan. Taking these averages with all the limitations inherent in them, it is clear that the rate of growth which is indicated by our development programme, falls very seriously short of our needs and no one can take this prospect as anything but depressing.

ACCELERATION OF THE RATE OF ECONOMIC GROWTH

The conclusion is inescapable that a much higher rate of economic growth has to be aimed at and achieved, but the fact that our population is growing and will continue to grow very fast is a clear warning, that we will not get anywhere in international race unless our rate of growth is stepped up from the present level of 3 to 5 per cent to 9 to 10 per cent per year, and this rate signifies not only that we have accelerated the rate of our growth but also that we are advancing towards socialism, i.e. domination of the propertied class is being ended, wrongs of the poor are being redressed and they have really come into their own. This rate of growth is the rate which most of the communist countries and also some non-socialist countries, e.g. Japan and West Germany have set up and sustained. Starting as we must from a low level of development, this rate does not, in absolute terms, mean much; but even then without achieving this rate of growth we will continue to occupy a very low economic position in the community of nations and our people will continue, comparatively speaking, to labour under serious disadvantages. Raising the rate of investment from 11 to 18 or 19 per cent of our national income will mean hardly any advance if our national income in 1976 continues to be less than one-seventh to one-eighth of that of the advanced countries in 1960, even this high rate of investment of our national income will not carry us far. We have to go ahead much faster, catch up with the countries which had a start over us and come up reasonably near their level even if we cannot attain it for two or three decades. Our whole economy is weak and vulnerable, and we have first to think of making it intrinsically sound and strong. But we have also to set up a high rate of economic growth and maintain it for a long time. If we lag behind, our internal difficulties will mount up and in international relations we will suffer a real eclipse. A much higher rate of economic growth is for us an absolute necessity.

This is our population problem in its immediate and compelling form. We must raise the rate of economic growth in India to more than twice the rate which we have achieved or are likely to achieve in the Third Plan. These rates obviously fall short of our need and the condition of our masses will not materially change if this rate is maintained and the distribution of income is not radically altered in their favour. Even for attaining this rate our economy has been subjected to very severe strain, our dependence upon foreign assistance has assumed embarrassing dimensions and our people are not only lacking in buoyancy and a sense of achievement but are suffering from sense of frustration and purposelessness which is producing very disquieting effects. It is, apart from the increasing pressure of population, absolutely essential to find a way out of the impasse. But the prospect of adding 107 millions to our existing population in the context of the world population growing at about the same rate and unavoidability of this increase makes the necessity of a much more rapid rate of economic growth all the greater. Contraception, though necessary and desirable, is no answer to this great challenge. We must, it may be repeated, do all that we can to make small families the rule in this country and do it through wide and increasing use of contraceptives. And yet the stubborn fact remains that this is not the answer to the problem of resolving the crisis which we are facing today. This can be resolved only if we can raise the productive effort of our people to a much higher level of intensity and effectiveness and produce income which may enable them to raise their standard of living to a much higher level and also produce the surplus needed for increasing rate of investment. This is the answer to the extremely critical situation in which the country finds itself owing to the prospect of our population growth having been so much accelerated.

MEASURES FOR DOUBLING THE RATE OF ECONOMIC GROWTH

How can the higher cumulative rate of economic growth of say 9 to 10 per cent be realized? Can it be realized if we proceed on the present working hypothesis of economic development? Answer of the Planning Commission has been referred to above. We can raise production say by about 5 per cent in the next plan and raise per capita income from Rs 385 in 1960-61 to Rs 570 in 1970. This is completely inadequate to meet the needs of the situation. We must do better and very much better.

But how? Answer to this question has already been given in the different chapters of this book. Our whole economy has to be fundamentally changed, its great potential has to be released, latent capacity of our people has to be realized and brought into action, a new institutional framework has to be set up and motive power of the economy has to be generated by changing alignment and balance of forces. Larger investment from our own resources is essential, *but the problem of breaking the chains in which our economy is held is not primarily the problem of increasing the investment,* essential though it is, but it is the problem of being aware that our economy is in chains and the will to break them has to be developed and made effective. Agricultural production can be greatly increased, minor irrigation works can be expanded, small industries, trade and agriculture can be co-operativized, labour, including agricultural labour, can be organized in defence of its own interest and more to make it the custodian of our future, internal and external trade can be socialized for fiscal reasons, but much more for reasons of economic strategy, we can make community effort through public ownership of banks and economic enterprises a means by which key positions in the economy can be under public control and used also for the expansion of our financial resources and lastly we can convert our enormous, idle man-power from a great liability into a great asset. All these results can be produced with a scale of investment not beyond our means. By these means we will generate and channelize the surplus needed for intensification and diversification of agriculture, investment in labour intensive industries, communications and minor irrigation works and rapid development of our social services. Foreign exchange and foreign assistance component of these measures is nil and their investment requirements fully within our own means. We do not need even foreign advice, much less assistance, for dealing with our population situation, which is only being made an occasion for foreign penetration and intervention in our economy. This is the answer to the need for greatly accelerating the rate of our economic growth. This, of course, presupposes that industrialization and modernization of our economy would continue, economic and social infrastructure would be developed with greater earnestness and the whole economy would be integrated and work according to a common purpose. The need for foreign exchange and foreign assistance will remain, but a shift to the full utilization of our own resources and productive assets would be brought about and village, area, district and regional planning would be the foundation of planned development. This would be the answer even if our population were not increasing at all and could be stabilized, say, at 440 million. Even then problems of mass hunger, poverty and distress would remain and need all these changes if it is to be solved in a reasonably short time. But the problem necessarily becomes much more urgent and compelling because of the situation created by the present and prospective fall in the death rate. Demographic crisis is a part of the crisis which already exists in the country; and if the latter can be resolved, the former will be resolved as a part thereof; and if the general crisis cannot be or is not resolved, there is no way by which demographic crisis can be resolved. This conclusion follows from an objective assessment of the facts of the situation and is inescapable.

PLANNING IN SPECIFIC TERMS

It also follows that because the rate of increase of population, incidence of its pressure, and the incidental results like the proportion of landless labourers and poor peasant, the extent of unemployment and the degree of unemployment and

under-employment vary from state to state, our planning has
to be placed on regional, state and sub-regional basis, and in
terms of their specific conditions and problems. The general
plan targets fixed in aggregate on the basis of departmental
and *ad hoc* estimates, besides being wrong in principle and unsuited to our actual needs and therefore inevitably ineffective,
are completely out of accord with the present and prospective
population situation. If we have to plan at all, we must plan
in specific terms[15] within the framework of directives, aims
and objects of our economy. This obvious necessity becomes all

15. Diversity in the density, rate of growth, composition by sexes and
age-groups, labour force participation and participation of women in different states and different parts of the same states is a matter of common
knowledge and recent studies in regional and sub-regional population situation have made it clear that these diversities are of profound importance
from the point of view of planned development of the country. Differences
in the rate of growth of population in different states have been referred
to already. The fact that these rates in 1951-61 vary from 11.85 per cent in
Madras, 15.65 per cent in Andhra to 25.80 per cent in Punjab, 26.88 per
cent in Gujerat and 34.45 per cent in Assam; and within each state the
variations also are very wide, e.g. in the Punjab 15.99 per cent in Jullundur
and 47.84 per cent in Hissar; in Gujerat 29.45 in Kaira and 51.41 in Dang;
in Rajasthan 26.83 per cent in Bharatpur and 84.66 per cent in Ganga
Sagar, clearly suggests how meaningless is planning in aggregate without
any co-relation with specific population situation in different parts of the
country. Density of population varied in 1961 from 155 per square mile in
Assam and 189 in Madhya Pradesh to 1,032 in West Bengal and 1,127 in
Kerala. Proportion of urban population to the total population in 1961
varied from 6.3 per cent in Orissa and 7.7 per cent in Assam to 26.7 per
cent in Madras and 28.2 per cent in Maharashtra. The percentage of working population to the total population of each state in 1961 varied from
33.16 per cent in Uttar Pradesh and 33.31 per cent in Jammu and Kashmir
to 47.9 per cent in Madras, 51.87 in Andhra and 52.30 per cent in Kerala
and these variations are largely due to the fact that active participation of
women in productive work was 9.43 per cent in Uttar Pradesh, 19.71 per
cent in Jammu and Kashmir, 38.10 per cent in Madras, 41.32 per cent in
Andhra and 43.99 per cent in Kerala. Projections of the future growth of
the working force in different parts of the country would depend as much
on the extent to which women can be drawn into it as on the rate of
growth of population or its age structure. All-India average of women's
participation since 1951 has increased from 23.30 per cent to 27.96 per cent
and largely accounts for increase in the percentage of total working force

the greater because of the wide differences in the existing and prospective pressures. The population situation greatly increases the invalidity of the methods, which we have adopted so far in framing and executing our plans. These methods are wrong in themselves and show a lack of understanding of the essentials of planning; and the fact that our population and the increase in it are so unevenly distributed makes them (methods) all the more unsuitable and ineffective. The need for a radical change in the methods and measures of planning in India is very greatly increased by the compulsion of the population situation.

to the total population from 39.10 to 42.98 per cent. The composition of population according to age groups has since 1911 changed, 0-14 age group has increased from 1911 to 1961 from 38 per cent to 41 per cent, of 15-59 age group has fallen from 60.2 to 53.3 per cent and 60 and over has increased from 1.0 to 5.7 per cent and age structure of different states shows variations within a wide range .

These are merely illustrative figures to show how wide are the variations in the population situation in different parts of the country and how very essential it is to have regional, sub-regional, area, sub-area and village plans if planning is to be directly related to the actual needs, resources and potentials of the country.

The Institute of Applied Man Power proposes to undertake Man power surveys in 30 districts in different zones of the country and a pilot survey in Meerut district of Uttar Pradesh has already been undertaken. The object of these surveys is to provide an assessment of the existing Man power situation, to indentify specific problems and pin-point specific conclusions for policy formulations. Surveys are in fashion in this country but surveys like those undertaken by the Pilot Projects of the Community Development Administration, the Gram Ekais of the Khadi and Village Industries Commission and the Rural Industries Projects of the Planning Commission have not yielded any worthwhile results for economic evaluation and policy formulation. The Surveys of the Institute of Applied Man Power seem to be better designed and may provide a sound basis for preparation and execution of a programme of development on a properly planned basis.

Chapter Fifteen

PLANNING

FUNCTIONAL ANARCHY

It has been pointed out in specific terms all through the book how planning in India has been and is inadequate, ineffective and lacking in comprehension of its essentials. The result is that, in spite of the fact that though considerable development in agriculture, industry and communications has taken place, the economy *as a whole* has not, even in its broad outlines, become a planned economy and the planning authorities have not been able to direct or steer its course towards the chosen goals. There is a considerable amount of state intervention in the economy and its working has been largely influenced by state policy and action; but owing to the lack of coordination, clarity of purpose and intelligent understanding of and devotion to it (the purpose) on the part of the administrators and the people, the economy has, broadly speaking, been operating in an unplanned manner in spite of this intervention and its course has been largely determined by a combination of circumstances and factors which have not been amenable to public regulation and control. Planning is and has to be a long-term undertaking, and its objects and full efficiency cannot but be realized by successive stages. This is much more true of a country like India in which poverty of the people is such a stupendous problem, and their ignorance, extremely limited loyalties owing to the existence and working of the caste system and heterogeneity, create such serious hindrance in the way of developing and applying an integrated approach to the problem of the country's future. In India, of all the countries, no miracles could have worked. Impatience in the face of these difficulties could be taken as an indication of irresponsible utopianism. This, however, does not mean that all serious failings in the formulation and execution of economic and social policies have to be condoned, "functional anarchy"[1] according to Gunar Myrdal, has to be taken as a substitute for planned economy and distortions and miscarriage of social objectives of planning have not to be viewed with a sense of grave concern.

Basic Requirements

These points have been stated clearly in their different aspects in the different chapters of the book, and their re-statement is not called for; but all the same it is necessary to state altogether the basic requirements of planning in relation to the essential considerations, and examine briefly the mechanism, technique and dynamism of planning in India with a view to appraising its objects, procedure, operation and results and indicate more specifically the causes of its inadequacies, ineffectiveness and lack of comprehension of essentials. Planning in any country is conditioned by its history, social inheritance, the strength, sweep and moving capacity of the forces that are at work in it, and, of course, the quality of the leaders who are thrown up at the crucial stage of its history. Planning has been forced upon us in this country by the magnitude and urgency of our problems and the necessity of consolidating our independence at a time when the whole world is in a state of very unstable equilibrium and great dangers so obviously lie ahead for our country on that account. That the Soviet Union had already shown how much could be done by planning, in spite of the tremendous difficulties created for her by her own history and the hostile forces arrayed against her owing to the impact of her achievements on the minds of the people and the course of events and, of course, the great errors, some of them clearly avoidable, which her leaders committed in shaping their objects and policies, had greatly influenced our choice of the path of planned economy. The impressive results which

1. Gunar Myrdal. *Beyond the Welfare State*, p. 90. (The Stork Lectures— Yale University 1958)

planning has produced in China and the countries of Eastern Europe has further demonstrated what can be achieved by planning also in face of enormous difficulties. That the regimes in the Soviet Union and these countries were authoritarian did suggest and does suggest the need for important reservations in the general assessment of the mechanism and methods of planning used in these countries. The fact that in India personal freedom and civic liberties in large measure have been maintained and parliamentary political system is being honestly tried and operated, is a very fundamental difference which gives a special meaning to our efforts and achievements—a meaning which the countries involved in cold war against the communist countries want to turn to their advantage and thereby make India indirectly a partner in their crusade against them. While we have to choose our own path and learn as much from the serious mistakes of the communist countries as from their substantial achievements, we would do well not to get involved in the futile controversies about totalitarian and democratic planning.

Our own experience since independence indicates the need for real humility in this respect. We have had three free and fair elections, civil liberties, as stated above, have been largely preserved and parliamentary procedure and practices have been followed; but otherwise the actual working of our political system has not shown that we can maintain high standard of political behaviour, our polity is healthy and capable of meeting the challenge of our almost baffling problems and the parliamentary system itself has, in the conditions prevailing in a country like India, made any significant contributions to the solution of the problems of planning about the necessity of which there is a large agreement of opinion. Civil liberties and a parliamentary political system have great virtues of their own, which definitely make it worth while for us to preserve both and derive from them all the benefits which they can give; and yet we know that the parliamentary system in India is functioning in a manner which makes its future a subject of serious anxiety; and as far as the introduction and development of planned economy goes, it not only contributes little, as just pointed out, to the solution of the problems of planning but also creates difficulties in the way of objective consideration of the points at issue and in some ways defeats the very purpose of planning. This is not an argument for replacing the parliamentary system by an authoritarian one; but it does show the urgent need for serious reconsideration and of necessary revision of the parliamentary procedure and practices and the development of conventions by which the substance of democracy and not merely its form can be realized. The ballot-box democracy, as stated in a previous chapter, does not in itself in practice mean real democracy and in an inequalitarian society it means serious distortion of its essential objects and purposes. The parliamentary system is not an end in itself, but a means through which government through pursuation is meant to be carried out and active consent of the people made the basis of the entire political system. To the extent to which these objects are not realized in practice in a parliamentary system, it has to be modified to make creative participation of the people in the formulation and execution of planning policies possible and effective. The main point which needs to be thought about is that the issue of democratic or non-democratic planning is valid only in specific historic contexts, and any general presumption in favour of parliamentary system as an instrument of planning is not justified by the facts of the case. In the communist countries the new trends show that planning through fiats from above is a factor of diminishing importance; and decentralization and democratization of their economies are in progress, and it is likely that what is called administrative planning will become largely obsolete by the course of events. The basic requirements of planning are, essentially speaking, not widely different in different countries though in the formulation and implementation of concrete plans, it is all important that specific conditions and problems of a country and its people should receive their due consideration and be given the very highest priority.

The most important basic requirement of planning is that its social goal should be clearly known, generally understood, faith in it be widely shared and the social imperatives inherent in it become the obligation of the men in authority and the people in general. Planning is not merely programming or project-making though the latter are an essential part thereof. In planning continuity with the past is preserved, i.e. even when planning is based on revolutionary social premises and involves fundamental changes in social relations, a sense of history is maintained and the best in social inheritance is consciously preserved and incorporated in the new scheme of things. Planning, however, in the context of contemporary facts and conditions, means taking the economy out of its old orbit and moving it into a new one and bringing about a revaluation of values. This, of course, cannot mean that an entirely new set of values is substituted for the old values, but it does mean that a new social vision definitely becomes the ruling motive of the community and is translated into new social norms and codes and a large majority of people make an earnest effort to live up to them and for them. This, of course, means discovery of new social frontiers because of the new emergent social horizons and high level of buoyancy owing to the people partaking consciously in a great adventure. At all times of mass awakening, men acquire a new sense of human unity and feel that they are all brothers; but in terms of planning it implies that a new institutional framework is purposively created and for expression and realization of new social relations and values. In this change it is postulated that in all economic relations are implicit the governing values of the community; and if planning involves, as it must, change of values it means not merely change in men's minds, but also in the way production is organized, resources are provided for its expansion and its fruits are shared and human dignity is maintained and enhanced. The new social goal need not necessarily be socialism. It can, for example, be new humanism or a more enlightened form of liberal society or a social welfare state or community living, a new religious dispensation or reliving an old one. But it is the distinctive feature of planning today that reorganization of economy is its most cardinal object and that means that power pattern based upon property and wealth loses its validity and it is realized that a new pattern based upon division of social functions in the interest of the community has to be substituted for it. Planning, which has captured the imagination of the people all over the world is planning in terms of a classless society, of social equality, of cessation of exploitation by property-owners, of a sense of common endeavour to utilize the enormous potential productive power which modern science has placed at our disposal for the benefit of the community as a whole. This does not mean socialism as a dogma, but it does mean new social vision in which man becomes the master of his future and his own redeemer primarily through radical reorganization of the economy. Social goal in such terms is necessary for planning and without it, it cannot have much meaning or substance.

Planning necessarily means that a planning apparatus has to be created through which can be prepared an over-all plan for the country, its major constituent units and their sub-units right down to each local, urban or rural unit, each enterprise, productive undertaking or each organ of life of the community like schools, hospitals, clubs, theatres, etc. This apparatus necessarily means chain of commands and controls at different levels, lines of communication from top to bottom or the other way about, provision for a continuous interchange of views and re-adjustment necessitated by changing conditions and circumstances and a considerable scope for initiative and autonomy at each level without creating internal contradictions and conflicts.

It is generally held that planning bodies as a rule perform advisory functions and major policy decisions have to be made by political authorities, the cabinets, elective assemblies or local communities, etc. There is a distinction between formulation of plans and major policy decisions. The planning bodies have to function within the framework of broad directives of the governments which should commend a large measure of assent of the community as a whole. Within the framework of planning, organ of each major constituent unit, sub-units, etc. has to prepare a plan for its own area or undertaking and take into account and provide for its own needs and develop fully its own internal resources. Central direction with centralized formulation and execution of plans is a rule which experience of all countries, in which planning has been seriously undertaken, has been found to be of great value and is generally observed. Over-all plan, however, acquires meaning and operative importance only when it is broken down in plans for regions, states, areas and basic units and undertakings and each planning organ knows clearly the part which it has to play in the preparation and implementation of the general plan of the country. It, of course, has to be directly responsible for carrying out its own plan, but it has nevertheless to be fully aware of its part in and relation with the general plan. Planning is a highly specialized function and its organs have to acquire technical competence for discharging it; but as it is not merely a technical undertaking, planning authorities have to keep in mind its broader aspects and give them their due consideration in the discharge of these functions. Planning has to be a two-way process, general directive and formulation and execution of plans in concrete terms have to be reciprocally interdependent and continuous cantact between the country's planning organs at all levels has to be maintained and made the basis for attaining a moving equilibrium in policy-making and implementation of plans. Planning is an advisory function in the sense that planning bodies cannot be given or assume the authority to lay down the direction or purpose of development; but as directives and purposes cannot be conceived and indicated in vacuum, the planning authorities, through thought, research, and experience, have to give positive content to the directives and purposes, evaluate them

in the light of practice through vigilant control of implementation of plans, assess their impact on and reaction of the
economy to them and avoid rigidity in throught and action.
Planning bodies cannot and should not be merely bodies of
technicians who merely carry out a set of instructions and
have little to do with their formulation. Whatever the formal
position may be, the planners must necessarily have a very
important share in policy-making and safeguard integrity of
the policy at all levels and stages and bring conviction and
ardour to the performance of their duties.

It is the essence of planning that it is comprehensive and
maintains balance between resources and needs, fixes an order
of priorities among the needs and allocate resources in such a
way as to maximize the benefits of utilizing them from the
point of view of the community as a whole. Principle of
proportion is the cardinal principle of planning, i.e. as far as
possible it is necessary to evolve and apply criteria with
reference to which balance can be maintained between investment in different sectors, industries and undertakings, between
development of different areas, communities and sub-communi-
ties, and between the currency in circulation and disposable
income of individuals and value of goods on which it can
be spent which also implies that the assortment of goods in
the market has to correspond to the pattern of demand.
These balances and the criteria, in reference to which they
have to be realized, cannot be based upon any clear-cut or
sharply defined rules or formulas. Decisions in regard to them
are, in a large measure, a matter of judgement, and though
they have to be taken *ex-ante*, i.e. before production is planned and resources are allocated, and therefore the risk of
their turning out to be mistaken in the light of events has
to be taken and incurred, decisions have to be taken on the
basis of the available data, and as the planning proceeds,
deliberate effort has to be made to collect, compile and analyse
the relevent statistics in order that appraisal, formulation and
execution of major policy decisions be largely supported by

the facts of experience. These decisions can never become data derived from mathematical equations—limitations of econometric approach in planning have to be clearly understood and borne in mind, but the element of "hunches" in planning has to be reduced as far as possible and it has to be guided both by logic of facts and logic of values. Planning and value judgement must go together at all stages and levels, and therefore all through it, value considerations must remain all important. The principle of proportion has therefore to be operated within the framework of values, but statistical data collected, processed and presented as scientifically as possible, has also to provide the framework for the excercise of value judgements, i.e. the logic of facts has to be combined with logic of values and both together have to become the basis for the operation of the law of balance. The planners on the occasion of every policy decision have to judge the situation as a whole and try to remove all imbalances which may have emerged or continue to exist. Comprehensiveness of planning consists in the fact that a sense of proportion backed fully by insight acquired by a careful analysis of statistical data becomes a guide to the preparation, execution and evaluation of the plan.

In planning on a socialist basis the principle of proportion naturally requires that the communities, classes, groups and areas, which through the blind working of historical forces, have relatively speaking, lagged behind, acquire an inherent right to receive high priority and consideration and allocation of resources which they receive vary inversely to their position in the scale of development and the capacity to help themselves. Their needs presumably are most pressing and their means exceedingly limited. This imbalance has to be purposively redressed, and it has obviously to be one of the foremost tasks of the planners to devise ways and means by which this object can be realized. All sections and areas have to keep in step; and before they march together, they have to be brought into line with one another. How to reduce these

historical gaps between nations is one of the urgent international problems today. Planning on a world-scale is yet a
remote prospect; but in every planned economy which sets
itself the task of righting historical wrongs — and a planned
economy which does not undertake this task largely forfeits
its right to be considered a planned economy — has to remove
these imbalances with the utmost solicitude for the well-being
of the retarded sections and areas and make them truly a
sacred trust of the country as a whole.

Planning in the complex and diversified economies of today
has, even in under-developed countries, to rely upon the price
system for regulating production, trade and distribution of
income. The calculus of the price system has to be used as
an instrument of planning and price policy based upon social
premises of planning has to be framed with a view to realizing
the essential objects of the plan. This means, as clearly stated
in an earlier chapter, that price-structure of a planned economy
has to be an integral part of its planned cost and income
structures. This implies that autonomism of prices can have
no place in a planned economy, prices cannot and should not
determine the working of the economy and its parts and
autonomy of prices has to be replaced by the directive principles
implicit in plan objectives. It has also been pointed out earlier
that integration of price, cost and income structures must
necessarily be a long-term undertaking and carried out empirically and in stages. But the need for this integration should
be one of the basic premises of planning, and even in earlier
stages steps should be taken to promote and realize this object.
This means that currency and credit system should be directly
linked to production plan at all levels and the country should
have inter-related investment, credit and cash plans, and the
price system should work in a co-ordinated manner and respond
to the needs of a planned economy. It also follows that the
techniques of currency and credit regulation and control suited
to an unplanned economy have to be progressively superseded,
and all institutions, which perform these functions, have not

only to be publicly-owned but also operated with a view to making them organs of introducing and developing a planned socialist economy.

A planned economy necessarily involves structural changes, i.e. shift in its power-pattern at all levels has to take place, a new set of social relations has to be established and developed, a new institutional framework has to be provided and, of course, new social values have to be made the basis of the new social structure. All these changes have to be planned, new social foundations have to be laid, in perspective as well as well as short term and current planning; the stages by which these structural changes have to be realized have to be broadly indicated and progress towards the goal has to be vigilantly watched with care and earnestness and provision made against the inevitable resistance to the realization of this object. Broad strategy and tactics of the process have to be clearly known, stated and planned for. This is really the most important aspect of planning, for without this change its social purpose is bound to be defeated and democratic processes through which advance towards socialism can be realized cannot be brought into play, i.e. the people who have not participated in the community life on the basis of equality or rather have been deprived of its benefit owing to their having laboured under serious disabilities, cannot be given the necessary confidence and capacity to play their part in making the future and power of money and its tools cannot be broken. Structural changes cannot be planned in the same way in which a programme, say, of constructing roads, can be planned and carried out. But nevertheless if serious thought is given to this aspect of planning, seats of power and authority of those who are for status quo and against a basic social change, can be indentified and a planned effort made for their removal from positions of power by developing and exercising the countervailing power at all levels. In a real political democracy, the Government itself, to use the words of Rural Credit Survey, becomes a combination of the weak, throw its entire weight in favour of the structural changes and create and strenthen the processes which may favour and promote these changes.

Planning, it was stated above, is a two-way process. It is a process of framing directives and general targets from above, but these directives, unless they are broken into plans going down to the very basic level and in specific terms, can have no content or operative meaning. In other words, what is called planning from below is an essential part of planning and there can be no real planning without it. Organs of planning at the basic level have, if this object is to be realized, to be created and acquire vitality and function not only with the consent but active participation of the people. In theory planning from below was to be made a reality in the communist countries, but as is generally admitted, in practice there was really no planning from below in these countries. Yugoslavia realized the error of this procedure and has been earnestly trying to retrieve the position. In other communist countries also similar attempts are now being made though as yet it is not clear as to what measure of success they have in fact achieved. Their experience is conclusive against highly centralized planning and is strongly in favour of the necessity of planning from below. Centralized planning defeats its own purpose, creates bureaucratic rigidities and saps the vitality of a planned economy. Planning from below can, however, succeed only if democratization of the economy is progressively realized and all monopolies of power and position are broken. This is not merely a matter of inviting proposals from the operative unit and building up integrated plans for villages, towns, areas and sub-areas and federalizing the whole planning structure. That can only be done if the whole economy is federalized, is polycentred and the smallest unit in practice excercises a large degree of autonomy. This means combining integration with decentralization and reverse the trends in favour of centralization which are at work everywhere. The whole economy needs to be planned from an entirely different point of view. Many political thinkers have in thought projected this economy, but it has not as yet been realized anywhere.

Planning, if it is to succeed, requires a spirit of consecration on the part of the community as a whole but particularly of its elite. If planning means, as it must, a profound social change, if it means an entirely new set of social relations, new social values and a new way of life, it can be effective only if at least the key men at different levels are full of a sense of mission, know and understand the future they are working for and acquire the competence to realize it not merely as a vision but as an operating reality. In the communist countries the communist parties were meant to assume and discharge this role; and with all their faults and failings, they have in fact shown what dedicated work for a new way of life can accomplish. The communist parties cannot be created in non-communist countries as ruling parties; but in all planned economies it can and should be realized that a spirit of dedication, a self-disciplined cadre of men, for whom social objectives of planning are the very breath of their life and who work for them without any thought for themselves, are needed to make their planned economy a success in the real sense. How to create this cadre is a problem in planning which so far has not received any attention in spite of the fact that thinkers like H. G. Wells made it a pivot of their thought. It is not possible to posit whether there is an answer to this problem; and if there is, what it is. But a dedicated self-disciplined cadre of men, who are not a sect and do not profess a cult and yet have a sense of purpose, a coherent outlook and capacity of concerted action, is needed, more particularly at the initial stages, to give a planned economy a good start and carry it through successive stages of growth. All this needs to be seriously thought about and planned for. It will not be possible to attain perfection in planning for this all-important object but an approximation to it may be attainable. Anyway, if the supreme importance of this object is realized, an earnest effort will be made to achieve it.

Democracy and planning are not only naturally compatible

out are both needed for the effective introduction and development of planned economy. But where doubts are expressed
as to whether both can be combined, what the sceptics have
in mind is the content and working of parliamentary democracy as it exists in India and other newly independent under-
developed countries. In a large number of them the parliamentary system has already been abandoned, military or political
dictatorships have been established and the outlook for the
restoration of parliamentary institutions is really dark. In
countries like India and Ceylon, in which these institutions
are still working, it is known that a position of stability has
not yet been attained and serious dangers lie ahead. Even in
a country like France, parliamentary system has broken down
and no remedy has been found for the grave evils arising
from the rivalries of many political parties. In India it is
known that deterioration of parliamentary democracy is in
progress, the dominant position of the ruling party is mainly
due to historical causes and until lately the outstanding position of its leader, and the political position is known to be
exceedingly unstable. In theory no way out is clear. The
people have to be activized and educated to participate in democratic processes, decentralized planning and administration has
to be introduced and the power of political machines and the
powerful interests, which are using them to promote their
own ends, has to be broken. All this is necessary and desirable;
and if it is realized in spirit and not merely in letter, a democracy which will make planning, not only possible, but give
it the necessary strength, vigour and social content, can and
will be brought into being. This is an immense task not
only for India but in all countries in which parliamentary
system is being given a trial and also even in countries in
which it has been established for a long time. Planning or
no planning, the system is being subjected to severe strain in
face of the immense problems which it has to face on a world
scale. In the countries in which it has already been eclipsed
or there is a serious risk of its breakdown, its failure is not

due to planning in excess but its own inherent weakness. Democracy in a country like India has its stresses not because an attempt to introduce a planned economy is being made but because our people are unequal to the task of making it a success. If it can be saved at all, it will be through integrated decentralized planning and regeneration of true spirit of democracy among the people. The question as to whether democracy and planning can be combined raises a false issue. The question really is as to whether democracy can survive without planning, i.e. without a purposive introduction and development of a socialist society. The essence of democracy has to be preserved, but as pointed out before, not necessarily the form. The way out is not easy, but a way out has to be found—not only for India but for democracy itself. Demagogy, mad passions, opportunistic manoeuvres and manipulations and, of course, sinister designs of interests entrenched in position of power which frustrate not only planning, but also undermine democracy and place its future in jeopardy, are the real hazards to which democracy is exposed. Democracy can be saved by more democracy and not less — by its true spirit; and if it can be saved, it not only can and will be combined with planning but both will be found indispensible for each other. The countries in which, for historical reasons, authoritarian regimes have been established, i.e. in the communist countries, it is being realized more and more that inner democracy has to be revived and strengthened, the people's initiative has to be made effective and fear eliminated. In Soviet Union it has already been recognized that the stage for a big move in this direction has been reached and it has to be made. In other communist countries what is called 'thaw" has already been at work and the process cannot be long delayed even in China. A drama of truly epic proportions is being enacted on a world scale, which has in it the possibility of a new world coming into being — a world of peace, co-operation and true democracy.[2]

---

2. The Sino-Soviet conflict, the split in the communist parties all over

No one can forecast what the course will be and what phases it will go through. Democracy and planning in terms of social-ism are an essential part of this drama since both are needed for carrying the world, including India, to its future.

MECHANICS OF PLANNING

In India the Planning Commission is the main organization of planning — really the only one and practically speaking there are no other planning authorities in the country. The Planning Commission in theory is an advisory body, but in practice it has a very effective share in policy making and its growing power and authority have been viewed with grave misgivings. All important policy decisions, all important programmes and projects at the central and state levels, as a rule, are considered and approved by it before they are sanctioned by the cabinet and funds are provided for it. Lines of demarcation between area of its responsibility and that of the Ministries are not clearly laid down.[3] The latter,

the world and the tensions which are thereby created, make the immediate outlook really gloomy from the point of view of social democracy. This dark cloud over international horizon may, however, before long pass away. Let us hope that it will.

3. The divergence of views over the appointment of the Education Commission, which has recently arisen between the Planning Commission and the Ministry of Education, illustrates this point very clearly. The fact that even the need for planning the development of education as an integral part of a developing socialist society has been no part of whatever thinking on education has taken place in India since independence has to be taken as one of the most clear indications of distortions in planning which has taken place in this country. That a socialist society must have its own system of education with new purpose, objects and operative techniques should be self-evident and it should also be self-evident that teachers in the new system have to be men of socialist convictions and apply their minds, energy and creative ability to the task of introducing and developing this new system. This evident proposition has, however, not received anything like its due consideration, and though there is a reference to a socialist pattern of society in the terms of reference of the newly appointed Education Commission and it is admitted that it is necessary to revolutionize the traditional educational system to create a new social order, it is fairly clear that, generally speaking, profound

besides implementing policy decisions, take an active share in their formulation, are associated with the deliberations of the Planning Commission in regard to matters falling within their competence and in theory the final decisions are taken on a co-operative basis and embody the largest measure of common agreement. When Jawaharlal Nehru was alive, when there was a wide difference of opinions, the view which could enlist his support, generally prevailed but the position in this respect is still very undefined and uncoordinated policy decisions, illustrated by the appointment of the Education Commission, are made and create anomalies.

Even in the communist countries the chairmen of the Planning Commissions are, as a rule, men of high political standing and other members are not merely technical experts. In the nature of things it is not possible to make planning merely a matter of technical advice. It is essentially a socio-economic process and politics is its very substance. But it is necessary

and far-reaching bearing of socialism on the future of education in this country is neither adequately and fully understood nor appreciated.

The fact, that there was not even consultation between the Planning Commission and the Education Ministry on the question of the appointment of the Education Commission, shows the extent of confusion of purposes and policies in the planning processes in India. This is not only a grave failure in co-ordination but infringement of the very essential objects of planning.

That there is a risk of extensive political and social indoctrination, if a dogmatic attitude is adopted towards the introduction and development of socialist education, has to be admitted; but indoctrination and creative socialist education are poles apart and it has to be one of the most important objects of creative thinking on the subject that this inherent risk should be fully provided against. But that does not in the least impair the validity of the point that socialism has a profound bearing on the future of education and, as a matter of fact, cannot be realized without a system of socialist education. For want of space (the subject really needs a book to itself) it has not been possible to include the treatment of the all-important role of socialist education in socialist transformation of the Indian economy, but nevertheless it has to be understood and clearly borne in mind that without an adequate and successful system of socialist education there cannot and will not be any socialism in this country, or in any other country.

to attain in plan-making a large measure of detachment, objectivity and capacity to view major issues in the perspective of their inter-relations, of their long-term consequences and of the economy as a whole. Social premises have to be clearly borne in mind in all planning decisions and conformity to them has to be the prime responsibility of the central organ of planning. These conditions cannot be fulfilled in India because neither the cabinet ministers nor the other members are in a position to acquire and exercise these qualities. The cabinet ministers are overburdened with the work of their ministries and being active politicians, they cannot have the inclination, even if they have the time, to take an over-all view of things and bring the necessary comprehension to the performance of their duties as members of the Planning Commission. They are outstanding men, their association with plan-making gives it political prestige, but it does not give the process the necessary qualities referred to above. Politics and planning are and have to be clearly co-related, but serenity and balance are two essential attributes needed for planning; and under a parliamentary system, participation in active politics does not help in acquiring or strengthening these attributes. This deficiency is not made up by appointment of some junior politicians and a number of administrators to the Commission. The latter though known for their ability have no special qualifications or experience for planning and generally not only do not support socialism but from all reports it appears they have really negative interest in it, i.e. are opposed to it. That they have been included at all in the Commission is its own commentary on planning in India. Recent inclusion of an economist of standing in the Planning Commission is a step in the right direction, but its significance in the whole context is obviously limited.

Ten years ago a beginning in planning had to be made, and it was necessary for the Prime Minister to make appointments to the Planning Commission which, under the circumstances, seemed to be most desirable. But experience has clearly shown that combination of senior ministers, junior politicians and retired capable administrators without any interest in wider social objectives and really out of accord with them is one of the very important reasons of the failure of planning in India. A complete overhaul of the central organ of planning as a necessary part of building up the new apparatus of planning is called for. The latter has to be developed as an integral constituent of new social institutional framework of the country. Planning apparatus in India has, owing to lack of real social change in the country, been merely a make-shift arrangement and has neither struck roots nor acquired a vitality of its own. The Planning Commission being really the only organ of planning in the country, displays all the faults of improvisation to the greatest degree. Improvisation at initial stage, as stated above, was unavoidable, but after fourteen years of experience in planning the necessity of making it a part of an over-all new social process has become obvious. The Planning Commission, if it is to be more than a complicated appendix, has to be backed by deep stirrings in the life of the people and their most positive expression at the top. In an economy, which is, from social standpoint, not only stagnant but also decadent, the Planning Commission cannot excercise the function of directing, steering and vigilantly watching the economy to advance towards socialism. It is doubtful whether collectively it itself is deeply concerned about it or is in a position to make its realization its primary obligation. The central organ of planning must not get deeply involved in day-to-day administration or in the inevitable complications of a developing and changing economy. Detachment is a necessary condition for its successful functioning, but it has to be central organ of new life and its most effective instrument and expression. The Planning Commission in India was constituted as an adjunct of government but should have grown into an institution with broadening and deepening functions and become really a nerve centre of integrated changes and development. The fact that it has not yet outgrown its initial limitations is due to, as stated above, the whole economy being unfavourable to the process which it should have initiated and developed.

The Planning Commission has a staff which, according to the available information, comprises of about a dozen administrators, the technical officers and secretariat and clerical personnel. It has ten general branches and twelve special subject branches. These branches consist of technical experts who collect the material on general and specific problems, analyse it from the point of view of planning and present the issues on which the decision needs to be taken. The ministries have their own technical officers, who practically do the same work and there is hardly any significant difference between their output and that of the technical staff of the Planning Commission. In theory the Planning Commission staff deals with major issues and from wider standpoint bring to bear experience of working in a different and wider context on the performance of their duties; but in fact, largely speaking, there is a duplication of work and most of it is of routine type and involves merely collection and compilation of data which should be readily available from the technical staff of the Ministries and the institutions like the Reserve Bank. The Planning Commission needs a staff of its own which could come into close grip with so many new and unsettled issues of planning for a socialist economy in the making and investigate intensively with earnestness and to a purpose all the challenging problems of changing Indian economy into a developing socialist economy. A staff of 50 instead of the present strength of technical officers of over 160 would suffice if it was understood that highly paid and well-qualified staff of the Planning Commission has really to function at a much higher level, do creative work in thinking and social analysis and present their contributions with a view to stimulating and developing new trends in economic growth and change. It would be really possible to go further and organize the work of the Economic and Statistical Staff of all ministries, the Reserve Bank, State Bank, etc. from this standpoint, co-ordinate the work of the senior staff and not waste ability of high order merely in duplication and routine work. It should be possible for the Planning Commission's technical staff really to give a lead in this re-organization and raise the work of the social scientists in government administration and public institutions to a much higher level of performance. As it is, there is under utilization and bad utilization of highly trained and well-paid social scientists on a large scale which, besides involving financial waste, means that many men of ability and promise are being placed in a position in which the best in them is being lost and they are being conditioned to adopt bureaucratic attitude to their work instead of striking new paths. This is a problem in planning the organization and work of the planners themselves — which could and should have been given thought to in the very early stages of planning. The fact that even the need for this departure was not understood is still another indication of the poverty of thinking in general and in planning in particular. The result is that the social scientists in a very large number have been turned into bureaucrats, i.e. made routine-minded, have no awareness of social issues and are experts in "making work" instead of dealing with real problems of our economy and thinking earnestly as to how they can be solved and injecting a new element in bureaucratic administration. This great loss has to be retrieved and will be when planning in the right sense becomes an instrument of the new economy.

The Planning Commission has also worked through a number of other agencies, some ad-hoc, others permanent, which have been given a role in planning. Among them what are called working groups are significant. For the Third Five Year Plan, for example, a large number of such ad-hoc groups were constituted and their reports were made available before the plan was finalized. They functioned at expert level, reviewed the position as it developed under the two plans, suggested measures for remedying the defects of development programmes and also indicated the line and extent of growth in particular

There is at the state level no planning machinery. The Planning Departments exist and the Chief Ministers generally are the ministers in charge, but otherwise there is no planning process in the states, their plans are a collection of departmental estimates and they (states) increasingly depend upon the Centre for financing them. As pointed out before, that has not given them greater internal consistency, or made any contribution to their being balanced in relation to the other states' plans. Negotiation with the Centre for allocation for five year and annual plans is a process of not even a very refined political bargaining without any reference to objective standard, criteria, tests or means. The ordinary administration of the states is responsible for the preparation and execution of plans and at all stages departmental rivalries, overlapping of jurisdictions, bottlenecks created by lack of effective over-all superintendence and control and, of course, lack of co-ordination have free play. In effect it means that at the state level, even much more than at the centre, there is no planning in the real sense, there are no planning boards or commissions and the administrators prepare and implement development programmes and projects without knowing and paying any heed to the essentials of planning. The Planning Commission is now trying to pursuade the states to constitute Planning Boards of their own; but even if it succeeds, it will mean that replicas of the Commission will be created at the state level and not that real planning will be introduced in the States or a planned economy will begin to operate in the country. As the states are responsible for about half the planned development expenditure and discharge the most important functions, absence of planning in the States obviously creates an insuperable barrier in the development and working of a planned economy in the country. At the Centre also planning machinery, as stated above, is working badly and disregarding in practice the basic requirements of planning; but the position is little better than in the States. It is necessary both at the Centre and in the States to realize that in India there is no real planning or planned economy at present and a radical change of approach and direction is needed if the position is to be materially improved from the point of view of planning.

The most fundamental defect of planning in this country has still to be mentioned. There has been a talk of planning from below since 1951, but no action has been taken to realize this object. There are planning bodies at the district and block level and village plans have been in the air for a long time, but there are no district, block or village development plans, and it has been pointed out before, the very idea of village plans has now been all but abandoned. Without plans for each village, a group of villages (area plans) and district plans in specific terms, planning in this country cannot but remain meaningless, and there can be, without them, an illusion of plan-making, but no real planning. This point has been duly stressed before, and it is not necessary to elaborate it here. The fact is that the very fundation of planning is lacking in this country. There is a plan for the country but a plan in terms of statistical aggregates and not an operative plan of a mandatory character in which every production or administrative unit knows its obligations and resources and is prepared to play its part with knowledge and determination. A plan must necessarily consist of targets of achievements and resources in concreate terms, all co-ordinated and inter-related, on an ascending scale of continuous co-operative efforts and achievements. Our plans have been and are void of real content because there is no planning from below in this country and in the Third Plan, in spite of the Panchayat Raj and increase in the number of co-operatives, the prospect of this process being started in earnest, is not at all bright.

Planning in the private sector is even more nebulous than in the public sector. As stated before there is no planning in agricultural production, small industries, trade, construction, etc., and it is not known how the targets of investment and production given in the plans are framed and actually realized. Of the total investment of Rs 4,100 crores in the

Third Plan, in the private sector, besides investment of Rs 1,050 crores in organized industries and mining, Rs 3,050 crores are to be invested in agriculture, power, village and small industries, transport and communications, social service and inventries. There is no way of knowing how these estimates have been framed, what criteria have been adopted for the purpose and what is the territorial distribution of this investment. The funds for this purpose, apart from the provision of co-operative credit, it is presumed, are to be privately raised and utilized, their sources are neither indicated nor is it known as to how they will be tapped or channelized. There is really not even a pretence of planning in nearly three-fourths of the planned investment in the private sector, it is more a matter of guess work than of planning, and no one can say how far actual investment will even approximate to the planned estimates. This amount of Rs 3,050 crores is nearly 30 per cent of the total planned investment under the Third Plan, and to the extent to which it is based upon amorphous considerations, it also affects the validity of the plan as a whole.

In regard to the investment of Rs 1,050 crores there has been consultation with the Chamber of Commerce and representatives of the private-sector industries and the Development Councils which have been set up by the Ministry of Commerce and Industries for important industries. What these discussions amount to in practice, how the targets of investment and production and how their distribution in different parts of the country are fixed is again not known. But it is extremely unlikely that any objective tests and criteria have been applied and industrial development in the private sector is planned with reference to them. Out of the total amount of Rs 1,050 crores, which the private sector is going to invest in industry nearly 60 per cent, i.e. Rs 600 crores are to be drawn from internal sources, i.e. accumulated reserves. On the utilization of this amount there is no public control and there is no way of ensuring that the actual investments will correspond to the planned estimates. Import control could be used to regulate the import of capital goods; but from what is known about the working of import control, it can well be posited that it cannot be depended upon to secure even broad correspondence between planned estimates and actual investments.

There are no organs of planning so far as the private sector is concerned. The only way in which planning can be effectively introduced in this sector is that in agriculture, trade and small industries, the co-operatives and their federations should be organized, and in relation to large organized industries, the organization of each major industry should function as an instrument of planning, implementation, regulation and control. It is when self-government in organized industry is introduced in this sense, and the organizations of major industries cease to be instruments of increasing pressure and become institutions through which economic administration of industries can be carried out, that the present chaotic state of things will end, and the private sector will be assimilated in the national plan and subjected to its discipline. At present not only investment and production in the private sector are planned in a nebulous way, but there is no means by which responsibility for the implementation of the plan can be devolved upon duly constituted organ of planned development. The federal co-operatives and the organization of major organized industries can, as self-governing institutions, be "invested with the public interest" and while protecting the legitimate interests of their members, can be assigned public obligations in the matter of planning, development, co-ordination, regulation and control.

In large industries, the private sector should be a factor of diminishing importance as the country advances towards socialism; but so long as it lasts, it has, through self-government in industry, to accept and discharge public obligations and function according to the new social values and standards. That is, it has to accept honestly socialism as the goal of the economy and live up to its requirements. This point is implicit in the view of the Planning Commission that th

have the first priority, i.e. the plan is a socialist plan.

The technique of planning in order to attain the above object has to be developed with experience and in the context of specific conditions of a country. In the First Plan the development programme, which was already in operation, was dressed up as a plan and given an orderly appearance. In the Second and Third Plans, however, more specious considerations were taken into account and planning was intended to have greater cogency and consistency. We should have given to synchronization, phasing and removal of imbalance more serious consideration and developed, if, planning was to be planning at all, objective tests, criteria and standards with reference to which the choice of relativities could have been made. Even at later stages our limitations of organization and technical resources circumscribed our freedom of action in this regard; but all the same an earnestness to attain some degree of objectivity in planning was called for. In all objective considerations the need for compromises due to pressures and counter-pressures has to be allowed for, and it is not possible to give it (objectivity) a complete sway over actual decisions; but even then it was necessary to adopt a technique of planning in which the choice of relativities based upon the logic of values and logic of facts could be made and express itself in the structure of the plan. Our most serious omission, as far as the technique of planning is concerned, has been that the need for objective criteria in the choice of relativities has not been understood or provided for and our plans have been, still are without an inner meaning of their own derived from the application of the principle of proportions in planning. It has to be repeated that owing to our organizational and technical limitations we could not have attained a high standard of performance. But even in the preparation of the Second and certainly of the Third Plan we should have made an earnest effort to develop and apply this technique within the limit of our capacity and tried to make planning a meaningful process in terms of needs, resources, relative position of different sections and areas and, of course, our social objectives.

This we have not done and not even attempted to do. The result is that our major decisions with regard to investment and production, choice of technique, provision for different purposes and areas have been made on an *ad hoc* basis, often through unedifying bargaining between the Centre and the States and the different central ministries, and no measuring rods have been found and used for developing an orderly pattern of investment, production and development. The result is that the daily results show that developments of different sectors, e.g. coal and railways do not keep in step with one-another, bottlenecks develop, we do not look ahead, advance planning in matters, in which foresight is essential, has not taken place, and we are all the time up against difficulties which could and should have been anticipated. If we examine our planned targets of, say, foodgrains, cement, steel, communications in financial and real terms, we will realize that these were adopted without any careful assessment of needs, possibilities and resources. In the Plan reports no indication is given as to why these targets have been adopted and how they all hang together. As a matter of fact they do not, the whole pattern is lacking in symmetry and consistency and it is clear that whatever relativities are implicit in it are not due to the adoption and application of any rational calculus. Owing to this fact in important fields like agriculture, small industries, internal and external trade there is no plan at all, and even in large industries both in public and private sectors our development plans as regards choice of industries, their location and their relative importance has been more or less made on an *ad hoc* basis. Pressures and counter-pressures are being applied, industries reserved for public sector are, without any adequate reason or explanation, being transferred to the private sector and we have planned for foreign assistance to nearly one-third of our required resources without counting its cost or risks and are finding to our discomfiture that plans of foreign assistance, which are, we should know, incidents of cold war, do not correspond to our pattern and timing of requirements. All this means that projects and programmes have not been rightly integrated and co-ordinated, which is another way of saying that the essentials of planning have been disregarded in the formulations of these programmes.

The technique of planning also requires that all methods of regulations and control should be used in a co-ordinated manner in the implementation of the plan and any compartmentalization of regulatory apparatus should be carefully avoided. We are not lacking in regulatory devices. Import and export control, regulation and licensing of industries, public fixation of prices of a number of essential commodities like steel, cement, coal, soda ash, etc., capital issues control, control over the formation and operation of the joint stock companies, control over the movement of food grains—to mention the most important controls, can, if they are operated not compartmentally but as instruments of planning in a co-ordinated manner, be of great importance in the operation of planning. But in fact it is clear that they are not being used in a co-ordinated manner. The foreign exchange crisis in 1958, which took us unawares, showed not only that our right hand does not know what our left hand is doing but even ordinary precaution of keeping a watch on the developing situation is not being observed, and all the foreign exchange sections of the Reserve Bank, the Finance Ministry and the Planning Commission could not warn us against this process of depletion of our foreign reserves while this process was under way. This dramatic demonstration of the lack of co-ordination of operation of controls, however, has not made any difference to their unco-ordinated operation. Not only are they still being administered in a vexatious manner, but continue to suffer from lack of co-ordination and means of bringing it about have hardly received any consideration.

Failure of price policy—or rather our inability to develop a price policy—to which an extended reference was made in a previous chapter, is a self-imposed limitation and shows our inability to grasp the obvious point that a planned economy and free price system cannot go together. Not that our prices are determined by free play of market forces, they are not. A large number of them are subject to regulation and control, but no principles of public fixation of prices have been evolved and applied and even no thought has been given to them. We have, on that account, plenty of public intervention in price system but no price-planning, and a technique, which, it is admitted, is needed for flexible operation of planned economy is, owing to the pressures of vested interests, being very ineptly used and with very harmful results. Planned price structure has to be an essential part of any planned economy. But as our economy, in spite of all intervention in its working, still remains an unplanned economy, we have not realized how essential it is that a planned price structure should be developed and made an effective instrument of the technique of planning.

Our technique of planning, it is clear, is as inadequate and ineffective as its mechanism; and this is due to the fact that this technique has not yet become a functional necessity. A technique is adopted and applied only when an organism feels it is needed for its operation. As planning in India is still its own negation, it cannot adopt a technique which is needed for genuine planning.

DYNAMICS OF PLANNING

Planning as a process needs a moving force—a momentum generated within the economy and growing at a cumulative rate. It is admitted that planning in India is lacking in this essential quality more than any other essential, and it has failed to produce results primarily on that account. Inadequacy of planning mechanism can be largely reduced by changes in commands and controls and understanding of its essentials. But if it is to become dynamic, i.e. if it is to move onwards by power generated within the economy, power pattern has to be changed, new social relations have to be established, leaders,

who owe their position to the confidence which they inspire
and capacity which they are known to possess, have to be
thrown up and a widely shared vision of the future has to
become the moving and sustaining spirit of the economy. The
fact that we are at present seriously handicapped owing to lack
of these dynamic elements is making our common endeavour
anaemic and unfruitful. There is no recipe for creating dynamism needed for making the planning process an attribute of
the economy as a whole. The economy itself has to be fundamentally changed, and it is the theme of this book that most
of the changes, which have taken place in the planning period,
have made the entire planning process less and not more
favourable for rapid growth, and the economy has been moving in low or rather reverse gear from the standpoint of socialist transformation of the economy. All the changes indicated
in the book are intended primarily to remove this fundamental
deficiency and bring into play forces without which planning
must remain only an exercise in econometrics and statistical
techniques not unoften of a doubtful value. As a life process it
is necessary to link it with the main springs of the economy—
movements in the minds and hearts of the people and patterns
of their social relations and behaviour.

Is it possible to plan that this dynamism may become common property of the life of our people? Is it possible to raise
them above the present level and get them to function on a
community basis and in its interest? Is it possible to tap their
hidden reserves by a process of social exploration and discovery
and making these available for the operation of the economy?
Is it possible to bring about these changes and let the people
go ahead with faith in themselves and without fear? No one
knows the answers to these questions, and yet we know that
springs of energy and social steam of our people have not been
even touched and the prevailing social inertia is a phase
and not a permanent quality of our national life. Social technique of overcoming this obstacle has to be known, acquired,
developed and exercised. We cannot and should not assume

that life in India will keep flowing at the low ebb at which it has been flowing for the last fourteen years and a new and swelling tide in it cannot rise and carry us forward to our future. We must assume that a real upswing in our community life is possible, and given the necessary insight and endeavour it can and will take place. This assumption has to be an act of faith, but we have to know that without new tide in our affairs planning will remain pursuit of very small men lost to any sense of national destiny or insight into the true inwardness of the core of socialist planning. There are priorities if this task is to be accomplished with success, and among them the highest is that the power of money at all levels has to be weakened and vanquished if we are to make any headway against our baffling difficulties. This has to be the primary purpose of our social strategy and tactics. Merely a change in power pattern, though of fundamental importance, is not enough. The technique of taming power itself has to be acquired and a deeper dynamism than the one needed for a shift in power pattern is needed if planning is to produce lasting results and carry guarantees for the future in itself. Transfer and taming of power are twin processes and have to operate at the same time; and the qualities needed for one can with understanding be used also for the other. At present our planning is ineffective and without any potential for the future because we have not put first things first—we really do not believe in the values which we profess, our declaration of these values has a hollow ring and convinces no one, not even the men in authority. The secret of this dynamism is that we should live these values and enrich them with living experiences. This may appear to be a commonplace conclusion of a complicated argument on planning but it is nevertheless a sound conclusion and is of profound significance.

This point has also a bearing on what is called perspective planning and a brief reference to it is needed. Our horizon in planning has to be wide and we have to know as best as we can what the shape of things is likely to be at least fifteen or twenty years hence and make our knowledge the basis of our plans. Among the projections which we have to make, the growth of population, its composition, distribution, age-structure and fertility rates are obviously of primary importance. Any long-term forecasts of population, when a deliberate effort is being made to restrict the rate of its growth, cannot but be speculative owing to the inevitable uncertainty attached to forecasts about the changes in human behaviour in the sphere of deep personal intimacies; but as all persons, who for the next fifteen years are going to join the working force, will have to be supported and can contribute to economic growth, have already been born, reasonable forecasts of the impact of their number on the working, needs and productivity of our economy can be made on the basis of long-term planning and our plans of housing, schools, hospitals, etc. and, of course, employment can be prepared on this basis. But it is also necessary to forecast the rate of economic growth in the country as a whole and in different areas and match it with the rate of population growth and its structure. This can be done on the assumption like the rate of investment, capital output ratio, needs and resources of different regions and states and the effect of our planning on their relative position. But even more important than these are assumptions about the structural changes in the economy, changes in property-relations, distribution of wealth and income and in social priorities of individual and community life. These assumptions make the task of perspective planning infinitely more complex and difficult, but as our perspective planning cannot possibly be a set of projections based upon static assumptions, we have to give due importance to this all-important fact in all our long-range plans. This can be done if there is a clear conception of what is to be done on a planned basis in the field of social dynamics, how the necessary forces are to be generated, directed and channelized and what is to be the shape of the social structure which has to be built up in place of the existing decadent social structure. All this makes the task of perspective planning, it may be said again, far more difficult and makes it necessary to take into account a large number of variables and their inter-dependence. But unless the scope of perspective planning is extended to the field of social dynamics, it will lose most of its meaning and practical importance. We are living not only in a fast changing world but also in a world which we want to change with a purpose and as rapidly as possible. Perspective planning has to be co-related to this fundamental fact and to acquire a realistic and deeper significance on that account. Our present exercises in perspective planning are mostly projections of the existing trends, i.e. they do not involve any planning at all, but make provision for the future on the basis of the general social framework remaining more or less the same. This is obviously a very wrong approach to a very important aspect of planning and has to be abandoned.

PARLIAMENTARY SYSTEM AND PLANNING

In conclusion a word may be said about the relation of parliamentary system to planning. For effective planning it is necessary to have an agreement among those who are in power on the essentials of policy, continuity in the formulation and execution of plans and broad support among the people for major decisions of development and social change. It is obvious that if there is discord on essentials in the cabinet, the change of government owing to one ruling party being replaced by another which is directly opposed to the other in matters of major importance and uses its political power to frustrate or reverse the policy decisions of the party ousted from power and the people are sharply divided over fundamentals and the divisions arouse passions and conflicts, planning in the sense explained above, cannot be introduced or carried out under a parliamentary system. In a country like France if the party conflicts make stable governments impossible the parties are not only in conflict with one another but are fundamentally antagonistic to one another. If the people are divided in their convictions and loyalties and prepared to resort to force to resist policy decisions unacceptable to them, there can be no planning. Under such conditions radical changes on an agreed basis in the working of the parliamentary system without negating the essentials of the government by consent have to be made if democracy and planning have to be combined for preparing and implementing comprehensive plans. Planning of the kind now being implemented in France under which she has, in spite of political instability, attained a high level of prosperity in the last few years, is possible and is being carried out by capitalist monopolies is not planning in a real sense. Even in advanced countries experience of parliamentary democracy has clearly shown that the system has created serious problems and if it is to meet the challenge with which every country is confronted, the working of parliamentary democracy has to be modified in order to avoid political instability, party conflicts and passionate politics. But experience has also shown that it is not easy to introduce the required modifications, and De Gaullism, as stated before, is not an answer to this problem even in France, much less in other countries.

In the undeveloped countries even short post-independence experience has discredited parliamentary democracy in most countries; and even in India, as is well known, this system is creating severe strain and the position is far from stable. The limitations of the parliamentary system from every point of view, but particularly from the point of view of planning, have to be realized and search for the necessary changes has to be seriously undertaken. A planned and largely agreed change in the parliamentary system is urgently called for. Alternative is a totalitarian monolithic regime; if that is to be ruled out, a system broadly supported by a large majority of the people and accountable to them and yet free from the more serious evils of the parliamentary regime has to be conceived, evolved and made a workable proposition. This matter requires all the earnest thought that it needs, and an early solution to it has to be found not to save the parliamentary system in these countries, but democracy itself. The problem, to repeat, is urgent; and it is a race against time and early action is called for.

But it is also necessary to add that our parliamentary system is in no way responsible for inadequacy of planning in India. As Congress has been continuously in power all these years at the Centre and in the States[5] its political authority to formulate and carry out policy decisions has never been in question and Congress could have, if it was so minded, planned on a comprehensive and integrated basis, implemented the plans with determination and vigour and mobilized the support of the people for the purpose. It also has not been prevented from carrying out effective planning owing to the quasi-federal character of our constitution. The States are not only amenable to central guidance and control owing to their having been under Congress rule, but also their increasing financial dependence makes it very difficult for them to adopt obstructive attitude in planning as in most other important matters. The failure of planning in India is not due to the parliamentary system but owing to the lack of understanding of its essentials on the part of the Government, unwillingness to take the necessary consequential measures to make planning a reality and more than the other causes, to the increasing concentration of economic and political power at all levels in the hands of the men of wealth and property and their growing control over the men in power in the Government, in political parties and all other key positions. If early action is not taken by all people and parties who care for planning and socialism to combat these trends, even such planning as we have in the country will become impossible and the future of both democracy and socialism will be seriously jeopardized. As stated above, an

5. This statement is subject to the exception that in Kerala the Communist Government was formed and functioned for some months. The latter (the communist government) however was prepared to carry out with greater sincerity and determination the programme of the Congress Party itself. This, it is well known, was made impossible for it. It was ousted and had to make way first for Presidential rule and later for a coalition, which was united on being anti-communist but on nothing else.

early revision of the tenets of parliamentary democracy is urgently needed, all ideas, energy, resources and organized strength of what are generally called progressive forces have to be pooled for effective action. Time, to repeat, is running out and unless the dangers looming ahead are met well in advance, there is no prospect of saving socialism and democracy in India. If the battle is lost in this country, it will, it is obvious, have a very unfavourable impact on all newly independent undeveloped countries and balance of forces in the world as a whole will be seriously disturbed.

Chapter Sixteen

THE PROSPECT

WE LOST our way when we started on the road to planning in 1951; and since then we have not been able to find it in spite of a large measure of state intervention, very considerable public investment, and the growing insistent affirmation that for India socialism is the only way to the future. With the passing away of Jawaharlal Nehru, the position has become even more uncertain. The problem of succession has, for the time being, been peacefully and smoothly solved and there is, as stated in the opening pages of this book, a basis for subdued optimism. That, however, is only a beginning of the post-Nehru era and in itself is no answer to our extremely difficult problems. We owe a lot to Nehru, but the situation, we are confronted with, has arisen because we have, in practice, shown very little understanding of the essentials of socialism, planning and the art of consolidation of political independence. Lack of clear policy and capacity to deal with actual problems is very clearly illustrated by our obvious inability to formulate and execute an adequate policy for arresting and reversing the course of inflation. The latter, being the result of the cumulative pressures generated by the mistaken social, economic, monetary and financial policies of the three plans, cannot be put an end to merely by a stroke of pen or bold declarations. Reassessment of the objectives, policies, processes, administrative apparatus, alignments, political organization and strategy has to be undertaken and corrective action taken with understanding, courage and determination. It is the purpose of this book to provide this re-assessment and indicate as clearly as possible what has to be done to regain our sense of direction and choose our new course on the basis of our experience and full grasp of the needs of the future.

Re-statement of the major conclusions of the book is neither necessary nor can it serve any useful purpose. It is, however, desirable to re-state very briefly the major premises of socialism which have been explained throughout the book, but particularly in its first three chapters. This brief re-statement of the first principles can serve as a frame of reference and put in relief the basic assumptions of socialism on which we can chart our course for the future. These are:

(1) Socialism, first and foremost, must mean equality and brotherhood in social relations and way of life and all barriers to the realization of these objects have to be removed by the state backed by the organized strength of the community.

(2) The greatest obstacle in the way of realizing this object is the existing class structure and the distribution of power which goes with it. A change in this social pattern has to be brought about in stages; but this change has to be given the very highest place in the programme of action for without it frustration of sound concepts, well-conceived policies and even devoted efforts is inevitable.

(3) A fundamental change in class structure can be brought about either by force applied by a party of determined, and well-organized revolutionaries or by mass awakening and effective organization of the exploited sections of the community to back the efforts of the parties unreservedly committed to socialism and state legislation sincerely devised to bring about the basic change in class structure. The latter course is definitely more desirable and under the actual conditions existing in India is likely to give better results though recourse to the first alternative, i.e. application of force, cannot and should not be ruled out if the entrenched interests make it unavoidable to adopt this course owing to their violent suppression of peaceful efforts to introduce fundamental changes in class structure.

(4) Private ownership of the instruments of production, distribution and exchange is and cannot but be a serious hinderance in the way of realization of socialism and has to be replaced by their progressive public ownership or co-operativ-

ization. In the transition period the operation of private enterprise in agriculture, industry, trade and finance has to be subjected to public regulation to reduce and remove the lack of harmony between public good and private interests and a framework of common values has to be established both for the public and the private sectors.

(5) Built-in safeguards have to be provided against the risk of totalitarian trends inherent in comprehensive public ownership of the economic apparatus through the appropriate institutional changes and firmly established social norms and mores.

(6) Socialism needs its own institutional framework, the creation and development of which requires a high order of constructive ability and social insight; and the provision of the framework has to be undertaken.

(7) Replacement of money values by social values is the primary task of socialism and it is absolutely essential that the whole system of credit, currency and price mechanism should be charged with socialist purpose, and express and realize it fully in its operation.

(8) Socialism has to mean full and rich personal and community life, both being reciprocally necessary and essential and any trends that repress the former or impoverish or degrade the latter have to be consciously negated.

(9) Democracy and socialism are really two aspects of the same life process; and one cannot be realized without the other. This involves:

(a) Government by consent,
(b) Accountability of the Government to the organized will of the people,
(c) Freedom of thought, expression and association,
(d) Entire participation of the people in the country's political system and the operative apparatus of the economy,
(e) And true fellowship as the prime concern of all political and economic organizations.

(10) Socialism and narrow exclusive nationalism in the

present context are completely incompatible with each other, and peace, establishment of international community and world government as early as possible are absolutely essential prerequisite of socialism and has to involve the end of colonialism in all forms and exploitation of some nations by other nations.

(11) A federalized social structure based upon the establishment and working of living and creative small communities is essential for successful realization of a socialist society.

The most highly developed modern techniques have to be used fully for economic growth, the conquest of hunger and poverty and reduction and elimination of soulless toil; but its use must be a social function and its utilization carried out within the framework of socialist values and not cause any social alienation and discords.

(13) Socialism can be sustained and enriched only if, generally speaking, internal reserves of the individuals and the community are built up and replenished by the understanding and cultivation of the substance of life, continuous social communion becomes an integral part of the personal and community life and the whole educational system and cultural life embody, express and realize this supreme value.

These premises have been already stated, amplified and elaborated in relation to the problems of socialist transformation of the Indian economy in its different aspects. Their brief restatement brings out clearly how greatly our efforts and achievements have fallen short of the needs of socialist transformation even in its initial stages and how very necessary it is to muster all the forces of social change to initiate the process in right earnest and carry it forward as fast and as far as we can. No miracles can be worked, and, as stated below, the prospect of even moderate success in achieving this object in the existing conditions is really not bright at all; and yet as it is necessary for our very survival that this process should be set into operation and carried forward in spite of all our limitations, it is necessary that we should know the content of socialism with as great clarity as possible. It is generally stated that there is no clear definition of socialism and disagreement in regard to it is very wide and a source of great confusion. The differences exist and sectarian trends make them wider than they actually are. In India, given the genuine desire to secure the largest measure of common agreement in theory and practice on the part of all earnest socialists, it probably would be possible to frame a common programme to which a large majority of socialists can give allegiance on the basis of the spirit of the social premises referred to above. This agreement must not merely be an agreement at verbal level but evoke consent, interest and enthusiasm of most of the earnest socialists. Analysis of the existing tendencies, as stated in Chapter 3, indicates that a point of convergence, though not identity of views and principles, is emerging and may, if full implications of agreed socialist premises are borne in mind, be reached as a basis for the implementation of a common programme.

Nehru's death creates a situation which makes it all the more imperative to secure this agreement in spirit and action. Jawaharlal Nehru remained steadfast in his loyalty to socialism since 1930—the Karachi resolution and at the end of his life conviction that without socialism there could be no future for this country and even the world became firmer and brighter than ever. He did all that he could to make his conviction the working hypothesis of his policy; and non-alignment, support of small industries, introduction of political decentralization, emphasis on industrialization, particularly the development of heavy industries, on the need of completing land reforms, social catholicity and readiness to receive assistance from all countries were the results of his abiding faith in socialism. The fact that India is now fully committed to the early realization of the socialist goal is largely due to his deepening conviction that if she does not traverse the socialist road and face the problems of the future with socialism as her guiding principle, she would certainly go astray and cease to be true to her appointed destiny. He could not transmit the intensity of this conviction to his immediate associates or the Congress organization as a

whole; and the sense of urgency, which he so transparently felt
in every fibre of his being in the last year of his life, was shared
in words but not in fact by the men in power in the Central
and State Governments, in key positions in policy making and
administration. This was his misfortune but not his fault; but
there is not the slightest doubt that he himself felt deeply and
keenly that the country had to advance towards socialism with
rapid strides, otherwise we all would land in a morass.

There is, however, another aspect of his socialist convictions
which has also to be taken into account in assessing the present situation. His own mind, owing to its deeply ingrained
habit of eclecticism, sensitivity to intimations of life which
elude verbal expression, innate distrust of fanaticism and in-
tolerance in all forms and shapes, his clear realization of the
constraints of the objective situation in India and his being
very markedly susceptible to the plastic stress of, for which the
only phrase is, time spirit, made him indecisive, ineffective and
even vaccilating on many very critical occasions. These are
great qualities and his outstanding stature in the country and
in the world was in no small measure due to them; and the
fact that his death has had such a powerful impact all over
the world is largely due to his having been known to have
possessed these qualities pre-eminently. But there were also
great faults of these qualities which account for the fact that
the country has not advanced towards socialism after independence to any significant extent, anti-socialist forces have
become stronger, socialist objectives have been frustrated in
the implementation of policies, and the men in high places in
government, administration and public life are men whose
loyalty to socialism, to say the least, is greatly in doubt. This
is not entirely or even mainly due to the faults of Nehru's
great qualities. The country itself has been found wanting in
essential respects, the new opportunities have evoked the lust for
power and narrow degrading loyalties based upon caste, language and regional antipathies, and the springs of idealism and
capacity for dedication to new social visions and the fountains

of capable and disinterested leadership in all walks of life have become feeble dribbles. These are the fundamental reasons which explain why the country has been let down in all these vital respects and a penetrating analysis of why this has happened, when the country is confronted with gigantic tasks, has still to be undertaken. But that we have been and are in a bad way in all these respects admits of no doubt whatever, Jawaharlal undertook and performed super-human tasks and it is clear that he shortened his life on that account. But he could not have accomplished what only a nation stirred to its depths, responsive to the needs of the country and led by hundreds of thousands of wise and capable leaders at all levels, particularly at the basic level, could have accomplished.

All this is true and yet it is also true that limitations of his great qualities have left us with a legacy which calls for the exercise of superb qualities on a mass scale by which the effects of his great limitations can be neutralized and the country can generate its own power on which it can move ahead on the road to socialism. Great men can work wonders and convert men of clay into heroes; but the only way in which the limitations of the entire social structure can be overcome is to create conditions and forces by which such limitations can be counteracted and surmounted. Jawaharlal Nehru intellectually was aware of this fact, but this awareness did not move him deeply enough and in spite of his deep interest in and love of the masses and great hold over them, he did very little to alter the class alignments of forces in this country and make the masses, whom he loved and who loved him, on account of his deep humanism, the moving force in the country and masters of their destiny. The enormous crowds that he attracted were a great tribute to his personal magnetism—charisma to use the current word—but these crowds remained only adoring crowds. They dispersed and nothing was left of their collective will or collective strength because they really did not have either the one or the other. They were really fortuitous concourse of individuals and when they dispersed they were completely atomized. They were merely crowds, and though bound together for the time being by a common emotion, they did not represent a common purpose or a common vision. These crowds, if Jawaharlal Nehru had the will and ability of a great artist in the making of men, could have been organized into masses in action, but that would have required a Lenin or a Gandhi and Nehru did not have qualities of either. He, as he often said, drew his strength from the masses. That he did and without exercising the arts of an ordinary demagogue. And yet he never gave them strength of their own or made them masters or instruments of their own destiny. This is the reason why after Nehru the masses are still inert, have not produced any great leaders who are moved by them and in their turn can move them. Yes, Nehru's hold over the masses was not converted and could not be converted into the strength of the masses.

This is the task, which he knew had to be performed, but he could not perform it owing to his own limitations, and, as just stated above, the country's inability to rise to the great need of the times. This is the task which has now to be performed by all who know how great is the need in a spirit of deep gratitude for what the departed leader has done for us. There is a danger that his name, like Gandhi's name, will be invoked by the men, to whom what he stood for, means less than nothing, to defeat the goal which he had set his heart upon all his life, and particularly, to repeat, in the last year of his life. This has happened before all through history and in all parts of the world. In other words, counter-revolution can become a menace and a reality in the name of revolution and with the flag of revolution flying overhead. This danger is very real in India, is clearly more than visible on the horizon and all the strength that can be, as stated above, mustered has to be mustered to meet it. This is our task, our compelling duty and has to be adequately and fully performed, not by invoking his name in vain, but providing social alchemy of the strength and spirit of the people and creating a situation in which counter-revolution will not be able to raise its ugly head, and even if it does, it will meet the fate that it deserves, i.e. be completely vanquished.

Jawaharlal Nehru did not define socialism as clearly and unambiguously as he should have and in the name of flexibility, which is undoubtedly needed, compromising decisions were taken and carried out whose dangerous implications were overlooked, and the spirit of socialism did not inform the plans and their implementation. The result is, as stated above, that the Government is being run by men, who in a large number of cases, are untrue to socialism, the whole administration largely manned, in higher echelons in particular, by able but self-seeking men with practically no allegiance to socialism and even the higher interests of the country, the economy is being dominated by the men of wealth for whom socialism is an anathema, and political organizations and parties are being operated by political machines and not by men of any great ideals and disinterested devotion to the needs of the future. Flexibility, which has to be the very soul of our socialist faith, and the need for which was rightly stressed by Jawaharlal Nehru on innumerable occasions, would in practice become a cloak for the most unscrupulous rank opportunism and really an instrument for impeding the advance of socialism and its eventual overthrow. In the name of pragmatism it is not unlikely that our whole future would be put in jeopardy and by steps dishonestly conceived and insidiously carried out, retreat from socialism will be beaten even in theory and much more in practice. 'Centrism', now in vogue, is really a beginning of this retreat and is being made purposely the vogue in order to hold in check the radical forces and prevent social change proceeding at the speed needed by the urgency of the situation. What the country really needs is not centrism but centre of power, energy and drive which will move the people, give them hope and faith and redeem them from the prevailing atmosphere of frustration and cynicism—a really social dynamo.

In a letter written by Jawaharlal Nehru to Gandhi in 1934, which is now being widely quoted, he said, "A strange way of dealing with the subject of socialism is to use the word which has a well-defined meaning in the English language, in a totally different sense—which is not helpful in the commerce of ideas." Jawaharlal Nehru exposed himself to the charge of making socialism amorphous and therefore, meaningless, to use his own words, "muddled humanitarianism" in spite of his fidelity to its spirit. He had no time, perhaps not even the inclination and aptitude, for mastering the vital details of the great task of building socialism in this country. His real strength and the greatest contribution lay in his being utterly true to his vision of the future. But it is almost certain that attempt will be made to make socialism void of all precise content and use it in a truly "strange" way which will not only be unhelpful in "the commerce of ideas" but also come in the way of understanding and realizing its essentials. All these difficulties are there and in this book they have been set forth with as much clarity and force as possible. They are truly formidable difficulties, but those who have faith in socialism and are prepared to work and live for it, should refuse to be daunted by them. *Real loyalty to the memory of Jawaharlal Nehru requires not that we should follow him but fulfil him by going beyond him by understanding not only his great qualities but also their limitations and truly transcending them.* We owe him so much that the only way to even very partly repay him is to do our best to accomplish what he did not accomplish, really could not have accomplished in spite of his great qualities and really super-human endeavour. "The people of India today with all their burdens and problems, live on the frontier of a new world which they are helping to build. In order to cross the frontier they have to possess courage and enterprise, the spirit of endurance and capacity for hard work and the vision of the future." This is what Jawaharlal Nehru himself put into Chapter I of the Third Plan. He did not live to take his people across the frontier on which they have been and are living.

They have to cross it yet and must. This is their immediate task, and, if they are true to the vision of the future, they will accomplish the task with success; otherwise all is dark for the immediate future. This alternative has to be and must be averted.

INDEX

INDEX

DATE DUE

NOV 10			
MAY 28 '72			
JAN 3 '84			
JAN 4 1984			
GAYLORD			PRINTED IN U.S.A.